Teach for the Sky

British Training Aircraft since 1945

Teach for the Sky

British Training Aircraft since 1945

James Jackson

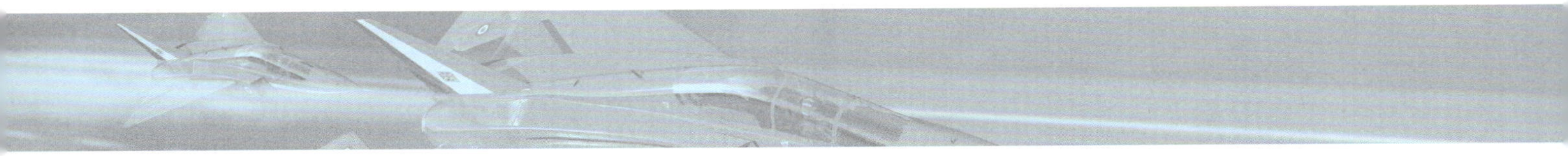

First published in 2021 by Crécy Publishing

ISBN 9781902109664

Printed in Turkey by Pelikan Print

Crécy Publishing Limited
1a Ringway Trading Estate, Shadowmoss Rd, Manchester M22 5LH
www.crecy.co.uk

Front cover top: XK037 during a training sortie around the Mach Loop in May 2018. The Mach Loop is within the RAF's Low Flying Area LFA7 which covers most of Wales. The markings are of No IV (Reserve) Squadron, one of the shadow squadrons belonging to No 4 FTS. *Chris Gibson*

Front cover profile: BAe Hawk T.1 XX226 of No 4 Flying Training School. *Rolando Ugolini*

Front cover bottom: Alternate history Red Arrows making a thunderous display in their BAC P.45s. Had the Air Staff not compromised on the provision of variable-geometry wings for AST.362, it is possible that the P.45 would have been developed instead of the SEPECAT Jaguar. *Luca Landino*

Back cover top: A manufacturer's model of the final design of the Hawker Siddeley HS.1182 Hawk. The Hawk's development was on time and on budget and led to an incredible sales success. *Author's Collection*

Back cover profile: BAE Systems Hawk T.2 ZK019 of No IV (Reserve) Squadron. *Rolando Ugolini*

Back cover middle left: The Avro Anson had been a training workhorse throughout the Second World War and remained so well into the 1950s. The Anson T.20 was developed for use in training schools in Southern Rhodesia. *Author's Collection*

Back cover middle centre: An early artist's impression of the Hawker Siddeley P.1174 Harrier Trainer which would enter service as the Harrier T.2. *Brooklands Museum*

Back cover middle right: Hawker Siddeley's SP.117-1 was designed to win export orders for the company and began an extensive series of design studies that led directly to the Hawk. *Via Chris Farara*

Back cover bottom: The Shorts Tucano T.1 was developed from the Embraer EMB-312 Tucano as a basic trainer and served alongside the Hawk until October 2019. Delivered in February 1989, ZF163 seen here was retired in July 2001. *Author's Collection*

Half title page: Scottish Aviation Bulldog T.1 XX534 of the East Lowland UAS at Turnhouse on 1st March 1974. By this time it had already served with the CFS and the Royal Navy EFTS and would not be retired until 2001. Today it flies in private ownership as G-EDAV. *Charles E. MacKay*

Page 3 top: Early production Tucano T.1s ZF138 and ZF139 are seen here in neat formation. *Author's Collection*

Page 3 bottom: Boulton Paul's promotional artwork offered the vision of a flight of P.119s. Sadly the emergence of the de Havilland Vampire Trainer in June 1950 destroyed any hopes of official interest due to the superior economics of utilising standard Vampire parts already in mass production and with export Vampire users already lined up as potential customers. *Author's Collection*

Contents

Acknowledgements

A book relies on the work of so many people beyond that of the author. Researching and writing *Teach for the Sky* has drawn together source material from a range of sources and archives and has involved many people along the way.

Firstly, I would like to thank my family, friends and work colleagues for all their support and encouragement throughout. I would like to give special thanks to Chris Gibson and Tony Buttler for all their kind assistance, not only in the supply of information and images but also for mentoring me through the process of writing my first major book.

The research for *Teach for the Sky* has relied on primary sources to a large extent from several archives. Many of these are run by volunteers and retired employees from the aviation industry. They are experts within their fields and should be given recognition for their efforts in curating and preserving these archives for future generations of historians. Thanks must go to Les Whitehouse for his generous assistance and knowledge of all things Boulton Paul. Chris Farara who tends the Hawker archive at the Brooklands Museum was an invaluable help in providing information and images relating the Kingston's varied array of training aircraft. Jeremy Graham provided much useful material and images from the Westland (now Leonardo) archives and Ralph Pegram provided material on Supermarine. Joe Cherrie has been an enthusiastic supporter of *Teach for the Sky* since I first raised the idea and has provided much material on Scottish Aviation. Dave Forster as an expert on the English Electric Canberra provided much useful information and images of the type in its various training guises. Paul Chapman kindly dug through his personal archive of SEPECAT Jaguar material. Thanks must also go George Jenks of Avro Heritage at Woodford, Peter Amos with his extensive knowledge of Miles Aircraft and the staff of The National Archives at Kew, London. I would also like to give a special mention for the Secret Projects Forum run by Paul Martell-Mead which is an invaluable resource on an eclectic mix of aviation and defence projects and which is a productive hub for aviation researchers from around the world.

Teach for the Sky would be incomplete without images to bring the aircraft to life on the page. It has once again been a pleasure to work with Luciano Alviani who was commissioned to paint three artworks of 'what-if' scenes of aircraft projects that remained on the drawing board and was so enthusiastic that he volunteered to contribute a fourth. It was an equal pleasure to work with Luca Landino who wonderfully brought two further projects to life in three-dimensional computer art. Terry Panopalis deserves special thanks for providing many excellent images from his collection. Many others also contributed from their personal collections, many of them being fellow Air-Britain members or family members and friends who are custodians of other collections. Thanks are due to; Glen Auld, Trevor Bartlett, Peter Berry, Chris England, Bill Fisher, Ken Haynes, Derek Heley, Mike Hines, Mike Hudson, Alan Kilham, Ian MacFarlane, Chares E. MacKay, Ralf Manteufel, David Miller, Tom Pharo, Glyn Ramsden, P. Michael Rhodes, Steve Ryle, Bill Teasdale, Liam Thomas, Robin A Walker, Dave Welch, John Wilkinson, Michael West and Bob Woolnough.

I must also thank those involved in the production of *Teach for the Sky*. Neil Lewis kindly edited the text and provided much needed guidance and support and it has been a pleasure to work with Charlotte Stear and Jeremy Pratt at Crécy Publishing.

James Jackson, Morecambe
April 2021

Introduction

Every pilot and aircrew member of the three flying services, the Royal Air Force, the Fleet Air Arm and the Army Air Corps, has one thing in common, they were all trained for their specialist roles. That training is an expensive investment of years of instruction and personal development that requires the right techniques and equipment to enable each student to achieve the best from their abilities and to ensure that the investment is not wasted. This book spans just over 70 years of training following the Second World War and charts the evolution of training aircraft as the gas turbine replaced the piston engine and demanded an evolution of training requirements to master the skills needed as performance of frontline aircraft increased to supersonic speeds. The continual improvement and multiplication of electronic equipment such as radar and Doppler navigation and weapon guidance systems required student pilots, navigators and bomb aimers to gain knowledge of how to operate these 'black boxes' to get the best performance out of them.

This book is not an in-depth history of training methods or unit histories, but rather focuses on the numerous types of training aircraft that have been used since 1945 and how and why they were selected and the numerous developments along the way. A lack of space sadly prevents the inclusion of the Air Cadets and the Air Training Corps and their associated gliding equipment which have given many young aviators their first taste of flying.

Training aircraft vary according to the stage of the training syllabus they are designed to be used on. The elementary and basic trainers have benign handling and low power suitable to get the ab initio pilot to solo standard and on which to learn the basics of good airmanship and navigation to gain their coveted 'Wings', the winged badge all British military pilots wear. Advanced trainers have performance approaching that of frontline aircraft that the pupil will encounter on their first posting to enable them to gain valuable experience of a wide range of flying conditions and flight profiles and gives the budding fighter pilot their first taste of releasing weapons. For the future multi-engined pilot the advanced trainer of choice has two engines on which to learn the vagaries of dealing with asymmetric flight with one engine inoperable. Student helicopter pilots require a trainer too in order to learn the rather different skills of juggling the collective pitch and specialist pilot techniques such as autorotation to deal with engine failures to make a safe power-off emergency landing using the lift from the rotor blades. For the student navigator, radio operator or observer, their advanced trainer has two engines too, but they are seated in the cabin where they learn how to carry out their tasks in small groups under the watchful eyes of the instructor. Finally, the conversion trainer prepares the pilot for their first tour of operations as a 'first tourist' with an operational squadron and finally they get their hands on the frontline aircraft, or something very similar to it, that they will be flying for their tour of duty. Their value can be judged when it is considered that at one point the RAF argued that the English Electric Lightning and

In the foreground of this 2010 photograph, Hawk T.1A XX167 is in No 208 Squadron markings alongside XX314 and XX218 from No 19 (Reserve) Squadron, both of these units have now disbanded and all three aircraft retired. *MoD/Open Government Licence, 2010*

BAC TSR.2 were too demanding to allow first tourists to fly operationally. For 'second tourists' embarking on another posting, perhaps switching to a completely different type of aircraft, the conversion trainer is just as vital to enable them to gain knowledge of the vagaries of their new mount.

Navigators in 1946 were still taught tried and tested manual methods such as dead reckoning but they had to also master a growing range of electronic aids. The creation of the jet-powered V-Force of nuclear bombers also created a new breed of aircrew, the Air Electronics Operator (AEO) to operate the electronic countermeasures (ECM) equipment, but the Nav-Plotter (Radar) still required skills in visual bomb-aiming. Even as late as 1982 the 'Mark One Eyeball' still proved a useful tool during the Black Buck raids of the Falklands War against the airfield at Port Stanley. The Panavia Tornado provided the swansong of the two-man pilot and navigator team, the fast-jet navigator absorbing the roles of bomb-aimer and Air Electronics Operator. Now that the Tornado has been retired it remains unclear whether artificial intelligence will completely make the 'back-seater' redundant or whether they may return one day.

The training syllabus has evolved over time to keep pace with the technological advances in aviation and often the choice of training aircraft has led the development of the syllabus. For the assessors of prospective training aircraft, a lot of pressure to select the right type was on their shoulders, for the trainer would shape the experience of every pilot and aircrew member for decades to come. Although simulators for flying training date back to the earliest days of powered flight, today the training syllabus makes increasing use of simulators which with artificial intelligence and life-like graphic displays and motion enable an increase of flight experience without the running costs of an aircraft and with increased safety. It is probable that simulators will continue to provide a valuable synthetic aid, but as long as the manned aircraft remains in the sky there will always be a need for trainers to enable future generations to gain their flight experience.

A common theme across many militaries and air forces around the world is that military budgets are never as generous as the militaries themselves hope for. In particular, since the end of the Cold War Western defence budgets shrank quite rapidly and many air forces were swiftly downsized which had knock-on implications for the number of trainee pilots and aircrew required. A desire to decrease spending on expensive capital costs and to maximise value for money has seen many Western air forces begin to shift military flying training to civilian providers. In Britain, the concept of Private Finance Initiative (PFI) has been widely applied since the mid-1990s where previously state-run services would be conducted or supported by private industry, the government avoiding upfront capital costs but paying fees over the duration of the contract. These budgetary policies coincided with increasing centralisation of flying training to create in 2002 the UK Military Flying Training System (UKMFTS) which would be completely operated and equipped by private providers to create a coherent training organisation. In 2003 BAE Systems were awarded the Advanced Jet Trainer contract, supplying the Hawk T.2 while in 2006 the main fixed-wing UKMFTS contract was awarded to Ascent Flight Training, a consortium which included Lockheed Martin and the VT Group, who then sub-contracted Elbit Systems and KBR operating as Affinity Flight Training Systems to provide the aircraft from 2018. After much delay, in 2016 Ascent were also selected to the helicopter training portion of UKMFTS, sub-contracting the provision of the helicopters to Airbus Helicopters with Babcock and Lockheed Martin supplying the infrastructure and ground-based training equipment. Britain's flying training organisation is settled until the contracts expire in the latter half of the 2030s. It cannot be denied that there were teething problems at the beginning, but such a financial model enables the Ministry of Defence to procure a new completely new training fleet every 30 years. The only downside is that those training aircraft are whatever off-the-shelf solutions exist, rather than being tailored to precisely what RAF or Fleet Air Arm require and the chances of future British military pilots training on aircraft produced in Britain beyond 2030 are small.

Note on Units

By the 1970s the British aviation industry and ministries had adopted metric measurements but for consistency imperial units will be given alongside metric conversions. Nautical miles (nm) have been used throughout this book. The RAF used statute miles until the 1960s and where these are quoted from original documents a conversion is given to nautical miles and kilometres. Speeds are given in knots (kt) and kilometres per hour (km/h), weight in pounds (lb) and kilograms (kg). Where possible aircraft weights quoted in the main text will be the all-up weight (AUW) which includes the weight of the aircraft's structure, engines, fuel, oil, crew and payload.

Note on Designations

All aircraft serving with the British armed forces are given an official designation outlining their role and a Mark number denoting any differences between variants. For training aircraft the letter 'T' is used as the prefix, for example T.Mk.1. In the main text the designations are presented in a shortened form, for example, T.1.

A map of the main airfields in the United Kingdom where RAF, FAA and AAC training units have been stationed during the post-war era. *Chris Gibson*

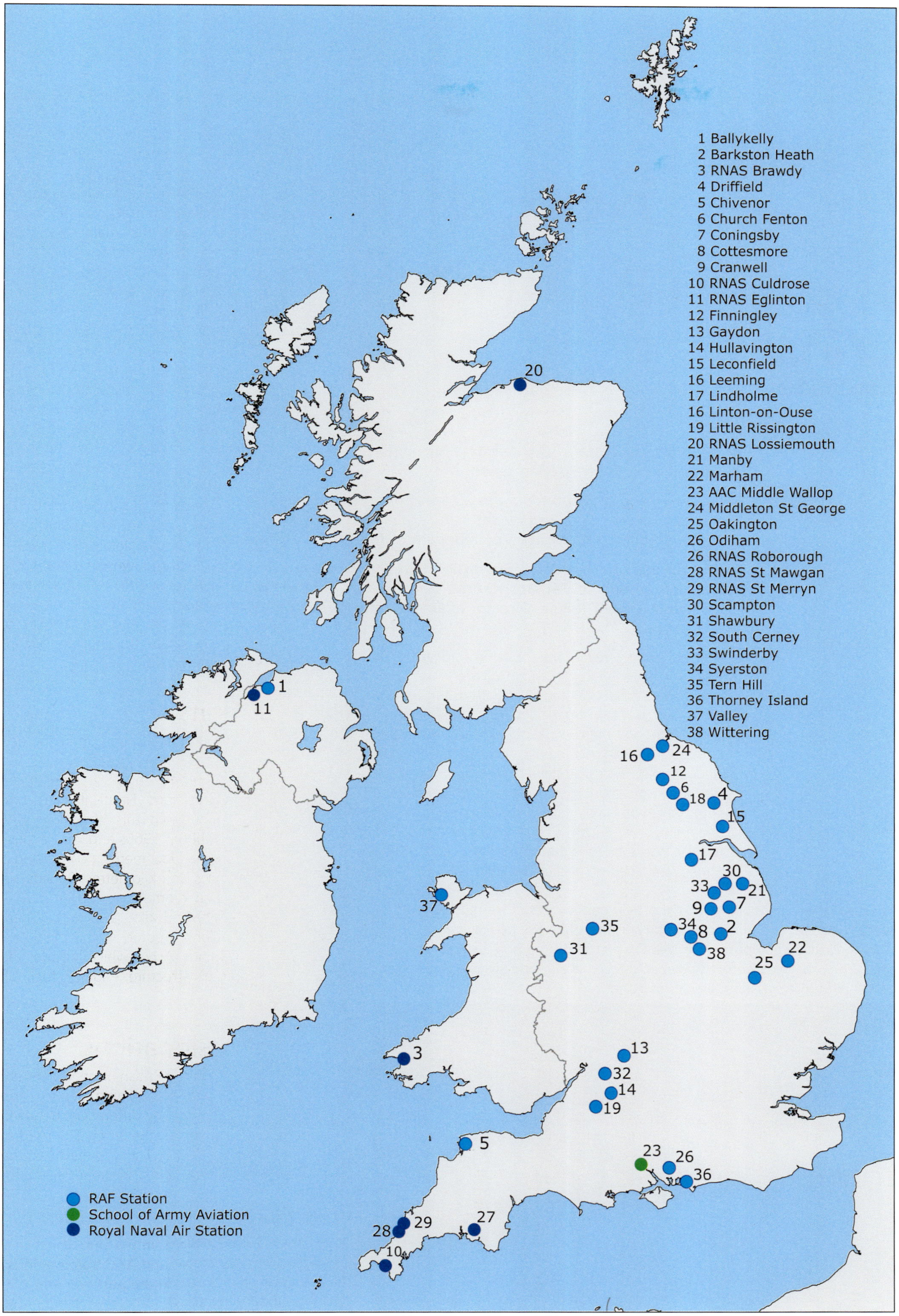
1 Ballykelly
2 Barkston Heath
3 RNAS Brawdy
4 Driffield
5 Chivenor
6 Church Fenton
7 Coningsby
8 Cottesmore
9 Cranwell
10 RNAS Culdrose
11 RNAS Eglinton
12 Finningley
13 Gaydon
14 Hullavington
15 Leconfield
16 Leeming
17 Lindholme
16 Linton-on-Ouse
19 Little Rissington
20 RNAS Lossiemouth
21 Manby
22 Marham
23 AAC Middle Wallop
24 Middleton St George
25 Oakington
26 Odiham
26 RNAS Roborough
28 RNAS St Mawgan
29 RNAS St Merryn
30 Scampton
31 Shawbury
32 South Cerney
33 Swinderby
34 Syerston
35 Tern Hill
36 Thorney Island
37 Valley
38 Wittering
RAF Station
School of Army Aviation
Royal Naval Air Station

1 Re-equipping the Training Schools

'Imprimis Praecepta' – 'Our teaching is everlasting'
Motto of the Central Flying School

'It was agreed that considered as an up-to-date replacement for the Tiger Moth, the Chipmunk was an excellent little aeroplane.'
Air Commodore E D Barnes, Commandant of the Empire Flying School

'The Air Staff are under the impression that the big canopy of the Prentice has done much to spoil this aeroplane. Perhaps you could advise as to whether this is true or not.'
Air Commodore T R Pine, Director of Operational Requirements, May 1948

The Central Flying School came into existence alongside the Royal Flying Corps and the Royal Naval Air Service, known initially as the Military Wing and Naval Wing respectively, on 13th April 1912. Although the CFS did not officially open until 19th June and did not begin its first course until 15th August, the CFS can lay claim to be one of the oldest military flying training schools in the world. The importance of training was understood from the beginnings of British military aviation, the CFS initially being given equal importance as the two armed branches of military aviation. The CFS was soon taken under the wing of the Royal Flying Corps as the Royal Naval Air Service became an independent force. With the outbreak of the First World War the expansion of flying training became inevitable as thousands of pilots and aircrew were trained. The creation of the Royal Air Force on 1 April 1918 centralised flying training once again, which has endured ever since to varying degrees even after the Fleet Air Arm (FAA) and Army Air Corps (AAC) re-emerged as independent forces. The Second World War resulted in the exponential growth of the RAF in terms of manpower and equipment. At the end of the war the RAF operated a vast training organisation spread across the globe with training schools in the United Kingdom (UK) and across the Empire in places such as Bermuda, Egypt and India. The Commonwealth Air Training Plan saw thousands of pilots and aircrew trained at 74 training schools in Australia, Canada, New Zealand and Southern Rhodesia and many others were trained under agreements with the United States of America. It was this wartime experience that formed the basis of the post-war training system that this book will examine in detail, in terms of the aircraft it operated and how those aircraft not only reflected changes in training requirements but how advanced in aviation led to new innovations for training.

Following the Second World War a new generation of training aircraft were required, including elementary trainers like the de Havilland Canada DHC-1 Chipmunk T.10. WB610 pictured here had a short service life of just six years before it was sold to Australia and civilian registered as VH-BSM in August 1956. *De Havilland*

Five Stages

At this stage it would be useful to briefly explain the training system. The terminology and the length of the syllabus flown and the types employed have varied over time and will be discussed in more depth in the relevant chapters in this book, but the basic structure is essentially identical today to that of 1945 (and earlier). During the first part of the period covered by this book, flying training was conducted by Flying Training Command, becoming Training Command in 1968 when it absorbed Technical Training Command that had been responsible for non-pilot aircrew training. In 1977 Training Command was subsumed into Support Command, training becoming the responsibility of No 21 Group. Later re-organisations saw a separate Personnel and Training Command re-emerge and in April 2007 that Command was merged with Strike Command to form a single, unified, Air Command. Training a pilot can take several years to accomplish and follows five stages;

- Primary: this is the first stage where the student is introduced to flying, also known as elementary training or grading. Elementary Flying Training Schools (EFTS) initially provided flying experience but were replaced in the 1950s by Basic Flying Training Schools for National Servicemen. Potential graduate entrants gain their air experience with a University Air Squadron (UAS), on graduation from university they are eligible to join the RAF College at Cranwell, where they are taught to be an officer as well as a pilot. In 1958 Air Experience Flights (AEF) were created alongside the existing Volunteer Gliding Schools to fulfil the same function for the cadets of the Combined Cadet Forces and the Air Training Corps.
- Basic: this is the core of flying training. The student having gained some experience now joins a Flying Training School (FTS) or the RAF College. The student now learns how to fly and navigate and good airmanship. The syllabus includes blind instrument flying, formation flying, basic aerobatics and flying at night. There is also a strong ground school element of classroom tuition and use of flight simulators to gain experience and indeed this applies to all stages of the training syllabus. This syllabus has varied in length but regardless the aim of every student is to gain their 'wings', the aircraft flying badge, variants of which all qualified British pilots and aircrew have been entitled to wear since 1913.
- Advanced: the RAF has long operated a 'streaming' policy, on completion of the basic flying stage the students are assessed by their ability, aptitude and their own preferences to begin training on the category of aircraft they are destined to fly operationally. The three streams are; fast jet for those destined for fighters and strike aircraft; multi-engine for those destined to fly transports or maritime patrol aircraft; helicopters. In the early 1950s the fast jet stream was further broken down into fighter and attack streams.
- Operational: this phase of training is to prepare the student to operate his category of aircraft. For example, fast jet students will undergo weapons training at this point to learn how to operate weapons systems, air-to-air combat techniques and air-to-ground strike profiles to launch bombs and rockets.
- Conversion: this is the final stage at the Operational Conversion Unit (OCU) where the student trains on the aircraft that they will use operationally to ensure that they are sufficiently skilled to attain operational standards on their first posting on a tour of duty, becoming known informally as a 'first tourist'. The classroom and flight simulator are still integral to this phase of training, synthetic training now making up at least half of all training time at an OCU. Today the training system and its equipment is of such quality that a pilot who successfully passes this final stage is possibly only six months away from flying a real operational sortie. In contrast, during the 1960s the Air Staff worried whether newly graduated first tourists could cope with flying aircraft like the English Electric Lightning.

It should not be thought that a pilot was stuck in his stream forever. The central tenet of the RAF's training syllabus was that all students would receive an identical basic training syllabus so that they could later receive advanced or conversion training onto a new type, for example helicopter pilots in a future posting could receive training to fly transport aircraft. Pilots destined for the FAA and the AAC received their basic training via the RAF but Service provided their own advanced training to train their pilots for their intended specialist operational roles. Today all military pilot and aircrew training is centralised as much as possible until the OCU phase. Qualified flying instructors (QFI) are taught by the CFS, which is also responsible for maintaining flying standards across all RAF units. For many years it was also responsible for basic flying training for all RAF helicopter pilots.

The training for navigators, signallers (formerly wireless operators), gunners and air engineers follows a slightly different path. They still go through the basic, advanced and conversion stages but at dedicated specialist schools such as Air Navigation Schools (ANS), Radio Schools and Gunnery Schools. Many of these specialist units have disappeared as aircrew roles changed, gunners being superfluous from the 1950s onwards and air engineers by the early 2000s were also redundant. New aircrew roles have emerged in their place, such as sensor operators, and many old roles have changed, navigators becoming weapons systems officers to reflect their much wider tasks operating a range of electronic systems such as radars and electronic warfare equipment.

Obtaining the Trainers

The procurement of training aircraft broadly followed that of all other military aircraft. The Air Staff at the Air Ministry (from 1964 absorbed into a unified Ministry of Defence (MoD)) would direct the Operational Requirements branch to raise Operational Requirements for new or modified aircraft based on requests for equipment from Flying Training Command or specialist training requirements raised by the experience of the operational Commands, for example Bomber Command would have much input into the training of bomb aimers. Following approval of the financial aspects by the Treasury, the technical aspects of the Operational Requirement were evaluated and drawn up into Specifications by the Ministry of Supply (MoS). The MoS was the interface between the Air Ministry (and the other two armed Services) and industry and was responsible for research and development as well as production of all military and many civilian systems. Reorganisations from the late 1950s have led to a bewildering array of successors to the MoS that feature in this book. The responsibility for aviation programmes was moved to a new Ministry of Aviation in 1959, which was merged into the Ministry of Technology in 1967, briefly becoming independent again as the Ministry of Aviation Supply before military procurement came under the direct control of the MoD's Procurement Executive (MoD(PE)) in 1972. The Specifications once agreed were issued to the aircraft manufacturers who would submit tenders with their chosen design and the estimated development and production costs. The MoS (and its successors) would evaluate these tenders on their technical and economic merits and following agreement from the Air Ministry and the Treasury, would negotiate the development and production contracts. As can be imagined the chain of committees and ministerial squabbles could result in progress taking years from the identification of a particular need to the actual aircraft materialising in service.

Taking Stock

At the end of the Second World War many of the training aircraft in use had been designed during the late 1930s as the expansion scheme came into full flow and their large production runs not only attested to the demand for pilots and aircrew, but also the high wastage rates due to accidents. As peace returned these pre-war designs still formed the backbone of Flying Training Command. The de Havilland DH.82A Tiger Moth had entered RAF service in November 1934 and during the war had equipped no less than 28 EFTSs in the UK, 25 in Canada (plus four Wireless Schools), twelve in Australia, four in Rhodesia (plus a Flying Instructors' School), seven in South Africa and two in India. Replacing the Tiger Moth was no easy task. The Miles M.14 Magister was another elementary trainer but was soon disposed of and all had gone by 1948. Advanced trainers had been the Miles Master series with a variety of engines and the North American Harvard supplied from the USA either from pre-war purchases or in larger numbers via Lend-Lease. Although many of the Lend-Lease examples were disposed of at the end of hostilities, the Harvard remained the main advanced trainer in the early post-war years, but a replacement was required. The Avro Anson had begun life as a coastal reconnaissance aircraft but soon became a bomber crew, navigation and radio trainer and production would not end until May 1952 with a grand total of 11,020 built of all marks built in Britain and Canada. The Airspeed Oxford was a purpose-designed bomber aircrew trainer and 8,586 had been built by the time production ended in July 1945. Both types formed the backbone of the multi-engine pilot training syllabus and were operated as navigation and radio operator trainers well into the 1950s; their replacements will be detailed in Chapter Eleven.

Post-war the requirement for new pilots and aircrew fell dramatically and Flying Training Command began to shrink in size. In 1947 Technical Training Command took over the specialist training units and Reserve Command took over the remaining EFTSs and reinstated the UASs to provide graduate officer entrants once again for the RAF College at Cranwell. The training sequence remained unchanged. Due to a surplus of piston-rated pilots most new entrants were trained by the FTSs to fly the new jet-powered fighters and the surplus meant that a graduated pilot could wait up to nine months before receiving their first operational posting. The specialised nature of naval flying was reflected by the 29 advanced and specialist schools that the FAA ran in 1946 using a mixture of trainers and operational types like the Supermarine Seafire and Fairey Barracuda.

Britain's post-war economy had many problems to solve and money was short. Flying training suffered from a lack of funds to invest in new aircraft but development programmes begun during the middle part of the war began to bear fruit and in 1950 this enabled the first major change in the syllabus. The introduction of all-through training meant that primary and basic training was now carried out at the same FTS, enabling pilots to remain with one school to progress from the Percival Prentice to the Harvard. The outbreak of the Korean War and the emergence of the Soviet Union as a nuclear power in 1949 resulted in a large rearmament programme and an expansion plan for the RAF. This plan involved flying training units to supply the necessary numbers of pilots and an additional 750 instructors a year to train all these new pilots. New Basic Flying Training Schools (BFTS) were set up to train National Service pilots and the AFSs were split into fighter, attack and multi-engine streams to bridge the gap between the piston-

The Miles M.14 Magister was the RAF's most advanced elementary trainer in 1939 and was still in widespread use in 1945. By 1948 the RAF had standardised on the older de Havilland Tiger Moth. *Author's Collection*

engined Harvards and the operational jet fighters at the OCUs. Reprising the pre-war expansion plans, civilian contractors were also brought in to run schools and Reserve Flying Schools (RFS) and Flying Refresher Schools were created to re-train called up reservists and reposted pilots to bring their knowledge and skills up to date. Following the end of the Korean War another inevitable contraction occurred with the Rhodesian Air Training Group, the RFSs and civilian contractor schools being closed.

Percival's Prentice

As wartime training needs became paramount, replacements were sought for the pre-war trainers then making up the bulk of the training fleet. On 28th November 1943 Specification T.23/43 was issued to meet Operational Requirement OR.131 for a replacement for the de Havilland DH.82A Tiger Moth. The requirement called for a fully aerobatic low-wing, fixed undercarriage aircraft of wood or metal construction; in June 1945 this was amended to all-metal construction. The requirements called for three hours endurance at a maximum cruising speed of 104kt (193km/h), a maximum stalling speed of 43kt (80km/h) and a service ceiling of 15,000ft (4,570m) that should be reached in five minutes. Initially two versions were planned; one for home-based schools with an unsupercharged de Havilland Gipsy Queen 32 and one for use overseas in tropical conditions with a supercharged Gipsy Queen 51. In July 1945 the Gipsy Queen 31 was selected for the home aircraft and operation in arctic conditions was also stipulated, presumably with an eye for possible use in Canada.

Learn to Test; Test to Learn: The Empire Test Pilot's School

The test pilot is highly respected for their ability and skill. But even test pilots need to be trained how to carry out their flying assessments safely and to fully understand the latest scientific and technical knowledge if they are to perform a worthwhile job. Test flying has always been hazardous and the death rate during the Second World War saw the formation of the Test Pilot's School within the A&AEE on 21st June 1943, the first dedicated test pilot training unit in the world. Becoming the Empire Test Pilot's School (ETPS) on 28th July 1944, it became part of the Royal Aircraft Establishment in 1947 before being privatised in 2001 and now working in a partnership between the MoD and QinetiQ. The ETPS runs fixed-wing, multi-engine and rotary-wing courses and began training flight test engineers from 1974. The ETPS has over 1,500 graduates, with many of its students coming from around the world. Test pilots need to be able to assess a wide range of aircraft and the ETPS fleet has reflected that with a range of non-RAF service. The eclectic fleet is too numerous to reproduce here in detail, but has included small airliners, jet fighters, training aircraft, gliders and helicopters.

Today the ETPS flies a mix of aircraft; the Grob G120TP, Pilatus PC-21, Diamond DA42, Saab Gripen D, an Avro RJ flying classroom, as well as Leonardo A109E Power and Airbus H125 helicopters.

The de Havilland DH.82 Tiger Moth is perhaps one of the most famous training aircraft used by the RAF. Replacing such a ubiquitous aircraft was no easy task, but the Air Ministry set out to achieve that with Specification T.23/43. *Crown Copyright*

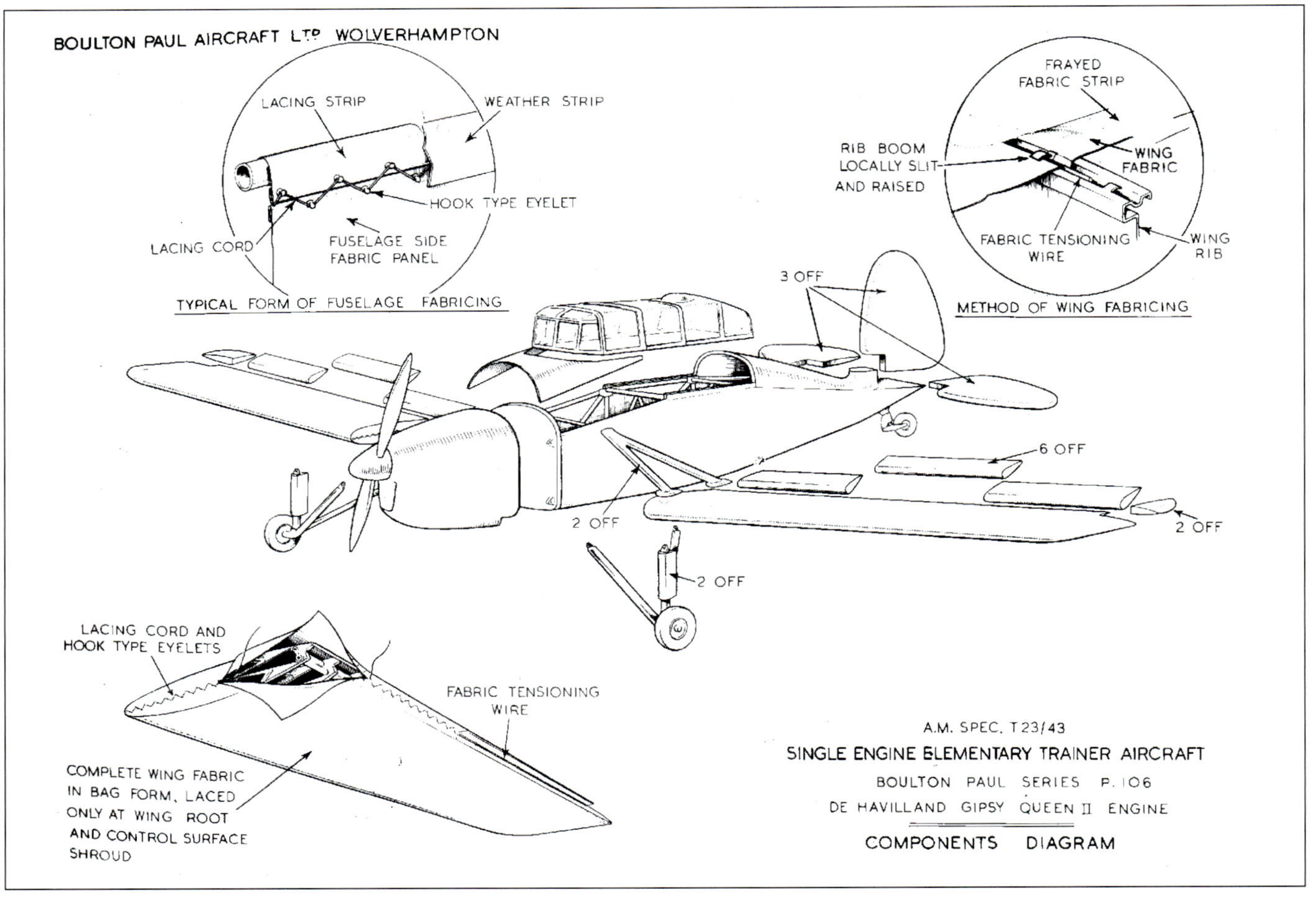

Elementary trainers had to endure rough usage and be easy to repair. Boulton Paul's chief designer J D North designed the P.106 with interchangeable wings, empennage and control surfaces and the wings were covered by an innovative canvas bag which slipped over the wing. *Les Whitehouse, Boulton Paul Archive*

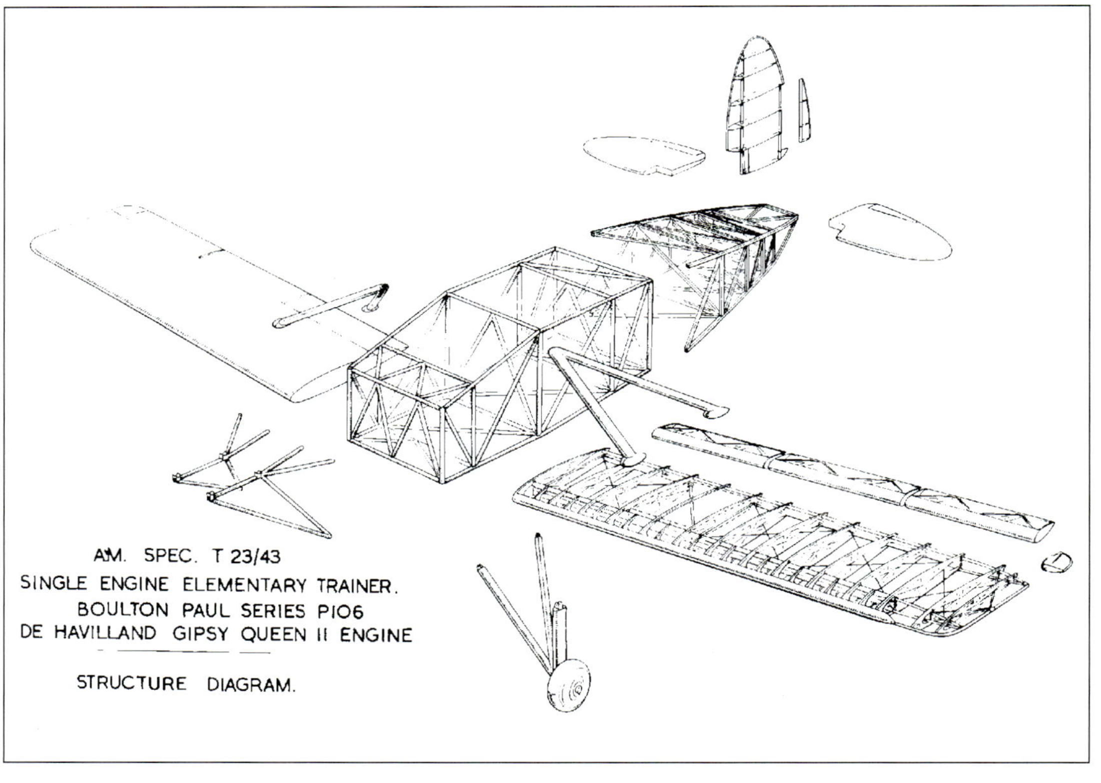

The structure of the P.106 was relatively basic even for 1943 with a fabric-covered all-metal structure. Simplicity was seen as essential for easy repair and maintenance. *Les Whitehouse, Boulton Paul Archive*

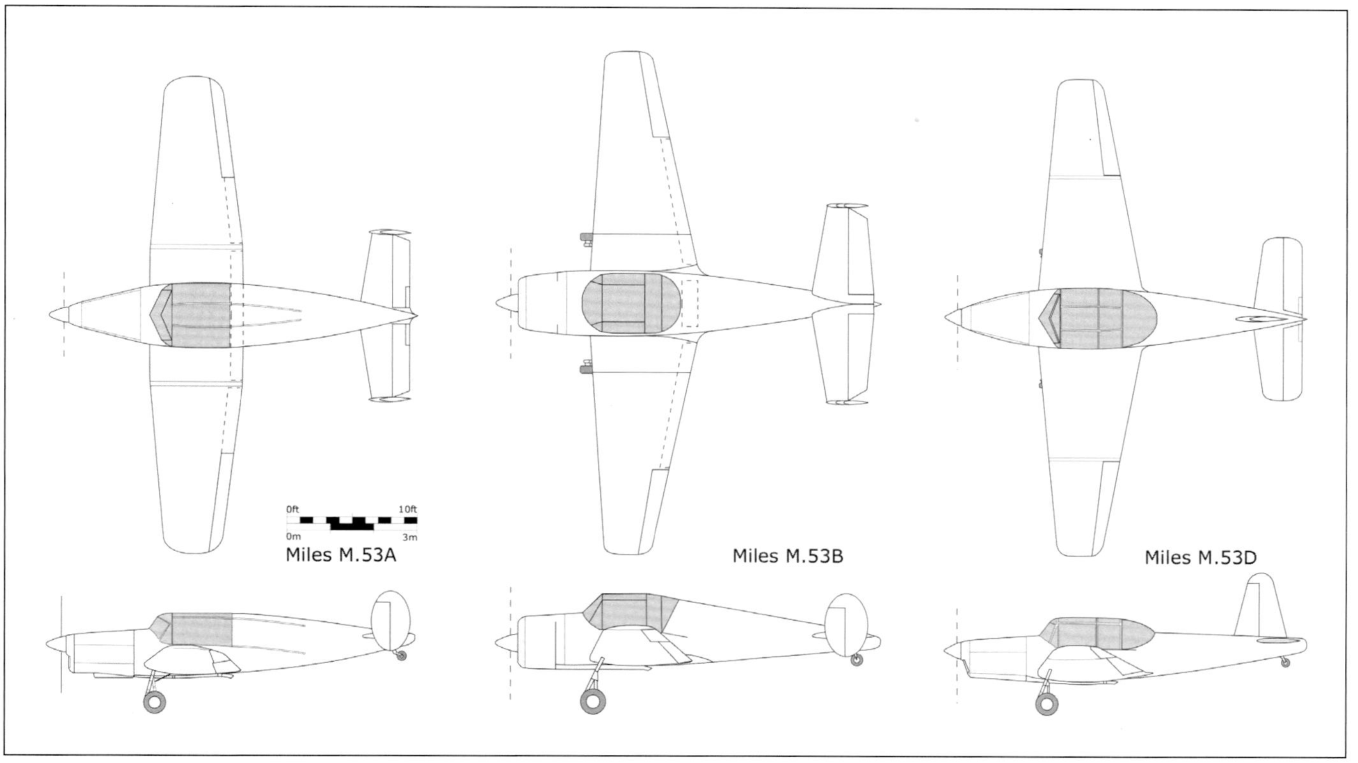

The Miles M.53 series was based on the M.38 Messenger. The large cockpit canopy covered the three seats required under Spec. T.23/43. From left to right are; M.53A with a Gipsy Queen series engine, M.53B with a Cheetah XIX and the M.53D with a Gipsy Six III. *Author*

A novel feature was the provision of side-by-side seating for the student and the instructor and provision for a third seat behind so that a second student could observe the cockpit procedures, in theory reducing training time. This layout was the result of a 1940 study by the Central Flying School (CFS) Examining Wing into training methods and a subsequent trial by the Empire Central Flying School at Hullavington with two Miles M.28 communications aircraft; the Mk.II, HM583, with side-by-side dual controls and a central rear seat and the Mk.III PW397 with triple controls for all three seats. The latter arrangement did not find favour. Although the third seat became policy for Specifications T.23/43 and T.7/45, in practice it was little used but side-by-side seating remained a feature of all future British training aircraft for the next forty years.

Four companies responded with tenders. Boulton Paul offered the P.106 which had a strut-braced low-wing monoplane powered by either a 210hp (156kW) Gipsy Queen II or a 200hp (149kW) Gipsy Queen III engine. The fabric-covered structure was designed for low cost and easy manufacture and repairability, the wings being easily covered by a fabric 'bag' that was slid over the wing. The tail fin and tailplanes were all-moving control surfaces and were fully interchangeable. The P.106A had side-by-side seating for the student and instructor, the P.106B added a third seat behind and the P.106C had tandem seating. Keen to provide a replacement for one of their products, de Havilland tendered the DH.105 which featured a bubble canopy for the cockpit. The Heston Aircraft Company offered the JC.1. Miles Aircraft Ltd. was another trainer specialist and in January 1944 submitted three designs powered by a mix of five engines. The M.53A made maximum use of M.38 Messenger parts and jigs and was offered with the Gipsy Six, Gipsy Queen II and Gipsy Queen IV engines. A twin-tail fin layout was proposed to offer the best spinning performance. The larger M.53B exceeded the requirements, being designed to be capable of carrying out advanced training and offered with a choice of powerplants; the Armstrong Siddeley Cheetah XIX, Gipsy Six and the Gipsy Queen IV. The larger cockpit had room for additional radio or navigation equipment if desired. The M.53C was basically a strengthened M.38 with a Gipsy Major III or an American Lycoming GO-435 as offered for the M.38. All three designs had the Miles extending aerofoil flaps to meet the low stalling speed requirement. In September 1944, George Miles offered the M.53D with a Gipsy Six III engine, an enlarged cockpit canopy and a single tailfin as tested on the M.38/28 prototype – a twin-fin unit was also offered.

The management of Percival Aircraft Limited had reached an agreement with F G Miles not to tender a design, in return for Miles not submitting their M.51 Minerva light airliner to the Brabazon 5B specification to allow Percival a clearer field for their P.48 Merganser. This gentleman's agreement did not last however, and T.23/43 Issue 2 covered Percival's private venture Type Aj design by Arthur Gage, which would become the P.40 Prentice. The Ministry of Aircraft Production assessors rated the P.40 and DH.105 highly enough to order five prototypes of each powered by a mix of Gipsy Queen 32 and 51 engines. The DH.105 prototypes were later cancelled and due to unavailability of the 296hp (220kW) Gipsy Queen 51, all five P.40 prototypes and six pre-production aircraft received the 251hp (187kW) Gipsy Queen 32.

Percival Prentice T.1 VR227 was completed in May 1948 and the majority of its RAF career was with the RAF College at Cranwell before being used by No 1 Air Signals School to train signallers between March 1954 and its retirement in August 1957. *Author's Collection*

The first prototype, serialled TV163, first flew on 31st March 1946 and before the trials programme was completed 444 Prentices had been ordered, 264 from Percival and 180 sub-contracted to Blackburn Aircraft at Brough to keep the factory in work following the cancellation of their Firebrand carrier-based torpedo-strike fighter. The third airframe built was a static test airframe, withstanding structural loads in excess of 10G during testing in 1947. Handling trials at the Aeroplane and Armament Experimental Establishment (A&AEE) at Boscombe Down and the Empire Flying School at Hullavington began in April 1947 and revealed that all was not well with the Prentice. The Prentice had poor lateral stability with the aircraft suddenly flicking inverted in even low-rate turns, poor spin recovery characteristics and aileron and rudder imbalances. The spin recovery problems proved the hardest to cure; anti-spin strakes made little difference, a lengthened rear fuselage was fitted to the fourth prototype, TV172, the first pre-production aircraft, VN684, received a new twin-tail unit and a series of raised tailplane positions were trialled on the second prototype, TV166. These trials lasted well into 1949. Later analysis showed that the large cockpit canopy had also caused aerodynamic problems – the cockpit was large; during the late 1950s Freddie Laker's Aviation Traders offered six and seven-seat civilian conversions! The low stalling speed requirement had also resulted in too many compromises in the design of the wings. The final solution was a combination of anti-spin strakes faired into the tailplane leading-edge, the rudder was increased in size, given greater movement and a trim tab and the new wingtips upturned by 30°. Spinning was only allowed with the canopy closed, flaps fully up and without an occupant in the rear seat but generally the recovery proved good after the modifications and there was good stall warning. Following instances of the flaps hitting the ground on landing at maximum deflection, the travel was limited to two stages.

The delays due to these design problems almost led to the cancellation of T.23/43 and the adoption of a revised elementary training syllabus using the Tiger Moth and de Havilland Canada Chipmunk instead. Although cancellation was avoided, the orders were reduced to 349 aircraft. The decision by de Havilland not to put the Gipsy Queen 51 engine into production meant that the tropical T.2 variant was limited to just one development aircraft, VR211 being built in late 1948. A further upgraded variant, the T.3 with a 345hp (257kW) Gipsy Queen 71, was developed for the Indian Air Force, twenty being completed by Percival and a further 50 by Hindustan Aircraft under licence. Several foreign air forces were interested in the Prentice and although successful winter trials in Canada failed to lead to an order from the Royal Canadian Air Force (RCAF), 100 were built for Argentina and three for the newly formed Lebanese Air Force, the company even designing their distinctive roundel.

Percival Prentice T.1 VR192 at the SBAC display held at Radlett in September 1947. This aircraft was the pattern aircraft supplied to Blackburn to aid the setting up of a second production line. Retired from RAF service in 1957 it was one of the few Prentices to be converted for civil use, as G-APIT. It went on display at the Brenzett Museum in Kent in 2019. *Terry Panopalis Collection*

Prentice T.1 VS639 at the SBAC Farnborough show in September 1949. This aircraft's service use was limited to its time with No 1 FTS between January 1952 and July 1954. *Terry Panopalis Collection*

The Prentice T.1 entered service with the Empire Flying School at Hullavington in August 1947 for service trials and the CFS at South Cerney re-equipping in July 1948, where the Prentice was used to train instructors. By 1949 the CFS was training 360 instructors a year. From September 1948, the RAF College at Cranwell began using the Prentice for basic training and soon five FTSs were equipped alongside ten RFSs providing refresher training as well as St Andrews, Edinburgh and Queen's UASs. Following the closure of all the RFSs in 1953 as an economy measure and replacement by the Percival Provost, the remaining Prentices were used for communications duties and the last RAF training unit equipped with the Prentice was the Air Signallers School until it closed in 1957. Although underpowered and sluggish, it proved a stable if uninspiring trainer and its cockpit was spacious with good all-around vision. Perhaps the last word should go to a No 7 FTS Operational Report which commented, 'It never really gained the affection of its pilots. The Prentice did not fail, it just did not inspire.'

Built by Blackburn, Prentice T.1 VS284 is seen here during its use by the RAF College at Cranwell during 1949-53. *Terry Panopalis Collection*

Canadian Chipmunk

Although the Prentice was being developed to replace the Tiger Moth as a basic trainer, it was clear that a new elementary trainer was also required to equip the numerous elementary and refresher training schools being reformed after the war. The Miles M.14A Magister during the war had equipped many of the EFTSs and had been used by every RAF Command, the FAA and even by the Army for training glider pilots. Most were quickly disposed of post-war and by the end of 1948 the last had departed RAF service. The Air Staff had issued Specification T.8/48 in January 1948 for a replacement, the Operational Requirement OR.260 not being finalised until May. The MoS invited tenders from industry for 100 aircraft with potential future orders bringing the total to 750. Two existing aircraft were tendered, the de Havilland Canada DHC-1 Chipmunk and the Fairey Primer. Boulton Paul and Percival considered tendering, but both companies instead focused their efforts on Specification T.16/48 for a Prentice replacement.

At the end of 1947 Boulton Paul's chief designer John Dudley North looked at converting the P.108 Balliol, developed to meet Specification T.7/45 for a turboprop-powered advanced trainer, into an elementary trainer. The resulting P.112 had a new fixed undercarriage and an Alvis Leonides Series IVM radial engine and retained the three-seat cockpit of the P.108 and around 80 percent of the original structure. The P.112A was similar but powered by a Pratt & Whitney R-1340 Wasp engine. By January 1948 it was clear that the Air Ministry was looking at the Chipmunk very favourably and as Specification T.8/48 was already written around that type, North considered that the larger P.112 was unlikely to win and formal tender was not made, although brochures were sent to the Ministries for informal feedback.

The RCAF's requirement for a modern monoplane Tiger Moth replacement had been met by de Haviland Canada's first indigenous design produced under the leadership of émigré Polish engineer Wsiewołod J Jakimiuk, the DHC-1 Chipmunk. The low wing monoplane had a fixed undercarriage and an enclosed tandem cockpit. The prototype, CF-DIO-X, was fitted with a 145hp (105kW) Gipsy Major 1C engine and made its first flight on 22nd May 1946 at Downsview, Toronto, piloted by seconded de Havilland test pilot Pat Fillingham. Development proceeded smoothly with

This General Arrangement drawing of the Boulton Paul P.112 shows the strong similarity with the P.108 Balliol on which it was based. *Les Whitehouse, Boulton Paul Archive*

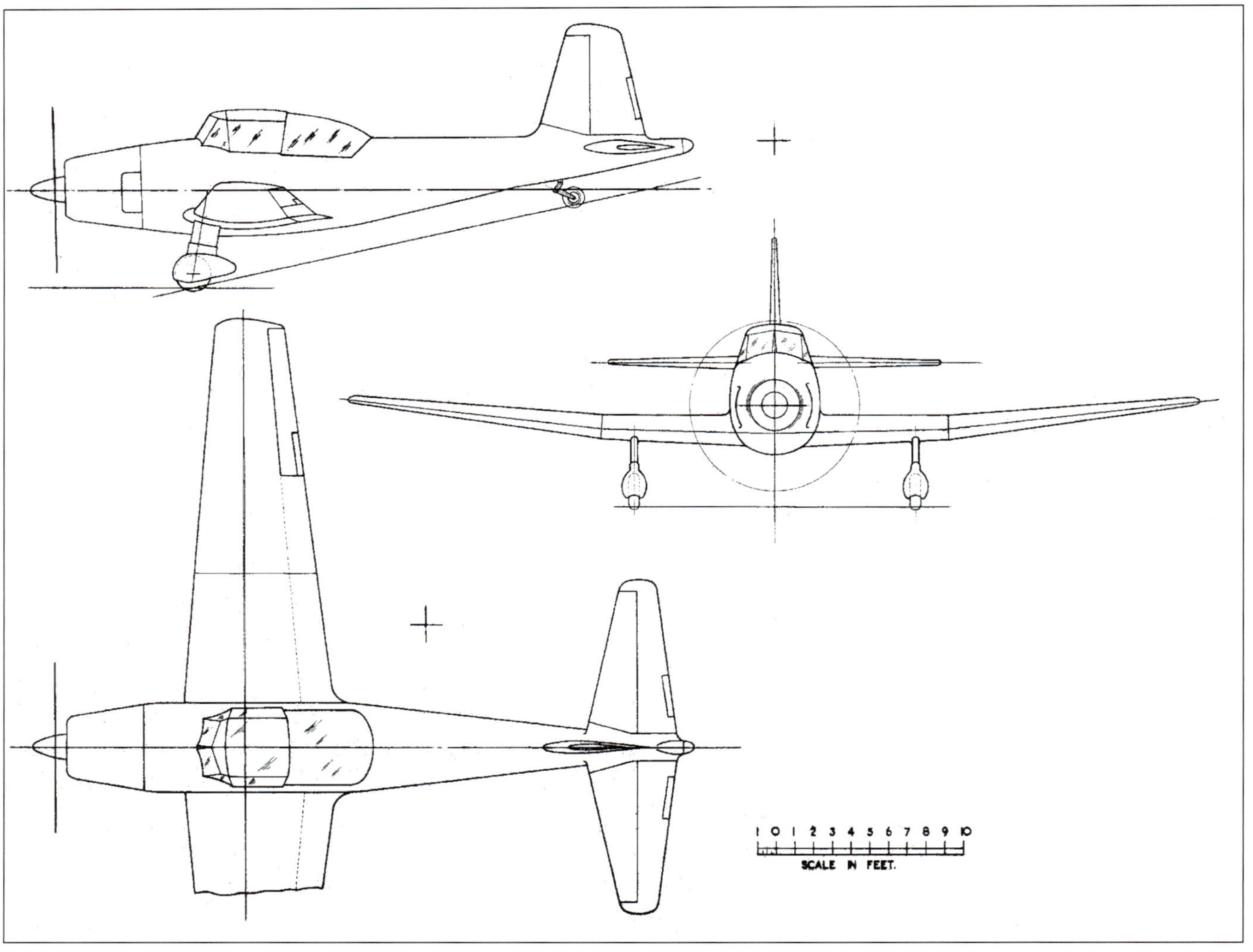

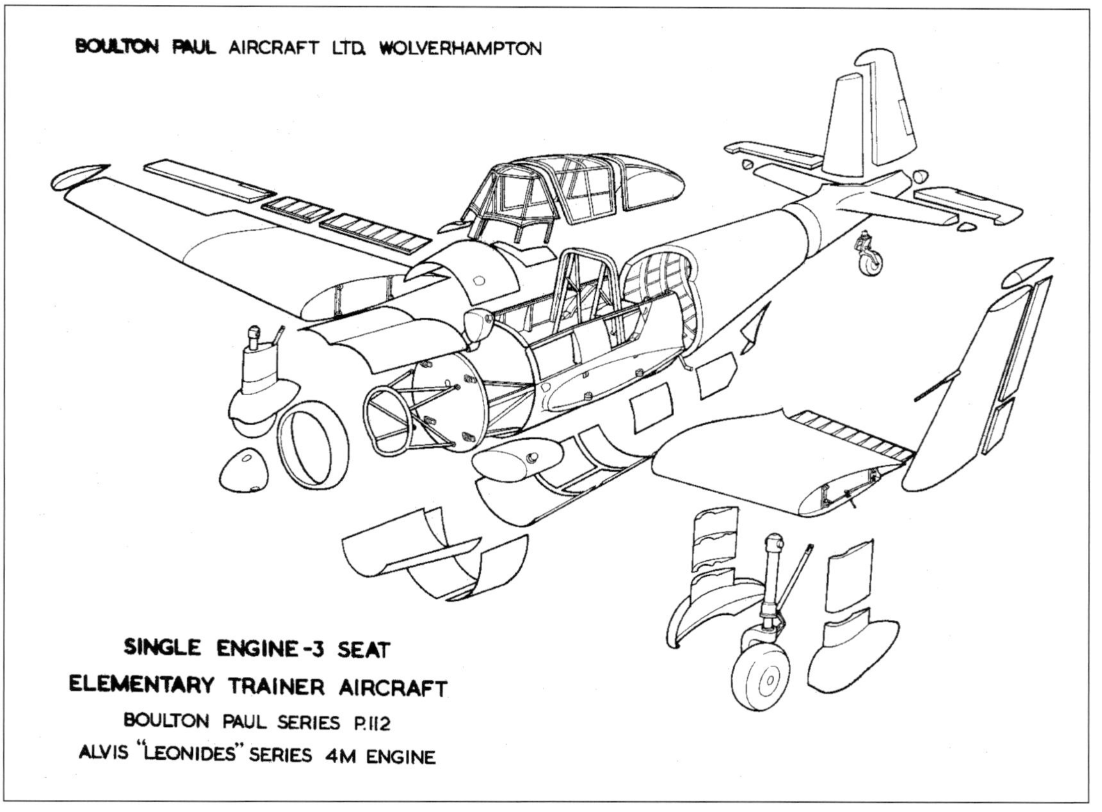

The P.112 shared 80 percent of its structural components with the Balliol, including its folding wings; originally designed for the Royal Navy's Sea Balliol and retained to ease ground handling and hangar storage. *Les Whitehouse, Boulton Paul Archive*

minor adjustments to the tailplane incidence, modified trim control gearing and inboard leading-edge stall strips to overcome an abrupt stall due to the use of the US 35B wing profile. The first of 113 production aircraft with Gipsy Major 10 engines ordered for the RCAF entered service in 1948. By this time the Chipmunk was already well known in Britain, indeed de Havilland had transferred CF-DIO-X to Hatfield as early as November 1946. The aircraft was reassembled, re-registered as G-AKEV and sent to the A&AEE at Boscombe Down for evaluation on 15 April 1947. The tenth production aircraft, serialled G-AJVD, undertook handling trials with the Empire Flying School's Research Flight at Hullavington in June 1947. Although some shortcomings were found with the instruments and the rudder effectiveness when flying aerobatics, it was rated by the Commandant Air Commodore E D Barnes as 'an excellent little aeroplane' which could be manoeuvred within safety limits suitable for elementary and reservist training alongside the Prentice. The eleventh aircraft, G-AKDN, was the first to be fitted with the Gipsy Major 10 engine and later acquired RAF specification instrument panels. This aircraft was demonstrated to the MoS and was evaluated by the A&AEE.

This airbrushed photograph of Balliol T.1 prototype VL892 by Boulton Paul's artists provides an impression of how the P.112 would have looked. The Alvis Leonides radial engine surprisingly does not mar the sleek lines of the Balliol. *Les Whitehouse, Boulton Paul Archive*

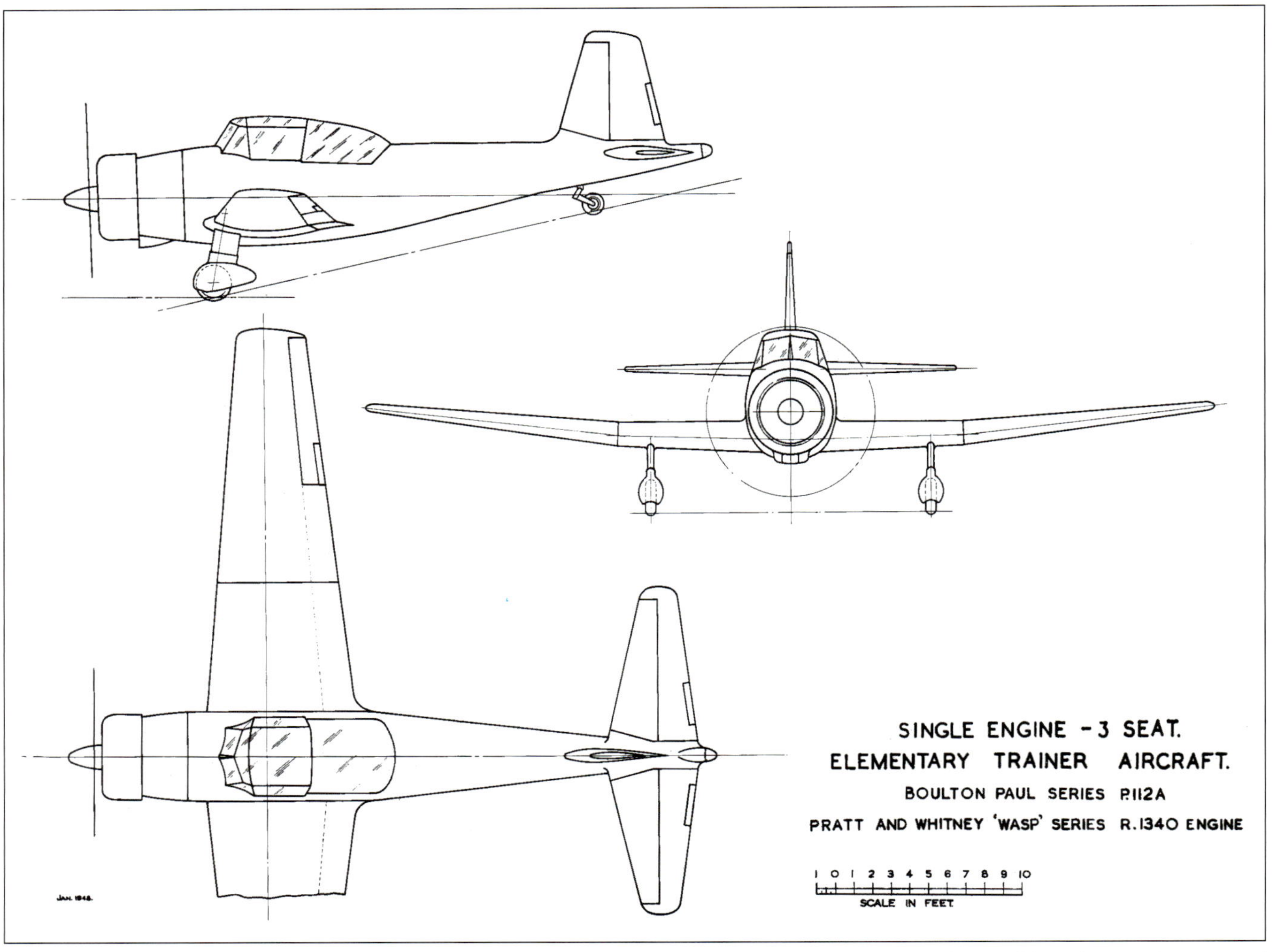

The P.112A was to be powered by a Pratt & Whitney R-1340 Wasp which was cheap to obtain on the world market, an important consideration for potential export buyers. *Les Whitehouse, Boulton Paul Archive*

Again, the assessment was favourable and the Air Ministry wrote Specification T.8/48 around the Chipmunk with suitable changes to meet RAF requirements. These included; the standard RAF instrument panel with full night flying equipment, a lightweight TR.1920 VHF radio and 'Two-Stage' amber blind flying training equipment using amber-coloured Perspex panels and blue-tinted goggles to simulate darkness for the student. The RAF had standardised its instrument panel layout in 1937, with a standard position for the six essential flight instruments; altimeter, airspeed indicator, turn and bank indicator, vertical speed indicator, artificial horizon and directional gyro/heading indicator. This minimised difficulties associated with blind flying during type conversion and the standard panel was fitted to everything from the Master and Anson to the Spitfire and Lancaster – but not the older Tiger Moth. Post-war, the arrangement was altered with the top row consisting of the airspeed indicator, artificial horizon and altimeter, and the bottom row having the turn and bank indicator, heading indicator and vertical speed indicator.

Fitting the more powerful 180hp (134kW) Blackburn Bombardier was briefly considered but rejected. There was only one major problem, insufficient structural strength factors at the required all-up weight (AUW). The strength factor was a measure of how the structure could withstand aerodynamic loads imposed during flight, especially during manoeuvres such as aerobatics while safely carrying a payload to ensure a good fatigue life and low risk of any structural failure. The quoted brochure figures were a strength factor of 9 at a maximum AUW of 1,562lb (708kg) for aerobatics and a factor 7.5 at 1,900lb (861kg) for both the normal flight and

Chipmunk T.10 WK642 of the Cambridge UAS, seen visiting North Weald in May 1961, shows well the anti-spin strakes that were added to the Chipmunk fleet from 1958. *John Wilkinson*

aerobatic categories. The MoS, however, estimated that a Chipmunk fitted with the necessary RAF equipment and with a student and instructor aboard would weigh 1,930lb (875kg). Even removing the instructor and all the fuel would only reduce the weight to 1,600lb (725kg), making the quoted strength factors impossible to attain! It was then discovered that it was not unusual for civilian Airworthiness Requirements Board aerobatic clearance to be issued at such impractically low weights. The MoS pointed out that the new generation of British trainers were designed for a strength factor of 10. Jakimiuk was summoned to Britain to see if the fuselage could be strengthened. After reassuring the MoS he returned to Canada and by March tests had confirmed that a fully aerobatic certificate of airworthiness could be issued for 1,930lb (785kg). This had been achieved by strengthening the wing spar and wing attachment points and redesigning elements of the fuselage centre section.

Further changes for the RAF included; additional fuel capacity, a redesigned canopy with repositioned release handles and repositioned undercarriage legs moved forwards by 9in (22cm) due to a forward shift in the centre of gravity. The selected engine was the Gipsy Major 8 with a Coffman cartridge starter, saving 3lb (1.3kg) over the Gipsy Major 10 with its electric starter. Most of these changes were incorporated into G-AJVD for evaluation during 1948.

The Fairey Primer was actually a pre-war design, the Tipsy M developed by Ernest Oscar Tips of Fairey Aviation's Belgian subsidiary, Avions Fairey. The Tipsy M was a conventional low-wing monoplane with a fixed undercarriage, the structure consisting of a welded metal frame with wooden ribs and stringers and fabric covered. The tandem cockpit was enclosed by a canopy. The prototype, OO-POM, was in Britain for flight tests even before the outbreak of the Second World War in September 1939 and remained at Fairey Aviation's Great West Aerodrome at Hounslow, although the drawings and jigs at Avions Fairey's Gosselies factory were destroyed during the German invasion in May 1940. Post-war, Fairey took OO-POM out of storage and decided to produce a batch of ten aircraft as the Fairey Primer.

Following modifications, including a 145hp (105kW) Gipsy Major 10 engine, the aircraft was re-registered G-AKSX but flown under Class B-Conditions markings G-6-1 until a certificate of airworthiness could be issued. Fairey supplied the aircraft for handling trials with the Empire Flying School and the A&AEE in May 1948. Like the Chipmunk it was found to be a pleasant aircraft to fly and good for aerobatics with benign stall characteristics. By the end of the summer G-AKSK had been dismantled to supply its engine and parts for the first two production Primers, G-ALBL which flew in October and G-ALEW (flown with B-Conditions markings G-6-5) which received a 155hp (115kW) Blackburn Cirrus Major 3 engine. The opportunity was also made to create a set of production drawings and jigs from the parts of G-AKSK to replace those destroyed in 1940. The MoS issued Specification T.17/48 to cover the Primer and in late November 1948 G-ALBL was sent to Boscombe Down for comparative trials against the Chipmunk. The Chipmunk was assessed to be more pleasant to fly, the Primer having a tendency to spin with a aft centre of gravity which could have been potentially dangerous when flown solo by an inexperienced pilot in rear cockpit. The 1930s-era steel and fabric structure was outmoded, it was easier to repair but was vulnerable to weathering, an important factor if used in tropical locations, and the fabric adhesive used was thought to be unreliable. Everything was in the Chipmunk's favour, except the costs.

In mid-May 1948 Fairey had tendered 100 Primers at £2,070 each and for further orders up to 750 this price would progressively fall to £1,320 for the final 250 aircraft with the first delivery within thirteen months of the contract award. De Havilland's bid was considerably more expensive at 100 Chipmunks for £4,400 with deliveries completed by March 1950, the price falling to £2,600 each for 750 over a five year production run. These prices were exclusive of MoS-supplied embodiment loan items such as engines, propellers, instruments and radios. By July both companies had re-estimated their bids. Fairey's price for 100 had increased slightly to £2,150 each and £1,380 each for the last 250 and by the end of the year had risen to £2,590 and £1,750. Desperate not to lose out on price, de Havilland finally offered a flat price of £2,100 each for any order over 100 aircraft. Although the MoS's Controller Air, Air Marshal Sir William Alec Coryton recommended ordering the Primer on the basis of cost alone, on 25th February 1949 an order was placed for 200 Chipmunk T.10s, all to be built in Britain at de Havilland's factory at Hatfield. Another order for another 100 followed in May and eventually 740 would be built, production later moving to Hawarden with Percival fitting out and assembling 100 Hatfield-built fuselages. The first production Chipmunk T.10 was WB549 flown on 26 August 1949. de Havilland Canada had switched to a broader chord rudder to increase the tail area before British production began, but Hatfield-built aircraft did not receive the modified rudder until 1951 and it took until 1954 to modify existing aircraft. The only other major aerodynamic change was the introduction of anti-spin strakes in 1958. de Havilland also built 217 Chipmunk Mk.20s for export with the Gipsy Major 10 and OGMA in Portugal licence-built another 66. The original de Havilland Canada production line at Downsview produced 217 Chipmunk T.1 and T.2 aircraft for the RCAF and export.

The initial deliveries began in February 1950 to the Oxford and Cambridge UASs and No 22 RFS at Cambridge. During the Korean War expansion five BFTSs and the Rhodesian Air Training Group were equipped with Chipmunks. The rapid reduction in training requirements after the war saw at least 200 Chipmunks put into storage and sold onto the civil market. Thirteen AEFs were formed with 60 of these stored airframes. The Chipmunk became ubiquitous across RAF units and airfields.

Left: Chocks Away! A student and instructor prepare to begin another training sortie. Chipmunk T.10 WK585 was shared between No 12 AEF and the East Lowlands UAS based at Turnhouse when this photograph was taken on 10th July 1977. With the canopy slid back, the snugness of the cockpit can be appreciated. *Charles E MacKay*

Below: The Chipmunk was a tri-Service aircraft, the FAA used the type for elementary flying grading before pilots joined the RAF's basic flying training course. Chipmunk T.10 WK635 was delivered to the RAF in June 1956 and was not transferred to the Navy until May 1971. It is seen here on the strength of Yeovilton's Station Flight. After being sold to private owners in the USA it returned to Britain in 2010 and today flies in its Royal Navy colours as G-HFRH. *Author's Collection*

Below: Chipmunk T.10s WB754 and WG432 in AAC service at Middle Wallop in 1961 in the standard 1960s trainer colours; all-over silver with 'dayglo' vinyl strips. Training aircraft during the latter 1950s began to receive 'dayglo' paint but this faded off in sunlight. To combat this the vinyl strips were used, although sometimes they peeled off! Sold in 1997, WB754 resides in South Africa as ZU-BJZ but WG432 is preserved with the Museum of Army Flying at Middle Wallop. *Bill Fisher*

No less than four members of the Royal Family would gain their wings on the 'Chippie'; Princes Michael, Philip, Andrew and Charles all flew T.10 WP903 between 1960 and 1969. The humble Chipmunk even became a spy plane. During the 1980s two Chipmunks, WB466 and WG486, of the Gatow Station Flight were used to conduct covert reconnaissance missions by BRIXMIS, the British Commander-in-Chief's Mission to the Group of Soviet Forces in Germany, flying within the 12nm (22km) radius of the Berlin Control Zone to obtain a bird's eye view of Soviet and East German military installations in the city. As the Chipmunk was replaced from 1973 by the Scottish Aviation Bulldog, the Chipmunk fleet was issued to the AEFs, the last leaving service in March 1996.

In 1953 eleven Chipmunk's were supplied to the Army's Light Aircraft School at Middle Wallop and when the Army Air Corps (AAC) was formed in September 1957, more were transferred from RAF stocks. The AAC operated a fleet of around 20 Chipmunks at the Elementary Flight at Middle Wallop until March 1997. The FAA did not receive their first Chipmunks until 1966 when twelve were issued to the Britannia Flight of the Britannia Royal Naval College at Dartmouth based at Roborough to provide air experience to naval officers (as late as 1956 the College had acquired four ex-civilian Tiger Moths for this role) and used the type until November 1994.

At the time of writing the Chipmunk remains in service with the RAF; Chipmunks WG486 and WK518 provide the pilots of the Battle of Britain Memorial Flight experience of tailwheel undercarriage aircraft. Until March 2019 the Royal Navy Historic Flight used WK608 in the same training role. Some still remain in use with Air Training Corps units and, incredibly, the Portuguese Air Force has been using six modernised Chipmunks for cadet pilot screening since 1997 at their Air Force Academy, clocking up 1,000 hours a year with no potential replacement yet offering the same economy of operation.

The AAC used the Chipmunk for training until 1997. T.10 WB693, seen here on display at Middle Wallop on 5th July 1984, was one of those retired in 1997 and headed to New Zealand as ZK-RFS. The red and white colour scheme was standard for RAF training aircraft from the 1970s to the late 1990s. *Don Hewins*

Training the Army

At the end of the war the RAF maintained the Airborne Observation Post (AOP) role using light aircraft like the Auster series. The AAC was formed in 1942 and by 1944 comprised the Glider Pilot Regiment, the Parachute Regiment, the Air Landing Regiments, the Special Air Service Regiment and the Air Observation Post Squadrons. In 1949 the Corps was broken up and the RAF took over responsibility for the AOP Squadrons. These were unique units with RAF groundcrews and staff but with pilots from the Army's Royal Artillery and working largely outside of RAF control as independent units supporting Army formations. This situation would last until the Glider Pilot Regiment was merged with the Air Observation Squadrons of the Royal Artillery

British Army aviation is closely linked to the Auster series of light aircraft and until the advent of helicopters remained an important asset for airborne observation. Auster AOP.6 WE559 is seen here at Middle Wallop on 23rd July 1960. The following year it was sold to Beagle Aircraft and rebuilt as an A.61 Terrier 2 and registered G-ASAD. *Robin A Walker*

The prototype Auster T.7 VF665 looks immaculate at the SBAC Farnborough show in September 1949. First flown on 20 April 1948, during 1958-60 it was converted into the Marshall MA.4 boundary-layer control research aircraft, being lost in a fatal crash on 9th March 1966. *Terry Panopalis Collection*

to reform an independent AAC in 1957. Basic flying training was conducted by the RAF. At Middle Wallop the RAF formed No 227 OCU as a dedicated AOP training unit to replace the former No 43 Operational Training Unit (OTU) at Andover, which had also gained a Helicopter Training Flight during 1945. The OCU became the Air Observation Post School in 1950 and the Light Aircraft School in 1952. To meet the demands for additional manpower during the Korean War, No 1912 AOP Flight was formed as the Continuation Training Flight to provide pilots with some continuation training after they graduated from the AOP School while they waited to be posted to a squadron overseas. During the 1960s, Airwork Limited operated the flying training fleet of Chipmunks and Hiller UH-12 helicopters at Middle Wallop.

In addition to the Tiger Moth, No 227 OCU would also receive a dual control variant of the Auster Type K, designated the AOP.6, which entered service in June 1946 to replace the wartime Auster Mk.V. The Type Q was the dual-control trainer variant with the same 145hp (105kW) Gipsy Major 7 engine and fitted with blind flying training equipment. The prototype, VF665, made its first flight in 1947 and 87 production Type Q aircraft followed as the Auster T.7. The T.7s were issued to also the AOP Flights for check flights. They were joined later by ten AOP.6s converted to a similar standard with dual controls, which were then re-designated as the T.10. The most famous T.7s were WE563 and WE600 which were modified as the Auster T.7 Antarctic for the 1956 Commonwealth Trans-Antarctic Expedition. They were fitted with extra radio equipment, larger tail surfaces, fittings for float or ski undercarriages and were painted bright orange to aid visibility. During 1958 VF665 was converted by Marshall of Cambridge into the Marshall MA.4 to meet Specification ER.184D to explore boundary-layer control by suction with the University of Cambridge. The aircraft received a new wing and a 60shp (44kW) Budworth gas turbine which drew air through 20,000 perforations in the wings, flaps and ailerons. A stronger undercarriage and an enlarged fin and rudder were also fitted. First flown in 1959, it sadly suffered a fatal crash near West Wratting, Suffolk on 8th March 1966 and was destroyed.

Developments during the latter part of the war and the early post-war years had set the training fleet on the right path and despite the early problem with the Prentice, elementary and basic training was soon being conducted on modern aircraft as the training organisation continually readjusted to the ebb and flow of the number of pilots required. The Chipmunk, Prentice and Auster were not advanced high-tech aircraft, they were simple but reliable aircraft intended to cope with the rough and tumble of training young students unused to flying and were designed for economy and reliability. In contrast, the Air Staff had something cutting edge planned for its future advanced trainer, an innovation that would prove to be far-sighted but too ambitious – the application of the gas turbine engine for training.

Chipmunk T.10 WK559 was delivered to the RAF in February 1952 and transferred to the AAC six years later. It is seen here at Middle Wallop in late 1961. In the background is another de Haviland Canada product, brand new DHC.2 Beaver AL.1s. These were used as liaison aircraft and for advanced flying training. Retired in 1997, WK559 is now preserved at the Military Aviation Museum, Virginia Beach, USA. *Bill Fisher*

2 The Turboprop Trainers

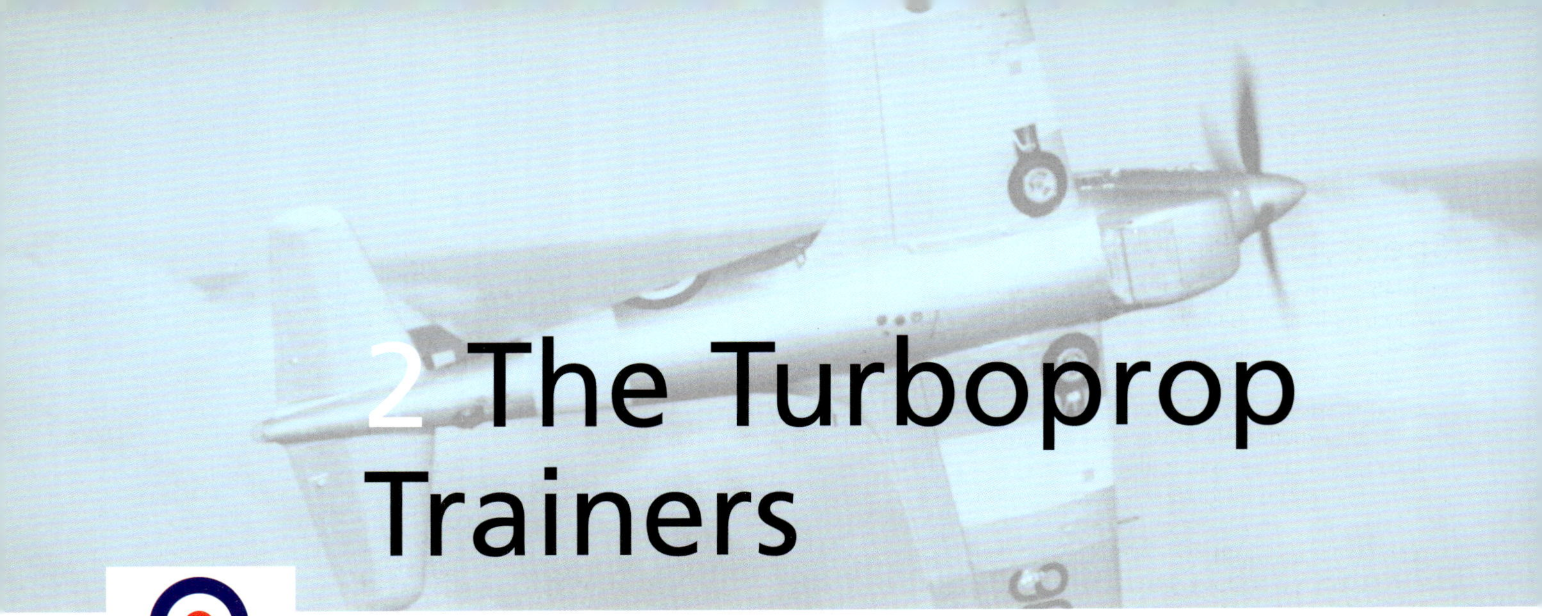

'If you accept our proposal, as I hope you will, for an advanced trainer with a turbine unit, you will only be anticipating the general introduction of turbine units for Service types.'
Air Vice-Marshal John Breakey, Assistant Chief of the Air Staff (Tactics and Requirements), April 1945

'We all were badly sold by the slogan "turbines for everything", which was the battle cry of the turbine prima donnas of about two years ago.'
Air Vice-Marshal John Boothman, Assistant Chief of the Air Staff (Tactics and Requirements), February 1947

'The set-back in the production of the T7/45 is, however, most disappointing as it means that our advanced trainers – whether they be Harvards or Martinets, will be getting pretty ropey by the time they are replaced by the T7/45. This, of course, has repercussions on maintenance as well as on morale.'
Air Chief Marshal Sir Leslie Hollinghurst, Air Member for Supply and Organisation, November 1946

Among the wartime specifications for new training aircraft, one was rather different in specifying a new form of propulsion. It would result in an advanced trainer that would form the backbone of the Flying Training Schools (FTS) during the early 1950s, but with a rather different engine from that originally planned. By early 1945 the Air Staff began to look towards the post-war replacement for its current advanced trainers; the Miles Master and the North American Harvard. Production of the Master had ceased in 1942 and decreasing stocks of spares would see the type retired beyond 1946. The Harvard had been supplied under a combination of pre-war direct purchases, taken-over French orders and Lend-Lease orders. With the country's Dollar reserves already strained, it was desirable to find a replacement from Britain's aircraft industry. The Air Staff approved Operational Requirement OR.159 and on 16th March 1945 Specification T.7/45 was issued to both A V Roe and Boulton Paul. The specification requested side-by-side seating for the instructor and the student but the novel feature was the powerplant; 'a propeller-turbine engine capable of 1,000 BHP at ground level', what today we would call a turboprop. This was the world's first turboprop-powered training aircraft and indeed the world's first single-engined turboprop-powered aircraft.

This promotional artwork of the Boulton Paul P.108 Balliol shows its close-cowled Armstrong Siddeley Mamba turboprop and the unusual three-seat layout that the Air Ministry had requested. In theory a newly arrived student could learn basic airmindedness from watching the instructor and the student pilot who was further along in training operating the controls. *Author's Collection*

Specifying the Future

In 1945 jet propulsion was the new cutting edge of aviation. It offered greatly increased performance and opened the way to high-speed flight at high altitudes. Dr Alan Arnold Griffith, the head of the Engine Department at the Royal Aircraft Establishment (RAE) had been experimenting with an axial-flow gas turbine that could be used to drive a propeller during the late 1930s and by 1945 Rolls-Royce were further developing work by Air Commodore Frank Whittle on turboprop engines with the RB.50 Trent, a converted RB.37 Derwent II turbojet fitted with reduction gear driving a 7ft 11in (2.41m) diameter Rotol five-bladed propeller. The main advantage of the turboprop over the early turbojets was that the propeller made it more efficient at lower altitudes, improved the power-to-weight ratio and decreased the take-off run. In April 1945 the Assistant Chief of the Air Staff (Tactics and Requirements) (ACAS(TR)), Air Vice-Marshal John D Breakey wrote a memorandum explaining the decision to use the turboprop engine on the RAF's future advanced trainer. He highlighted that out of the programme of new aircraft then being developed for post-war use, 18 out of the 22 aircraft were to be powered by either turbojets or turboprops. He considered that in future piston engines would only be considered for basic training and communications aircraft. Breakey, not unreasonably, made the case that since the fighter squadrons would be rapidly re-equipped with jet fighters like the Gloster Meteor and de Havilland Vampire, students should learn the new techniques of how to operate a jet engine in flight. The engine controls would be much simpler and Breakey dismissed concerns that students should learn the more complicated throttle, mixture and radiator controls of piston engines in case the new jet fighters were delayed in service. He proposed that if that did prove necessary, that obsolete piston-engined fighters could be used to provide such experience and argued that; 'the retention of a reciprocating engine in our advanced trainer solely for the enjoyment of engine complexity would be the height of conservatism.' Even though Breakey was writing five months before the converted Gloster Meteor F.1 EE227 made the world's maiden turboprop-powered flight with two RB.50 Trents, he would probably have been surprised that another 43 years would elapse before future RAF fighter pilots would get their hands on a turboprop-powered trainer, the Shorts Tucano.

Designing the Trainer of the Future

On 7th August 1945 Issue 2 of Specification T.7/45 was issued, calling for an advanced trainer capable of incorporating naval features such as folding wings and arrester gear. The requested roles were; dual flight instruction, advanced pilot training, dual gunnery training and dual bombing training using low-level, gliding and dive bombing profiles. The maximum speed was to be at least 182kt (337km/h) at 10,000ft (3,050m) with an endurance of at least 2.5 hours at the same altitude. A climb to 15,000ft (4,570m) should take no less than twelve minutes with a service ceiling of not less than 25,000ft (7,620m). Dive brakes would be used for a diving speed of not more than 489kt (563km/h). Provision for drop tanks was required as was a single 0.303in Browning machine gun with 1,000 rounds, a Mk.IID gyro gunsight and two light series carriers for eight 8lb (3.6kg) practice bombs. As well as the side-by-side seating, like Specification T.23/43 before it, provision for a third seat so a second student could observe the cockpit procedures was also requested.

The turboprop-powered trainers to Specification T.7/45 were to replace the piston-engined advanced trainers like the Miles Master Mk.III. DL630 was used by the A&AEE for trials on cylinder cooling, gun sights and the flaps. *Author's Collection*

Two turboprop engines then being developed proved suitable to meet the requirements; Armstrong Siddeley's ASMa Mamba and the Rolls-Royce RB.53 Dart. The production standard ASMa.3 Mamba was rated at 1,010shp (753kW) and had a 10-stage axial compressor, six combustion chambers and a two-stage axial power turbine. The epicyclic reduction gearbox was incorporated into the propeller spinner. The early prototype RDa.1 Dart was aimed at use in the T.7/45 trainers and soon achieved 1,250shp (932kW) (plus 300lbf (1.34kN) residual thrust). The Dart was developed using experience gained from the more powerful RB.39 Clyde and had a two-stage centrifugal compressor, seven combustion chambers and a two-stage axial turbine. Although the specification was originally only issued to Avro and Boulton Paul, both Blackburn Aircraft and Miles Aircraft also submitted tenders.

Avro submitted the Type 701, a sleek low-wing monoplane with retractable undercarriage and side-by-side cockpit seating and an all-metal structure. Given the inevitable uncertainties about which engine would be successful or be ready in time for production, Avro selected both the Mamba and Dart for the prototypes. The Mamba's jet exhaust ran beneath the cockpit floor and exited from the starboard side of the rear fuselage to counteract the propeller torque, the Dart's exhaust exited from a centrally-mounted ventral orifice. The two-spar wing was built in five sections and its aerofoil section was based on that of the Hawker Tempest fighter. The wing contained the undercarriage and the two 65gal

(295lit) fuel tanks. The armament training equipment consisted of a single 0.303in Browning machine gun with 300 rounds and two light bomb racks and the wing also had provision to carry two 45gal (204lit) drop tanks. A vertical F.24 camera could be carried in the rear fuselage.

Boulton Paul's P.108 was very similar in layout to Avro's design with a low-wing layout and a large cockpit for three seats. The third seat initially faced starboard but was soon moved to the centreline facing forwards to enable a better view of the instrument panel. This also enabled a larger canopy providing all-round vision, although the third seat was never fitted. Boulton Paul favoured the Dart and this was fitted in the nose with the exhaust on the starboard side of the rear fuselage. The all-metal structure was sturdy and designed to withstand a wheels-up landing with minimal damage. For commonality with the naval version, all production aircraft would have the facility for folding wings, which could carry two 45gal (204lit) drop tanks. To improve maintainability the tail fin, tailplanes, ailerons, elevators and main undercarriage legs were all interchangeable. No hydraulics were fitted – except to operate the windscreen wipers – as Boulton Paul believed that a pneumatic system was easier to maintain. The armament training equipment consisted of a single 0.303in Browning machine gun with 300 rounds and two light bomb racks. Fittings were also provided in the rear fuselage for glider towing. Boulton Paul also submitted a backup plan in case the turboprops failed to materialise in time, the largely identical P.109 which was powered by a Bristol Perseus radial engine.

Blackburn seems to have offered their B-52 design powered by either a Rolls-Royce Merlin or a Bristol Perseus radial piston engine.

The Miles M.70 was not an attractive looking design but had something that most trainers then lacked, staggered tandem cockpits. The instructor's cockpit was mounted higher for good all-around vision, especially during gunnery practice and landing. Although the Alvis Leonides was an interim solution until the turboprops were ready, several design changes were required; a tailwheel undercarriage, Miles Master-type rearward retracing mainwheels and reduced wing dihedral. *Author*

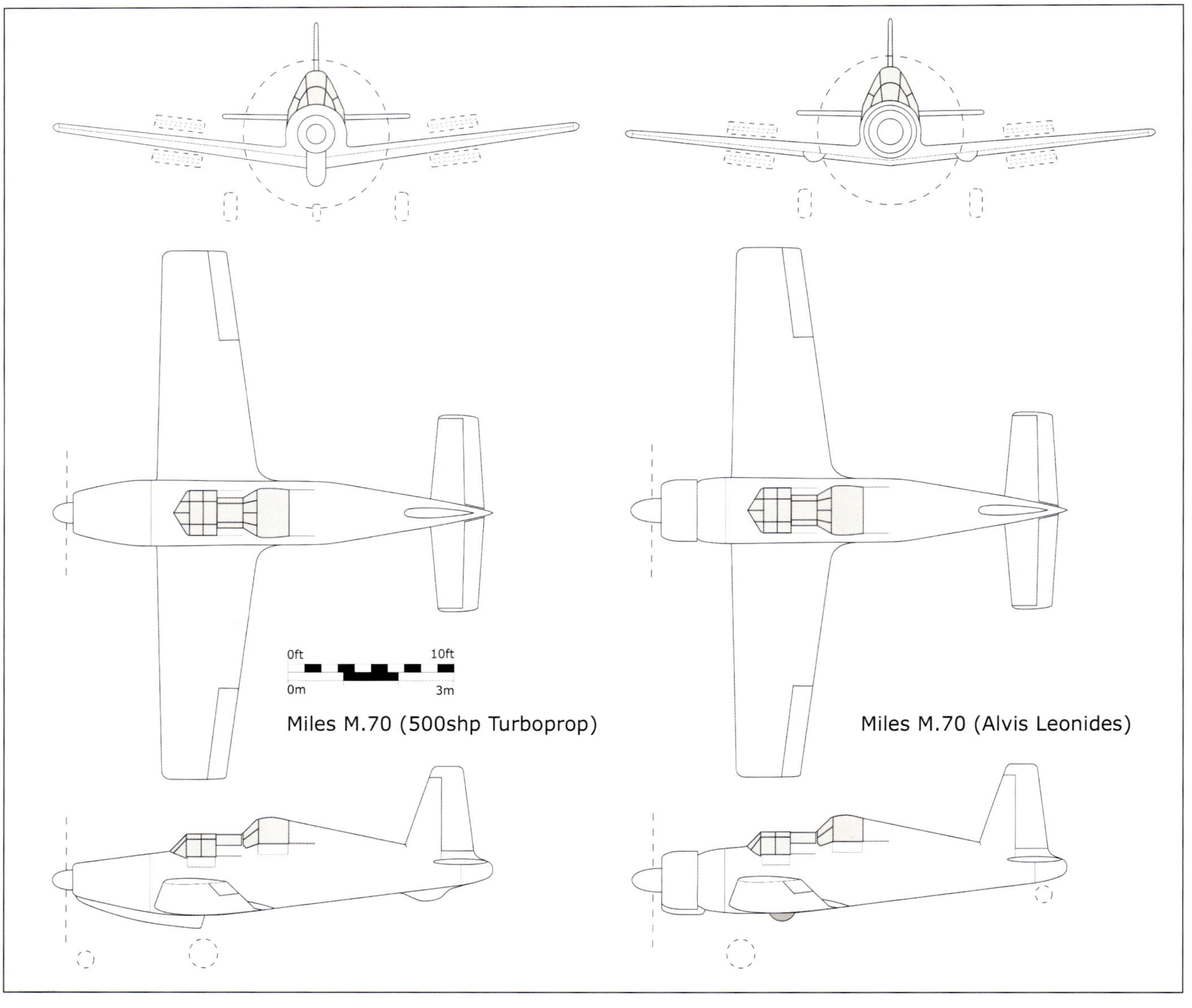

Miles took a different approach with their M.70 design. George Miles believed that a cheaper trainer was required with lower power. Accordingly the M.70 was designed around a 500shp (372kW) turboprop engine, either the Napier E.127 Nymph then being readied for bench testing or a similar unnamed design from Bristol. Showing prescience, Miles also offered an alternative Alvis Leonides radial engine installation should development of the turboprops be delayed. The instructor and student were in separate tandem cockpits, both cockpits being identical but the instructor's cockpit being mounted further aft and higher than the front cockpit. This layout had its roots in the M.29 Master V project of 1940 via the wartime M.31 Master IV and the M.37 Advanced Trainer which provided much useful aerodynamic and practical experience. The construction was all-metal, the wings having pneumatically-operated dive-brakes. The training equipment included a single 0.303in Browning machine gun with 300 rounds, a gyro gunsight, a G.24 gun camera and two light bomb racks. Full night flying instruments and two-stage amber blind flying equipment were fitted. The M.70 was not selected and neither of the small turboprops progressed beyond bench testing.

Avro and Boulton Paul had been the favoured companies to fulfil the specification from the beginning and on technical grounds the Air Staff and the Ministry of Supply (MoS) found little between the Type 701 and the P.108, although the P.108 was the favoured choice. Handling could only by judged by actual flight trials so prototypes of both types were ordered. Contracts for four prototypes of each type were issued to Boulton Paul on 27th August 1945 and to Avro on 11th September. In keeping with the Air Ministry's educational theme for training aircraft names, the P.108 was named the Balliol (after the Oxford University college) and the Type 701 the Athena (the Greek goddess of learning). Orders for a pre-production batch of 20 of each type followed in August 1946. Given the urgent need to start replacing the Harvard from 1948, the Air Ministry had no compunction about ordering two sets of production jigs and discarding a full set if either of the designs proved a failure after testing despite Britain being the midst of serious economic difficulties.

Interim Solutions

The main concern during the development of both aircraft was not the airframes but the engines. The Mamba was progressing the quickest, the Dart did not start bench trials until 1946 and did not fly until October 1947 in the nose of converted Avro Lancaster NG465. While the pre-production batches were split evenly between the two engines, all four P.108 prototypes were planned to receive the Mamba, Avro kept their prototype options open with an equal split between the two engines. Both the engines required a degree of redesign following early testing, the failure of the Mamba's reduction gearing being a particularly serious setback. Air Vice-Marshal John N Boothman, the new ACAS(TR), was concerned about the impact that any development delays would have on replacing the Harvard in time, it was estimated that there were sufficient numbers of Harvards to fulfil the training requirements until 1948, or 1949 at the latest. From the latest reports it seemed unlikely that either engine would enter pre-production until mid-1948 and given the need to have a fully reliable engine for training, it would be at least spring or summer 1949 before the training schools could start to receive the new aircraft.

During 1946 Boothman asked the MoS to issue a contract for Miles to convert two M.25 Martinet target tugs into advanced trainers as an interim type until the T.7/45 trainers were ready. A conversion programme would also provide much needed work for the Miles factory at Woodley. Miles had already been working on a conversion for the Fleet Air Arm (FAA) (see below) during 1945 and brushed off the plans as the M.37 Advanced Trainer. The conversion was identical to the earlier proposal for the Navy and the 870hp Bristol Mercury 30 radial engine was retained. With an all-up weight (AUW) of 5,600lb the maximum design diving speed would be 321kt (595km/h) with an endurance of 2.75 hours. Martinet HP413 was modified with a dummy rear cockpit for aerodynamic trials before JN725 completed its conversion and made its first flight as an M.37 on 11th April 1946. The second prototype JN668 followed in May. The flight trials went smoothly and no problems were encountered with

Table 2.1 – Avro Athena and Boulton Paul Balliol variants

	Miles M.70 (Napier E.127)	Miles M.70 (Leonides)	Avro Athena T.1	Avro Athena T.2	Boulton Paul Balliol T.1	Boulton Paul Balliol T.2
Wingspan	31ft 4in (9.55m)	31ft 4in (9.55m)	40ft (12.19m)	40ft (12.19m)	39ft 4in (11.98m)	39ft 4in (11.98m)
Length	26ft 2in (7.97m)	26ft 2in (7.97m)	37ft 3in (11.35m)	37ft 3.4in (11.36m)	?	35ft 1.5in (10.70m)
Wing Area	172ft² (15.97m²)	172ft² (15.97m²)	270ft² (25.08m²)	270ft² (25.08m²)	250ft² (23m²)	250ft² (23m²)
All-Up Weight	?	4,150lb (1,882kg)	7,191lb (3,621kg)	8,130lb (3,687kg)	7,845lb (3,558kg)	8,410lb (3,815kg)
Powerplant	E.127, 500shp (372kW)	Leonides, 500hp (372kW)	Mamba ASM.3, 1,010shp (753kW)	Merlin 35, 1,245hp (928kW)	Mamba ASM.3, 1,010shp (753kW)	Merlin 35, 1,245hp (928kW)
Max Speed/ Height	215kt (399km/h) at 10,000ft (3,050m)	212kt (394km/h) at 10,000ft (3,050m)	252kt (468kmh) at 20,000ft (6,100m)	254kt (471kmh) at 20,000ft (6,100m)	266kt (494km/h)	250kt (463km/h) at 9,000ft (2,700m)
Service Ceiling	42,600ft (12,985m)	28,000ft (8,535m)	?	29,000ft (8,840m)	?	32,500ft (9,900m)

Above: Some Martinets survived as target tugs until at least 1950. Two are seen here at Gibraltar on 5th February 1949, the same day that 773 NAS arrived aboard HMS *Theseus* and reformed as a Fleet Requirements Unit. In the background is an Avro Lancaster GR.3 of No 210 Squadron. *Author's Collection*

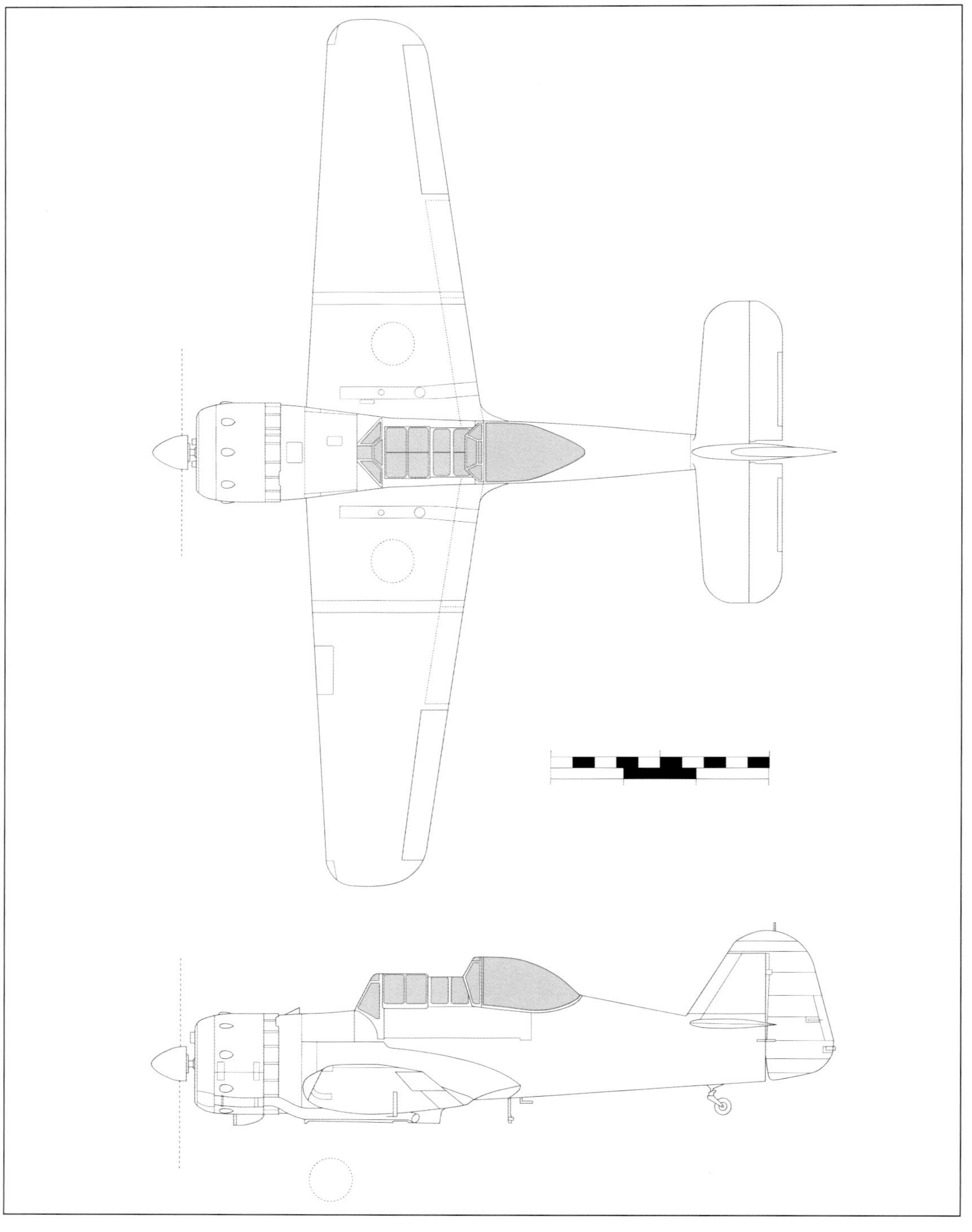

Both the RAF and the FAA looked at converting surplus Martinets into advanced trainers. The raised rear cockpit for the instructor was developed from two earlier projects based on the Miles Master; the M.29 Master V of 1940 and the M.31 Master IV. The resulting M.37 Advanced Trainer differed only in detail to the original proposal shown here. *Author*

the new cockpit profile during aerobatics, spinning or stalling. The Air Ministry's Air Member for Supply and Organisation, Air Chief Marshal Sir Leslie Hollinghurst, argued that converting Martinets was unjustified given that sufficient Harvards were available and pointed out that having two types in service would complicate servicing. Also, the Martinet was of wooden construction and many were rapidly deteriorating in condition while stored. By February 1947 another 177 Harvard IIA and Harvard III trainers had been brought back from South Africa as the Commonwealth Air Training Plan wound down and the need for a conversion programme passed and the M.37 was abandoned.

Delays to the Mamba turboprop forced Boulton Paul to redesign the engine mountings and forward fuselage of the first prototype Balliol T.1, VL892, for a Bristol Mercury 30 radial engine. The engine was removed from a Miles Martinet target tug that the company was using at the time. The original vertical tail and cockpit canopy seen here were later altered following the handling trials carried out with VL892. *Author's Collection*

Misled by the Turbine Prima Donnas?

Boothman and the aircraft companies were becoming increasingly concerned with the slow development of the turboprops despite the MoS arguing in February 1947 that the airframe delays were more serious and promising that engines would be available for the prototypes. This was proved untrue when Boulton Paul was forced to redesign its first prototype Balliol T.1, VL892 to fit a Bristol Mercury 30 radial engine taken out of a surplus Martinet. With this engine VL892 made its maiden flight at Pendeford on 30th May 1947 in the hands of the company's test pilot Lindsay Neale. The ability to test the handling and aerodynamics paid dividends as VL892 later received a new canopy and a dorsal fin extension. It would take almost a year before the second Balliol prototype, VL917, with a Mamba became the world's first single-engined turboprop aircraft to fly on 24th April 1948. Unfortunately, this aircraft soon suffered an accident when the propeller pitch-change mechanism failed as Neale was coming in to land, the aircraft ending up on its belly with the aircraft suffering a broken tail and Neale a broken leg. Avro's first prototype Athena T.1 powered by a Mamba, VM125, first flew from Woodford on 12th June 1948, followed by the only Dart-powered Athena T.1A, VM129, on 17th September 1949.

The Avro Athena with its intended Mamba turboprop was a sleek looking aircraft, this is the first prototype Athena T.1, VM125. *Blue Envoy Collection*

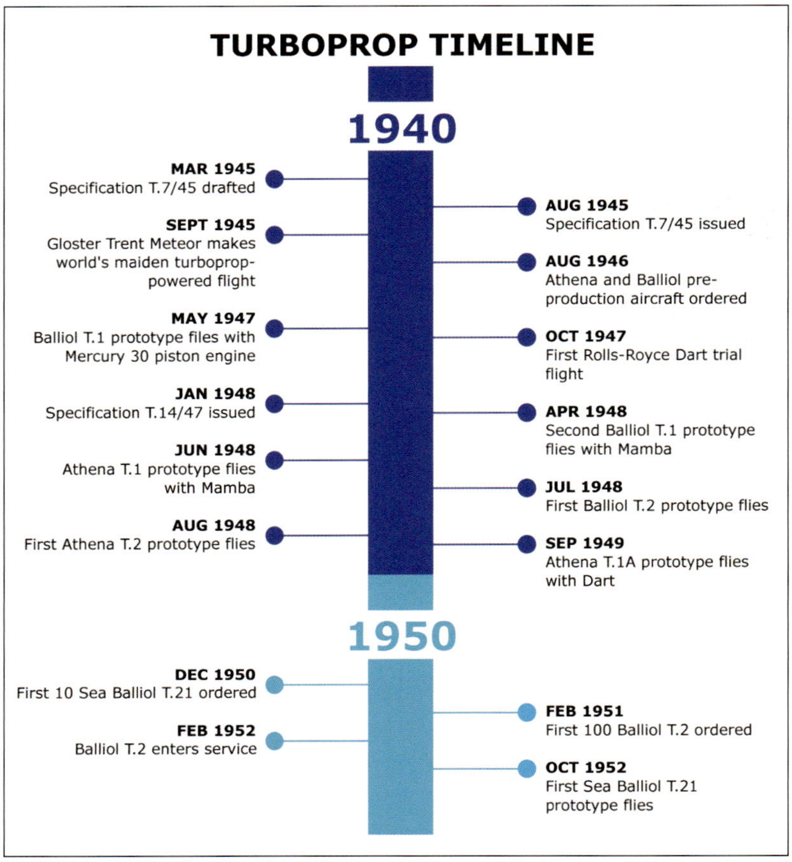

By the time the prototypes had flown Boothman had become completely disenchanted with the turboprop due to its increasing complexity and cost and outlined an alternative plan in a strongly-worded memorandum in February 1947. A single Mamba needed 2,500 compressor and turbine blades and at a price of between £1 and £7 for each blade these alone would cost at least £2,500! Boothman estimated that a complete production Mamba would cost between £7,000 to £8,000. At this time the Rolls-Royce Merlin only cost £2,000 and was still in production with plentiful stocks of engines and spares. Thousands of Bristol Pegasus and Mercury radials were still held in storage too. Using stocks of the stored Merlin 24 in 700 aircraft would save £3.5 million. Boothman pulled no punches in advocating a change in powerplant; 'We all were badly sold by the slogan "turbines for everything", which was the battle cry of the turbine prima donnas of about two years ago. At that time the turbine was promised as a less complicated piece of mechanics and cheap to produce, and easy to design. Since that day the prima donnas have retired somewhat from the scene and have left the practical engineers to further their projects. It is now that we are finding out the troubles.' Unknown to Boothman then, it would be another year before the Mamba would complete its 150-hour type test.

Sir Alec Coryton, the MoS's Controller Air, outlined three modification options for the Merlin 24; Scheme I fitted the supercharger from the Merlin 32 with 0.471 ratio reduction gear and an

Athena T.1 VM125 on the ground shows the relatively tall landing gear and the jet exhaust port in the rear fuselage. *Author's Collection*

improved overhaul life of 360 hours, Scheme II was identical but with a 500 hour overhaul life and Scheme III would also use Merlin 621 cylinder blocks with the latest valves for an anticipated 1,000 hour overhaul life – a similar upgrade being carried out on the Merlin 24s fitted to Avro York transports to increase their overhaul life. The more expensive Scheme III was not considered worthwhile as it seemed unlikely that the trainers would last in service long enough to accrue 1,000 hours between overhauls and Scheme II was selected instead. This resulted in the 1,280 hp (954 kW) Merlin 35.

The Merlin Works Its Magic

On 16th January 1948 Specification T.7/45 was superseded by T.14/47 which specified the use of the Merlin 35, the Merlin-powered variants being designated T.2. The speed at maximum cruising power was to be at least 183kt (338km/h) at 10,000ft (3,050m) with an endurance of 2.5 hours. Provision for the third seat was eliminated but the hydraulic air brakes were retained. The fourth Balliol and Athena prototypes were cancelled and the pre-production batches were cut to seventeen aircraft each. The price of the Merlin 35 worked out nearer £4,000 following modification and in September the MoS tried to convince the Air Staff that the Mamba could now be procured for £5,500 but Boothman's successor, Air Vice-Marshal Claude Pelly declined as; 'the RAF has no real need to train itself in the use of the turbine/propeller type.' The need for a turboprop trainer raised in 1945 had already proved to be illusory. The lustre of jet power had forced the premature adoption of novel technology before the RAF even had any frontline aircraft powered by turboprops. The RAF's first purpose-built turboprop-powered aircraft would be the Armstrong Whitworth AW.660 Argosy tactical transport which entered service in 1960.

The Balliol and the Athena required varying degrees of redesign to accommodate the heavier Merlin, not least losing their sleek cowlings and gaining bulky looking chin radiators. The Balliol had relatively few changes beyond the new engine mounts and cowling; the underfloor space for the jet exhaust piping being used for the relocated fuselage fuel tank and the rear fuselage vent being becoming an access panel for maintenance. The Athena required more significant redesign; the wing was moved forwards by 27in (68.5cm) to restore the centre of gravity, the flying control layout also being changed. The ventral access doors for ground servicing were removed and access to the electrical services and flying controls provided via the undercarriage doors. The fuselage fuel tank was moved to the wing centre section between the spars which simplified the fuel system and removed the need for a selector cock. The opportunity was also taken to remove the third cockpit seat and reposition the radio equipment to the space freed up, which also allowed the canopy to be shortened to reduce drag. The prototype Balliol T.2 VW897 was first flown on 10th July 1948, the first Athena T.2, VW890, following on 1st August 1948. Handling tests with the Athena revealed that greater fin and rudder area was required and T.2 VW891 tested a new taller fin with a dorsal fin and a balanced rudder. These modifications were incorporated to the production aircraft. The Balliol had also gained a dorsal fin and the tailplane incidence was altered.

The Rolls-Royce Merlin with its chin-mounted radiator turned the sleek P.108 into a pugnacious looking aircraft. This is the third prototype Balliol T.2, VW899. ***Author's Collection***

Trials of both types were marred by accidents. Balliol T.2 prototype VW897 was destroyed during tests to cure elevator reversal in out-of-trim dives at speeds above 278kt (514km/h). Whilst diving at 347kt (643km/h) the windscreen collapsed and the plane dived into the ground near Wolverhampton, killing both test pilots aboard, Lindsay Neale and Peter Tisshaw. The first Athena T.2 prototype, VW890, suffered an undercarriage collapse in August 1948 and during handling trials at the Aeroplane and Armament Experimental Establishment (A&AEE) at Boscombe Down in June 1949, it lost part of its tail fin and rudder during the first spinning test. The first Athena T.1 prototype VM125 was written off in an accident shortly afterwards on 30th August.

The main A&AEE assessor, Wing Commander Tom Neil, found that both types generally handled well, although the Balliol suffered from pitching during spinning. The Boscombe Down evaluation was a competitive trial to decide which would be ordered into service. The Central Flying School (CFS) carried out their evaluation in October 1949 on two aircraft of each type and considered that the Balliol had crisper handling that allowed the student to exploit their ability better and to learn how to fly with precision. The Athena had high weathercock stability but less effective ailerons and the heavy rudder foot loads prevented smooth aerobatics. The A&AEE thought that the Athena's longitudinal stability was too great at high speed with trim changes during diving and that there was inadequate stall warning, both of which would require fundamental design changes to cure. Spinning to port was equally unpleasant on both types but the Balliol was preferred. The Balliol was also faster but the CFS felt that the Athena was superior above 20,000ft (6,100m). The Handling Squadron of the RAF Flying College at Manby also made an assessment. The results of gunnery trials at Central Gunnery School at Leconfield were also evenly rated but the Balliol's wing folding which gave easy access to the gun for servicing and reloading was preferred. A request by the School to consider fitting two 0.5in calibre machine guns was resisted. Despite numerous changes agreed with the Air Staff, both cockpits were still not entirely satisfactory, the Athena's instrument panel being too close and low to the pilot and the assessors having problems flying blind with pupil's instrument in the Balliol. From an engineering perspective the servicing man-hours per flying hour were a third higher for the Athena and tyre wear was also greater. Tropical and hot-and-high trials were successfully held at Khartoum, Sudan and Eastleigh, Kenya, in temperatures up to and exceeding 35°C (95°F).

Satisfied that the Balliol was the superior choice, the MoS placed an order for 100 T.2s on 20th February 1951 and as the rearmament programme got into full stride another 138 were ordered from Boulton Paul and 120 from Blackburn. The Air Staff's expansion and rearmament plan in response to the Korean War, Plan H of July 1951, briefly boosted the required numbers of Balliols to 502 before the subsequent, and smaller, Plan K of 1952 cancelled all 120 Blackburn-built and 225 Boulton Paul-built Balliols. This was partly to save money and partly because Flying Training Command was now settling into its Percival Provost and de Havilland Vampire T.11 flying training syllabus. The delays from the switch of engines meant that by the time production was underway that the Balliol was becoming overtaken by other developments as the use of turbojets for advanced training had now

The second prototype Athena T.2, VW891, is seen here at the A&AEE, Boscombe Down, on 25th August 1949. It was used for trials at Avro and at the Telecommunications Research Establishment, being scrapped in 1952. *Author's Collection*

Balliol T.2 VR596 is in the standard early post-war training colour scheme of all-over silver with yellow bands on the wings and rear fuselage. This aircraft was in use with the Central Fighter Establishment when it was involved in a fatal accident on 14th August 1952. Following engine failure the crew attempted to bail out, the navigator, Flying Officer Michael Frank Wheatley, jumped clear but his parachute failed to deploy correctly and he was killed. The pilot, Major C H Fairburn, USAF, was forced back into the cockpit by an unexpected surge of engine power but survived the resulting crash east of Castle Rising, near Kings Lynn, Norfolk. *Author's Collection*

become possible. Only 161 Balliols were completed by Boulton Paul and 30 by Blackburn. The Athena had already received a contract for 20 aircraft in August 1946, three had already been cancelled in January 1948 but eighteen were completed as T.2s, the last two airframes being cancelled in 1951. Eleven were used for armament training at the RAF Flying College at Manby equipped with underwing racks for four 3in (76mm) rocket projectiles between June 1950 and September 1955. The Empire Test Pilots School made use of two Athenas for short periods separately in 1950 and 1951. The Athena was pleasant to fly and the equal of the Balliol, but its small production run hindered any chance of intensive use and the switch to an all-jet training fleet in 1953 spelled the end of both the Athena and the Balliol within a few short years.

Originally intended as the RAF's main advanced trainer, the Balliol's delayed entry into service from 1948 to 1952 coincided with the shift to jet-powered advanced training and only No 7 FTS at Cottesmore was completely equipped with the type, operating it until its disbandment in mid-1954. Others served in varying numbers with No 2 FTS at Hullavington and No 6 FTS at Tern Hill. Students flew a syllabus of 120 hours following their initial 60 hours on the Percival Prentice. The aircraft's main vice was the vicious torque stall if engine power was applied too quickly, especially during overshoots on landing when a wingtip could hit the ground. The last major user was the RAF College at Cranwell until the end of 1955. Other training roles saw around twenty Balliols progressively used by No 288 Squadron – the Fighter Command Control and Reporting School – at Middle Wallop, the Civil Anti-Aircraft Co-operation Unit at Exeter and the School of Flying Control at Sopley, the latter Balliol fleet being operated and maintained by Airwork Limited under contract. The Durham University Air Squadron also received surplus Balliols, No 228 OCU at Leeming only used Balliols in a support role while thirty Balliols were used as airborne targets with No 238 OCU which trained all-weather fighter radar operators.

The third Athena T.2, WV892 at the 1949 SBAC Farnborough show. First flown on 25th August 1949, it was written off when accidentally landed with the undercarriage retracted at Boscombe Down on 10th April 1952. *Terry Panopalis Collection*

Balliol T.2 WG178 is seen here during its tenure with No 238 OCU, where it was used as an airborne target for the OCU's student all-weather fighter radar operators flying in Bristol Brigands. The yellow canopy Perspex is part of the two-stage amber blind flying equipment, which combined with the pilot's blue-tinted goggles gave an excellent impression of a dark nocturnal sky during the daytime. *Terry Panopalis Collection*

This airbrushed photograph of Balliol T.2 prototype VL899 provides an impression of how the Balliol T.2A would have looked with the Pratt & Whitney R-1820 Cyclone radial engine. The T.2A was aimed at potential export customers looking to replace their North American Harvards.
Les Whitehouse, Boulton Paul Archive

Boulton Paul devised a further Balliol variant, the T.2A powered by a 1,200hp (894kW) Pratt & Whitney R-1820 Cyclone radial engine. The T.2A was intended for export; the cancellation of RAF orders required the company to look at ways of selling surplus airframes on the production line. Interest in the Balliol from the Middle East and India required an engine with better hot-and-high performance and many of these nations were already satisfied Harvard operators, making the Cyclone an attractive choice. India also looked at the Mercury as fitted to T.1 VL892 but events conspired against the T.2A. North American restarted Harvard production which undercut the T.2A on cost and the number of surplus T.2 airframes were much less than forecast. This lack of surplus airframes complicated an order for twelve T.2s for the Royal Ceylon Air Force, which required five aircraft diverted from the production line (the MoS ordering five replacements for the RAF) in addition to seven transferred from RAF stocks at No 9 Maintenance Unit at Cosford. Athena T.2 VR569 was loaned back to Avro with the civil registration G-ALWA for a demonstration tour of India in early 1950, but no interest resulted. A six-month long trial with the Balliol at Nellis Air Force Base, Nevada, in cooperation with the US Air Force during 1950 failed to convince them of the efficacy of the side-by-side layout compared with the new North American T-28 Trojan with tandem seating. One of the aircraft, VR601, crashed at Nellis due to engine failure on 5th October during the trials. Ironically, three decades later the US Air Force would insist on side-by-side seating for its Next Generation Trainer for basic flying training while the RAF would staunchly revert to tandem seating.

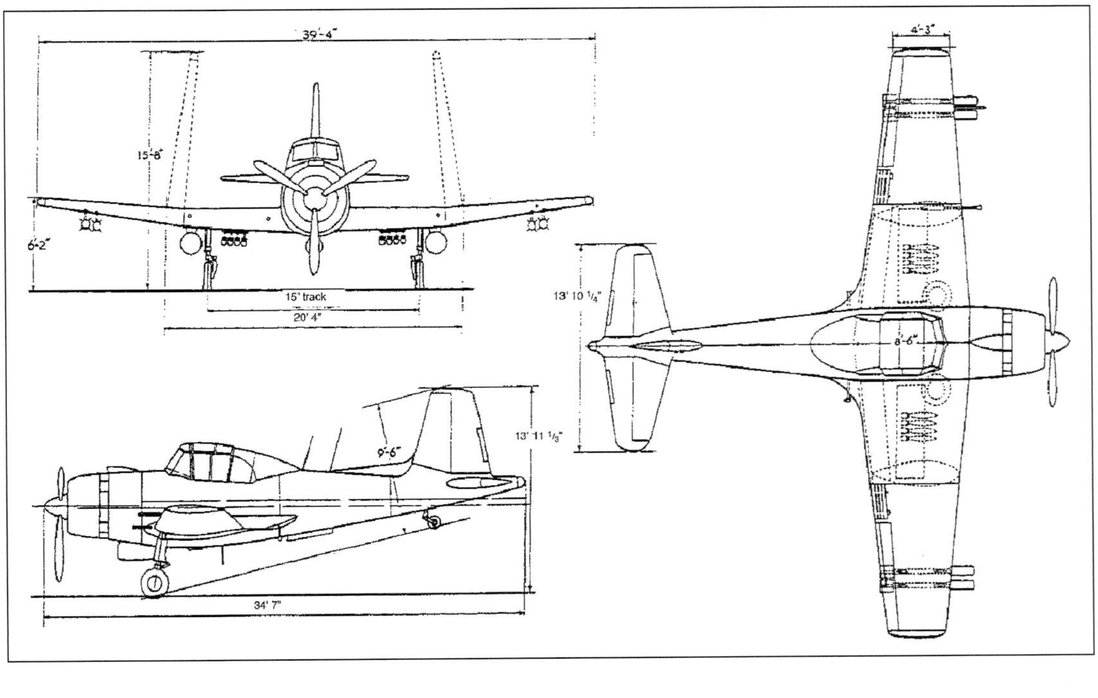

This general arrangement drawing shows the range of armament options that could be fitted to the Balliol T.2A; one machine gun in the port wing, four 3in (76mm) rocket projectiles and racks for up to eight 20lb (9kg) bombs as well as two drop tanks.
Les Whitehouse, Boulton Paul Archive

Balliol T.2 VR599 was converted to become the prototype Sea Balliol T.21. The most obvious visible difference is the arrester hook beneath the tail. *Author's Collection*

Fly Navy, Train Navy

From the beginning T.7/45 had included provision for naval use with folding wings and arrester gear for use with the FAA and naval representatives had met with Avro and Boulton Paul in December 1945 to discuss their requirements. The Navy was keen to keep the provision for towing a glider or target. The main additional requirement was taking off from an aircraft carrier flight deck, the maximum run being 250ft (76m) into a 27kt (50km/h) headwind at the normal AUW. Provision for Rocket-Assisted Take-Off Gear (RATOG) or tail down accelerating (catapult launching) was not required. The Admiralty agreed to choose whichever design the RAF selected. The width and height with the wings folded was important for hangar stowage aboard an aircraft carrier; the P.108 had a folded width of 24ft (7.3m) and a height of 14ft 9in (4.5m), the Avro Type 701 being slightly smaller at 18ft 6in (5.6m) and 14ft 9in (4.5m) respectively. The Navy was worried that the Type 701's original twin jet exhausts would affect the deck crew safely disengaging the arrester wire from the hook unless a remote or piloted-operated release was used. The fourth Balliol and Athena prototypes were originally planned to be fitted with arrester gear but in October 1946 the Navy changed its requirements, no longer planning to operate the trainers from its carriers. Boulton Paul elected to keep the folding wings for all production aircraft and the Navy retained the arrester hook for use on dummy landing decks equipped with arrester wires on dry land for deck landing training role.

On the release of Specification T.14/47 with the change to the Merlin 35, the Admiralty issued the equivalent Naval Requirement NR/A.11 and Specification N.102D, which was issued on 26th August 1950. The differences were mainly related to equipment; the addition of a homing beacon receiver, navigation using an ATMC.III compass and a chart board, provision for a G Type compass, full naval night flying equipment, an extra oblique F.24 camera and provision for a Type J target towing winch. Light series racks were provided for eight 25lb (11.3kg) With the RAF selecting the Balliol, Boulton Paul now finalised the Sea Balliol's design. The propeller diameter could not exceed 10ft 6in (3.2m) and fitting a new five-bladed Rotol propeller was not cost effective so the blades of the existing de Havilland four-blade propeller were cropped. A beefed up undercarriage capable of withstanding a descent of 14ft/sec (4.2m/sec) was also required and this led to further redesign of the inboard wing leading-edge. Material shortages delayed the completion of the undercarriage and the naval prototype by six months. By July 1950 the Treasury

Sea Balliol T.21 WL721 is seen here at Lee-on-Solent on 31st August 1957 when it was assigned to 781 NAS, the Royal Navy's Southern Communications Squadron. Stored from 1960 it was scrapped four years later. *Robin A Walker*

had approved ten production Sea Balliol T.21 aircraft, soon increased to 20 which were ordered in December (another ten followed in February 1951) and two pre-production Balliols, VR596 and VR598, were modified with arrester hooks. Following tests at the RAE to prove the modification, they were used for deck landing trials during November 1950 aboard HMS *Illustrious*, which was at that time serving as the Navy's dedicated training and experimental research carrier. Another pre-production aircraft, VR599, received all the intended naval modifications to serve as the Sea Balliol T.21 prototype, making its maiden flight on 23rd October 1952. Although the estimated requirement was for 60 aircraft, only 30 were actually ordered and these equipped several training and Royal Naval Volunteer Reserve squadrons.

Conversions Galore

The Navy had shared the same worries about replacing the Harvard, especially since they lacked the option to switch to the Miles Master, all of which belonged to the RAF. The FAA did have a fleet of Miles M.25 Martinet target tugs, however, and they asked Miles to develop a conversion to enable them to be used as advanced trainers. The conversion involved removing the outer wing fuel tanks and the installation of a separate cockpit with a bubble canopy for the instructor replacing the former winch operator's cockpit. The cockpit would be mounted higher to give the instructor excellent all-round vision and had identical controls to the front cockpit. The 870hp Bristol Mercury 30 radial engine was kept and conversion would take around 1,500 man-hours to complete. The Admiralty's Director of Air Warfare and Flying Training was in favour of the Martinet conversion but by October 1945 no decision had yet taken whether the Navy would take over its own basic flying training from the RAF. A tentative Training Aircraft Establishment of 200 aircraft to be maintained until 1948 would have required a total of 450 aircraft to cover the likely wastage rates. At that time only 215 Harvards, 43 Master Mk.II and 168 Martinets were held in Britain, with another 116 Martinets returning from overseas. A conversion plan for 120 Martinets was outlined but the Admiralty became worried that the RAF might have the same idea and try to take over the available stocks of Martinets, seemingly unaware that the Air Staff had indeed asked Miles for the same conversion as the M.37 Advanced Trainer. Inspection of the available stored airframes at Evanton and Renfrew Airport did not begin until April 1946. Many of them had been stored outdoors or had seen service in the harsh conditions of the Mediterranean or South Africa and accordingly were in very poor condition; of the 462 available airframes only 84 were deemed suitable for conversion. Shortly afterwards it was decided to rely on the Harvard for as long as spares could be obtained and the conversion programme was abandoned.

The Fairey Firefly two-seat carrier-based fighter had been briefly considered for conversion in 1945 but rejected due to the greater cost and time that would be incurred compared to the Martinet. Fairey Aviation went ahead on a private-venture basis. The conversion consisted of a new rear cockpit raised by 12in (30.5cm) with a separate windscreen and canopy replacing the original observer's cockpit. Early production Firefly FR.1 Z2033 was given a mock-up rear cockpit for aerodynamic trials and was flown on 29 May 1946. FR.1 MB750 was converted into the true prototype fitted with a complete and fully equipped rear cockpit with dual controls and was flown in July. From 1947 Fairey converted 34 F.1 and FR.1 airframes that had been earmarked for repair. The first nine conversions retained two 20mm Hispano cannon but the remainder had all armament removed and all received 1,720hp (1,282kW) Rolls-Royce Griffon XII engines. They were first issued to 736 Naval Air Squadron (NAS), the Naval Air Fighter School at St Merryn, being replaced in February 1950 by the Sea Fury T.20. They were passed to 764 NAS and 766 NAS at Lossiemouth, being used on a syllabus of 70 hours of advanced training until the mid-1950s.

The T.1 was followed by the T.2 for tactical weapons training. Similar to the T.1, it retained two 20mm Hispano cannon and well as underwing racks for 500lb (226kg) bombs, practice bombs, mines flares and smoke floats. Both cockpits were fitted with gunsights. Fairey's Stockport factory carried out 57 conversions from 1949. The main user was 737 NAS, the Naval Air Anti-Submarine School at Eglinton, where they were used for the instrument flying and anti-submarine weapons phases of the Operational Flying School Training Course. They were replaced by the Fairey Gannet AS.1 and T.2 in the mid-1950s. Others were issued to 764 NAS and 766 NAS at Lossiemouth and 765 NAS at Culdrose, the Piston Engine Pilot Pool, still had T.2s on strength as late as 1957. The T.3 and T.7 conversions were for anti-submarine observer training and will be discussed in Chapter Twelve.

The Hawker Sea Fury T.20 was originally developed as a private venture by Hawker in late 1946 as part of an export order from Iraq for 30 non-navalised 'Baghdad Furies'. The prototype Iraq Dual Trainer 1 (IDT 1) had separate windscreens and canopies for the tandem cockpits. Before completion, the Admiralty had already seen the value of the proposed trainer for its own use. Accordingly the IDT 1 airframe was purchased and allocated serial VX818 and Specification N.19/47 was issued. Iraq was offered the flight test data and a replacement production T.20 aircraft. The arrester hook was removed and the retractable tailwheel replaced by a fixed wheel. For gunnery training only two 20mm Hispano cannon were retained, the empty gun bays being filled by equipment removed from the rear fuselage to make space for the second cockpit. Underwing racks for bombs were also fitted. The instructor's cockpit was equipped with a gunsight and

Hawker's prototype Sea Fury T.20 first flew on 13th July 1948 and was written off in a crash landing following engine failure on 22nd June 1954. *Terry Panopalis Collection*

a periscope to aid the forward field of vision when gun aiming. The prototype T.20 made its maiden flight on 15th January 1947. During early flight testing the windscreen of the instructor's cockpit collapsed, so Hawker devised a modification which removed the rear windscreen and linked both cockpits by a Perspex tunnel. A total of 60 T.20s were used as advanced trainers and as conversion trainers by the Royal Navy Volunteer Reserve squadrons until they were withdrawn in 1956. Some were released for export, three being sold to the Union of Burma Air Force, two to Cuba and fourteen were converted as target tugs for the West German company Deutsche Luftfahrt Beratungsdienst as the TT.20.

The Navy's Turboprop Trainer

Despite the existence of the 'jet prima donnas' within the RAF, arguably the Fleet Air Arm embraced the turboprop more enthusiastically, being impressed by its lower fuel consumption and superior economy over turbojets. Turboprops were specified for four anti-submarine aircraft; the re-engined and heavily modified Short SB.3 Sturgeon, the Short SB.6 Seamew, the Blackburn B.88 and the Fairey Gannet – the only one to actually reach operational service. One strike-fighter was also to be re-engined, the Westland Wyvern. In December 1945 it had been decided to replace the 3,500hp (2,610kW) Rolls-Royce Eagle 24-cylinder piston engine with the Rolls-Royce RB.39 Clyde. The Clyde's development was soon delayed and in May 1946 the Armstrong Siddeley ASP.3 Python was chosen as an alternative. The Wyvern was redesigned to accommodate the new engines, the larger Python requiring an increase in fuselage length by 21in (53cm) and greater depth to fit the bifurcated exhaust. Rolls-Royce soon abandoned the Clyde to focus on the AJ.65 Avon turbojet but by that time 20 Python-powered TF.2 pre-production aircraft and a single T.3 two-seat trainer to Specification T.12/48 had been ordered in September 1948.

The Admiralty had begun a policy of developing conversion trainers for its frontline fighters following the purchase of the Hawker Sea Fury T.20. Specification T.12/48 called for a Python-powered Wyvern TF.2 modified with a tandem cockpit for an instructor and student with fully duplicated flying and engine controls and each having a gunsight. The trainer was to have a weapons training capability consisting of two 20mm cannon and underwing racks for bombs, the Boot Leg toss-delivered rocket-propelled torpedo, Red Angel anti-ship rockets and 3in (76mm) rocket projectiles. Endurance was to be 360nm (666km) with drop tanks and in addition to the usual naval radio equipment an ASV.16N surface-search radar was also required. Westland began work on the W.38, deepening the rear fuselage for the instructor's cockpit. Initially Westland planned a new framed canopy over both cockpits, but the final design had a separate canopy for the instructor and a periscope to improve the forward view when gun aiming. The prototype VZ739 would be the only T.3 built and first flew on 11th February 1950. Its test flying career with Westland was short, force-landing on the Axe estuary following a turbine blade failure in the Python. On 22nd December 1950 the Admiralty cancelled the T.3, citing no need for a two-seat Wyvern, the fighter version of which was still struggling in development due to engine and propeller problems.

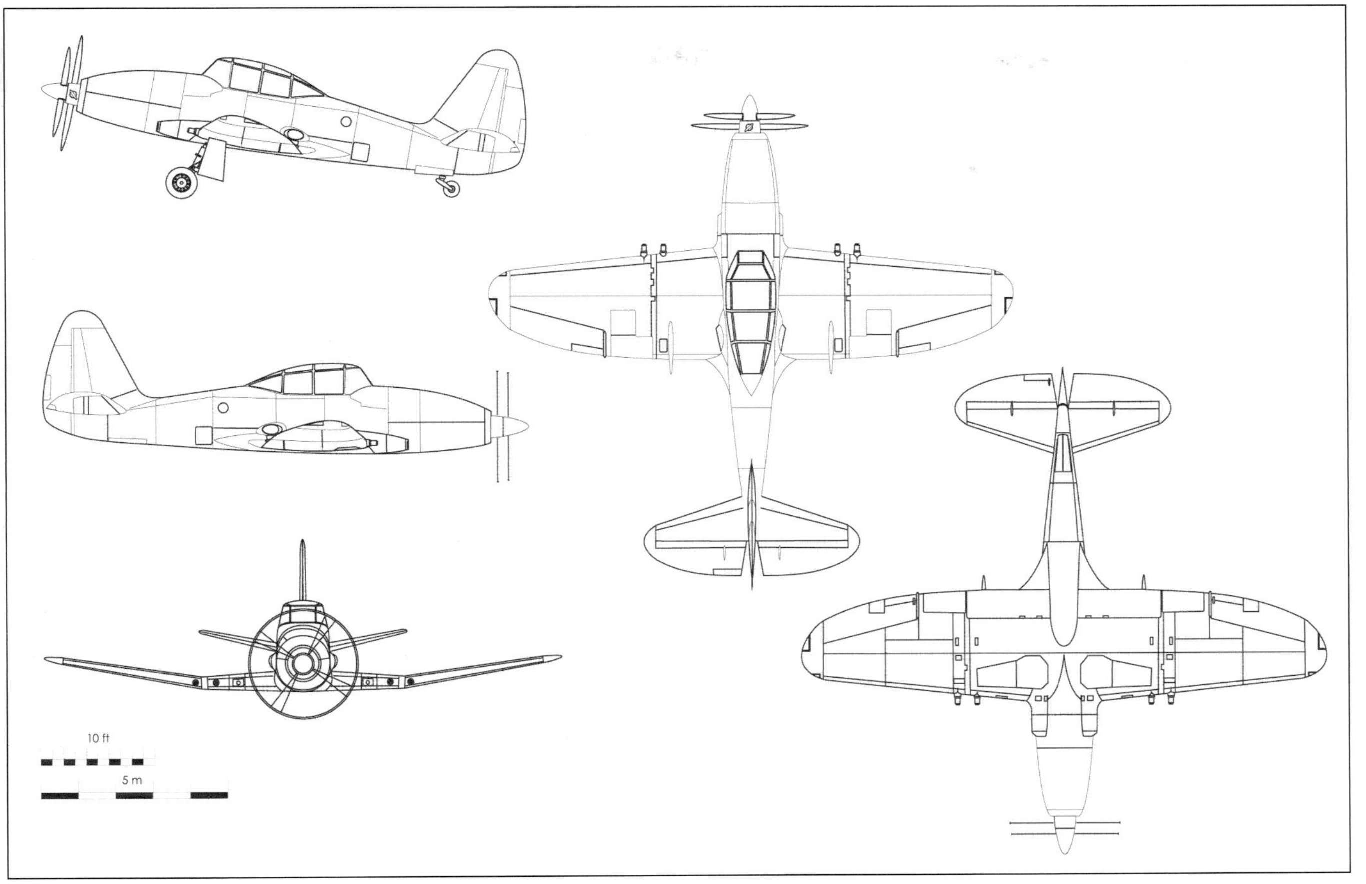

This drawing illustrates Westland's original proposal for a turboprop-powered trainer based on the Westland Wyvern strike fighter. These proposals would later crystalise into Spec. T.12/48. *Jens Baganz*

After so much development work on the aircraft and their engines at the behest of the Air Ministry and the Admiralty, the end result of untamed enthusiasm for an arguably immature technology was that turboprops would not feature in future training aircraft until 1988. They were superseded by more reliable and economical turbojets. The Merlin-powered Balliol and Athena were probably the right aircraft for the job but appeared at the wrong time.

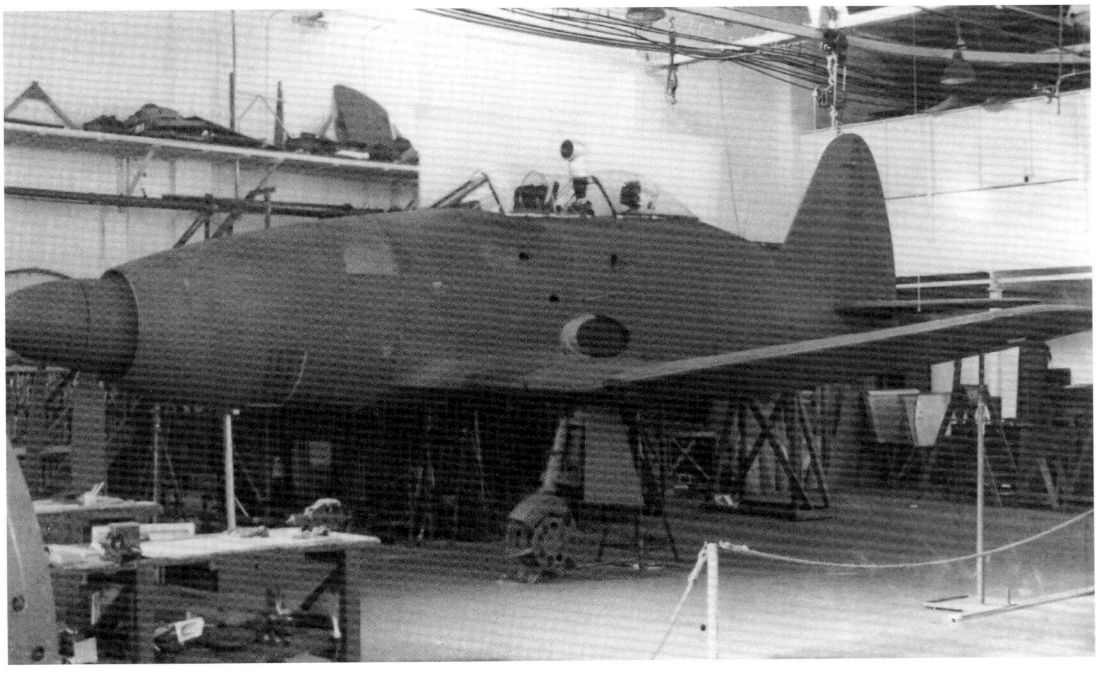

Westland built a full scale mock-up of the Wyvern trainer. The periscope for the rear cockpit is obvious. *Leonardo*

Prototype Wyvern T.3 VZ139 is pictured here shortly after its roll out at Yeovil in January 1950. At this time the aircraft lacked the rear cockpit periscope. *Leonardo*

This close up photograph of the Wyvern T.3's cockpits provides excellent detail of the periscope mounting and the large mirror housing, which presumably gave a good field of vision forwards. *Leonardo*

Prototype Wyvern T.3 VZ139 was the only example built and had a short flying career. On 3rd November 1950, during a test flight a turbine blade failure forced Squadron Leader Derek Colvin to make a forced landing on the marshland of the Axe estuary in Devon. A successful recovery proved impossible but the Admiralty had already decided not to proceed with the T.3. *Leonardo*

Wyvern T.3 VZ139 was one of only a handful of British first-generation turboprop-powered trainers to fly. Arguably ahead of their time, the Balliol, Athena and Wyvern sadly emphasised that turboprops were at that time immature for service use. *Leonardo*

3 Replacing the Prentice

'If the Department's actions give the public the impression that policy was restrictive in this way, the Minister might face some awkward questions to answer in Parliament. Thus, the Department's policy must not only avoid being restrictive but must also avoid giving the appearance of being restrictive.'

Mr E Thornton, Technical Director of Plans, October 1948

'The Chairman pointed out that some firms had submitted designs purposely based on a low powered engine estimate and had introduced other features to ensure a 'light' Aircraft... but apparently because of his preference for the Cheetah engine D.O.R. did not want a light aircraft.'

Minutes of the Tender Design Conference, 14th April 1949

'Group Captain Broad reported that the Percival design was found to be a very pleasant and thoroughbred little aircraft which handled extremely well.'

Minutes of a Ministry of Supply meeting, January 1951

During early 1948, the Air Staff issued Operational Requirement OR.257 for a replacement for the Percival Prentice basic trainer. The Air Staff had been disappointed with the Percival Prentice due to the difficulties with its spinning characteristics and although it had escaped cancellation and was proving to be a useful training platform, the RAF was keen to find a better replacement. In addition, the decision to curtail Prentice production to 349 aircraft had made it impossible to replace the remaining Tiger Moths in service in South Rhodesia and the number of operational Prentices at home could only be maintained until mid-1953. This made it essential that the replacement should be in service by 1953 and to meet this date the service trials would have to begin no later than spring 1951. The prospect of large orders for the selected aircraft attracted a complete cross-section of Britain's aircraft industry, from established companies like A V Roe and Percival to little-known newcomers like Chrislea and Planet, who were gambling on the chance of success to propel themselves to become established manufacturers. At this time training aircraft were still seen by many aircraft designers to be relatively basic aircraft similar to civilian light aircraft. No requirement before or since had thrown up such a range of contenders and is all the more remarkable considering that the industry was still rebuilding itself and adapting to post-war circumstances.

Who Should Apply?

Specification T.16/48 to meet OR.257 called for a single-engined two-seat basic trainer suitable for worldwide use with side-by-side seating for the instructor and pupil. The aircraft was to be fully aerobatic with good manoeuvrability, no handling vices and easy recovery from any stage of a stall, spin or unusual condition. The maximum continuous cruising speed was to be at least 110kt (203km/h) with two hours endurance. The stalling speed was to be no higher than 55kt (101km/h) with flaps down – a considerable relaxation from Specification T.23/43 to avoid some of the problems that had troubled the Prentice. Good climbing performance was required, the time to 5,000ft (1,520m) and 10,000ft (3,050m) was not to exceed seven and twelve minutes respectively. The service ceiling was to be not less than 10,000ft (3,050m) and preferably 15,000ft (4,572m). The required take-off and landing distance to clear a 50ft (15m) obstacle was not to exceed 500yd (457m). A fixed undercarriage was specified to save weight and cost. Given the intention for overseas use, maintainability and reliability was important to allow semi-skilled personnel to service the aircraft. The engine had to have an 800 hour running life between overhauls and an engine change was to take three groundcrew no more than four hours.

The third Percival P.56 Provost T.1 prototype WG503 was completed as the P.56 Mk 3 with the Alvis Leonides engine in order to comply with the Air Staff's wish to fit the more modern and powerful engine than the Cheetah. *Author's Collection*

The Ministry of Supply (MoS) had to decide which companies should be invited to tender to avoid the dispersion of scarce resources. The general policy was to reduce the number of aircraft companies which relied on MoS contracts to those which had the resources and experience to design modern fighters and bombers. The aircraft companies, however, had the right to see any specification with a security grade of Restricted or lower and could submit a tender even if they were not on the Ministry's approved Trade's List, although a contract for development or production could not be awarded until they were listed. Air Marshal Sir Alec Coryton, the Controller of Supplies (Air), considered awarding tenders on a private venture basis but eventually it was decided to apply the usual procedure to avoid any complaints or public criticism of the MoS's procurement policies. Percival, Boulton Paul, Fairey and Blackburn received formal invitations to submit tenders, but Folland and Chrislea had already made known their intention to go ahead and submit tenders.

The Contenders

The MoS subsequently received tenders from fifteen companies totalling no less than 31 designs powered by nine different engines. Although they differed in details and cockpit layout, all of the design tenders were low-wing monoplanes with side-by-side seating and the majority had a fixed tailwheel undercarriage. Air Service Training Ltd was experienced in training, having been formed in January 1931 by John D Siddeley as a flying school for civil and military pilots. It had become part of the Hawker Siddeley group in 1934 and in 1947, its wartime Civil Repair Organisation was reorganised as the AST Aircraft Division, designing and undertaking conversions and modifications for civilian aircraft but having no experience in the design and manufacture of complete aircraft. Their submission to T.16/48 was to be the only aircraft that they would design, although later they developed the C.4 target drone. Their conventional design had an all-up weight (AUW) of

3,050lb (1,383kg) and had two engine options; the 245hp (182kW) de Havilland Gipsy Queen 32 or the 295hp (219kW) Gipsy Queen 50. The latter engine enabled the 10,000ft (3,050m) climb requirement to be met and increased the service ceiling from 16,700ft (5,090m) to 21,000ft (6,400m). The wings were of conventional two-spar construction with detachable wingtips and the starboard wing held two lightweight crash-resistant fuel tanks with a combined capacity of 36gal (163lit). The fuselage was designed in three sections with a stressed-skin covering and the main cockpit bulkhead served as a crash pylon and carried the radio and electronic equipment for easy accessibility when being serviced. The tail control surfaces were fabric covered, which was considered unsuitable for tropical use. The MoS considered the use of nested channel-sections for the spar booms and longerons to be unnecessarily complicated but double curvatures had been avoided as far as possible in the design to aid fabrication. The company estimated that they could build five aircraft a week with their existing facilities, which the MoS considered a feasible estimate. The tendered price for two prototypes was £50,000 with a price of £3,200 per aircraft for a production run of 500 aircraft, with delivery of the first prototype fourteen months from the date of contract.

Airtech Ltd was another company attempting to expand into aircraft construction. The company had been formed on 16 February 1947 by the charter airline Chartair to carry out aircraft maintenance, conversions and the manufacture of freight panniers for Handley Page Halifaxes, Avro Lancastrians and Tudors. Their submission had an AUW of 3,500lb (1,587kg) and was the only design tendered to feature a twin-fin tail unit. The wing had a main plate web spar with a false spar carrying the Frise ailerons and split flaps. Two leading-edge fuel tanks held a combined capacity of 40gal (181lit). The fuselage was designed in two sections, the rear section being of semi-monocoque construction and the main spar frame was used as a crash pylon. The main control run underneath the cockpit was accessible for maintenance via a ventral hatch. The engine was a Gipsy Queen 31 which gave sufficient estimated performance to meet the five minute climb to 5,000ft (1,520m) requirement, but not the 10,000ft (3,050m) requirement. The tendered price for two prototypes was £41,000 and the price per aircraft for a production run of 500 aircraft was £3,500, with delivery of the first prototype nine months from the date of contract. The MoS rated Airtech's facilities and experience as inadequate for aircraft design and production without extensive expansion.

The Avro Type 714 was based on the Type 704 Athena but with a fixed undercarriage and a smaller-capacity piston engine. The variant shown in this original artist's impression has the de Havilland Gipsy Queen 50. *Avro Heritage*

Auster Aircraft Ltd submitted their A.9 design. The construction was unorthodox with one-piece single spar wings, single-piece pressed frames and the use of swaging on the fuselage skin panels to give them additional stiffness to eliminate the need for stringers to save structural weight. To ease servicing, the instruments, electrics and hydraulic header tank were all accessible via a single panel ahead of the engine firewall. Auster selected the 180hp (134kW) Blackburn Bombardier but had decided to use a Gipsy Major 8 in the first prototype to avoid development delays. The climb to 10,000ft (3,050m) was estimated at eleven minutes and the take-off and landing distances clearing a 50ft (15m) obstacle were 352yd (321m) and 350yd (320m) respectively. The assessors rated the cockpit layout as the third best of all the submissions and Auster had also offered the cheapest tender with a price for two prototypes of £90,000 and a price of £1,400 per aircraft for a production run of 500 aircraft, with delivery of the first prototype sixteen months from the date of contract. The planned rate of production was up to ten aircraft per week, but the assessors felt that some re-equipping and expansion would be required to double the production capacity from the five Auster T.7s then being produced a month.

A V Roe offered the Type 714, a development of the Type 701 Athena advanced trainer then being developed meet Specifications T.7/45 and T.14/47. The Type 714 was offered with two engines, the 410hp (305kW) Armstrong Siddeley Cheetah X – which was out of production – or the 295hp (219kW) Gipsy Queen 50. The wing was of conventional two spar construction with the centre-section integral with the fuselage and detachable wingtips. The cockpit featured a crash pylon built into the fuselage bulkhead aft of the pilots' seats, aft of this was a 50gal (227lit) fuel tank. The AUW with the Cheetah X was 4,200lb (1,905kg), decreasing to 4,066lb (1,844kg) with the Gipsy Queen. With the Cheetah, the Type 714 would take just over five minutes to reach 5,000ft (1,520m) but the 10,000ft (3,050m) climb still exceeded the requirement. The Gipsy Queen proved underpowered for the design and was unable to meet the 5,000ft (1,520m) minimum requirement but despite this it was judged to be the best for all-round performance but the spinning qualities were estimated to be the worst. The MoS rated Avro's cost estimates as the most reliable and realistic offered. The tendered price for two prototypes was £50,000 and £3,350 per aircraft for a production run of 500 aircraft at the rate of 35 per month, with delivery of the first prototype six months from the date of contract. Avro was already

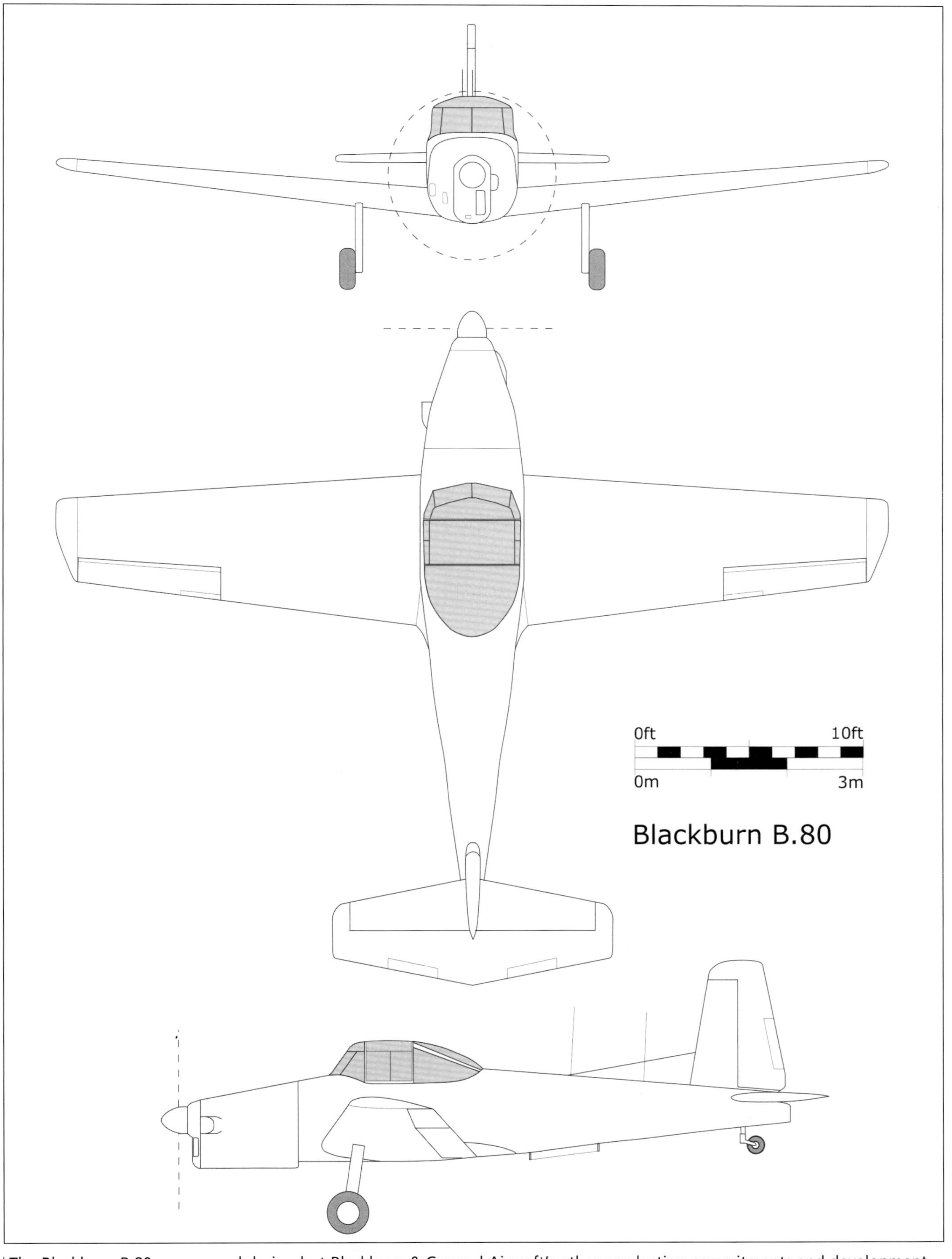

The Blackburn B.80 was a good design but Blackburn & General Aircraft's other production commitments and development programmes counted against its chances of entering production. *Author*

overloaded with design work but spare production capacity was potentially available if no more Athena T.2s were ordered (which proved to be the case) and Anson T.21 navigation trainer production was scheduled to end in March 1953.

Blackburn and General Aircraft Ltd. submitted their B.80 design with an AUW of 3,187lb (1,445kg) and a low stalling speed of 50kt (92.5km/h). The wing had detachable wingtips and was fitted with pneumatically operated single split flaps. Two wing fuel tanks held a combined 60gal (272lit). The one-piece fuselage was of monocoque construction with skin plating using pre-fabricated stringers to reduce assembly time. Both the Gipsy Queen 30 and Gipsy Queen 50 were offered, the latter offering a marginally better rate of climb and service ceiling. The tendered price for two prototypes was £69,200 and £2,300 per aircraft for a production run of 500 aircraft, with delivery of the first prototype a year from the date of contract. Blackburn estimated that up to a 100 a month could be completed with their existing facilities when its Prentice T.1 sub-contract was completed in March 1949. The MoS could not ignore, however, that Blackburn were working on – and could have potential future orders for – the C.3/46 Universal Transport, the GR.17/45 anti-submarine aircraft and the X30/46 glider (of these only the Universal Transport would enter production as the Beverley).

Boulton Paul utilised its experience with the P.108 Balliol trainer then being developed to meet Specifications T.7/45 and T.14/47. Rather than offering one design with a choice of engines, the company decided to submit two designs; the P.115 with the 345hp (257kW) Gipsy Queen 71 and the P.116 with the 295hp (219kW) Gipsy Queen 51. The wings of the P.115 were fitted with fuel tanks totalling 49gal (222lit) capacity. At 4,106lb (1,862kg) AUW the P.115 was capable of just meeting the 5,000ft (1,520m) and 10,000ft (3,050m) climbing requirements. The P.116 was smaller and lighter with an AUW of 3,839lb (1,741kg) with a reduced fuel capacity of 42gal (190lit). With less power, the P.116 had inferior climbing performance which failed to meet the climbing requirements but the longer take-off and landing distances still met the minimum

Boulton Paul applied much of the experience it had gained from the P.108 Balliol into the P.115 and the result was a very similar, but smaller design. *Les Whitehouse, Boulton Paul Archive*

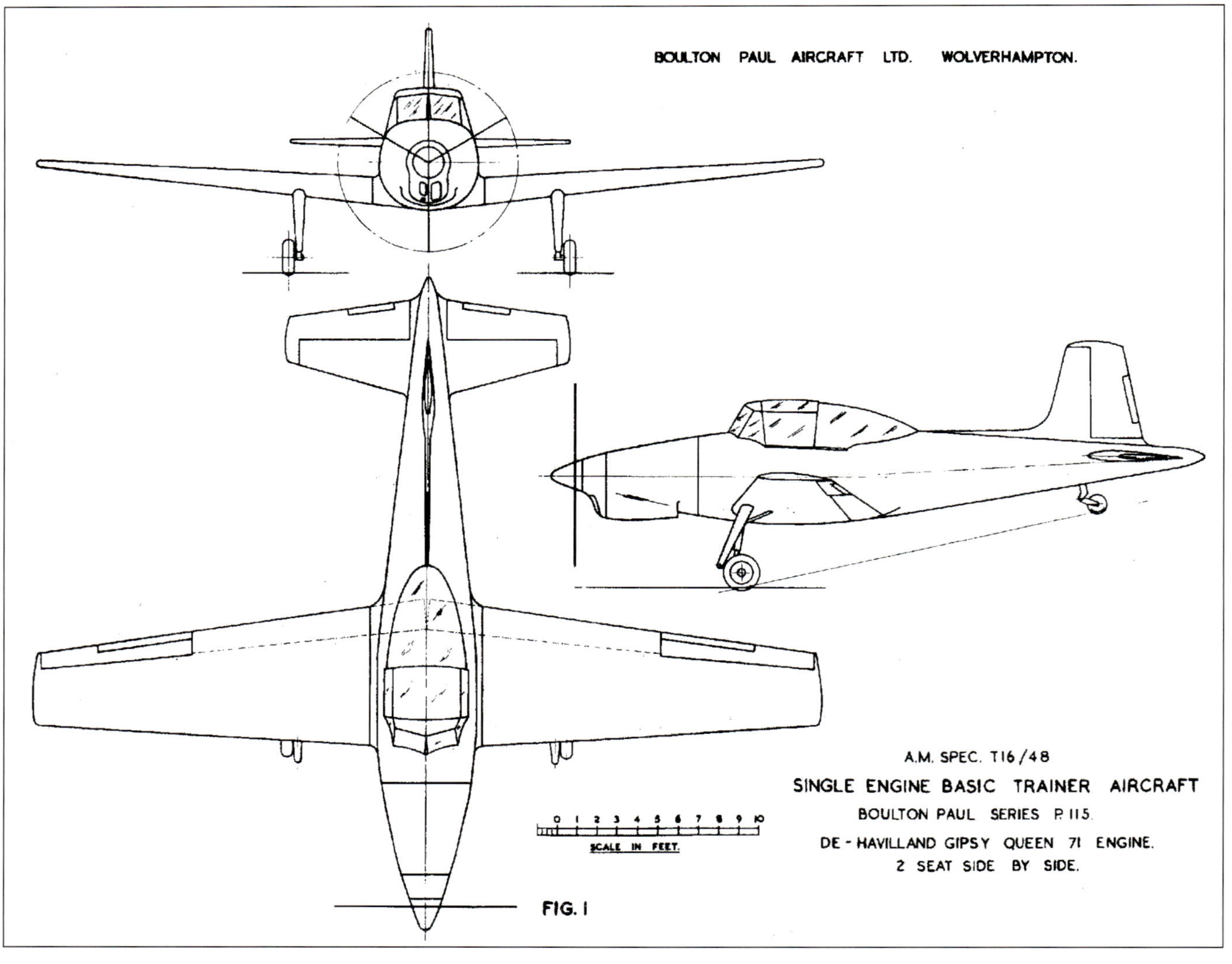

FIG. I

requirements. The cockpit layout was based on that of the Balliol. Both designs shared a common structure with a light alloy stressed skin forward fuselage and a circular cross-section monocoque rear fuselage. The aircraft could be broken down into sections for easy transportation but the MoS discovered that applying Balliol production experience did not lower the costs as much as hoped. The tendered price for two prototypes was a rather expensive £226,000 with delivery of the first prototype eighteen months from the date of contract and a price of £3,500 each for a production run of 500 aircraft delivered at the rate of 40 aircraft a month. Boulton Paul would have ample production capacity available with production of pre-production Balliols and Vickers Wellington T.10 conversions being completed by July 1950, but the MoS warned that future Balliol T.2 orders would use up this capacity. Boulton Paul were ranked in third place overall, reflecting the company's experience following the Balliol development programme.

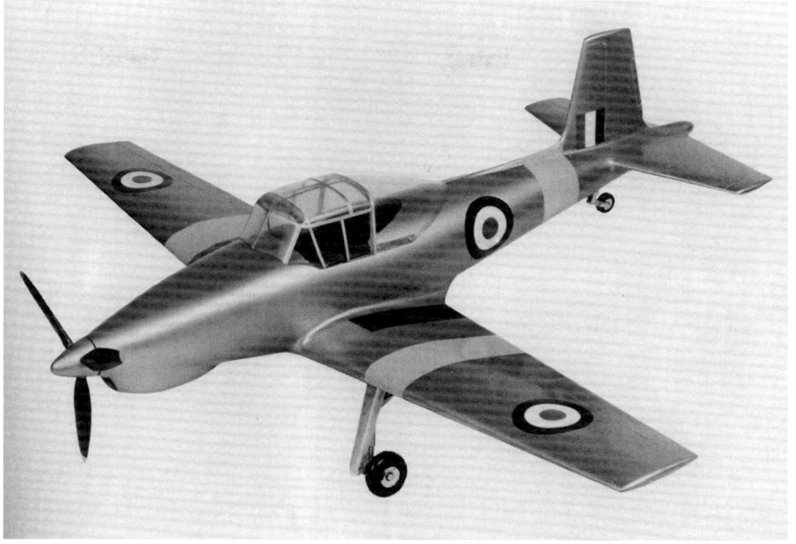

This model of the P.116 in standard RAF training colours shows the sleek design to good effect. *Les Whitehouse, Boulton Paul Archive*

The P.116 was very similar to the P.115 but was smaller and lighter to use the de Havilland Gipsy Queen 51 engine. Not clearly specifying the engine the Air Staff wanted in the Specification meant that all the Gipsy Queen powered submissions were effectively wasted effort as the RAF wanted more powerful radial engines. *Les Whitehouse, Boulton Paul Archive*

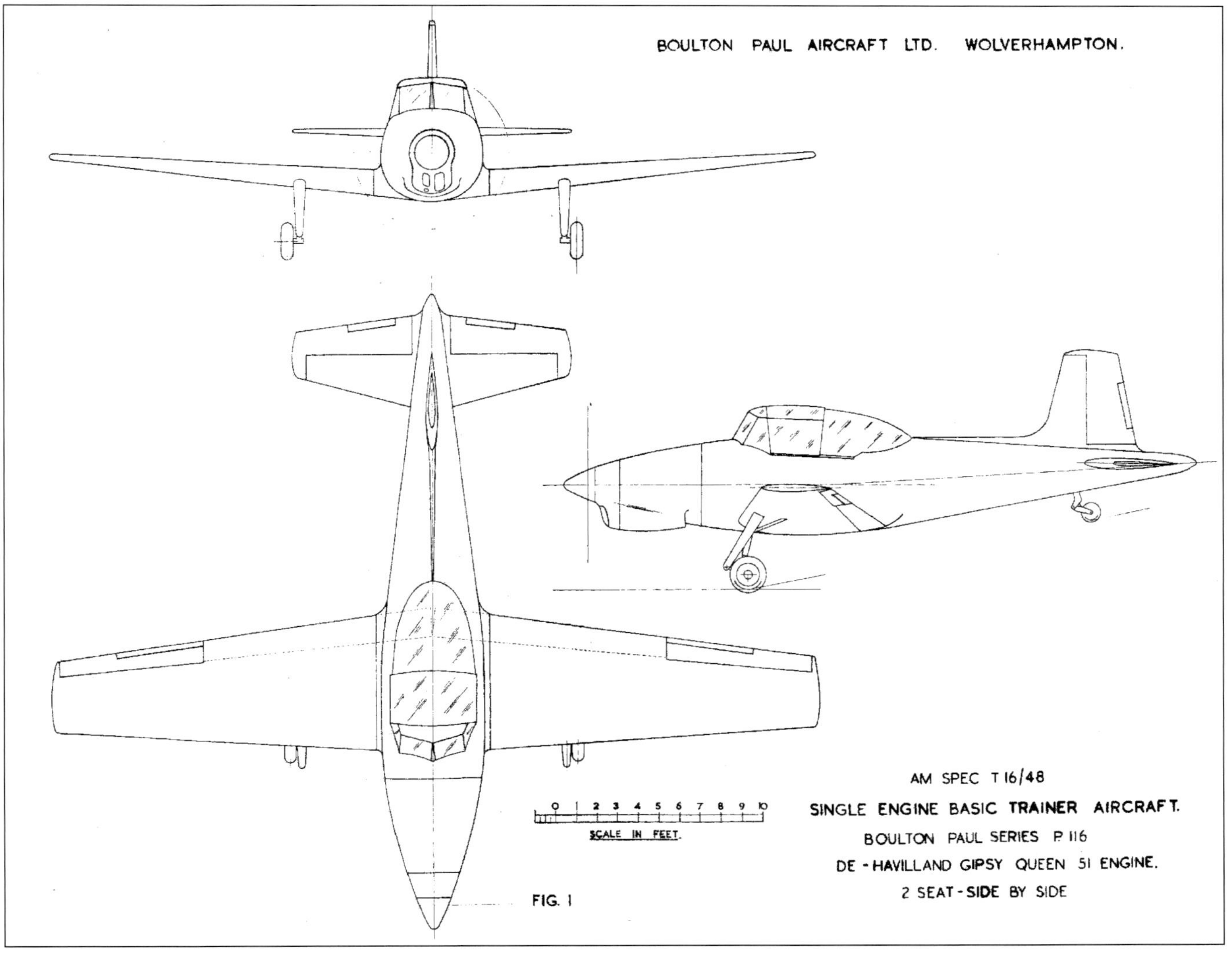

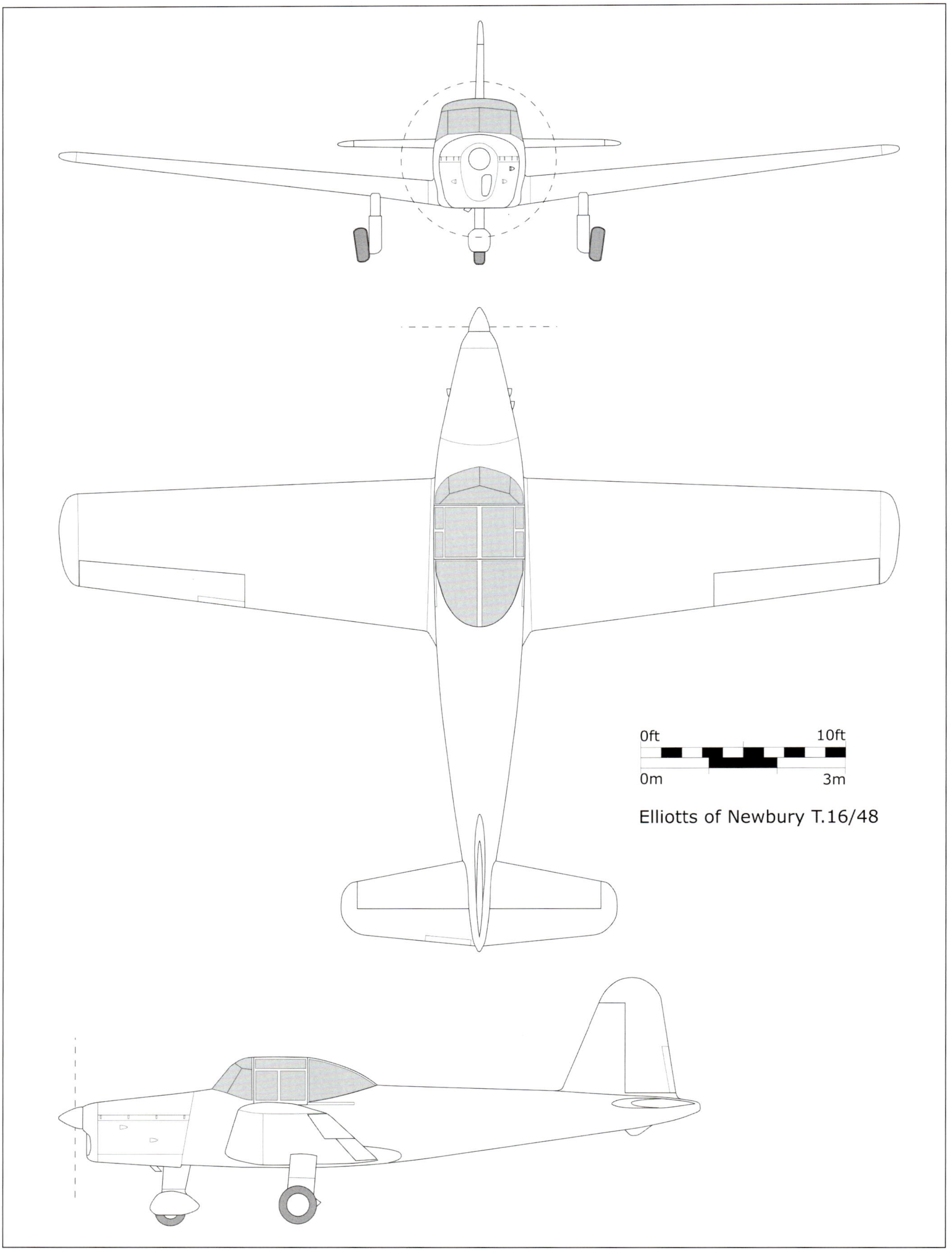

Elliotts of Newbury was an unlikely contender but its tender was based on the A.P.4 light aircraft. Elliotts had no success with powered aircraft and returned to gliders, until the company exited aviation entirely in 1965. *Author*

The Chrislea Aircraft Company saw T.16/48 as a means to obtain a large order and possible export success following the poor sales of their Ace series, with its unusual wheel control and floor-mounted pedal control system. Chrislea's design was a low-wing monoplane with a single tail and a tailwheel undercarriage. The straight-tapered wing was built in four sections with detachable wingtips with fabric covering aft of the spar and the light alloy covering at the leading-edge formed a torsion box with the D-shaped spar. The wings also held two 15gal (68lit) fuel tanks. The monocoque fuselage was split into three sections for ease of production. A low wing loading resulting from the 2,465lb (1,118kg) AUW in conjunction with slotted flaps gave a low stalling speed of 43kt (79km/h) and take-off and landing distances of 325yd (297m) and 370yd (338m) respectively. The selected engine was the 180hp (134kW) Blackburn Bombardier, which the MoS felt was unsuitable as it offered insufficient power to provide sufficient margins to allow for future weight growth, the weight estimates proving to be rather optimistic. The tendered price for two prototypes was £51,580 with a price of £1,970 per aircraft for a production run of 500 aircraft delivered at the rate of five a week, with delivery of the first prototype fifteen months from the date of contract. The MoS assessed Chrislea's facilities and production experience as being inadequate without extensive expansion for production. Fully acknowledging their fledgling status, Mr E Doran of Chrislea wrote to the several contacts at the MoS asking for a critique of their brochure and taking the opportunity to ask for any advice they could give regarding the export prospects for their Series 3 Ace light aircraft. Overall it seems that the MoS was satisfied with the quality of the brochure, but the MoS declined to comment on the Ace's export prospects. The cool response was perhaps a sign that the MoS were not keen to encourage a small entrant firm and doubtless the pressures of military development programmes were occupying the officials' minds with light aircraft not really fitting into their remit.

The furniture maker Elliotts of Newbury had switched to large-scale production of aircraft components and gliders during the war. Gliders remained Elliotts' main products, with the exception of an attempt to enter the light aircraft market with the four-seat EoN A.P.4. Their submission to T.16/48 was essentially a scaled-up A.P.4 in the hope of reducing the development time. The two-spar wing had removable leading-edge sections and wingtips to ease repairs and the fuselage was easy to build with a rectangular cross-section. A 34gal (154lit) fuel tank was fitted in the wing centre-section. Both tricycle and tailwheel undercarriages were offered and the estimated AUW was 3,330lb (1,510kg). The 245hp (182kW) Gipsy Queen 32 was underpowered for the aircraft, taking over six minutes to reach 5,000ft (1,520m) and sixteen minutes to 10,000ft (3,050m), the service ceiling being 17,000ft (5,181m). Elliotts considered fitting the more powerful Gipsy Queen 50 but no performance estimates were produced. The tendered price for two prototypes was £68,580 and £2,950 per aircraft for a production run of 500 aircraft at the rate of five per week, with delivery of the first prototype 21 months from the date of contract. Any production was reliant on replacing the non-aircraft commercial production that the company was then undertaking and retooling for aircraft production but the MoS held a favourable impression of the company's competence based on their wartime record.

Fairey applied the useful experience gained from the Fairey Primer and submitted three designs; Scheme A with a 245hp (182kW) Gipsy Queen 32, Scheme B with a 295hp (219kW) Gipsy Queen 50 and Scheme C which was Scheme B with a tricycle undercarriage. All three had a common single-spar wing and an orthodox monocoque construction fuselage. Scheme A had an AUW of 3,100lb (1,406kg), Scheme B 3,350lb (1,519kg) and the tricycle undercarriage added 70lb (31kg) to Scheme C. The MoS, however, considered that these weights had been underestimated. Scheme A had provision for 36gal (163lit) of fuel in two leading-edge tanks, Schemes B and C having larger capacity tanks for 44gal (200lit). The Gipsy Queen 32 provided climbing times of almost six minutes and fifteen minutes to 5,000ft (1,520m) and 10,000ft (3,050m) respectively, the increased power of the Gipsy Queen 50 improving those figures to almost six and twelve minutes. The main negative point in the MoS assessment was the below average spinning qualities. The tendered price for two prototypes was £130,000, with an initial flight of the first prototype ten months from the date of contract. The price per aircraft was £3,020 for a production run of 500 aircraft delivered at the rate of 30 per month. The MoS was concerned that Fairey was predicted to be busy with Firefly production until March 1953 and after that was the prospect of winning Specification GR.17/45 for an anti-submarine aircraft which would place additional workload on the design and production staffs (Fairey did indeed win to produce the Gannet).

The Folland Aircraft Company had submitted a tender despite the MoS declining to send them an official invitation due to the company's limited production capacity. At that time, Folland was producing de Havilland Vampire components under sub-contract and non-aviation products such as refrigerators and electric trucks. The Fo.132 was a conventional design with a straight tapered wing and the fuselage structure was designed to be built in two halves with a longitudinal joint and covered with aluminium alloy sheets. Two 15gal (68lit) fuel tanks were fitted in the wing roots. The out of production 410hp (305kW) Cheetah X was again an odd choice, perhaps with the intention of making use of left over stocks. The MoS felt that the quoted AUW of 3,300lb (1,496kg) was grossly underestimated, the assessors' estimate being 4,230lb (1,918kg). At this revised weight the wing area would be too low which would have consequences, in particular the landing distance requirement would be exceeded by 150yd (137m), although the other performance requirements would still be met. In its favour, the simple construction of the wings and fuselage made the Fo.132 easy to produce and the estimated costs were only high due to Folland's lack of facilities. The tendered price for two prototypes was £20,000 with a price of £2,700 per aircraft for a production run of 500 aircraft, with delivery of the first prototype fifteen months from the date of contract.

Handley Page (Reading) was formed when Handley Page acquired the assets of Miles Aircraft Limited's Reading site following their bankruptcy. The former Miles team had endured a difficult period and were therefore highly enthusiastic about T.16/48 when it was announced, starting work just after Christmas 1948 with a team of eight completing the brochure and building a mock-up before the end of February 1949. Two designs were submitted, the HPR.1 and the HPR.2. The HPR.1 was offered in two versions with the 295hp (219kW) Gipsy Queen 51 and the 345hp (257kW) Gipsy Queen 71, the latter offering a marginally better performance. The AUW with the Gipsy Queen 51 was 3,593lb (1,629kg). The wing had a single spar and stressed skin construction with a detachable leading-edge and was fitted with pneumatically operated Handley Page slotted flaps. The fuselage was of semi-monocoque construction with three main assemblies and a 45gal (204lit) fuel tank was located in the centre-section aft of the main spar. The larger HPR.2 of 4,282lb (1,942kg) AUW was powered by a 475hp (354kW) Cheetah 27, giving sufficient performance to meet the climbing requirements and the fuel tank was enlarged to 55gal (250lit) capacity. The cockpit layout was judged to be the best of all the designs based on the examination of the mock-up. The cockpit controls and services could be easily serviced on the ground via ventral panels. For the HPR.2, Handley Page quoted a price of £73,000 for two prototypes with delivery of the first prototype eleven months from the date of contract. The first prototype would be a flying shell with the fully equipped second prototype following two months later. With a production run of 500 aircraft, the price was estimated at £4,350 per aircraft for the HPR.2 or £3,800 for the HPR.1. The very high tooling costs and estimates of man-hours and production costs baffled the MoS assessors given the previous experience the team had at Miles, although it must be said that some of Miles' previous production costs had been high so the tender might have reflected that. The HPR.2 however, met all the specified requirements and was rated second overall.

Percival was another company with extensive trainer experience and they had already been working on their P.56 private venture design before T.16/48 had been issued; indeed the MoS had compared the draft specification against the P.56 during its formation. Percival submitted a range of four designs. The first was powered by a 245hp (182kW) Gipsy Queen 32 and the others had a smaller wing and were powered by the 295hp (219kW) Gipsy Queen 51, 307hp (228kW) Blackburn Grenadier and the 420hp (313kW) Cheetah XV respectively. The AUW varied from 3,150lb (1,428kg) with the Gipsy Queen 32 to 3,765lb (1,707kg) with the Cheetah XV. The wing had slotted flaps and the fuselage was of conventional semi-monocoque construction built in two sections. Two 20gal (90lit) capacity fuel tanks were fitted in the wing leading-edges, inboard of the undercarriage. The Gipsy Queen 32 proved underpowered, the Gipsy Queen 51 and Grenadier giving slightly improved performance but the Cheetah XV provided sufficient power to meet all the performance requirements and became the favoured version. Along with the Blackburn B.80, it was judged as having the best spinning characteristics and Percival was judged to have the best design and production capability, especially as Prentice production was due to finish by March 1950. The tendered price for two Gipsy Queen-powered prototypes was £129,000 and £3,545 per aircraft for a production run of 500 aircraft, with the first prototype estimated to fly by June 1949. The price for the Cheetah XV variant was £800-£1,000 more expensive due to the cost of the engine and propeller. Even so, it was the Cheetah-powered P.56 that emerged as the leading contender.

Perhaps the most surprising tender was received from the Planet Aircraft Company Ltd., founded during 1947 by Major John Nelson Dundas Heenan to design and build the futuristic Satellite light aircraft with a streamlined fuselage, a V-tail and a buried mid-fuselage engine driving a pusher propeller. Major Heenan had secured financial backing from the Distillers Company Ltd. (who by 1950 owned Magnesium Elektron Limited), Imperial Chemical Industries and Blackburn and General Aircraft Ltd. He was convinced of the utility of using magnesium alloys to save airframe weight and saw T.16/48 as a further opportunity to demonstrate its advantages. The new design was quite unlike the Satellite and was conventional in layout and powered by a 250hp (186kW) Gipsy Queen 32 (the Gipsy Queen 51 was also considered). A single 51gal (231lit) fuel tank was fitted behind the forward spar in the inboard wing section. The structure though very similar to the Satellite, the single-spar wing, fuselage and tail surfaces were of monocoque construction using Magnesium-Zirconium alloy which reduced the number of wing ribs and fuselage frames, estimated to require 40 percent fewer parts compared with a conventional aluminium skinned airframe. The MoS was impressed by the simple construction, although they felt that forming certain structural sections (in particular wing leading-edge panels) with current presses and providing adequate corrosion protection would be problematic. By the time of the assessment there were also doubts regarding magnesium's torsional strength following the fracturing of the Satellite's main fuselage keel following an undercarriage collapse, the Air Registration Board requesting a complete re-stressing of the Satellite's airframe. Planet quoted a price of £68,315 for two prototypes but did not provide any cost estimates for production and the predicted weekly output of four to six aircraft seemed unlikely unless the company could acquire suitable production facilities.

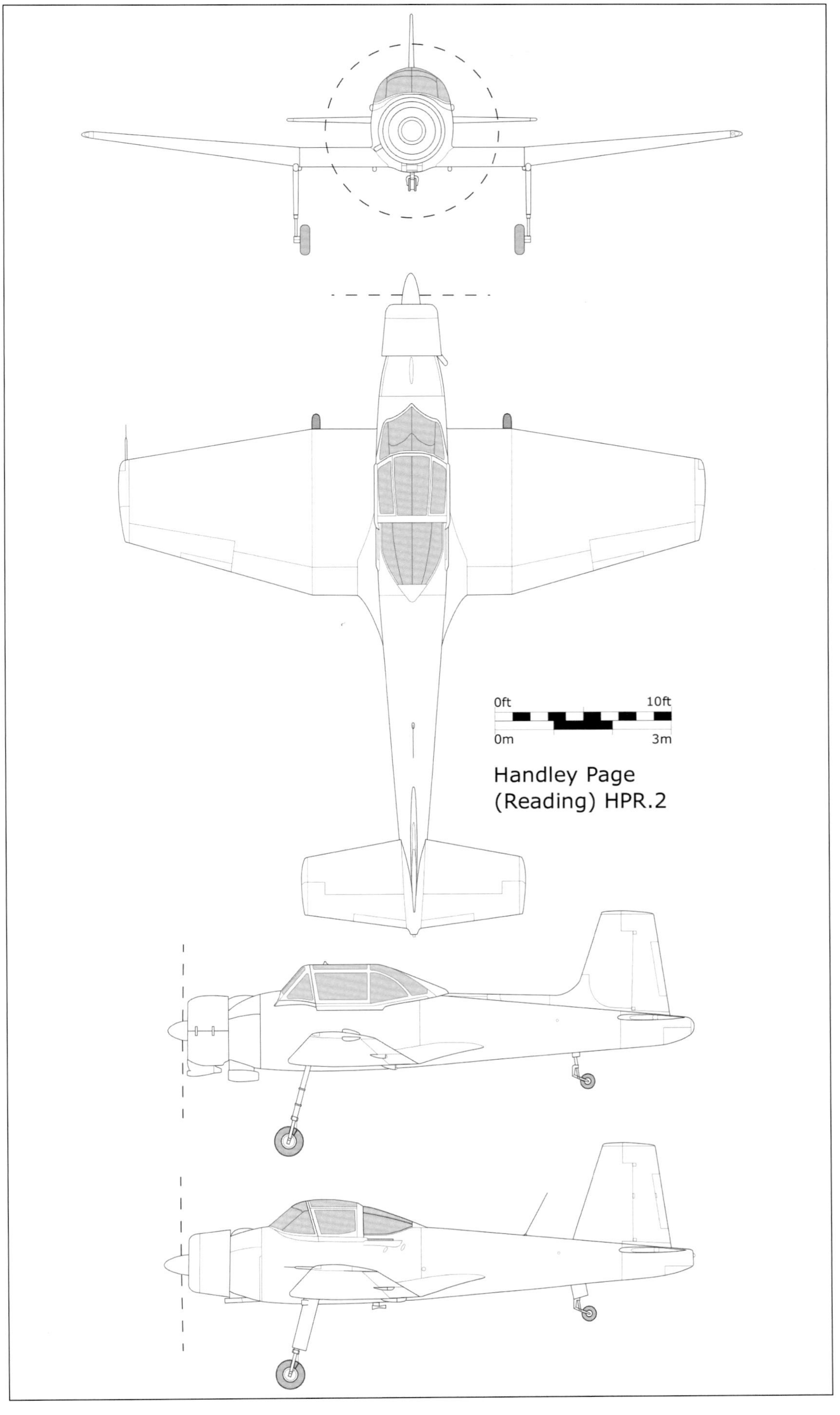

The main drawing shows the second prototype HPR.2 WE505 powered by the Alvis Leonides, the upper side view is the first prototype WE496 with the Cheetah engine. The company put in a lot of effort in an attempt to rectify all of the many shortcomings of their design. *Author*

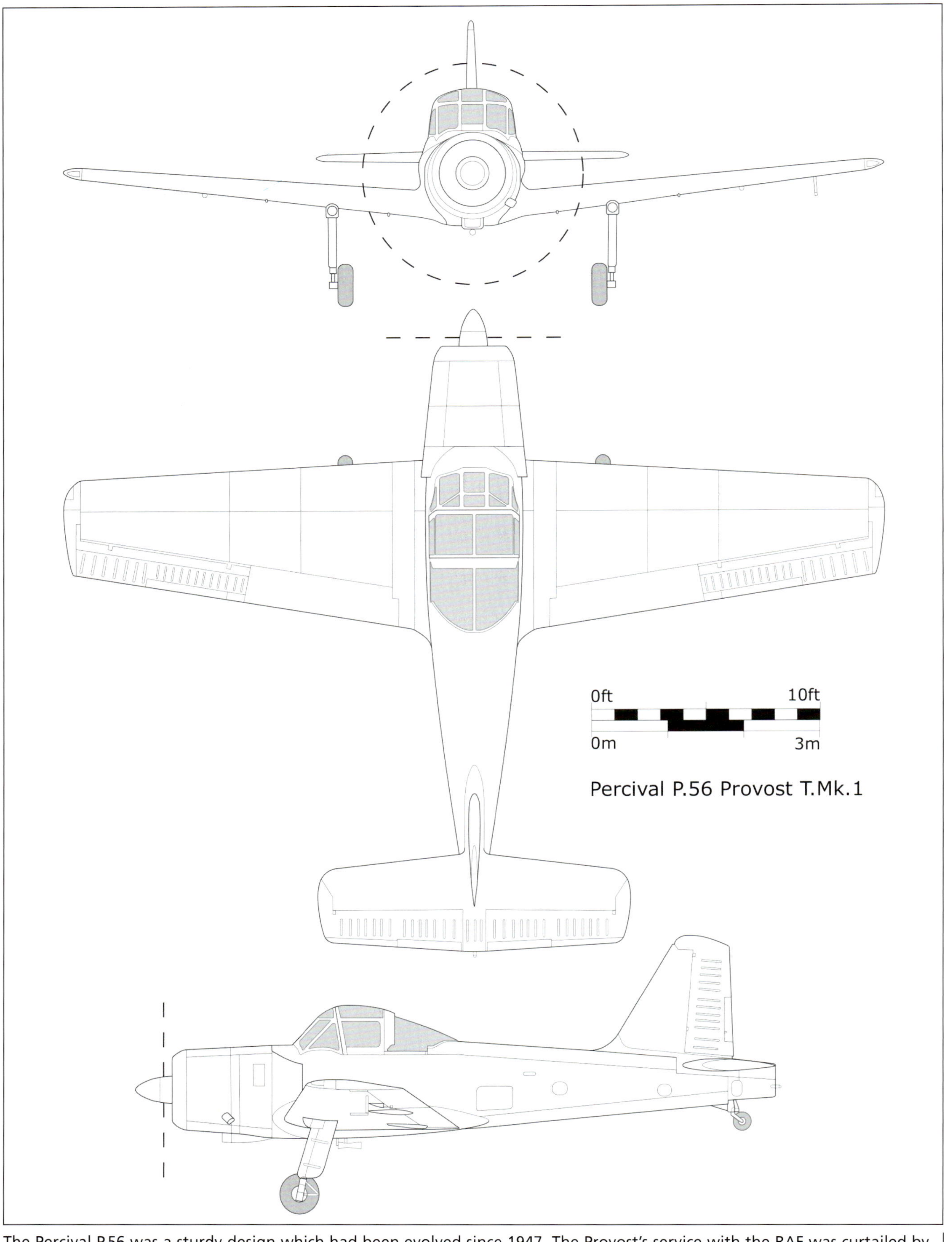

The Percival P.56 was a sturdy design which had been evolved since 1947. The Provost's service with the RAF was curtailed by the P.84 Jet Provost. Remarkably, the Provost's airframe would prove adaptable to a different form of propulsion without this intention being built into the original design. *Author*

Table 3.1 – Specifcation T.16/48 Contenders

	Air Service Training Design 1	Air Service Training Design 2	Airtech	Auster A.9	Avro 714	Avro 714	Blackburn B.80	Blackburn B.80
Wingspan	36ft 0in (10.97m)	36ft 0in (10.97m)	41ft (12.49m)	31ft 4in (9.57m)	40ft 2in (12.24m)	40ft 2in (12.24m)	36ft (10.97m)	36ft (10.97m)
Length	27ft 3in (8.30m)	27ft 3in (8.30m)	31ft (9.44m)	22ft 8in (6.94m)	31ft 9in (9.67m)	34ft 4in (10.46m)	29ft (8.83m)	29ft (8.83m)
Wing Area	165ft^2 (15.32m^2)	165ft^2 (15.32m^2)	250ft^2 (23.22m^2)	124ft^2 (11.51m^2)	261ft^2 (24.24m^2)	261ft^2 (24.24m^2)	190ft^2 (17.65m^2)	190ft^2 (17.65m^2)
All-Up Weight	3,050lb (1,383kg)	3,100lb (1,406kg)	3,500lb (1,587kg)	2,260lb (1,025kg)	4,200lb (1,905kg)	4,066lb (1,844kg)	3,187lb (1,445kg)	3,272lb (1,484kg)
Powerplant	Gipsy Queen 32, 245hp (182kW)	Gipsy Queen 50, 295hp (219kW)	Gipsy Queen 31, 235hp (175kW)	Bombardier, 180hp (134kW)	Cheetah X, 410hp (305kW)	Gipsy Queen 50, 295hp (219kW)	Gipsy Queen 30, 245hp (182kW)	Queen 50, Gipsy 295hp (219kW)
Stalling Speed	?	?	50kt (92.5km/h)	47.5kt (88km/h)	51kt (94km/h)	52kt (96km/h)	50kt (92.5km/h)	50kt (92.5km/h)
Time to 5,000ft (1,520m)	6.02min	4.67min	6.6min	4.67min	5.2min	7.5min	5.9min	5.5min
Time to 10,000ft (3,050m)	14.84min	9.85min	14.5min	11.3min	11.8min	16.8min	14.7min	11.5min
Service Ceiling	16,700ft (5,090m)	21,000ft (6,400m)	16,500ft (5,029m)	?	19,400ft (5,910m)	17,500ft (5,330m)	17,300ft (5,270m)	21,400ft (6,520m)
Take-Off over 50ft (15m)	442yd (404m)	?	420yd (384m)	352yd (321m)	460yd (420m)	435yd (397m)	370yd (338m)	?
Landing over 50ft (15m)	?	?	345yd (315m)	350yd (320m)	420yd (384m)	410yd (374m)	470yd (429m)	?
	Boulton Paul P.115	**Boulton Paul P.116**	**Chrislea**	**Elliotts of Newbury**	**Fairey Scheme A**	**Fairey Scheme B**	**Fairey Scheme C**	**Folland Fo.132**
Wingspan	38ft 10in (11.83m)	32ft 6in (9.90m)	36ft (10.97m)	40ft 6in (12.34m)	37ft 6in (11.43m)	37ft 6in (11.43m)	37ft 6in (11.43m)	36ft (10.97m)
Length	32ft 6in (9.90m)	30ft 8in (9.34m)	28ft 1in (8.55m)	30ft 4in (9.24m)	29ft 4in (8.94m)	29ft 4in (8.94m)	29ft 4in (8.94m)	26ft 4in (8.02m)
Wing Area	215ft^2 (19.97m^2)	193ft^2 (17.93m^2)	195ft^2 (18.11m^2)	240ft^2 (22.29m^2)	218ft^2 (20.25m^2)	218ft^2 (20.25m^2)	218ft^2 (20.25m^2)	200ft^2 (18.58m^2)
All-Up Weight	4,106lb (1,862kg)	3,839lb (1,741kg)	2,465lb (1,118kg)	3,330lb (1,510kg)	3,100lb (1,406kg)	3,350lb (1,519kg)	3,420lb (1,551kg)	3,300lb (1,496kg)
Powerplant	Gipsy Queen 71, 345hp (257kW)	Gipsy Queen 51, 295hp (219kW)	Bombardier, 180hp (134kW)	Gipsy Queen 32, 245hp (182kW)	Gipsy Queen 32, 245hp (182kW)	Gipsy Queen 50, 295hp (219kW)	Gipsy Queen 50, 295hp (219kW)	Cheetah X, 410hp (305kW)
Stalling Speed	52.5kt (97km/h)	54kt (100km/h)	43kt (79km/h)	49kt (90km/h)	46kt (85km/h)	48kt (88km/h)	?	51.2kt (94km/h)
Time to 5,000ft (1,520m)	4.9min	6.22min	6.1min	6.3min	5.9min	5.7min	?	3.3min
Time to 10,000ft (3,050m)	9.8min	13.3min	14.7min	16min	15.1min	12min	?	7.1min
Service Ceiling	22,000ft (6,705m)	20,500ft (6,250m)	15,400ft (4,690m)	17,000ft (5,180m)	17,500ft (5,330m)	21,000ft (6,400m)	?	20,000ft (6,090m)
Take-Off over 50ft (15m)	400yd (365m)	460yd (420m)	325yd (297m)	430yd (393m)	435yd (397m)	460yd (420m)	?	460yd (420m)
Landing over 50ft (15m)	460yd (420m)	475yd (434m)	370yd (338m)	350yd (320m)	390yd (356m)	?	?	480yd (438m)

Table 3.1 – Specifcation T.16/48 Contenders (continued)

	Handley Page (Reading) HPR.1	Handley Page (Reading) HPR.1	Handley Page (Reading) HPR.2	Percival P.56	Percival P.56	Percival P.56	Percival P.56	Planet Aircraft
Wingspan	35ft (10.66m)	35ft (10.66m)	37ft (11.27m)	41ft (12.49m)	35ft 6in (10.82m)	35ft 6in (10.82m)	35ft 6in (10.82m)	37ft (11.27m)
Length	30ft 3in (9.22m)	30ft 6in (9.29m)	29ft 11in (9.11m)	30ft 9.5in (9.38m)	28ft 7.5in (8.72m)	28ft 7.5in (8.72m)	27ft 4in (8.33m)	28ft (8.53m)
Wing Area	192ft² (17.83m²)	192ft² (17.83m²)	223ft² (20.71m²)	208ft² (19.32m²)	208ft² (19.32m²)	208ft² (19.32m²)	208ft² (19.32m²)	202ft² (18.76m²)
All-Up Weight	3,593lb (1,629kg)	3,889lb (1,764kg)	4,282lb (1,942kg)	3,150lb (1,428kg)	3,195lb (1,449kg)	3,205lb (1,372kg)	3,765lb (1,707kg)	3,040lb (1,378kg)
Powerplant	Gipsy Queen 51, 295hp (219kW)	Gipsy Queen 71, 345hp (257kW)	Cheetah 27, 475hp (354kW)	Gipsy Queen 32, 245hp (182kW)	Gipsy Queen 51, 295hp (219kW)	Grenadier, 307hp (228kW)	Cheetah XV, 420hp (313kW)	Gipsy Queen 32, 245hp (186kW)
Stalling Speed	50.5kt (93.5km/h)	52.2kt (96km/h)	51kt (94km/h)	47.8kt (88.5km/h)	48.1kt (89km/h)	48.1kt (89km/h)	53.2kt (98.5km/h)	51.5kt (95km/h)
Time to 5,000ft (1,520m)	6.6min	5.5min	4.5min	6.6min	5.1min	5.1min	3.7min	5.2min
Time to 10,000ft (3,050m)	14min	11min	10min	17min	10.8min	10.7min	8.7min	12.75min
Service Ceiling	17,300ft (5,270m)	21,800ft (6,640m)	21,800ft (6,640m)	14,900ft (4,540m)	20,320ft (6,190m)	20,300ft (6,190m)	20,500ft (6,250m)	14,500ft (4,420m)
Take-Off over 50ft (15m)	427yd (390m)	403yd (368m)	323yd (295m)	382yd (349m)	316yd (288m)	312yd (285m)	315yd (288m)	410yd (374m)
Landing over 50ft (15m)	422yd (385m)	415yd (379m)	406yd (371m)	373yd (341m)	376yd (343m)	376yd (343m)	385yd (352m)	430yd (393m)
	Portsmouth Aviation	**Westland (Design 1)**	**Westland (Design 2)**	**Westland (Design 3)**	**Westland (Design 4)**	**Westland (Design 5)**		
Wingspan	36ft (10.97m)	46ft (14.02m)	46ft (14.02m)	46ft (14.02m)	46ft (14.02m)	46ft (14.02m)		
Length	27ft 6in (8.38m)	33ft 8in (10.26m)	33ft 8in (10.26m)	33ft 8in (10.26m)	33ft 8in (10.26m)	33ft 8in		
Wing Area	194ft² (18m²)	300ft² (27.87m²)	300ft² (27.87m²)	300ft² (27.87m²)	300ft² (27.87m²)	300ft² (27.87m²)		
All-Up Weight	3,500lb (1,587kg)	3,800lb (1,723kg)	3,900lb (1,769kg)	4,200lb (1,905kg)	4,300lb (1,950kg)	4,500lb (2,041kg)		
Powerplant	Gipsy Queen 50, 295hp (219kW)	Gipsy Queen 31, 235hp (175kW)	Gipsy Queen 51, 283hp (211kW)	Gipsy Queen 71, 330hp (246kW)	Cheetah X, 410hp (305kW)	Cheetah XV, 420hp (313kW)		
Stalling Speed	52kt (96km/h)	47kt (87km/h)	47.5kt (88km/h)	49.5kt (91km/h)	50kt (92.5km/h)	51.5kt (95km/h)		
Time to 5,000ft (1,520m)	6.1min	7.9min	6.4min	6.1min	5.6min	4.4min		
Time to 10,000ft (3,050m)	12.9min	20.2min	13.8min	12.4min	12.7min	10min		
Service Ceiling	19,300ft (5,880m)	16,300ft (4,970m)	22,700ft (6,920m)	24,800ft (7,560m)	20,700ft (6,310m)	25,200ft (7,680m)		
Take-Off over 50ft (15m)	420yd (384m)	480yd (438m)	420yd (384m)	410yd (374m)	400yd (365m)	360yd (329m)		
Landing over 50ft (15m)	370yd (310m)	345yd (315m)	350yd (320m)	365yd (333m)	370yd (338m)	390yd (356m)		

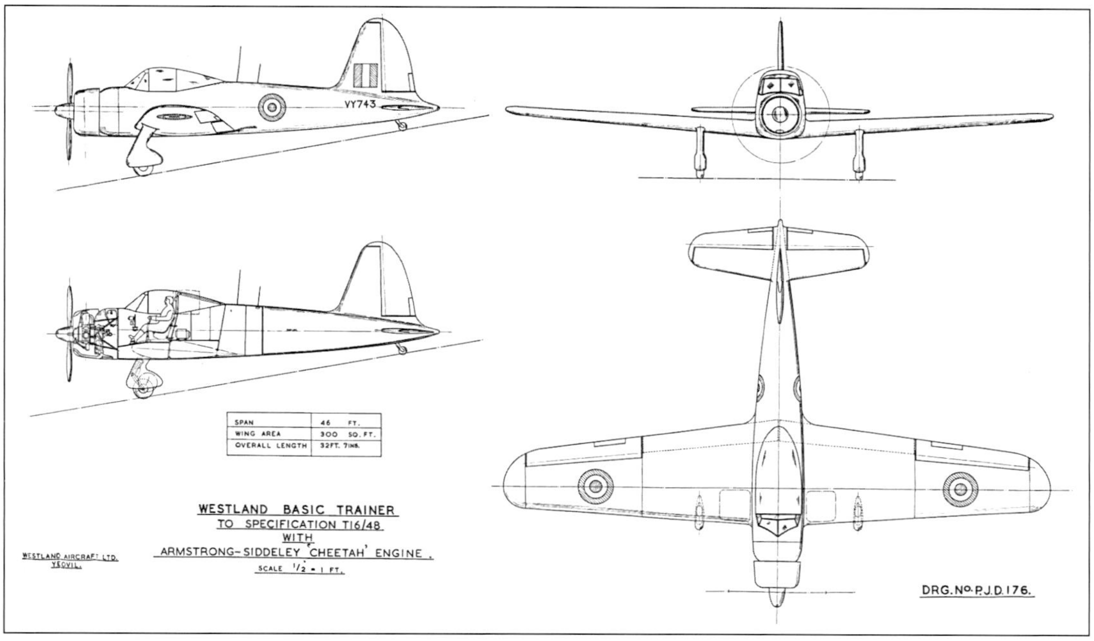

This Westland design on drawing sheet PJD176 was one of two Armstrong Siddeley Cheetah-powered designs tendered. All five of Westland's submissions shared the same airframe. *Leonardo via Chris Strainer*

Portsmouth Aviation had been formed out of Portsmouth, Southsea and Isle of Wight Aviation during the war to concentrate on repair and modification work. Post-war, the company had attempted to enter the commercial aircraft market with its twin-engine Aerocar light aircraft (which would fail to enter production). T.16/48 provided the company with another chance to become a fully-fledged manufacturer. Their tendered design featured an all-metal tapered wing with two spars was fitted with split flaps and fabric covered ailerons. Two 20gal (90lit) fuel tanks were fitted in the wing centre-section. Good rollover protection was provided by a robust crash pylon in the cockpit and the cast magnesium alloy windscreen frame which was connected to the fixed rear portion of the canopy by a central member. The horizontal tailplane was provided with variable incidence. The MoS assessor felt that the weight estimates were optimistic, the likely true weight would result in a higher wing loading and landing distance than forecast. The tendered price for two prototypes was £83,750 and £7,068 per aircraft for a production run of 500 aircraft, with delivery of the first prototype sixteen months from the date of contract. The MoS, however, felt that the company could not build up a production team in time to meet these proposed schedules.

Westland Aircraft Ltd. submitted no less than five designs, three powered by Gipsy Queen series engines and two with Cheetahs but all five shared an identical airframe, which was largest and

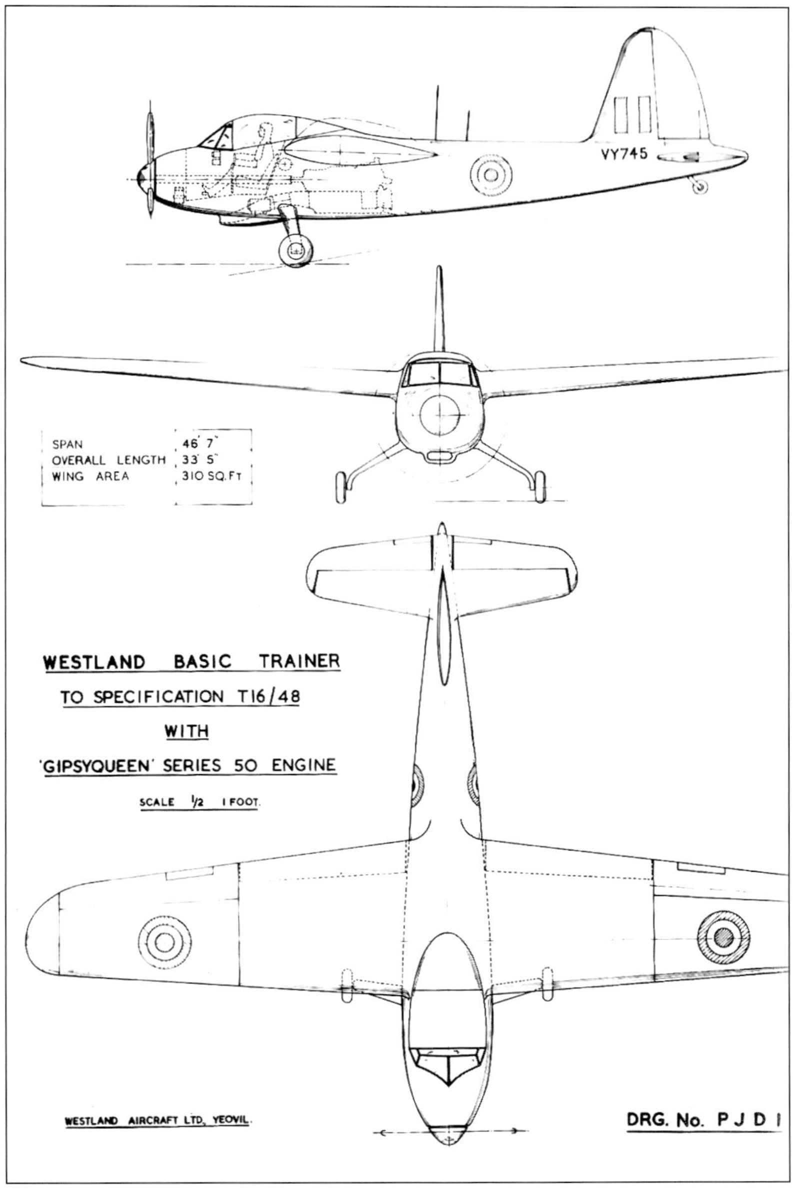

Westland drew up, but did not submit, this unusual design with a Gipsy Queen engine buried in the forward fuselage driving a tractor propeller via an extended driveshaft. The aim was to give the best possible view forwards and downwards for the student and instructor, the wing being above and behind the canopy. *Leonardo via Jeremy Graham*

heaviest of all the submissions tendered. Two 30gal (136lit) wing fuel tanks were fitted in all five designs. Westland also studied an unconventional arrangement with the Gipsy Queen 50 mounted in the centre fuselage beneath the wing with the propeller driveshaft running forwards between the side-by-side seats. Presumably this design was considered to improve the forward view from the cockpit on take-off and landing and drew on experience with the original design work for the Wyvern naval fighter. This interesting design was not submitted as part of the final tender. Indeed, Westland's brochure was found to be incomplete on submission, but the performance estimates were judged by the MoS to be reliable and the company was judged to have sufficient design capacity. Westland quoted a price of £125,674 for two prototypes, the first with an estimated delivery date of eighteen months from the date of the contract, and a price of £3,940 per aircraft for a production run of 500 delivered at the rate of twenty per month. Similar to the situation at Fairey, Yeovil had existing commitments for 163 Wyvern TF.2 torpedo-fighters and 43 WS-51 Dragonfly helicopters which would keep its workforce occupied until at least 1953. In addition, Westland was also undertaking Gloster Meteor and Supermarine Spitfire conversion work, all of which made it unlikely that adequate production facilities would be available in time.

Head-to-Head

All the tenders and the outcomes of the technical and industrial assessments were discussed at the Tender Design Conference held on 14th April, 1949 at Thames House, Millbank, the home of the MoS. Rather brusquely, the meeting opened with a statement that no representative had been invited from the Admiralty and that because all basic training of its pilots was conducted by the RAF it was not thought necessary for them to be present. One can only imagine how the Fleet Air Arm felt not having a say regarding how its pilots were being trained. There was also some discussion of whether the same aircraft might be selected to fulfil the role of a light communications aircraft, but this was not factored into the selection process. The Assistant Chief of the Air Staff (Operational Requirements), Air Vice-Marshal Geoffrey Tuttle, recommended that two companies should be approached to construct prototypes to stimulate a spirit of competition, although given the number of tendered designs it was obvious competition was already strong. Tuttle now also strongly favoured the use of the Cheetah radial engine, which narrowed the field of contenders considerably as most of the manufacturers had been trying to design the lightest possible aircraft to meet the performance requirements. Armstrong Siddeley were also relying on the potentially large order to keep their Cheetah production line open.

In this photograph the second prototype Provost T.1 WE530 stands alongside the third prototype WG503 in August 1955. By this time WE530 had been modified with an Alvis Leonides. *Author's Collection*

This left the Percival P.56 and the HPR.2 as the most suitable designs, the P.56 having been a frontrunner since T.16/48 had been written. Both were selected for comparative trials, it was stipulated that the trials and a production contract must be completed by November 1950 to ensure that the first production deliveries began during 1952. Despite a proposal to abandon the comparative trials to save money, orders for two prototypes of each type were placed on 13th January 1950. Percival P.56 WE522 was first to fly, making its maiden flight on 24th February at Luton. The first HPR.2, WE496, followed on 1st May (the canopy was lost just after take-off due to a faulty lock). Two days later a group of RAF pilots who had already flown P.56 WE522 were invited to Woodley to fly the HPR.2. Initially the Air Staff had selected the 385hp (287kW) Cheetah XVIII due to its reliability and good spares availability but they soon switched to the new Alvis Leonides which offered more power and less weight. They were unwilling, however, to completely abandon the Cheetah until competitive trials had been completed, despite the risk of delaying the development programme and delivery dates, the latter having previously been the Air Staff's main concern. Both companies were requested to fit one of their prototypes with the Leonides; Percival modified their third prototype, WG503, with a new engine mount as the P.56 Mark 2 and Handley Page acquired an engine directly from Alvis and installed it into the second HPR.2, WE505, having intentionally designed the engine mount to fit both engines – Alvis having pressed Sir Frederick Handley Page during 1949 to use the Leonides, even suggesting a third prototype aircraft as a Leonides testbed.

The Aeroplane and Armament Experimental Establishment (A&AEE) at Boscombe Down undertook the comparative handling trials and engineering assessment before the Cheetah-engined prototypes were handed over to Flying Training Command for operational assessment by the Central Flying School (CFS) at Feltwell during December 1950-January 1951. The P.56 proved to be pleasant to fly and required no major design changes and was judged to have slightly superior ground handling characteristics. The HPR.2, however, was delayed due to the design changes which were required to solve several handling problems that had become apparent during manufacturer's trials with WE496. Fitting revised ailerons proved unsuccessful in improving the entry into spins and eventually the area of the elevators, rudder and tailfin were increased. Elevator reversal at the stall with the flaps down and power on was cured by adding a mechanical interconnection between the flaps and elevator balance tab. Other problems included poor fore and aft control, which caused pupils to approach too fast during landings and the heavy controls made flying aerobatics tiring. The unacceptable spinning characteristics resulted in the CFS pilots being prohibited from intentionally spinning WE496. On the ground, the HPR.2 suffered from tail-lightness which resulted in a slight tendency to nose over when the brakes or full throttle was applied. The heavily modified WE505 cured some of these faults but missed the CFS trials entirely due to the length of time needed to make the modifications.

The first prototype HPR.2, WE496, is seen here with the original vertical tailfin and canopy at Woodley around the time of its first flight on 1st May 1950. During the flight the canopy broke free, luckily missing the tail. ***Author's Collection***

The first HPR.2, WE496, is seen here sporting several changes; a new canopy with a fixed rear section and a taller fin with the tip chord reduced by 9in (23cm) in an attempt to improve the poor spinning characteristics. The wing also has increased dihedral. *Author's Collection*

The A&AEE did have a chance to carry out preliminary handling trials with WE505 and found that the spinning characteristics had been improved, but now the rudder was deemed too heavy for most other flight conditions and required further tuning. The A&AEE's cockpit assessment was satisfied with the P.56, except for some suggested minor changes to switches and ancillary controls, but the assessment criticised the HPR.2's poor rearward view and lack of headroom. The CFS, however, criticised the P.56's unorthodox sliding throttle control, which was hard to operate precisely from the right-hand seat during aerobatics and the grouping of the instruments, despite Percival having followed the advice of the MoS Cockpit Layout Committee throughout its design.

On 30th January 1951 an MoS committee met to decide which aircraft to recommend for production on the basis of the A&AEE and CFS assessments. Although the Leonides-powered prototypes had not yet been assessed, it was judged that there would be no impact on the outcome apart from that the additional power from the Leonides might help to improve the sluggish performance of the HPR.2. Given the results of the assessments and its relatively trouble-free development, the committee concluded in favour of the P.56. An initial order for 200 aircraft followed on 29th May, the name Provost being chosen the following month. From 28th May to 5th July A&AEE pilots flew both the Cheetah and Leonides-powered Provost prototypes at Nairobi in Kenya and Khartoum in Sudan during tropical trials which amassed a total of 211 flying hours.

This view of WE496 shows better the increased wing dihedral which provided much needed pre-stall buffet to warn the student of an impending stall. *Author's Collection*

Designed with the benefit of the company's experience and the advice of the Ministry of Supply's Cockpit Layout Committee, the instrument panel was designed to be logically laid out under the 'Standard Six' layout for the student. The Central Flying School, however, criticised unorthodox sliding throttle control, which was hard to operate precisely from the right-hand seat during aerobatics and the grouping of the instruments. Evaluation by the instructors was invaluable to getting everything right. *Author's Collection*

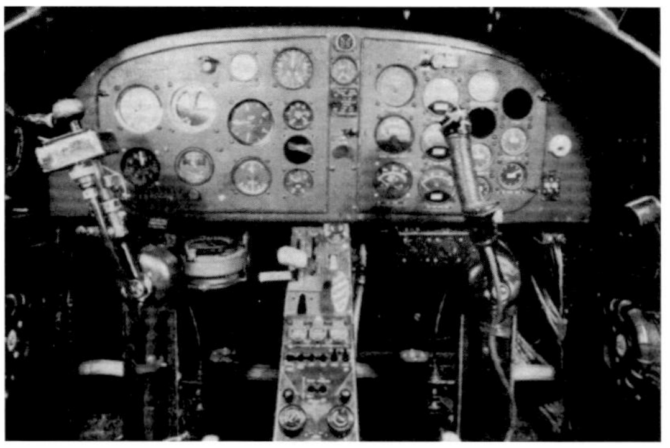

Although the HPR.2 looked good on the ground, in the air a host of aerodynamic problems delayed the A&AEE and RAF's evaluations and although it had some good points, the Percival P.56 was far superior. *Author's Collection*

The second prototype HPR.2, WE505, was fitted with all of the aerodynamic improvements that had been tested in WE596, including another revised vertical tail with the tip chord reduced by 6in (15cm) and the Alvis Leonides radial engine. *Author's Collection*

The Provost Arrives

In December 1952 Flying Training Command unveiled its new training sequence based around its new Provost. Previously students had progressed from the de Havilland Chipmunk T.10 to the Prentice before going to a Flying Training School (FTS) for basic training on the North American Harvard or the Balliol to earn their wings, those students destined for the fighter stream progressing to an Advanced Flying School to fly the de Havilland Vampire T.11 to prepare them for operational conversion training. The performance of the Provost enabled the Balliol phase to be deleted entirely so that students would complete all their basic training on Provost before graduating to fly the Vampire T.11 at an FTS. This saved training time, cost and reduced the multiple types used by the Command. The Provost's performance and agility, including a 90° per second rate of roll, and its similar cockpit layout to the Vampire T.11 soon endeared it to students and instructors alike. The first production Provost T.1s were delivered to the CFS at South Cerney in May 1953 for intensive service trials and instructor training before No 6 FTS at Tern Hill started to re-equip in July with their first course beginning on 1st October. There were some initial teething problems and restrictions until the Leonides was modified to allow up to 90 seconds of inverted flight and thicker gauge metal used on the mid-span wing sections at to cure skin wrinkling following heavy landings. The last Provost T.1, XF913, was delivered on 9th April 1956 and by then four FTSs and the RAF College had been re-equipped and they were soon also issued to several UASs as well. In 1957 the CFS formed an aerobatic team, *The Sparrows*, which had Provosts with modified engines to obtain the original rating of 550hp (410kW) and a quicker-opening throttle – in service the Leonides had been given reduced boost settings to preserve engine life and reducing the power to 520hp (387kW). Although exactly what the RAF wanted and a superb trainer, the Provost would be soon superseded by Percival's private venture to convert the Provost for the jet age as the Jet Provost. In early 1960 No 2 FTS began to convert to the Jet Provost and in August 1962 No 6 FTS was the last to give up its Provosts. Other examples soldiered on with the College of Air Warfare at Manby until April 1964 and with the Central Air Traffic Control School at Shawbury until October 1968.

As originally planned for when OR.257 was drawn up, Provosts would be operated in Rhodesia despite the closure of the Rhodesian Air Training Group in 1953. In May 1953 the Southern Rhodesian Air Force ordered four export-standard Provost T.51s followed by twelve T.52 armed trainers, all converted from ex-RAF aircraft. The Provost proved easy to adapt for armament training with underwing racks for practice bombs, machine gun pods and rockets and the student and instructor could both have a reflector gunsight. Other exports were made to; Ireland with four T.51s and six T.53s (including the last two of the 461 Provosts built), Burma with twelve T.53s, Sudan with four T.53s and later five ex-RAF aircraft as unarmed T.52s, Oman also received a total of eight unarmed ex-RAF T.52s, Iraq ordered 15 T.53s and finally Malaysia received a total of 24 T.51s, many of them reconditioned ex-RAF aircraft.

The success of the Provost more than redeemed Percival's reputation following the rather lacklustre Prentice. The Provost was a

Provost T.1 WV471 at the 1953 SBAC Farnborough show. Retained by Alvis for engine testing, it later served with the RAF College, No 6 FTS and CFS before becoming ground instructional airframe 7952M in 1967. *Terry Panopalis Collection*

Provost T.1 XF558 during its use with the Royal Air Force Flying College at Manby during the early 1960s. The aircraft was sold to the Royal Malaysian Air Force in 1968, a total of 24 ex-RAF Provosts being supplied between 1961 and 1968. *Author's Collection*

successful trainer but was at the cusp of the jet age overtaking pilot training but would itself form the basis of a successful line of jet-powered trainers to secure Percival's place as the premier trainer provider for the RAF. The tendering process to OR.257 is interesting in itself as it presents to us a snapshot of the state of the British aircraft industry in 1949, an industrial sector still short of skilled manpower, both in the workshops and in the design offices, as well as battling material shortages. It also show how ambitious the post-war newcomers were, alas unlike some of the new aircraft companies that flourished after the First World War, there was to be little success for new manufacturers. Arguably the industry was already too large, the MoS already grappling with how to streamline the industry but lacking effective means to do so. Within five years rationalisation would appear and with it even companies like Percival would lose their independent identities.

Southern Rhodesia was not just a sunny location to train RAF aircrew. The Southern Rhodesian Air was itself a satisfied customer of Percival aircraft for flying training and transportation duties. Seen here in 1955 is Provost T.52 SR136 along with Pembroke C.1 SR133. *Blue Envoy Collection*

4 Introducing the Jets

'I have not included the Avro scheme for a trainer with a Derwent V engine, as that is in a different category and is even more advanced than the Advanced Trainer as we know it.'
Mr E W Johnston, AD/RDL.1, Ministry of Supply, June 1948

'I think that in so far as using a jet trainer is concerned, we will rely on the dual Meteor which Glosters are producing for us. The firm requirements have been issued now for some time and Glosters are getting down to the project. They seem quite keen to do this because they have so many foreign enquiries for a machine of this nature.'
Air Vice-Marshal John Boothman, Assistant Chief of the Air Staff (Tactics and Requirements), January 1947

'It seems to me there is a great deal of force in your argument. However, the policy on these matters is, of course, for the Air Staff to decide.'
Mr A E Woodward-Nutt, Director of Research and Development (Aircraft), July 1952

'The R.A.F. can be justifiably proud of its pioneering in Flying Training. One of the most interesting innovations in this field is the introduction of the Jet Provost as an ab initio trainer.'
Air Commodore D M Somerville, Director of Flight Safety, September 1956

In October 1959, the RAF introduced the world's first 'all-through' training syllabus using jet-powered aircraft for both basic and advanced flying training. A series of experimental courses since 1955 had proved the value and the arrival of the Percival Jet Provost provided the perfect tool to enable students to go from grading flights on the de Havilland Canada Chipmunk T.10, to earning their wings on the Jet Provost T.3. Although future fighter pilots would step up to more powerful jet trainers for their advanced training, the most important factor was that every RAF pilot, regardless of whether they went on to fly propeller-driven Blackburn Beverley and Lockheed C-130 Hercules transports, Avro Shackleton maritime reconnaissance aircraft or Westland Wessex helicopters, had the knowledge and skills to fly a jet-powered aircraft. It would become a central tenet of the training syllabus. This policy was arguably the result of industry providing the right aircraft and proving their value rather than being a process actively led by the Air Staff. As we have seen in Chapter Two, the Air Staff by 1945 had grabbed the opportunities that jet engines offered and had foreseen future advanced trainers being powered by turboprops. This effort ultimately faltered through lack of reliable engines and high operating costs and the Air Staff had already written off the turbojet as being uneconomic to operate for training. Despite the arrival of the Gloster Meteor and de Havilland Vampire fighters and the future prospect of the English Electric Canberra and the V-Force of nuclear bombers, the need for a turbojet-powered advanced trainer was not immediately foreseen and the idea of using turbojet-powered basic trainers was resolutely opposed. The various aircraft companies submitted several private-venture proposals for basic and advanced jet trainers. Some of the latter were selected as their need became apparent but it would not be until the arrival of the Percival P.84 Jet Provost which coincided with a growing interest in an 'all-through' jet syllabus in the early 1950s, that the jet basic trainer would be brought into RAF use.

Self-Learning Pioneers

The early post-war jet fighter pilots undertook their operational conversion flying at No 226 Operational Conversion Unit (OCU) at Bentwaters. Without any dedicated jet-powered training aircraft then in existence the unit relied on a motley collection of Supermarine Spitfires, Hawker Tempests, de Havilland Hornets and Mosquitoes, North American

The Percival Jet Provost enabled the RAF to operate the world's first all-through jet training programme, being used for both basic flying and navigator training. Jet Provost T.4 XP581 is seen here in July 1967 with No 3 FTS taxying to begin a training sortie. Only two years later it was retired and scrapped. *Terry Panopalis Collection*

Harvards and a handful of standard Meteor and Vampire fighters. The early courses comprised a mix of students destined for the wide array of piston and jet-powered fighters. The instructors themselves had few jet flying hours and the lack of any dual-control trainers meant that good ground instruction was essential. Pilots destined for the Meteor were given one hour on the Airspeed Oxford to provide some basic instruction on twin-engine handling and asymmetric flying. Conversion was reliant on reading the Pilot's Notes, any sage advice from those few instructors who some jet flying hours and the sole hour spent flying the pedestrian Oxford. The new and faster Meteor F.4 with a pressurised cockpit and lighter ailerons proved even tricker to master. Unsurprisingly, conversion training was both inefficient and dangerous with a high accident rate. Future Vampire pilots approaching their first flight were given cockpit drills which included a blindfolded test, a written test and finally they sat in the cockpit while members of the groundcrew sat on the tail booms to demonstrate the correct flight attitude for landing. By 1949 the syllabus had been formalised as experience grew and included; familiarisation exercises, stalls, low altitude flying, height climbs, aerobatics and high-speed runs. The need for more structured training was still obvious, however.

Gloster Takes the Lead

By 1947, Gloster Aircraft Ltd with its eye on the export market had already begun design work on the G-43 two-seat conversion trainer based on the Meteor F.4. The Air Ministry gave its backing to the project and in February 1947 announced their interest before the Preliminary Mock-Up Conference was held on 23rd March. Operational Requirement OR.238 had been drawn up as early as December 1946 and Specification T.1/47 was issued on 16th May to cover development and production for the RAF as the Meteor T.7. The trainer was based on the standard F.4 airframe but with a 30in (76cm) fuselage extension to insert a second seat into the lengthened cockpit, the pupil and instructor sitting in tandem, the instructor's seat being raised by 2in (5cm). An extra fuel tank was fitted and provision was made for a 180gal (818lit) ventral tank and two 100gal (454lit) drop tanks. The armour plating was retained as it was built into the structure and retaining it avoided additional design work. The new canopy was heavily framed and initially no ejection seats were fitted, the RAF having deemed them as desirable but not essential. Once flight testing began it was discovered that the extended nose offered additional directional stability and Gloster capitalised on this to produce the improved F.8 fighter variant. In return, later production T.7s received the F.8's new enlarged area tail surfaces to compensate for the forward shift of the centre of gravity and also received the same 3,500lbf (15.6kN) Rolls-Royce Derwent 8 engines. The RAF wanted to acquire the T.7 to enable fighter pilots to gain familiarisation in operating turbojets before going solo. It would also be used for instruction in aerobatics, ground attacks and air-to-air fighting tactics. The Air Staff requested that the conversion was as simple as possible with the minimum amount of equipment required for flying instruction to be provided in the instructor's rear cockpit. No guns were fitted but the pupil had a retractable G.4B gyro gunsight which was harmonised with the G.45 gun cine-camera. Detachable two-stage amber panels for blind instrument flying training were provided for the front cockpit.

Gloster Meteor Trainer G-AKPK was the private venture prototype that was the template for the Meteor T.7. Rebuilt from the crashed F.4 demonstrator G-AIDC, it made its maiden flight on 19th March 1948. After touring several countries it was sold to the Royal Netherlands Air Force in November 1948. *Author's Collection*

Gloster's private venture prototype G-AKPK (later re-registered G-AIDC) made its maiden flight on 19th March 1948 in the hands of test pilot Bill Waterton. The first production T.7, VW410 (converted from F.4 airframe EE530), made its first flight on 28th October. Performance was good, the rate of climb being improved due to the T.7's lighter weight and handling trials at the Aeroplane and Armament Experimental Establishment (A&AEE) at Boscombe Down with the second production T.7, VW411 (formerly F.4 EE573), showed a similarity in flying characteristics to the F.4. But the marginal longitudinal stability, poor spinning characteristics and large changes of trim associated with increased speeds and thrust were not ideal for a trainer. In January 1952 Specification T.1/47 Issue 2 was issued to cover production for the Royal Navy. Orders for the RAF and Fleet Air Arm (FAA) eventually totalled 682. The type proved equally popular with export nations flying the Meteor with no less than 72 new-build and 75 ex-RAF aircraft being delivered to Belgium (Avions Fairey also converted 20 F.4 airframes), Brazil, Denmark, Egypt, France, Israel and the Netherlands. In addition to helping to improve the F.8 fighter, the T.7 also went on to form the basis of the Meteor NF.11 night fighter developed to Specification F.24/48.

On 26th August 1949 No 226 OCU was transferred to Flying Training Command to become No 203 Advanced Flying School (AFS) and was re-equipped with the T.7. The students having completed their basic instruction at the Flying Training Schools (FTS) on Prentices and Harvards would receive their first jet experience. Five days later the former No 203 AFS at Stradishall was transferred to Fighter Command and reformed as No 226 OCU and split into Meteor and Vampire Flights which covered the gunnery and tactics phases of the 25 hour syllabus respectively. Ten AFSs were equipped with T.7 and they also served with the Central Flying School (CFS), Empire Central Flying School and two Air Navigation Schools for training fast jet navigators. Most frontline squadrons also received a couple of T.7s for check flights and continuation training. The Meteor was a demanding aircraft to fly, especially when flying on asymmetric power and for those pilots who had come straight from the Harvard without any prior asymmetric handling training. The leg rudder forces were high and simulated engine failure after take-off and single engine overshoots were physically demanding. There was also the phenomenon of the 'Phantom Dive' if the airbrakes were accidentally selected open with the undercarriage and flaps down due to the increased drag. With many T.7s lacking ejection seats, any mishap at low level could be potentially fatal and T.7 crashes contributed to the horrifying statistic that 890 Meteors of all marks were lost in RAF service with the death of 450 pilots, many of them during training.

Above: Meteor T.7 WA672 preparing to depart for a display during the Battle of Britain open day at Leconfield on 19th September 1959. At the time WA672 was attached to No 19 Squadron, a Hunter F.6 unit based at the airfield. *Ian MacFarlane*

Below: The Meteor T.7 had a long training career. This example, WH166, was delivered in 1952 and is seen here at St Mawgan at the Battle of Britain Display on 14th September 1968, when it was operated by the Central Flying School. Retired a year later, this aircraft is today is part of the Birlingham Jet Aircraft Collection. *Chris England*

Vampire Trainers

As the demand for fighter pilots increased in response to the unexpected outbreak of the Korean War, the single-seat fighters, in particular the Vampire, had to maintain their share of the training burden. On 15th December 1950 No 229 OCU was formed for day fighter pilots at Leuchars with Vampire FB.5s and FB.9s to provide 26 hours of tactical flying before the pilots progressed to frontline squadrons. More units followed; No 202 AFS at Valley in April 1951 with a mix of Vampire F.1 and FB.5 fighters and Meteor T.7 trainers, No 206 AFS at Oakington in December 1951 and No 208 AFS at Merryfield in February 1952. At Pembrey No 233 OCU completed no less than 46 Vampire and eight Hunter courses between September 1952 and July 1957. The Air Ministry returned to its pre-war policy of allowing private companies to run flying training schools and Flight Refuelling Ltd. received a contract to provide the logistical organisation for No 210 AFS at the company's airfield at Tarrant Rushton. As reservists were recalled, No 102 and No 103 Refresher Flying Schools began providing six week-long courses being providing 20 hours on Spitfires and 15 hours on Vampires during April 1950 to November 1951.

de Havilland had soon recognised the need for a two-seat trainer variant of the DH.100 Vampire and shared Gloster's concern with both the export and home markets. In June 1950 the company decided to proceed with the project as a private venture and since the Hatfield design team was fully occupied, the work was passed to their subsidiary Airspeed Ltd. at Christchurch. The Chief Designer at the time was George Miles, who had moved to Airspeed following the collapse of Miles Aircraft in 1947 and the design team was led by R C Gilbert. Gilbert's team soon settled on side-by-side seating for the instructor and pupil for its advantages in instruction and this also saved design time as the forward fuselage could be based on that of the NF.10 night fighter, the mock-up of the latter being moved from Hatfield to Christchurch. The fuselage design was slightly altered, the canopy side rails were lowered to give a cockpit width of 44in (111cm) at shoulder level, which unlike the NF.10 allowed both seats to be installed level with each other. The standard fighter spade-grip control columns were replaced with hand-grip control columns and the instrument panel layout was redesigned. A new canopy was fitted, but no ejection seats were initially fitted. The wings, tail booms and tail unit were from the Vampire FB.5 fighter. Provision for four 20mm Hispano Mk.V cannon with 150 rounds per gun was retained but only two were normally fitted. A G.45 gun cine-camera was fitted in the nosecone and two retractable Mk.4E gyro gunsights were fitted in the cockpit. The use of the standard Vampire FB.5 wing meant that the full range of underwing store options were available, including; eight 60lb (27kg) rocket projectiles and eight 25lb (11kg) practice bombs, two 500lb (227kg) bombs with or without rockets or two 1,000lb (453kg) bombs.

Vampire T.11 WZ419 was part of the first production batch of fifty aircraft for the RAF.
Author's Collection

The prototype Vampire T.11, G-5-7 on show at the SBAC Farnborough show in September 1950. At this stage the aircraft had not yet flown, but de Havilland was keen to begin marketing the type. G-5-7 (later serialled WW456) made its first flight on 15th November 1950.
Terry Panopalis Collection

The prototype, assigned Class B-Condition markings G-5-7, was ready for static display at the 1950 SBAC Farnborough Show but did not make its maiden flight until 15th November at the hands of test pilot John Wilson. The Air Staff soon became very interested in the Vampire trainer as a more representative airframe for converting Vampire pilots, who were currently training on the twin-engined Meteor T.7. Service trials at No 203 AFS at Driffield commenced in March 1951 following initial delays due to armament problems. Two students, Pilot Officer Michael Warrington and Officer Cadet Kenneth Harvey were selected to undertake a trial flying training course and they went solo after 6 hours 55 minutes and 8 hours 35 minutes respectively. On 2nd April the Central Gunnery School carried out armament tests before handing the aircraft to the A&AEE at Boscombe Down for two phases of evaluation. These evaluations went well and Specification T.111P was issued on 17th April 1952 to cover production of the Vampire T.11. Apart from confirming the armament fit, the specification stated that the aircraft must be cleared to perform four-turn spins. An order for 142 aircraft followed, all of which were built at Christchurch. The first production aircraft WZ414 made its first flight on 19th January 1952 and was retained for trials at the A&AEE alongside several other early production aircraft, WZ418 being used for armament and operational trials with the Central Fighter Establishment over the summer. The first delivery was WZ426 to No 202 AFS at Valley on 2nd September 1952.

Two pre-production aircraft, WW458 and WW461, were ordered for naval evaluation on 5th July 1951 and were delivered to RNAS Culdrose. This was followed by Specification T.111P2 issued on 28th May 1952 for the Sea Vampire T.22. This was identical to the Vampire T.11 except for the fitting of a TR.1936 radio transmitter/receiver and ABX radio beacon equipment, a pilot-operated signal discharger and fixed fittings for anti-G suits. No navalised features such as an arrester hook or folding wings were required as the trainers were intended for shore-based training only. A contract for 53 aircraft was issued on 19th February 1952 and the first T.22 aircraft, XA100, was completed in April 1953. The Vampire trainer also emulated the export sales success of its fighter stablemate; 232 T.55 export variants and eight refurbished ex-RAF T.11s were sold and another 390 were built under licence-production agreements in Australia, India and Switzerland. In all 24 nations either brought or evaluated the type.

Continual improvements were made to the aircraft in the light of service experience. Early aircraft were criticised for poor spin recovery and rudder overbalance as well as poor visibility from the heavily framed cockpit and poor emergency escape facilities. In early 1953 the tailplane fin acorns were removed and the lower leading-edge of the fin moved forwards by 6in (15cm) which improved the spin recovery and cured the rudder overbalance. By April 1952 a new moulded single-piece canopy with direct vision windscreen panels, a new single blind-flying panel and manual Martin-Baker Mk.2 ejection seats were ready for testing. With further modifications, including the fitting of automatic Martin-Baker Mk.3B ejection seats, these changes were introduced on the production line from the 144th aircraft and Marshall of Cambridge was awarded a contract to refit the older aircraft to the same standard.

The first Vampire T.11s were delivered to No 202 AFS on 2nd September 1952 and alongside the introduction of the Percival Provost T.1 in mid-1953 allowed the introduction of a new flying training syllabus. The old system of students undergoing basic training at an FTS and advanced jet training at an AFS was replaced now that students could be given jet experience at the FTS stage. Students would now complete 130 hours of basic flying on the Provost T.1 followed by 100 hours of advanced flying on the Vampire T.11. The new syllabus was trialled by No 206 AFS starting with No 101 course on 21st April 1954, with Pilot Officer David Clegg becoming the first to solo on the Vampire T.11 on 15th May. The only downside of the new syllabus was its £10,000 greater cost per pilot. On 1st June Flying Training Command was reorganised and the AFSs were disbanded and reformed as FTSs. The RAF College at Cranwell replaced its Boulton Paul Balliol T.2s with Vampire T.11s in January 1955, but their first Provost/Vampire syllabus students did not graduate until April 1957. The CFS, responsible for training flying instructors and maintaining flight standards, was also reorganised for the Provost/Vampire syllabus with CFS (Basic) at South Cerney with Provost T.1s and CFS (Advanced) at Little Rissington with two Meteor squadrons and a Vampire flight. During May 1957 the two elements merged at Little Rissington with Provost and Vampire squadrons delivering a semi-specialised course with intakes of 42 students every nine weeks. The students would undergo 51 hours on the Provost, then the course

Sea Vampire T.22 XG775 is seen here at the Yeovilton Naval Air Day on 9th September 1967, resplendent in the colours of the Flag Officer Naval Flying Training, the personal aircraft of Rear-Admiral David W Kirke. This senior post was responsible for all naval flying training from 1945 until it was abolished in November 1970. XG775 survives today in private ownership. *Liam Thomas*

The Vampire T.11 had a relatively long service life despite being a first-generation jet trainer. T.11 XD550 served from August 1954 to July 1969 and is pictured here in September 1966 sporting CFS markings and the ubiquitous dayglo vinyl strips which adorned most of the training fleet. *Terry Panopalis Collection*

split; 40 students receiving 40 hours on the Vampire before being posted as Qualified Flight Instructors (QFIs) to fighter squadrons and the remainder completing their training on the Provost. There were also changes to training for FAA pilots. The disbandment of the Royal Navy's Volunteer Reserve squadrons in March 1957 had drastically reduced the training requirements and on 27th January 1958 No 7 FTS lost its role as the dedicated Naval Jet Flying School, this duty being transferred to No 1 FTS at Linton-on-Ouse which graduated its first mixed RAF and FAA course on 3rd April.

Sea Vampire T.22 XG768 was being used by the Lossiemouth Station Flight when it was photographed visiting Odiham for a Battle of Britain open day on 9th September 1962. Visible in the lower fuselage are the cannon firing ports carried over from the NF.10 for gunnery training, although Vampire trainers were only fitted with two 20mm Hispano cannon. *Robin A Walker*

The Vampire T.11 also equipped the Central Gunnery School for six years from September 1952 – the School later transferred to Fighter Command as the Fighter Weapons School. The T.11 was used on the Pilot Attack Instructors' course, the syllabus of which included 55 flying hours. Following experience gained during the Korean War, there was a renewed emphasis on fighter weapons training, in particular air-to-air gunnery. The T.11 proved to be eminently suitable, retaining the stable gunnery platform characteristics of its fighter origins, modern jet performance and the full range of air-to-ground ordnance used by frontline Vampire and Venom squadrons. The side-by-side pupil and instructor seating and individual gun sights increased safety during practice missions and enabled easier debriefings.

The arrival of the Folland Gnat T.2 into Flying Training Command use from November 1962 saw the T.11 being gradually replaced, having trained over 3,000 pilots. In July 1963 No 4 FTS gave up the last of its Vampires but the need train foreign pilots from Jordan, Lebanon, Iraq, Kuwait and Saudi Arabia saw the Vampire Training Flight being retained during 1965. The Flight lived a nomadic existence, forming out of No 1 FTS before lodging with No 7 FTS at Church Fenton in January 1966 and then No 3 FTS at Leeming from November until its task was completed in January 1968. The final T.11s in British service were the aircraft of No 3/4 Civilian Anti-Aircraft Cooperation Unit at Exeter Airport which were used as high-speed ranging and tracking targets across Southern Britain and in naval exercises until 31st December 1971.

The Avro 704 of 1947 still looks futuristic today with its twin 'bug eye' canopies and a wide fuselage containing two Rolls-Royce Derwent 5 turbojets. An ambitious design, its advanced nature put it far beyond Air Staff requirements at that time. *Avro Heritage*

Private Venture Proposals

Equally as keen as the Services to adopt the new jet turbine technology, the aircraft industry saw the need for jet-powered trainers and thoughts soon turned to developing an advanced trainer that might attract the attention of the RAF. In hindsight, Gloster and de Havilland were in the preeminent position of being able to offer variants of existing frontline jet fighters, which quickly proved attractive to the Air Ministry when they were offered. One of the earliest attempts to enter this market was made by Avro in early 1947 when Chief Designer Stuart Davies began work on an advanced trainer powered by the Rolls-Royce Derwent turbojet. The Type 704 was a futuristic looking advanced trainer powered by two Derwent 5 engines fed via wing root intakes and with a single tailpipe exhaust. The student and instructor sat side-by-side but both had individual 'bug-eye' canopies. The compact design was smaller than the Type 701 Athena with a span of 37ft 8in (11.4m) and a length of 34ft 6in (10.5m) with an estimated all-up weight (AUW) of 9,245lb (4,193kg). This was soon superseded by the Type 704B based on the Athena, following an approach from Rolls-Royce in January 1947. With the intended Armstrong Siddeley Mamba and Rolls-Royce Dart turboprops being delayed, Rolls-Royce enquired whether Davies had considered fitting a Derwent to the Athena instead. The resulting Type 704B had a single Derwent mounted behind the cockpit fed by extended wing root intakes and with a bifurcated exhaust exiting the rear fuselage.

The Avro Type 704B design came about when Rolls-Royce enquired whether Avro's Chief Designer Stuart Davies had considered fitting their Derwent turbojet to the Athena. The resulting design had a Derwent behind the cockpit fed by wing root intakes and exhausted via a bifurcated jet pipe. Heat and vibration problems on the rear fuselage would have been likely with this layout. *Author*

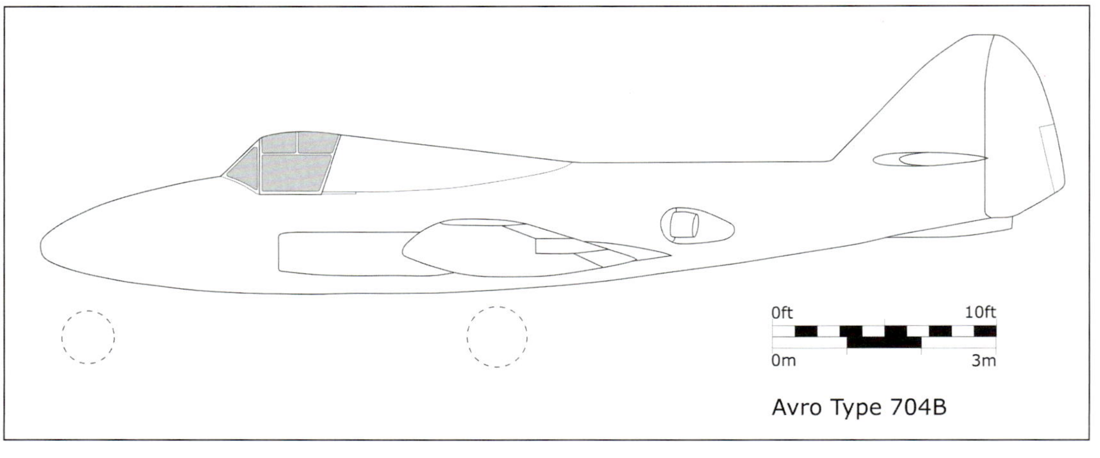

Alternative paths. Two Boulton Paul P.119 Brasenose T.1s streak in over the ranges at Kirkcudbright, releasing a salvo of 3in rocket projectiles against the tank hulks. The P.119 was a contemporary private venture with the de Havilland Vampire Trainer but lost out due to the latter being based on a frontline fighter. *Luciano Alviani*

The revised undercarriage would use a standard Meteor nosewheel. It had a span of 40ft (12.1m), a length of 39ft 6in (12m) and an AUW of 9,429lb (4,276kg). Unofficially presented in early 1947 to meet T.7/45, Air Vice-Marshal John N Boothman, the Assistant Chief of the Air Staff (Tactics and Requirements) argued that the Meteor Trainer then on the drawing board offered a better prospect and that piston engines offered the better economy for the T.7/45 trainers. A refined design completed in April 1948 was again offered against the Meteor T.7 that June and also figured in the early discussions of Operational Requirement OR.257 which would result in the Percival Provost. By then the RAF was committed to the Meteor and the Type 704B was in a different class from the relatively basic type wanted for OR.257.

In February 1950 Boulton Paul became the next company to propose an advanced trainer. Whilst developing the Balliol they had come to the conclusion that the RAF would need a suitable jet-powered advanced trainer. The P.119 was an attractive moderately-swept low-wing design with side-by-side seating with ejection seats and powered by either a single Rolls-Royce Derwent or a Nene depending on the desired level of performance. It could be armed with two 20mm cannon and underwing racks for bombs or rocket projectiles The P.119 is notable in being one of the few aircraft proposed with the NACA duct low-drag flush intake – one notable example from America being the North American YF-93 fighter – which Chief Designer John Dudley North selected for its low drag properties which removed the need for draggy wing root intakes and wing fillets. The NACA scoop proved difficult to scale up with problems with poor pressure recovery, poor flow volume and airflow issues at high angles-of-attack, but today it is ubiquitous as a ventilation intake. The P.119N was a proposed for naval variant with folding wings and an arrester hook. The aircraft was designed with economy of operation and maintenance in mind, like the Balliol it relied on a pneumatic system and the rear fuselage could be detached to give access to the engine with an engine change estimated to take an hour. It was hoped that the speed of 412kt (764km/h) at 22,000ft (6,705m) with the Derwent and 482kt (893km/h) at 10,000ft (3,050m) with the Nene, combined with excellent manoeuvrability would make the P.119 a good trainer for future fighter pilots. A full scale mock-up was built at Pendeford but the emergence of the private-venture Vampire trainer four months later removed any chance of production as the Vampire had the bonus of offering production and parts commonality with its fighter stablemates.

The Boulton Paul P.119 was a conventional design and except its intake configuration. The NACA duct proved difficult to scale up into an intake for jet engines due to problems with poor pressure recovery, poor flow volume and airflow issues at high angles-of-attack. However, it proved ideal as a ventilation intake and can be seen on countless aircraft today.
Les Whitehouse, Boulton Paul Archive

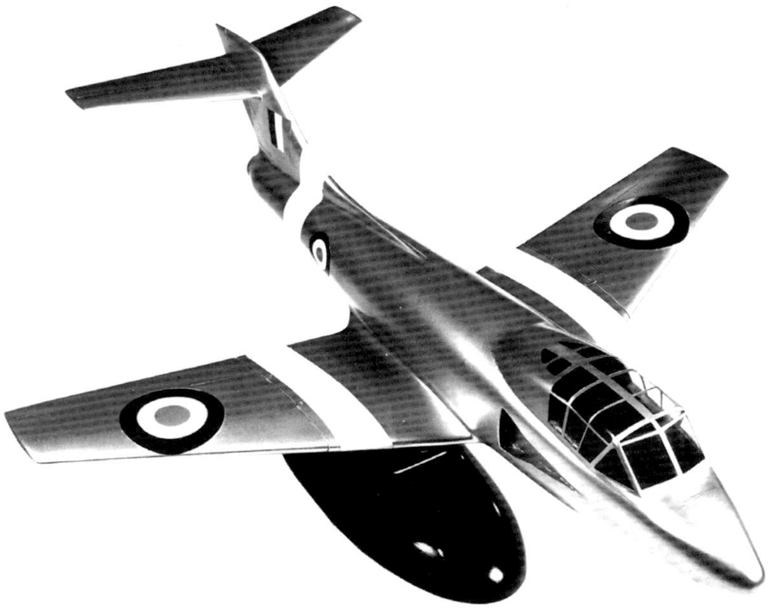

Above This frontal view of the P.119 mock-up shows to good effect the flush NACA duct intake which reduced drag and enabled a performance approaching that of frontline fighters of the time.
Les Whitehouse, Boulton Paul Archive

Left: A model of the P.119 in standard early 1950s RAF training colours. Just visible on the upper surface of the wing is the hinge line for the folding wings which would have been shared with the fully navalised P.119N for operations aboard aircraft carriers.
Les Whitehouse, Boulton Paul Archive

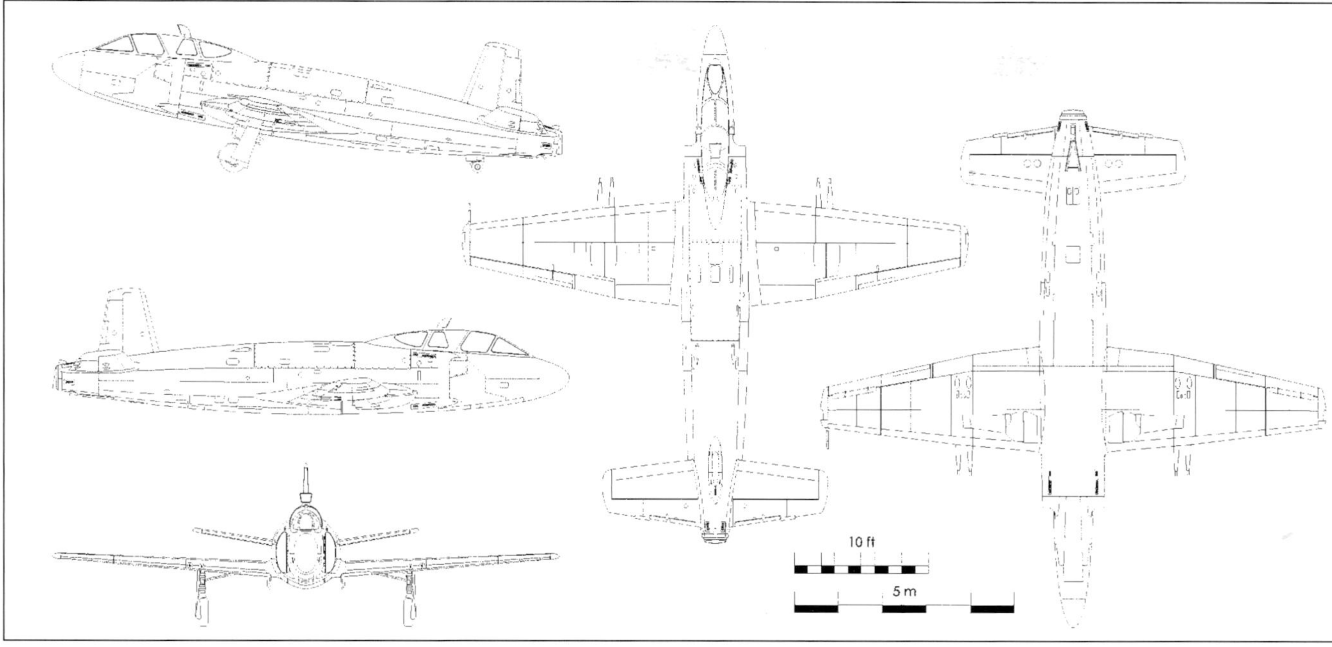

Vickers-Supermarine had the same idea as de Havilland; make a trainer out of their latest fighter. The Attacker's forward fuselage and intakes were slightly lengthened to insert the instructor's cockpit. The result was surprisingly attractive. *Jens Baganz*

Naval Fighter-Trainers

During 1950 several companies proposed two-seat trainer variants of naval aircraft and projects that were then underway. There seems to be no formal requirement from the Admiralty but the timing and capability of these designs suggests that they were offered to meet a potential need for an armed operational conversion trainer for the Fleet Air Arm. All of these designs were somewhat more powerful and heavily armed than RAF trainers of the period, indeed these predate the Air Staff's Operational Requirement OR.318 for an advanced transonic trainer by five years.

During April 1950 Westland designed a jet-powered successor to its W.35 Wyvern naval torpedo strike-fighter, the W.37. The W.37/1 was powered by a 7,500lbf (33.3kN) reheated Armstrong Siddeley Sapphire turbojet and had an internal weapons bay, the W.37/2 having a slimmer fuselage and carrying its weapons externally. Both had moderately swept wings with wing root intakes and a T-tail. Although based on current Admiralty specifications, these designs were a private-venture and they were also offered as two-seat operational trainers. A mock-up was built but no official interest was forthcoming and the W.37 designation was re-used in 1951 for a carrier-based all-weather fighter project submitted to Specification N.114T.

Around the same time as de Havilland began work on the Vampire trainer, Vickers-Supermarine offered a trainer variant of its Type 398 Attacker carrier-based fighter. The Attacker had just entered production for the Navy and shortly afterwards Pakistan ordered 36 land-based Type 538 fighters. Probably with an eye on export orders a trainer was designed and a model was displayed at the Brussels International Aeronautical Exhibition in June 1950. The major change to the fuselage was the tandem cockpit with a lengthened nose and the intakes for the single Nene turbojet were slightly moved forwards. The instructor's cockpit was fitted with a periscope to improve forward vision for the gunsight and both cockpits had ejection seats. The Attacker's four 20mm Hispano cannon and arrester hook were retained. Supermarine also developed the Type 539, a conversion of the Type 525 swept-wing carrier-based fighter that had been submitted in June 1949 to meet Specification N.9/47. The Type 539 retained the Type 525's airframe, 45° swept wings and V-tail and the twin 6,500lbf (28.9kN) Rolls-Royce Avon RA.3 turbojets. The nose was modified with a very similar tandem cockpit to the Attacker Trainer and the fixed armament was reduced to two 20mm Hispano cannon, but the ranging-radar in the nose was retained and two F.24 cameras could be fitted in the rear fuselage. Two fuselage fuel tanks were removed to make room for the instructor and equipment displaced from the nose respectively, but No 2 fuselage tank was slightly enlarged to compensate. The Type 539 would have been a formidable conversion trainer with frontline fighter performance but no interest was forthcoming. Redesigned with a conventional tail, the Type 525 led to the Type 544 Scimitar day-fighter which entered service in 1958 and its pilots would receive their operational conversion training on the Sea Vampire T.22.

This poor quality but interesting photograph shows the model of the Attacker Trainer displayed at the Brussels International Aeronautical Exhibition in June 1950. Despite Supermarine planning to use the Class B-Conditions marking G-15-7, no prototype was ever built.
Via Tony Buttler

The work on the Attacker Trainer was not wasted. An identical solution was applied to the Type 525 swept-wing naval fighter. The result was a formidable aircraft which looks much more like a radar-equipped night-fighter than a trainer in capability.
Via Ralph Pegram

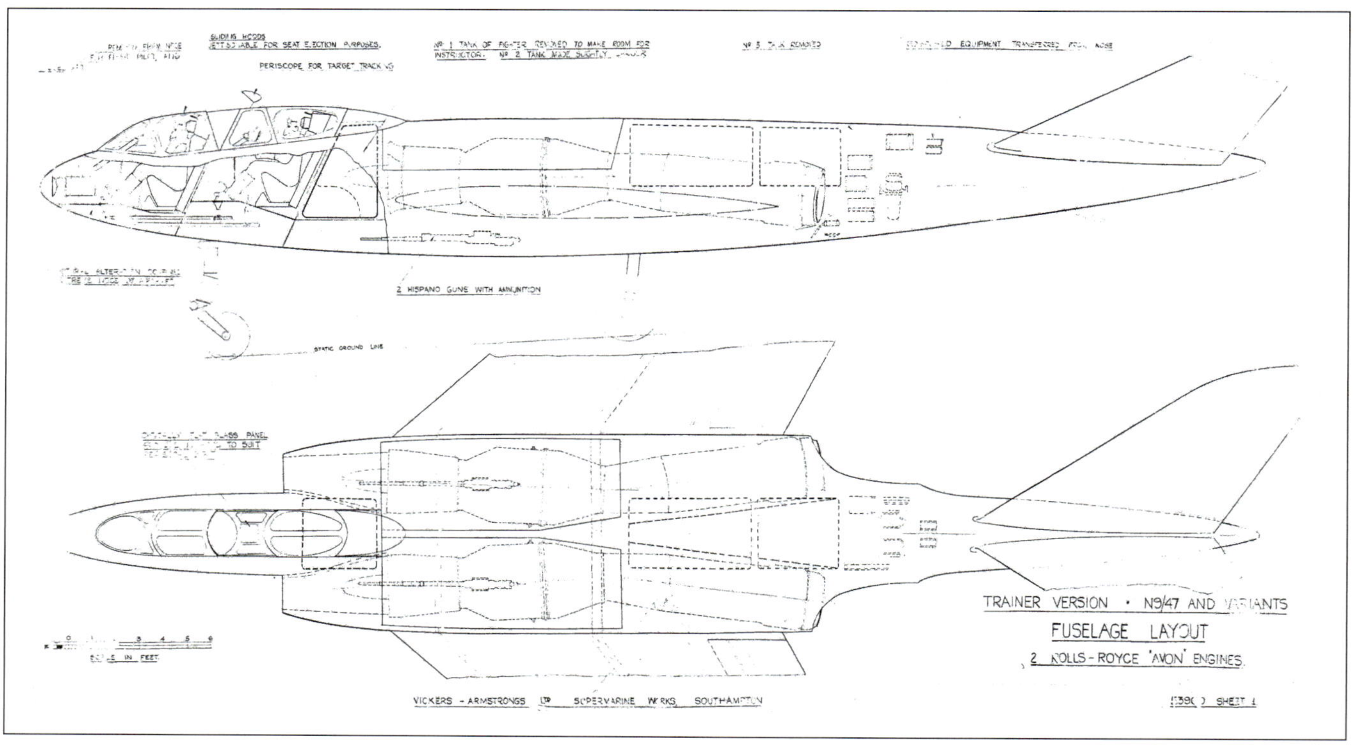

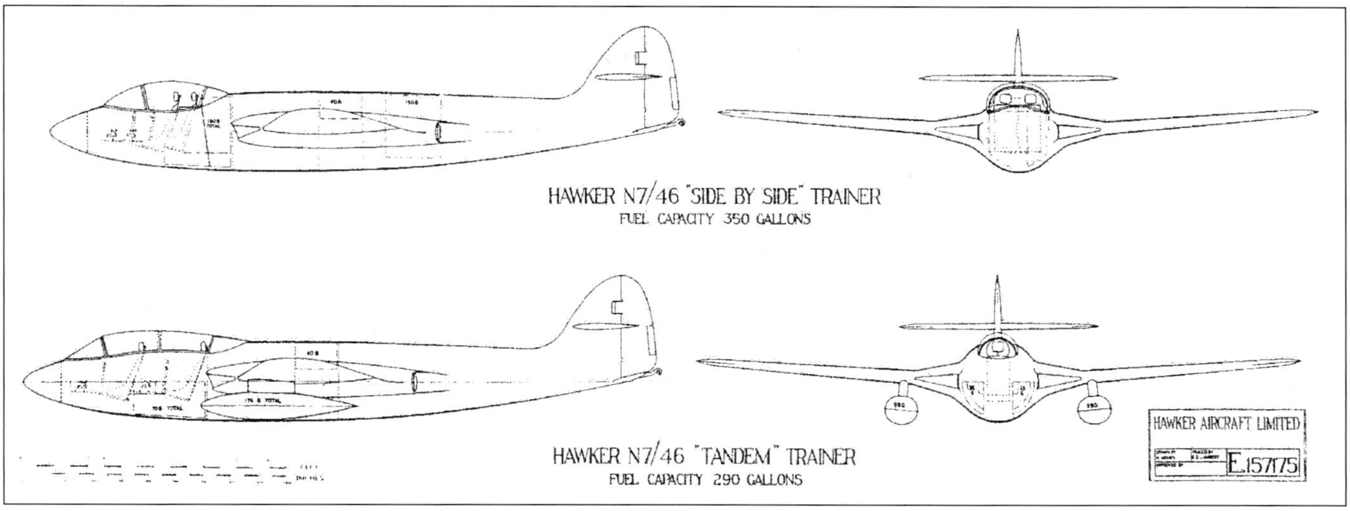

Hawker's design office studied two trainer variants of the P.1040 Sea Hawk with side-by-side or tandem seating, the latter requiring external fuel tanks to restore range. No armament was offered as fuel tanks replaced the 20mm Hispano cannon and ammunition bays. *Chris Farara*

Hawker also proposed a two-seat trainer variant of a naval fighter, in this case the P.1040 Sea Hawk. The proposal married a new cockpit and forward fuselage section to the standard Sea Hawk airframe and folding wings. The new cockpit had slightly staggered side-by-side seating for the instructor and student and the total internal fuel capacity was 350gal (1,591lit). A second proposal had a new forward fuselage with tandem seating, this entailed removing the forward fuselage fuel tank; two smaller 35gal (159lit) tanks being placed either side of the instructor's seat in the former cannon armament bays. To maintain the centre of gravity the rear fuselage tank was also removed and to compensate, two external 88gal (400lit) tanks were fitted to provide a total system capacity of 290gal (1,318lit). Neither proposal carried any armament, but the arrester tailhooks were retained, which suggests that both were intended for possible naval use as advanced pilot trainers.

This diagram shows all the major structural components of the Sea Hawk trainer. Only the forward fuselage differed from the original fighter and the naval features of an arrester hook and folding wings were retained. *Tony Buttler*

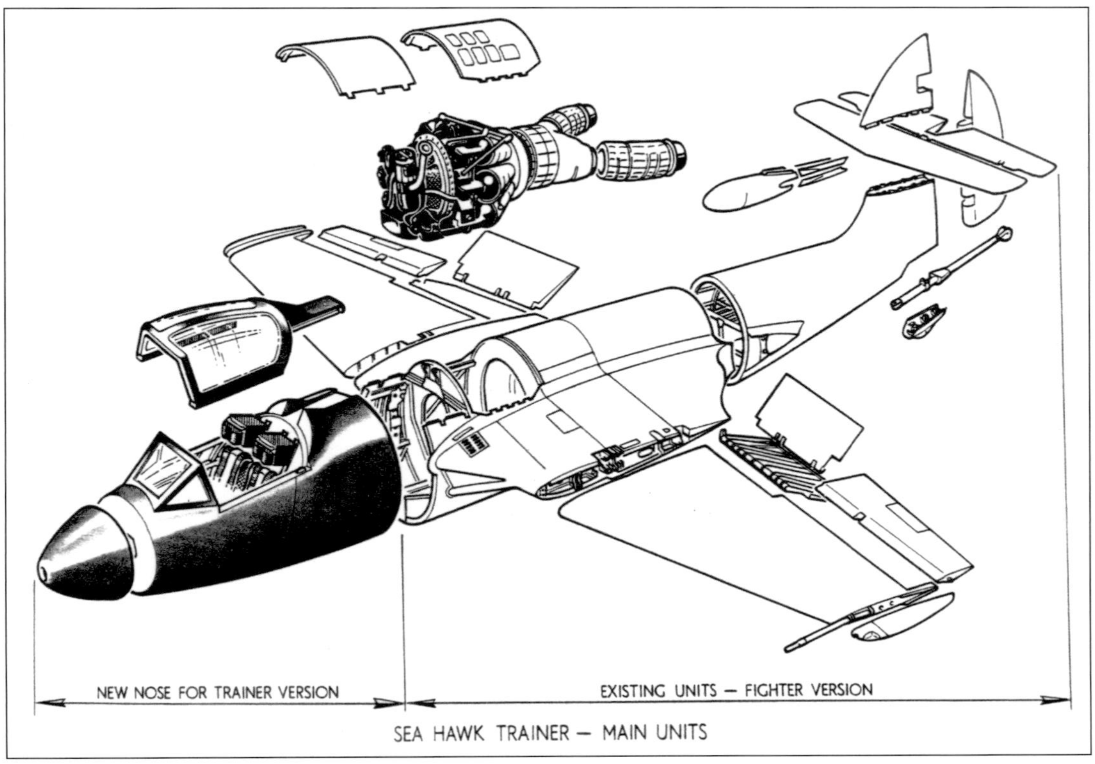

The Basic Trainer Market

With the Meteor T.7 and Vampire T.11 fulfilling the advanced trainer roles, the industry switched to proposing basic trainers to take advantage of a new generation of smaller, lighter and more economical turbojets. Armstrong Siddeley in 1948 had developed a turbojet variant of the Mamba turboprop as the ASA.1 Adder. From the Adder they had developed the 1,145lbf (5.09kN) ASV.1 Viper as a short life expendable engine for the Australian Government Aircraft Factory's Jindivik target drone, but quickly had appreciated the potential for manned applications and began work on the longer life 1,640lbf (7.29kN) ASV.5 Viper 101. Bristol in 1952 had been approached by designer William 'Teddy' Petter to develop a simple lightweight engine for his Folland Midge lightweight fighter project. The resulting BOr.1 Orpheus was first run in December 1954 rated at 3,285lbf (14.6kN) and by Spring 1955 was attaining 4,050lbf (18.0kN). With further development, both of these engines went on to power numerous fighters and trainers. In France, Turbomeca was developing a series of small engines, the 243lbf (1.07kN) thrust Piméné of 1949 led to the 350lbf (1.27kN) Palas, the 1,760lbf (7.8kN) Ossau and in 1952 the 880lbf (3.9kN) Marboré II, which powered the Fouga CM.170 Magister, Europe's first jet-powered basic trainer. Seeing a gap in the market without any direct British competitor, Blackburn and General Aircraft's Engine Division acquired a licence from Turbomeca in October 1952 to produce a range of the light turbojets and turboshafts.

The emergence of the Magister in 1952 also sparked interest within NATO for jet trainers and in mid-1952 the Standard Jet Trainer Working Party was formed to study potential aircraft that could be used across NATO countries. In July 1952 the Air Training Advisory Group was formed to advise on flying standards and how best to use available resources. A joint squadron was based at Villacoublay Air Base in France, staffed by qualified flying instructors from across NATO to visit flying training schools throughout Europe to check the standards of training and to suggest possible improvements. In the absence of concrete interest from the Air Ministry the NATO developments were to provide further impetus to the private venture work then being undertaken.

The two Blackburn P.92 designs were very similar but the P.92/2 was larger and heavier and was Blackburn's favoured solution to the jet training problem. ***Author***

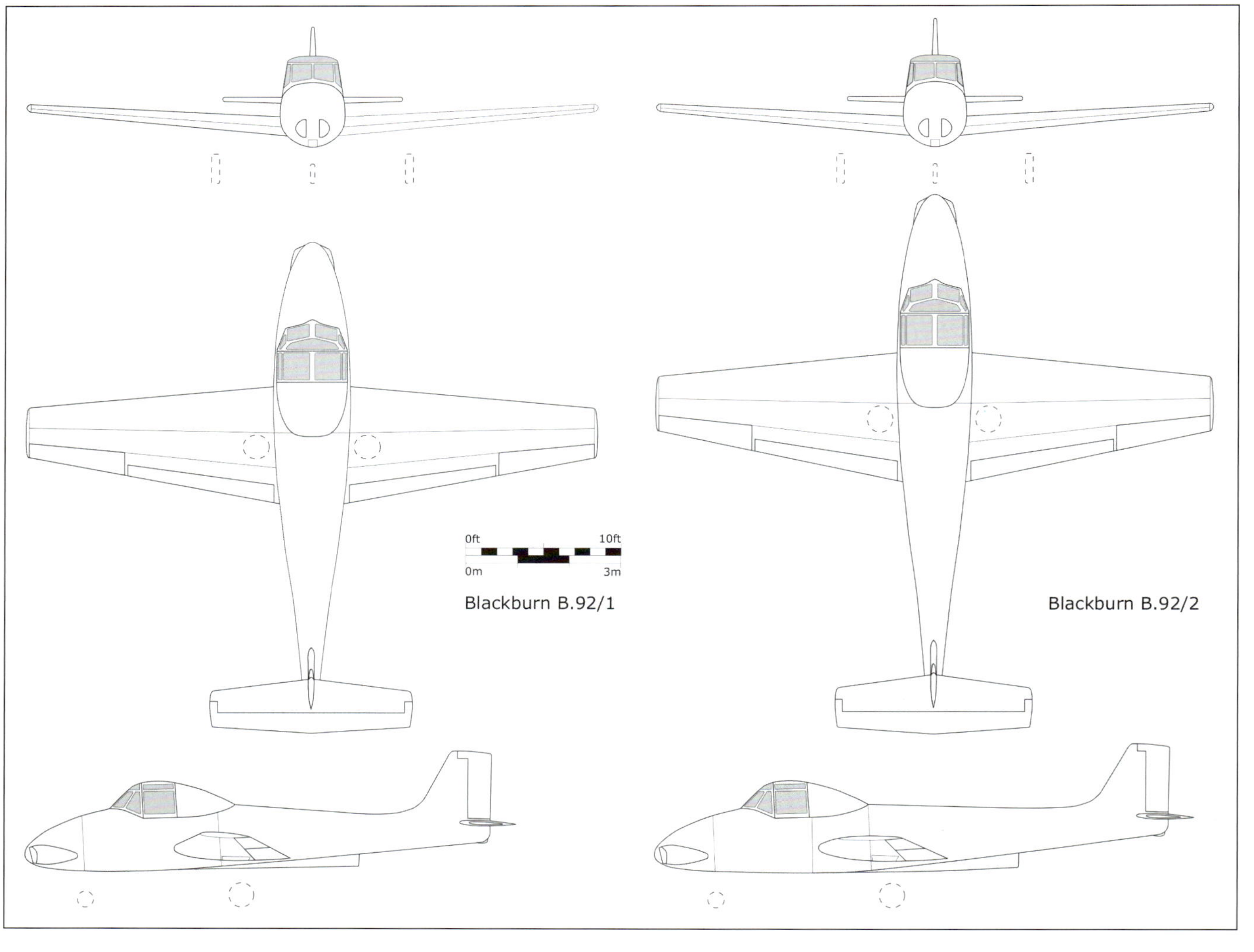

Table 4.1 – Blackburn B.92

	B.92/1	B.92/2
Wingspan	36ft 5in (11.1m)	35ft 5in (10.79m)
Length	31ft 3in (9.52m)	34ft 4in (10.46m)
Wing Area	200ft² (18.5m²)	220ft² (20.4m²)
All-Up Weight	3,989lb (1,809kg)	5,732lb (2,600kg)
Powerplant	Marboré II, 880lbf (3.9kN)	Ossau, 1,760lbf (7.8kN)
Max Speed/Height	246kt (455km/h) at 10,000ft (3,050m)	355kt (657km/h) at 10,000ft (3,050m)

NATO's Military Standardization Agency in 1954 recommended the Magister as the common trainer but – as with nearly all NATO attempts at standardisation – several new jet trainers subsequently appeared including; the Cessna T-37, Macchi MB.326 and the Percival Jet Provost, which alongside the Magister would dominate the Western market for the next 20 years.

Blackburn Aircraft began work on their B-92 jet trainer in July 1951. By July 1952 this had evolved into the B-92/1 powered by the Marboré and the B-92/2 with the more powerful Ossau, both engine being part of the licence agreement with Turbomeca. Both aircraft shared a common design with a low-wing monoplane wing, side-by-side seating and the jet engine was mounted behind the cockpit in the lower fuselage with a bifurcated nose intake to clear the nosewheel bay and a ventral exhaust under the rear fuselage. Gunnery or rocket training equipment could be fitted and sufficient fuel was carried for two consecutive sorties totalling 2.75 hours. Blackburn argued that the small jet engines gave comparable fuel costs to the piston-engined Provost, especially when a syllabus with reduced flying hours was factored in. The B-92/1 had an estimated AUW of 3,989lb (1,809kg) and was aimed at a like-for-like Provost replacement in terms of power loading, wing loading and take-off and landing distances even in tropical conditions. The estimated maximum speed was 242kt (448km/h) with an initial rate of climb of 1,710ft/min (8.6m/sec). The B-92/2 with increased power and better performance was Blackburn's ideal future basic trainer with an AUW of 5,732lb (2,600kg), maximum speed of 346kt (640km/h) and an initial rate of climb of 3,400ft (17.2m/sec). This level of performance would enable students to learn how to handle jet engines and relevant flying characteristics whilst closing the gap in performance between the basic and advanced trainers. Blackburn was selling a concept as much as an aircraft, their brochure suggesting that Flying Training Command should begin experiments with jet basic trainers. Blackburn actually declined to submit the B-92 to the NATO Working Party, claiming that the requirements were too vague and that they lacked the time to prepare a more detailed study. Blackburn's technical director, Mr N E Rowe (who had been the Director of Technical Development at the Ministry of Aircraft Production during the Second World War), explained to Mr A E Woodward-Nutt, the Ministry of Supply's (MoS) Director Military Aircraft Research and Development, that 'our objective was to put to the Air and Training Staffs a note which has an approach to the problem of the basic jet trainer from the designer's point of view, in the hope that this might help them in their own thinking on the problem.' Woodward-Nutt seemed convinced by Blackburn's arguments but it was up to the Air Staff to decide if they wanted a jet basic trainer. Copies of the brochures were sent to Assistant Chief of the Air Staff (Training) and while Blackburn's ideas might have added to the Air Staff's evolving thoughts on the subject, no further interest in the B-92 itself was shown. Blackburn also drew up the B-92A powered by a Mamba turboprop and the B-92B with two Mambas.

Boulton Paul's artist has again doctored a Balliol in flight to give a convincing impression of how the P.125 'Jet Balliol' would look. The nose intake and ventral exhaust was the easiest conversion but Percival's Jet Provost proved to be the more practical transformation of a piston-powered airframe. *Les Whitehouse, Boulton Paul Archive*

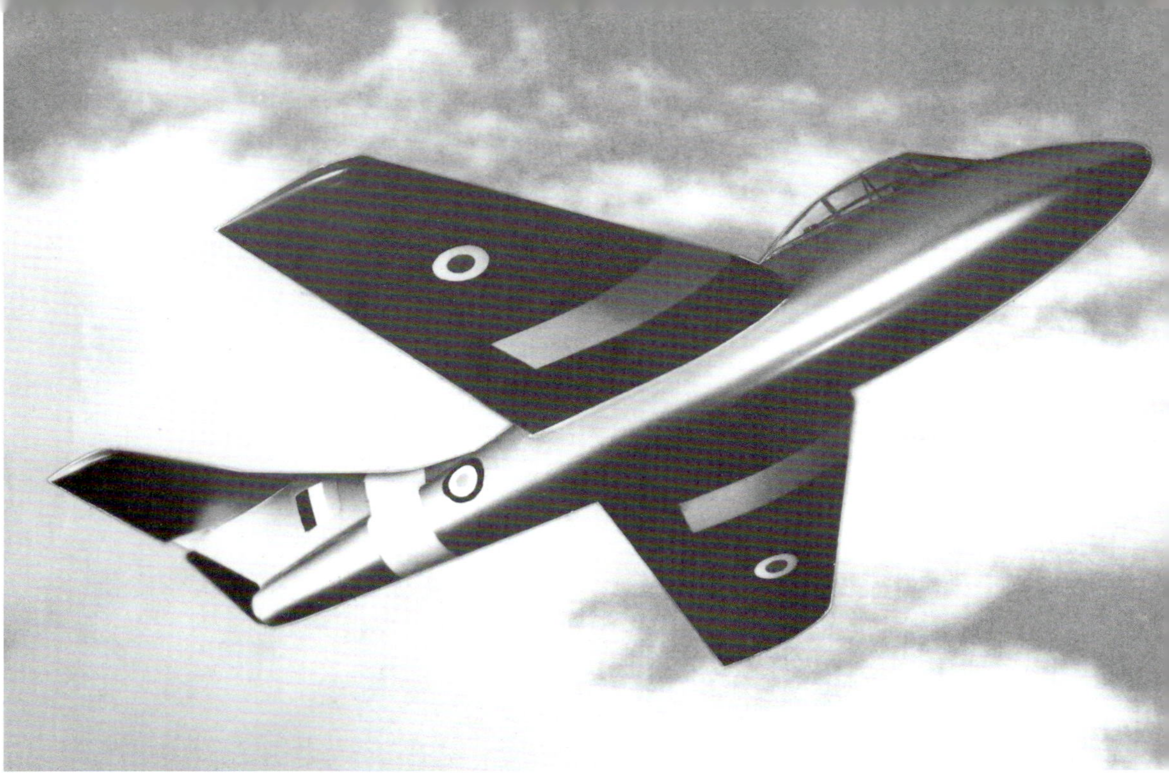

The Boulton Paul P.124 was the result of MoS discussions and was proof that the Air Staff was keeping its options open. The ten Percival Jet Provost T.1s were purely for evaluation and a further order was not guaranteed. The MoS opened its planned tender competition, the P.124 may well have been built, at least in prototype form. *Author's Collection*

Surprisingly, it took until 1952 before Boulton Paul submitted a jet-powered Balliol, the P.125 which was proposed to meet the NATO Working Party requirements. The P.125 was powered by a Rolls-Royce Derwent fitted in the nose with a ventral fuselage exhaust and the undercarriage was revised with a tricycle layout with the nosewheel offset to port. The P.124 was submitted to a draft MoS specification in July 1954, but Percival's Jet Provost was already undergoing evaluation with the RAF by this time. The P.124 had side-by-side seating, a moderately swept wing and was powered by a single 1,640lbf (7.29kN) Armstrong Siddeley ASV.5 Viper turbojet with wing root intakes. It had an estimated AUW of 5,380lb (2,440kg) and maximum speed of 330kt (611km/h). With little chance of an RAF order the P.124 was modified with a Bristol Orpheus turbojet as the P.131 and tendered to the Royal Australian Air Force's Operational Requirement OR/Air/37 issued in May 1954, again without success.

English Electric in June 1954 proposed their P.9 design, a small basic jet trainer with side-by-side seating and powered by a 880lbf (3.9kN) Marboré II. Work stopped in October, but the design would later be revisited a decade later as a starting point when work began on an advanced trainer to succeed the Folland Gnat.

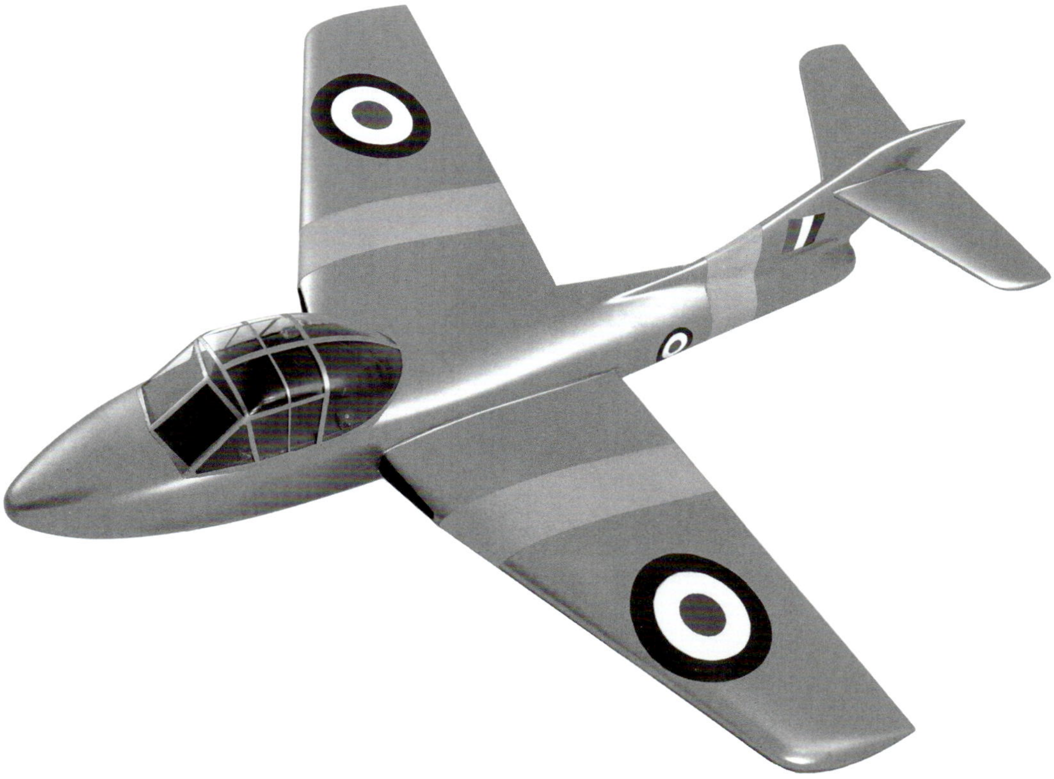

Although shown here in RAF training colours, the P.131 was a revised P.124 with a Bristol Siddeley Orpheus and was intended mainly for the Royal Australian Air Force. *Les Whitehouse, Boulton Paul Archive*

This unknown design was from a Boulton Paul publicity department negative. Although similar to the P.124 it differs in several respects with a low-mounted wing and tailplane. Despite further research the identity of this project is unknown. It may depict an early P.124 proposal or is a speculative sketch by the company's artist Eric Evans or one of his young protégés. The serial VR177 is fictitious but dates it as the early 1950s. *Author's Collection*

Not defeated after the collapse of Miles Aircraft, in December 1948 F G Miles formed F G Miles Ltd. at Redhill Aerodrome in Surrey. In 1951 the company moved to Shoreham Aerodrome in West Sussex and the Miles brothers were reunited when George left Airspeed on its merger with de Havilland. Having gained experience by converting the prototype M.5 Sparrowhawk into the M.77 Sparrowjet racing aircraft with two Turbomeca Palas turbojets between 1951 and 1953, the Miles brothers began to design an economical jet-powered basic trainer, the M.100 Student. The M.100 was powered by a single 880lbf (3.9kN) Marboré IIA fed by a dorsal NACA flush intake above the wing centre section to limit the possibility of foreign object ingestion. This led to some engine airflow problems at certain incidences of flight, especially on take-off and Rolls-Royce later estimated that the engine efficiency was reduced by 20 percent. The Marboré was fitted in the upper fuselage behind the cockpit and exhausted over the rear fuselage, the tail having twin fins to allow the efflux to pass through. The student and instructor sat side-by-side in the cockpit with large car-type

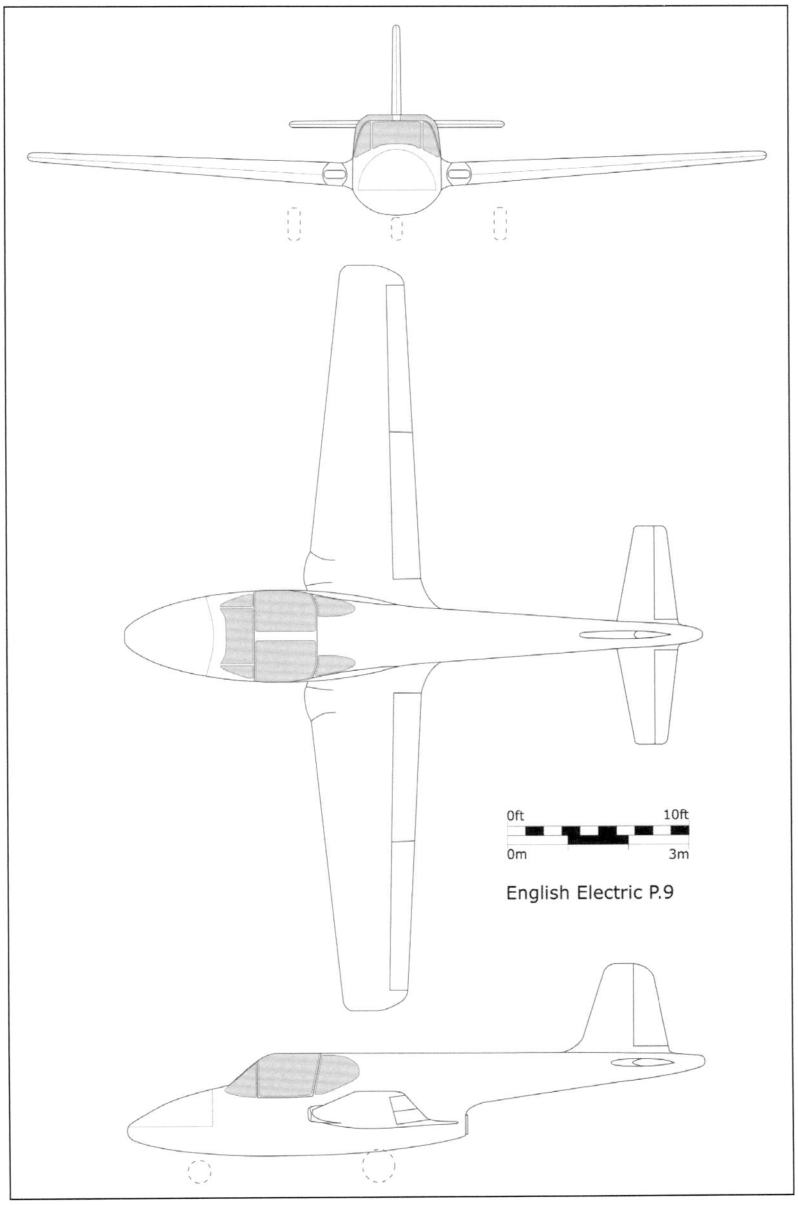

English Electric was more famous for its Canberra tactical bomber and Lightning interceptor but the company also designed a small basic jet trainer with side-by-seating, the P.9. *Author*

The prototype Student made its initial flights during 1957 under temporary B-Conditions markings as G-25-4 before it was registered as G-APLK. It is seen here at the Baginton (Coventry Airport) Air Show in April 1961 when FG Miles Limited were marketing the Student to private pilots. *Terry Panopalis Collection*

doors for access and without ejection seats but with an excellent field of vision. The modest weapons capability was designed with armament training in mind but also as a cheap close support aircraft, the options being; two pods each with 35 50mm Oerlikon rockets, four 60lb (27kg) or six 25lb (11kg) rocket projectiles or eight 25lb (11kg) bombs. Two 7.7mm machine guns could also be fitted to the weapons pylons. Begun as a private venture in 1953, the prototype, later registered G-APLK, did not make its maiden flight with George Miles at the controls until 15th May 1957. By this time the Jet Provost was entering RAF service and the relatively poor performance compared to the Viper-engined Jet Provost prevented any official interest in the Student. A navalised version was also promoted as a communications aircraft, the small wingspan enabling it to be struck below on aircraft carrier lifts without the need for wing folding. Miles tried to market the Student to the civil market in its original two-seat and enlarged four-seat Mk.3 Centurion forms, but again without success. In early 1964 G-APLK was modified to Mk.2 standard and proposed for the counter-insurgency role. The RAF conducted trials, allocating serial XS941, but it was again rejected with the Provost as the armed Strikemaster fulfilling the role.

Around this time Westland also designed a basic jet trainer with side-by-side seating and was powered by a single turbojet fed by wing root intakes and with a ventral exhaust under the rear fuselage. This design never went any further.

Evaluating the Jet Provost

On the back of their success with the P.56 Provost, in 1951 Percival began design studies of a jet-powered variant with an emphasis on handling qualities rather than performance and making the best use of existing Provost parts. The wing, fin and tailplane were used, with strengthening where necessary, and married with a modified fuselage with a 3ft (0.9m) longer rear section to house a 1,640lbf (7.29kN) ASV.5 Viper 101. The cockpit was moved forwards and a tricycle undercarriage with a new nosewheel leg was fitted. Initial studies had the Viper in the forward fuselage, this was then moved beneath the nose into a nacelle and a twin-engine version with podded engines was also studied before the final arrangement with the engine in the rear fuselage fed by 'ear' type intakes either side of the cockpit was agreed. As flown the intakes were moved to the wing roots. Armed with their P.84 sketches the company approached the Air Ministry who agreed that the idea had merit. Percival utilised their relationship with RAF Flying Training Command to thoroughly analyse the likely advantages of a 120 hour Jet Provost syllabus; cost savings by replacing both the Percival Prentice and Vampire T.11 for basic and advanced training, students would not have to unlearn propeller techniques were converting

Low cost was the key aim for the M.100 Student and this diagram shows all the main structural components and the location of the Turbomeca Marboré IIA behind the cockpit. *Miles Aircraft*

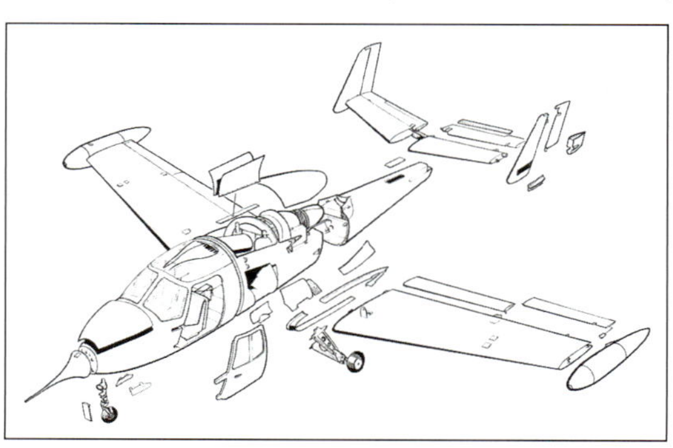

This illustration from a 1958 brochure for the Student shows well the good field of vision from the cockpit. *Miles Aircraft*

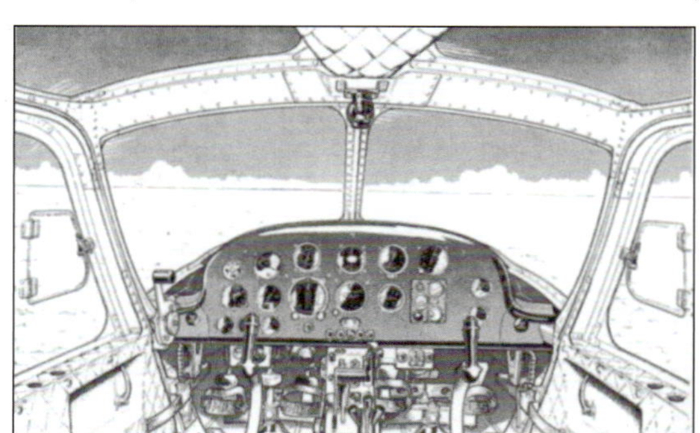

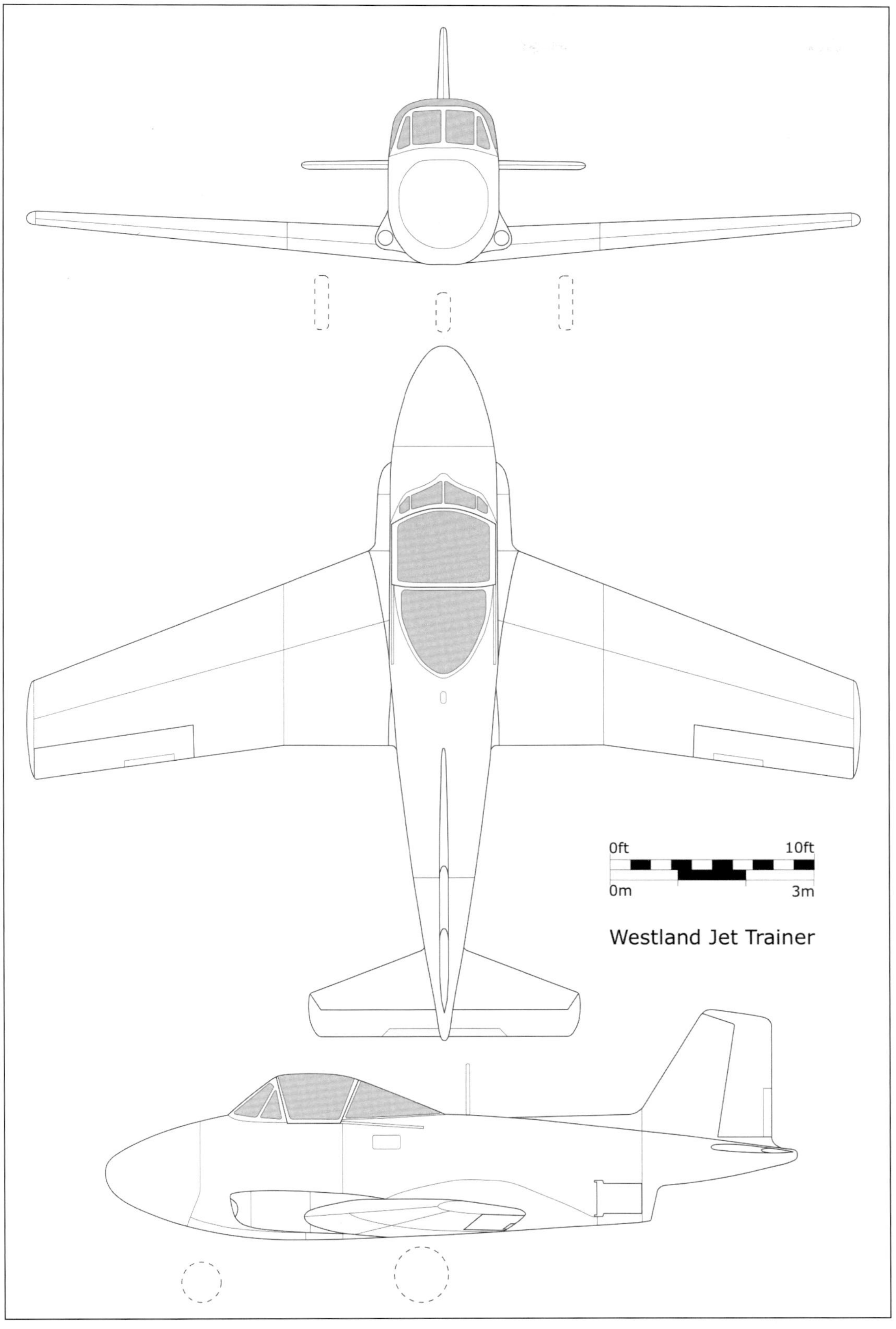

Westland joined the race to interest the RAF in a basic jet trainer. Their design was similar in many ways to the Jet Provost and had two lateral airbrakes and side-by-side cockpit seating. *Author*

to jets, the handling and controls would be closer to operational types and that jet ab initio training would weed out unsuitable fast jet pilots quicker. The P.84 was also thought to be particularly well suited to deck landing training with the Navy. Percival was also tapping into the MoS's own thoughts around this time. In February 1952 the Ministry had examined a proposal from the Air Ministry to re-engine the standard Provost with a lightweight Turbomeca Aspin II or ASA.1 Adder turbojet in the nose replacing the Alvis Leonides piston engine. This was rejected as impracticable given the resulting forward shift in the centre of gravity due to the much lighter turbojets and the effects on the aerodynamics.

The birth of a dynasty. The first prototype Percival Jet Provost T.1 XD674 following a test flight. Uniquely for a prototype from this era, it has survived, being preserved at the RAF Museum Cosford. *Author's Collection*

With the industry heavily promoting basic jet trainers, French and NATO policy influences and the RAF's own experience with the Meteor T.7 and Vampire T.11, the Air Staff began to move towards evaluating a suitable trainer. The easy convertibility and relatively low development cost of the P.84 was attractive to the Air Staff, as was the low operating cost of £61 per flying hour compared to £161 for the Vampire T.11. On 12th March 1953 the Secretary of State for Air announced that the RAF would trial the Jet Provost and an order for ten aircraft was issued. The Air Ministry issued Operational Requirement OR.321 and the Ministry of Aviation issued Specification T.16/48 Issue 4 on 27th May to cover the development. The required stalling speed with flaps and undercarriage down was to be 65kt (120km/h) and 180gal (818lit) of fuel were required for 60 minute sortie at 20,000ft (6,100m) plus take-off and climb, descent and landing with a 10% reserve.

The first prototype Jet Provost T.1 XD674 made its maiden flight on 16th June 1954 with Chief Test Pilot 'Dick' Wheldon at the controls. After successfully completing the manufacturer's development programme within 123 flying hours, the aircraft was submitted for A&AEE trials in November. Minor changes including a small ventral fin, modified nosewheel undercarriage doors and a drooped wing root leading-edge extension reduced the stalling speed by 6kt (11km/h), increased lift at low speeds and reduced the take-off run. In July, XD674 was displayed at a NATO Convention in Paris and the next month flew at the SBAC Farnborough Show. The RAF began its assessment at the CFS at South Cerney totalling 111 flying hours over five months using three Jet Provosts. From August 1955, No 2 FTS at Hullavington ran two courses with three – ultimately nine – Jet Provosts. On 17th October Pilot Officer R T Foster became the first student to solo on the type after 8 hours 20 minutes flying time. Solos would soon average 10 hours 10 minutes, compared to the current Provost average of 11 hours 15 minutes. The course was observed by the NATO Air Training Advisory Group and observers from Austria, Peru and Thailand. In September 1955 a Royal Canadian Air Force evaluation was carried out at Percival's Luton airfield. There was even interest from America, the Chief of the Navy's Bureau of Aeronautics, Admiral Russell, expressed interest in purchasing an evaluation batch of 20 with the possibility of future orders or licence-production. West Germany was another potential interested user.

The wastage rate during the evaluation was comparable to the Provost with five students per course dropping out. All the students on the first course passed out as 'high-average' rating and some pilots progressed to the Vampire T.11 after just 90 hours. Having a cockpit layout very similar to the Vampire helped in this regard. The training syllabus evolved to 23 weeks of ab initio training with 85 flying hours and 22 weeks of basic training with 75 flying hours. This was 40 hours more than the Provost syllabus but with experience it was reduced to 145 and then 120 hours. Despite some serviceability issues with the undercarriage, the pneumatic system and the Viper, No 2 FTS flew 4,000 hours in eighteen months and a total of 50 pilots were trained by November 1957. The T.1 had been completely free of fatal accidents, accidents from undershoots and overshoots,

The prototype Jet Provost T.2 was initially flown under B-Conditions markings as G-23-1 and later registered as G-APVF to Percival Aircraft. Some of the improvements over the T.1 can be seen here; single-piece canopy, a dorsal fin, wingtip tanks and the increased span flaps and correspondingly decreased span ailerons. *Author's Collection*

spinning troubles and loss of control. In 6,229 flights totalling 4,399 hours between 1st May 1955 and 31st March 1957 there had been ten major and eighteen minor accidents, mainly due to engine flame-outs during aerobatics and undercarriage defects. The write-off accident rate was 10 percent of the major accident rate, compared with 13 percent for the Vampire T.11 and 44 percent for the Provost T.1 during 1956 alone! The trials also showed savings of £3,000 on flying costs. From late 1957 the CFS slowly received most of the T.1 fleet, using them to form the *Sparrows* aerobatic team in 1958 for the SBAC Farnborough Show and reforming in 1959 as the *Redskins*.

Percival's third private venture Jet Provost T.2, G-AOUS was demonstrated to the Royal Canadian Air Force before being used to trial the 2,500lbf (11.1kN) ASV.11 Viper 202 for the T.4 variant. Seen here coming in to land during the SBAC Farnborough show in 1959, G-AOUS went on to be evaluated by the Portuguese Air Force. During diving tests on 16th November 1960, the nose wheel was inadvertently lowered, leading to severe upward pitching and a complete structural failure. Percival test pilot John Overbury was sadly killed. *Terry Panopalis Collection*

The T.1s were evaluation aircraft and still had some rough edges. Percival took the experience gained to develop the T.2. Percival and Armstrong Siddeley jointly funded three production 1,750lbf (7.78kN) ASV.8 Viper 102 engines for the T.2. The rear fuselage received better streamlining, a circular cross-section and a dorsal fin while the problematic and expensive to maintain pneumatics were replaced by a hydraulic system with a common jack to operate all three undercarriage legs. The main undercarriage legs were strengthened to cope with a terminal velocity of 12ft/sec (3.6m/sec) and shortened by 22in (55cm) to allow them to retract into the wings, which required the redesign of the inboard wing structure. These structural changes saved weight and the flaps were increased in span with the ailerons correspondingly shortened with reduced deflections. The wingtips could accommodate optional 50gal (227lit) fuel tanks. The ninth T.1 XD694 was converted on the production line and flew on 1 September 1955 and undertook trials with A&AEE and No 2 FTS. Percival and Armstrong Siddeley funded three more T.2s themselves which conducted winterisation trials in Scandinavia and G-AOHD spent six months with the Royal Australian Air Force for evaluation with 1 Basic Flying Training School at Point Cook. No orders from this evaluation or sales tours across Europe, North and South America materialised. An evaluation with the Portuguese Air Force during 1959 resulted in the order for Cessna T-37 due to the generous provisions of the US Mutual Defense Aid Plan. The third T.2 with an 2,000lbf (8.9kN) ASV.9 Viper undertook ground attack trials during 1958 as XN117 with No 85 Squadron in Aden alongside the Folland Gnat and the Hawker Hunter. The Hunter was selected but the Jet Provost's stable platform for gunnery and rocket firing ultimately lead to the dedicated Strikemaster. One of the T.1s, XD693, was earmarked in 1956 for conversion by Handley Page as the HP.103 laminar flow wing testbed with a new wing using engine bleed-off air to create a smooth laminar flow over the wing surfaces to reduce drag. This interesting project went no further, however.

JET PROVOST TIMELINE

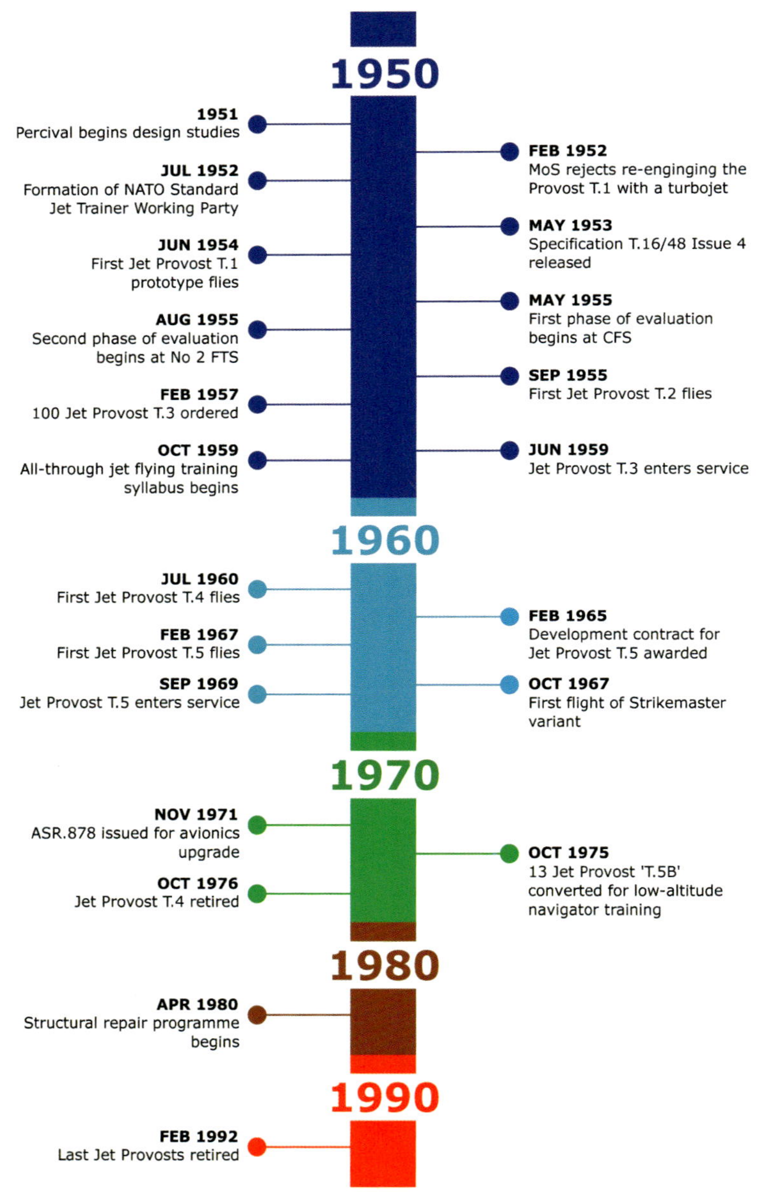

Jet Provost in Service

The T.1s were ordered purely for evaluation of jet ab initio training and a production order was not a given. In March 1954 the MoS issued a draft specification to industry, Boulton Paul submitting the P.124 and Miles the M.100. With no clear outcome by late 1955, F G Miles raised the ante politically, getting the local Member of Parliament for his Shoreham works, Captain Henry Kerby, to ask the Minister of Supply, Reginald Maudling, a Parliamentary Question about the selection of the T.1 and its reliance on pneumatics rather than hydraulics. Miles also asked Wing Commander Bullus, the Parliamentary Private Secretary to the Minister of State at the Board of Trade, to raise the contract during the Estimates debate. This had little effect on the outcome. In December 1955, the Director of Operational Requirements, Air Commodore Herbert Kirkpatrick, proposed equipping one flying school with 50 Jet Provosts and then tendering a quick competition to a revised OR.321. The Deputy Chief of the Air Staff, Air Marshal Sir Thomas Pike, categorically ruled out the M.100 and backed the Jet Provost following its successful evaluation and having potential export orders behind it. All that was required was Treasury approval and political protection for Maudling to deflect any criticisms for not inviting industry to tender. With the Hawker P.1101 Hunter trainer and Folland Gnat trainer also being developed, the Treasury needed convincing about this new request but finally an order was placed for 100 production Jet Provost T.3 on 8th February 1957. On 21st May Specification T.16/48 Issue 5 was issued, calling for a climb to 30,000ft (9,145m) within 25 minutes and a maximum speed of 260kt (481km/h) up to 30,000ft (9,145m). Lightweight ejection seats were to be fitted.

The Jet Provost T.3 was the first RAF jet-powered basic trainer and enabled the retirement of the Percival Provost. Shown here is XM384 shortly after its delivery to No 2 FTS on 1st January 1960. *Author's Collection*

On 29th June 1959 the first four T.3s were handed to the RAF at Luton and issued to the CFS at Little Rissington the same day. The arrival of the first T.3s trainers at No 2 FTS at Syerston in June led to the first course in October, students gaining their wings after 79 hours of dual and 41 hours of solo flying in June 1960. Soon the training sequence was changed with students being streamed after obtaining their wings onto the Vampire T.11 for fast jet pilots or the Vickers Varsity T.1 for multi-engine training. A total of 201 T.3s were built and remained in service until No 125 Course at No 1 FTS at Linton-on-Ouse graduated in June 1993. By this time several Jet Provost airframes had amassed over 9,000 hours. From 1984 No 1 FTS, and its fleet of Scottish Aviation Bulldogs and Jet Provosts, had been operated under contract from the Ministry of Defence by Airwork Limited. The Jet Provost became known to the public via a series of aerobatic display teams including the *Red Pelicans* formed by the CFS, which became the RAF's 'official' team in 1964, only to have their crown taken by the Gnats of 4 FTS's *Yellowjacks* the following year.

The T.3 was agile but its performance was sluggish so Percival fitted the 2,500lbf (11.1kN) ASV.11 Viper 202 into T.2 G-AOUS and two late production T.3 airframes, XN467 and XN468, to create the T.4 in 1960. Fuel tankage was increased with a higher 7,400lb (3,356kg) gross weight – later cleared for aerobatics with full tip tanks at 7,250lb (3,288kg). Percival test pilot Reginald Stock carried out high rotation spinning trials with one full and one empty tip tank on a production T.4, he was forced to take an unconventional recovery after about seventeen turns in the spin. Attempts to increase performance by reducing drag were also made. Production was switched over to the new variant in July 1960 and 198 were built. The T.4 with its better climbing performance soon replaced 40 hours of Vampire T.11 flying training on the syllabus and its increased power was found to improve training standards. This increased usage rapidly used up the T.4s fatigue life, the reintroduction of the Chipmunk T.10 for some ab initio training in 1965 helped a little but the last was retired from pilot training in October 1976. Two were used by the Tactical Weapons Unit at Brawdy to train Forward Air Controllers and others carried on in the more sedate environment of the Central Air Traffic Control School at Shawbury until the school was disbanded on 6 July 1989. Export versions of the T.3, as the T.51, and the T.4 as the T.52, saw sales success, many of them receiving stronger wings with provision for underwing hardpoints for 250lb (113kg) bombs and six 60lb (27kg) rocket projectiles. A total of 72 of both marks were sold to; Sri Lanka, Kuwait, Sudan, South Yemen (these were ex-RAF T.4s), Venezuela and Iraq. A potential order in 1964 from South Africa for 250 T.52s was prevented by the arms embargo then in place.

Jet Provost T.4 XP686 flew as part of the *Macaws* flying display team during its time with the College of Air Warfare at Manby during 1965-70. *Terry Panopalis Collection*

Following their change of ownership to become Hunting Percival, the company continued to explore armed developments of the T.4 for counter insurgency work such as the H.156 developed in 1963. The H.159 was a further development powered by two 1,635lbf (7.3kN) Turbomeca Aubisque turbofans mounted in rear fuselage nacelles. In 1958 Percival had drawn up a tandem seat trainer based on the Jet Provost as the H.127 powered by a 2,750lbf (12.2kN) Rolls-Royce RB.145 turbofan, a single-seat ground attack variant being the H.128. These studies, including the 1961 H.143 swept wing Jet Provost, went no further.

As part of these private venture developments, in 1961 Hunting Percival proposed a pressurised cockpit to improve the high-altitude training capability in response to an Air Ministry request for a study on pressurising the T.4 in production and converting T.3s to the same standard. Despite this, no further official interest was forthcoming at this stage and the H.145 project (becoming the BAC.145 when Hunting Percival became part of the British Aircraft Corporation) proceeded as private venture for export customers. BAC offered to fit the new cockpit to existing T.4s but the fleet was already nearing the end of its fatigue life. By 1964 the increased utilisation of the T.4 for high altitude training and the resulting physiological restrictions placed on the instructors forced the RAF to revisit the proposal. A development contract was issued in February 1965. The cockpit had automatic pressurisation from 8,000ft (2,240m) with a redesigned canopy featuring miniature detonating cord to shatter the Suntex safety glass on ejection. Initial plans to fit lighter wings for the RAF aircraft were abandoned and all production aircraft received the sturdier export wing with provision for weapon hardpoints to save development costs and improve fatigue life. The Viper 202 was retained but the internal fuel capacity was increased to 270gal (1,227lit) to remove the need for the tip tanks.

Table 4.2 – Jet Provost

	Jet Provost T.1	Jet Provost T.2	Jet Provost T.3	Jet Provost T.4	Jet Provost T.5
Wingspan	35ft 5in (10.79m)	35ft 2in (10.71m)	36ft 11in (11.25m)	36ft 11in (11.25m)	35ft 4in (10.76m)
Length	31ft 11in (9.72m)	31ft 10in (9.70m)	32ft 5in (9.88m)	32ft 5in (9.88m)	34ft (10.36m)
Wing Area	213.7ft² (19.8m²)	213.7ft² (19.8m²)	213.7ft² (19.8m²)	213.7ft² (19.8m²)	213.7ft² (19.8m²)
All-Up Weight	6,750lb (3,061kg)	6,830lb (3,098kg)	7,092lb (3,216kg)	7,400lb (3,356kg)	9,200lb (4,173kg)
Powerplant	Viper 102, 1,750lbf (7.78kN)	Viper 8-102, 1,750lbf (7.78kN)	Viper 8-102, 1,750lbf (7.78kN)	Viper 202, 2,500lbf (11.1kN)	Viper 202, 2,500lbf (11.1kN)
Max Speed/Height	262kt (485km/h)	286kt (531km/h)	282kt (524km/h)	356kt (659km/h)	355kt (658km/h)
Service Ceiling	31,000 (9,450m)	31,000 (9,450m)	31,000 (9,450m)	31,000 (9,450m)	36,750 (11,200m)

Jet Provost T.5 XW374 of the RAF College flying a sortie in July 1987. The pressurised cockpit of the T.5 brought with it a larger canopy for better visibility. *Terry Panopalis Collection*

The two development aircraft were modified from the last two T.4 airframes on the production line. The first to fly was the 3,000lbf (13.3kN) Viper 500-powered BAC.166 XS231 on 16th March 1965, the BAC.167 aerodynamic prototype XS230 making its maiden flight on 28th February 1967 at Warton with Reginald Stock (now BAC's Jet Provost Project Pilot) at the controls. Specification 265 issued on 2nd April 1968 called for a low stalling speed of 75kt (139km/h) which required BAC to trial XS230 with fillets around the wing root, engine intakes and wing leading-edge. Other aerodynamic refinements included nose strakes for improved low-speed handling, wing root slats and sealed flap and rudder hinges to reduce high-speed flutter. The maximum level speed between sea level and 30,000ft (9,145m) was to be 320kt (593km/h) and the aircraft was to be capable of climbing to 20,000ft (6,100m) in not more than 9.5 minutes and to 30,000ft (9,145m) in 17.2 minutes. Following successful trials an order was placed for 110 production Jet Provost T.5 aircraft. Following the closure of the Luton factory in 1966, the Jet Provosts were built at Hurn and the fuselages and tailplanes at Warton, where final assembly was also carried out. The CFS took delivery of its first aircraft on 3 September 1969. While RAF instructors felt there was little difference in terms of handling apart from a slower spin rate and a faster rate of climb, the T.5 provided a quieter and more comfortable environment. The only export T.5s were the first five production aircraft delivered to the Sudanese Air Force.

With modest avionics updates to enable it to meet civil requirements for flights in controlled airspace, the Jet Provost T.3A had a long and successful career with the RAF. XM466 had been delivered as a T.3 to the RAF College at Cranwell in July 1960. Upgraded to T.3A standard in late 1974, it was retired in 1992. XM424 had joined the CFS in May 1960 and was modified to T.3A standard in early 1975 before being retired in 1993. Both aircraft were the dedicated display aircraft of No 1 FTS for 1992 and still survive today. XM466 is registered in the USA as N7075U and XM424 still flies in the UK as G-BWDS. *Blue Envoy Collection*

Successful as the Jet Provost was, the training environment continued to change. By 1971 improved avionics were required for instrument and procedural training and to meet mandatory civil requirements for flight in controlled air space. Air Staff Requirement ASR.878 was drafted and in response to BAC's feasibility study submitted in November 1971, Specification 284D&P was issued on 7 December 1972 for the improved T.3A and Specification 285D&P for the T.5A. Between 1973 and 1976 a total of 177 aircraft were upgraded with Decca VOR/ILS, RCA DME, Sperry CL.6 compass and a standby Ferranti FH.31 attitude indicator. Thirteen other T.5s were reassigned to low-level navigation training and were modified at Leeming during late 1975 with 48gal (218lit) tip tanks, losing their nose strakes in the process. They were unofficially called 'T.5B' and were operated by No 6 FTS at Finningley and served until replacement by the Short Tucano T.1 in January 1992. During late 1978 an increase in training commitments saw 21 stored T.5A airframes being reactivated for the RAF College at Cranwell and in September 1979 7 FTS was reactivated with two squadrons of T.3As and T.5As. As can be imagined, this heavy usage soon led to plans to extend the Jet Provost's life into the 1990s until a replacement could be found. In April 1980 fatigue cracks were found in several T.5 tail fins due to the stresses of high-speed low-altitude flying, leading to flying restrictions until the fleet had their fins re-riveted. The RAF had used 38 spare sets of wings to extend the fatigue life but in January 1982 20 new sets of wings were ordered and were fitted at 5 Maintenance Unit at Kemble. Others received new front spars and centre fuselage bulkheads at Warton. Jet Provost T.3A XN548 was the first to be reflown by test pilots Reginald Stock and Eric Bucklow following refurbishment at Warton on 8th November 1982. Typical of the heavy use of the type, XN548 had already accumulated 19,000 take-offs and landings in 22 years before its refurbishment. This life extension programme saw the Jet Provost through until its replacement by the Tucano T.1 in 1993. Few other trainers served the RAF for so long or so well, providing flying skills to several generations of RAF pilots and completely vindicating the shift to using jet aircraft throughout the training sequence.

Jet Provost T.5s XW320 and XW321 being put through their paces. *Blue Envoy Collection*

5 Training the Fighter Pilot: Pushing the Boundaries

'Want to fly a Lightning, want to occupy the single seat in the single seater, all weather night and day, highflying supersonic, supernormal Lightning?'
Streaked Lightning, recruitment film, 1962

'We do not consider that the possibility should be ruled out of producing a satisfactory trainer developed as a variant of a future fighter.'
Air Commodore Glynn Silyn-Roberts, Director of Military Aircraft Research and Development, March 1953

'In fact in some cases one gets the impression that the OR has not been taken very seriously. We have not approached the firms concerned on these differences pending the meeting with the Air Ministry in the hope that at least some of the aircraft will be eliminated.'
Mr W S Johnston, RD Projects, May 1954

'The whole basis on which the Gnat case has been fought is that of a pure flying training aircraft to bridge the gap from Jet Provost to dual F.23. Had armament been seriously proposed at an earlier stage it is unlikely that the Gnat would have been selected. This late change may appear to the Financial people as a "fast one".'
Brief for the Chief of the Air Staff, July 1957

As we have seen in the previous chapters, the advent of jet propulsion changed the RAF in numerous ways from the aircraft it flew, how it flew them and how students were trained to master them. The advances in aviation during the post-war years were staggering. In 1946 a fresh faced Fighter Command pilot might still be strapping into a late mark Spitfire, with a Rolls-Royce Griffon providing a maximum speed around 390kt (722km/h) and using the 'Mark One Eyeball' to aim his four 20mm cannon. By 1960 the English Electric Lightning F.1 was capable of Mach 2.0 (2,450km/h) with twin reheated Rolls-Royce Avon turbojets and the pilot needed to be able to simultaneously fly the aircraft and successfully manipulate the controls of the Ferranti AI.23 AIRPASS radar to search and achieve a lock-on onto a target for his two de Havilland Firestreak (codenamed Blue Jay) infra-red guided air-to-air missiles (AAM). This was potentially such a tricky task that although the Lightning was used in recruitment films, the Air Staff in reality worried that newly qualified pilots on their first tour of operations as a first tourist would be overwhelmed and initially it was considered that they were not to fly it. The tactical bomber pilots of Bomber Command were eagerly waiting to trade-in their subsonic English Electric Canberras for the British Aircraft Corporation (BAC) TSR.2 which had the prospect of automatic supersonic terrain-following flight. During the mid-1950s the fast jet stream students following the completion of basic training went on to an Advanced Flying School (AFS) flying the Gloster Meteor T.7 and later the de Havilland Vampire T.11 and then progressed to the Operational Conversion Unit (OCU) to fly their future operational aircraft to learn the skills necessary to get the best from the aircraft and how best to fly and operate it in combat. In addition the Central Gunnery School (later becoming the Fighter Weapons School) taught the necessary techniques of air-to-air and air-to-ground gunnery with cannon, rockets, bombs and AAMs. The continual progression of frontline aircraft and their performance and complexity required a new generation of advanced trainers.

Learning to Fly a Triangle

During 1950 the Air Staff issued Operational Requirement OR.278 to cover dual-control training variants of the de Havilland DH.110 and Gloster Javelin all-weather fighters which were being developed under Specification F.4/48. Specifications T.116D and T.118D were released for each type

This formation flown on the 20th anniversary of the Battle of Britain shows the rapid post-war progression of aviation technology and training requirements to enable student pilots to master these fighters. The difficulty of that task is reflected by the fact that of the fighters shown here, all but the Hurricane had dedicated two-seat conversion trainer variants. From bottom to top are; Hawker Hurricane IIc LF363, Supermarine Spitfire PR.XIX PM631, Gloster Meteor F.8 WL164, Hawker Hunter FGA.9 XE610, Gloster Javelin FAW.9R XH894 and English Electric Lightning F.1 XM137. *MoD/Open Government Licence, 2018*

respectively on 21st October 1951. The Air Staff wanted a dual-control variant to enable pilots to practice instrument flight approaches and landings to ensure proficiency in night and poor weather operational flying and for gunnery practice to maintain standards. This need was especially true for the Javelin, which was the RAF's first delta-winged fighter which, because of its delta wing configuration, had unique low-speed handling characteristics during approach and landing – in particular the high angle of attack at low airspeeds required to maintain lift. At one point the DH.110 was among the most important British fighter projects for the RAF and the Fleet Air Arm (FAA) with further projected variants for long-range escort fighters and naval strike. By the end of 1950 economic pressures and indecision by the Admiralty regarding their all-weather fighter requirements had scaled back the proposed development phase. The RAF favoured the more advanced Javelin and by early 1953 the RAF had reversed its earlier interest in the DH.110 and Specification T.116D was cancelled.

Gloster continued work on the Javelin trainer, subcontracting the development to its subsidiary Air Service Training Ltd. The former navigator/radar operator's rear cockpit was modified for use by an instructor was fitted with full controls, a flight instrument panel, a bulged canopy to improve visibility and a periscope to enable the instructor to monitor gunnery practice and which also proved helpful to provide extra vision when supervising landings and taxying. The standard armament of four 30mm ADEN cannon was retained in the wings and a more streamlined nose contained a more basic ranging radar for training, rather than the long-range AI.18 radar of the operational fighter. Changes from the standard Javelin FAW.1 included a lengthened fuselage to compensate for the altered centre of gravity caused by removing the original radar, which coincidentally provided room for additional internal fuel. Production Javelin T.3s also received the all-moving tailplane as fitted to the improved Javelin FAW.4 variant to ease the stick forces at high airspeeds. The prototype, WT841, made its maiden flight on 20th August 1956 and was followed by 21 production aircraft, with the first, XH390, making its maiden flight on 6th January 1958. The majority of the Javelin T.3s were issued to No 228 OCU at Leeming and all fifteen frontline Javelin squadrons also received at least one each for continuation training duties, the T.3 would remain in service until the last of the Javelins retired in 1968.

Delivered on 30th December 1958, Gloster Javelin T.3 XH392 was still a relatively new airframe when it was photographed at Gaydon on 19th September 1959. XH392 met its end at Catterick Fire School following its retirement from flying duties in December 1962. *P. Michael Rhodes*

Javelin T.3 XH392 is pictured here at Leuchars in August 1966 whilst on the strength of No 238 OCU. This aircraft also met its end at Catterick Fire School in 1967. *Terry Panopalis Collection*

Delivered to the RAF on 5th May 1959, Javelin T.3 XH445 is pictured here at Tengah, Singapore in the markings of No 64 Squadron in 1966. The aircraft was written off when it ran off the end of the runway at Tengah following brake failure on 11th July 1966. *Terry Panopalis Collection*

Trainers for the New Generation

In early 1953 the Air Staff and the Admiralty identified the need for an advanced jet trainer with similar performance to the new Hawker Hunter and Vickers-Supermarine Swift transonic swept-wing fighters then entering service and the planned supersonic fighters, among them the P.1B Lightning. The Air Staff's Operational Requirements branch had a preference for converting one of these fighters into a suitable trainer given that the desired in-service date was 1959. The Ministry of Supply's (MoS) Director Military Aircraft Research and Development, Air Commodore Glynn Silyn-Roberts, also supported this approach and suggested calling for design studies of two-seat variants of the Lightning and the Type 545 Swift Development, arguing that a conversion should be cheaper and quicker to design. He estimated that the costs of a supersonic trainer would probably be equivalent to the cost increase of supersonic fighters over subsonic designs.

A joint Air Staff/Admiralty Operational Requirement OR.318/NA.45 was raised during March 1953. The proposed trainer was to be used for instruction of handling high-speed aircraft by day and night, instrument flying including automatic approaches, tactics and weapon and search radar training at both OCUs and frontline squadrons. It was not required to be convertible into an operational fighter. Side-by-side seating for the student and instructor was preferred, but it was accepted that using a fighter as the basis might mean having to accept tandem seating. The maximum speed at the 50,000ft (15,240m) service ceiling was to exceed Mach 1.0 while attaining at least Mach 0.9 below that altitude in level flight. The climb to 50,000ft (15,240m) was not to exceed ten minutes without

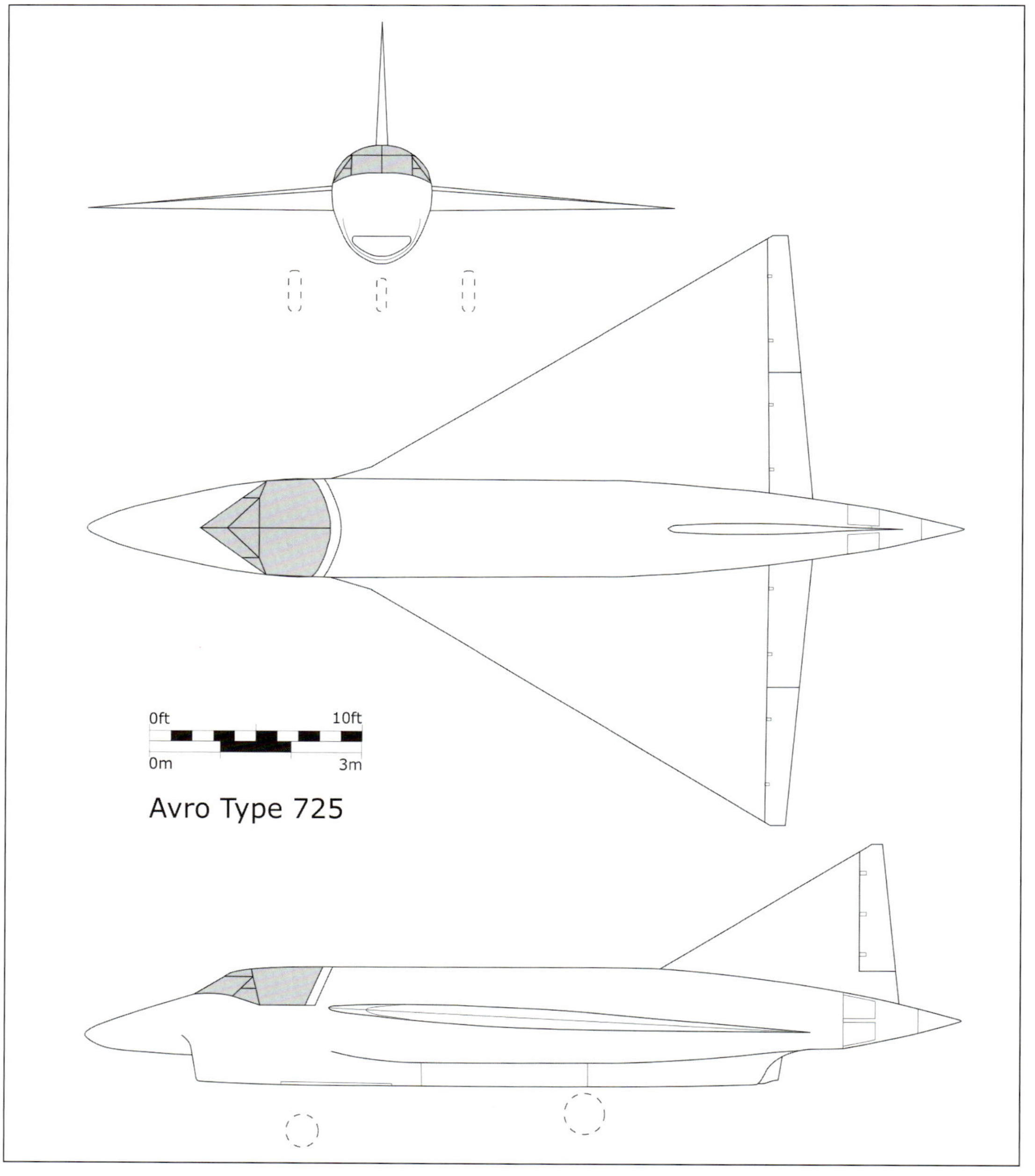

The Avro Type 725 looks almost identical to the Type 720 rocket-powered interceptor. The main external differences are the larger cockpit canopy and the jet intake extended further forwards to ease access to the cockpit with the Bristol BE.26R Orpheus running. *Author*

external tanks or stores. The required sortie endurance was one hour fifteen minutes plus a ten percent fuel reserve and the ferry range was to be at least 1,200nm (2,220km). Take-off to 50ft (15m) with full equipment, weapon load and internal fuel was not to exceed 1,500yd (1,370m), the same distance being specified for the landing run from 50ft (15m). The aircraft was to be fully aerobatic and capable of spinning for four turns without external stores or tanks. The armament would consist of a single 30mm ADEN cannon with ammunition for 20 seconds of firing and provision for a Blue Jay acquisition round (a fixed dummy Blue Jay missile body with a live infra-red-seeker) and underwing hardpoints for air-to-air and air-to-ground rockets, two 1,000lb (453kg) bombs or 25lb (11kg) practice bombs. A Radar Ranging Mk.3, ultimately an AI.23 AIRPASS, set would be fitted and the student and instructor would each have a gyro gunsight. Specification T.147T was issued and four companies responded to the invitation to tender; A V Roe, English Electric, Hawker and Vickers-Supermarine.

Avro submitted the Type 725 based on the Type 720 rocket-powered point-defence interceptor then under development to meet Specification F.137T. The emphasis of Avro's design was on retaining as much of the 720's structure as possible to reduce production costs by using standard jigs for both aircraft. The wings, elevons, tailfin and rudder, main undercarriage and the majority of the fuselage were unchanged. Avro considered the metal honeycomb sandwich construction to be both cheap and easy to manufacture but also offered good structural strength combined with low weight. The main structural change involved the new cockpit with side-by-side seating, but still retaining the existing fuselage diameter and canopy contours, although the MoS in its assessment was less optimistic that extensive changes could be avoided and that structural strengthening would be required. The jet intake was extended forwards to allow the crew to enter the cockpit while the engine was running.

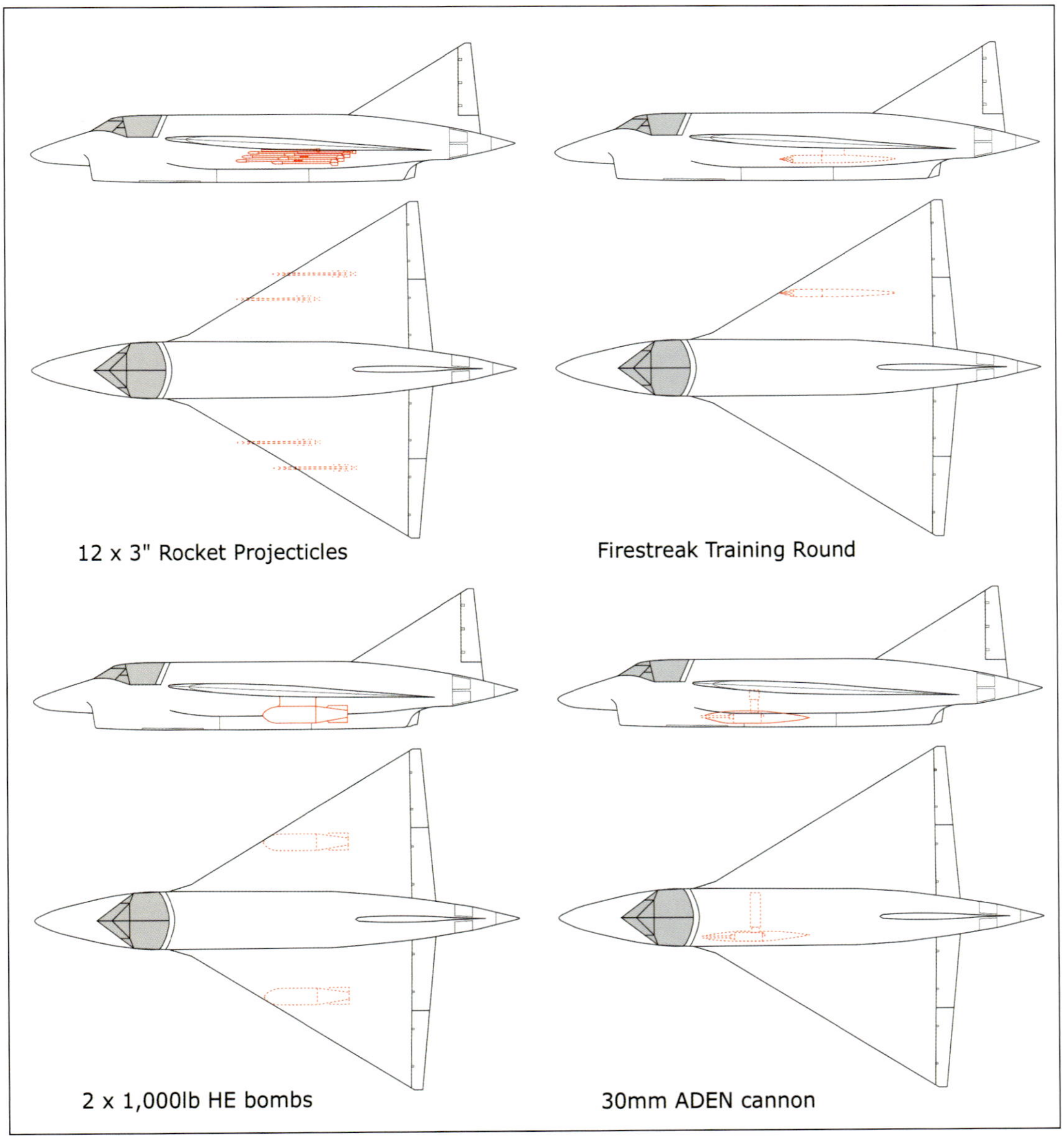

The weapons options for the Type 725. Clockwise from top right; Firestreak acquisition round (a pod-mounted IR-seeker), a 30mm ADEN cannon in an external pod, two 1,000lb (453kg) HE bombs, twelve 3in (76mm) rocket projectiles. *Author*

The other major change was the replacement of the 8,000lbf (35.6kN) de Havilland Screamer liquid-fuelled rocket engine and the 1,640lbf (1.7kN) Armstrong Siddeley ASV.8 Viper 101 turbojet. The two available engine choices were the 6,500lbf (28.9kN) Bristol BE.26R (later to become the Orpheus) and a proposed development of the de Havilland PS.32 called the DH.10 with 2,000°K reheat to achieve 6,500lbf (28.9kN). To avoid any delay that might arise from specifying a new engine that would need development alongside the airframe, the DH.10 was replaced with the higher-rated 10,750lbf (47.8kN) PS.37 Gyron Junior, which Avro also specified for another Type 720 variant, the Type 726 NATO light fighter. Retaining the same delta wing and aerodynamic shape as the 720 meant that performance was estimated to be good with a cruising speed of Mach 1.0 using reheat and Mach 1.2 to 1.4 in shallow dives. Avro conceded that one performance requirement could not be met; it was impossible to spin a 60° swept delta wing. The cockpit with its two side-by-side lightweight ejection seats was pressurised to give a cabin altitude of 25,000ft (7,620m) at 45,000ft (13,715m). The seats were located slightly further aft than the pilot's seat in the 720 to counteract the shift in the centre of gravity. The control columns, instrument panel and flying controls were all stock items from the 720. Any radar with a dish diameter up to 18in (45cm) could be fitted in the nosecone. A 30mm ADEN cannon could be mounted externally on the port side of fuselage adjacent to the nosewheel bay, where the ammunition boxes would be fitted. With the B.E.26R the all-up weight (AUW) was 11,472lb (5,203kg), the maximum speed was Mach 1.02 at 40,000ft (12,190m) with a service ceiling of 48,000ft (14,630m) and 45,000ft (13,715m) being reached in just over seven minutes. With the larger and more powerful PS.37 Gyron Junior, the AUW was 16,030lb (7,271kg) with a maximum speed was Mach 1.15 at 40,000ft (12,190m) with a service ceiling of 52,000ft (15,850m) and 50,000ft (15,240m) being reached in five-and-a-half minutes using reheat.

English Electric submitted a variant of their new P.1B Lightning interceptor then under development to meet OR.268. The P.11 was essentially the standard P.1B, retaining the same twin 14,000lbf (62.2kN) Rolls-Royce Avon RA.24R turbojets but with a new cockpit with side-by-side seating. At this point the P.1B had a quartet of 30mm ADEN cannon and removing the upper pair provided enough room for the wider cockpit. The P.1B's original engine choice, two 10,500lbf (46.7kN) reheated Armstrong Siddeley Sapphire Sa.5 turbojets, was also offered. The MoS assessors noted, however, that the brochure had made no mention of the trainer requirement for normal landings at take-off weight, which may have required additional structural strength. With an AUW of 28,658lb (12,999kg), the estimated maximum speed of the Avon-powered version was Mach 2.0 at 40,000ft (12,190m) with a service ceiling of 49,000ft (14,935m) without reheat or 53,000ft (16,154m) using reheat.

Hawker submitted the P.1101, a development of the Hunter with a new forward fuselage with side-by-side seating. The estimated AUW was 16,613lb (7,535kg). The selected engine was the 10,500lbf (46.7kN) Avon RA.23 to achieve at estimated Mach 0.92 at 40,000ft (12,190m), a service ceiling of 47,000ft (14,325m) and a climb of eleven minutes to 50,000ft (15,240m). Hawker also offered the 8,025lbf (35.8kN) Avon RA.21 as an alternative engine, with reduced performance.

Vickers-Supermarine submitted the Type 554 based on the supersonic Type 545 Developed Swift with its high aspect ratio cranked wing and nose intakes, which being developed under Specification F.105D.2 and at that time was estimated to be six to twelve months away from flying. The Type 554 retained much of the Type 545's design and the main external difference was a wider cockpit canopy covering the side-by-side seats. Two engine choices were offered based on the likely engine selections for the Type 545 to boost commonality; the 17,500lbf (77.8kN) Avon RA.19R and the 21,750lbf (96.7kN) Rolls-Royce RB.106R. The AUW was estimated as 22,010lb (9,983kg) and 26,000lb (11,793kg) respectively. The estimated performance with the Avon RA.19R was Mach 1.0 at 40,000ft (12,190m), a service ceiling of 53,300ft (16,245m) and a climb of just over five minutes to 50,000ft (15,240m). The more powerful RB.106R offered a greater performance with Mach 1.2 at 40,000ft (12,190m) and a climb of four minutes to 50,000ft (15,240m).

Table 5.1 – OR.318 Contenders

	Avro 725	Avro 725	EE Co. P.11	Hawker P.1101	Vickers 554	Vickers 554
Wingspan	27ft 3.6in (8.27m)	27ft 3.6in (8.27m)	34ft 10in (10.62m)	33ft 8in (10.26m)	39ft (11.89m)	39ft (11.89m)
Length	40ft 9in (12.42m)	40ft 9in (12.42m)	55ft 3in (10.62m)	45ft 10.5in (13.98m)	46ft 3in (14.12m)	46ft 3in (14.12m)
Wing Area	256ft² (23.78m²)	256ft² (23.78m²)	474.5ft² (44.08m²)	349ft² (32.4m²)	381ft² (35.43m²)	381ft² (35.43m²)
All-Up Weight	10,965lb (4,973kg)	11,405lb (5,173kg)	28,658lb (12,999kg)	16,613lb (7,535kg)	22,010lb (9,983kg)	26,000lb (11,793kg)
Powerplant	BE.26R, 6,500lbf (28.9kN)	DH.10/ PS.37, 10,750lbf (47.8kN)	two Avon RA.24R, 14,000lbf (62.2kN) dry	Avon RA.23, 10,500lbf (46.7kN)	Avon RA.19R 17,500lbf (77.8kN)	RB.106R, 21,750lbf (96.7kN)
Max Speed/Height	585kt at 40,000ft (12,190m)	660kt at 40,000ft (12,190m)	1,155kt at 40,000ft (12,190m)	530kt at 40,000ft (12,190m)	575kt at 40,000ft (12,190m)	690kt at 40,000ft (12,190m)
Service Ceiling	48,000ft (14,630m)	52,000ft (15,850m)	49,000ft (14,935m)	47,000ft (13,325m)	53,500ft (16,305m)	56,500ft (17,220m)

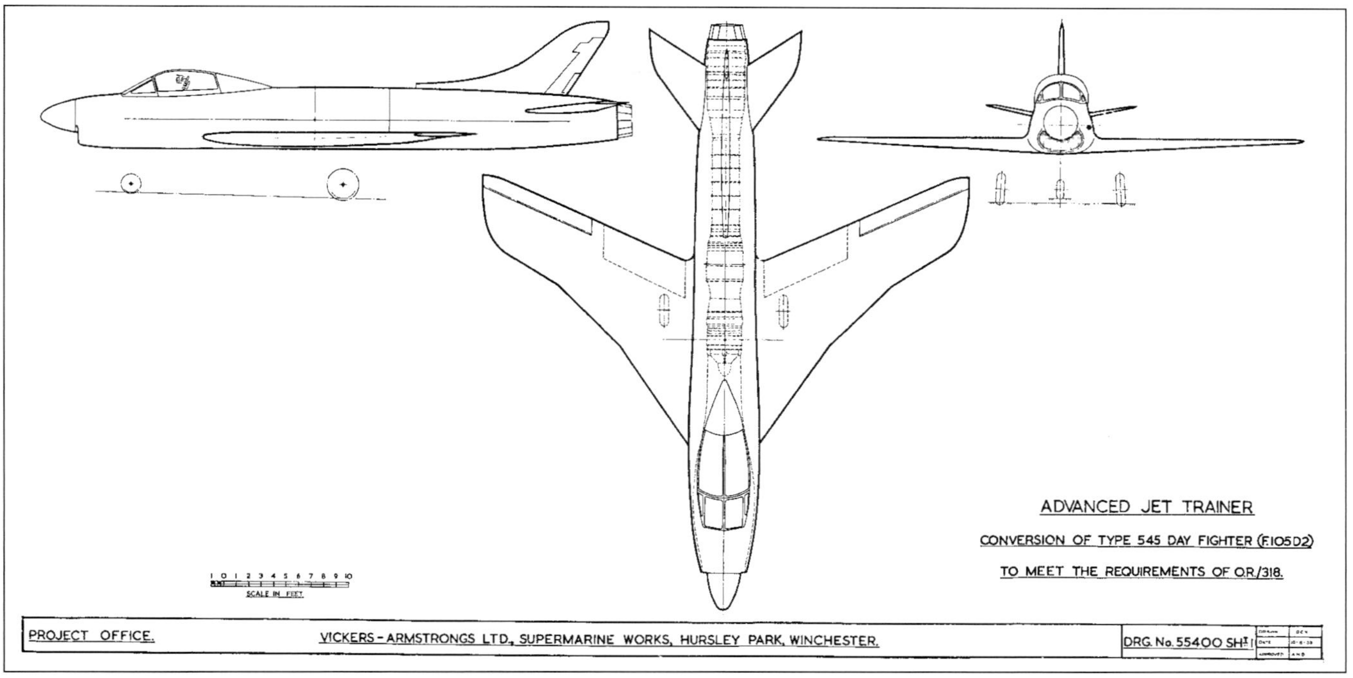

The Vickers-Supermarine Type 554 was based on the Type 545 Swift Development optimised for transonic performance. *Via Ralph Pegram*

The Type 557 applied the side-by-side cockpit and intake of the Type 554 to the Swift F.1, one of two 'Superpriority' fighter programmes along with the Hawker Hunter. The Swift proved to be a disappointment and the Type 557 would never leave the drawing board but Hawker's very similar idea to adapt the Hunter proved a great success. *Via Ralph Pegram*

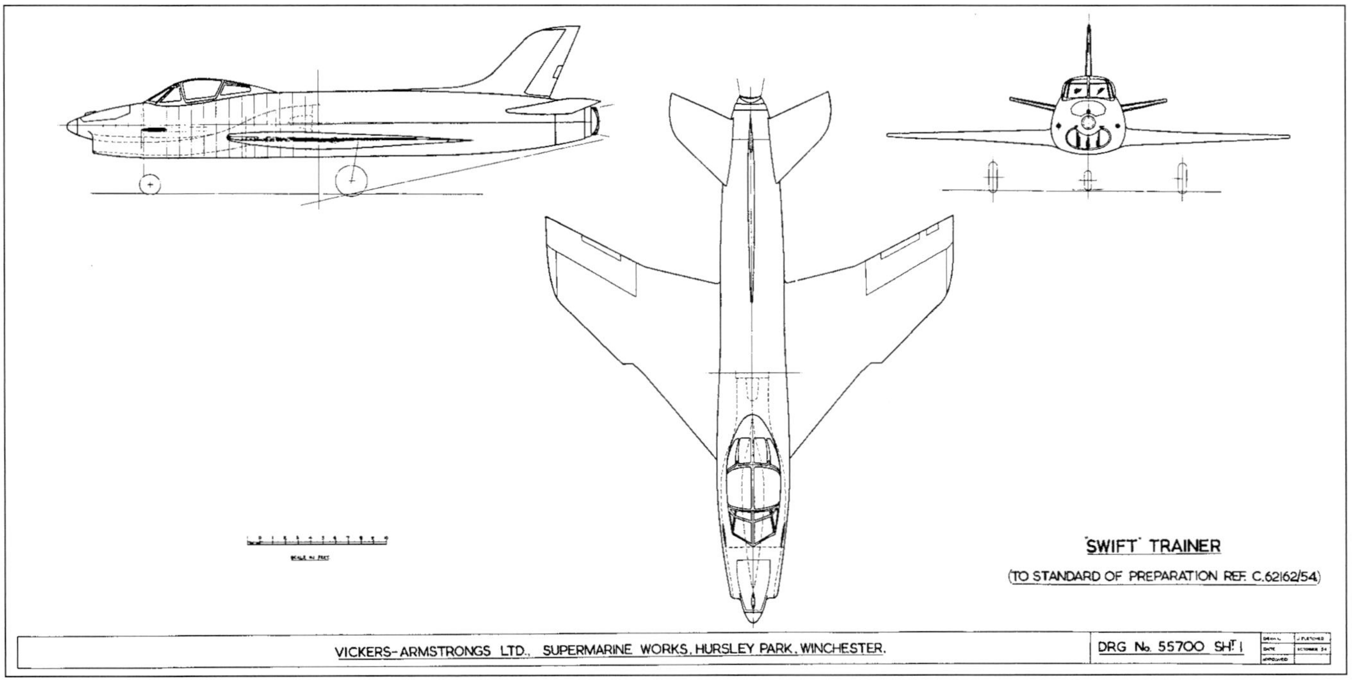

The MoS was not very impressed with the submissions with RD Projects, Mr W S Johnston, gaining the impression that the manufacturers had not taken the operational requirements seriously. The MoS weight assessments for all the submissions came out higher than the tendered figures and Johnston worried that the modified fuselages may have lacked structural strength. The lack of a suitable engine for the Avro 725 had ignited strong interest at both de Havilland and Bristol for a new 7,000-8,000lbf (31.1-35.5kN) class lightweight turbojet, that could be used in the OR.318 trainer, the Type 720 and Saunders-Roe SR.177 rocket-powered interceptors and the NA.39 naval strike aircraft (which was won by the Blackburn Buccaneer). But any new engine would take at least four years to enter production. None of the submissions met the requirements in full and the MoS felt that the final choice would depend on which performance aspect was most desirable to the Air Ministry.

The P.1101 had approximately the required performance except for being subsonic while the P.11 had performance equivalent to the P.1B but at the expense of endurance and was the most expensive option. The Director of Operational Requirements, Air Commodore Wallace H Kyle, rejected the 725 due to its engine choices and there were doubts about using a tailless aircraft for training when the frontline fighter force all had conventional tail surfaces. The Type 554 was judged to be the best all-round design which nearly met all the requirements and would be ready for delivery by the end of 1958. Interestingly, although the P.1101 was judged unsuitable, Kyle felt that it might have a role within Flying Training Command anyway. The OR.318 and NA.45 requirements went unfulfilled, being withdrawn in October 1954 and during 1955 the Avro 720 and Vickers-Supermarine 545 fighters themselves were cancelled. Interestingly, the same month that OR.318 was abandoned, Vickers-Supermarine drew up a very similar design to the Type 554, the Type 557 based on the Swift F.1 airframe but with a side-by-side cockpit. It was to be equipped with radar and an armament of two or four 30mm ADEN cannon and was also offered as a night-fighter. Again, this private venture went no further, the Swift would soon become mired in development problems and the rather rushed production programme was cancelled in 1955. Two of the OR.318 contenders would come back to life, however.

Rebirth: Hunter Becomes Teacher

Hawker continued work on the P.1101, partly as a private venture. Like Gloster and de Havilland before them, they had a close eye on the need to support the training needs of export Hunter operators. Air Commodore Kyle's comment must have struck a chord. The RAF still needed a more modern trainer representative of its latest frontline types; the Meteor T.7 had a terrible accident rate and the Vampire T.11 was outdated. The Air Ministry issued Specification T.157D in 1954 to cover development for the RAF with the aim of introducing the Hunter trainer during 1958. The aircraft was to have an endurance of at least one hour with sufficient fuel for a training sortie comprising and take-off, climb to 43,000ft (13,715m), ten minutes at full power and ten minutes at cruising power followed by a ten-minute descent. Twenty minutes were for time spent in the circuit at cruising power, followed by an approach and landing which included a second circuit and landing. The prototype Hunter T.7, XJ615, flown on 8th July 1955 was a standard Hunter F.4 fitted with a new cockpit section fitted forward of the front fuselage transport joint which had side-by-side seating. For armament training the cannon pack was replaced by a single 30mm ADEN on the starboard side (originally two had been specified and export T.7s also received a twin-gun pack) and underwing hardpoints were retained for rocket projectiles and two 1,000lb (453kg) bombs. The dog-tooth leading-edge and tailplane modifications as fitted to the F.6 were also applied and a brake parachute was fitted in an extended fairing above the jet exhaust – the first Hunter to receive this feature. The second prototype, XJ627, was converted from an F.6 fuselage but all subsequent T.7s used F.4 fuselages and were fitted with the Avon Mk.122, each conversion costing £75,000. Development took time, with aerodynamic airflow problems resulting from the new canopy dorsal fairing causing the maximum speed to be limited to Mach 0.88 until the fairing was redesigned. The production orders covered 45 new-build aircraft and 28 conversions from surplus F.4 aircraft and deliveries to No 229 OCU began in mid-1958. For the training of future fighter pilots, it was the T.7s and F.6s of the Tactical Weapons Unit (TWU) with No 1 TWU at Brawdy and No 2 TWU at Chivenor that were used to teach the necessary combat skills for air-to-air and air-to-ground combat. Students were trained in aerial combat manoeuvres, gunnery and night flying – around 40 percent of an air defence pilot's sorties would take place at night. The selection process was rigorous, only the top students were posted to air defence, a less than average instrument flying rating would see them posted to two-seater strike or ground attack roles. The Hunter formed the backbone of the TWU until No 1 TWU received its first BAe Hawks in July 1977, No 2 TWU not replacing its Hawker Hunters until 1981.

The Royal Navy was also seeking a replacement for its Sea Vampire T.22 fleet as a fighter lead-in trainer. Hawker adapted the P.1101 with an arrester hook for airfield dummy carrier landing practice. Satisfied with the proposal, Specification N.157D&P was issued on 20th August 1957, changes from the standard T.7 including revised radio equipment and the capability to carry two Martin AGM-112 Bullpup air-to-surface (ASM) missiles for weapons training. Production orders for the Hunter T.8 covered ten new-build aircraft diverted from the RAF's T.7 order and 31 F.4 conversions. The converted T.8 prototype, WW664, was flown on 3rd March 1958 and the first unit to receive the T.8 was 726 Naval Air Squadron (NAS) at Lossiemouth.

In October 1956, the Air Ministry issued OR.946 for a standardised flight instrument display for all fighters and strike aircraft. As the new standard instrument panel for fighters and strike aircraft, students had to become familiar with the new instruments and the IFIS was soon specified for future training aircraft and a small number of T.7s and T.8s were earmarked for upgrading. Hawker in October 1956 also proposed the P.1120, a modified P.1101 with the full OR.946 IFIS display and without the ADEN cannon, the space presumably being used to house the additional avionics required. The original engine of the T.7 was retained, a Rolls-Royce Avon Mk.122.

Delivered in September 1958, Hunter T.7 XL594 was on the strength of No 19 Squadron at Leconfield when it was photographed in September 1960. At this time the squadron flew Hunter F.6s. To the left is the tail of Supermarine Swift FR.5 WK277.
Terry Panopalis Collection

The Hunter T.7s served worldwide with the RAF. XF321 pictured here was serving with No 1417 (Fighter Reconnaissance) Flight with No 8 and 43 Squadron markings at Khormaksar, Aden. In 1970 XF321 was transferred to the FAA and written off in an accident in 1984.
Terry Panopalis Collection

Standard F.6 and FGA.9 Hunters served as operational trainers with the TWU until the early 1980s. F.6A XG225 is pictured here in August 1979, a year before its final flight on 9th September 1980. Today XG225 is probably better known as the gate guardian at the RAF Museum, Cosford.
Terry Panopalis Collection

A nice ventral view of Hunter T.8 WW664. The wider forward fuselage did nothing to mar the beautiful lines of the Hunter, but the larger canopy did create some aerodynamic problems with severe buffeting at high speed that took time to solve. In 1969 WW664 was sold to the Republic of Singapore Air Force. *Author's Collection*

The Integrated Flight Instrument System

The ubiquitous 'Standard Six' instrument panel that had been refined from the 1937 original concept was fast becoming outmoded during the 1950s as supersonics required more accurate instruments that could be read and the information mentally digested quickly by the pilot. The Air Ministry issued Operational Requirement OR.946 in October 1956 for a standardised flight instrument display which would be fitted to all future fighters and strike aircraft. Unlike its analogue predecessor, the only training aircraft it would be fitted to would be advanced flying and conversion trainers. The Integrated Flight Instrument System (IFIS) replaced several analogue dials, using an air data computer that fused speed and altitude data from pitot/static pressure signals via an air data system and pitch, roll and heading data from a master reference gyro which was fed to a standardised display. Indicated air speed and Mach number was displayed on two moving horizontal tapes; altitude and vertical speed were shown on a height and rate of climb/descent display which used a single pointer and digital display for height and a traditional pointer for vertical speed. The attitude indicator used a roller-blind display, divided into grey and black horizontal sections. In steep climbs or dives beyond the horizon, the display showed a zenith star, the long tails indicating the nearest horizon, angle of roll markings were also provided. Fitted beside the attitude display was the navigation display combining the functions of a gyro, ILS, TACAN range and bearing display and an offset TACAN display. A small set of standby-flight instruments were also provided in case of a technical failure affecting the IFIS displays.

This proposal lost out to converting existing T.7s, the inclusion of IFIS only adding £10,000 to the conversion cost. The first Hunter T.7A conversion was carried out on XF289. Four further conversions (WV318, XL568, XL614 and XL616) were used for IFIS trials before being issued to Lightning squadrons for instrument flying practice and instrument rating pending the delivery of the Lightning T.5 which featured the full IFIS display.

Four Hunter T.8s (WV322, XE664, XF967 and XF995) were also modified to a similar standard as the T.8B, lacking the ILS which FAA aircraft did not require but gaining an airstream direction detector that was used to provide accurate speed and angle of attack data during final approaches for practice carrier landings. Eleven T.8s were upgraded with TACAN but without the IFIS as the T.8C for 759 NAS at Brawdy, being used on Phase 1 of the Advanced Flying Training Course. Students would then progress to 738 NAS at Lossiemouth for weapons training on the T.8 or 849 NAS for Airborne Early Warning training on the Fairey Gannet. In 1965, 759 NAS was awarded the annual Boyd trophy for its outstanding work in converting Jet Provost trained pilots to the Hunter. Both the T.8B and T.8C lost their ADEN cannon on conversion and received Harley lights in the nosecone. The Harley light was to make the aircraft more visible to trainee gunners aboard Royal Navy warships during simulated attack runs to aid tracking, the light being turned off when training more experienced gunners. The T.8Bs were issued to 764 NAS which undertook air warfare Instructor training and 736 NAS, the Buccaneer operational training squadron. After a

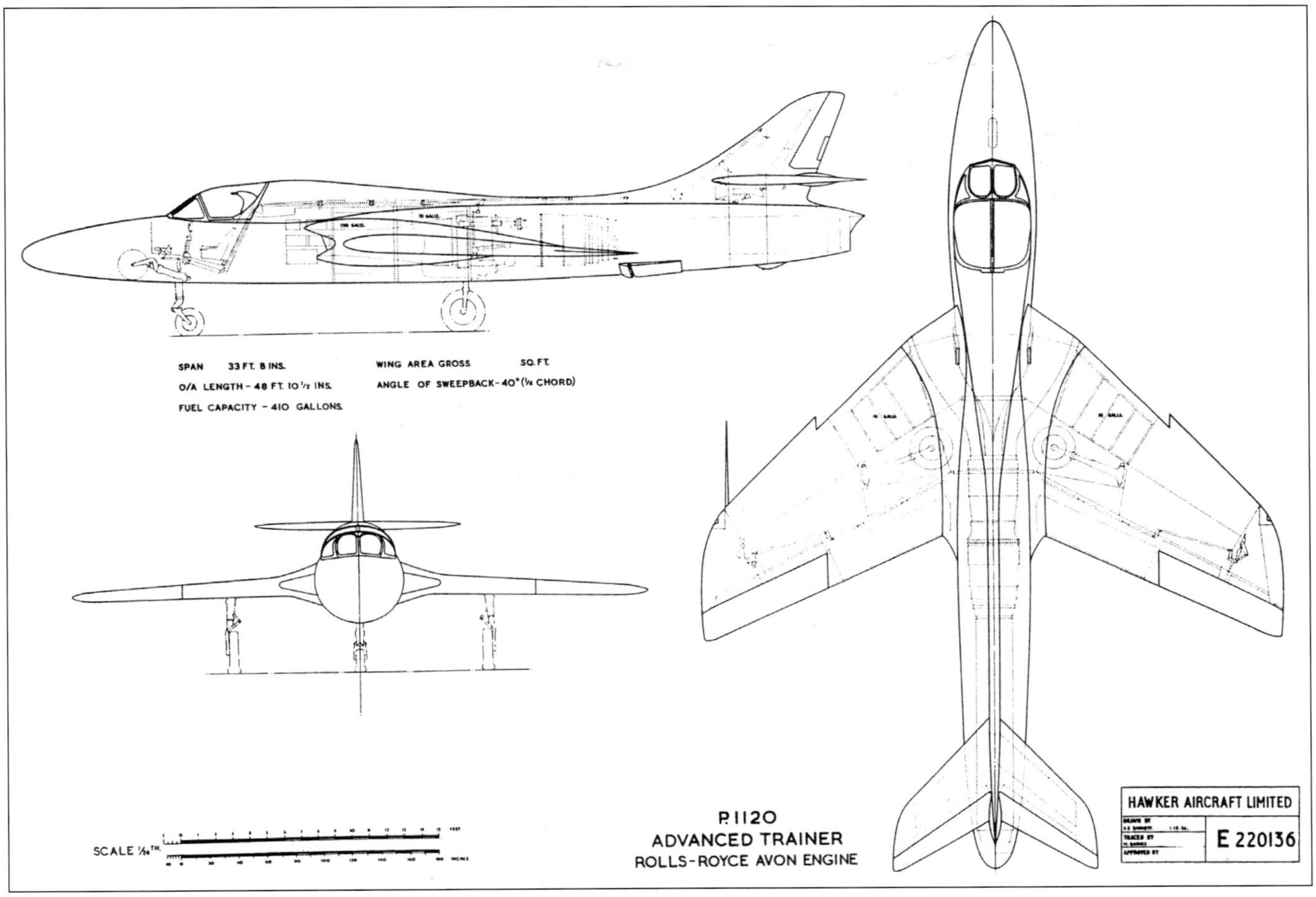

The Hawker P.1120 was identical in all respects to the Hunter T.7 except for full IFIS cockpit instrument displays and no provision for a 30mm ADEN cannon. The Air Staff opted to instead add IFIS to its T.7 conversions at an additional cost of £10,000. *Via Chris Farara*

period of storage and trials work, three RAF T.7s were issued to No 12 Squadron at Honington in October 1969 for instrument flying practice and instrument rating for the Buccaneer S.2A, the RAF's much resisted alternative to the cancelled TSR.2 and from the early 1970s a composite T.7, T.7A and T.8B fleet was used by frontline squadrons and No 237 OCU. These were the last training Hunters to retire when they were withdrawn alongside the Buccaneer on 31st March 1994.

A cutaway drawing of the proposed P.1120. *Via Chris Farara*

This photograph of Hunter T.7 XL571 shows the single 30mm ADEN cannon fitted beneath the cockpit for gunnery training. Delivered to No 229 OCU in June 1958, it was on the strength of No 1 Tactical Weapons Unit (TWU) when it crashed off Strumble Head into the St. Georges Channel on 8th September 1977 following engine failure. Both pilots aboard ejected safely; Flight Lieutenant S Parfirt landed in the sea and Flight Lieutenant H E Spirit landed on the clifftop, luckily not being dragged over the edge by his parachute. *Author's Collection*

A line up of Fleet Requirements and Air Direction Unit Hunter T.8s at Yeovilton. At the head of line is XF985, converted to T.8C standard and which crashed at Roman Farm, Charminster, Dorset on 10th April 1990, when a jammed aileron forced pilot Rick Lea to eject. *Author's Collection*

After their duty as testbeds for the Ferranti Blue Fox radar was completed, the Hunter T.8Ms were used by 899 NAS as radar trainers for Sea Harrier pilots. XL603 is seen here in October 1985. *Terry Panopalis Collection*

Three Hunter T.8s (XL580, XL602 and XL603) were converted for the Ferranti Blue Fox ARI.5982 radar development programme for the Hawker Siddeley Sea Harrier FRS.1 V/STOL naval fighter as the T.8M. These aircraft would also serve as airborne intercept and operational weapons trainers on completion of the trials. Specification 288D&P was issued to Hawker Siddeley on 30th July 1976 for the conversion work. The design changes included grafting the Sea Harrier FRS.1's complete radome and nose section onto Hunter along with updated avionics including two Head-Up Display units and a radar scope in the right-hand seat position. The outer underwing pylons could either carry two pods for 22 2in (50mm) rockets or two AIM-9L Sidewinder acquisition training rounds to simulate live firing. Structural modifications were also made to allow the use of two 230gal (1,045lit) underwing drop tanks. On completion of the Blue Fox programme, XL580 and XL603 were converted as planned for the training role and were delivered to 899 NAS in August 1981 alongside another eight conversions.

The FAA also used the standard single-seat Hunter for training. The Hunter GA.11 was a converted F.4 with an Avon Mk.122, an arrester hook – for use with airfield arrester equipment – and TACAN for use in the Fleet Requirements and Air Direction roles as a high-speed target to simulate aircraft and missiles for training radar operators and gunners aboard the Navy's ships as well as weapons training. The ADEN cannon were removed and some later received a Harley light in the nosecone to make them more visible to trainee gunners during simulated attack runs. The interchangeable camera nose from the FR.10 tactical reconnaissance version could also be fitted and when any of the 40 GA.11s were so fitted, they were designated PR.11. The GA.11 was used alongside the T.8 by 738 NAS at Brawdy where it operated Phase 2 of the Advanced Flying Training Course covering fighter tactics and weapons release, until its disbandment on 8th May 1970. Airwork and – from December 1972 – Flight Refuelling Ltd. undertook the Fleet Requirements and Air Direction roles using GA.11s and T.8s, also forming the *Blue Herons* display team on behalf of the FAA. Today the Hunter is still supporting training, Hawker Hunter Aviation using a small fleet of ex-Swiss Hunter F.58s as threat simulators and equipment test and trials platforms under Ministry of Defence and NATO member contracts, the Hunter proving more economical than using advanced trainers for this role.

Rebirth: Lightning

The English Electric P.1B Lighting F.1 was released to the Central Fighter Establishment in December 1959 and No 74 Squadron took delivery of the first fully-equipped F.1s on 30th July 1960. The Lightning was the RAF's first supersonic fighter, the only one of the initial generation to survive the development woes and policy changes that saw its contemporaries successively cancelled. The need for a suitable conversion trainer was still very apparent despite the demise of OR.318. Specification T.178D&P was issued on 15th July 1957 for a dual-control Lightning and English Electric dusted off its work on the P.11. Earlier, in 1955, the Warton design team had considered a tandem cockpit but it was decided to retain the side-by-side seating arrangement of the earlier P.11 study. The canopy profile was modelled on that of the Hunter T.7 due to its proven aerodynamics following Hawker's extensive work to solve drag issues which affected the Hunter T.7 at first. The 30mm ADEN cannon were deleted to provide room for the wider cockpit, but otherwise the Lightning T.4 was fully combat capable with two Firestreak AAMs and AI.23 AIRPASS radar and had almost identical performance. Both the instructor and the pupil had a gyro gunsight and radar scope but the full IFIS panel was not fitted. The first of two T.4 prototypes, XL628, first flew on 6th May 1959 at Warton and was followed by 20 production aircraft (another 10 were cancelled). The Lightning Conversion Squadron at Coltishall received its first examples in June 1962 and several were issued to the frontline squadrons to maintain currency and standards until they were withdrawn from service during 1976. The second T.4 prototype, XL629, served with the Empire Test Pilot School from 1966 to November 1975. Two aircraft were converted during 1966 to similar T.54 standard for Saudi Arabia under the *Magic Carpet* contract.

English Electric Lightning T.4 XM972 of No 226 OCU taxying out on a training sortie carrying a pair of Firestreak AAMs. The Tiger Moth in the background is only separated by thirty years of development from the Lightning but shows both ends of the spectrum of training aircraft. *Author's Collection*

With the planned introduction of the improved Lightning F.3, Specification T.205D&P was issued to English Electric on 5th December 1960 for a similarly improved trainer. The maximum speed was not to be less than Mach 1.8 and the endurance was to be greater than one hour for a subsonic training sortie or greater than 35 minutes when supersonic, 150nm (278km) from the base. The two prototypes, XM666 and XM667, were converted T.4s, the work being undertaken at Filton and XM666 making its first flight as a T.5 on 29th March 1962. The T.5 shared the same basic airframe and Avon 301R turbojets as the F.3 but with the forward fuselage of the T.4 and the avionics included the full IFIS instrument panel (though layout was completely different to the single-seat F.6) and was fully combat capable.

Chain Lightning. T.4s and F.3s of No 226 OCU awaiting the start of the day's flying at Coltishall on a murky day in May 1968. In the front Lightning T.4 an instructor and student fighter pilot prepare to begin a training sortie. *Terry Panopalis Collection*

The new Stage 3 increased area vertical tail fin to maintain stability when carrying the improved Red Top AAM was also fitted. The need for the modified tail fin had also become evident during trials with the T.4 when XL628 was lost following a major fin failure on 1st October 1959 during a 360° maximum starboard aileron roll at Mach 1.7. BAC chief production test pilot Johnny Squier successfully ejected – becoming the first British pilot to eject whilst supersonic – but the search-and-rescue operation failed to locate him following the failure of his homing beacon and Squier finally paddled ashore after a gruelling 28-hour ordeal. The prototype T.5 XM666 was also lost during flight trials when the new Stage 3 fin failed following a 3g turn at Mach 1.82 over the Irish Sea on 22nd July 1965. Luckily both BAC Deputy Chief test pilot Jimmy Dell and Flight Test Observer John Elkington survived. The airframe was salvaged and as a result the defect was discovered and the fin was reinforced.

Originally 30 aircraft were wanted but the Air Staff at one point considered cancelling the T.5 to put the funding towards a BAC TSR.2 operational trainer variant. The Air Staff, however, eventually gave approval to continue with 20 aircraft. A subsequent order for five aircraft was cancelled. The production T.5s were all built at Filton and entered service with No 226 OCU during April 1965. A 1965 proposal to fit the T.5 with the 600gal (2,727lit) ventral tank and cambered leading-edge wing of the ultimate F.6 fighter along with improved radio and navigation avionics was cancelled in June 1966 as insufficient aircraft could be released from service to enable a viable conversion programme to take place. BAC Warton proposed a T.5 variant for TSR.2 lead-in training (see Chapter Six) and another T.5 proposal was to fit a variable-geometry wing as a research aircraft and then possibly forming the basis of a carrier-based Lightning for the FAA. The T.5 was exported as the T.55 and these did receive the new wing and ventral fuel tank from the F.6. The last production T.5, XS460, was converted as the first of six T.55s for Saudi Arabia under the *Magic Palm* contract and two T.55Ks were built for Kuwait.

Lightning T.5 XS457 of No 226 OCU basking in the summer sun at the Armed Forces Day at Upper Heyford on 14 June 1969. The aircraft first flew on 8th November 1965 and following its time with No 226 OCU served with No 11 Squadron, the Lightning Training Flight and No 5 Squadron before retirement in 1986. It was broken up for scrap in 1988, although the forward fuselage survives as an exhibit at Binbrook. *David Miller*

On its introduction to service, the Air Staff felt that the Lightning was too much of a leap for first tourist pilots fresh from training. This made the provision of a suitable conversion trainer more pressing and only pilots with 1,000 flying hours on fast jets were initially selected until the first T.4s were delivered. For most of its service life, only the top ten percent of students at the TWU were selected for posting to Lightnings; they were the elite of the RAF pilots. The Lightning Conversion Squadron had been formed on 4th January 1960 as part of the Central Fighter Establishment, initially using borrowed aircraft to convert Lightning pilots until the dedicated T.4s arrived. It became an autonomous unit in June 1962 and a year later was reformed as No 226 OCU at Middleton St. George. The OCU also obtained single-seat F.1s and F.1As released as the fighter squadrons re-equipped with improved marks and in 1971 gained a reserve war role as No 65 Squadron for its F.1s and T.4s. As well as the trainers,

The Lightning T.5 was fully combat capable, XS417 of No 23 Squadron is loaded with two Firestreak AAMs for its next sortie in June 1967. *Terry Panopalis Collection*

As they were replaced by newer marks, older Lightning F.1, F.1A and F.2s were passed to three Target Facilities Flights as radar targets for practice interceptions and surface-to-air missile engagements. Lightning F.2 XN797 photographed here served with the Target Facilities Flight at Binbrook. The unit was formed in February 1966, originally as part of the Fighter Command Trials Unit before becoming independent. It was disbanded on 31st December 1973. *Blue Envoy Collection*

there were simulators for the ground school phase, the size of the equipment filling an entire room! The cockpit had no visual display and the canopy was painted white inside so the training was strictly instrument flying. By 1965 the OCU had three squadrons; 1 Squadron for ab initio and conversion training, 2 Squadron for AI.23 radar training and 3 Squadron using T.5s for advanced radar training and Intercept Weapons Instructor courses. Pilots destined for West Germany only flew the F.1 and T.4 as the upgraded T.5's cockpit layout bore no resemblance to the F.2 in use by the West German-based squadrons. As the training task declined in size as the McDonnell Douglas Phantom FGR.2 took over much of the air defence role, it was disbanded on 30th September 1974 and from October 1975 was replaced by the Lightning Training Flight formed from 'C' Flight of No 11 Squadron at Binbrook, initially using three F.3s and three T.5s, until its disbandment on 1st April 1987 as the Lightning fleet was withdrawn from service. By the early 1980s the Lightning was entering its twilight years but there was still a need to maintain a cadre of Lightning pilots. Training new first tourists was impractical so the emphasis was on keeping existing Lightning pilots current on type and during 1981 the Lightning Augmentation Flight operated as a refresher unit for ex-Lightning pilots who were serving ground tours to keep their type ratings up to date.

Petter's Diminutive Trainer

Three years after the cancellation of OR.318, the Air Staff revisited their requirements for a Vampire T.11 replacement. The Vampire's 1940s origins were becoming obvious now that frontline fighters featured swept wings, powered controls and transonic – shortly to be supersonic – performance. This more demanding performance required a comparable advanced trainer to maintain pilot standards. The Air Officer Commanding Flying Training Command, Air Marshal Sir Richard Atcherley, recognised that a gap existed between the Jet Provost and the Hunter T.7. With a new generation of supersonic fighters forthcoming, a new trainer was desired for introduction in 1960. At this time it was envisioned that the bulk of the pilot graduates would go to Fighter Command but the 1957 Defence Review radically changed personnel requirements. Flying Training Command estimated that in 1961 the destinations of pilot graduates (excluding naval graduates and second tourists) would be: 36 to day fighters, 16 to all-weather fighters, 48 to Canberras, 20 to reconnaissance squadrons, 24 to Coastal Command as second pilots, 48 to Transport Command as second pilots and 40 as V-bomber second pilots. This led to some discussion whether tailoring the new trainer with avionics and performance matching that of frontline fighters was still valid given these wider needs, ignoring Fighter Command's call that all pilots should gain 350 flying hours before reaching squadrons. A like-for-like replacement for the Vampire T.11 would require 185 aircraft to maintain an operational training fleet of 135 aircraft.

A draft operational requirement was drawn up to form the basis of an MoS sponsored design study by Folland on whether it was possible to convert the small Gnat lightweight fighter into a trainer. By October 1956 the MoS had completed its technical appraisal and Specification T.185D was drawn up in January 1958. The maximum speed was to be Mach 0.96 in level flight at 36,000ft (10,970m) with the capability to exceed Mach 1.0 in a shallow dive – the airframe was stressed for Mach 1.2 above 36,000ft (10,970m). The operational ceiling while maintaining a 1.5g turn without external tanks was to be 46,000ft (14,020m) and the climb to 40,000ft (12,190m) was not to exceed 6.5 minutes. Endurance with internal fuel was to be one hour fifteen minutes with external fuel tanks providing an additional hour's endurance. The Gnat trainer was to have docile handling but also be fully aerobatic, cleared for intentional spinning up to four turns without and with empty external tanks. The take-off to clear a 50ft (15m) obstacle was not to exceed 2,600ft (792.5m) and landing at full fuel load from 50ft (15m) on a wet runway was not to exceed 3,600ft (1,097m).

Folland's chief designer, William E W 'Teddy' Petter, had to make some changes to the basic Gnat to create the Fo.44 Gnat Trainer. The take-off and landing distance requirements required a larger wing with a 40 percent increase in wing area and separate ailerons and flaps replaced the flaperons of the Gnat fighter. The tail fin was also enlarged to ensure directional stability. Fuel capacity inside the small airframe was borderline and because of the tight centre of gravity limits, the rear fuel tanks were removed which resulted in a ten minute shortfall in the requested sortie endurance. External slipper tanks were fixed to the underside of the wing because conventional drop tanks on underwing pylons would impact both performance and stability. The small cockpit also raised some concerns. Following an inspection of the mock-up,

The first production Gnat T.1, XM691, heading for the heavens. Petter's small but nimble Gnat gave a generation of pilots their first taste of fast jet flying. XM691 had an unusual fate following its retirement; the Orpheus engine, tail and other parts found their way into Donald Campbell's Bluebird K7 jet-powered boat for his ill-fated attempt to break the world water speed record while the airframe was destroyed during filming at Shepperton Studios in July 1969. *Author's Collection*

Pictured shortly after its inaugural roll out ceremony at Folland's factory at Hamble, Gnat T.1 XM691 shows its clean lines. *Blue Envoy Collection*

the Institute of Aviation Medicine recommended an additional 1in (2.5cm) of upwards seat adjustment, raising the canopy headline by 0.5in (1.2cm) to give a 9in (22.8cm) vertical distance between the eye to the inside of the canopy when wearing a 'bonedome' helmet and finally an increase in the range of rudder adjustment. Lightweight Folland 4GT ejection seats would be provided for both crew members. Even so, concerns remained. Group Captain Baldwin of Flying Training Command rang the Operational Requirements branch to record that he had had three tall students who had struggled to fit in the larger Vampire and Meteor and who had grown since entering the service! Another Flying Training Command officer, Medical Officer Flying Squadron Leader Bobey, was also concerned about the available room in the front cockpit for a fully equipped pilot, especially if they had to eject. Although the Air Staff requested a full IFIS instrument panel for the Gnat, the small cockpit made this impossible. Indeed, Petter resisted fitting TACAN because it was difficult to find space for it. In the event only the navigation display was fitted alongside normal analogue flight instruments.

Flying Training Command also suggested providing a weapon training capability but this proposal was not supported by the Ministry of Aviation's Training Staff. Folland already offered a pod containing a single 0.30in machine gun with 126 rounds and a Ferranti lightweight sight for the front cockpit for its export Gnats. The Operational Requirements branch rejected this proposal, considering that guns were an almost dead requirement from 1960 onwards and that gunnery practice could be taught more effectively with simulators. At this time, simulators were generally

A photograph of the third production Gnat T.1 XM693 shortly after its completion. Although developed from a fighter, no armament was ever fitted to the Gnat T.1. Its role was purely as an advanced flying trainer. *Terry Panopalis Collection*

Gnat T.1 XR951 of No 4 FTS seen on public display day during August 1967 alongside Percival Jet Provost T.3s and a McDonnell-Douglas Phantom FGR.2. *Terry Panopalis Collection*

regarded as only useful for specific training tasks, such as gunnery practice or cockpit drills. Simulators were largely static object and if they made any attempt at representing external vision, a small television camera moving over a terrain model was about the height of sophistication possible in the analogue electronics era. The Air Staff still preferred 'hands on' training, although advanced full mission simulators were being planned for the 1970s in which student pilots could undertake operational training, flying 'real' sorties against simulated targets.

A pre-production batch of fourteen aircraft was approved by early 1958 for development work and the first, XM691, made its maiden flight on 31st August 1959. Six months previously Specification T.185P had been issued to cover production, the first order for 30 Gnat T.1 trainers being placed in February 1960 and successive orders bringing the production total to 106. The first eight pre-production aircraft were used for performance and handling trials and the first production examples entered service with the CFS in February 1962 and in November No 4 FTS at Valley received its first Gnats. The school became the major user, replacing all its Vampire T.11s by July 1963 and students flew a 70 hour Gnat syllabus, increased to 85 hours by 1973. Students also spent thirteen hours on the flight simulator. These simulators were built as fully mobile vans so that they could be redeployed but given the harsh weather conditions in North Wales they were eventually enclosed in a building! It was No 4 FTS that first brought the Gnat to wider public attention when it informally formed the *Yellowjacks* aerobatic team with their distinctive all-yellow aircraft under the leadership of Flight Lieutenant Lee Jones during 1964. They performed at that year's SBAC Farnborough Show and shortly afterwards the RAF decided that it would be safer if one official display team was formed under the CFS flown by skilled Qualified Flying Instructors. The following year the *Red Arrows* began public performances and soon became the quintessential part of any air show. The Gnat remained in service with No 4 FTS until the last course graduated on 29th November 1979, the school having received its first Hawker Siddeley Hawk T.1s in 1976. By that time the Gnats of No 4 FTS had accumulated 157,000 flying hours and 1,421 students pilots had passed though the school. The *Red Arrows* also said goodbye to the Gnat at the end of the 1979 display season. Possessing good performance and handling, except for pitch control problems, the Gnat was generally liked by the students but it had some shortcomings that hampered its utility. Students had to learn specific emergency drills associated with various specific systems fitted to the Gnat, which did not apply to other frontline fighters and made this portion of the training less valuable. The instructor's limited view hampered weapons instruction and the small cockpit remained an issue for larger pilots, after a number of unfortunate leg and knee injuries following ejections, taller pilots had to be trained on the Hunter T.7. Of the 89 Gnats issued to No 4 FTS during that period, 28 were written off in accidents.

A row of Gnats on the No 4 FTS flightline at Valley on Anglesey, Wales. The School operated the Gnat for seventeen years on the fast jet advanced flying training syllabus. *Blue Envoy Collection*

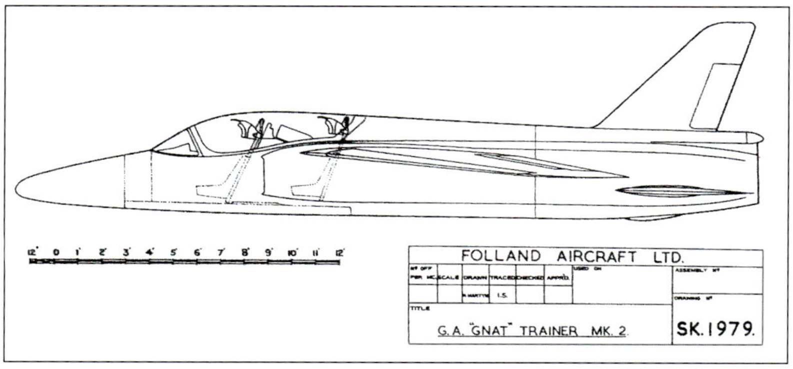

The Gnat Mk.2 looked very similar to the T.1 but its new wing and reheated Bristol Siddeley Orpheus were designed to achieve supersonic performance. *Brooklands Museum*

'Teddy' Petter continued to push his cheap lightweight fighter concept and set his sights on obtaining supersonic performance with a new wing with a thickness-chord ratio of six percent and a reheated turbojet for a maximum speed of Mach 1.2. The Fo.143 Gnat Mk 2 was offered as a single-seat day fighter with AI.23 radar and Firestreak or Sidewinder AAMs and in two-seat night fighter, single-seat carrier-based fighter, photoreconnaissance and two-seat trainer variants. Originally planned with a 4,850lbf (21.57kN) Bristol Siddeley Or.4 Orpheus 701 with a Swedish 1800°K reheat system for a 30 percent boost in sea level static thrust, Bristol began work on the Or.6 Orpheus with 20 percent more thrust with an afterburner based on that of the Ol.22R Olympus fitted to the TSR.2. The Gnat T.1 had a substantial influence on the supersonic Gnat Mk.2; the new 40° swept wing had a similar planform but slightly less wing area and the tailplanes, vertical tail and the undercarriage were all utilised. The forward fuselage was also adapted, the rear cockpit space being used for fuel and avionics in the single-seat versions. In the trainer the rear seat would be raised by 3in (76mm). The low-speed handling was to be as good as that of the Gnat T.1. The trainer could climb to 45,000ft (13,715m) and be used for high speed periods both with and without reheat for a one hour sortie of 145nm (270km) radius. Folland again offered the machine gun pod and Ferranti gyro sight for armament training. Some wind tunnel work and structural tests on two specimen wings was carried out. Despite some interest from the Air Staff, who considered drafting an Operational Requirement for the fighter, this private venture ultimately went no further.

So by 1960 Flying Training Command and Fighter Command had a range of advanced and operational trainers suited to its current generation of fighter aircraft but of course technical progress was still continuing and the 1960s would see a new range of technologies and operating concepts such as vertical take-off and landing flight and aircraft were becoming integrated weapons systems with their sensors and weapon systems. No sooner had the Gnat entered service the Air Staff were thinking about an advanced supersonic replacement. There is no denying however that the Hunter, Lightning and Gnat trainers had long and successful careers and provided much needed experience that could be applied to future training aircraft.

A pair of Gnat T.1s from the CFS on the break, XM709 leading XM706. They were retired in 1979 and 1977 respectively. *Blue Envoy Collection*

6 Training to Strike

The advent of jet propulsion did not just affect fighter pilots; bomber crews would have to master the new technology too. In 1944, before he moved from Westland Aircraft to set up English Electric's new design team, William E W 'Teddy' Petter had begun studying a twin-jet tactical bomber. These studies quickly evolved into the English Electric Canberra to Specification B.3/45 for a high-speed high-altitude tactical bomber. The Canberra introduced Bomber Command to speeds beyond 470kt (870km/h) and altitudes to 48,000ft (14,630m), making the stalwart Avro Lincolns decidedly pedestrian in performance. The heavy bombers would soon join the revolution. As Britain began developing its independent nuclear deterrent, the jet bomber was selected to deliver it. The V-bomber trio of the Vickers Valiant, Avro Vulcan and Handley Page Victor would also feature advanced aerodynamics such as delta and crescent-shaped wings for high subsonic cruising speeds. Pilots had to learn how to cope with handling jet engine flame outs, asymmetric thrust and the effects of high-altitude flight on their bodies. The arrival of the V-bombers brought several changes; expanded airfield facilities, new organisation for ground crew servicing, new ancillary and ground equipment, new flying suits, new weapons handling procedures and a plethora of training simulators to name but a few. Within a decade the arrival of surface-to-air guided missiles (SAMs) would force a return to high-speed low-altitude sorties, although Canberra interdictor pilots were already beating up the West German countryside at low level. Arguably the most important member of a bomber crew was the bomb aimer, it was their responsibility to get the bomb load onto the target accurately and they needed the skills for high-speed high-altitude bombing runs using blind bombing equipment such as the H2S ground mapping radar as well as visual bombing from lower altitudes. Although highly destructive, nuclear weapons were expensive in short supply so the RAF could not afford to waste them in inaccurate attacks. Finding a suitable operational trainer for bomber crews was to be a headache throughout the 1950s. During the 1960s the Canberra aircrews of Bomber Command – from 1968 Strike Command – were eagerly waiting to upgrade to the British Aircraft Corporation (BAC) TSR.2 which had the prospect of automatic supersonic terrain-following flight. This was not to be, but the ageing bombers required replacement and the arrival of the Panavia Tornado in the early 1980s would bring not only new technology, tactics and weapons but a new multinational method of training too.

Honing Accuracy

During the early 1950s the strategic bomber fleet was comprised of Avro Lincoln B.1 and B.2s supplemented by the Washington B.1, Boeing B-29s supplied by the US under the Mutual Defense Aid Plan. Both of these types would be partially replaced by the Canberra from 1951 as an interim solution until the V-bombers were ready. In 1948 Bomber Command had reduced all operational and conversion training units to just one; No 230 Operational Conversion Unit (OCU) Scampton equipped with the Lincoln B.2 and Mosquito B.35. The Central Bombing Establishment,

The Avro Lincoln was the mainstay of bombing training during the first half of the 1950s and finding a suitable replacement that could carry the latest H2S Mk.9 radar proved a complicated task. Lincoln B.2 SX953 of the Bomber Command Bombing School is seen here at Lindholme during 1956. The aircraft is fitted with a large radome enclosing the 6ft (1.8m) 'whirligig' scanner of the H2S Mk.IVA radar. *Dave Welch Collection*

which had been formed in 1945 to train bombing and gunnery leaders as well as carrying out research trials, was disbanded the following year. The Bombing Trials Unit and the Blind Bombing Unit were retained for experimental trials work as the Command geared up for radar-guided blind bombing and the ballistics for the new Blue Danube nuclear bomb. The Washington during its short service life with the RAF gained its own conversion unit, the Washington Conversion Unit being formed out of No 35 Squadron at Marham.

As important as pilots and aircraft were, the measure of a bombing force's effectiveness was its accuracy of weapons delivery. It mattered little how well trained a pilot was or how technically advanced the bomber was if the bombs missed the target. The advent of nuclear weapons and their importance as the national deterrent increased the pressure for accuracy despite their unprecedented destructive capability. In a 1952 minute on bombing training, the Deputy Director of Operational Training, Group Captain J R Gordon-Finlayson, highlighted the problems faced during the early 1950s. During the Second World War, Bomber Command had used 'saturation' or 'shot-gun' methods with an average accuracy of 4,000yd (3,657m), Gordon-Finlayson calculated that if accuracy had been improved to 500yd (457m), a 1,000 bomber raid could have been accomplished by less than 100 aircraft. This was important in terms of the cost of equipment and manpower; the cost of a bomber had risen from £30,000 to £300,000 and its bomb aiming equipment from £100 to £50,000. The ideal visual bombing average accuracy in 1939 was 100yd (91m) at 120kt (222km/h) and 10,000ft (3,050m), in 1952 it was 1,000yd (914m) at 500kt (925km/h) and 50,000ft (15,240m). The bomb aimer was now part of a sequence of radar, navigation and bombing techniques in which even the slightest human error would multiply mechanical errors inherent in even the best equipment.

As the 1950s dawned the Air Navigation Schools (ANS) were still following the wartime syllabus and providing every navigator with basic bomb aiming instruction. This was becoming expensive both in terms of aircraft utilisation and equipment, especially bombsights. The large increase in navigator requirements during the rearmament expansion programmes stretched resources to breaking point. Therefore, in April 1952 bombing training was transferred to Bomber Command and, as an economy measure, Lincoln operational training moved from No 230 OCU to frontline squadrons, freeing the unit to run visual and H2S blind bombing training with nine Lincolns. The frontline squadrons were already obtaining poor accuracy and these changes had little positive effect and Bomber Command was soon asking for additional aircraft and resources. In October, the Bomber Command Bombing School was formed at Scampton (soon moving to Lindholme) from the assets of the former Central Bomber Establishment. Due to dissatisfaction with the Bombing Instructors' Course at the Central Gunnery School, no candidates had been sent for several months and the Bombing School therefore had to also train its own Instructors. The training reductions made problems worse, the No 230 OCU bombing school syllabus had reduced 35 hours of H2S training to just thirteen.

The theoretical accuracy using the H2S Mk.4 and Mk.9 radars was 500yd (457m) but the average Command error was 1,100yd (1,005m), while 900yd (822m) was considered the minimum acceptable for peacetime training. During the war the serviceability of H2S sets was about 75 percent with large numbers of trained radar tradesmen. With reduced numbers of tradesmen this had reduced to only 50-60 percent, meaning that in wartime half of the bombing force would be effectively bombing blind. Given that the Lincoln fleet cost £8 million annually to run, in theory the poor accuracy and serviceability reduced its monetary value to just £840,000. The remedy was to

Lincoln B.2 SX946 in use with the RAF Flying College at Manby is seen here visiting West Malling on 3rd October 1959. The Flying College was formed at Manby on 1st June 1949 to combine aspects of the instructional work of the Empire Flying School, the Empire Air Navigation School and the Empire Air Armament School. *Robin A Walker*

ensure that students could attain 1,200yd (1,097m) before reaching the OCU by increasing the syllabus to 38 hours and providing technical knowledge to enable in-flight rectification of problems to improve serviceability by 20 percent. The theoretical accuracy of Gee-H fitted to the Canberra was 100yd (91m) or less but the average Command error was 350yd (320m) with the desired maximum being 250yd (228m). To achieve this Canberra crews would need six hours ground training to achieve 300yd 9274m) before reaching No 231 OCU. The Bombing School would also run refresher courses for eight Lincoln H2S Mk.4 and eight Washington AN/APQ-13 operators every two weeks.

An acute shortage of replacement Rolls-Royce Merlin engines cast doubt on whether all of Bomber Command's Lincolns could be kept serviceable into 1953, including the Bombing School's aircraft. The H2S Mk.9 had been developed for the V-Force bombers and was designed to form the Navigation and Bombing System when combined with the Navigation and Bombing Computer (NBC) and Green Satin Doppler radar. Green Satin enabled highly accurate and completely automatic measurements of wind speed and direction, allowing the NBC to perform dead reckoning calculations with a very high degree of accuracy. This automated the navigation process to the point where separate navigators and bomb aimers were no longer needed and would therefore eventually merge the bomb aiming training syllabus into navigator training.

Obtaining new equipment was not easy. An October 1952 proposal to modify the Lincolns with H2S Mk.9 was abandoned as the scanner required extensive bomb bay modifications and fitting radar and a visual bombing station seemed unlikely as it had proved impossible in the Avro Ashton, a jet-powered development of the Tudor airliner which had been converted for the Royal Aircraft Establishment for bomb aiming trials. The Lincoln also lacked any facilities for a radar instructor. The Commander-in-Chief Bomber Command, Air Chief Marshal Sir Hugh Lloyd, requested twelve Varsity T.1s but an earlier attempt to fit the H2S Mk.4 radar had been cancelled in 1950 due to several technical issues, including the need for a smaller 3ft (0.91m) diameter radar scanner and reduction of fuel to maintain the all-up weight. Fitting the larger and heavier H2S Mk.9 seemed impossible and a new smaller scanner would take years to develop as the scanner originally intended for the Canberra had been cancelled. In March 1953, the Assistant Chief of the Air Staff (Operational Requirements), Air Vice-Marshal Geoffrey Tuttle, warned that, 'we must consider very carefully what we are training for.' He considered that all bombing would be carried out blind irrespective of altitude and would be using powered guided weapons by 1962. Getting a bomber trainer suitable for ab initio and advanced bombing training would be difficult given the widely different performance required for each role, even if the equipment was largely identical. Air Vice-Marshal George Harvey of Bomber Command confirmed the need for an aircraft capable of carrying a crew of four and three students with performance equal to operational bombers and equipped with current navigation and bombing equipment. Harvey suggested a modified Handley Page Hastings transport with H2S Mk.9 as an interim type until an converted jet or turboprop airliner became available. In the absence of new equipment a Bomber Command request to the Air Staff for approval to use three Lincoln squadrons from mid-1954 for H2S training for the V-Force was approved – albeit reduced to two squadrons. These squadrons were used on an expanded range of refresher and new entrant courses alongside ground courses, Lindholme receiving new buildings for additional simulators.

The Avro Ashton Mk.3 conversions were completed to aid development of the H2S Mk.9 radar and NBS equipment intended for the V-bombers. Some consideration was given to using them for V-bomber crew training. This photograph shows Avro Ashton Mk.4 WB494 which had a pressurised ventral pannier for a bomb-aimer for visual bombing research. The two outboard wing nacelles each held four 100lb (45kg) practice bombs. First flown on 18th November 1952, WB494 was later converted for Armstrong Siddeley Sapphire turbojet trials before being scrapped in 1963. ***Terry Panopalis Collection***

In mid-1954 a Lincoln replacement with H2S Mk.9 radar, NBC Mk.2 and the Visual Sight Attachment bombsight (later cancelled) was back on the agenda. The aircraft required the payload and space for the H2S equipment and radar scanner, four 6kW electric generators for sufficient power and a service ceiling of at least 20,000ft (6,100m) for realistic training. The Handley Page Reading HPR.1 Marathon was rejected as completely impractical on all counts. The Varsity, as noted above, was unsuitable for conversion. A Mk.9 scanner could be fitted into the nose of a Bristol Type 170 Freighter but there would be serious weight and balance problems to overcome and fitting four generators to a twin-engined aircraft was problematic. Avro had already studied fitting a Mk.9 scanner to the lower nose of the York as fitting a ventral radome was impossible given the low ground clearance. The result was limited to 200° coverage but not unfeasible. A Lincoln conversion remained in contention but the favoured choice was the Hastings, one conversion having already been made for the Radar Research Flying Unit.

A decision was finally made and eight Hastings C.1 transports were converted as the T.5 and served with the Bombing School (becoming the Strike Command Bombing School in 1968) from 1959 until its disbandment. Four T.5s continued with the Radar Flight of No 230 OCU until June 1977, even seeing use as maritime reconnaissance aircraft during the 'Cod Wars' over fishing rights with Iceland during the mid-1970s. The search for an ideal crew trainer with the performance similar to a jet-powered V-bomber and identical avionics was dropped as unfeasibly expensive. The Air Staff saw the way forward as using standard bombers at the OCUs alongside static ground pilot and radar simulators for the aircrews. However, in February 1957 a proposal emanated from within Bomber Command to convert Vickers Viscount airliners as Lincoln replacements. But Group Captain I G Esplin of the Operational Requirements Branch discovered few within the Air Ministry, including the Assistant Chief of Air Staff (Training) or the Group Captain Training at Headquarters Bomber Command, knew anything about the proposal and Esplin dismissed it as a 'red herring' and the proposal soon vanished.

Left: The ventral H2S Mk.9 ground mapping/bombing radar radome is obvious on this photograph of Hastings T.5 TG511. After much discussion, converted Hastings C.1 transports were seen as the most cost effective solution to providing a bombing trainer. *Author's Collection*

Below: Handley Page Hastings T.5 TG503 is seen here in July 1974 during its time with No 230 OCU, where it was used to train maritime reconnaissance radar operators. On 30th June 1977, the remaining four Hastings with the OCU's Radar Flight (TG503, TG505, TG511 and TG517) were retired. *Terry Panopalis Collection*

Above: The Air Staff might have been surprised when they selected the Hastings as a bombing trainer that it would still be in service two decades later. Here Hastings T.5 TG517 is seen accompanied by Vulcan B.2 XL320 of No 230 OCU. The four red cod painted on the nose are from its time flying maritime patrols hunting for Icelandic patrol vessels during the 'Cod War' in 1975-76. *Terry Panopalis Collection*

Conversion to Canberras

The Canberra T.4 was evolved from the Canberra B.2 bomber which had entered service with Bomber Command in January 1951. The Canberra powered by two 6,500lbf (28.9kN) Rolls-Royce Avon turbojets could attain a maximum speed of Mach 0.82 at 40,000ft (12,190m). This was a large difference from pilots used to flying the Avro Lincoln and even the de Havilland Mosquito. It was clear that a conversion trainer would be required to enable pilots to become proficient in handling the new bomber and to learn the necessary operational handling and tactics. Specification T.2/49 was released on 28th March 1949 and called for a variant of the Canberra with dual controls, but it was not intended to fly the aircraft solo from the instructor's seat. Two Rolls-Royce Tay turbojets were specified, but in June 1950 the standard two Avons were reinstated. The resulting Canberra T.4 was almost identical to the standard B.2 except for having a solid nose and a new cockpit with side-by-side seating for the student and instructor, the navigator was retained on the port side aft. Fitting side-by-side ejection seats required the additional seat to slide on rails to allow access to the navigator's position. Prototype WN467 first flew on 6th June 1952 with English Electric's Chief Test Pilot Roland Beamont at the controls, development and construction having cost only £178,900. The T.4 entered service with No 231 OCU in 1954.

The Canberra T.4 lacked any weapons capability and was intended purely as a conversion trainer for Canberra pilots. Canberra WH841 is seen here soon after its delivery in March 1954. It was struck off charge in 1971. *via Dave Forster*

The Canberra T.4 looked almost identical externally to the standard bomber variants, except for the solid nose cone. Pictured here is the prototype Canberra T.4, WN467. *Author's Collection*

This unit had been formed at Bassingbourn on 1st December 1950 with Mosquito T.3s and Gloster Meteor T.7s. To give the first crews experience of handling jet engines the Bomber Command Jet Conversion Flight at been formed on 15th December 1950 with two Gloster Meteor F.4 and two Meteor T.7 trainers. The Flight rotated around the airfields to provide instruction to the Canberra squadrons as they formed up until the task was taken on by No 12 Flying Training School in October 1954. Canberras assigned to the 2nd Tactical Air Force in West Germany had a dedicated tactical bombing role and to prepare the crews for this demanding low-level flying role the Tactical Development Unit was established at Ahlhorn in 1953 with standard B.2 bombers.

English Electric built 75 T.4 production aircraft and seventeen B.2s were later converted to T.4 standard. The T.4 saw extensive use and equipped no less than five OCUs as well as the RAF College, the Central Flying School (CFS), the Empire Test Pilots School and dozens of other squadrons and specialist training units. Some airframes saw up to 40 years of service. Export Canberra purchasers also acquired small numbers of T.4s for conversion training; seven went to India, two to Venezuela and Southern Rhodesia received three ex-RAF aircraft. New Zealand received two new-build aircraft with minor changes as the T.13 and the Royal Australian Air Force converted seven of its B.20 bombers to a similar standard as the T.21.

Canberra T.4 WH849 was delivered to the RAF on 27th May 1954. It was finally retired by No 39 Squadron in 2002 and is today preserved at the Laarbruch Museum at Weeze, Germany. *Author's Collection*

Delivered to the RAF in October 1954, Canberra T.4 WJ866 served with the Royal Navy's Fleet Requirements and Air Direction Training Unit (FRADTU) during 1971 to 1986. WJ866 is seen here approaching Yeovilton in September 1974. Sadly WJ866 was the last operational Canberra loss in RAF service, when it crashed at Marham during a night time touch and go on 2nd September 2004. The crew ejected outside the envelope of the Martin-Baker ejection seats; the navigator was injured but sadly both pilots were killed. *Terry Panopalis Collection*

No 231 OCU remained associated with the Canberra until its disbandment on 23rd April 1993, in later years supporting the photo-reconnaissance PR.7 fleet as the Canberra Standardisation Training Flight. By the late 1960s the OCU's Canberra fleet was getting long in the tooth and increasingly unrepresentative of later Canberra variants like the PR.7. It was decided to modernise the navigational equipment of four Canberras (WH919, WJ637, WJ731 AND WJ677) at No 60 Maintenance Unit at Leconfield. The modernisation entailed extensive work, complete stripping of the current equipment and fitting ILS/VOR, IFF/SSR and TACAN with new aerials and a new panel for the navigator. An additional inverter was required for the power needed and the lower inboard port wing skin had to be cut to fit a Green Satin Doppler radar. The trials installation was fitted to WH919 in 1970, with the others following during 1971-72. On completion they received the B.2T designation.

Canberra T.4 WJ863 is seen here in September 1973 at Cottesmore, home of No 360 Squadron, which conducted electronic countermeasures (ECM) training for the RAF and Royal Navy until 1994. *Terry Panopalis Collection*

By the late 1960s the navigation equipment fitted to the Canberra B.2 bombers used by No 231 OCU was unrepresentative of equipment in later operational marks of Canberra, such as the PR.7 and T.17. Four Canberras were reworked to B.2T standard by No 60 Maintenance Unit, including WH731 which was converted during 1971-72. *Author's Collection*

V-Bomber Training

Planning the training requirements for the forthcoming V-bombers began in mid-1951, in particular for the Valiant which would enter service first. Pilots and navigator/bomb aimers would need a suitable advanced trainer. Using a Valiant for these roles seemed uneconomic so early thoughts turned to the Canberra for pilot training and perhaps a converted de Havilland Comet, Ashton or Viscount for crew training. The lack of a clear policy or technical requirements at this stage frustrated the Director of Operational Requirements, Air Commodore Harold V Satterly, who pointed out that a specialised aircraft would not be ready until after the Valiant entered service. Even so, he asked the Ministry of Supply (MoS) to advise on suitable aircraft. The Deputy Director Military Aircraft Research and Development's study concluded that design and production of a new aircraft was impossible given the timescale, production effort and costs. The desire for performance similar to the Valiant eliminated all propeller-driven aircraft from contention. The experimental Type 663 Tay Viscount with two Rolls-Royce RB.42 Tay turbojets was rejected as impractical as the Tay was not in production. The Ashton was a possibility but Avro already had production commitments for the Canberra and the Vulcan. The Comet would need substantial redesign to accommodate the radar scanner and was expensive to build and operate. The Shorts SA.4 Sperrin, the often forgotten V-bomber back-up, was more suitable – the prototype had just flown – but Shorts had production capacity problems too. A Valiant variant would just take production capacity away from the bombers. The MoS was prepared to make detailed investigations into the Comet and Sperrin if asked to by the Air Staff but they were unenthusiastic about this and felt that the answer lay in ground-based simulators which would be ready before an aircraft; the simulator company Redifon was already working on a prototype for completion in 1953. The matter was quietly dropped and the standard Valiant was used for operational training alongside the Canberra.

The creation of the V-Force required detailed planning, including the provision of suitable operational training aircraft. It soon became clear that using frontline aircraft was the only practical choice. Pilots would step up from the Canberra T.4 to the four-engined V-Bombers. Seen here are three Vulcan B.1As of the Waddington Wing in 1957.
MoD/Open Government Licence, 2018

Looking every inch like a mini-Vulcan, Avro 707C WZ744 was the two-seat member of the experimental Type 707 family and considered as the basis of a dedicated conversion trainer for Vulcan pilots. In the event this proved unnecessary as the delta wing resulted in fewer handling problems than originally feared. WZ744 is seen here in September 1969 at Finningley where it was preserved as instructional airframe 7932M. *Terry Panopalis Collection*

Avro's futuristic Type 698 Vulcan with its large delta wing broke new ground and the company planned both the Type 707 one-third and Type 710 half-scale scale flying models to aid development. The 710 was soon abandoned but the 707 programme went ahead under Specification E.10/49, although subject to its own development delays it contributed comparatively little to the final design of the Vulcan. Issue 2 of E.10/49 added two dual control 707C aircraft, WZ739 and WZ744, featuring wing root intakes and a bulged cockpit canopy to accommodate two seats side-by-side. Another two were also ordered, it was hoped to use all four as operational conversion trainers for the Vulcan. The 707 research flying programme identified that the Vulcan's layout created no unusual handling vices and therefore it was decided to use standard Vulcans for training. Three of the 707Cs were cancelled but WZ744 was completed and used for research, including the development of fly-by-wire electrically signalled hydraulic controls.

In 1952 Bomber Command had selected Gaydon as the location for the Valiant OCU and the following year the runways and buildings were extended. The conversion unit started life as the reformed No 138 Squadron on 1st January 1955; in July the squadron became operational and moved to Wittering and Gaydon was officially redesignated No 232 OCU. This unit's experience would form the pattern of V-bomber operational training for all three types. The first Commanding Officer was Wing Commander G W Oakley who had been the liaison officer with Vickers for three years and had flown many hours as co-pilot with test pilot Brian Trubshaw in the second prototype WB215. The selection of crews followed a new process given the level of experience and responsibility required to fly a bomber armed with nuclear weapons. Aircraft captains were required to have 1,750 flying hours as captains and at least one Canberra tour and equally desirable was four-engine piston experience. Co-pilots needed 700 flying hours as captains and a full Canberra tour. Navigator/bomb aimers had to be recommended by their Commanding Officers and needed to complete the Bombing School syllabus. Signallers had to have completed a tour in either Bomber, Coastal or Transport Command. Unlike the rest of the RAF, a V-bomber tour was five years long rather than two and a half. Ground crews were also trained at Gaydon at the Valiant Servicing School with extensive training carried out at Vickers, Boulton Paul and Rolls-Royce on the airframe, powered flight control system and engines respectively. Alongside the few Valiant B.1s on strength, Canberra T.4s were also used for handling training and circuits and bumps. Following the decision to employ the Valiant as a refuelling tanker aircraft, Flight Refuelling Limited used converted Canberra B.2 WH734 with a prototype Mk.16 Hose Drum Unit in its bomb bay both for trials work and to assist in the training of the first air and ground crews at Tarrant Rushton. Once No 214 Squadron at Marham began re-equipping with tanker Valiants in early 1956, flight crews were sent to Tarrant Rushton and Boscombe Down for flight training.

This parade at No 232 OCU at Gaydon on 19th March 1956 shows the first aircraft delivered to the unit; Vickers Valiants WZ364, WZ372, WZ377, WP216, WZ365, WZ374, WZ362 and WZ361. *Author's Collection*

The squadron's role conversion flight was 'A' Flight with Valiant B(K).1s XD689 and XD780 to train the tanker crews, while 'B' Flight used two standard probe-equipped Valiant B.1s with 1,650gal (7,500lit) external tanks for receiver training, pilots learning how to make contact with the hose drogue. These early training sorties were 'dry', the squadron not making its first 'wet' fuel transfer until January 1959. It was one of No 232 OCU's aircraft, the second production B(PR)K.1 WP217, which on 6th August 1964 suffered a cracked rear spar during a training sortie. Being the second such event within two months, all Valiants were grounded and with re-sparring deemed uneconomic, all but one were scrapped.

Long before this, No 232 OCU had been earmarked to also serve as the Victor conversion unit, its first Victor B.1 being collected on 28th November 1957. The OCU was then split into 'A' Squadron with the Victor and 'B' Squadron with the Valiant. The first Victor course was completed in April 1958 and the crews were posted to the newly reformed No 10 Squadron at Cottesmore. The OCU completed a concentrated 1,000 flying hour trial in August to test the operational durability of the Victor. This revealed fatigue cracks in the tailplane, which although due to a manufacturing flaw, led to the entire fleet being fitted with new tailplanes as a precaution. During early 1958 No 232 OCU also took delivery of three Victor B.1s equipped with Yellow Aster reconnaissance radars intended for No 543 Squadron, the crews being trained on the OCU's Valiant B(PR).1s. A new 'C' Flight moved to Cottesmore to being conversion training with the improved Victor B.2 in April 1961, completing its task in June 1965 leading to the disbandment of No 232 OCU. It reformed in May 1970 from the Tanker Training Flight at Marham operating converted Victor K.1 tankers. Before No 232 OCU severed its links with the Victor on its disbanding on 30th June 1986, it had played its role in the famous BLACK BUCK missions of 1982, providing an air-to-air refuelling instructor to each Vulcan crew for day and night training flights over the Irish Sea and Western Isles.

The Vulcan gained its own conversion unit, No 230 OCU reforming at Waddington on 31st May 1956. Its allocation of B.1s XA897 and XA895 lasted barely two months before they were sent on a goodwill tour to New Zealand and the Vulcan Operational Reliability Unit at Boscombe Down respectively. Not until 3rd January 1957 did it receive XA898, but the return of XA895 on 19th January enabled the first course to begin on 21st February. This first course graduated on 21st May and formed 'A' Flight of No 83 Squadron, the first to equip with the delta-winged bomber. The next course became 'B' Flight and then the following courses were used to form No 101 Squadron at Finningley. The OCU's Vulcan B.1s were all early production aircraft with 11,000lbf (48.9kN) Bristol Olympus 101 engines but no problems were encountered during training and the introduction of the Vulcan into service went very smoothly for a new type. In October, No 230 OCU sent three Vulcans to participate alongside two Valiants from Nos 138 and 214 Squadrons in the US Strategic Air Command (SAC) Bombing Competition at Pinecastle Air Force Base, Florida. It was essential to see how the V-bombers compared to the US bomber fleet and the results certainly provided much needed experience for the fledgling training syllabus and the RAF has continued to participate in USAF exercises ever since. In the 1974 SAC Bombing Competition, a No 230 OCU Vulcan B.2 crew won the Mathis Trophy for the best bombing and navigation result for a single crew, despite the navigation systems malfunctioning shortly after take-off and the navigators forced to rely on the old methods of pencil and map. In July 1960 the OCU received its first example of the improved Vulcan B.2, XH558, and had four more before the end of the year B.2s. The first B.2 qualified crews went to No 83 Squadron in November and from 1965 the OCU operated solely with the B.2 until its disbandment on 31st August 1981.

A Handley Page Victor K.2 of No 232 OCU taking off. This OCU had a long association with the Victor from 1958 to 1986. *Author's Collection*

This painting illustrates what might have been had the TSR.2 not been cancelled. A BAC TSR.2 Eagle T.2 and Hawker Hunter T.12 of No 237 OCU are seen flying over the Ballistic Missile Early Warning System site at Fylingdales during a training sortie. Behind is the prototype Hunter T.12 XE351 and a TSR.2 operated by the Royal Aircraft Establishment. *Luciano Alviani*

Training for TSR.2

The planned OCU for the BAC TSR.2 fleet was to be No 237 OCU based at Coningsby. It was to be equipped with seven TSR.2 trainers and twelve Hawker Hunter Mk.66 (referred to by the Air Ministry as the T.66) trainers powered by a higher-thrust Rolls-Royce Avon 203 turbojet, similar to aircraft sold to the Indian and Jordanian Air Forces. The OCU would also possess two ground flight simulators. The initial plan was to begin Hunter training in June 1967 to coincide with the first TSR.2 delivery, but this was postponed due to the development delays until April 1968. Each course would last 40 weeks consisting of 76 hours on the simulator and 45 hours of TSR.2 flying time (the initial plan was for 70 hours). The first courses would only have been open to experienced Strike Command pilots only and they would have logged 300 hours on trainers, including the Hunter, before arrival. It was hoped that the flight simulators would be ready in August 1967 but a planned Land Mass Simulator which would use cameras moving over a detailed scale model of the target terrain for low-level strike training was suspended to save development costs.

Due to the advanced nature of the TSR.2 and its different handling characteristics and flight profile, it was decided that a dedicated trainer would be a cost-effective training solution. The expense of a trainer would outweigh the cost of losses of frontline aircraft due to training accidents. The trainer would be used for instruction, standardisation checks of flying and operational techniques, including weapons delivery. BAC made its first preliminary proposals in early 1960 and constructed a forward fuselage mock-up. Some level of easy conversion of training airframes to fully operational configuration was also desired. The Air Staff had specified side-by-side seating for the pupil and instructor but the estimated costs of the airframe changes and the loss of easy conversion meant these that plans were shelved. Instead, in September 1960 the Air Staff changed their requirements to tandem seating to allow for full conversion to an operational aircraft. BAC modified its mock-up and estimated that a design study would cost £12,000.

No further work was carried out until May 1962 when BAC carried out a full design study, but the Air Staff was still trying to convince the Defence Research Policy Committee (DRPC) for the need for a dedicated trainer. The discussions took months and

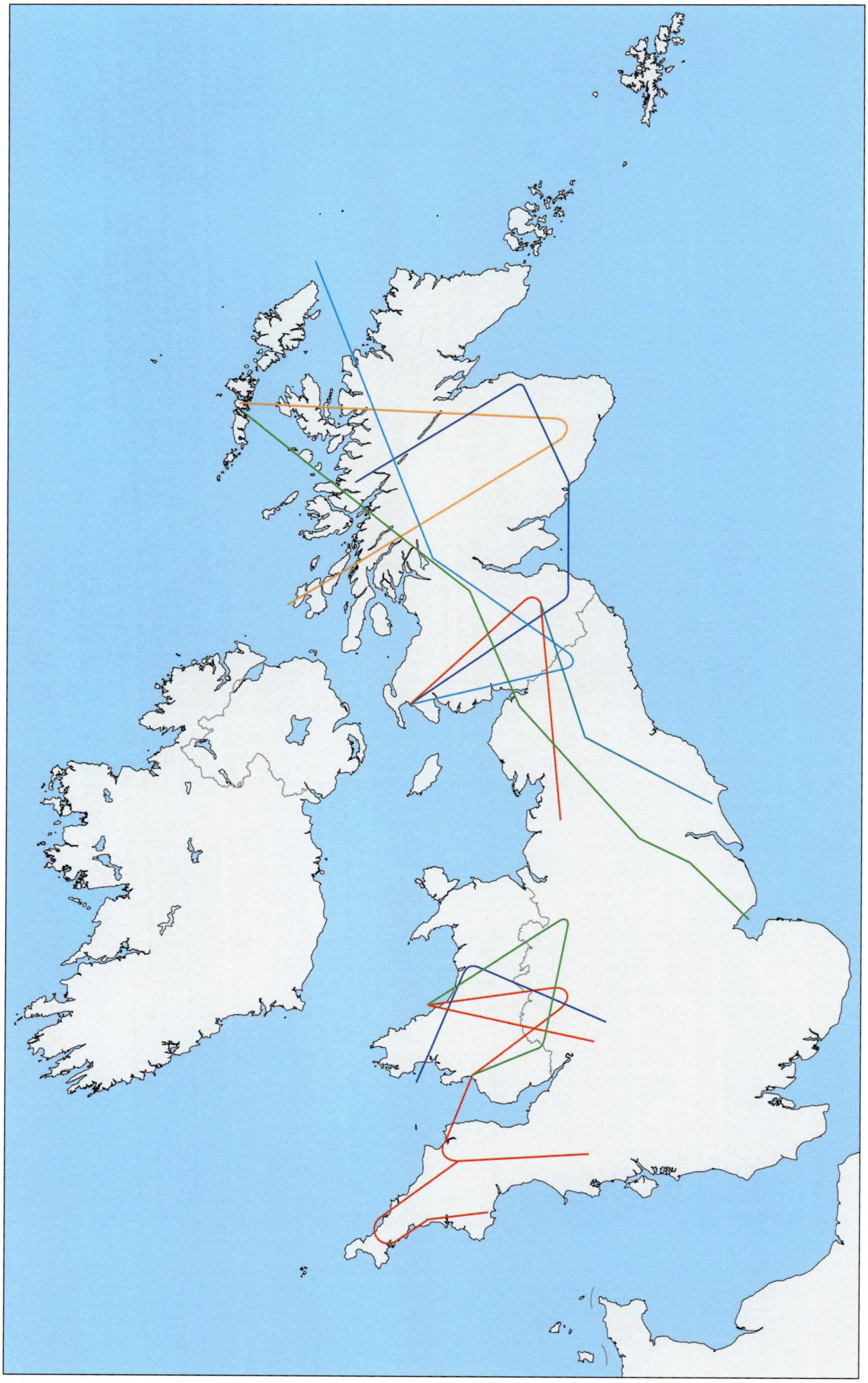

This map shows the official low level flying routes across the United Kingdom as of December 1962 when discussions began on future training requirements for TSR.2 crews, who would need to train low and fast. *Chris Gibson*

involved in-depth analysis of the proposed syllabus and comparisons with the Fleet Air Arm's (FAA) method of establishing operational squadrons with intensive shore-based training as an operational unit. It was not until May 1963 that the DRPC agreed and BAC was awarded a contract for the design study. At a meeting with the Air Staff on 24th October, the current requirements and the size of the required training fleet was discussed. The RAF wanted nine aircraft, seven for the OCU with two for use as strike aircraft with the capability to be converted into trainers if required. The rest of the trainer fleet was to be capable of conversion to full strike standard within a week using modification kits with the concession that the trainer canopy could be retained as long as some strike missions could still be flown with it in place.

Following the signing of the contract in March 1964, the design team at Weybridge began detailed work on the Type 595. Warton assisted with experience gained with the Canberra T.4 and Lightning T.3 and T.5 trainer conversions and wind tunnel tests commenced in September. The brochure was ready in January 1965 but unfortunately coincided with the review of the TSR.2's future and in February the Air Staff once again postponed the idea. The Type 595 shared the same airframe as the strike variant but with a single clear-view canopy. The Central Computing System for navigation and computing weapon delivery flight profiles was not required. It was agreed that a CC.11 compass, Doppler, moving map display, E Type compass, a direction indicator and TACAN provided sufficient navigation data and could be used for weapon delivery manoeuvres.

The Type 595 mock-up was inspected by a group from the Air Staff in September 1964. The mock-up was positioned both horizontally and raised to 15° incidence to approximately the landing approach configuration on a 3° glideslope. Wing Commander Croshaw of the Operational Requirements branch was concerned at the restricted view in landing configuration, which he felt was equivalent to the Gloster Javelin T.3 (which had a similar high approach attitude due to its delta wing), which was the minimum acceptable standard. Following another meeting at Weybridge on 24th November, Croshaw requested further assessment of the instructor's cockpit by pilots with Javelin T.3 experience including A&AEE pilots, Fighter Command instructors and CFS Examiners. These included Wing Commander P Smith of the Air Plans division who found it impossible to see the simulated runway and approach lights using either 3° or 2° landing glideslopes. Croshaw suggested using a periscope like that fitted to the Javelin T.3 periscope, which had been designed for gunnery training but was also useful for in flying in the landing circuit and ground manoeuvring at night.

Three strike trainers; the BAC Type 595 TSR.2 Trainer, the General Dynamics TF-111K and the Panavia Tornado GR.1T. All were designed for partial or full weapons capability for operational training and frontline use in wartime. The immense size of the TSR.2 is apparent compared to its US rival and the Tornado, illustrating the effect of rapid miniaturisation of electronics and aerodynamic and propulsion advances in just two decades. *Chris Gibson*

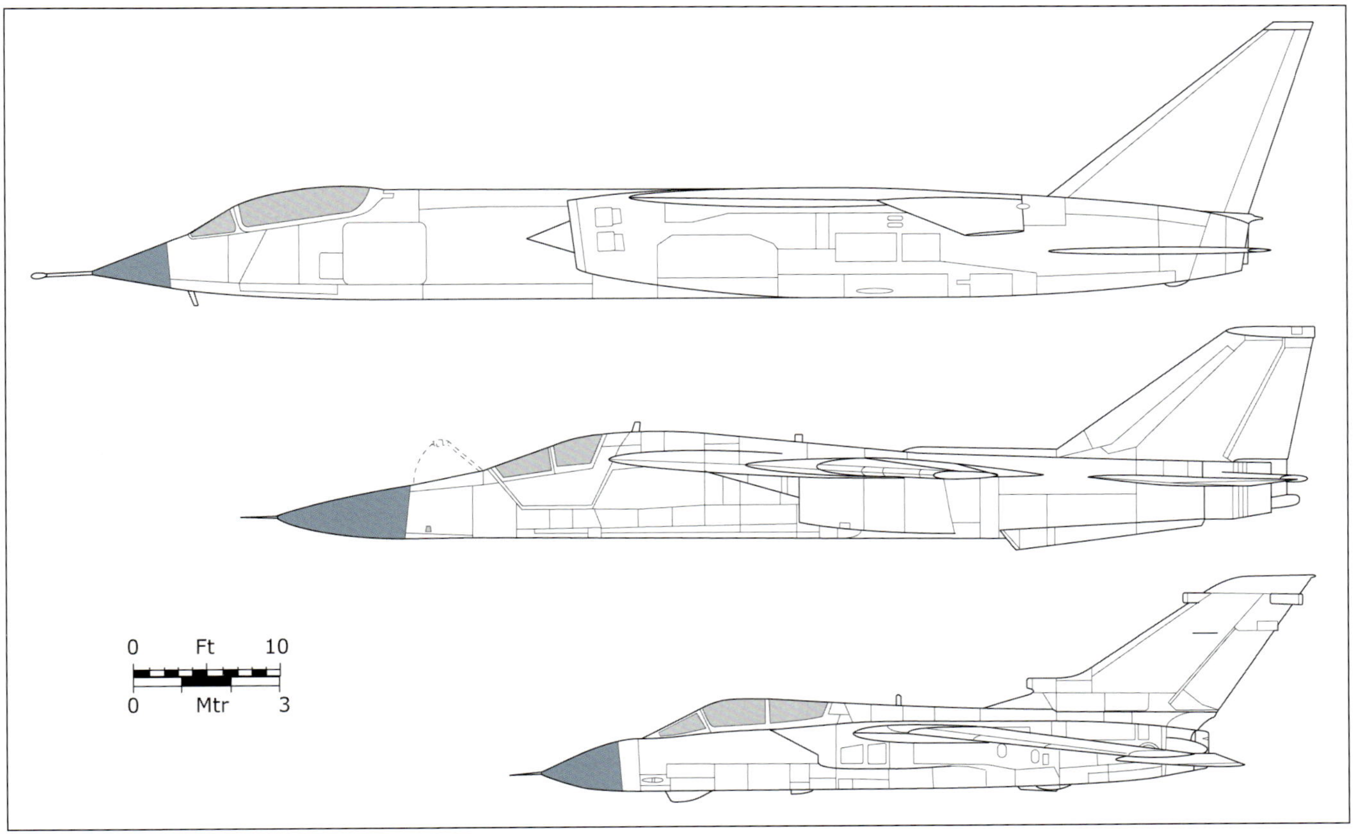

The Weybridge team suggested that the strike navigator's ventral periscope could be retained instead. Overall Croshaw was unhappy with the proposed layout and considered that simulator training might be more cost effective. On 20th January 1965, Flight Lieutenant E Stewart of the Handling Squadron visited Weybridge for his assessment. Stewart had 150 hours experience on the Javelin T.3, 900 hours on the Meteor T.7 and some recent limited experience on the Folland Gnat T.1. The left hand side of forward headrest had been cut away to improve forward visibility but the results of Stewart's evaluation was the same, with no forward visibility and only limited visibility to the sides. Stewart assessed the approach and landing from the back seat as being 'extremely difficult and probably hazardous if not impossible.' BAC was informed that their proposal was currently unacceptable and it was recommended that the navigator's periscope be reinstated and a larger, perhaps two-piece, canopy fitted. The mock-up's windscreen had also been modified with one similar to the Javelin. The Air Staff were prepared to accept some performance limitations; a maximum speed of 450kt (835km/h) at sea level or Mach 1.4 at altitude and a maximum altitude of 40,000ft (12,000m). The requirement for conversion was also relaxed has it was realised the airframes were unlikely to be converted in practice. BAC was asked to bring forward new proposals but no further work was done before cancellation of the TSR.2 programme on 6th April 1965.

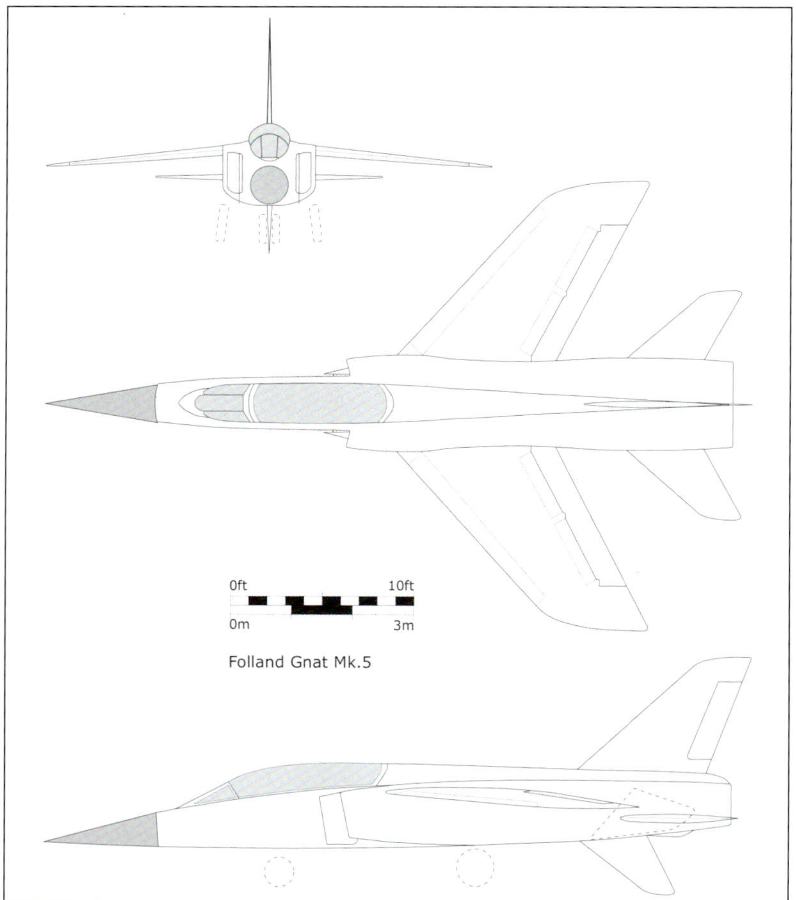

Folland Gnat Mk.5

Lead-In Trainers

Other lead-in trainers were looked at before the selection of the Hunter T.66. By the end of 1959 the Gnat T.1 or Hunter T.7 had been assessed as being more suitable than the Canberra due to the latter's subsonic performance. The Gnat was not considered suitable due to its limited avionics fit, but in mid-1960 Folland proposed a Gnat T.2 with improved navigation equipment including a master reference gyro to give a partial Integrated Flight Instrument System (IFIS) fit. The RAF remained unenthusiastic and in September Folland offered the Gnat Mk.5. This developed Gnat had a five percent thickness/chord ratio wing powered by two reheated RB.153Rs and could accommodate an AI.23 radar in the nose and had an estimated maximum speed of Mach 2.4 and a maximum ceiling of 60,000ft (18,290m). The Air Staff still considered it to be inferior to the Hunter or Lightning and developing a new trainer was an unwanted additional expense.

The Lightning T.4 was considered suitable for conversion training in concert with ground simulator training. It was pointed out that take-off and landing techniques using blown flaps would be different but the Navy had not experienced any difficulties with the lack of a dedicated trainer for converting Blackburn Buccaneer pilots. In January 1961 BAC proposed a modified Lightning T.5 with the TSR.2 terrain-following radar repackaged to fit into the AI.23 AIRPASS radome with the electronics stowed in the forward armament bay. A simple Head-Up Display (HUD) would replace the Light Fighter Sight and a simplified navigation suite using Decca Doppler and a radio altimeter would be located in the main equipment bay. The large ventral fuel tank developed for, but never used by, the T.5 would also be fitted. In late 1963 the proposal was submitted by Warton to Weybridge for consideration, leading to worries whether the proposal might mean the rejection of a dedicated TSR.2 trainer. The Air Staff, however, felt that the modified T.5 was not as attractive as a dedicated TSR.2 trainer variant.

The Air Staff's preferred lead-in trainer was the Hunter T.66. The plan was to provide twelve for the OCU and two for each frontline TSR.2 squadron. In May 1961 RAF pilots and navigators undertook five sorties in Hawker's Mk.66A demonstrator G-APUX (the rear fuselage was from a former Belgian F.6) from Dunsfold for low-level sorties. The trials demonstrated some of the handling and navigational challenges posed by high-speed low-level flying. The crews involved praised the T.66's usefulness as a lead-in trainer. However, the flights proved less popular with the residents of Somerset, Devon and Cornwall and numerous telephone calls and 30 letters of

The Folland Gnat Mk.5 was the last attempt to develop a supersonic derivative. Although sharing a family resemblance to earlier Gnats, the Mk.5 was powered by two RB.145 engines and had a large retractable ventral fin for stability at speeds up to Mach 2.4. *Author*

The English Electric Lightning T.4 was the only training aircraft that the RAF possessed which could come close to matching the TSR.2's supersonic performance. T.4 XM987 of No 226 OCU is seen here coming in to land at St Mawgan on 16th May 1972. First flown at Warton on 13th July 1961, XM987 was retired in October 1974. *Chris England*

complaint were received. This prompted the Air Staff to re-examine the suitability of low-level flying areas in the UK and whether overseas locations might be preferable. The Assistant Chief of the Air Staff (Policy) argued that a Hunter lead-in trainer was generous and that No 229 OCU at Chivenor could accommodate the necessary training. The differing avionics required compared to the Hunter T.7 and the increase in TSR.2 flying hours required made this impractical however and the small TSR.2 OCU offered a more cost effective solution.

Hunter F.6 XE351 was converted to Mk.66 standard as the T.12 (initially the T.7A designation was considered – later assigned to upgraded T.7s) with a T.7 forward fuselage section. The aircraft would be both a trials aircraft for TSR.2 equipment with the Royal Aircraft Establishment and a prototype for future conversions. The main scope of the trials was the development of the planned HUD and the FX.126 surveying camera, which was mounted in the nose, its size requiring a distinctive 'bump' on the top of the nose. Other avionics included distance-measuring equipment, Green Salad UHF homer, the full OR.946 IFIS which was linked to the HUD and a small 'side-stick' controller for the Flight Director. The flight trials programme throughout 1963 was very successful and it was considered feasible to use the equipment in the T.66, albeit with some additional tactical navigation equipment and reinstatement of the original yaw damper to improve handling at high speed in turbulent conditions. In the event, the cancellation of the TSR.2 saw all these training and equipment plans shelved.

Hawker created the Hunter T.66 variant as an export private venture with the more powerful Rolls-Royce Avon 203 turbojet. Had the TSR.2 not been cancelled, several T.7s would have been upgraded to T.66 standard. XE531 was the sole RAF aircraft to be modified, becoming the T.12 for TSR.2 avionics trials. XE531 is seen here in 1978, still in RAE use as a testbed. *Terry Panopalis Collection*

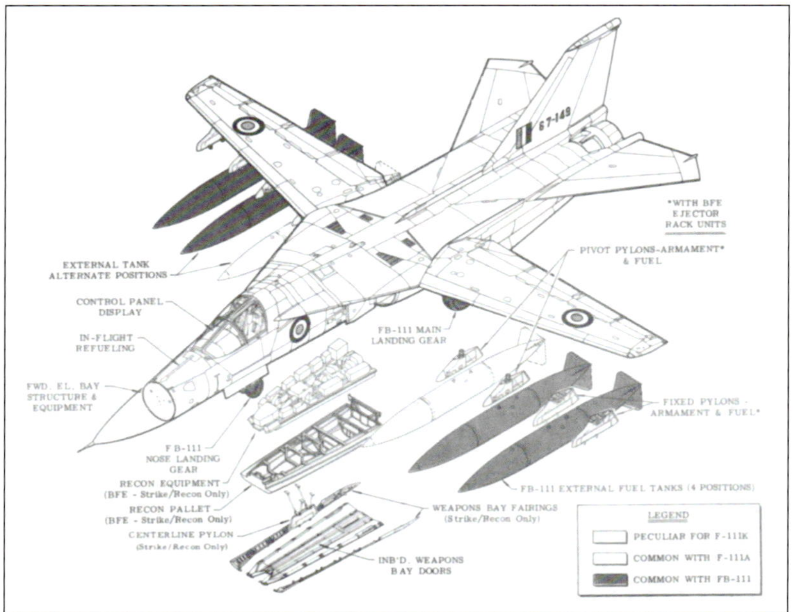

The F-111K was based on F-111A and FB-111A components. The four TF-111K trainer/strike aircraft would have lacked lack the capability to carry the reconnaissance pallet in the bomb bay.
General Dynamics via Joe Cherrie

Strike Trainer Cancelled (Again)

With the TSR.2 cancelled, the Canberra had to soldier on until a replacement could be found. During the summer of 1965 Air Staff Requirement ASR.343 was rewritten around the TSR.2s direct competitor, the General Dynamics F-111K, as Defence Secretary Denis Healey confirmed the selection of the American aircraft. The F-111K was developed from the standard American F-111A but fitted with the undercarriage of the FB-111A, developed for SAC, for a higher gross weight take-off capability and some specific British avionics. Two nearly identical variants were ordered, 46 F-111K for strike/reconnaissance and four TF-111K for the trainer/strike role. The latter had similar avionics but lacked the capability to carry the reconnaissance pallet in the bomb bay, instead having an additional centreline ventral pylon for a Martel TV-guided air-to-surface missile (ASM) datalink pod. Dual controls were also fitted to the trainer/strike aircraft. The proposed structure was four operational squadrons and one OCU, No 237 OCU again being the likely unit. On 18th September 1967 the first two airframes to enter construction included the first TF-111K trainer/strike aircraft, 'UK2', serialled XV884, which was intended for avionics testing and weapons release trials before being converted to production standard. In May 1965 collaboration on the Anglo-French Variable Geometry Aircraft (AFVG) led by Britain was agreed, specifically as an interceptor of the RAF but the FAA and the French were also interested in its potential for the strike role. Ironically, having foreseen the need for a VG wing trainer and given up the requirement (see Chapter Five) the RAF was now potentially to be equipped with two VG winged aircraft. The desire to limit spending on foreign purchases saw the TSR.2 ground simulators repurposed for the F-111K, including the Land Mass Simulator and Visual Attachment for low-level training and elements of the digital computer and visual equipment were also used in the McDonnell Douglas F-4 Phantom FGR.2 simulators. In the event, on 29th June 1967 the French withdrew from the AFVG programme and on 16th January 1968 the F-111K order was also cancelled due to the economic effects of the devaluation of the Pound which had inflated the unit cost to £3.02 million. The aircraft the RAF had spent the best part of two decades avoiding, the Blackburn Buccaneer, was the only option left. For the Buccaneers the Hunter T.7 and T.8 proved more than capable for type conversion.

Of the first two airframes under construction, 'UK2' was to be the first of four TF-111K aircraft, XV884. The original plan was for XV884 to be an avionics testbed for integrating British avionics as well as weapons separation testing. Following the UK government's cancellation of its order on 16th January 1968, both were broken up for parts recovery.
General Dynamics via Joe Cherrie

The strike/recon F-111K, unlike USAF F-111As, would have lacked provision for any duplicated flight controls at the right-hand position where the navigator would have sat. Only the TF-111Ks would have had this feature.
General Dynamics via Joe Cherrie

Three T.7s were issued to No 12 Squadron at Honington in October 1969 for instrument flying practice and instrument rating. Following the handing over of all FAA Buccaneers to the RAF in 1972, the T.7A and T.8B fleet was combined alongside some standard T.7s and issued to RAF Buccaneer squadrons and No 237 OCU and were retired when they were withdrawn alongside the Buccaneer on 31st March 1994.

Tri-National Tornado Training

Following the demise of AFVG, the national-only UKVG programme was proposed in July 1967 but barely lasted into the autumn after West Germany declined to collaborate. In 1968 the programme, rebranded as the Advanced Combat Aircraft, began to make inroads into the 'F-104 Consortium', the various European operators of the Lockheed fighter now looking at possible replacements. Britain was invited to join in May 1968 and Air Staff Target AST.392 was drawn up. Renamed the Multi-Role Combat Aircraft, the MRCA was to be in service by 1975. Several of the initial members dropped out (Belgium, Canada and the Netherlands) but BAC, Messerchmitt-Bölkow-Blohm and Fiat formed a joint company in September 1969 to develop the MRCA, Panavia Aircraft GmbH. Following the first flight of prototype P01 at Manching in Germany on 14th August 1974, the MRCA was named Tornado.

The planning for MRCA training began in June 1972 when the Joint Operational Training Study Group was created by the four operators, the RAF, Luftwaffe and Marineflieger and the Aeronautica Militare Italiana (AMI). Their report in March 1975 laid out the future training plan for combined joint operational training. This was not unnatural given the collaborative development of the Tornado itself and the similar missions and training requirements air forces had for their production GR.1 and IDS fleets. Out of the operators the RAF had by far the most extensive experience of OCUs. The AMI carried out its own operational training for its Fiat G.91 and F-104 Starfighter pilots, but had no experience of fast jet navigator training. The Luftwaffe was reliant on training facilities in the USA for its G.91, F-104 and F-4 Phantom pilots and Weapons Systems Operator training for the F-4. The German Marineflieger abandoned its initial plans for independent training and instead would rely on the Luftwaffe. The forecast training task for the three nations was 150 crews annually during the force build-up for six years and subsequently 120 replacement crews annually. The study focused on a joint OCU and a joint Weapons Conversion Unit (WCU).

The OCU would train crews in basic operating techniques, conversion training, system and radar familiarisation and self-defence training. Three courses were envisioned; a main thirteen week-long course for crews suitable for experienced and first tourist pilots providing 63 flying hours per crew (40 for the pilot and 27.5hrs for the navigator) with eight courses per year; a four-week instrument rating examiner course for RAF and German instructors with up to six pilots on each of three or four courses per year; and short ten week courses for around ten RAF senior officers per year destined for Tornado stations including ground school and simulator training with sixteen flying hours for pilots and fourteen hours for navigators. Aircraft and instructors would be pooled from all three nations, national crews would fly national aircraft but would also swap, the same holding true for instructors. RAF and German instructors would require at least 500 hours fast jet experience, with AMI instructors having 200 hours on F-104s. For Navigator/Weapon Systems Officer instructors the RAF would have to bear the brunt until enough experienced German and Italian instructors were available and the RAF and Luftwaffe discussed aligning their syllabus to ease training. Airfields were reviewed in all three nations but it was agreed that the RAF could provide the best engineering support and as all teaching would be in English it would also solve language problems. Cottesmore was identified as the most favourable location and could also accommodate the RAF Ground Servicing School as well as two British simulators which would help the ground school and simulator training phases.

The Tri-national Tornado Training Establishment at Cottesmore had a fleet of Tornados and personnel drawn from all three partner nations. Each aircraft carried an identification code denoting its home nationality; B for Britain, G for Germany and I for Italy. On display here at the North Weald Fighter Meet in May 1995 is B-51, GR.1 ZA327. All aircraft assigned to TTTE carried national markings but could be flown by a student and instructor of any of the three nations. *Alan Kilham*

The WCU would run a six week course with 56 aircraft hours per crew eight times a year. The syllabus would cover low flying, laydown, dive and toss delivery and radar attacks. Again, RAF experience heavily influenced the syllabus. Training on each nations' specific ASMs (Martel, Kormoran and Jumbo) would be given on operational units. The concept of operations was the same with pooled aircraft, instructors and, hopefully, common practice weapons. The Luftwaffe offered to supply a simulator to provide each crew with fifteen hours of instruction. Engineering support would also be pooled, but the German groundcrews would be withdrawn to the Central Front in the event of a Warsaw Pact attack. The likely location was Decimomannu in Sardinia with ranges at Capo Frasca. The airfield was being expanded and was already used for NATO exercises and weapons training and benefited from good weather.

Like the TSR.2, much development also went into ground simulators to reduce training costs and technological developments offered some attractive savings as simulator capability grew. The OCU would have two flight simulators in which each crew would spend 35 hours and one avionics systems trainer which would have navigation/attack system modes to save flying simulator time and would use some actual Tornado 'black boxes' to give the full experience (other non-essential switches and panels would be representative only), each crew receiving fifteen hours training. The cockpit procedures trainer was a simple device train the crew in cockpit drills before entering the simulator. It was essentially a mock-up with photographs for the instrument panels and the working elements were restricted to necessary switches and lights. The RAF had just introduced the Radar Videotape Recorder (RVR) training for navigators and it much impressed the other MRCA partners with its capability and relatively low cost. The OCU would have one RVR and a library of MRCA radar video tapes on which to train the crew to teach them how to operate the radar and interpret the scope.

The training units were to be equipped with Tornados fitted with dual controls with minimal flight instruments in a rear cockpit to act as operational conversion trainers and to maintain flying standards on frontline squadrons. The aircraft were otherwise fully combat operational. The dual control variant of the RAF's standard GR.1 was unofficially known as the GR.1(T) and 36 were built and many were upgraded to GR.4 standard during the 1990s. The first production Tornado flown from Warton was GR.1(T) ZA319 on 10 July 1979, flown by BAe's Chief Test Pilot David Eagles. The concept of a joint OCU was accepted and a memorandum of understanding was signed in 1979, although the joint WCU did not come to fruition. The Tri-national Tornado Training Establishment (TTTE) was formed at Cottesmore on 1st April 1979, but not formally established until 29th January 1981 when the initial ten-year agreement began. The TTTE began its first course on 1st May 1980 and the first RAF Tornados arrived on 1st July; GR.1(T)s ZA320, flown by BAe's Executive Director of Flight Operations Paul Millett with co-Chief Designer Ollie Heath in the rear seat and ZA322 flown by David Eagles and BAe's Chief

This Tornado GR.4 is in its element on a training sortie from Marham as it flies along the Mach Loop, one of the RAF's low-flying training routes within a series of valleys in west-central Wales. It lies within Low Flying Area LFA7, which covers most of Wales. *MoD/Open Government Licence, 2015*

Navigator Ray Woollett. The first Luftwaffe aircraft followed in September but the first Italian aircraft did not appear until April 1982. Among the first aircraft supplied, the RAF used early production single and dual control GR.1s from the first batch of 23 aircraft which lacked the laser target-seeker and retained their original RB.199-101 engines. Three GR.Mk.1A reconnaissance variants were briefly used during 1987-88. At its peak size, the TTTE had a pool of 22 German, 21 RAF and seven AMI Tornados and was training 300 crews annually. The TTTE operated a ground school and four multinational squadrons, A, B, C and S (S Squadron's role was to train the instructors and maintain standards), and trained all strike Tornado crews until disbandment on 24th February 1999, the RAF element having been absorbed by No 15 (Reserve) Squadron at Leuchars in June 1998. The end of the Cold War shortly after the renewal of agreement for another ten years saw more diverse national mission requirements and the three nations agreed it had become more cost effective to train at home and so the agreement was terminated early. The Tornado Weapons Conversion Unit had been formed at Honington on 1st January 1984, becoming No 45 (Reserve) Squadron in November 1987 and No 15(R) Squadron in April 1992 to become the RAF's main Tornado training unit until 31st March 2017, two years before the Tornado's retirement.

When the Tornado Air Defence Variant (ADV) was developed for the RAF, again provision was made for a dual-control operational training variant. Eight of the eighteen F.2s built were fitted with dual controls and issued to No 229 OCU at Coningsby, the first two, ZD901 and ZD903 arriving from Warton on 5th November 1984. During March and April 1985 BAe ran two Service Instructor Aircrew Training courses at Warton headed by the Tornado ADV test pilots and navigators. The courses comprised a ground school and a month of flying before the instructors returned to Coningsby to set up the OCU's course. Later the OCU would receive 31 'two stick' F.3 aircraft, unofficially called the F.3(T). Saudi Arabia's Tornado ADV pilots were also trained at No 229 OCU and six of their ADVs acquired under *Al Yamamah* 1 contract were fitted with dual controls.

The provision of trained pilots and aircrews for Bomber and Strike Commands had been a huge task and had been met with a mixture of innovative approaches to training organisation and equipment. Steady improvements were made and new advances in technology adopted along the way. It had been an evolution fraught over problems finding suitable training aircraft and programme cancellations and changes in strategy and defence policies caused much dislocation, but by the mid-1970s the RAF was by far the most experienced air force in operational conversion training in Western Europe. Its leadership of the TTTE paved the way for more multinational collaborative training programmes and underlined the success of the reforms required to hone the V-force as a credible nuclear deterrent during the 1950s and 1960s.

A Tornado F.3 releases flares on an operational sortie over Iraq during Operation Telic in 2003. Tornado ADV pilots and navigators had to be trained for a completely different combat role, tactics, weapons and radar from those crews destined for the Tornado IDS and consequently No 229 OCU was completely separate from the TTTE. *MoD/Open Government Licence, 2003*

7 Going Supersonic and Vertical for the 1970s

'Both firms are applying to the concept the principle of variable sweep which, of itself, would provide the aircraft industry with invaluable technological expertise in this field.'
Brief for the Deputy Chief of the Air Staff, December 1963

'There is a possibility therefore, of the development of an aircraft on the lines of A.S.T.362 being undertaken as a joint Anglo/French venture if the necessary initial political steps can be taken.'
Brief for the Deputy Chief of the Air Staff, December 1963

'Training pilots to master, first its V/STOL techniques, and then its wide variety of weapons and sensors, will be a formidable task.'
Introduction to Operational Requirement OR.382 (Issue 2) for the Hawker Siddeley P.1154 trainer

The arrival of the supersonic English Electric Lightning into Fighter Command service in 1960 had required Flying Training Command to seek new trainers to cope with the increased training demands on pilots' flying abilities. By 1962 two good transonic trainers were in service; the Folland Gnat T.1 and Hawker Hunter T.7, but aviation was still progressing and the replacements for the English Electric Canberra, Hawker Hunter, de Havilland Sea Vixen and Blackburn Buccaneer were all to be far more sophisticated supersonic aircraft. The British Aircraft Corporation (BAC) TSR.2 was designed for supersonic automatic terrain-following flight and the supersonic Hawker Siddeley P.1154 added vertical/short take-off and landing (V/STOL) capability and the need to master Bristol Siddeley's innovative 'four poster' thrust vectoring nozzles to transition to and from vertical flight. Future pilots faced the prospect of not only flying their aircraft at twice the speed of sound but also operating modern radars and weapons systems utilising a range of air-to-air (AAM) and air-to-surface (ASM) missiles. A future advanced trainer to bridge the gap between the firmly subsonic Jet Provost on which the student earned their wings and these advanced operational aircraft was required for the 1970s. By the early 1960s, aircraft designers had a new trick up their sleeve to give an aircraft the aerodynamics to be docile and safe at low speeds for take-off and landing and have low drag for sustained supersonic

Had the Air Staff not compromised on the provision of variable-geometry wings for AST.362, it is possible that the BAC P.45 would have been developed instead of the SEPECAT Jaguar. Certainly the P.45 would have made a very attractive, if expensive, mount for the Red Arrows. *Luca Landino*

performance – the variable geometry (VG) wing. An aircraft could decrease the leading-edge sweep for low-speed flight and to provide high lift for take-off and landing and at altitude the wings could be swept back to decrease the leading-edge sweep and wing area with reductions in drag for supersonic flight. Aircraft were also becoming more expensive to develop, the rationalisation of the industry following the cancellation of several expensive projects in the 1957 Defence Review reflected that the UK could not afford to develop several advanced military and civil aircraft by itself. International collaboration to share research and development efforts and costs and to increase production runs for more economic production became increasingly popular with the Government, the Ministry of Aviation (MoA) and the Air Ministry. Both themes were to feature heavily in the search for a new generation of trainers.

The Swinging Sixties

The Folland Gnat T.1 had entered Flying Training Command service in February 1962 but already thoughts had turned to its replacement with a desired in-service date of 1972. Based on the experience with previous trainers, for example the de Havilland Vampire T.11, it was estimated that a trainer became unrepresentative of frontline types within twelve years. By 1972 the Gnat's basic design would be thirteen years old and the Hunter even older, the Air Staff worried that the generational gap would be serious. The new American Northrop T-38A Talon supersonic advanced trainer was influential in highlighting the kind of capability that the RAF was looking for. In December 1961, the Air Ministry began drafting a new Air Staff Target (AST) for a Variable Geometry Pilot Training Aircraft for advanced and operational conversion training. The required speed with the wings in the forward position was 400kt (740km/h) between sea level and 10,000ft (3,050m) and Mach 0.75 between 10,000ft to 30,000ft (9,145m). Enough internal fuel was required for two 50 minute sorties. With the wings swept back, the speed would be Mach 0.95 at sea level and Mach 1.2 at 40,000ft (12,190m) with enough fuel for a 50 minute sortie. By June 1962, the desired performance was greater still; with the wings forward Mach 0.9 at sea level and Mach 1.2 at the tropopause with an endurance of 60 minutes; with the wings swept the speeds were Mach 0.93 and Mach 2.0 respectively with a sortie length of 45 minutes. It had to operate from a 6,000ft (1,830m) wet runway, sustain a 1.5g turn at 48,000ft (14,630m) (later increased to 1.75g) and even a Vertical Take-Off and Landing (VTOL) capability was desired. The inclusion of a secondary counter-insurgency role had the side effect of immediately requiring AST.362 to be classified Secret. Cost was another important factor and AST.362 sought more value for money. The rear cockpit would be used not only by instructors but also trainee navigators to teach crew co-operation. It was argued that by the early 1970s live armament and radar training would be less commonplace as cheaper simulators took over these roles. Even so, the estimated cost per flying hour of £200 was far greater than the Gnat at £84 or the Hunter at £90. The annual running costs for a fleet of AST.362 aircraft would be £4.74 million compared to £1.26 million for the Gnat.

Although VG wings were desirable, there was still much research to be done. The Air Staff had withdrawn from the joint Operational Requirement OR.346 with the Navy that had begun in 1959 – with strong backing from the MoA – for a research programme which would lead to a two-seat strike aircraft. The British Aircraft Corporation's (BAC) former Vickers and Hunting design teams were progressing on a private-venture basis following the winding up of OR.346 in January 1963.

As the Hawker Siddeley P.1154 supersonic V/STOL fighter saga unfolded (see below) during 1963, AST.362 was pushed back with a revised in-service date of 1975. This had implications for the Gnat fleet. It was originally intended to maintain 44 Gnats at No 4 Flying Training School, nine at the Central Flying School (CFS) and seventeen at the School of Refresher Flying until 1972. To delay introducing the new advanced trainer until 1975 it was proposed to extend the Gnat to 1980 by reducing the Refresher School to nine aircraft or replacing all its Gnats with Jet Provost T.4s. But this would lead to excess Gnats, perversely the Air Staff seeking ways to use up excess Gnats; reintroducing sixteen Gnats to the refresher role, increasing the advanced syllabus from 70 to 95 hours using nine extra Gnats and using Gnats instead of Hunters as BAC TSR.2 lead-in trainers. That would still leave 40 excess Gnat airframes, some could replace the ten Vampire T.11s being used for Air Traffic Controller training or disposed of as unmanned drone targets. The AST.362 trainer would replace 50 Hunters at the Operational Conversion Units (OCU) and up to another 45 if the Royal Navy also brought the new trainer. On top the estimated capital costs of £47 million for research and development the £460,000 unit cost meant buying 150 aircraft could total up to £92.5 million. While some offset could be gained from selling surplus Gnats and Hunters on the export market, with additional training costs of £24.1 million the total expenditure between 1966 and 1980 could total £116 million.

Folland, now part of the Hawker Siddeley Aviation group, was eager to promote a successor to its Gnat. Fate now played a hand. To this point, most of the VG wing studies in had been conducted by BAC. But in 1960 Maurice Brennan left Weybridge, where he had been working on the OR.346 studies, to take up position as a Director and Chief Engineer at Folland at Hamble. Hawker Siddeley's Technical Director, Stuart Davies, suggested that Brennan should put his knowledge into further developing the Gnat. In October 1960, the single-engined Fo.146

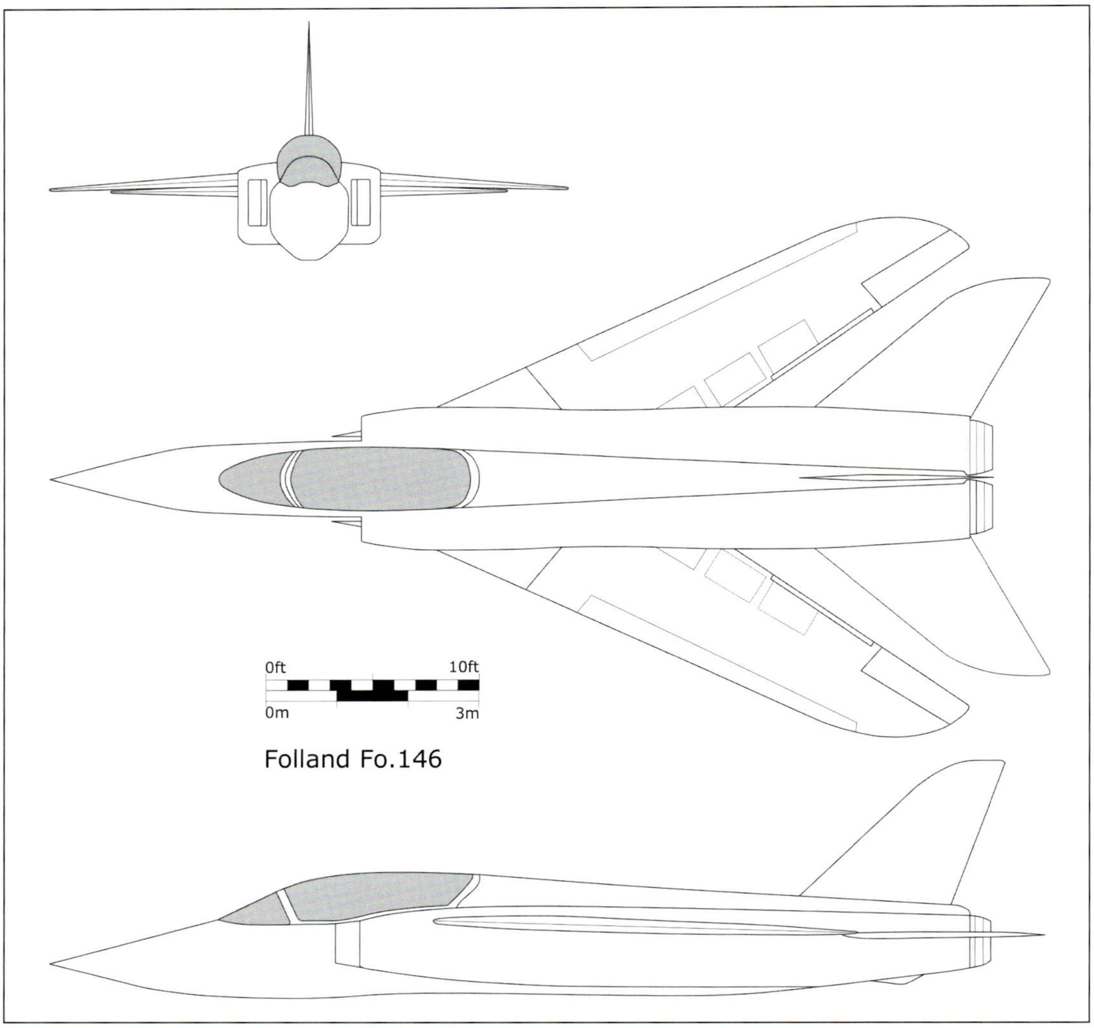

The Folland Fo.146 was the end of the Gnat lineage, incorporating design work from the Mk.5 and variable-geometry technology thanks to Maurice Brennan becoming Chief Engineer at Hamble and bringing with him a wealth of experience from BAC Weybridge. *Author*

was proposed as a trainer with a VG wing and was redesigned as a light strike aircraft in January 1962 with two Rolls-Royce RB.153 turbofans. At the time of Brennan's arrival, Folland had been working on the Gnat Mk.5, a more advanced supersonic development with a five percent thickness/chord ratio powered by two reheated RB.153Rs as a fighter with AI.23 AIRPASS radar and as a two-seat trainer. The maximum speed was Mach 2.4 with a time to 50,000ft (15,240m) of three minutes and a maximum ceiling of 60,000ft (18,290m). Brennan added a VG wing to create the Fo.147. The wings could be swept between 0° and 25° at low speeds, allied with slotted trailing edge flaps to give the same low-speed performance as the Gnat T.1. Sweeping the wings to 60° to 70° would allow speeds up to Mach 2.2 – the brochure optimistically claimed that speeds up to Mach 3 might be possible with further development. The wing sweep mechanism consisted of three tracks in the fuselage, ball-screws driven by duplicated hydraulic motors; as the sweep lessened the leading-edge of the wing moved down the track along the fuselage. The main design replaced the horizontal tailplanes with a rotating retractable all-moving foreplane beneath the forward fuselage for trimming combined with all-moving wing tip elevons, the second design had a conventional set of all-moving tail surfaces. The estimated all-up weight (AUW) for the tailless design was 18,500lb (8,392kg). The basic design was pitched as an advanced trainer and capable of flying simulated operational flight profiles, but actual weapons training was proposed for a dedicated two-seat fighter variant with radar and up to 2,500lb (1,133kg) of AAMs or ASMs and other air-to-ground weapons.

In May 1962 the Fo.148 appeared, further refined for the training role and closer to its Gnat origins. The wing sweep mechanism was similar in concept to the Fo.147 but was now a 'pivot and shoe' arrangement and the wing gained full-span leading-edge flaps. The Fo.148 was offered in three versions; Stage 1 was a primary trainer with an unreheated RB.153 and the wings fixed in the forward position, Stage 2 was the Gnat replacement with an unreheated RB.153 and operable VG wings, finally Stage 3 had full equipment, radar, two fuselage pylons for Bullpup ASMs or Red Top AAMs and a reheated RB.153-61 with a thrust reverser to reduce the landing run. The estimated radius for training missions was 330nm (611nm). With a planned first-flight date of 1963 or 1964 it looked a capable design, but as AST.362 took shape it seems that no interest was received and so Folland's last 'Fo'-designated design remained on the drawing board.

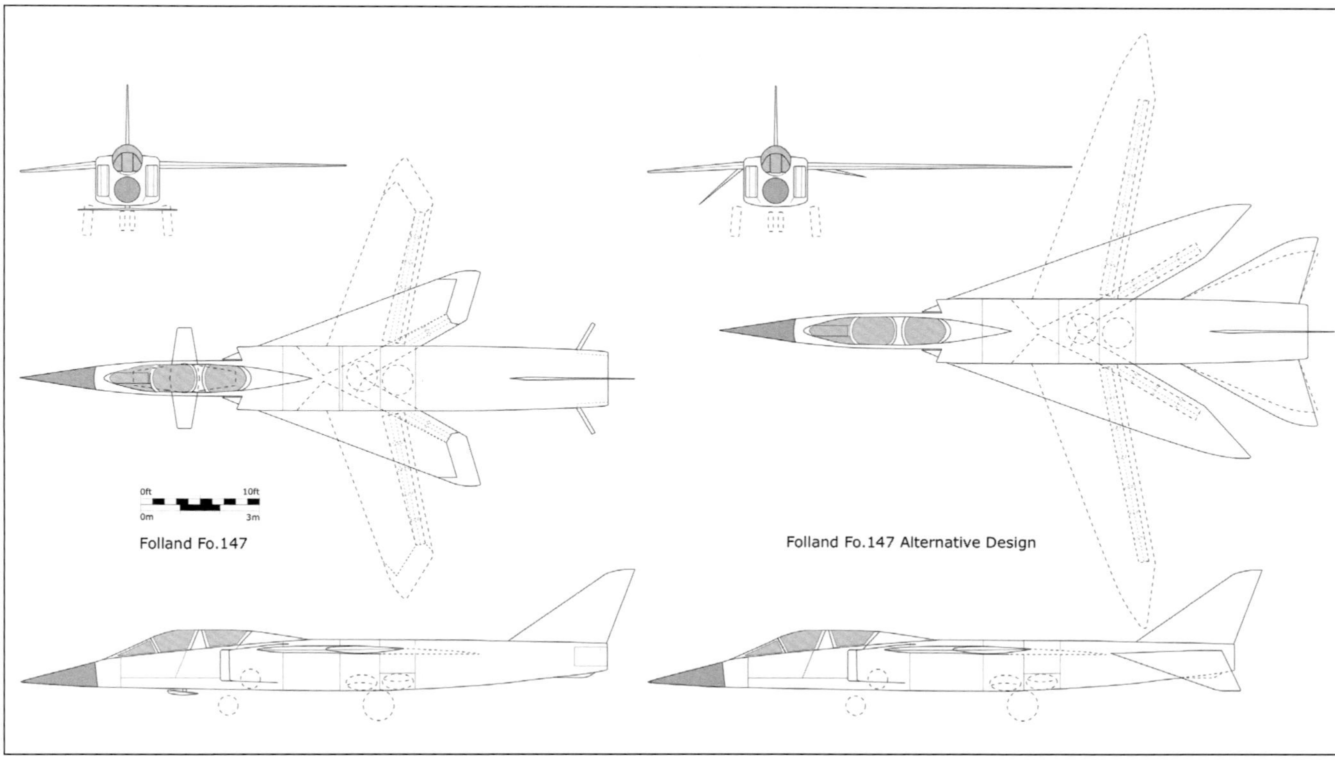

The Folland Fo.147 was studied in two variants. The main design had a retractable foreplane under the forward fuselage and tip ailerons. The alternative design used tailerons which required longer-span wings and a relocated wing to compensate for changes to the centre of gravity. Both were very ambitious designs, and like many private venture studies, tended to blur the lines between advanced trainer and frontline fighter. *Author*

AST.362 Choices: Going it Alone or Collaboration?

International collaboration in the aviation sector was increasing, notably the signing of the Anglo-French agreement for the development of Concorde on 29th November 1962. As early as December 1963 there was interest from the French and the Deputy Chief of the Air Staff was informed by the Ministries that an Anglo-French programme was possible if the necessary initial political steps could be taken. The Armeé de l'Air's new Dassault Mirage IIIB operational conversion trainer appeared to be very expensive to operate and their Ecole/Appui ECAP requirement was very similar to AST.362, being a trainer/strike aircraft with an in-service date of 1968. Soon the French Air Ministry replaced ECAP with ECAT, the Ecole de Combat et Appui Tactique, which was issued in January 1964 calling for a light tactical trainer with good rough field take-off performance, a maximum speed of Mach 0.9 at sea level, a range of 269nm (500km) at 450kt (834km/h) and excellent handling. At least five designs were seriously considered; the Breguet Br.121, Dassault MD 911 Cavalier, Nord 3600 Harpon, Potez CM.173 Super Magister and the Sud Aviation SA.125 (for more details see *French Secret Projects: Cold War Bombers, Patrol and Assault Aircraft*). With the existence of ECAT, AST.362 was paused while the political discussions took place. In March, the British and French governments agreed to collaborate on two programmes; a new trainer based on the ECAT requirement led by the French and the multi-role Anglo-French Variable Geometry Aircraft (AFVG) led by the British.

BAC and Hawker Siddeley had already been informally working on AST.362 studies since late 1963 and during the summer of 1964 submitted their designs. The former Folland design office at Hamble proposed the HS.1170B developed from the HS.1170 subsonic V/STOL fighter designed by the former Hawker design office at Kingston upon Thames to meet a German requirement for a nuclear strike fighter. The HS.1170B had a fixed wing with 40° leading edge-sweep with leading-edge slats and full-span slotted flaps, the fuselage had a bicycle main undercarriage layout with outriggers. The 13,500lbf (60kN) Bristol Siddeley BS.94/5 turbofan had 'mild' Plenum Chamber Burning (PCB) for 19,000lbf (84.4kN) to enable the aircraft to reach Mach 1.1 at sea level and Mach 1.7 at 36,000ft (10,970m). PCB enabled all four swivelling jet nozzles of the BS.94/5 to exhaust 'hot' air; the rear nozzles were fed by the turbine stage but the front nozzles were fed from the compressor stage and the air ejected from the forward pair of nozzles was therefore 'cold'. PCB acted like an afterburner by burning fuel inside the forward plenum chamber feeding the forward nozzles to increase the thrust available. Alongside this design,

Table 7.1 – AST.362 contenders

	Fo.147	Fo.148	HS.1170B	HS.1171	HS.1173	BAC P.45 EAG.3411	BAC P.45 EAG.3409	BAC P.45 EAG.3397 MP.2	SEPECAT Jaguar T.2
Wingspan		35ft (10.67m)	25ft (7.62m)	?	25ft (7.62m)		24ft 4.5in (7.45m)		28ft 6in (8.69m)
forward	36ft 6in (11.13m)					36ft 7in (11.15m)		36ft 7in (11.15m)	
swept	18ft (5.49m)					20ft 2in (6.15m)		20ft 2in (6.15m)	
Length	51ft (15.54m)	47ft (14.33m)	50ft (15.24m)	?	35ft (13.72m)	45ft 2in (13.77m)	45ft (13.71m)	48ft 11in (14.92m)	57ft 6.25in (17.53m)
Wing Area		?	200ft² (18.6m²)	?	210ft² (19.5m²)		305ft² (17.3m²)		260.27ft² (24.18m²)
forward	186ft² (17.3m²)					160ft² (14.8m²)		160ft² (14.8m²)	
swept	195ft² (18.1m²)					138.5ft² (12.8m²)		138.5ft² (12.8m²)	
All-Up Weight	18,500lb (8,392kg)	16,500lb (7,848kg)	20,850lb (9,458kg)	20,000lb (9,072kg)	20,250lb (9,185kg)	18,830lb (8,541kg)	18,830lb (8,541kg)	18,560lb (8,418kg)	24,150lb (10,954kg)
Powerplant	two RB.153 reheated	RB.153-64, 11,750lbf (52.2kN) reheated	BS.94/5, 19,000lb (84.8kN) with PCB	Two RB.172 Adour	RB.72-57AR, 13,000lbf (57.8kN) reheated	Two scaled RB.172-54R, reheated	Two scaled RB.172-54R, reheated	RB.168-1R Spey, reheated	Two Adour 102, 7,305lbf (32.5kN) reheated
Max Speed/Height	Mach 2.2	Mach 2.05	Mach 1.7 at 36,000ft (10,970m)	?	Mach 2.4 at 36,000ft (10,970m)	Mach 2.2 at 36,000ft (10,970m)	Mach 2.2 at 36,000ft (10,970m)	Mach 2.2 at 36,000ft (10,970m)	Mach 1.6 at 36,000ft (10,970m)
Service Ceiling	?	60,000ft (18,290m)	?	?	?	?	?	?	46,000ft (14,020m)

Hamble returned to the VG wing and proposed the HS.1171 as a private venture, powered by two Rolls-Royce RB.172 turbofans. Not to be outdone, Kingston designed their own private venture, the HS.1173. This was a conventional fixed wing aircraft with tandem seating and a large dorsal spine for fuel, the trainer's capacity totalling 580gal (2,637lit) (the single-seater had 700gal (3,3183lit)) to enable a good supersonic range and leaving the four underwing hardpoints free for weapons. Two 30mm ADEN cannon were fitted beneath the intakes and were intended for ground attack strafing only. The wing had a 'dogtooth' leading-edge with two-part slats and double-slotted trailing-edge flaps, ailerons and spoilers which augmented the ailerons at high speeds. Powered by a reheated 13,000lbf (57.8kN) Rolls-Royce RB.172-57AR fed by two-shock intakes, the aircraft could reach Mach 1.4 at sea level and Mach 2.4 at 36,000ft (10,970m) with reheat. In truth Kingston had their eye on the single-seater as a Hunter replacement and without any official interest the project was abandoned in March 1965.

With the demise of OR.346, BAC had moved their VG wing design team from Weybridge to Warton. The submission to AST.362 was the P.45 for the trainer and strike roles. The definitive P.45 design was powered by two reheated RB.172-49R or RB.172-54R engines and was offered in two versions. The main proposal featured a VG wing which pivoted around vertical pins in the fuselage and which could be altered from 25° to 68° sweep. The VG wing root was sealed by two overlapping hinged metal doors closing upwards and inwards with rubber edges forward and inflatable rubber tubes on the aft edges. At low sweep angles the wing took advantage of its leading-edge slats and full-span Fowler flaps for good take-off and landing performance. A fixed ramp intake was used as reheat would only be used during take-off and supersonic flight. The student and instructor sat in tandem with the rear cockpit elevated in a gracefully humped profile. The fixed wing variant had a delta wing of 58° leading-edge sweep developed from that of the TSR.2 and fitted with part-span blown flaps for high-lift at low speeds. BAC also proposed single-engine trainer and strike versions, both having the VG wing and a Rolls-Royce RB.168 Spey engine. In all cases, the single-seat strike versions lacked reheat for their engines. BAC emphasised the low cost and that it could be immediately placed into development as a VG wing research aircraft. BAC estimated that from an Instruction to Proceed in early 1965 that the first flight would take place 39 months later, with service release for the trainer by the end of 1970 and for the strike version in early 1972. BAC foresaw the P.45 being a multi-role aircraft suitable as an interceptor for overseas use, light strike and reconnaissance. Two ventral 30mm ADEN pods could be fitted on ventral hardpoints, a centreline ventral hardpoint could accommodate an AS.30 ASM and there were two underwing hardpoints for use when the wings were at minimum speed. Several configurations of dorsally-mounted and overwing pylons were considered for the VG and fixed wing designs.

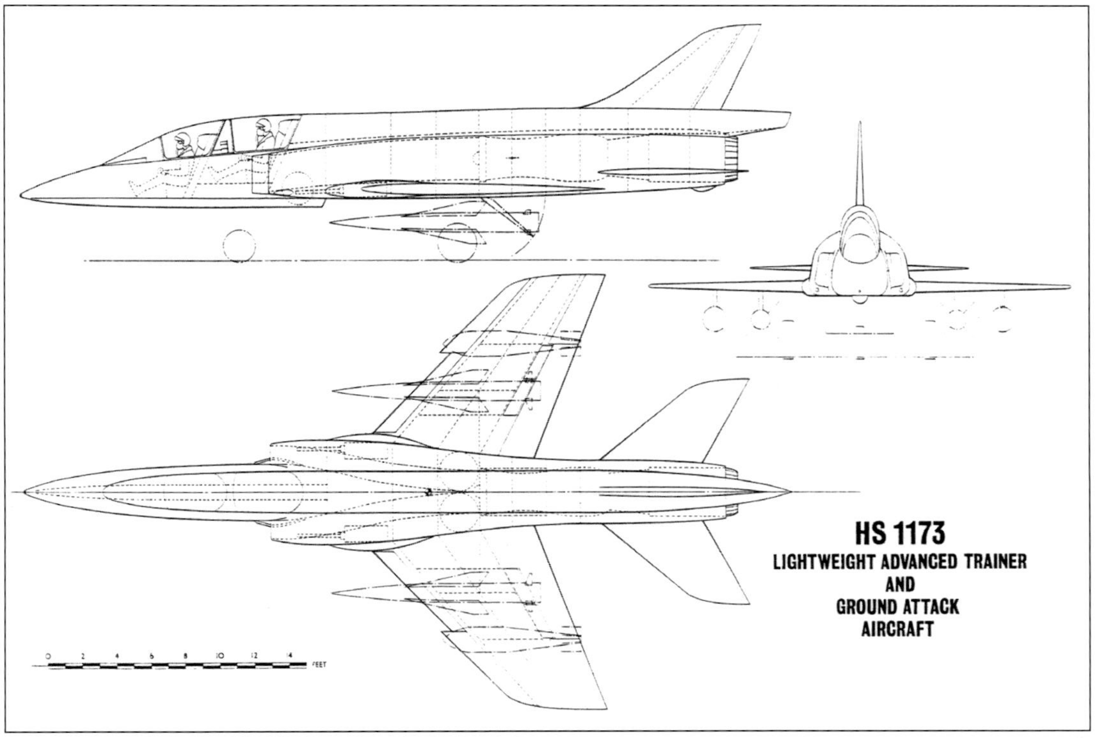

In early 1965 Hawker Siddeley's Kingston design team pitched the HS.1173 as a private venture. It was an attractive Mach 2 capable design. The fat dorsal spine contained more than half of the internal fuel. The ventral spine beneath the cockpit was an unusual feature and carried the control rods as there was no load carrying structure beneath the cockpit floor. *via Tony Buttler*

The BAC design team at Warton began its P.45 series with a single-engined variable-geometry design, EAG.3397. The trainer EAG.3397 MP.2 was to be powered by a RB.168-1R Spey. The single-seat MP.3 lacked reheat but gained two ventral cannon packs and a pylon for a single AS.37 Martel ASM. *Author*

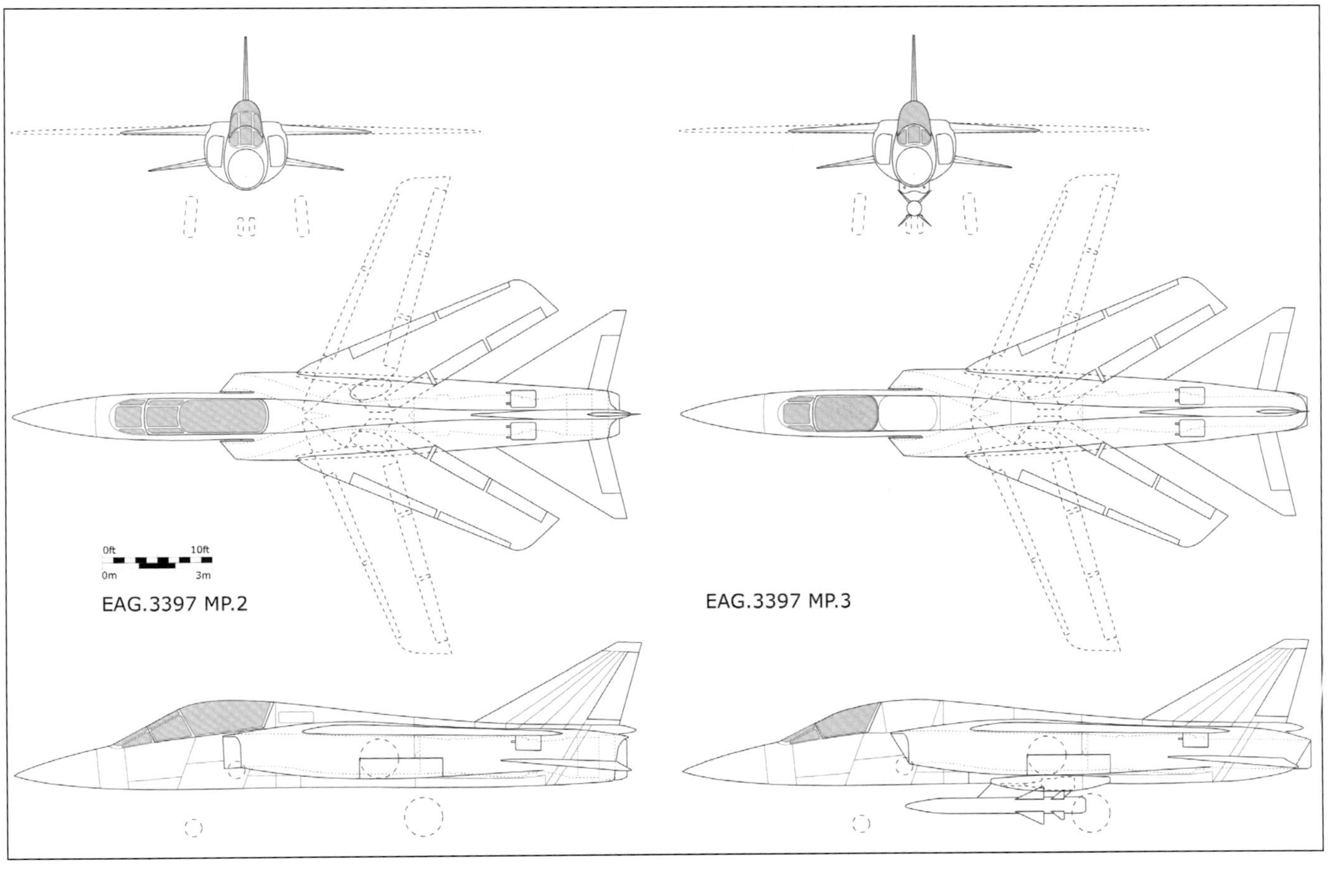

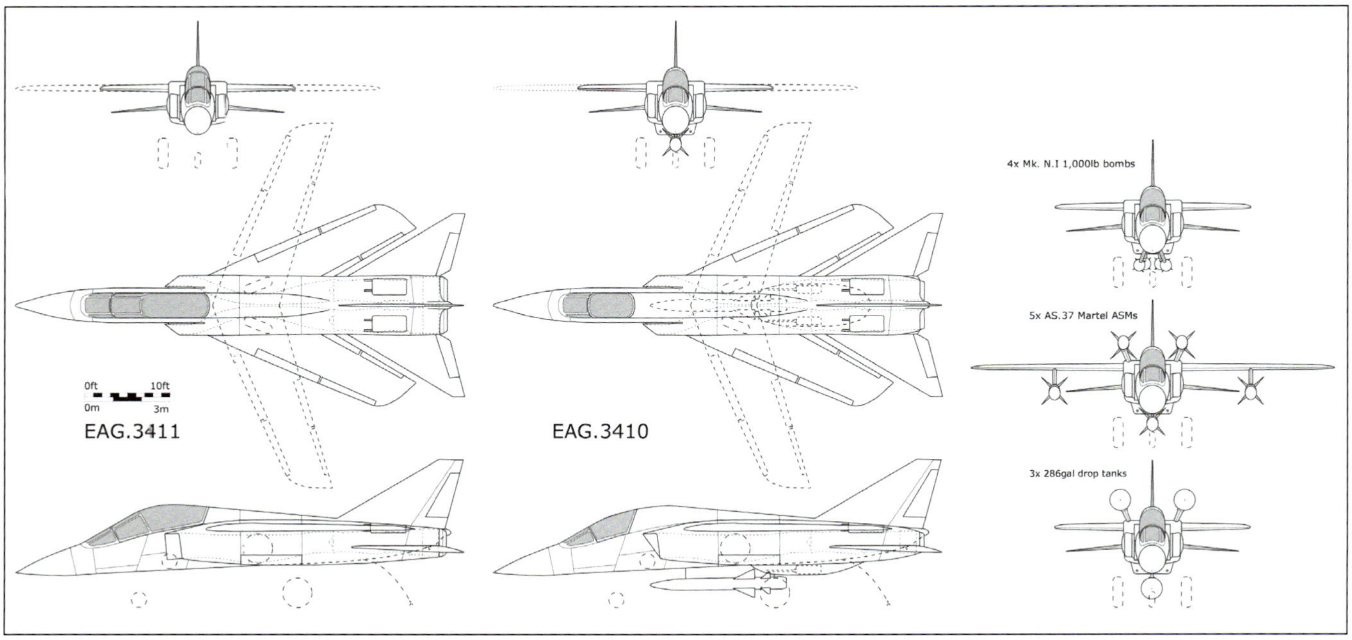

The favoured P.45 design to fulfil AST.362 was EAG.3411 powered by two scaled RB.172-54R. The single-seat strike variant EAG.3410 had non-reheated Adours and had a revised intake boundary layer splitter and a smaller diameter rear fuselage cross section. A ventral weapons pack carried two 30mm ADEN cannon. Having a variable geometry wing complicated the choices for external weapons so ventral and dorsal pylons were planned. *Author*

Warton's two-seat P.45 study EAG.3409 and the single-seat EAG.3408 looked like mini-TSR.2s with a very similar wing planform. They had identical engine choices as EAG.3409 and EAG.3410. The strike EAG.3408 had several unusual features; the 30mm cannon were mounted in pods near the wing tips and the wings boasted a mix of underwing and overwing pylons, the latter presumably in an attempt to reduce drag. Similar overwing pylons would appear on the Lightning F.6 and the Jaguar. *Author*

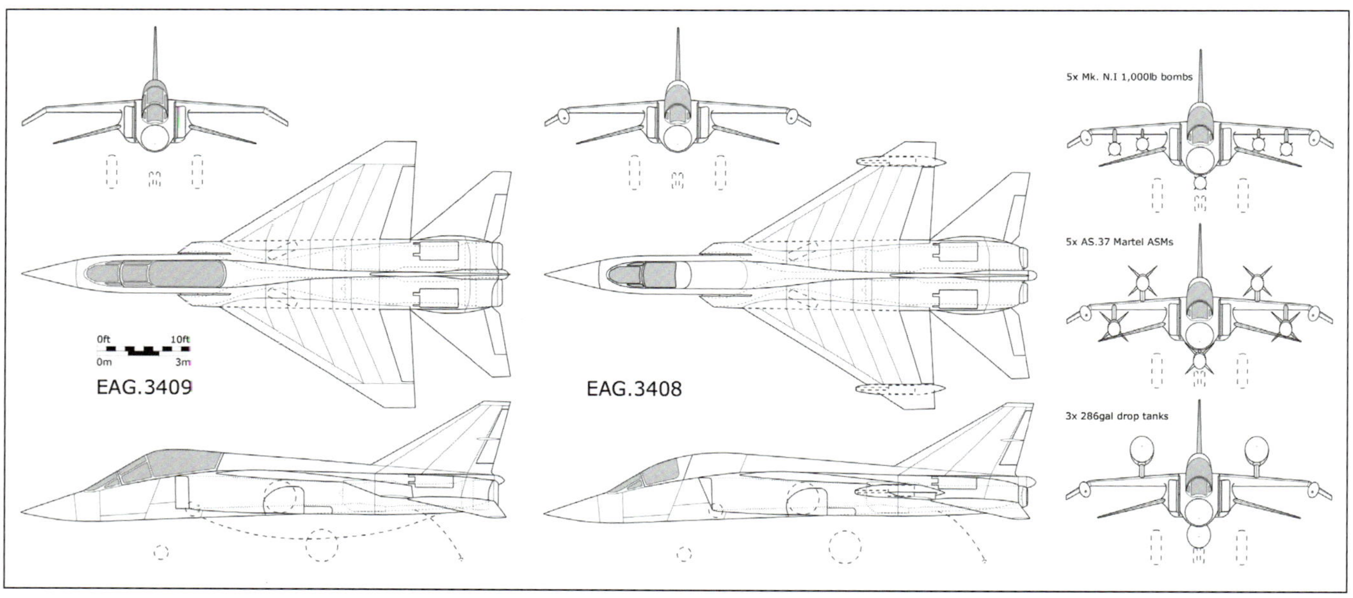

BAC even proposed a 30in (76cm) diameter radar with a pulse-doppler guided version of the European HM.45 AAM (a licence-built Hughes GAR-11 Falcon) for the fighter version. While the RAF's views on what made a good fighter differed from BAC's, with an estimated £15 million research and development cost, the RAF were increasingly interested in the strike role. In November, the Dutch Air Attaché, Colonel Fucquin de Grave, made enquiries about the P.45 while studying potential replacements for its Lockheed F-104G fighters. In hindsight, a BAC report on the P.45's export potential written in December 1964 might have been optimistic at foreseeing a 25 percent market penetration of 1,000 aircraft by 1975.

The MoA carried out their assessments in September 1964, confirming that the HS.1170B and P.45 could successfully meet the trainer and strike requirements. The MoA liked that the VG wing gave the ability for the instructor to vary the handling characteristics to cover a wider training syllabus as the student progressed towards operational capability and offered superior performance and flexibility to the HS.1170B's thrust vectoring. Thrust vectoring was also expensive and lacked any no engine-out safety. In hindsight, the provision of a VG wing for such a small aircraft with relatively low performance seems to outweigh the benefits given the cost (it was estimated VG wing research would cost an additional £6 million) and weight penalties involved. However, BAC saw this as the only remaining platform at that time to make use of its VG wing expertise. In any case, the political developments were leaving these contenders on the side-lines.

Enter the Jaguar

On 18th February 1965, the French Air Ministry announced the selection of the joint Rolls-Royce-Turbomeca RB.172/T.260 Adour engine for the ECAT and the following month both nations agreed that a VG wing was not required for economic reasons. AST.362 became a formal requirement as ASR.362 in April 1965 as a common requirement with France and on 17th May a Memorandum of Understanding between the two nations was signed. The fulfilment of the RAF's future supersonic trainer was now in the hands of France and gone were hopes of a VG wing trainer. France wanted ECAT in service by 1970 and felt that the VG wing would take too long to develop. The Air Staff saw the VG wing as only essential for developing the P.45 as a fighter but they were unable to immediately decide on future fighter needs and going it alone risked losing French co-operation on other projects, for example the negotiations then underway on helicopter development. Without the required support the British efforts were abandoned in the hope of a cheaper solution.

Meanwhile industry began to seek out French partners and Breguet's Br.121 design was selected in partnership with BAC. BAC had the prospect of a Br.121 workshare and leadership of the AVFG programme to keep its VG wing research alive. The Br.121 was officially named Jaguar at the Paris Air Show in 1965, the trainer cockpit mock-ups were accepted in November and in December design work was frozen. The trainer variant would be 2ft 11in (90cm) longer and the rear seat was raised by 15in (38cm) and had forward visibility of 8.5° below the horizontal datum, which was judged acceptable, and the RAF proposed fitting inertial navigation equipment. The RAF wanted 150 Jaguar B trainers and the Armeé de l'Air would take a mixed fleet of 75 Jaguar E trainers and 75 Jaguar A ground-attack aircraft. A proposal for the RAF to use French Jaguar E trainers until production Jaguar B aircraft were ready was rejected. In March 1966 the joint technical requirement was agreed and French funding was approved. During May the Société Européenne de Production de l'Avion (SEPECAT) was formed as a partnership between Breguet and BAC (Breguet merged with Dassault in 1968).

This drawing from the official brochure shows well the overall design and structure of the two-seat Jaguar B and Jaguar E for Britain and France respectively. ***SEPECAT via Paul Chapman***

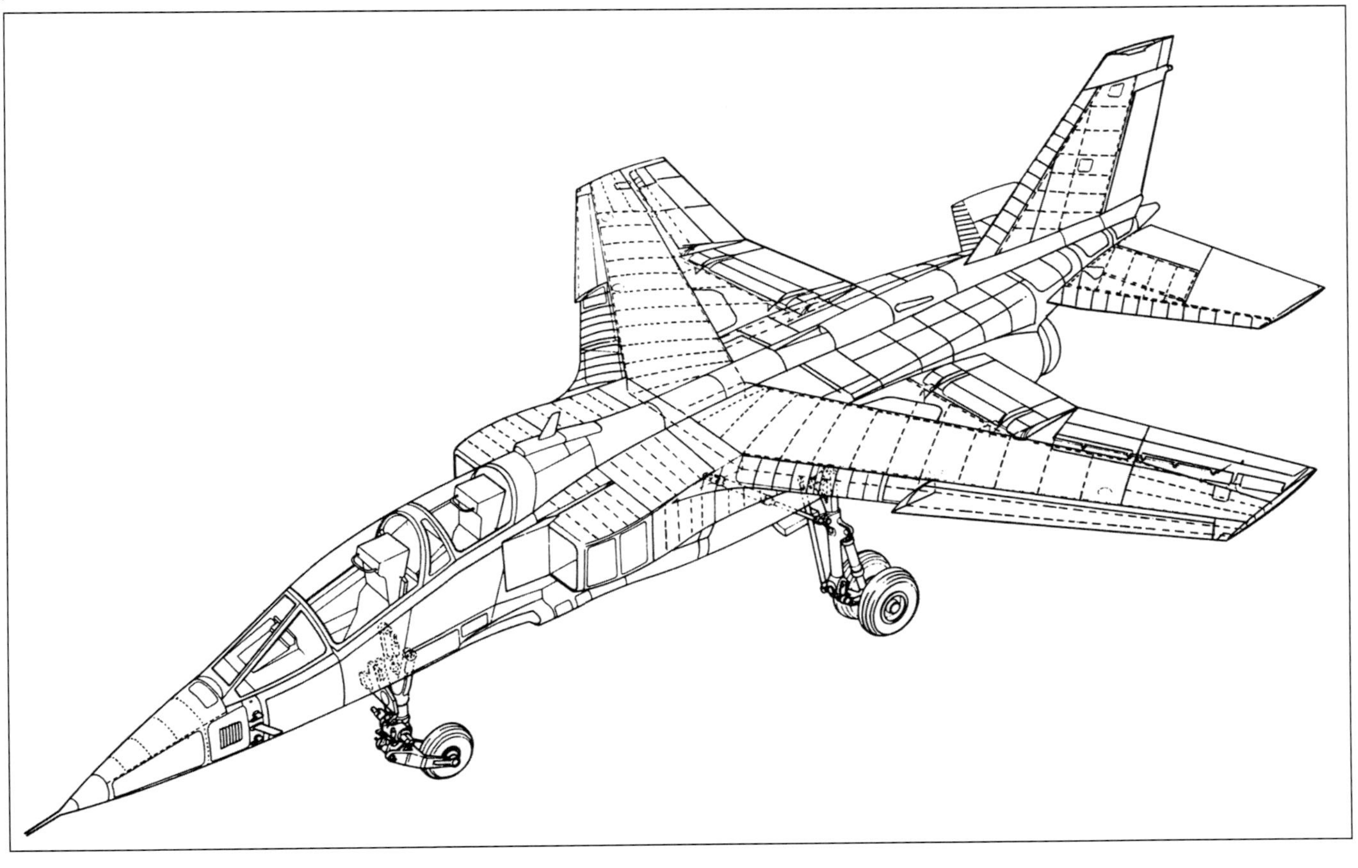

The prototype Jaguar E-01 was the first Jaguar prototype of any variant to fly. It made its maiden flight on 8th September 1968. E-01 can be distinguished from later production aircraft by its shorter tailfin and intake splitter plates. It was destroyed in a crash attempting to land at Istres following an engine fire on 26 March 1970. The pilot, *Commandant* Brossier ejected safely. *SEPECAT via Paul Chapman*

BAC was responsible for manufacturing the wings, tail surfaces, rear fuselage and assembly of British aircraft at Warton. Breguet built the front and centre fuselages and assembled French Jaguars at Toulouse-Colomiers. The Jaguar was the first RAF aircraft to be completely designed in metric units. On 22nd June Rolls-Royce Turbomeca Limited was formed to develop and manufacture the Adour. Strong interest was received from Japan, who were also looking for a supersonic trainer. SEPECAT offered to lease 30 trainers during 1971-74 and discussions regarding licence-production were also held. In the event these talks broke down over the level of royalty payments and instead Japan developed the very similar Mitsubishi T-2. BAC also made presentations to the Royal Australian Air Force and the Royal Canadian Air Force, without sales success, during the summer of 1966.

On both sides of the Channel the Jaguar quickly fell from favour as a trainer. The French felt that it was too large and they sought a new collaboration with West Germany in 1970 which would result in the Dassault/Dornier Alpha Jet. The Air Force Board in July 1970 agreed to remove the Jaguar from the pre-OCU training pattern and replace it with a new cheaper subsonic advanced trainer, which would result in the Hawker Siddeley Hawk (see Chapter Eight). The leap from the Jet Provost to the Jaguar was large, but the real reason was the more pressing need to boost the number of frontline squadrons and using a cheaper trainer would buy the RAF four squadrons of ground attack Jaguars. The planned purchase changed to 165 Jaguar S fighters and 35 Jaguar B trainers (a single Jaguar B attrition replacement was built in 1982). First UK prototype, the single-seat S-06, XW560, was flown by BAC test pilot Jimmy Dell on 12th October 1969 at Warton, followed later by trainer prototype B-08, XW566, on 30th August 1971 flown by BAC's Chief Test Pilot Paul Millett. B-08 had been built with 80 percent production parts and was used to assess the two-seat cockpit and the nav-attack avionics and was also used for rough field undercarriage tests, external weapons and gun firing trials. The Jaguar Operational Requirements Liaison Officer attached to the project to oversee that the RAF was getting what it wanted, Squadron Leader John Preece, got his first flight in a Jaguar aboard B-08 on 20th June 1972.The first production Jaguar T.2, XX516, was first flown on 22nd March 1973 by test pilots Reginald Stock and John Cockburn. The Jaguar T.2 was provided with full navigation and attack avionics to allow operational use but they lacked the laser target seeker, radar warning receivers and the provision for an in-flight refuelling probe. Fourteen were updated during the 1980s to T.2A standard with a new Ferranti FIN 1064 inertial navigation system and upgraded Adour 104 engines.

Following recent practice with the organisation of operational conversion training for the Harrier (for details see later in this chapter), at Lossiemouth

The second French Jaguar E prototype, E-02, made its maiden flight on 11th February 1969 and was used for Adour development trials as well as flutter and spinning tests. It would be another two years before the British Jaguar B-08 trainer would fly. *SEPECAT via Paul Chapman*

the Jaguar Conversion Team was formed on 1st July 1973, initially training the required instructors. As part of this process, BAC ran a two-week conversion course which involved the highly experienced test pilots Paul Millett, Tim Ferguson and John Cockburn. The type conversion of the initial frontline unit, No 54 Squadron, began in March 1974 and in October 1974 the Jaguar Conversion Team became No 226 OCU. At its height, the OCU was split into two Squadrons to handle the training workload. From 1st November 1991 the OCU became No 16 (Reserve) Squadron, still at Lossiemouth, until its disbandment in 2007. The T.2 and T.2A were also issued in small numbers to the eight frontline Jaguar squadrons to maintain standards. Two T.2s were also ordered for the Empire Test Pilot's School at Boscombe Down to conduct part of the School's demanding syllabus. Both were later written off in accidents and replaced by aircraft transferred from the RAF. In partnering with the French the RAF had lost its planned supersonic trainer, soon realising that it would be too expensive to operate and instead gaining a Hunter FGA.9 replacement to release the McDonnell Douglas F-4 Phantom FGR.2s for air defence duty. Although successful as a ground attack aircraft, the supersonic trainer proved itself to be an expensive luxury. The P.45 was sacrificed to keep France as a partner in aviation but it is perhaps telling that Jaguar is, to date, the only Anglo-French fighter or strike aircraft developed and after its takeover of Breguet, Dassault favoured the export potential of its Mirage and F1 series of fighters, although British efforts through SEPECAT did secure several export orders.

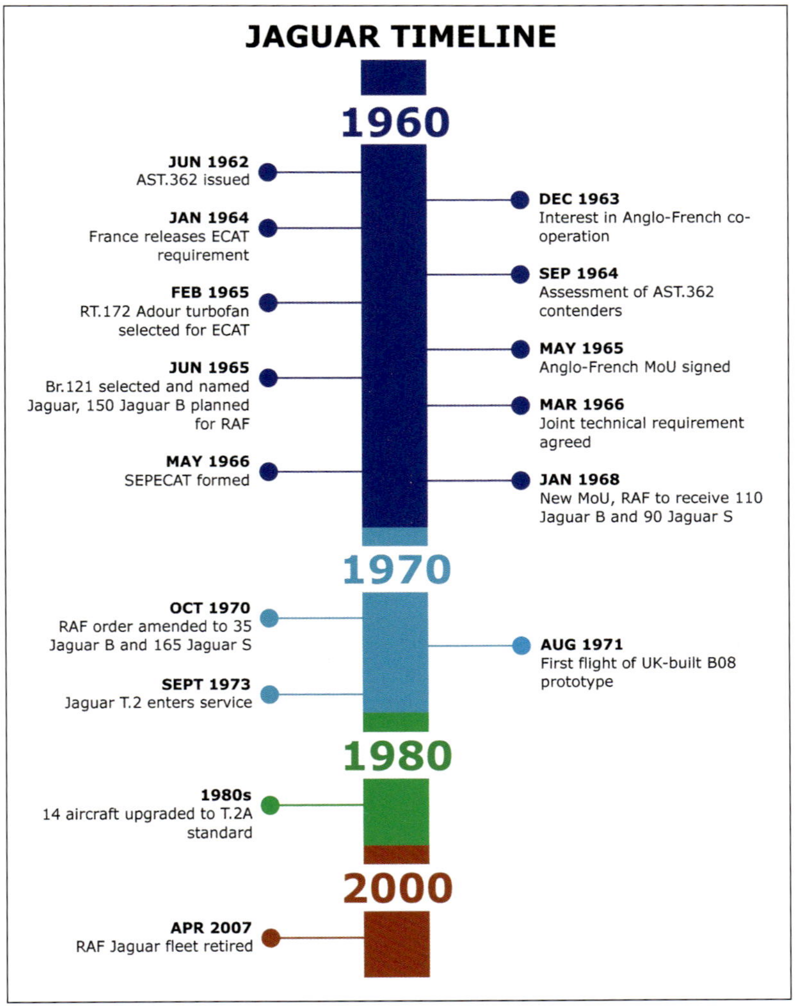

The Jaguar was intended as a supersonic trainer but soon found itself operating as a tactical strike operational trainer. Here a Jaguar T.2 of No 226 OCU is being marshalled out of its Hardened Aircraft Shelter at Lossiemouth prior to a training sortie. *Blue Envoy Collection*

A Jaguar T.2 on display during a wet day at Finningley in 1980 showing the wide range of weaponry that could be carried by the Jaguar. The inclusion of a dummy Harpoon anti-ship missile was perhaps wishful thinking, the only aircraft in the RAF inventory to carry Harpoons were Hawker Siddeley Nimrod MR.2 maritime patrol aircraft. *Chris Gibson*

Training Goes V/STOL

During the 1950s the concept of fixed-wing aircraft capable of Vertical and Short Take-Off and Landing (V/STOL) took hold among aircraft designers, air forces and commercial airlines around the world, including Britain. In the nuclear age, fleets of fighters and strike aircraft that did not rely on vulnerable large targets like airfields to operate from looked like a wise military concept for the future. V/STOL aircraft could in theory operate from any small piece of open ground (or ship's deck). The Hawker P.1127 with its revolutionary Bristol Siddeley Pegasus turbofan with four swivelling jet nozzles in a 'four poster' configuration offered the most practical method of translating from vertical to horizontal wing-borne flight. The first untethered hover on 19th November 1960 would lead in time to the RAF operating a V/STOL fighter. The P.1127 soon proved a success and was further developed into the militarised Kestrel FGA.1 for tripartite evaluation of the V/STOL fighter concept by the RAF, US Air Force and the West German Luftwaffe. As ever, the Air Staff were already looking ahead to the next generation capable of supersonic horizontal flight, but the transition from vertical to horizontal flight (and vice versa) was not easy, with pilots in the vertical flight phase having to control and balance their aircraft on the column of air from the Pegasus, using 'puffer' jets for changes in azimuth and pitch. The P.1127 was among the easiest of the V/STOL designs to fly with only three essential controls; the control column, the throttle and the nozzle lever which controlled the position of the nozzles. That still meant three controls to manipulate with two hands and the Air Staff quickly understood pilot conversion training would not be an easy task but was one that the RAF would have to face with the use of dedicated training aircraft.

Two projects that illustrate well the supersonic and VTOL trainer dreams of the Air Staff during 1960s are brought to life here; the twin-engined Folland Gnat Mk.5 proposed as a Mach 2.4 capable development and the Hawker Siddeley P.1154 trainer. Neither would leave the drawing board but here an assortment of Gnat T.2s and P.1154 Harrier T.2s of the Royal Aircraft Establishment head out on their test sorties. *Luciano Alviani*

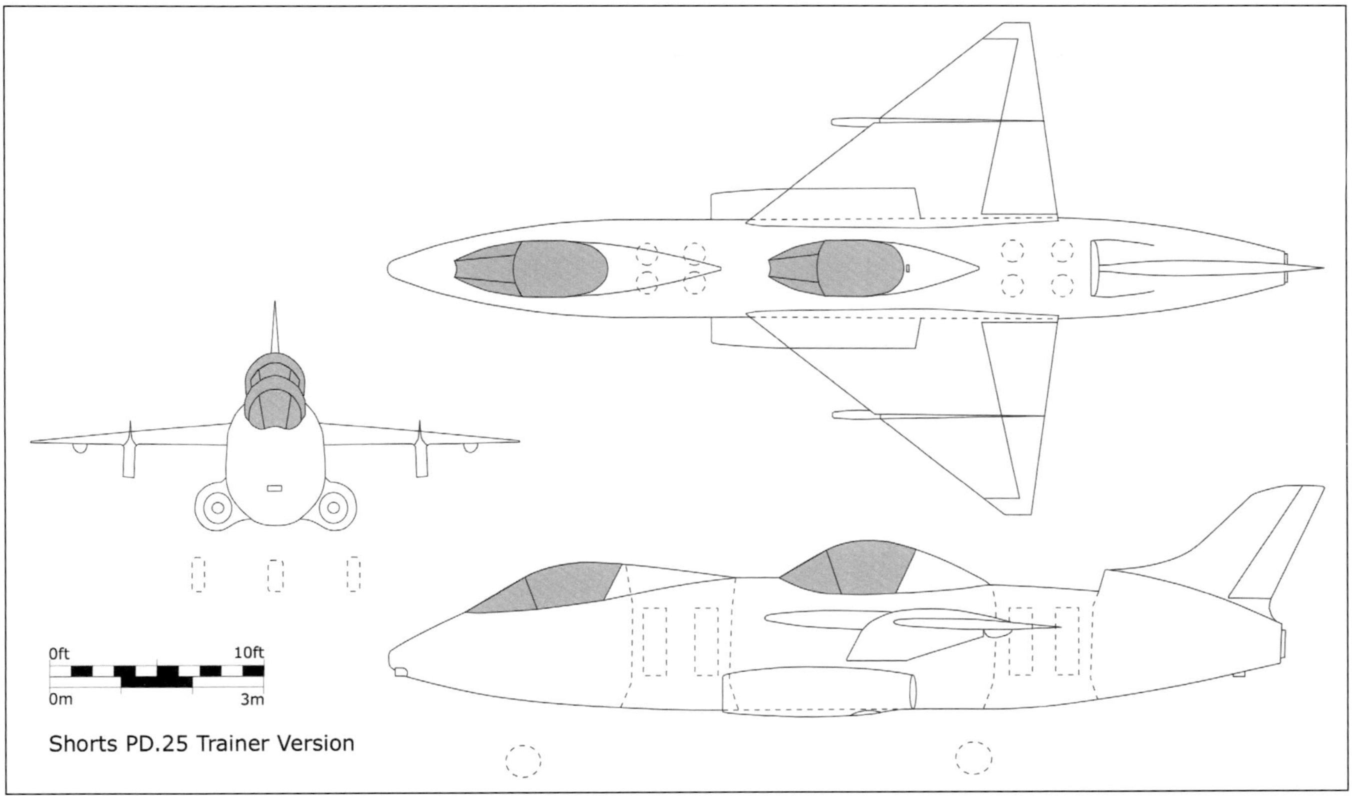

Short Brothers in Belfast worked on a series of VTOL fighters during the 1950s and 1960s, including the PD.25. Shorts decided to go one step further and turn the PD.25 fighter into a trainer with the instructor shoehorned between the two banks of four Rolls-Royce RB.108 lift-jets in the fuselage. The resulting reduced fuel capacity must have provided a pitiful range, probably only sufficient for the couple of VTOL hops. *Author*

One early VTOL trainer project was from Short Brothers in Belfast. They had developed the delta-winged PD.25 VTOL ground-attack fighter from experience gained with their SC.1 VTOL research aircraft. The PD.25 had eight Rolls-Royce RB.108 lift-jets in the fuselage in four pairs either side of the wing centre section plus three more for horizontal flight; two in lower fuselage nacelles and one in the tail cone. Shorts quickly devised a trainer variant, putting the instructor into a second cockpit inserted in the wing centre section at the centre of gravity. Presumably, what little fuel capacity was left was in the wings and lower fuselage. Endurance would have been pitiful but presumably sufficient to show the student pilot some vertical take-offs and landings, although the delta wing prevented the instructor from seeing the ground around the aircraft. The two wing hardpoints that doubled as wing fences were also retained.

The Hawker Siddeley P.1154 was a supersonic V/STOL fighter intended to replace the Hawker Hunter FGA.9 in RAF service as a single-seat ground attack fighter able to carry a tactical nuclear weapon and the Sea Vixen in Fleet Air Arm (FAA) service as a two-seat interceptor. Developed from Hawker's revolutionary P.1127 research aircraft, the P.1154 shared the same basic configuration but used the Bristol Siddeley BS.100 turbofan with PCB for supersonic performance. Originally submitted to NATO Basic Military Requirement NBMR.3 in 1961, two variants were developed under the Air Ministry's Operational Requirement OR.356 and the Admiralty's requirement AW.406. With the P.1154 expected to be available in squadron use by January 1968, thoughts naturally turned to a conversion trainer to enable current and future 'first tourists' – newly graduated pilots – to master the new handling techniques and combat tactics.

There were two options available; develop a two-seat trainer from the proven and subsonic P.1127 or to develop a third variant of the P.1154 airframe. The Air Staff immediately rejected the P.1127 as a suitable platform, the Deputy Director of Operational Requirements stating that it would 'contribute very little to training task.' Partly this was because the Air Staff saw the cheaper P.1127 as a potential threat to the entire P.1154 programme. Elements within the Admiralty and the FAA began to favour the American McDonnell Douglas F-4 Phantom as a far superior interceptor and this further convinced the Air Staff of the need to press its support for the P.1154 programme. Attempts by the Defence Research Policy Committee to force a common airframe in mid-1963 saw the resulting single-seat fighter with naval features suit neither party and in February 1964 the Admiralty went its own way and ordered the F-4 Phantom. The Air Staff could now focus on an RAF-specific ground attack fighter and issued OR.356 Issue 2 and Specification SR.250, followed in 1964 by OR.382 for a two-seat trainer variant.

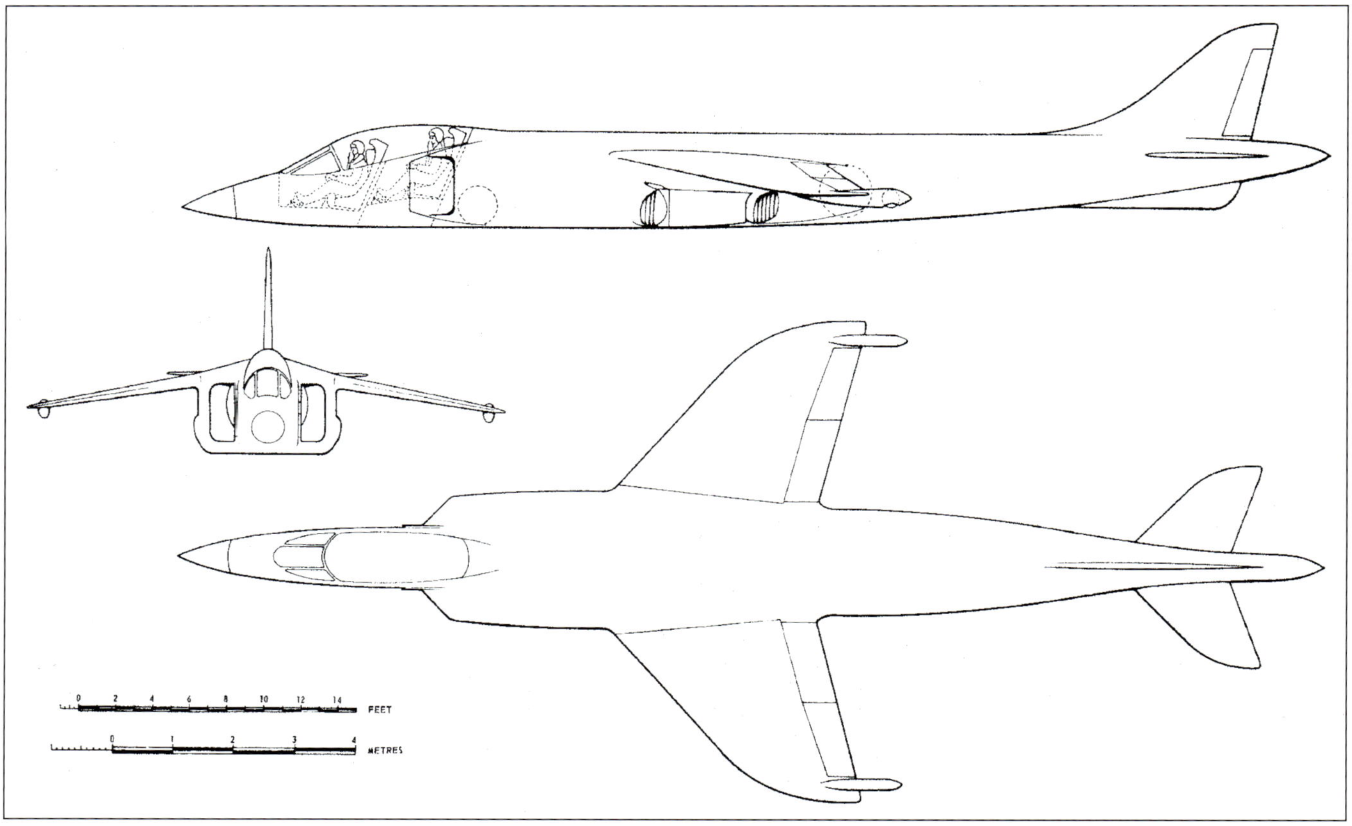

The two-seat P.1154 interceptor for the Royal Navy is well known, the two-seat RAF trainer variant is less well known. This three-view drawing of the early P.1154-6 was basically the RAF ground-attack fighter airframe with a lengthened fuselage and a two-seat cockpit. *Via Chris Farara*

The P.1154 trainer would be used for; type conversion with emphasis on V/STOL techniques and high-speed low-level flight; systems training for the strike, reconnaissance and air defence roles; instrument and night flying training; squadron continuation training in general handling, operational practices, and emergency drills; flight checks by instructors and examining pilots and weapons training. The Air Staff admitted that this complex training task would be expensive, although the training simulator then being developed to Air Staff Requirement ASR.348 would reduce some of the training costs. A trainer variant would also be more effective and economical than using standard single-seat P.1154s. OR.382 called for a trainer as representative as possible of the operational version with an in-service date of 1968. The engine, performance and handling and avionics fit was to be as close as possible to the standard P.1154, although for the sake of economy the rear cockpit would be equipped with repeaters rather than a fully duplicated navigation/attack system. The main change was the provision of the second cockpit for an instructor, but it had to also be possible to fly the aircraft with only front seat occupied.

The tandem cockpit was based on the experience of the P.1154RN intended for the Royal Navy. The instructor had surprisingly good all-round visibility despite the large intakes on either side of cockpit. *Brooklands Museum*

A General Arrangement drawing of the P.1154 conversion trainer. *Author's Collection*

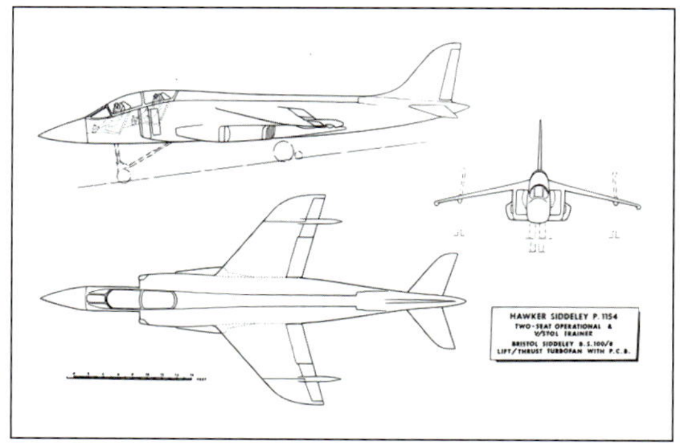

Hawker Siddeley based the forward fuselage on that of the two-seat naval variant. The main design changes included 26in (58cm) forward and 15in (38cm) rear fuselage extensions and a 915lb (415kg) increase in structural weight, although the increase in the AUW was only 87lb (39kg). The rear cockpit required 124gal (563lit) of fuel to be moved from the front and rear tanks to maintain the centre of gravity. The navigation/attack system was moved from behind the cockpit to underneath the rear seat. The cost of development was estimated at £35-37 million. Fitting a rear cockpit that met all the requirements was difficult due to the design restraints imposed by need for adequate instrument panel areas and clearances for emergency ejection. The Air Ministry's Human Engineering Division estimated that the downward view ahead was 15° relative to the longitudinal axis, reducing during landing to 7-10°. Surprisingly, given their size, the intakes would not significantly interfere with sideways visibility. The Royal Aircraft Establishment's (RAE) Aero Flight at Bedford made detailed calculations of P.1154 transition and landing attitudes using the P.1127, because at that time even the industry's best flight simulators could not present the outside world in a realistic way to investigate the problem of the pilot's view out of the cockpit. Most simulators relied on a small television camera moving over a scale model containing features such as airports or potential targets. Research into computer generated displays was ongoing but limited to very basic and stylised frame images with little detail. Using laser scanned photo transparencies, motion picture systems and computer generated images to simulate low-light conditions were other research areas. The P.1154 trainer had a short life, with development of the fighter being delayed, the 1968 in-service date looked unlikely to be achieved and with rising costs the government cancelled the programme on 2nd February 1965. Instead the RAF would receive the F-4 Phantom and the P.1127, developed from the Kestrel into the operational Harrier GR.1.

Two-Stick Harriers

The selection of the P.1127 did not alter the fundamental need for a V/STOL conversion trainer as long as such aircraft were part of the RAF frontline inventory and Ralph Hooper and his design team began studying a two-seat P.1127. In September 1965 Hawker Siddeley had submitted a feasibility study for the P.1174 trainer variant to the new Ministry of Technology (Mintech), which had absorbed the MoA. The Operational Requirements Committee endorsed ASR.386 for a Harrier trainer on 21st April 1966 and Hawker Siddeley was awarded a £12 million project definition phase contract, the political approval not being confirmed until January 1967. The requirements in ASR.386 were for an advanced trainer with the ability to join single-seater Harriers in ground attack operations in wartime.

This early artist's impression of the P.1174 Harrier Trainer shows some differences compared to the final design, most notably the boundary intake splitter vents behind the cockpit. *Brooklands Museum*

This diagram shows the extent of the changes required to the Harrier's structure, the new parts required for the HS.1174 are shown in red. The smaller view at the top compares the overall size of the Harrier GR.1 and T.2. *Brooklands Museum*

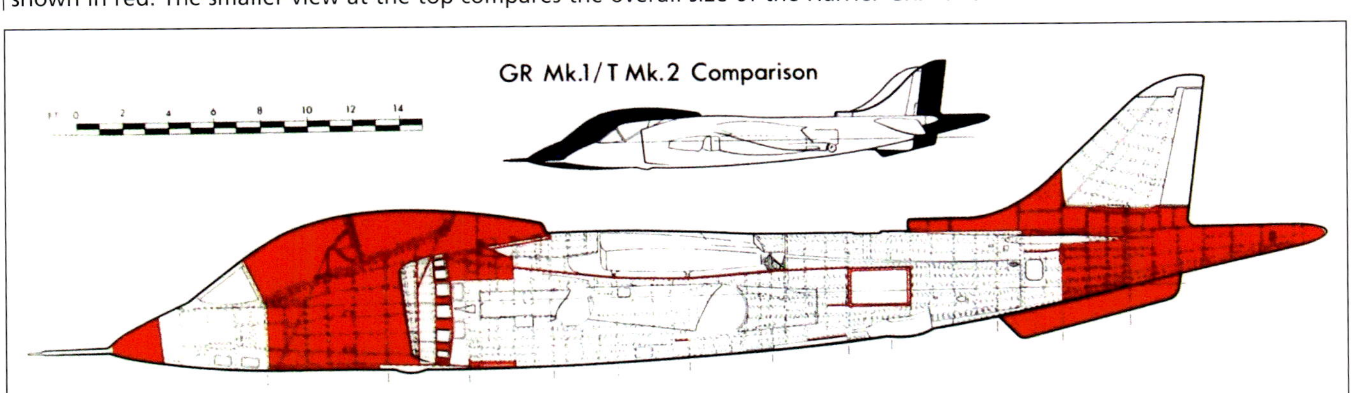

The wings, tailplanes, control surfaces, intakes and undercarriage were unchanged. The front cockpit was almost identical except for higher canopy head clearance and the front pilot was located 3ft 6in (1m) further ahead of the centre of gravity and 1ft (0.3m) higher when on the ground. Visibility was deemed acceptable, the Kingston design team initially considered a periscope mirror for better rearward vision in the solo combat role but actually found the over-the-shoulder visibility was better than the standard Harrier when the cockpit mock-up was built. The rear cockpit was new with the rear bulkhead moved 7in (17cm) backwards and a high floor to avoid changes to the nose undercarriage and the required 10° view over the student's head was achieved. An internal windscreen was fitted to protect against ejection seat blast. Mintech were worried about the effects of ejecting through the canopy and bird impacts but it was acknowledged that weapons sighting through the top of the canopy would affect accuracy from the rear seat. The only major equipment change was a more powerful air conditioning system with 80 percent more airflow to enable use worldwide. As well as the 3ft 9in (1.1m) forward fuselage extension and re-faired fuselage lines, the rear fuselage was extended by 5ft 9 1/2in (1.7m) with 60lb (27kg) of fixed steel ballast and 130lb (59kg) of removable ballast was added when flown solo. Due to the increased side area of forward fuselage the vertical tail was enlarged and moved 2ft 9 1/2in (0.85m) further back and was 3in (76mm) higher due to the new position of the fin post fittings. Scale model transonic wind tunnel tests showed inadequate directional stability at moderate incidences and small range of sideslip angles so the decision was made to raise the tail fin by another 8in (20cm) to restore stability. A larger ventral fin was also fitted. Fortuitously, or perhaps with a shrewd eye on the future, the trainer could still be accommodated on aircraft carrier lifts. The weight when flown with two pilots was 13,565lb (6,152kg), which was 1,482lb (672kg) heavier than the standard Harrier GR.1. The trainer would have identical avionics, navigation and attack systems as the GR.1, but would lack a moving map display in the rear cockpit, and would be fully combat capable when flown as a single-seater. One oblique F.95 Mk.7 camera was required as well as the capability to carry a reconnaissance pod with cameras and data link for real-time transmission of reconnaissance information.

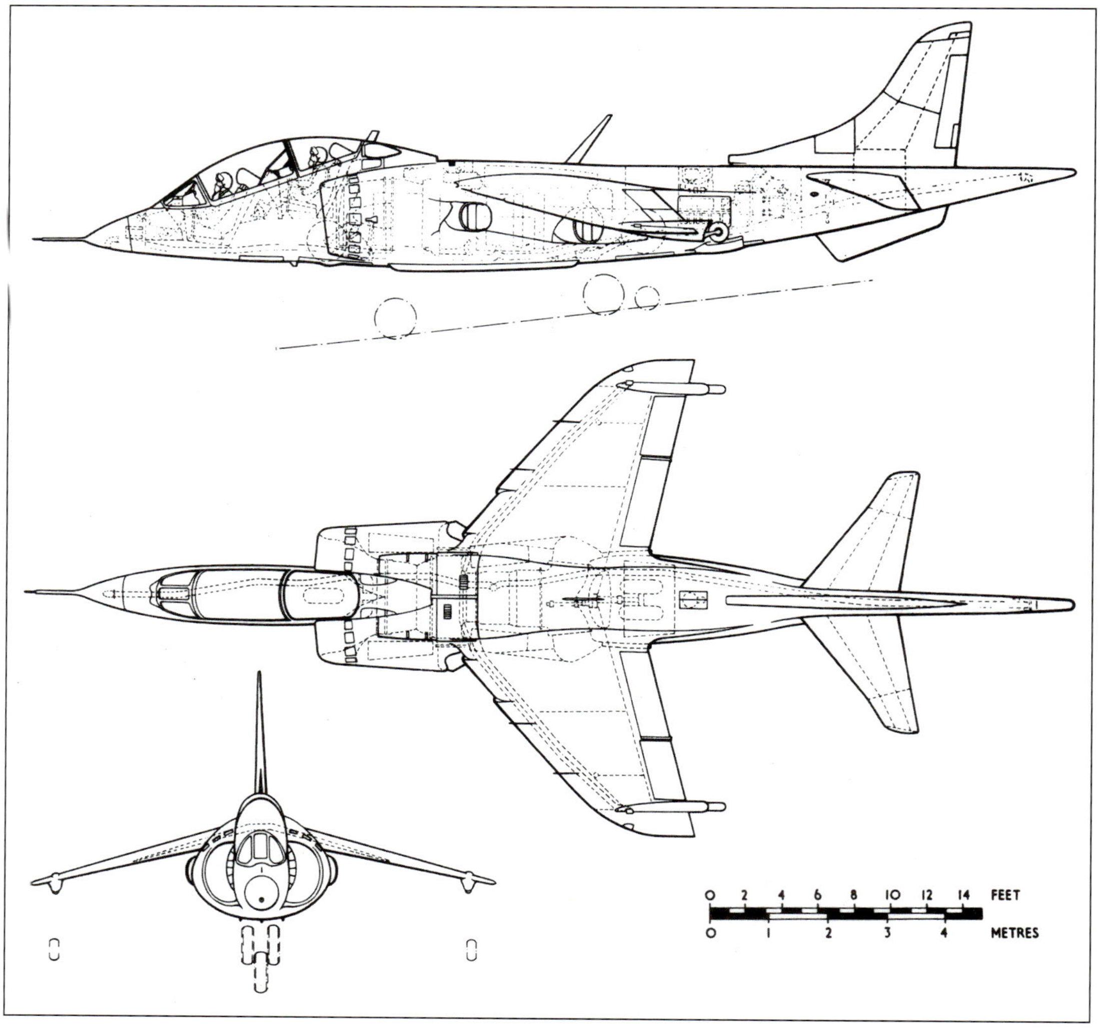

This is the final design of the P.1174. The drawing shows the larger vertical tail intended for export customers and initially fitted to the RAF's Harrier T.2s. aircraft. The big fin gave better high alpha handling for the training role but the smaller fin was better for the operational role which the RAF required.
Via Chris Farara

In December 1966, the RAF began planning the Harrier training syllabus. The forecasted OCU build-up would see the first Harrier GR.1 delivered in April 1969 with 30 aircraft by February 1970 and the first Harrier T.2 arriving in the last quarter of 1970. The flight simulators would be ready for March 1969. Conversion and work-up flying for twelve OCU instructors would to be carried out during first. Re-equipment training for frontline pilots would take place from November 1969 to the third quarter of 1971 with an intake every seven weeks for a seventeen-week course. The intakes would be restricted to second tourists with current high or above average jet ratings. Following experience gained with the Kestrel Evaluation Squadron, all pilots were given five hours of helicopter instruction to give pilots an introduction to hovering and to enable early suspension if they failed to reach the required standard. The initial second tourists would be given a reduced 72 flying hour syllabus plus 42 hours on the simulator, first tourists requiring the full 86 flying and 86 simulator hours. Instructors transferred from No 229 OCU at Chivenor with Hunter experience would only need 60 flying hours given their low-level flying experience. The first pilot attack instructors and instrument flying examiners came from No 229 OCU, which also later provided Harrier first tourists with Hunter lead-in training totalling 72 flying hours covering tactics, low-level and night flying and all forms of air-to-ground gunnery and bombing.

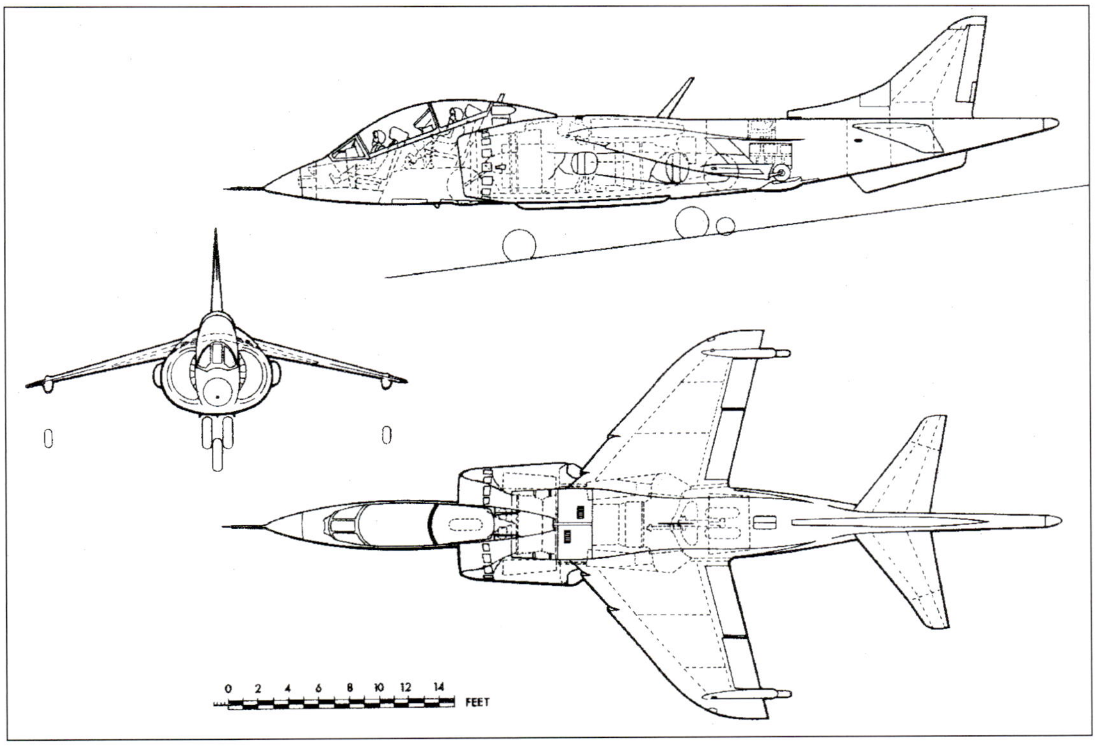

This three-view drawing shows the final P.1174 design with the smaller Harrier fin, which the Harrier T.2 later reverted to for better handling in the operational role. *Via Chris Farara*

Harrier T.2 XW268 joined the Harrier OCU on 7th January 1971 and is pictured here the following November. It was later modified to T.4 and then T.4A standard during the late 1970s. In February 1983 XW268 spent a month with the Indian Navy Training Unit at RNAS Yeovilton to train Indian Navy Sea Harrier pilots. In 1990 the airframe was further modified as a T.4N and transferred to the FAA. *Terry Panopalis Collection*

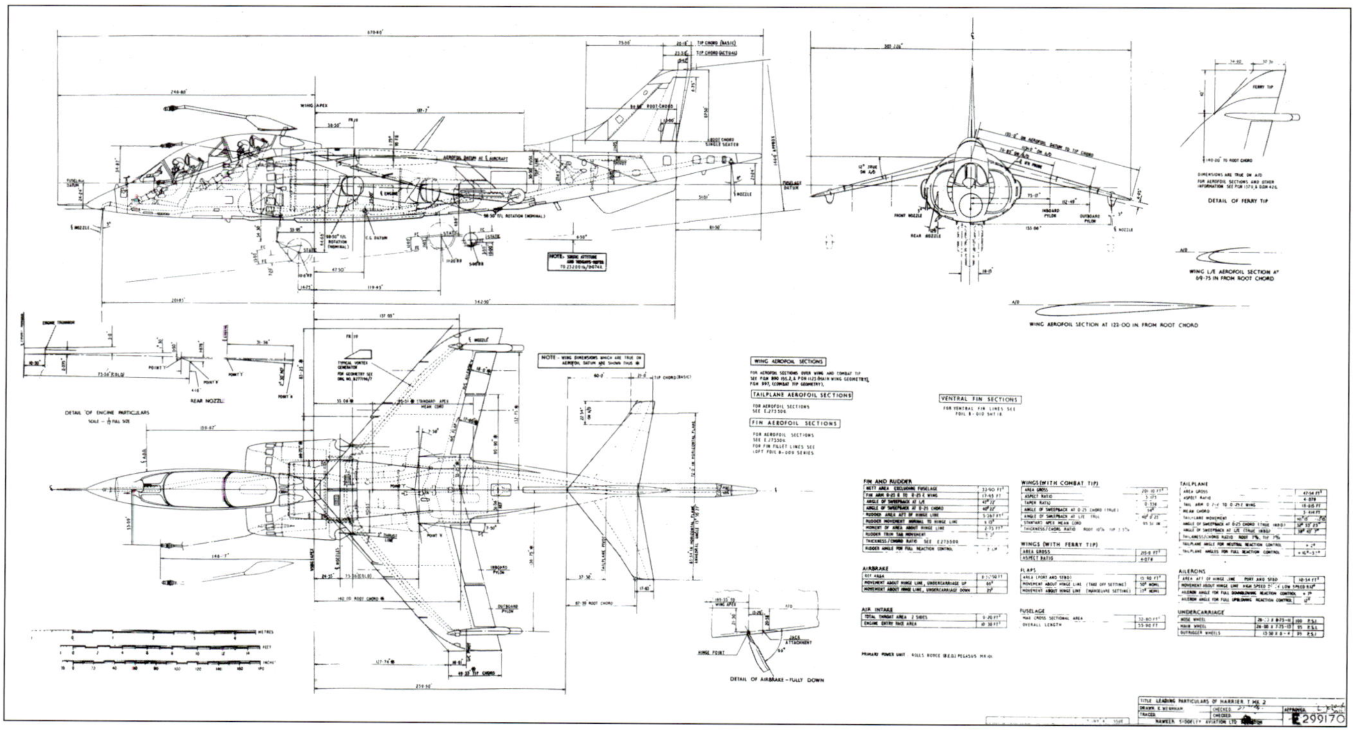

This detailed structural diagram reveals that the Harrier T.2 could be fitted with the same detachable inflight refuelling probe as the Harrier GR.1 and GR.3 to extend range. *Via Chris Farara*

The MoD and the Treasury seemed satisfied with the estimated £1.15 million unit cost (compared to £0.85 million for a standard GR.1) and Mintech issued Specification T.259D&P on 1st July 1968 and ordered two prototypes, XW174 and XW175 and nine production T.2s (later three more were ordered). Hawker Siddeley also funded their own two-seater, registered G-VTOL, which became famous for its many demonstrations and research flights at the hands of test pilot John Farley. The prototype XW174 made its maiden flight at Dunsfold on 22nd April 1969 with test pilot Duncan Simpson at the controls. XW175 had its first flight on 14th July and first production T.2 followed on 3rd October.

Rather than forming an OCU immediately, on the first day of 1969 the Harrier Conversion Team was stood up at Wittering to begin the task of training the instructors. It would not be until July 1970 that the first T.2 arrived, until then Hunter FGA.9 and standard Harrier GR.1 aircraft being used. Shortly afterwards in October 1970 the unit was redesignated as No 233 OCU. The last four production aircraft (XW926, XW927, XW933 and XW934) were completed to T.2A standard with the improved 20,500lbf (91.2kN) Bristol Siddeley Pegasus 10 Mk 102 turbofan instead of the original 19,000lbf (84.6kN) Pegasus 6 Mk 101. The first ten aircraft were later upgraded to T.2A standard and received an enlarged tail fin which had been developed for potential export aircraft to provide better high alpha handling for the training role.

Harrier T.4 ZB600 of No 233 OCU flying low over the Lincolnshire countryside. The Harrier T.4 was fully combat capable and was fitted with a LRMTS in the nose. Delivered to the RAF on 10th March 1983, in September 2002 it was one of two sold to the Indian Navy as attrition replacements. *Author's Collection*

Harrier T.4A(N) XZ445 of the FAA is seen here in air defence Barley Grey and carrying a full weapons load of ventral cannon pods, LAU-5003 rocket pods and drop tanks. *Author's Collection*

When the GR.1 fleet was upgraded to GR.3 standard with a 21,500lbf (95.6kN) Pegasus Mk 103 and a Ferranti Laser-Ranging Marked Target Seeker (LRMTS) in the nose, thirteen T.2As were modified to the same standard, being redesignated as the T.4. They were joined by twelve new-build aircraft between 1976 and 1987. The T.4 reverted to the original smaller tail fin which proved superior for the operational role. Five No 233 OCU aircraft later had the LRMTS removed to save weight and increase flight endurance, being redesignated as the T.4A. One T.4, XW268, was funded by the Royal Navy but operated by the RAF until 899 Naval Air Squadron (NAS) was formed. In October 1976 McDonnell Douglas and British Aerospace began the Harrier II development programme with a new enlarged wing for better handling and lift and a revised fuselage utilising more composite materials to save weight and increase payload.

Initially the Harrier accident rate was very high despite the provision of a dedicated conversion trainer. Part of the problem was that pilots used to the Hunter tended to handle the Harrier in the same way, fine once in the air but during the tricky vertical flight phases, going outside the narrow parameters could be fatal. The main problem was that during the transition the pilot had to operate three different controls simultaneously; the stick in the right hand and both the throttle and the jet nozzle level with the left hand. This needed excellent dexterity but even good pilots could accidentally mix up the nozzle and throttle controls with potentially dangerous results. By the late 1970s, the RAE was looking at computer-aided flight and propulsion control systems to simplify the pilot's workload. The planned joint RAE/British Aerospace V/STOL Displays and Advanced Controls programme would see Harrier T.2 XV175 heavily modified with fly-by-wire controls to investigate the concept of unified control – the control system working with one mode covering all aspects of the flight. Due to the high costs the programme was scaled back, but the resulting Vectored-Thrust Aircraft Advanced Flight Control programme between 1986 and 2007 resulted in the unified control method using the stick and throttle for all phases of flight being applied to the Lockheed Martin F-35B Lightning, which has so far proved much easier to master than the Harrier.

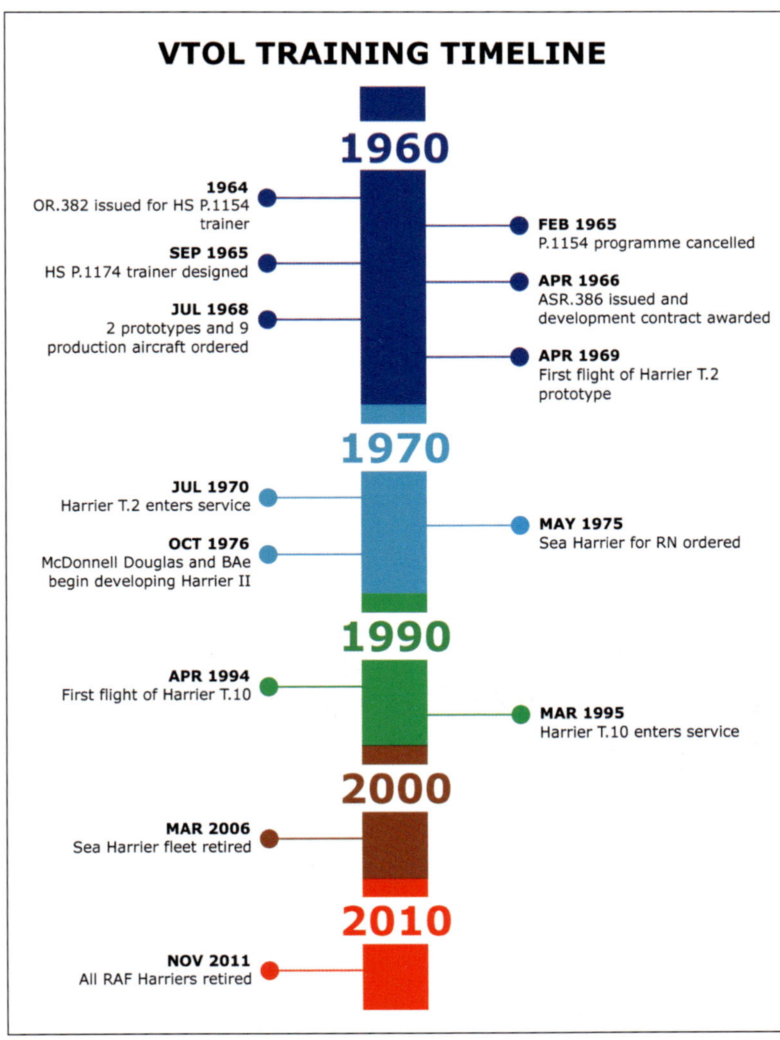

Harrier II

In the mid-1970s Hawker Siddeley and McDonnell Douglas had begun collaborating on an improved Harrier airframe with a new larger wing of supercritical profile with greater use of carbon-fibre composites to save weight for increased payload and range while leading-edge root extensions would improve manoeuvrability. Following trials with two rebuilt YAV-8B Harrier II aircraft from late 1978 the MoD formally selected Harrier II in 1981, the resulting GR.5 entering RAF service on 1 July 1987 when No 233 OCU at Wittering received its first examples. At this time there were no dedicated Harrier II trainers or simulators. During the late 1980s, as Spain looked to reduce training costs for its AV-8S Matador pilots they leased time on Wittering's Harrier simulator. In a reversal of fortunes a few years later, the MoD brought training time on Spain's new EAV-8B Harrier II simulator before the GR.5 simulator was ready for installation at Wittering. A decade later the GR.5 was supplanted by the improved GR.7 which had a full night attack capability with a GEC-Marconi forward-looking infra-red camera in the nose and a GEC-Marconi FIN 1075/1075G inertial navigation system and a moving map display in the cockpit.

A proposal during the late 1980s to refit the T.4 trainers with the night attack avionics of the GR.7 to create the T.6 was eventually abandoned when the performance and capability differences between the original design and the Harrier II were realised. Instead a dedicated trainer variant was approved in February 1990, the T.10 being based on the two-seat TAV-8B trainer being developed for the US Marine Corps. Due to the improved airframe and aerodynamics of the Harrier II the airframe changes were relatively easier than the original HS.1174. The forward fuselage is lengthened by 3ft 11in (1.19m) and the tail fin is increased in height by 1ft 5in (0.43m) and has slightly broader chord to give the required directional stability. In early 1992 thirteen T.10 aircraft were ordered and ZH563, serving as the prototype, first flew on 7th April 1994.

A trio of Harrier T.10 trainers from No 20 (Reserve) Squadron, the Harrier OCU based at Wittering. With the formation of Joint Force Harrier and the decision to withdraw the FAA's Sea Harriers in 2006, the squadron became a joint RAF/RN unit, manned by each service, before the Harriers were retired in 2010. *Blue Envoy Collection*

Unlike the TAV-8B, the T.10 was fully combat capable with the avionics of the GR.7 and retained all eight underwing hardpoints. By the time of the T.10's introduction into service on 1st March 1995, No 233 OCU had been rebadged as No 20 (Reserve) Squadron. The last RAF Harrier trainer variant was the T.12, a conversion of all twelve surviving T.10s to the same weapons, avionics and software standard of the upgraded GR.9. The conversions were undertaken between 2003 and 2006 and served a relatively brief career post upgrade until the Harrier fleet was disbanded following the 2010 Strategic Defence and Security Review in November 2011 and the surviving airframes sold to the US Marine Corps as spares sources.

Harriers at Sea

The P.1127 made its first landing aboard the aircraft carrier HMS *Ark Royal* on 28th September 1963, at the time that the P.1154 and the F-4 Phantom were at the forefront of the Navy's mind. The defence cuts during 1966 as the withdrawal from 'East of Suez' began saw the planned CVA-01 aircraft carrier cancelled and the progressive running down of the carrier fleet. The Command Cruiser, part of the escort force for the CVA-01, escaped cancellation and with its 'through-deck' for Westland Sea King HAS.1 helicopters offered a means to get the Navy back into fixed-wing aviation with the Harrier. In May 1975, an order was placed for 24 P.1184 Sea Harrier FRS.1 fighters and the FAA had to build up a training organisation, facing many of the same training requirements the RAF had planned for nearly a decade earlier. The Sea Harrier fleet would require 30 pilots and instructors initially with a smaller number of new pilots annually. Naval pilots first took the RAF's conversion course at No 233 OCU to learn how to fly the Harrier before progressing to 899 NAS at Yeovilton to begin operational conversion training on the Sea Harrier. The two Services had completely different training needs beyond the basics of learning how to fly the Harrier. The RAF's Harrier pilots were ground attack specialists, the Sea Harrier required fighter pilots skilled in aerial combat and was equipped with Blue Fox radar, which required up to 50 hours of training time. The strike role was a secondary mission. The Sea Harrier Operational Conversion Course consisted of over a hundred sorties including navigation, weaponry, air combat, interception and reconnaissance. There were subtle differences in take-off and landing techniques, especially with the use of the ski-jump aboard the aircraft carriers to enable a heavily laden Sea Harrier to use a rolling take-off and gain additional lift from the jump before swivelling the jet nozzles to enter the climb. A ski-jump was built at Yeovilton on which to practice take-offs and a dedicated pilot simulator facility was also constructed.

Harrier XW268 again, this time in T.4N guise and sporting special 899 NAS 50th anniversary markings. This photograph was taken in 1993; on 27th June 1994 an accident while landing at RNAS Yeovilton ended XW268's flying career. The aircraft is now on display at the City of Norwich Aviation Museum. *Terry Panopalis Collection*

To complement the sole T.4 XW268 three T.4N trainers were ordered, basically a T.4A with corrosion-resistant Pegasus 104 turbofan of the FRS.1. The T.4N was incapable of being stowed below in the *Invincible*-class anti-submarine aircraft carriers. The squadron also operated eleven Hawker Hunter T.8M airborne intercept and weapons trainers. Two of these, XL580 and XL603, had been converted for the Ferranti Blue Fox radar development programme. On completion of the radar trials they had been converted to the training role and joined by another eight conversions. Four Harrier T.60s were ordered by India as trainers for their Sea Harrier FRS.51 fleet, being standard T.4N airframes but fitted with Sea Harrier avionics, except for Blue Fox.

With the introduction of the improved and vastly more capable Sea Harrier FA.2 in 1993 the FAA had the need for an updated trainer with the glass cockpit and improved Hands-On Throttle and Stick controls. The FAA upgraded their three T.4Ns and two ex-RAF T.4s, which following upgrade with FA.2 avionics – but lacking the GEC-Marconi Blue Vixen multi-mode radar – entered service in 1996, redesignated as the T.8N. They also received the new 21,500lbf (95.6kN) Pegasus 11 Mk 106 These remained in service until the Sea Harrier force was withdrawn in March 2006.

By 1972 the RAF had a supersonic and a V/STOL-capable trainers, but both were conversion trainers rather than being used in the advanced phase of flying training. The enthusiasm of technological progression was much in evidence and out of the package of supersonics, VG wings and thrust-vectoring VTOL, two had been achieved but arguably the Air Staff had again been seduced by the future without really taking stock of the economics and feasibility. With scaled down ambitions however, the scene was set for a for Gnat replacement that would define many future generations of pilots – the Hawker Siddeley Hawk.

Harrier T.12A ZH657 under a moody sky in July 2010, five months before its retirement. As part of the Joint Force Harrier ZH657 carries the markings of 800 NAS. *Terry Panopalis Collection*

8 The Hawk Story

'Please convey my good wishes to assembled designers this evening. Are anticipating yet another winner. I marvel at their powers of self-punishment knowing that the eyes of the world are on them yet again. They must get it right first time to keep our health.'
Ralph Hooper on the eve of the selection of the HS.1182 Hawk, 4th October 1971

'One of the worrying features of British aviation prospects is that the traditional markets built up in the 1950's are being lost. The sort of supremacy which the Vampire and Hunter had in certain sales areas has faded and may never be recovered.'
Hawker Siddeley SP.117-1 Brochure, 1968

'For the time being we are keeping all our irons in the fire, ready to jump in the direction of maximum advantage.'
Minute by Under Secretary (Air), Ministry of Technology, January 1970

During the late 1960s attention shifted to replacing the Folland Gnat T.1, Hawker Hunter T.7 and T.8 and the Jet Provost fleets with a new low-cost advanced trainer. The supersonic SEPECAT Jaguar trainer to Air Staff Target AST.362 had proven to be a short lived and expensive experiment. In a time of increasing costs and decreasing military budgets an economical trainer became ever more desirable. Hawker Siddeley (from 1977 part of the nationalised British Aerospace (BAe)) saw its design efforts result in the HS.1182 Hawk T.1. The Hawk remains in service today with potentially decades of service yet to come and which has been very successful on the export market, even breaking into the American market, a feat few that British military aircraft have achieved. The Hawk was notable for several other reasons; it bucked the trend of the time by being a purely national project and indeed was the last all-British military aircraft to be developed; it was ordered off the drawing board without any dedicated prototypes and yet entered service on time and on budget. The Hawk has been a very successful swansong of the British aircraft industry.

Replacing the Gnat and Hunter

In July 1970, the Air Force Board removed the expensive Jaguar from its planned pre-Operational Conversion Unit (OCU) training role and instead looked for a more economical aircraft to replace the Gnat T.1 and Hunter T.7 from 1976, offering the prospects of large savings in flying training costs. The British Aircraft Corporation (BAC) and Hawker Siddeley Aviation had already begun private venture studies as early as 1968, but international collaboration was still on the cards as other NATO and Commonwealth air forces had similar requirements over similar timescales. In 1969 the Ministry of Defence (MoD) had invited proposals from industry which emphasised the need for a light strike version for the export market to boost the scale of economy as the RAF only needed 150 aircraft. The Central Flying School (CFS) had also been thinking along similar lines and Group Captain W E Martin, the Deputy Director of Operational Requirements, circulated an outline Air Staff Target AST.397 in September 1970. The new aircraft would be used for pilot training in the following roles; high, medium and low-altitude general handling day and night, instrument flying, formation flying, high and low-altitude pilot navigation and weapons training. The maximum speed would be Mach 0.84 with an optimum cruising speed of Mach 0.60 at 30,000ft (9,145m) with a climb to 30,000ft (9,145m) from brake release in seven minutes, a service ceiling of 40,000ft (12,190m), an endurance of 1.5 hours at low level and take-off and landing from a 4,000ft (1,219m) runway. The configuration of the aircraft was left open with either tandem or side-by-side seating (but if the latter was used the view from the front seat had to be 15° below the horizontal datum and 5° from the rear seat), single or twin engines,

Two Hawker Siddeley HS.1182 Tercel T.1s of No 4 FTS during a training sortie. This was almost a reality, the P.1182-30 was the main submission to ASR.397, but slightly failed to meet the requirements. Two redesigns resulted in the Hawk we know today. Obvious differences are the single-piece canopy, high-mounted intakes and a 7.62mm machine gun in the port wing root. Tercel was the winning name of Hawker Siddeley's staff newsletter naming competition, but the management had no objections to the Air Staff's choice of Hawk. *Luca Landino*

swept or straight wings, powered or manual flying controls and a maximum all-up weight (AUW) of 10,000lb (4,535kg). Once the initial proposals had been received from both companies, these requirements were formalised as Air Staff Requirement ASR.397 in October 1970 and formal tenders by Hawker Siddeley and BAC were resubmitted to fully comply with the requirements in November.

Industry Sees a Market

In August 1968, Hawker Siddeley's Special Projects team at Kingston upon Thames, Surrey, led by R S Williams had drawn up Special Project SP.117-1 because they saw a genuine market for a new basic trainer and Kingston urgently needed work to keep its technical team employed as the Harrier entered the production phase. Their market survey showed that early production Fouga Magisters, Cessna T-37s and Percival Jet Provosts would need replacing from 1974 due to attrition and obsolescence and the replacement of piston engine trainers might see demand for turbofan-powered trainers reach 6,000 aircraft by 1983. Hawker Siddeley worried that Britain's market share built up during the 1950s on the back of the Hawker Hunter and de Havilland Vampire families was being lost and might never be recovered. Their aim was to capture a ten percent share of 600 aircraft and they favoured a national development programme. The new design had to be started in 1968 to be ready for introduction in 1975. Only a moderate advance in aerodynamics and performance was planned to reduce the development cost and technical risk. The SP.117 was a tandem seat design with a straight high-wing layout using manual push-rod flying controls and was powered by a single unreheated 4,750lbf (21.1kN) Rolls-Royce/Turbomeca RB.172 Adour for a maximum speed of Mach 0.84 and 3.75 hour endurance on a take-off weight of 9,090lb (4,123kg). Four underwing hardpoints could carry weapons and drop-tanks. Group Captain Martin's similar outline requirements of 1969 were clearly influenced by this design. The Adour was expensive but provided good performance and by 1975 would be proven in service on the Jaguar and have good spares supplies. Tandem seating was now back in favour due to its superior all-round view for the student. The wing had root intakes for the Adour and a wing section similar to the 1950s P.1040 Sea Hawk naval fighter with laminar flow to 30 percent of the chord and a fatigue life of 6,000 hours. Cockpit instruments and systems would vary to suit the customer and RAF aircraft would have the OR.946 Integrated Flight Instrument System (IFIS) in both cockpits.

A single-seat fighter with two 20mm cannon replacing the forward cockpit and the SP.117-3 with an area-ruled fuselage to achieve Mach 1.25 were also studied, the latter being pitched to fulfil

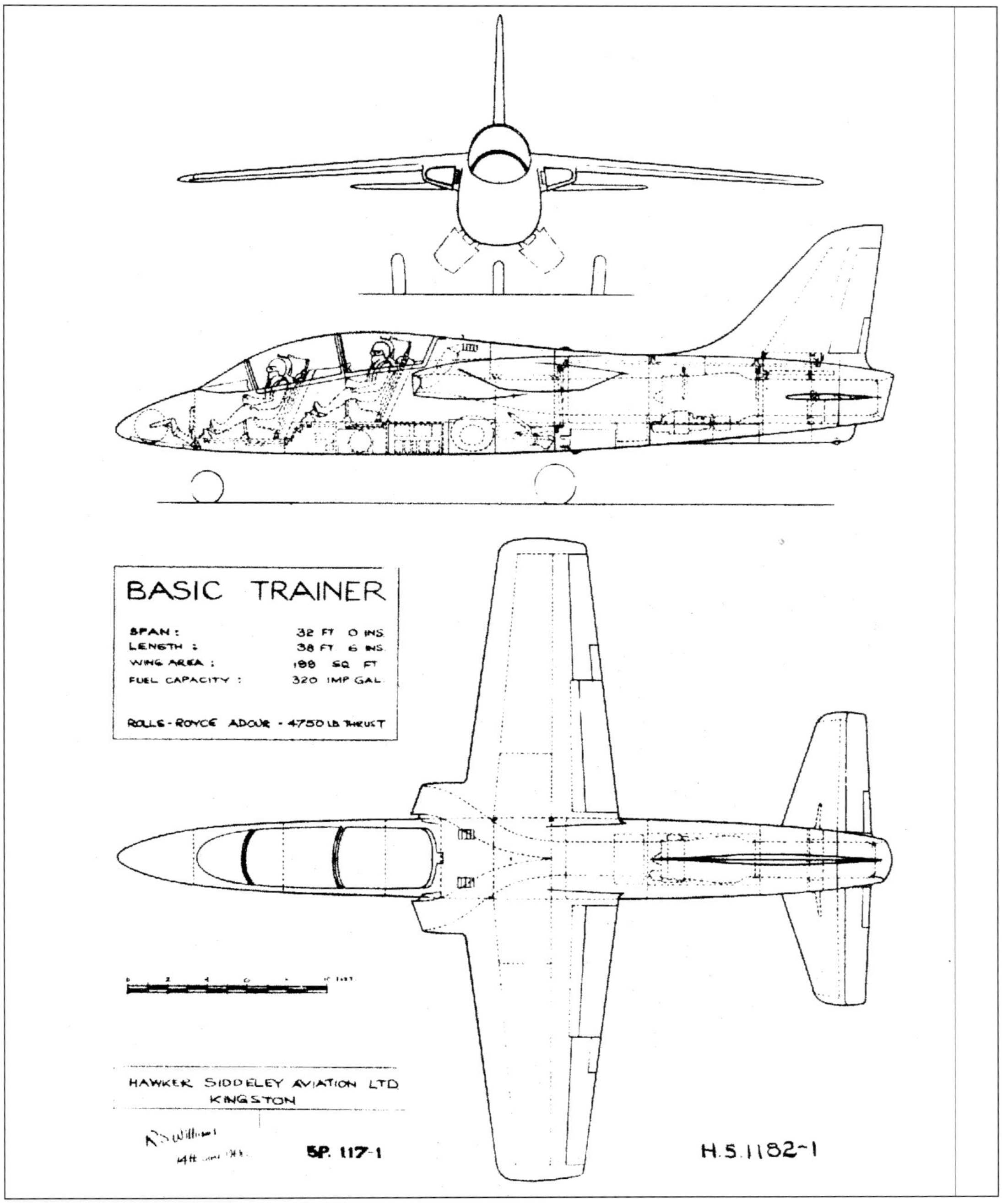

The birth of the Hawk. The SP.117-1 was designed in 1968 to win back export orders. The design eschewed advanced aerodynamics for lower development cost and risk. *Via Chris Farara*

Australian requirements for a strike lead-in trainer. With two prototypes and two static test airframes, an initial production run of 300 would allow a production unit price of £370,000, reflecting the £80,000 price of the Adour, but it was hoped to reduce the price of export aircraft to £250,000. In response to the MoD's invitation for proposals this design work was formalised as the HS.1182 by March 1969 with an emphasis on low purchase and operating costs, ease of manufacture and servicing and easy adaptation for role changes. The Project Office had experience with the Hunter and Gnat and Assistant Chief Engineer R B Marsh visited several Flying Training Command units to gain their opinions and requirements. Both high and low-wing layouts were considered and maximum speed and take-off weight had slightly increased to Mach 0.85 and 9,400lb (4,263kg) respectively. The weapons capability was now six hardpoints for a total of 5,000lb (2,268kg) with a take-off weight of 14,600lb (6,622kg). It was the HS.1182 that would be offered to ASR.397 following an exhaustive series of studies.

BAC's design team at Warton offered two families of designs in response to the invitation for proposals. The first step was to dust off the English Electric P.9 basic trainer design as a starting point, as was the inherited Jet Provost. The P.55 was a development of the Jet Provost T.5 with Strikemaster features for an improved fatigue life, a 4,000lbf (16.3kN) Bristol Siddeley Viper 600 and improved avionics. Wing tip tanks would again be required and the climb to 30,000ft (9,145m) would take eight minutes. The P.55 had little export potential and showed that the Jet Provost had been pushed beyond its limits.

The P.54 was a new design and offered in several versions; the P.54/3 had a 4,620lbf (20.5kN) unreheated Adour and the P.54/6 had the Viper 600 but other versions were studied with the Bristol Siddeley BS.153, the French SNECMA Larzac M49 and the Canadian-built General Electric J85-15. The Viper 600 offered superior climbing ability but had higher fuel consumption and insufficient thrust. The estimated production cost for 300 aircraft was £315,000 for the P.54/3 and £246,000 for the P.54/6 but these designs were soon superseded.

The Australian-Italian Job

In July 1969 BAC had begun talks with the Italian manufacturer Macchi, who had achieved considerable success with their MB.326 trainer since the late 1950s, including penetrating Commonwealth markets such as Australia and South Africa in a way that the Jet Provost had failed to. Unlike Hawker Siddeley, BAC sought collaborative partners to increase the potential production run to secure a profit. In December 1969, the First Secretary at the Italian Embassy, who specialised in technical collaborations, had meetings with Allen Greenwood, Assistant Managing Director at BAC Weybridge and Fabrizio Ferosio of Macchi and representatives of the Ministry of Technology (better known as Mintech). The proposal was a BAC-Macchi partnership; Macchi leading development of the MB.326 and BAC developing the AA-107, a joint project by BAC Warton and Commonwealth Aircraft Corporation of Australia which had begun in September 1968. The AA-107 had been the first collaborative project since the Plowden Committee Report of 1965 which had recommended that the industry should make greater use of collaborative programmes. The AA-107 was a supersonic trainer with a variable-geometry (VG) wing and a reheated Adour for a maximum speed of Mach 1.45. The Royal Australian Air Force (RAAF) wanted thirty as strike lead-in trainers for the General Dynamics F-111, a type that the British government had just cancelled its order for. The Australian government would only fund half of the estimated £30 million development cost, so BAC proposed putting up £7.5 million of its own money alongside a £7.5 million contribution from the UK government. BAC would build both prototypes but at least 100 aircraft were required to make the programme viable, their world market survey estimating a market share of 300 aircraft despite the high unit price of £350,000. The problem was that the RAF was already committed to the Jaguar, the potential RAAF order was too small and the Australian government was lukewarm towards the project. Therefore BAC sought customers from the other Multi-Role Combat Aircraft (MRCA) partners, Italy and West Germany, who would need a suitable lead-in trainer.

A meeting between the Assistant Chief of the Air Staff (Operational Requirements), Air Vice-Marshal Michael Giddings and his Italian counterpart General Colagiovanni soon hit major obstacles. The Italians foresaw retaining the MB.326 as a basic trainer until the 1980s and the RAF wanted a more advanced Jet Provost replacement,

The Commonwealth Aircraft Corporation AA-107 was a modern looking jet trainer and briefly looked likely to become an international collaboration between Australia, the UK and Italy. *Author's Collection*

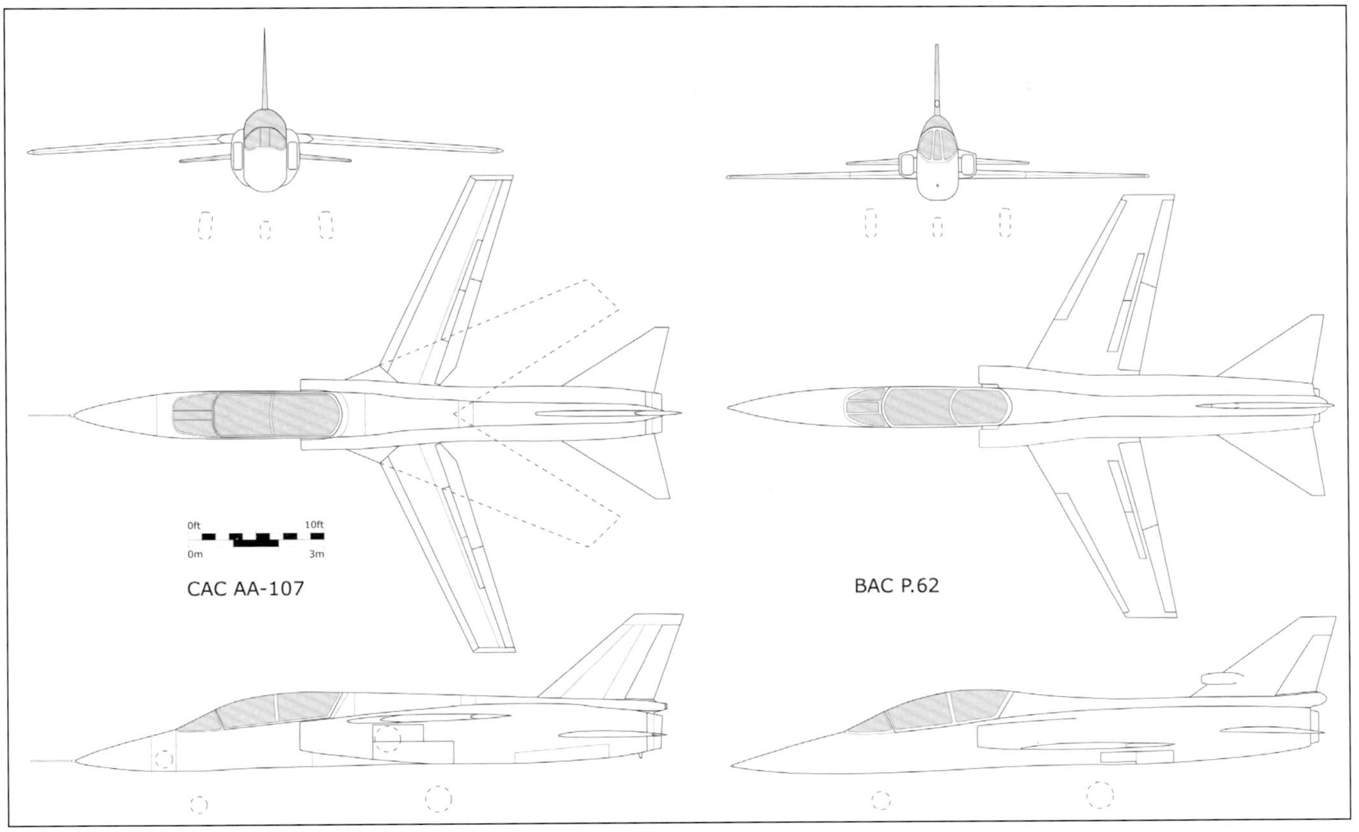

The AA-107 certainly captured the imagination of BAC's design team at Warton who developed a whole family of trainers and fighters from the basic design. This drawing compares the original AA-107 with one of the last of the BAC 107 family, the P.62 which used the fixed wing of the P.59 and was also offered as a single-seat fighter. *Author*

for the supersonic trainer role the RAF already had the Jaguar and the Italians had no requirement for a supersonic trainer, although the Italian Chief of Air Staff, General Fanali, was interested in the concept. Mintech was enthusiastic given the export successes of the MB.326, Jet Provost and Strikemaster and FIAT was interested in licence-building the Viper 600. Mintech favoured a package deal with the MRCA partners, although involving the Germans seemed unlikely due to the Franco-German trainer – soon to become the Alpha Jet – and any advanced trainer deal would have to accommodate the Australians. An agreement would also counter US and French moves towards Italian industry but there was no hope without actual Italian requirements and the agreement lapsed in January 1970.

BAC attempted to interest its other MRCA partner, Messerchmitt-Bölkow-Blohm (MBB). The Counsellor (Defence Supply) at the British Embassy in Bonn had an unofficial farewell meeting with his contact at MBB just before Christmas in 1969, which he dutifully cabled back to the Foreign Office in London. His unnamed contact confirmed that the German military/industrial complex was inclined towards co-operation with Britain but disquieting rumours that Rolls-Royce were unable to maintain the timescale and performance requirements for the RB.199 turbofan for MRCA were ammunition for the pro-French lobby within the Bundestag's Defence Committee to attack the MRCA programme. BAC wanted talks with MBB to share ideas on training aircraft but MBB feared French accusations of breaching the Franco-German training aircraft agreement, causing political trouble in Bonn and prejudicing their Alpha Jet submission in partnership with Nord. If they lost the Alpha Jet, MBB was happy to fall back onto BAC and Italian collaboration as they doubted whether the Alpha Jet would be suitable as an MRCA lead-in trainer. Hawker Siddeley had already visited MBB in November to discuss the HS.1182 and MBB-Nord trainers, but lukewarm interest and a statement that BAC would need to be involved in any collaborative deal ended further conversation. The Dassault/Dornier team did secure the Alpha Jet and any hopes of German collaboration vanished. Giddings had discussions with his French and German counterparts regarding the Alpha Jet, as did Mintech officials with Dassault and Dornier, but it was clear that British industry had little to gain from joining the programme other than being a sub-contractor. World trainer market surveys by all the various interested parties fluctuated from 5,000 to 2,600 aircraft and the UK share from 500 to 400 aircraft, but it was clear that getting any slice of the market for the UK was desirable, the Jet Provost and Strikemaster having already earned £21 million of exports by September 1970. From this point Mintech casted aside the Plowden Report and wanted a purely national programme.

The first prototype Dassault/Dornier Alpha Jet taking off from a rough field strip. The Alpha Jet was the main competitor to Hawk for much of its life. Britain found it could not join the programme even if it had wanted to. *Author's Collection*

The Warton Family

BAC Warton further developed the AA-107 into two families; trainers to meet ASR.397 which resulted in the P.57 and P.62, and the BAC 107 family including the P.60 and P.61 fighter and close support aircraft designs, the latter including co-operation with the MRCA partners via Panavia Aircraft GmBH as the Panavia New Aircraft Project. The P.57 was developed from the AA-107 and retained commonality in fuselage components and had substantially the same wing but now fixed rather than being variable-geometry. The engine would be an unreheated RT.172-06 Adour. The side-effects of basing the P.57 on an existing design were a compromise on larger dimensions, greater weight and higher production costs compared with a clean sheet design. The heavier weight reduced endurance and the estimated production cost for 300 aircraft was £335,000, Mintech's estimate being closer to £392,000. Without the Italian and German collaboration to increase the production run, building 150 RAF and 300 export aircraft would be uneconomic.

The BAC P.59 was similar in approach to the HS.1182 and proved superior in terms of economy compared to the more supersonic variable-geometry P.60 family. *Author's Collection*

By June 1970 the BAC 107 family comprised a range of aircraft from basic trainers to ground attack fighters and were of two distinct designs with either a fixed wing or a VG wing, echoing the earlier P.45. The P.60F1 was a basic/advanced trainer with a fixed thin wing with 35° leading-edge sweep and fitted with full-span flaps and slats and spoilers. The remaining control surfaces were the all-moving tail surfaces and the engine was a single unreheated Adour. The P.60F2 was a close support aircraft with advanced trainer capability and had a reheated Adour and provision for a 30mm DEFA cannon and two wing and four fuselage hardpoints for weapons. The French cannon was selected for export reasons but the Royal Aircraft Establishment's (RAE) Weapons Division criticised the choice. The P.61F1 was very similar to the P.60F2 but was powered by an unreheated RB.199. Other P.61F developments like the F2 were fighters. The P.60V1 basic/advanced trainer had a unreheated Adour and a VG wing with variable 27-69° sweep (but the inboard sections were fixed) with full-span flaps and slats and spoilers. The P.60V2 advanced trainer with close support capability had a full VG wing, a reheated Adour and the armament options of the P.60F2. The P.60V3 was the original AA-107 but the VG wings were now pivoted so the wing pylons needed to swivel. The P.61V1 was the F1 with the VG wing. The P.61 was approaching the F-86 Sabre fighter replacement market, but BAC did not consider the trainer to be the most attractive portion of market anyway and they were looking towards a mini-MRCA. Even so, BAC admitted that full development of P.60/61 family was unlikely and worried that it would endanger Jaguar exports.

The P.59 would become BAC's lead submission for ASR.397 and was developed from the P.54/6 with the Viper 600 and was regarded as the minimum aircraft to meet ASR.397 while still having some export potential. As such it was the closest competitor to the HS.1182. The P.62 was the strike variant with a reheated RT.172-06 Adour to enable supersonic flight, deemed an essential feature given the increased price. The P.62 drew on experience with the BAC 107 family but was separate from it to avoid any design compromises and retained the P.59's fixed wing. BAC also offered a modified Jaguar 'T' as an alternative. Detailed analysis by BAC and Mintech revealed that both the P.60F1 and P.59 narrowly failed to meet the requirement to climb to 30,000ft (9,145m) within seven minutes and although the P.60F1 was heavier it had superior speed due to the increased wing sweep and thinner wing. Using common wing structures throughout the BAC 107 family had led to weight and design compromises and therefore the increased performance did not make the P.60F1 more desirable than the P.59 in terms of unit and lifetime costs.

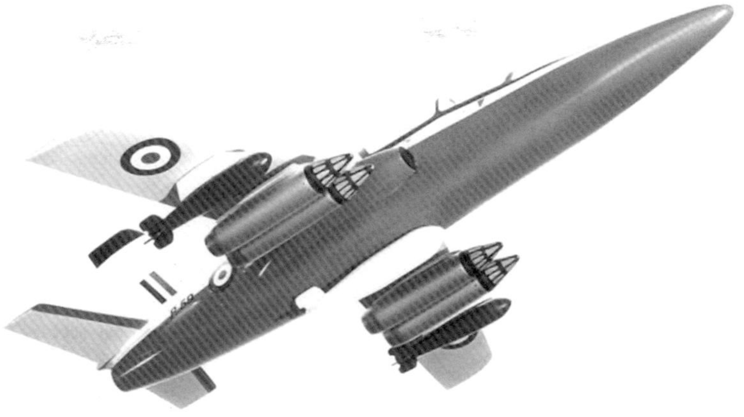

The P.59 was also designed to succeed the Strikemaster as a low-cost ground attack aircraft for export. The manufacturer's model is shown here carrying two 1,000lb (453kg) bombs and four Matra rocket pods. *Author's Collection*

Kingston Gets It Right

Kingston's work on the SP.117 quickly became formalised under the HS.1182 designation. With the outline requirements being flexible in regard to cockpit arrangement, number of engines and wing planforms, it is no surprise that Kingston's Project Office drew up around 20 designs covering a variety of types with combinations of single and twin engines, tandem and side-by-side seating, straight and swept wings and low, mid or shoulder mounted wing configurations. The HS.1182 was the first British military aircraft to be designed entirely using metric units. While BAC was concentrating on families of designs, the early HS.1182 studies all looked quite different despite having the unmistakably Kingston style in their elegant curving wing and tail surface leading edges. Some of them resembled the contemporary Aero L-39 Albatros and the slightly later Aermacchi MB.339. The twin-engined studies were perhaps the most interesting with the engines mounted in nacelles on the sides or the rear fuselage or the fuselage centre-section above the wing roots. Another had the engines under the wing roots with a T-tail and closely resembled the SAAB 105. These feasibility studies enabled several design decisions to be made; straight wings were rejected because they were restricted to Mach 0.80, twin engines increased drag for little benefit and offered only marginally improved reliability, fuselage-mounted main undercarriages offered insufficient track and low-mounted intakes had potential foreign object debris issues. The tandem cockpit was favoured due to its better visibility and lower drag and the low and mid-mounted wings were favoured for easy servicing and high-speed flight. A full scale forward fuselage mock-up was fitted on hydraulic jacks on a lorry trailer so that it could be moved from 2° to 7° nose up attitude, 4° representing the 100kt (185km/h) threshold speed at 5,070lb (2,299kg) landing weight.

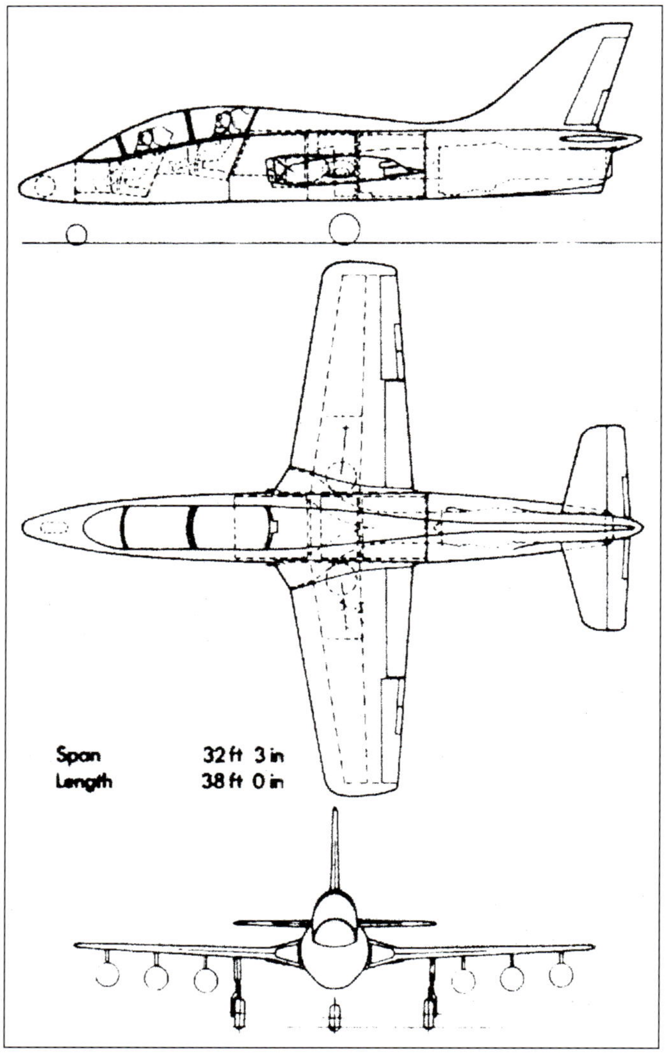

The HS.1182-4 was one of the first design studies, powered by a single Adour fed by wing root intakes. The result looks remarkably similar to the Aermacchi MB.339 that would fly a decade later. Note the six underwing hardpoints for the export strike role. *Via Chris Farara*

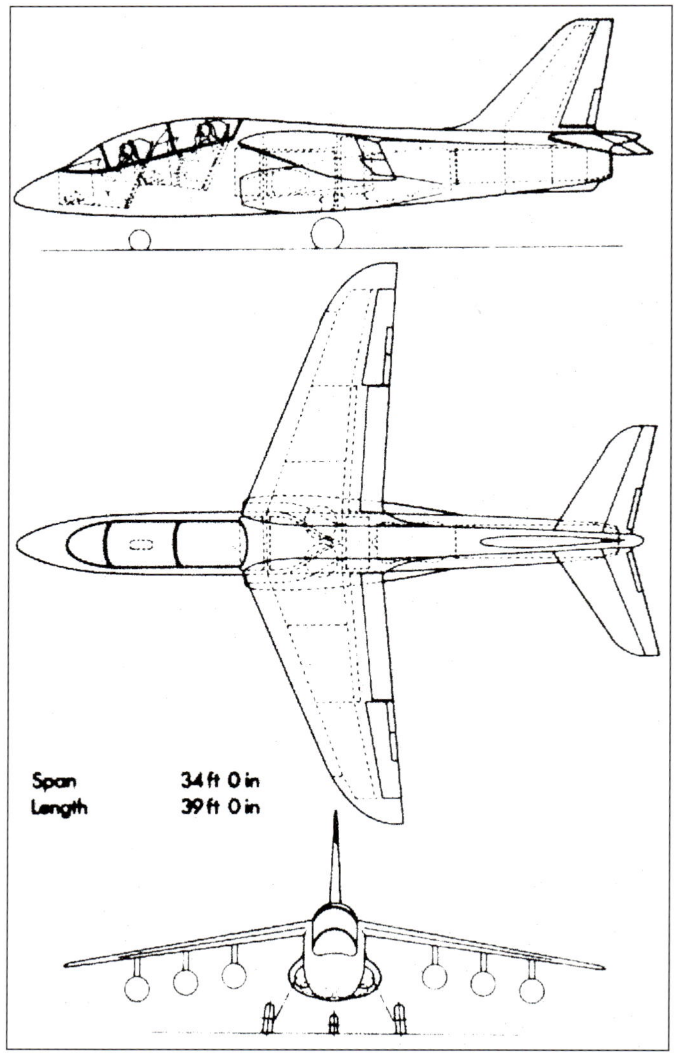

The HS.1182-7 had a moderately swept wing mounted high on the fuselage to minimise drag. Foreign object debris entering the low intakes might have been a problem on rough fields. The engine was a single Adour and the undercarriage was fuselage mounted. *Via Chris Farara*

As many pilots as possible were invited to try the cockpit during September 1969 and their comments were passed directly to the Head of Preliminary Design and the pilots' dimensions were recorded to ensure that the cockpit was comfortable for all sizes of pilots.

Most of the single-engine designs had the RT.172-06 Adour, while the twin-engined ones had either the BS.153 or the Larzac but a much wider choice of engines had been studied. For a single engine the studies had investigated the 7,575lbf (33.6kN) Rolls-Royce Mk.121/122 Avon, the unreheated RB.199 and SNECMA M 45H and at the lower end the 4,400lbf (19.5kN) Bristol Siddeley Orpheus 101, the Viper 600, Viper 21F and even the Czechoslovak Walter Titan as fitted to the L-39 Albatros – its 26 percent lower fuel consumption than the Viper 600 despite having similar thrust ratings being particularly impressive. Engines considered for the twin engine designs also included the Pratt & Whitney 5,760lbf (25.6kN) JT15D-3 and the 5,440lbf (24.1kN) General Electric J85-13. With the twin-engine designs rejected, the choice fell on the Adour with the Viper 600 as a reserve choice due to its low cost. No less than seventeen designs went forward for the final whittling down to just one ideal configuration.

The result was the HS.1182 submitted in October 1970 in Brochure HSK27. A full-scale mock-up was also built. The design had a low-wing layout but the intakes were mounted high on the fuselage just behind the cockpit canopy. The higher performance now envisioned saw the manual flying controls replaced by irreversible hydraulic-powered controls. The wing had an aerofoil based on that of the Harrier and could accommodate a 7.62mm machine gun in the wing root. The full export strike variant would have five hardpoints for up to 5,000lb (2,268kg) of weapons as well as two ventral 30mm ADEN cannon pods.

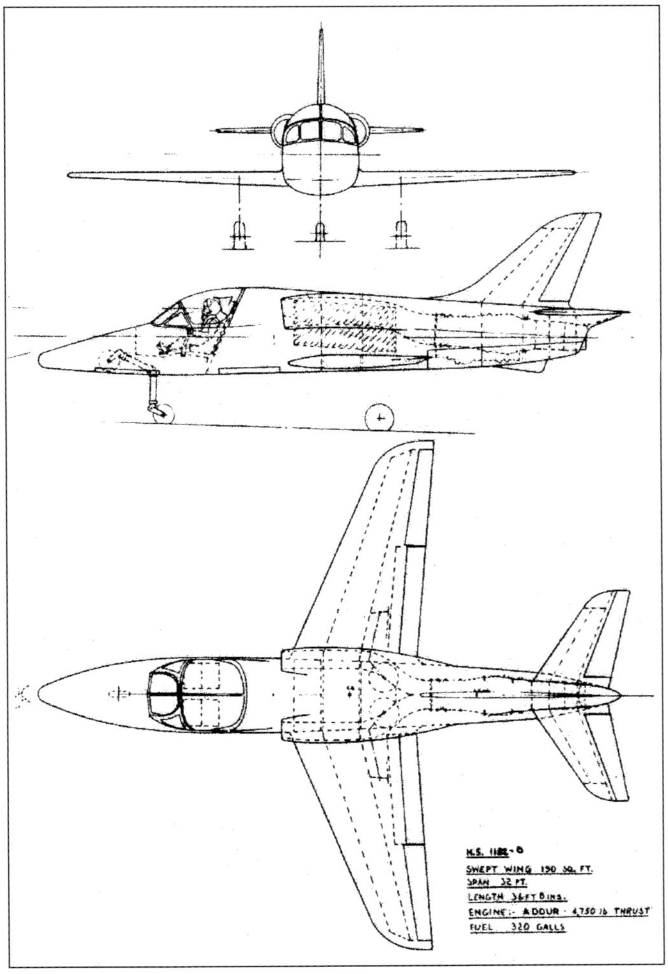

The HS.1182-8 of May 1969 was very similar in most respects to the other Adour-powered designs except for side-by-side seating for the student and instructor in a wider fuselage. *Via Chris Farara*

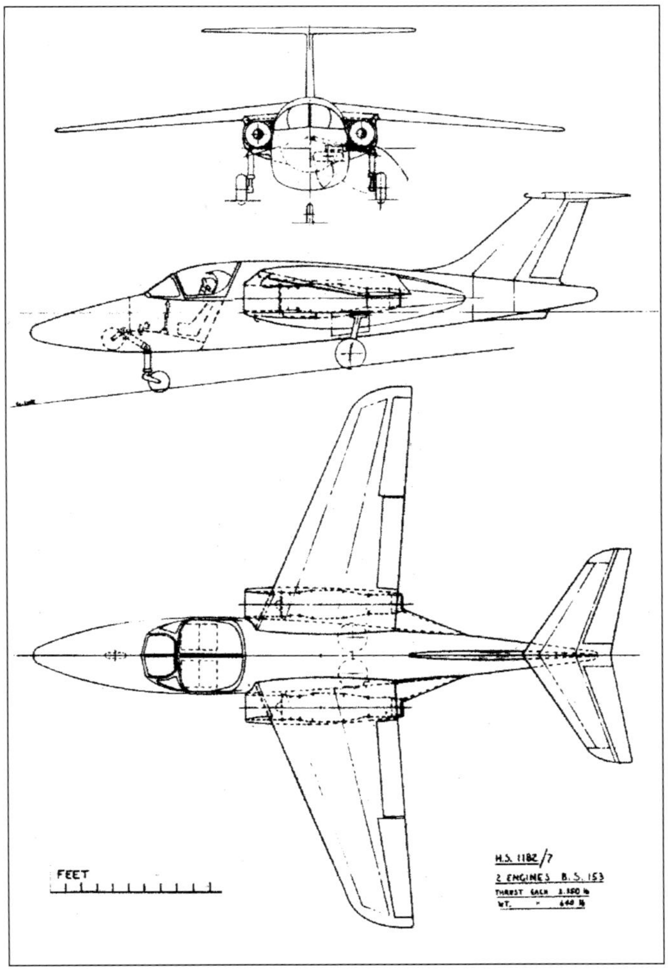

The HS.182-7 with two BS.153 engines and a T-tail and side-by-side seating looks like Kingston's answer to the SAAB 105. *Via Chris Farara*

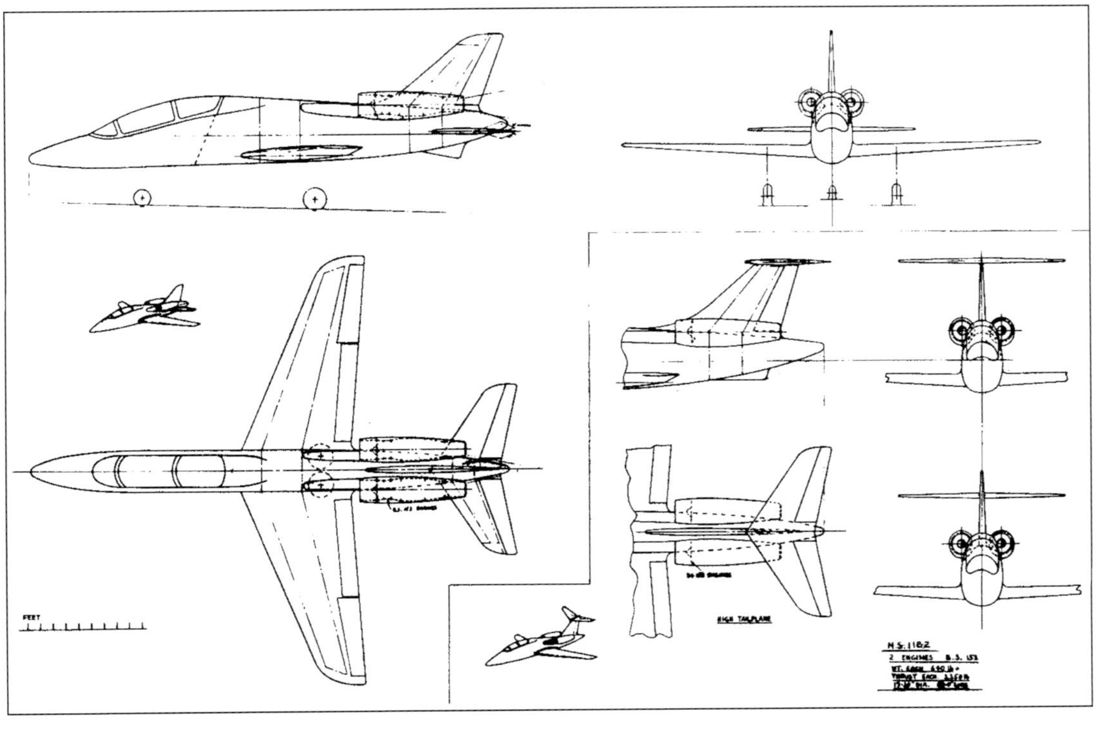

This twin-BS.153 powered design was more radical in having the engines mounted in pods on the rear fuselage (a layout later seen on the Fairchild A-10 Thunderbolt II) with either a conventional or T-tail arrangement. *Via Chris Farara*

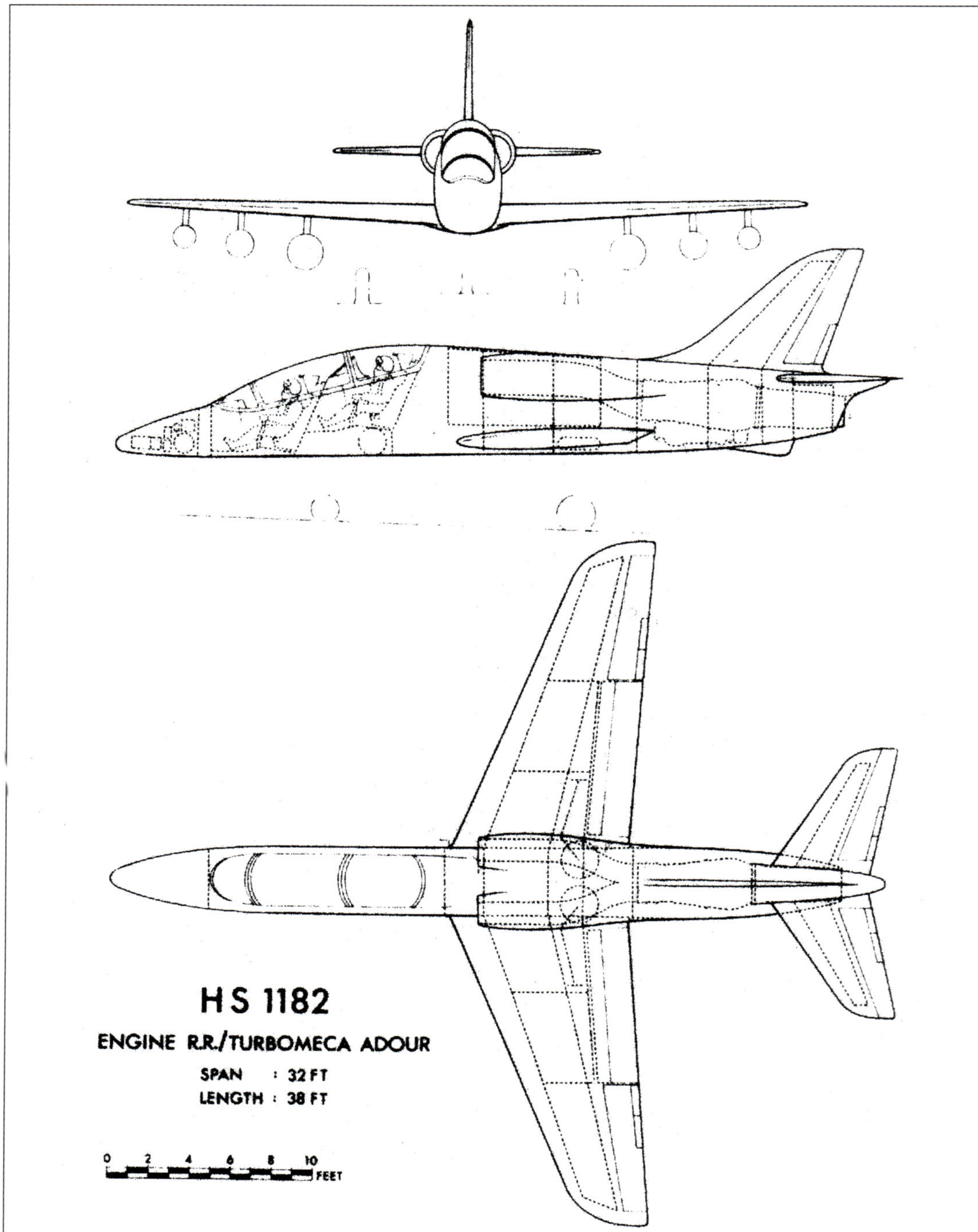

The HS.1182-29 of March 1969 was the selected baseline design with a take-off weight of 9,420lb (kg) as a trainer or 14,600lb (6,622kg) with a full warload of four 1,000lb (453kg) and two 500lb (226kg) bombs in the strike role. *Via Chris Farara*

The fuselage had a fatigue life of 6,000 hours and was stressed for 8g (12g ultimate load factor) with a design diving speed of 550kt (1,018km/h) or Mach 0.9. The stepped tandem cockpit provided a view from the front seat of 15° below the horizontal datum and 7° from the rear seat and the student and instructor had Folland F4 GT2 Mk.2 ejection seats as fitted to the Gnat T.1 to save weight. In size the cockpit was very similar to that of the Jaguar T.2 except for being slightly shorter and compared to the Gnat it was larger in length, width and headroom. Hawker Siddeley estimated that from a go-ahead in January 1971 that the first aircraft would be available in June 1973 and with four production aircraft used for 600 hours of flight testing, Controller Air (CA) Release would be in March 1976. The planned production rate for 175 aircraft for the RAF and as many as 464 for export was four per month.

Another version of ASR.397 was issued around the same time and it became clear that the design narrowly failed to meet some of the requirements; the maximum speed was only Mach 0.83, the landing speed was 112kt (207km/h) and the time to 30,000ft (9,145m) was eight minutes and the endurance was ten minutes short. Previous work on a smaller version, the HS.1182A, was now prioritised. The HS.1182A was 220lb (98kg) lighter and intensive high-speed wind tunnel tests on a 1/30th scale model led to several aerodynamic

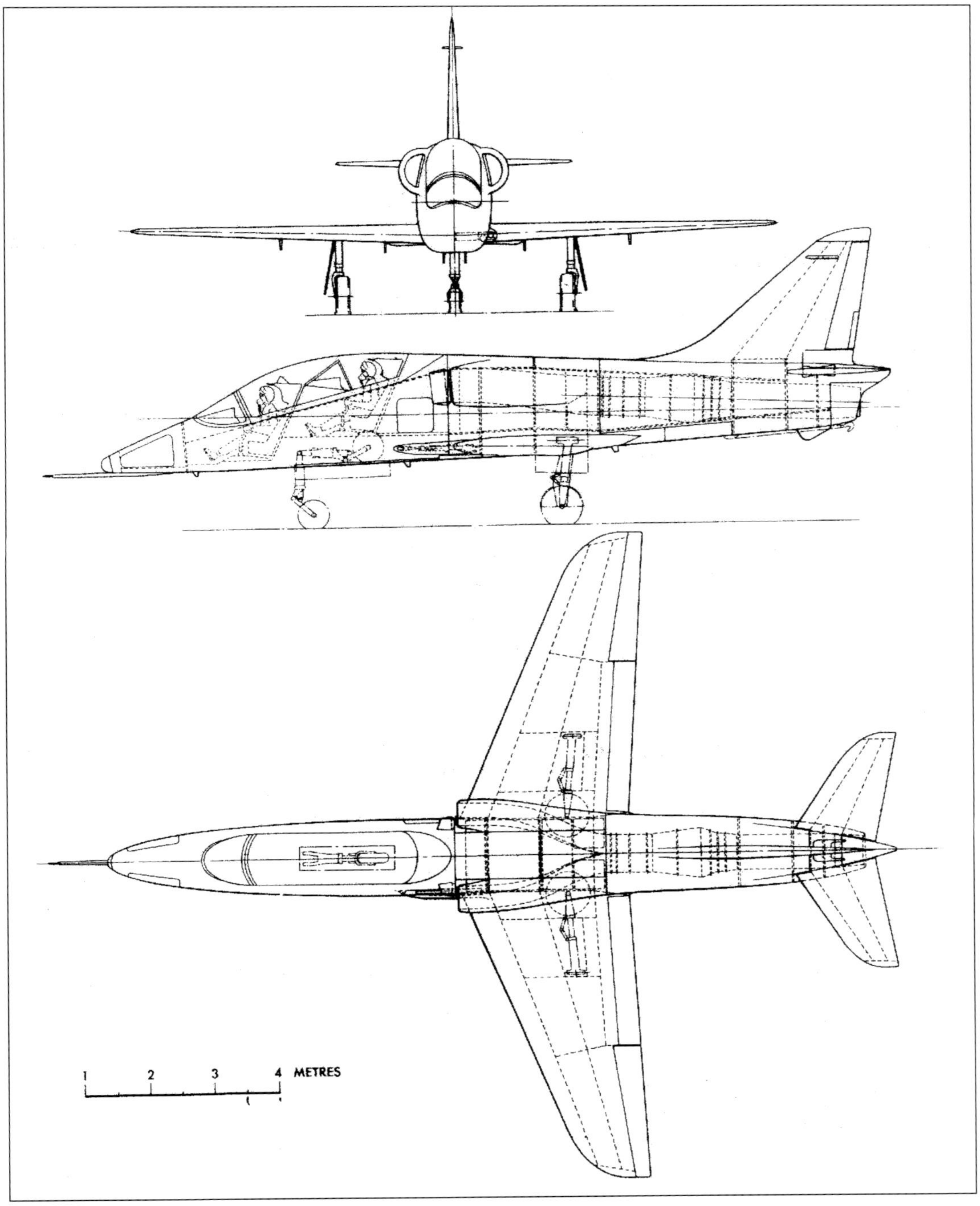

The HS.1182-30 was the submission in brochure HSK27 to meet ASR.397. The high intakes were designed for rough field operations. *Via Chris Farara*

refinements with the intakes moved to the wing roots, an increase in leading-edge wing sweep to 26° and anhedral for the tailplane. The Adour had proved temperamental with some intake configurations and Rolls-Royce and the RAE favoured a short intake and German aerodynamicist Dr Dietrich Küchemann (inventor of the drag-reducing 'Küchemann Carrots' fitted to the Convair CV-990 and Handley Page Victor B.2) favoured the lower intake position and he advised on several other aerodynamic features. The undercarriage was relocated ahead of the main wing structural box to improve rough field performance, the wing box became an integral fuel tank to increase total fuel capacity by sixteen percent. This required the Adour to be moved backwards by 13in (33cm) to maintain the centre of gravity and now only one 30mm ADEN cannon pod (taken from the Harrier) could be fitted on the centreline. The new undercarriage bays were used to assist engine removal and for access to the gearbox and auxiliaries. The cockpit was also moved 39in (99cm) aft and the fuselage side area was reduced to cut drag. The HS.1182V was a low-cost weapons trainer with an even smaller airframe powered by the 4,000lbf (16.3kN) Viper 632-11 and reduced avionics. It could carry a 30mm cannon pod and had two underwing hardpoints for two 1,000lb (453kg) bombs including the Hunting BL.755 cluster bomb, but would need extensive modifications to carry a 5,000lb (2,268kg) load. It just met ASR.397 but had no further growth potential and was unattractive for export.

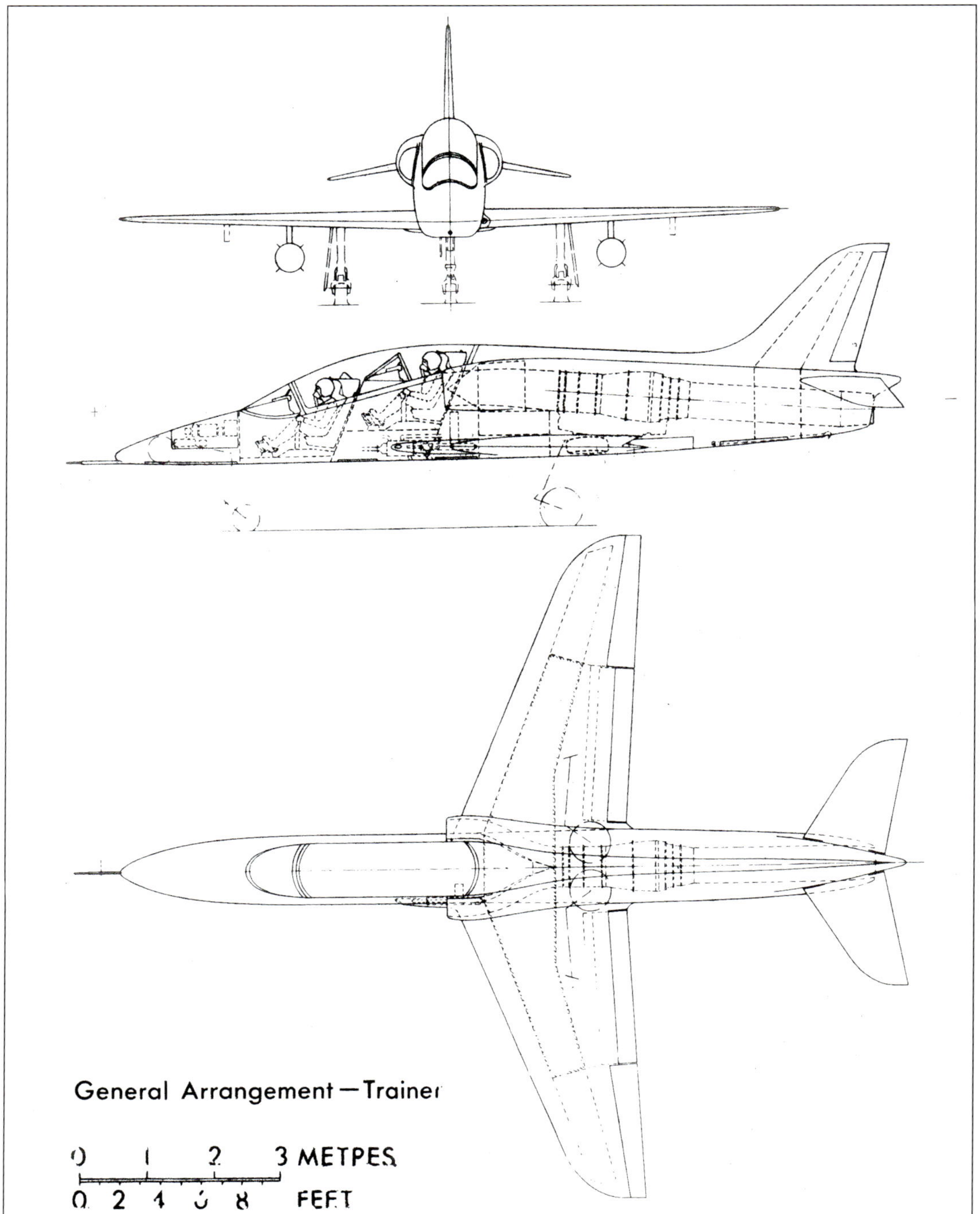

The HS.1182-30 could not quite meet all the requirements for ASR.397, so Hawker Siddeley asked for time to refine the design. The resulting HS.1182A of October 1970 was 220lb (99kg) lighter and had reduced fuselage and wing area to reduce drag. *Via Chris Farara*

The clean lines of the final configuration are evident on this manufacturer's model of the HS.1182. Despite the economic fallout of the 1973 Oil Shock and labour unrest, development, the start of production was only delayed by six months and was on budget. *Author's Collection*

The HS.1182AT swapped the Adour for the Viper for a smaller and lighter airframe. The Adour-powered HS.1182AJ was between the A and AT in size, allowing for good performance and avionics and fully met ASR.397 and became the final submission. There was a reprise to Australian involvement with Hawker Siddeley offering Commonwealth Aircraft of Australia a production licence for the HS.1182V or the HS.1182AT. The UK government insisted that the HS.1182AJ was offered too and a 70/30 percent split production agreement was proposed, the Australian facility also supplying sets for RAF aircraft. Negotiations during the summer of 1971 came to nothing, but in time Australia would become a customer for UK-built Hawks.

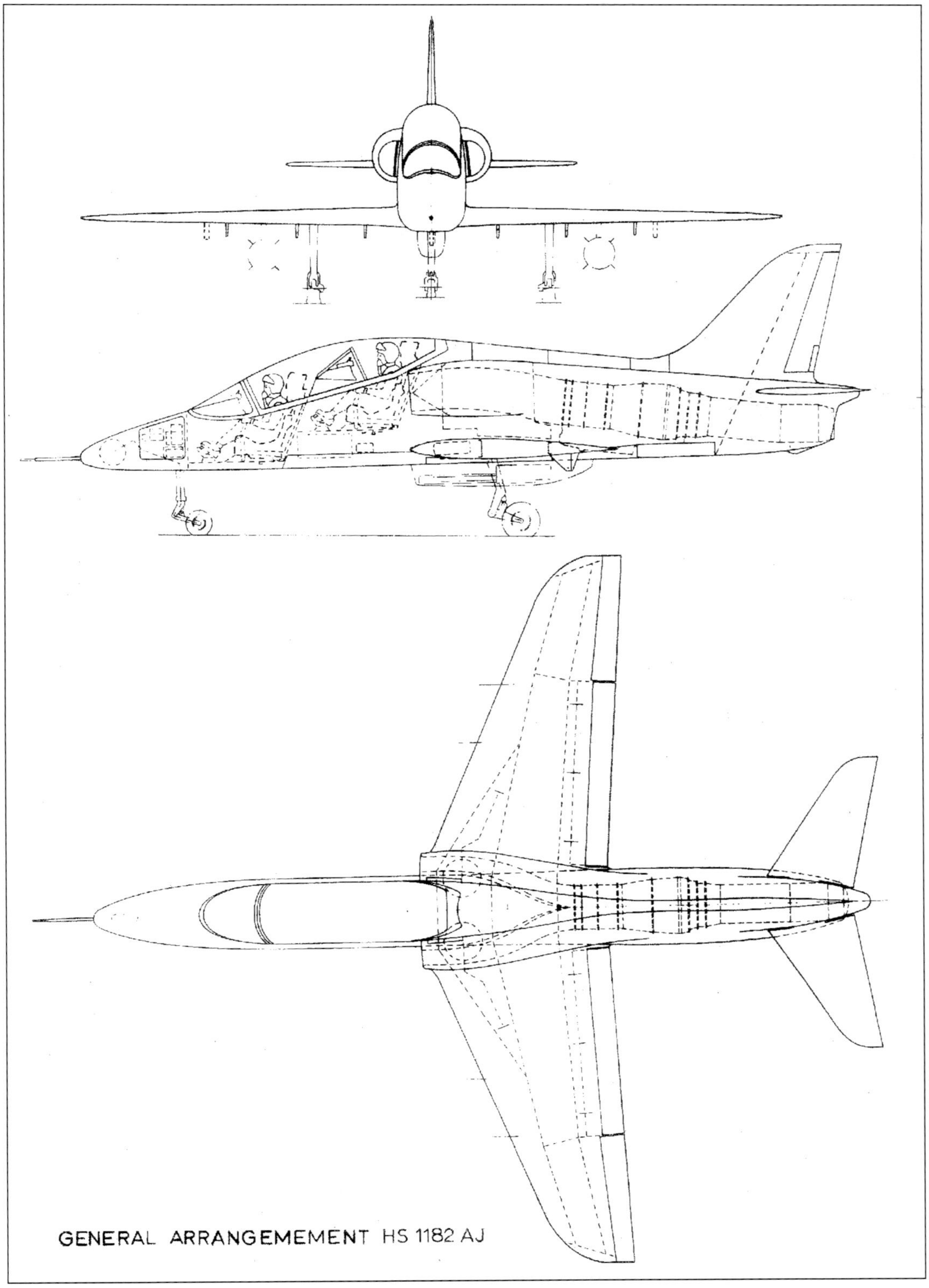

The HS.1182AJ was smaller than the HS.1182 but larger than the Viper-powered HS.1182AT and had a take-off weight of 9,794lb (4,443kg). It was the final design for submission in October 1971 and won ASR.397. Under the fuselage can be seen the 30mm ADEN cannon pod. Doubts over the intake position would see it later lowered to the wing root. *Via Chris Farara*

These were not the only projects that Hawker Siddeley were working on. The Gnat made a reappearance as the HS1182G powered by a Viper 600. This further development had an AUW of 8,300lb (3,764kg), a modified wing with lower aspect ratio and increased leading-edge sweep and fitted with full span leading and trailing-edge high lift flaps and slats. The original cockpit arrangement was retained and only four weapons hardpoints could be fitted with a capacity of 3,000lb (1,360kg). The HS.1182G was uncompetitive and emphasised the advantages of using the more powerful Adour. During the development of the baseline HS.1182 it was found that the export strike version had a very long take-off distance when carrying the maximum weapons load. To overcome this the HS.1183 was drawn up in October 1969 powered by two Viper 600s in the rear fuselage fed by wing root intakes and looking very similar to the Northrop F-5 family. Using two engines provided transonic performance and it was offered as a single-seat ground attack fighter with an armament of two internal cannon and five hardpoints and as a two-seat advanced trainer, but was too expensive to be suitable for ASR.397.

As early as August 1970 the MoD and Mintech had begun assessing the various contenders, in particular the HS.1182 and P.59, as they kept track of progress of the development programmes. The final submissions in November allowed the final assessments to be weighed up. Since the convoluted discussions with potential European partners, foreign solutions had largely disappeared from the scene but in February 1971 Fairey Company Limited, the independent remnant of the now long merged Fairey Aviation, offered the SAAB 105X licence-built in Belgium by Fairey SA. No interest was forthcoming given that the offer missed the submission deadline.

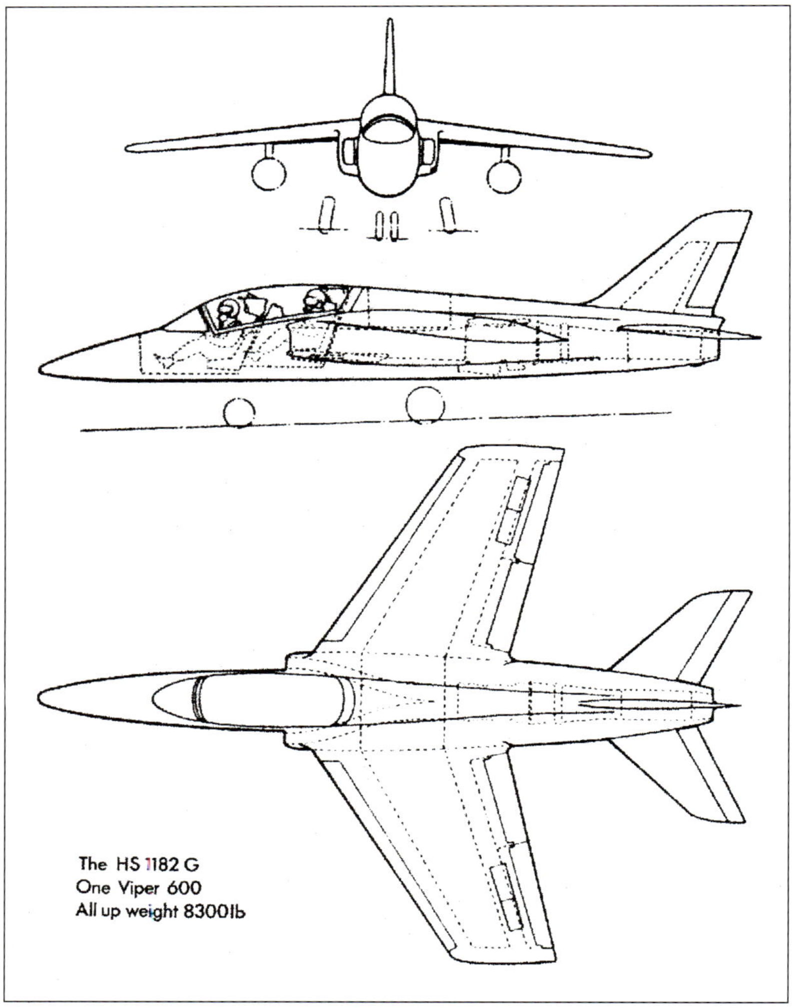

Left: Unexpectedly the Gnat was revisited as the HS.1182G powered by a single Viper Mk.600. The result was uncompetitive and proved the wisdom of going for a fresh design powered by a single Adour. *Via Chris Farara*

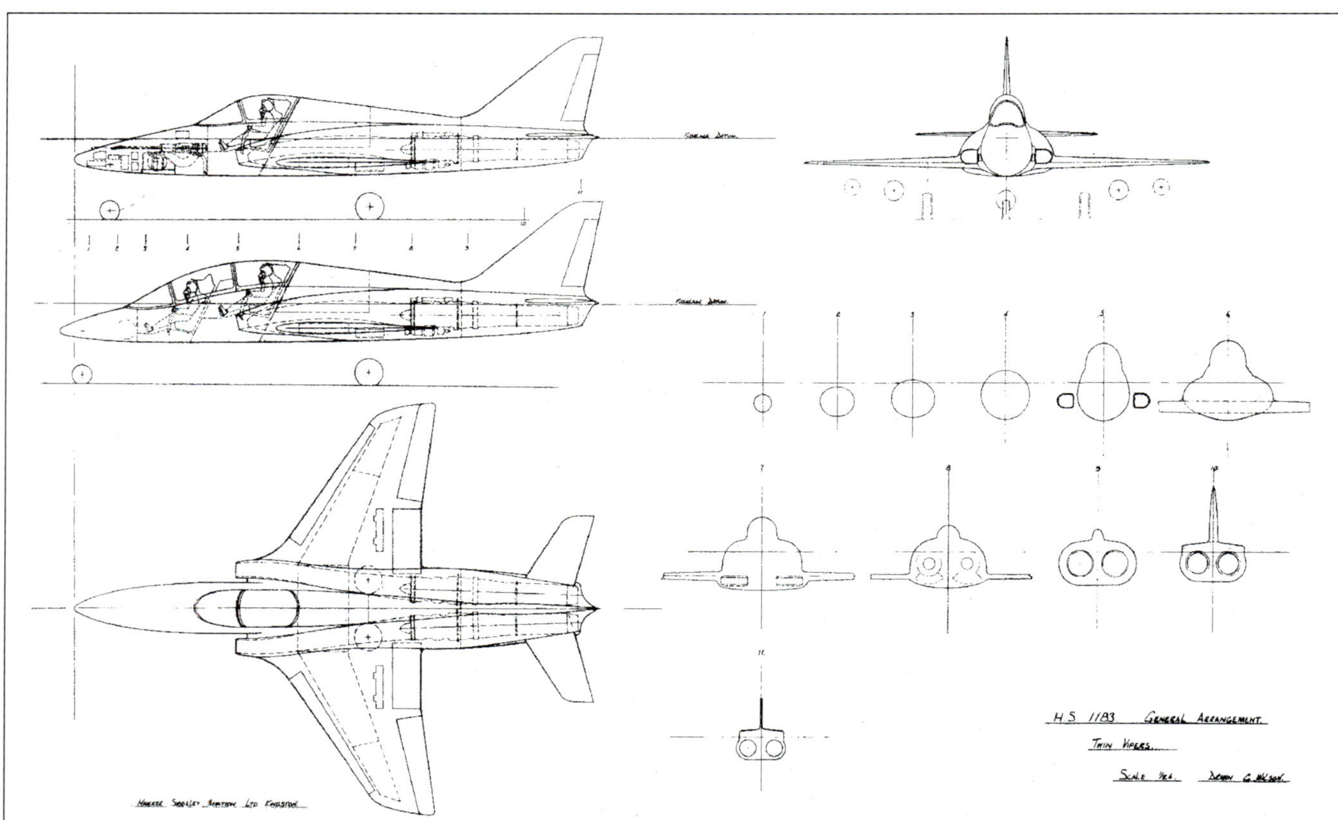

Below: The HS.1183 was aimed at the export market for light fighters and advanced trainers and was powered by two Viper Mk.600 engines. The result was a cross between the Hawk and the Northrop F-5. *Via Chris Farara*

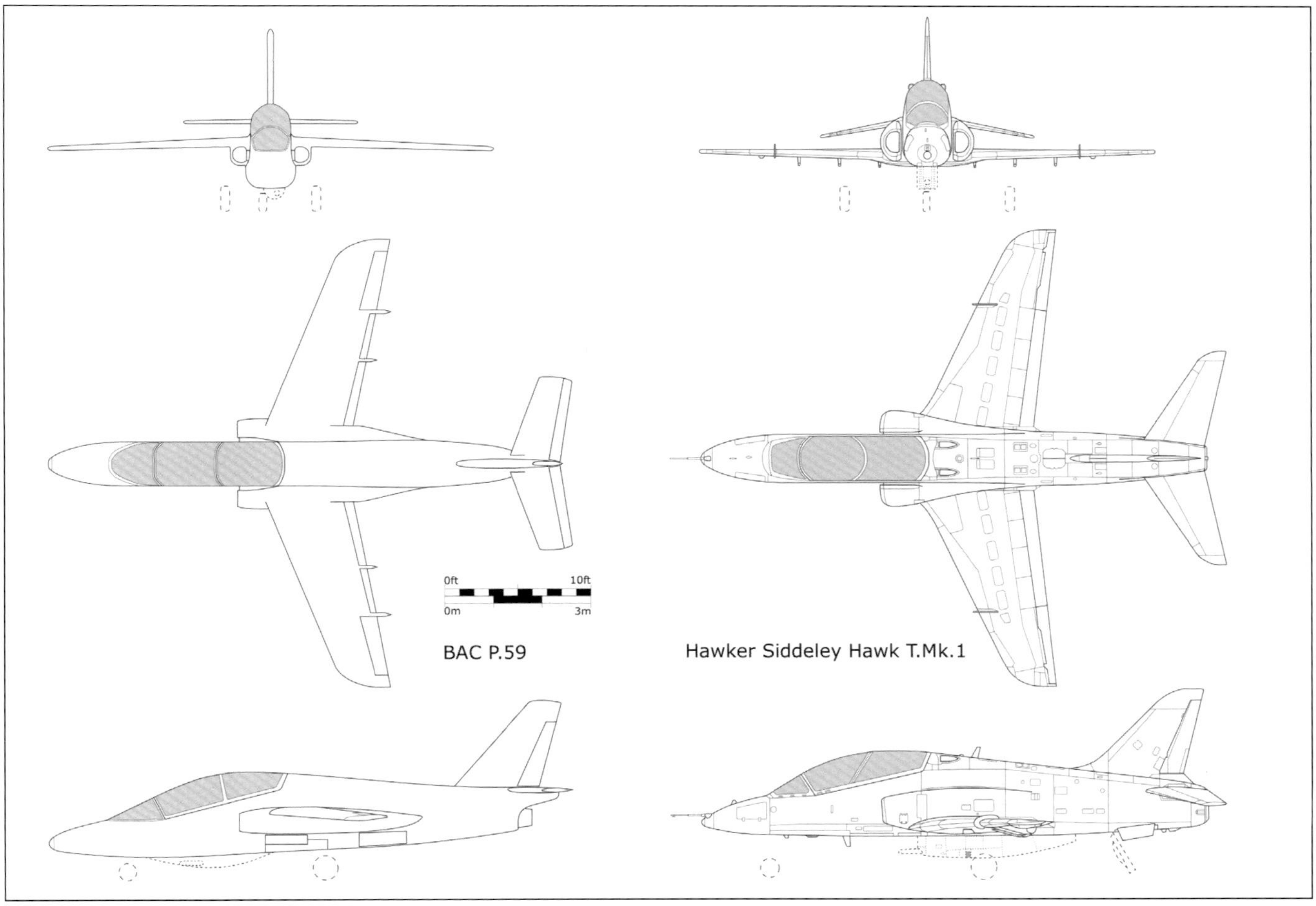

A comparison between one of Warton's P.62 designs and Kingston's HS.1182 Hawk. Both offered basic aerodynamics for straightforward handling and performance and an external cannon pod for armament training. *Author*

The MoD recognised that the HS.1182 had been designed more rigorously around AST.397. Compared to the P.59 the Adour-powered HS.1182 was heavier but had reduced fuel consumption and greater endurance and although it had a larger wing it did not require the P.59's sophisticated flaps and flying controls for good low-speed handling. Mintech estimated that the HS.1182 development programme could cost up to £24 million, around £6 million cheaper than the BAC P.60F1. On submitting their formal proposal in November 1970, Hawker Siddeley estimated a development cost of £19.8 million with 175 aircraft costing £72.1 million to produce. A meeting chaired by the Vice Chief of the Air Staff, Air Chief Marshal Sir Denis G Smallwood, in February 1971 assessed submissions. There was little between them in terms of performance but the HS.1182 had more growth potential although the P.59 had a slight edge in the training role. The Air Staff still had some doubts about the HS.1182's intake design but they liked that it had a ram-air turbine emergency power system. The MoD's preliminary assessment of ten year operating costs favoured the P.59 with savings of £26 million, mostly due to the £20,000 cheaper price per aircraft. The situation at Rolls-Royce with its financial collapse and subsequent nationalisation and its potential to disrupt the Adour programme played a part in delaying the final decision until early October 1971 when the HS.1182AJ was declared the winner. On 12th March 1972 Specification 281D&P was issued to cover development and production of 175 aircraft on a fixed price contract basis. As originally planned, there were no prototypes and all aircraft were built using production jigs and tooling. The start of production was delayed by six months following the effect of the Oil Crisis but no other delays were encountered.

Success at Birth

On 1st August 1973 the HS.1182 was formally named the Hawk. In the haste to find a name Hawker Siddeley had not had a chance to run their own staff competition, which narrowly favoured the name Tercel, but the management had no objections to their namesake being chosen. A year later, on 12th August 1974, the first aircraft, XX154, made its maiden flight at Dunsfold at the hands of Chief Test Pilot Duncan Simpson. Flight testing was undertaken by the four early production aircraft (XX154, XX156, XX157 and XX158) and later the company's export Mk.50 demonstrator G-HAWK (also serialled ZA101). The handling and performance trials generally went well but uncovered a few aerodynamic issues that needed rectification; a sudden leading-edge stall with little warning; a phantom dive when recovering from a stall with full flap and undercarriage up with a forward centre of gravity; and directional wander at high speeds making weapon aiming difficult. All of these were fixed relatively easily and high-speed rolling performance was improved by adding vortex generators to the upper wing surface.

Table 8.1 – AST.397 Contenders: HSA

	HSA SP.117-1	HS.1182 (HSK 13 March 1969)	HS.1182 (HSK 27 October 1970)	HS.1182A	HS.1182V (June 1971)	HS.1182AT	HS.1182AJ	Hawk T.1	Hawk T.2
Wingspan	32ft (9.75m)	32ft (9.75m)	32ft 5.5in (9.89m)	32.04ft (9.77m)	27.68ft (8.43m)	29.51ft (9m)	30.83ft (9.4m)	30ft 9.75in (9.39m)	32ft 7in (9.94m)
Length	40ft (12.19m)	38ft (11.58m)	39ft 8in (12.09m)	38.2ft (11.64m)	36.7ft (11.18m)	33.2ft (10.12m)	33.9ft (10.33m)	37ft 3in (11.45m)	40ft 9in (12.43m)
Wing Area	199ft² (18.48m²)	190ft² (17.65m²)	199.2ft² (18.51m²)	194ft² (18.02m²)	157.02ft² (14.58m²)	164.7ft² (15.3m²)	180ft² (16.72m²)	179.6ft² (16.69m²)	179.64ft² (16.70m²)
All-Up Weight	9,090lb (4,123kg)	9,420lb (4,272kg)	12,375lb (5,613kg)	10,570lb (4,795kg)	9,185lb (4,166kg)	9,279lb (4,209kg)	9,794lb (4,443kg)	11,000lb (5,000kg)	20,000lb (9,100kg) (max TO)
Powerplant	RT.172 Adour, 4,750lbf (21.1kN)	RT.172 Adour, 4,750lbf (21.1kN)	RT.172-06 Adour, 5,000lbf (22.2kN)	RT.172-06 Adour, 5,000lbf (22.2kN)	Viper 632, 4,000lbf (16.3kN)	RT.172-06 Adour, 5,000lbf (22.2kN)	RT.172-06 Adour, 5,000lbf (22.2kN)	Adour Mk 151-01, 5,200lbf (23.13kN)	Adour Mk 951, 6,500lbf (28.91kN)
Max Speed/Height	Mach 0.84 at 36,000ft (10,970m)	Mach 0.83 at 30,000ft (10,970m)	Mach 0.83 at 30,000ft (10,970m)	Mach 0.85 at 30,000ft (10,970m)	Mach 0.83 at 30,000ft (10,970m)	Mach 0.83 at 30,000ft (10,970m)	Mach 0.85 at 30,000ft (10,970m)	Mach 0.87 at 30,000ft (10,970m)	Mach 0.84 at 30,000ft (10,970m)
Service Ceiling	?	?	45,000ft (13,715m)	46,000ft (14,020m)	46,000ft (14,020m)	48,000ft (14,630m)	47,000ft (14,325m)	50,000ft (15,240m)	44,500ft (13,565m)

Table 8.2 – AST.397 contenders: BAC

	BAC P.54-3	BAC P.54-6	BAC P.55	BAC P.57	BAC P.59	CAC AA-107	BAC P.60F1	BACP.60F2	BAC P.60V1	BAC P.60V2	BAC P.60V3	BAC P.61F1	BAC P.61V1
Wingspan forward swept	28ft (8.53m)	28ft (8.53m)	35.3ft	29ft (8.83m)	29.6ft (9.01m)	29ft 10in (9.14m) 16ft 9in (5.15m)	28.2ft (8.58m)	28.2ft (8.58m)	28ft (8.53m) 16ft 6in (5.03m)	28ft (8.53m) 16ft 6in (5.03m)	28ft (8.53m) 16ft 6in (5.03m)	26ft 10in (8.18m)	28ft (8.53m) 16ft 6in (5.03m)
Length	35ft 6in (10.82m)	35ft 6in (10.82m)	34ft (10.36m)	37ft 6in (11.43m)	35.8ft (10.87m)	41ft 2in (12.57m)	41.5ft (12.64m)	41.5ft (12.64m)	?	?	?	40ft (12.19m)	40ft (12.19m)
Wing Area	130ft² (12.07m²)	130ft² (12.07m²)	223ft² (20.71m²)	130ft² (12.07m²)	145ft² (13.47m²)	?	160ft² (14.86m²)	160ft² (14.86m²)	?	?	?	160ft² (14.86m²)	?
All-Up Weight	8,500lb (3,855kg)	8,476lb (3,844kg)	8,377lb (3,799kg)	9,650lb (4,377kg)	9,800lb (4,445kg)	16,000lb (7,258kg)	10,957lb (4,970kg) loaded, ground attack	?	?	?	?	15,000lb (6,803kg)	15,000lb (6,803kg)
Powerplant	RT.172 Adour	Viper 600, 4,000lbf (16.3kN)	Viper 600, 4,000lbf (16.3kN)	RT.172 Adour, 4,750lbf (21.1kN)	Viper 600, 4,000lbf (16.3kN)	RT.172 Adour, 7,350lbf (32.6kN)	RT.172-06 Adour, 5,000lbf (22.2kN)	RT.172, reheated	RT.172-06 Adour, 5,000lbf (22.2kN)	RT.172, reheated	RT.172, reheated	RB.199, 8,394lbf (37.3kN)	RB.199, 8,394lbf (37.3kN)
Max Speed/Height	Mach 0.84	Mach 0.83	Mach 0.72	Mach 0.83	Mach 0.82	Mach 1.25	Mach 0.96	Mach 1+ at SL	?	?	?	Mach 1+ at SL	Mach 1+ at SL
Service Ceiling	44,000ft (13,410m)	44,000ft (13,410m)	40,000ft (12,190m)	40,000ft (12,190m)	?	50,000ft (15,240m)	?	?	?	?	?	?	?

Initial CA Release was achieved on schedule on 18th October 1976 and production Hawks T.1 XX162 and XX163 were delivered to No 4 Flying Training School (FTS) at Valley on 4th November, only 27 months after the first flight. The first No 4 FTS unit to fully re-equip was the CFS's 1 Squadron responsible for instructor training and standards. In September 1976, nine Hawks performed a formation display at the SBAC Farnborough Show, the first of many public shows to come. In July 1977 No 1 Tactical Weapons Unit (TWU) at Brawdy received its first Hawks, No 2 TWU at Chivenor not replacing its Hawker Hunters until 1981. Due to the fixed price contract some items had been omitted such as stopwatches, no rear cockpit directional gyro and no standby compass or UHF radio. These were rectified over time and the wheel brakes improved.

This Hawk T.1A is XX232 in No 4 FTS/ 208 (Reserve) Squadron colours on 15th June 2003, four years before its retirement. In the background is a Shorts Tucano of No 207 (Reserve) Squadron of No 1 FTS. The selection of the Tucano was heavily influenced by the Hawk as the two aircraft had to form a seamless progression from the basic to advanced flying training phases. *Author's Collection*

Hawk T.1 XX292 is shown here resplendent in No 4 FTS colours in the late 1980s. Later assigned to the Red Arrows, the aircraft had been in storage since 2009 before it was sold in 2020 to the Pima Air & Space Museum in Arizona. *Author's Collection*

The Hawk's reliability was soon confirmed. In 1978 after 3,000 flying hours, all the defects and servicing history were assessed were found to be far lower than the estimated contractual rate, resulting in a substantial payment to BAe and this reliable performance has been maintained throughout the type's life. By 1991 the Hawk fleet had amassed 300,000 hours and on 5th July 2006 the millionth hour had been flown. This heavy use led to several structural improvements; between 1988 and 1995 144 aircraft received new Mk.50 export-standard wings and from 2000 the Fuselage Replacement Programme refitted 80 aircraft with new Mk.60 centre and rear fuselages to extend the fatigue life beyond 10,000 hours.

In 1988 the Hawk design office and initial production moved to the former Blackburn works Brough and in 1992 Dunsfold was closed and all final production stages moved to Brough with the wing attachment and final assembly stages at Warton. Although Brough's airfield was made operational again in 2008 to allow Hawks to be flown to Warton, final assembly soon returned to Warton. With the introduction of the more advanced T.2 (see below), the final T.1s and T.1As serve on with No 100 Squadron and 736 Naval Air Squadron in the target facilities and threat simulation role as 'Red Force' aggressor aircraft and flying targets as well as for Joint Tactical Air Controller training. The most famous Hawks of course are those used by the *Red Arrows*. Having been formed on the Gnat T.1, Treasury approval in 1974 to continue funding the team beyond 1977 included a commitment to re-equip with fifteen Hawks in 1979 – interestingly the team's requirements had been considered during the design phase as far back as 1969! The *Red Arrows* began type familiarisation in April 1979; XX253 was the first aircraft delivered to Kemble on 29th August and XX251 underwent aerobatic testing at the Aeroplane and Armament Experimental Establishment at Boscombe Down. Thirteen aircraft were assigned for the 1980 season, including XX227 which had been used to trial the smoke generator installation at Dunsfold. The engine was upgraded to the 5,200lbf (23.1kN) Adour Mk.151-01 with a modified fuel system for a faster throttle response time. Many of the Hawks have had long careers with the *Red Arrows*, but nine aircraft have been lost in accidents. Current plans are to maintain the current Hawk T.1s until at least 2030 but there is uncertainty over what will replace them.

Exports had been at the core of the technical requirements from the very beginning and the Hawk has been continually marketed and developed for export customers. Alongside the RAF Hawk T.1s a private venture batch of 24 airframes were laid down, eight of which went to Zimbabwe. By April 1981 deliveries had already been completed to Indonesia and Kenya and Finland was receiving four complete aircraft along with 46 kits for assembly by Valmet. The stiffest competition was from Dassault and its Alpha Jet and the Middle East was a key market to break into. BAe funded the improved Mk.60 for Middle Eastern buyers with a more powerful Adour 861, provision for AIM-9 Sidewinders, drop tank capability, a tail braking parachute and better avionics. At that time BAe had little enthusiasm for a single-seat Hawk which would need a minimum of 50 sales to make it viable. A long-running proposal to licence-build up to 150 Hawks in Iraq under the SA'AD 25 project, possibly leading to production of the Hawk-derived P.1125 fighter, came to nothing, but Saudi Arabia was the key to topple the Middle Eastern market away from the Alpha Jet. Dassault was offering lower support costs but BAe redoubled its efforts and were rewarded with orders from Saudi Arabia, the United Arab Emirates and Kuwait totalling 91 aircraft and these were later followed by 22 Series 100 aircraft for the United Arab Emirates and Oman, the latter also receiving twelve Mk.208 single-seat fighters. Other Mk.60 sales included Switzerland and South Korea. No previous British trainer had ever been so successful in so many markets.

The new Hawk T.1 alongside its fast-jet flying training brethren; the Hunter T.7, Jet Provost T.5 and Gnat T.1. This collection of aircraft shows a variety of aerodynamic layouts and the switch from side-by-side to tandem seating. The Gnat looks particularly small compared to its contemporaries. *Blue Envoy Collection*

For export purposes British Aerospace cleared a wide range of stores for use on the five weapon hardpoints. One of the weapons cleared by 1981 was the BAe Sea Eagle anti-ship missile, a dummy of which is seen here carried on the ventral hardpoint on Hawk T.1 XX258 belonging to the Tactical Weapons Unit. *Author's Collection*

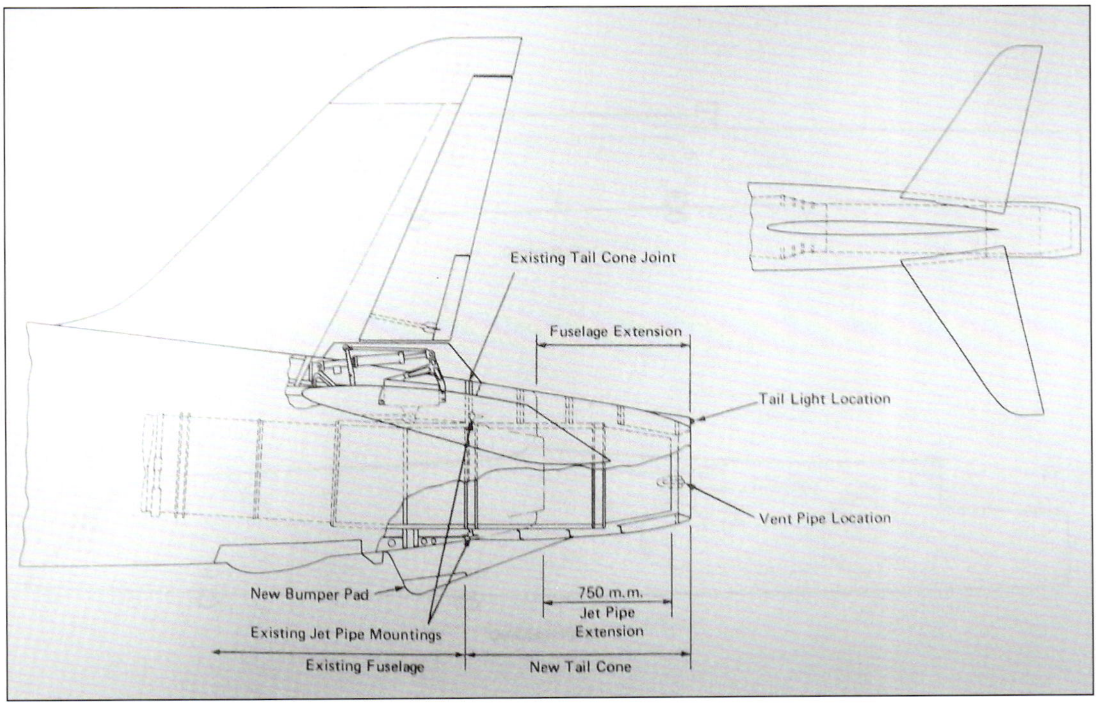

Plans for the cancelled Hawk T.2 with weapons capability included an extended tailpipe to reduce the threat from Soviet shoulder-fired SAMs such as the SA-7 *Grail*. The result was a slight loss of thrust in return for increased protection from IR-seekers. *Brooklands Museum*

The Hawk Gains Talons

Development of the Hawk has continued since its inception. Early proposals to use the Hawk T.1 for radar calibration with improved Decca Mk.19 navigation equipment and a pod-mounted radar augmentation device to increase the radar signature were not taken up due to the expensive modification cost of £90,000 per aircraft. A proposal to use the Hawk for the target facilities role was also rejected because it could not tow targets, unlike the Canberras then in use.

The first RAF armed Hawk was the proposed T.2 of 1975 with a wartime strike role. The T.2 was a T.1 brought up to Mk.50 export standard with an improved gunsight, a ventral 30mm ADEN cannon pod and modified pylons for four BL755 cluster bombs or two Sidewinders and two BL755s or Matra rocket pods. The Adour would be re-rated to provide 30 minutes of maximum thrust. Another interesting modification was the provision of a 29.5in (75cm) longer jet pipe to reduce the chance of a heat-seeking missile jamming the tailplane – or at worst hitting the aircraft – based on experience from Vietnam and recent Yom Kippur War against the Soviet SA-7 *Grail* shoulder-fired surface-to-air missile. The extension would reduce the angle the tailpipe could be externally seen by an infra-red missile seeker by 45° at the cost of a slight 13lbf (57Nm) loss of thrust and 0.25 percent greater fuel consumption. Initial plans to convert 60 or even all 175 T.1s were reduced by 1979 to eight T.2s as part of an order for eighteen additional Hawks and ten conversions. In peacetime they would serve with the TWUs at Brawdy and Chivenor. The order was postponed in 1980 to 1985 but was never placed.

Thoughts of using the Hawk as a secondary air defence asset were not far-fetched. In this photograph a Hawk T.1 of the TWU on detachment to Cyprus is seen escorting a Soviet Ilyushin Il-38 *May* maritime patrol aircraft over the Mediterranean during the early 1980s. *Blue Envoy Collection*

Rather than gain dedicated armed Hawks, during the production run a decision was reached that some aircraft would be delivered for the pure flying training role, this being facilitated by the removal of the aircraft's weapons control boxes. The capability to refit these boxes was maintained and these airframes were designated by the RAF as the T.1W.

Not long after the demise of the T.2, the T.1A was developed as a standby point defence fighter equipped with the ADEN pod and two outer pylons for Sidewinders. A total of 88 conversion kits were supplied from January 1983 and were mainly issued to the TWU, 72 of them being declared to NATO and if the Cold War had turned hot they would have been flown by instructors and paired with Panavia Tornado ADV interceptors which would use their AI.24 Foxhunter radars to guide the Hawks to their targets. Alongside two standard Hawk T.1s, the Empire Test Pilots School received one modified Hawk as the Advanced System Training Aircraft (ASTRA), which was converted by the Cranfield College of Aeronautics in 1986. This replaced the School's Beagle B.206 Basset CC.1 aircraft and was equipped with a digital variable-stability simulator able to give the Hawk different handling characteristics to mimic different aircraft.

Upgraded Hawk T.1A XX221 seen here sports the new air defence grey camouflage that adorned the NATO-declared reserve interceptor fleet operated by the TWU. On the wing pylons are Air Combat Manoeuvring Instrumentation (ACMI) pods used for tracking the aircraft during aerial combat training and recording in-flight data for subsequent analysis. *Author's Collection*

The ventral pod fitted to the Hawk contains a 30mm ADEN Mk.4 cannon and 120 rounds of ammunition. *Author's Collection*

At the sharp end. The drogue target has been the main method of gunnery training for at least a century. Here Hawk T.1W XX289 of No 63 (Reserve) Squadron, part of No 2 TWU is engaged on gunnery practice against a drogue, using its 30mm ADEN Mk.4 gun pod. The gun shows no sign of losing its importance in aerial warfare. *Blue Envoy Collection*

Alongside two standard Hawk T.1s, the Empire Test Pilots School had its third Hawk T.1, XX341, modified by the Cranfield College of Aeronautics in 1986 as the Advanced System Training Aircraft (ASTRA). The aircraft was equipped with a digital variable-stability simulator able to give the Hawk the ability to mimic the different handling characteristics of different aircraft. *Blue Envoy Collection*

The Hawk Evolves

Although not used by the RAF mention must be made of further export developments as they would feed into further improvements to the RAF fleet. The first major development was the T-45A Goshawk developed for the US Navy's VTXTS advanced carrier-capable trainer. BAe teamed up with McDonnell Douglas against variants of the Dassault/Dornier Alpha Jet, Aermacchi MB.339 as well as designs from General Dynamics, Rockwell, Ling-Temco-Vought, Fairchild and Northrop. The design was based on that of the Mk.60 but changes included; revised control surfaces and airbrakes, a larger tailplane and tail fin, a modified wing with leading-edge slats, structural strengthening for a 14,400 hour fatigue life and a stronger undercarriage and an arrester hook. A more powerful 5,854lbf (26kN) Adour 871 (known in US service as the F405-RR-401) was fitted. The BAe/McDonnell Douglas team were announced the winners on 18 November 1981 and full scale development began in 1984 with the first of two prototypes, BuNo 162787, flying on 16th April 1988. The first carrier landing aboard the USS *John F. Kennedy* occurred on 4th December 1991 but development delays meant that the first US Navy students only began training on 11th February 1994 with the first solo achieved on 23rd March. Avionics updates with a modern 'glass' cockpit known as 'Cockpit 21' were delivered from October 1996 and the last of 174 aircraft (300 had originally been planned) was completed in 2003. A land-based T-45B was offered to the USAF and for export, but without success.

The Hawk saw off the Alpha Jet and several US rivals to win the US Navy's VTXTS programme in 1981. This artist's impression of the T-45TS (as then it was then designated) is from 1984. The first prototype would not fly until 16th April 1988. *Author's Collection*

This photograph of T-45C Goshawk BuNo. 165641 of Training Air Wing 2 at Naval Air Station Kingsville, Texas, shows several of the design changes from the Hawk. These include the twin-wheel nose undercarriage with catapult strut, full span leading-edge slats, relocated airbrakes under the tail, arrester hook, a single enlarged ventral fin and tailplane canard vanes ('SMURFs') to prevent stalling of the horizontal tailplane. *Lt. Michelle Tucker/ US Navy*

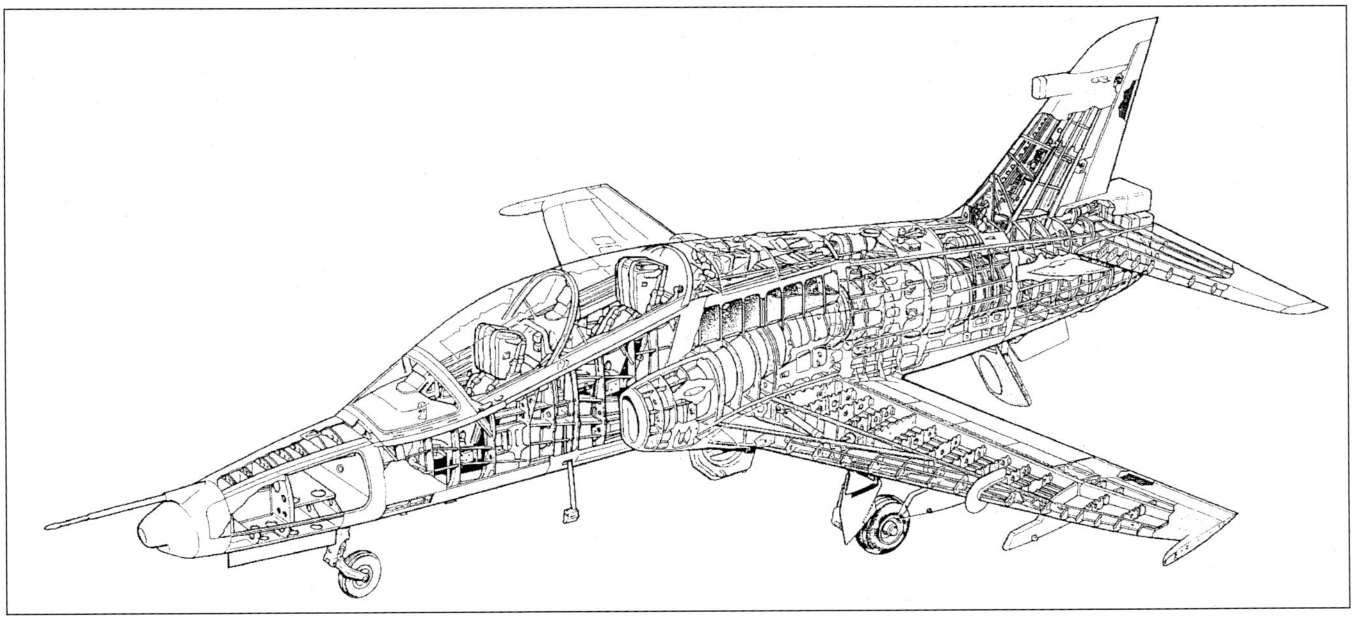

The Hawk 100 boasted several improvements over the original design. The obvious changes on this cutaway drawing are the extended nose with space for a laser rangefinder or FLIR and the wingtip rails for Sidewinder AAMs. Less obvious is the new cambered wing leading-edge and the modern cockpit avionics. *Via Chris Farara*

The Series 50 and Series 60 export aircraft were further developed into the Series 100 with a 5,990lbf (26.6kN) Adour 871, a cambered wing leading-edge, modern cockpit avionics including the first colour CRT displays in a military aircraft, laser inertial navigation (the first in a British military aircraft), provision for a laser rangefinder or FLIR in the nose and new wing tip rails for Sidewinders – which had been partially developed by the Swiss company F&W as part of the Hawk Mk.66 deal with that nation. The demonstrator G-HAWK was converted and flew as the Series 100 demonstrator on 1st October 1987. Given the enhanced combat capability, BAe carried out further stalling tests in all operational configurations and spinning tests in the air defence configurations. Interestingly the Hawk 100 saw its FLIR put into operational use before the Tornado. The Hawk 100 was further developed during the 1990s as a Lead-In Fighter Trainer (LIFT) with modern LCD cockpit displays, avionics like the terrain-matching Ground Proximity Warning System and Traffic Collision Avoidance uprated Adour engines. A new wing with a fixed drooped leading-edge to improve lift at high speeds was married to modified forward and centre fuselage sections with a 12,000 hour structural safe life and the empennage was also modified. In June 1997 the RAAF ordered 33 LIFT Mk.127, 21 of which were built in Australia and which since 2014 have been modified to Mk.128 standard. South Africa selected the LIFT Mk.120 in December 1999 with a 6,500lbf (28.9kN) Adour Mk.951, which has digital engine controls from the Eurojet EJ200 as fitted to the Eurofighter Typhoon. India and Saudi Arabia also purchased LIFT Hawks in deals which split the order between UK and local production lines for the Mk.132 and Mk.165 respectively, the latter having the Adour Mk.951. Bahrain received six Mk.129 during 2006-07 which were based on the Mk.127.

The Hawk 100 was further developed into a lightweight fighter. Despite the earlier reluctance to develop a single-seater, it was decided to in June 1984 to use the 100 Series as the basis of the Hawk 200. The prototype, ZG200, first flew on 19th May 1986 but was lost on its 43rd flight eight weeks later due to G-induced loss of consciousness, killing test pilot Jim Hawkins. Two more demonstrators were built, ZH200 which flew on 24th April 1987 and ZJ201 which followed on 13th February 1992, was fitted with full avionics and Westinghouse APG-66H multi-mode radar. Oman ordered a dozen in July 1990 and the first was delivered in 1993 and Indonesia and Malaysia brought the order book up to 46. The use of twin-store carriers allowed up to eleven weapons to be carried up to a total weight of 6,800lb (3,084kg) and the fuselage was modified to allow the fitting of two internal 30mm ADEN Mk.4 or 27mm Mauser BK27 cannon, although no buyer has specified these. The Hawk 200 had the distinction of being the last indigenous British-built fighter, albeit one not used by British forces.

In May 1986 BAe met with the MoD to discuss future Hawk requirements ranging from building attrition replacement aircraft, rebuilding programmes for life extension, the supply of Hawk 200 as a target facilities aircraft, fitting radar pods to enable the T.1A to be used for navigator/weapon systems operator training, fitting modern reconnaissance systems from the Tornado GR.1A and even modifying the type with in-flight refuelling as a replacement for the Blackburn Buccaneer in the maritime strike role. By 1989 BAe Brough was working on the Hawk 2000, a further development of the Series 100 to the needs of 1994-2000 as a stepping stone to a new design for the 21st Century.

The Hawk 100 and 200 were designed to be capable of multirole combat. Here at Farnborough a large array of dummy weaponry is on display, among them BAe's ALARM anti-radar ASM, Active Skyflash AAM, both of which were in development in the late 1980s and the tail of a Sea Eagle anti-ship missile can also be seen. *Author's Collection*

The new Rolls-Royce RTM.543-49 would be used with 25 percent more thrust than the Adour 871. A rear fuselage extension would improve balance and increase fuel capacity and a new wing would provide high lift and improved high subsonic handling and supersonic capability. As early as 1984 studies had begun for a supersonic 'High Speed' Hawk with a thin wing, reminiscent of the 'thin wing' Hunter and Javelin projects of the 1950s. Modern cockpit avionics and sensors would enable use of simulated virtual sensors and training in Beyond-Visual-Range missile attacks and electronic warfare. The Hawk 2000 could be armed with modern AIM-132 ASRAAM and AIM-120 AMRAAM AAMs for anti-helicopter and air defence roles and ASMs such as the NATO Modular Stand Off Weapon programme then in development for the close air support.

Another interesting proposal was to convert a standard Hawk T.1 with a supine seating position on a non-ejecting fixed reclined couch as part of the High Acceleration Cockpit programme connected with the development of a new fighter to AST.403 – work that would lead to the Agile Combat Aircraft, the Experimental Aircraft Programme (EAP) and the Eurofighter Typhoon. The new seat was reclined by 45° and would be in the forward cockpit, some of the controls would be repositioned to enable the pilot to reach them, the main penalty was a reduced 11° view over the nose. The BAe test pilots were willing to fly such an aircraft, but following static rig trials, the disadvantages of the highly reclined position outweighed the benefits and the EAP received a less substantial angle of recline.

The Hawk 2000 was a late 1980s concept of a modernised Hawk 100 for the 21st Century. Some of these desired improvements would be seen in the 120 LIFT-series of the 1990s. *Brooklands Museum*

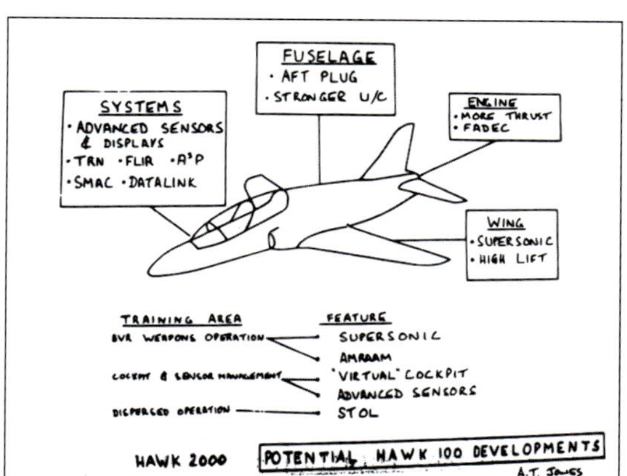

The 45° reclined seat would have required repositioned controls and a modified instrument panel, the opportunity being taken to introduce some digital multi-function displays. *Brooklands Museum*

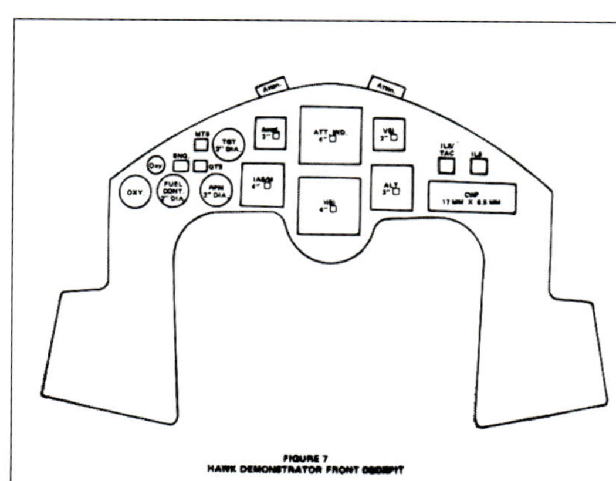

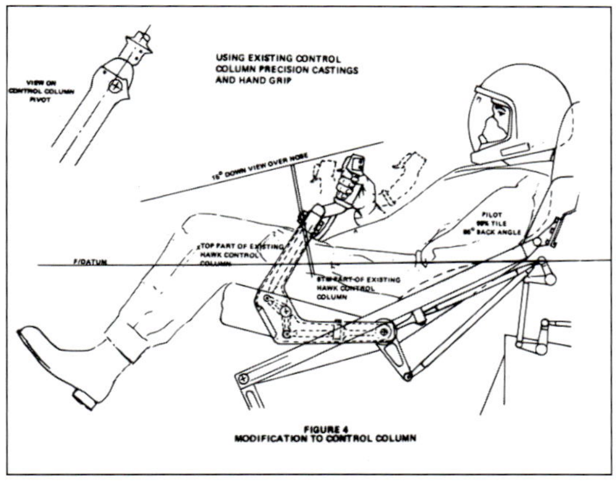

The Hawk was considered as a technology demonstrator for the High Acceleration Cockpit programme as part of researched linked to AST.403 for a new fighter. The new non-ejecting seat would be reclined by 45° and fitted in the forward cockpit. BAe's test pilots were willing to fly such an aircraft, but static rig trials revealed that the highly reclined position had too many disadvantages. *Brooklands Museum*

Hawk T.2: The Next Generation

At the turn of the century the MoD had begun looking at future training requirements and in 2001 BAE Systems – as BAe had now become – made an unsolicited proposal to supply the latest Series 100 LIFT to replace the T.1. Avionics and weapons systems had progressed a long way since the T.1s introduction in 1976 and students now needed to learn skills in enhanced situational and tactical awareness and gaining experience with modern digital 'glass' cockpits, sensors and smart weapons in order to progress to modern fighters like the Eurofighter Typhoon and Lockheed Martin F-35 Lightning. The MoD released its requirements for an Advanced Jet Trainer (AJT) in 2001 with a proposed in service date of August 2008. BAE Systems offered the Mk.128 based on the LIFT Mk.127 developed for the RAAF with an open architecture mission computer, sensor and weapon simulation equipment, a TCAS II Traffic alert and Collision Avoidance System and the Adour Mk.951 from the South African LIFT Mk.120. A potential deal worth £1 billion for up to 31 Hawk Mk.128 was soon in jeopardy, however. The MoD wanted a Private Finance Initiative deal, buying 11,000 flying hours annually and letting BAE Systems take on the development costs and risks, something the company was understandably not keen to do. Baulking at the high quoted prices, the MoD and the Treasury wanted to evaluate a cheaper bid from Alenia Aermacchi for the new M-346 Master (which had not then flown). The Chancellor of the Exchequer, Gordon Brown, lost however against the Prime Minister, Tony Blair, and the Minister of Defence, Geoff Hoon, who wanted to award the contract to BAE Systems to save Brough from closure and because of the Hawk's export potential, in particular the large Mk.132 contract from India. A revised deal of £800 million for 44 aircraft was still expensive, but on 30th July 2003 the Hawk was selected. A £158 million design and development contract was awarded on 22nd December 2004 for two T.2 aircraft; ZK010 making its maiden flight eight weeks ahead of schedule on 27th July 2005 with BAE System Chief Test Pilot Paul Hopkins and Hawk Deputy Project Pilot Peter Wilson aboard. The second aircraft, ZK011 followed on 6th June 2006. On 19th October 2006, a production contract was placed for another 26 T.2 aircraft, but an option for 24 more was not taken up.

HAWK TIMELINE

1960

AUG 1968 Hawker Siddeley Kingston designs SP.117-1

NOV 1969 Hawker Siddeley has abortive talks with MBB

1970

JAN 1970 BAC-Macchi AA-107 agreement lapses

JUL 1970 RAF decides Jaguar B will not be an advanced trainer

OCT 1970 AST.397 issued and submissions received

NOV 1970 AST.397 revised and improved tenders submitted

OCT 1971 HS.1182AT selected over BAC P.59

MAR 1972 175 HS.1182AT ordered

AUG 1973 Hawk name annouced

AUG 1974 First Hawk makes maiden flight

MAY 1976 First flight of Hawk Mk.50 export variant demonstrator

NOV 1976 Hawk T.1 enters service

AUG 1979 *Red Arrows* receive their first Hawk T.1

1980

NOV 1981 BAe/McDonnell Douglas team wins VTXTS with T-45

MAY 1986 First flight of Hawk 200

OCT 1987 First flight of Hawk 100

APR 1988 First flight of T-45A Goshawk

2000

AUG 2003 Hawk T.1 structural upgrade programme completed

JUL 2003 MoD selects Hawk Mk.128 LIFT as Hawk T.2

JUL 2005 First flight of Hawk T.2

JUL 2006 RAF Hawk T.1 fleet amasses 1 million flying hours

AUG 2008 Hawk T.2 enters service

2010

SEP 2010 Hawk Mk.128 LIFT unsuccessfully offered for USAF T-X requirement

FEB 2017 Advanced Hawk displayed at Aero India

JUN 2017 First flight of Advanced Hawk

DEC 2020 End of Hawk production at Brough

Service release was obtained on schedule on 30th August 2008 and Valley received its first aircraft in April 2009, No 19 (Reserve) Squadron (redesignated No IV (Reserve) Squadron in November 2012), using T.1s until full operational capability was achieved. The powerful mission computer and software is the key element of the Hawk T.2. It can simulate sensors such as radar and radar warning receivers, the deployment of chaff and flares, firing of guns and the release of bombs and missiles and can even provide realistic ground threats. The whole mission can be de-briefed and analysed using computers after the flight by the student and instructor. The first Operational Capability 2 software update was released in 2010, the software being developed alongside a new training syllabus. Since it is software based, the system is easily reconfigurable and updateable and does not rely on 'real' sensors that can fail or require maintenance. The seven weapons hardpoints can carry a wide range of stores including AAMs, BDU-33 practice bombs and Paveway laser-guided bombs. BAE Systems as a contractor under the UK Military Flying Training System looks set to maintain the T.2 for RAF use until at least the mid-2030s.

The Hawk LIFT/AJT was a sales success and in September 2010 was proposed for the USAF's T-X requirement to replace the Northrop T-38 Talon, but failed to reach the final round of the selection process. During 2011 a navalised Mk.132 variant for the Indian Navy was briefly considered and the AJT was also marketed to Japan in 2012. The same year Oman ordered eight AJT Mk.166 based on the Mk.128 as part of a deal for twelve Typhoons and in 2018 Qatar concluded a similar deal for nine Hawks and 24 Typhoons. In October 2020 the possibility of a joint RAF-Qatar Emiri Air Force squadron was raised, mirroring the formation of No 12 Squadron at Coningsby which provides training to Qatari Typhoon pilots and ground crew. Sales negotiations with Kuwait to replace its older Mk.64s as part of the BAE Systems-run Air Training College ended without success, however, in 2019. In June 2020 BAE Systems and the Australian Defence Department completed a major structural testing programme on the Hawk Mk.127 to achieve clearance for up to 50,000 flying hours, five times the current limit and potentially extending the life of the Hawk LIFT family into the 2040s.

Further development of the AJT led to the Advanced Hawk as a joint venture with Hindustan Aeronautics Limited. Improvements include improved cockpit displays and a BAE LiteHUD head-up display, increased weapons capability and a radar warning receiver. The main change is a new wing, giving the Hawk an improved turning rate, high angle-of-attack capability and take-off and landing performance. A single demonstrator, ZJ951, was built and displayed at the Aero India show in Bengaluru in February 2017 before its first flight on 7th June from Warton. BAE Systems estimates that up to 300 Advanced Hawks may be sold but at the time of writing neither the RAF or the Indian Air Force have shown any interest and after 104 years of operation Brough ceased aircraft manufacture in December 2020 with the completion of the Qatari order. For nearly fifty years the Hawk has more than vindicated Hawker Siddeley's original plan back in 1968 for a cheap but capable trainer aimed at the export market and has trained over 20,000 pilots worldwide so far.

The Hawk has served with No 4 FTS at Valley on Anglesey since 1976 and looks set to continue its association with the type until at least the mid-2030s. Two Hawk T.2s are seen here, ZK032 and ZK025, both equipped with ACMI pods on the wingtip rails. *MoD/Open Government Licence, 2010*

9 The Bulldog and Tucano

'The Bulldog effect is to train effectively.'
Scottish Aviation advertisement

'It would now prove cost effective to replace the Jet Provost with a more modern aircraft type.'
Air Force Board paper, April 1983

'You will be aware of considerable public interest which is already focused on the subject of the basic trainer and consequently there are a number of political issues which are likely to influence Ministers views and decisions in directions which are not necessarily predictable.'
I H Johnston, DCA, to the Vice Chief of the Air Staff, August 1983

The de Havilland Canada Chipmunk T.10 had a long life, indeed the RAF Battle of Britain Memorial Flight still uses it today to convert pilots to tailwheel undercarriage aircraft. By the 1970s the Chipmunk was still capable of teaching students the basics of flight in the air experience role, but it was becoming outdated in terms of avionics, was draughty and its tandem seating was less suitable for ab initio training. A suitable replacement was on hand in the Beagle Bulldog, but it was a lucky survivor of the collapse of its designer and as the Scottish Aviation Bulldog would faithfully provide air experience for nearly 30 years. Originally intended to replace the Percival Jet Provost, the Hawker Siddeley Hawk T.1 on its introduction in 1976 replaced the Folland Gnat T.1 but supplanted rather than replaced the Jet Provost. The Jet Provost was more suited to the basic flying syllabus and soldiered on until the limits of structural fatigue and service life would allow. The replacement for the 1990s would prove to be a politically controversial decision, but the Shorts Tucano T.1 was an effective trainer over the next thirty years. Together the Bulldog and the Tucano would admirably fulfil the vital roles of basic flying training to form the bedrock of the pilot training syllabus.

A Pup is Born

In 1960 Peter Masefield – the former Chief Executive of British European Airways – decided to act on his dream of winning back Britain's share of the light aircraft market from the mighty American manufacturers Beech, Cessna and Piper. Finding his fellow directors at Bristol Aircraft decidedly lukewarm about his ideas, he found financial backing from Pressed Steel Limited and in October created British Executive and General Aviation Limited – BEAGLE.

The Scottish Aviation Bulldog was a modern looking aircraft that had inherited the good handling and performance of its Beagle Pup predecessor. Today many ex-Service Bulldogs are enjoyed by private owners. Bulldog T.1 XX514 was the second production Model 121 aircraft for the RAF and was just four months old when photographed with the CFS at Little Rissington on 18th June 1973. It had previously been used for handling trials at the A&AEE. In 1976 it was involved in CA release trials for inverted flight. While in use with the Royal Navy EFTS it struck a tree during a simulated forced landing near Thirsk in September 1986 and was struck off charge. *Bob Woonough*

Not long afterwards Rolls-Royce agreed a licence deal with the American manufacturer Continental for suitable piston engines. The subsequent fortunes of Beagle were not good. A mix of poor business decisions, personal feuds, technocratic tinkering and an uphill battle for sales in the face of complete American dominance resulted in Beagle becoming nationalised under the Ministry of Technology (Mintech) in 1966 and then collapsing in December 1969 when the government refused to keep the ailing company afloat.

The Beagle B.121 Pup was designed as a sports aircraft and a trainer. Being stressed for aerobatics up to +4.4g made the airframe overweight and uneconomic to produce but it had excellent flying characteristics. The prototype G-AVDF first flew on 8th April 1967. In April 1969 it flew with a Lycoming IO-360 engine as part of the B.125 Bulldog development programme. G-AVDF has recently been restored to airworthiness. *Beagle*

Beagle's business plan envisioned a range of civilian aircraft from twin-engined executive aircraft like the B.206 to two-seater single-engine sports aircraft. In 1964 design work began on the B.121 Pup (given the company's name it was inevitable that its products bore the names of canine breeds) under the design leadership of John Larroucau. The Pup was designed to be suitable for flying schools and private-owner touring with a wide cockpit for side-by-side seats and, unusually for its class, stressed for aerobatics up to +4.4g, which made the airframe overweight and uneconomic to produce. Its main advantage was its very pleasant flying characteristics. The Pup would form a family of designs, including the military B.121T Pup Major based on the two-seat B.121C but swapping the 100hp (74.5kW) Continental O-200 engine for a 160hp (119kW) Continental O-300 and featuring a larger sliding bubble canopy. The B.121M would have a 210hp (156kW) engine and clipped wings for improved aerobatic capability. Beagle also planned to fit a device that simulated twin-engine handling and asymmetric power handling to enable multi-engine students to be trained.

The B.121T was also aimed at the College of Air Training at Hamble who, like the RAF, wanted to replace its Chipmunks. A full scale mock-up was built and further refinements altered the engine to the 150hp (111kW) Continental O-320. Mintech's focus was making Beagle profitable and they decided that the best course of action was to develop the standard Pup-100 civil aircraft first. In March 1968 Beagle presented to Mintech the Series 4 Pup-180 with a 180hp (134kW) Continental O-360 engine and a revised wing with a retractable undercarriage. The Pup-180 also formed the basis of the military B.123 with a 200hp (149kW) engine, an increased span wing with increased centre-section chord, full aerobatic capability including larger anti-spin strakes, larger tailplanes and a ventral fin, increased flap deflection and a bubble canopy. Later the retractable undercarriage was abandoned. Needing launch funding of around £660,000 the Pup-180 had been abandoned by December.

In March 1968, the Aeroplane and Armament Experimental Establishment (A&AEE) at Boscombe Down carried out a preview assessment of Pup-150 G-AVLN, and was impressed with the handling and performance. The RAF was also interested in the Victa Airtourer 150 as a Chipmunk replacement and in October the A&AEE flew a comparative trial against G-AVLN. The Airtourer's major failing was an inability to spin, the aircraft simply going into a tight spiral dive with increasing speed that risked structural damage. The Army Air Corps also evaluated G-AVLN in February 1969 at Middle Wallop and considered it ideal to replace its Chipmunks.

In January 1971, about a year after the collapse of Beagle, Peter Smith of the Ministry of Aviation Supply assessed the remaining uncompleted Pups to see if they could be completed for the RAF for the Air Experience Flights (AEF) providing flights to Air Cadets and possibly the University Air Squadrons (UAS). The RAF had been looking at powered gliders but these were affected by poor weather conditions and were less likely to enthuse the young cadets. There were 21 uncompleted Pup-150s at Shoreham plus a dozen Pup-100s which could be converted, six virtually complete aircraft at Radlett and 20 sets of parts at Prestwick. The RAF could obtain 59 Pups for £6,210 each on a ministry-to-ministry transfer deal as long as Scottish Aviation Limited, who had acquired the Pup rights, agreed to undertake the work. The MoD decided to complicate matters by requesting cost estimates to refurbish the Chipmunks as well as data on all suitable single-engine aircraft and quotations for powered gliders. Chipmunk modernisation could cost between £7,500-14,000 for each aircraft and the Sportavia RF5 and Scheibe Falke motor gliders would cost £4,800-6,000 and £3,758 respectively. It was discovered that one in seven air experience flights exceeded 4.5g but the Pup was only stressed to 4.4g, so a g-meter would have to be fitted. Scottish Aviation looked at improvements to the doors and brakes and using Bulldog parts to create a 'Bullpup', but frustrated with the MoD's delay in making up its mind, the Receivers began selling off the Pups and others were broken up at Prestwick for spares. The powered glider did not enter service with the AEFs, but 40 Slingsby T61 Ventures, a licence-built Falke, equipped thirteen Volunteer Gliding Schools from 1977, providing air experience to Air Cadets until 1990.

Scottish Aviation Bulldog T.1 XX665 of the Edinburgh UAS at its Turnhouse home on 30th May 1980. XX665 spent most of its life in Scotland until it was damaged in a forced landing following a loss of power on 20th September 1997. It was not repaired and became an instructional airframe. Today it is a cockpit simulator at Wellesbourne Mountford. *Derek Heley*

The Pup Grows into a Bulldog

The RAF had already shown interest in the Pup but it was Sweden's requirements that would drive the evolution of the Pup into the B.125 Bulldog. Sales Manager Alexander Gunn had taken G-AVLN to Sweden in November 1968 for an assessment as an ab initio trainer, the Royal Swedish Air Force writing their specification around a stronger Pup stressed for +6g/-3g aerobatics. The resulting B.125 married the 33ft 3in (10.13m) span Pup-180 wing with a modified Pup-150 fuselage with a sliding bubble canopy and a 200hp (149kW) Avco Lycoming IO-360-AIC engine. On 12th June 1969 Sweden ordered 58 trainers for the Air Force with an option for 45 for the Army in the short take-off and landing reconnaissance role armed with two Bofors Bantam anti-tank missiles at the wingtips. Almost immediately two more orders were received, the Foreign Office Aid Budget funding eight Bulldogs for Zambia and Kenya ordered five, bringing the order book to over £1 million. A Pup airframe was converted into the prototype, G-AXEH, which made its maiden flight at Shoreham on 19th May 1969 flown by chief test pilot John 'Pee Wee' Judge and flight test observer David Cummings. Preliminary flight testing had been completed by November, shortly before the collapse of Beagle. On 24th November 'Pee Wee' Judge and Bill Greenwood demonstrated the Bulldog to the Central Flying School's (CFS) Examining Wing at Little Rissington, one of whose officers was writing the new training syllabus around the Bulldog. The aircraft impressed the CFS examiners with its handling and ability to fly aerobatics with a full fuel load. The next day CFS and Red Arrows member, Squadron Leader Dunn of the Royal Australian Air Force, made another assessment at Shoreham, followed three days later by another by an Iraqi Air Force Chief Flying Instructor.

Bulldog T.1 XX702 of the Edinburgh UAS at Turnhouse on 30th May 1980. Behind is its predecessor, a Chipmunk T.10. In 1993 XX702 went to the CFS before being shared by No 7 AEF and East Midlands UAS, ending its service with the Liverpool/Manchester UAS in March 2001. Today it flies in private ownership as G-CBCR. *Derek Heley*

The collapse of Beagle threatened the Bulldog programme. Mintech's decision to declare Beagle bankrupt aborted talks with the American manufacturer Ling-Temco-Vought and Beagle was handed over to the Receivers to sell either as a going concern or piecemeal. The Bulldog purchasers were not happy, especially the Swedish Air Force who had faced intense public criticism from SAAB for not buying their MFI-15, which was technically inferior and more expensive – although Beagle had agreed a substantially undercut price to secure the sale. The Swedish government demanded the aircraft and threatened to cancel military orders from the UK worth £15 million. Although the Foreign Office was paying the bill, Zambia cancelled its orders for Bulldogs and Shorts Skyvans and they brought nine SIAI-Marchetti SF.206SMs instead as Zambia turned to Italian technical assistance for its air force. Prospective customer Thailand also went for the SF.206. Strong political pressure managed to save the Kenyan order and that for BAC Strikemasters. Scottish Aviation Limited had suffered from the collapse of Handley Page earlier in 1969 which had halted the Jetstream executive aircraft programme and they saw the Bulldog as a lifeline and acquired the Bulldog and Pup rights for £175,000, forming Scottish Aviation (Bulldog) Limited (SABL) and receiving £493,236 from Sweden's compensation payment from Mintech. The second prototype, G-AXIG, was completed and flown on 14th February 1971 as the programme restarted. Sales tours of Canada, Chile, Europe, the Middle East and Africa and were rewarded by an order in May 1971 worth £320,000 from the Royal Malaysian Air Force for fifteen Bulldogs. Further orders came from Ghana, Jordan, Lebanon, Hong Kong and Botswana.

What SABL really wanted was an order from the RAF. The RAF wanted the Bulldog and the A&AEE trials in February and May 1970 had gone well but the government refused to guarantee a future order. Not until 23rd November 1971 did the Chancellor of the Exchequer, Anthony Barber, confirm that an order would be placed. This was followed by contract KA/C/147 for 132 aircraft – the last two aircraft were later cancelled, however. On 15th August 1972 Air Staff Requirement ASR.401 was issued to cover the roles of primary pilot training for UAS graduate entrants and naval helicopter specialist pilots, primary instructor training at the CFS and miscellaneous roles within Strike Command and RAF Germany. SAL received Specification 282D&P for the Bulldog Series 100 Model 104 on 7th July 1972, specifying a maximum level speed of at least 124kt (230km/h), a continuous cruising speed of at least 110kt (204km/h), a rate of climb to reach 4,000ft (1,219m) within five minutes and 10,000ft (3,050m) within fourteen minutes. These RAF requirements and the need for improved structural strength resulted in the Series 120 Bulldog T.1, the first aircraft XX513 flying on 30th January 1973. Four Bulldogs were used during A&AEE trials. The spinning trials found some reluctance to recover if the recovery was delayed, the Aircrew Manual being updated with this warning. A strake was also fitted over the flap leading edges to cure premature asymmetric airflow separation in the fully down position. After the trials XX513 was issued to the Southampton UAS. Soon deliveries were being made at the rate of six per week and the London UAS at Abingdon was the first to fully re-equip with the Bulldog.

Left: Bulldog T.1 XX536 of the East Lowlands UAS at Turnhouse in May 1975 with its upper engine cowling removed for maintenance, exposing its Lycoming IO-360-A1A engine. *Charles E MacKay*

Below: The Bulldog was reasonably successful in the export market but some potential customers never placed an order. In this promotional artwork the Bulldog appears in the colours of the Hellenic Air Force. *Scottish Aviation via Joe Cherrie*

Two Bulldogs of the Birmingham UAS resting in the spring sunshine at Cosford in May 1982. Like many Bulldogs, both XX671 (foreground) and XX670 were sold for civil use in 2001. The former is in the USA as N50UP and the latter resides in Sweden, serving as a source of spares. *Trevor Bartlett*

An underspend in the 1977/78 financial year saw an Air Staff study to buy additional Bulldogs for additional training or a scheme to increase pilot recruitment and general air mindedness. The Chipmunk, of which there were many surplus airframes, was deemed more effective for grading flights and with sufficient Bulldogs to last until 1995 the long-delayed Boeing Vertol CH-47 Chinook transport helicopters were purchased instead. Beginning to reach to end of their service lives in 1989 the Bulldogs were slowly retired, filtering down to the AEFs during the 1990s and the last being withdrawn by No 10 AEF at Woodvale in 2001. Many of these still fly today with private owners.

The Bulldog was further developed by SABL, but most of these projects remained on the drawing board. The four-seat Series 200 Stag had been developed in February 1971 and grew into a family of variants with fixed or retractable undercarriages and 260hp (193kW) or 300hp (223kW) engines as the Series 300. The military variants could be fitted with four underwing hardpoints. These designs were further developed into the military Bulldog Series 2100 alongside the civilian Bullfinch Series 2200. Ongoing Bulldog and Jetstream production delayed the programme and only the prototype Bullfinch, G-BDOG, was flown in 1976 but no military interest was received.

By the early 1970s tandem seating was once again in vogue for training aircraft and Scottish Aviation hoped that Model 440 Bullfinch would be attractive. This promotional artwork shows the Bullfinch armed with a couple of 68mm rocket pods, again being promoted in Hellenic Air Force colours. *Scottish Aviation via Joe Cherrie*

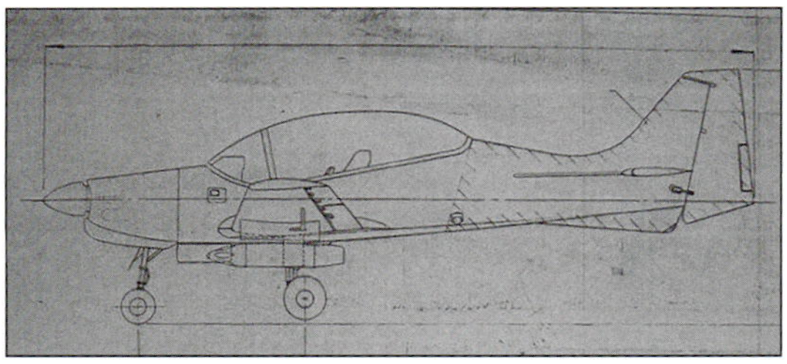

This side-view of the Model 440 shows the extent that the rear fuselage was carried over from the Bulldog. Sadly the lack of space for the rear cockpit and duplicated flying controls resulted in poor ergonomics for the instructor's legs. *Scottish Aviation via Joe Cherrie*

In 1973 the Series 3100 Stag two/three-seater trainer was drawn up with a retractable undercarriage and a 260hp (193kW) Lycoming IO-540, but again went no further. New Bulldog variants emerged in 1981 with the Series 420 with a retractable undercarriage and a 260hp (193kW) Lycoming IO-360 and the Series 440 with a modified fuselage with tandem seating inspired by the Embraer EMB-312 Tucano then being considered by the RAF. The short and wide cockpit entailed an unusual arrangement; the student's legs were astride the nosewheel gear but the instructor's cockpit had no room for rudder pedals or indeed the instructor's legs! The solution was to use the front cockpit side consoles to accommodate the instructor's rudder pedals and feet as well as mounting his flight instruments and a control stick. Altogether a very unusual and probably uncomfortable solution. The Series 440 was a stretch too far and was soon abandoned.

Chipmunk Upgrade

Although the RAF was settled with its training fleet during the 1970s, industry was still producing new private venture designs, some for export and others to hopefully attract the MoD's attention. The Chipmunk T.10 had not been entirely replaced by the Bulldog and numbers were still flown by AEFs and the Elementary Flying Training Squadron at Swinderby and the Naval Flying Grading Flight at Roborough would retain theirs until the early 1990s. In the late 1970s, Aero Bonner Limited had developed the 200hp (149kW) Super Sapphire V-6 engine based on a car engine and in 1979 converted Chipmunk G-ARWB, fitting a new water-cooled radiator under the rear fuselage. The aircraft was flown with the new engine on 2nd July 1979 and displayed at the SBAC Farnborough Show later that year, where it caught the interest of the RAF. A possible conversion programme by Rolls-Royce was investigated during 1980 but Rolls-Royce was divesting itself of its piston engine interests at that time and the MoD decided that the conversion was too expensive.

The West Country Hopeful

The most surprising birthplace of a potential Bulldog replacement was a department store. Mike Robertson, the millionaire owner of the West Country Trago Mills retail chain was a keen aviator and had financed the construction of Bodmin Airfield and the Whittaker MW2 ultralight aircraft designed by Mike Whittaker. Sydney A Holloway, who had worked at Fairey, Airwork and Edgar Percival, was later engaged to improve the MW2 but with Robertson's backing began a new aerobatic trainer working alongside an experienced design team and with Air Vice-Marshal Geoffrey Cairns, a former Commandant of Boscombe Down and a former Assistant Chief of the Air Staff (Operational Requirements) as test pilot.

The Trago Mills SAH-1 was a good performer and an attractive design but was hampered by a lack of manufacturing capacity to achieve any sales momentum. The prototype G-SAHI is seen here in its original colour scheme at the General Aviation Manufacturers and Traders Association exhibition at Cranfield in September 1983. *Bill Teasdale*

Partly aimed at replacing the RAF's Bulldogs, Holloway devised a cheap all-metal low-wing fixed undercarriage design powered by a 118hp (88kW) Lycoming O-235-L2A engine. The 4ft (1.21m) wide cockpit had a sliding bubble canopy and the airframe was stressed for aerobatics with a +6/-3g capability, a roll rate of 100° a second and could reach 5,000ft (1,524m) in under five minutes. The prototype SAH-1, G-SAHI, was flown from Bodmin Airfield by Cairns on 23rd August 1983. The SAH-1 was evaluated by Airwork, Hunting Aviation and British Aerospace's (BAe) Brough Division, who noted that with a 160hp (119kW) engine it would be a suitable replacement for the Bulldog and similar trainers such as the Cessna T-41 Mescalero with potential sales of 100 annually by 1990. Further development with a 200hp (149kW) engine would allow the use of four underwing hardpoints for machine gun pods, light bombs or six Matra F2 unguided rockets or it could be stretched into a four-seat civil aircraft. Robertson sought backers for production; a BAe offset manufacturing deal in Hungary connected with a BAe 146 feederliner purchase came to naught but Orca Aircraft acquired the project in 1988.

Orca went bankrupt the following year and the project was sold to FLS Aerospace, becoming the Club Spirit. The MoD then announced its plan to centralise and privatise elementary flying training at a new Joint Elementary Flying Training School at Topcliffe. Keen to bid, FLS developed the improved Sprint 160 and G-SAHI was modified with a 160hp (119kW) Textron Lycoming AEIO-320-D1B engine with a Hoffman constant-speed propeller. It first flew as the Sprint 160 on 8th April 1992. FLS lost the contract, however, to Hunting Aviation who had tendered the Slingsby T67M120 Firefly and of the initial production batch of five aircraft, only three were completed by 1998 and FLS went bankrupt. From then on plans for production have passed through several hands and remained stillborn. Currently John Edgley (famous for designing the distinctive Edgley Optica surveillance aircraft) has plans to market the type as a homebuilt kit aircraft. The SAH-1 was a bold attempt to break into the market. Pilots loved its handling and it was similar to the Slingsby T67 Firefly and the Grob G115, except for lacking their composite construction. Sadly, the lack of a substantial production and spares support organisation prevented any chance of success.

Firecracker

The Oil Shock in 1973 following the Yom Kippur War caused economic ripples across the world due to the huge increase in the price of oil. Air forces and airlines began searching for better fuel economy; for training that meant transferring more jet flying hours to more economical turboprops. Engine manufacturers also began developing small high-bypass turbofans to replace the previous generation of small turbojets like the Viper. The RAF had already decided its future trainers before the Oil Shock and was tied to the Jet Provost and the Hawk and the piston-powered Chipmunks and Bulldogs. Desmond Norman, one of the founders of Britten-Norman, foresaw that strained military budgets would require a low-cost trainer and founded NDN Aircraft Limited at Sandown on the Isle of Wight. Norman developed the NDN-1 Firecracker,

Desmond Norman having revolutionised the economical passenger light STOL aircraft with the Britten-Norman Islander, turned his attention to doing the same with the trainer market. The prototype Firecracker G-NDNI shows its modern stepped tandem cockpit to good effect. The reliance on a piston engine hampered potential sales, but the Turbo-Firecracker was already being planned. *Author's Collection*

a sleek low-wing monoplane of conventional all-metal construction with tandem seating and powered by a 260hp (193kW) Lycoming AE10-540 engine. It had a retractable undercarriage and an airbrake. The prototype G-NDNI first flew on 26th May 1977. In late February 1979 at NDN's request, CFS carried out an evaluation at NDN's site and at Leeming by CFS Chief Flying Instructors. The report by Air Commodore A W Fraser was glowing, describing the Firecracker as a leading contender in its class, having performance approaching that of the Jet Provost T.3A at 10,000ft (3,050m) and being perfect for aerobatics. Some minor improvements were highlighted to enable potential RAF use; improved stall warning, a higher rate of roll and a better equipped rear cockpit. NDN were already planning to fit a Lycoming LTP 101 turboprop and Fisher felt that this would make the Firecracker a perfect lead-in for the Hawk. But without any formal requirement at that time the matter rested.

Turbofan Versus Turboprop

By the mid-1970s competition from small jet and turboprop trainers was becoming strong and Scottish Aviation's thoughts turned to a 'Jet Bulldog'. This concept led to eight studies during 1974; Type 1 was a two/four-seat aircraft powered by unspecified 400lbf (1.77kN) turbojets; Type 2 was a two-seat trainer with side-by-side seating and a Turbomeca Marboré VI turbojet; Type 3 was a four-seater with a 285hp (212kW) Continental O-285B turbocharged piston engine; Type 4 had a turbocharged 300hp (223kW) Continental O-320; Type 5 had the O-320 powering a Dowty-Rotol ducted fan; Type 6 was a two-seat trainer with an unspecified 904lbf (4kN) turbofan; Type 7 was a two-seat trainer with a 1,289lbf (5.7kN) Lycoming AT170 turbojet and finally the Type 8 was a four-seat Type 7. The Type 1 was selected in May 1974 for development as the Don, the 30ft (9.1m) span and 42ft (12.8m) length being not much greater than the Bulldog. The Turbomeca Palas was a possible engine choice, although a twin small turbojet solution was favoured before design work stopped in November 1975. By 1975 the concept of a Light Utility Multi-Purpose System in the USA for a light jet trainer suitable for weapons training and ground attack kickstarted fresh design work. During 1976 and 1977 Scottish Aviation further developed the Don with a two-seat cockpit with side-by-side seats and a single Lycoming ALF101G turbofan as the Series 1100 Sapphire. Several designs were studied including low and high-mounted wings. When Scottish Aviation became part of the nationalised BAe, its military work and the Sapphire passed to Brough. A cockpit mock-up was built for a presentation to the RAF but no interest resulted and the project was abandoned in February 1980.

In early 1976 George Miles was back on the scene with yet another attempt to revitalise the M.100 Student; this time using The Lord Strathcona, the Shadow Minister of Defence, to channel his proposals for an intermediate trainer between the Bulldog and the Hawk. The proposal was fit the M.100 with one of the new generation of small turbofans then being produced by Williams International in the USA to offer superior economy and up to 870nm (1,610km) range on just 91 gal (413lit) of fuel and a unit cost of £70,000-£130,000. Miles claimed interest from El Salvador, the Philippines and a US/Swiss business group trying to interest the USAF. While The Lord Strathcona was impressed, the MoD technical branches were unconvinced about the claimed figures and there was no requirement for an intermediate trainer, the Chief of Air Staff, Marshal of the RAF Sir Andrew Humphrey confirming that the Jet Provost would remain in use until the 1990s. This was still not quite the end of the M.100 Student, in 1978 Scottish Aviation as part of BAe was asked to assess the type as a potential BAe product but Prestwick's assessment was equally unenthusiastic.

Throughout the 1980s and early 1990s BAe Brough became the centre of the company's military trainer efforts. In a similar development to the Sapphire, Brough further developed the Strikemaster as the Eaglet with a Garret TFE 731-2 turbofan requiring a new rear fuselage with a shorter tailpipe exhausting under the tail. The turbofan provided a maximum speed of 370kt (685km/h) at 24,600ft (7,500m) and a rate of climb of 5,265ft/min (1,605m/min). Advertised as a low-cost trainer it remained a study. Brough's main effort was the P.164 series which covered a range of new designs with both turboprop and turbofan engines and tandem and side-by-side seating arrangements. The original 1982 P.164 design was the culmination of two years design work and strongly resembled the Jet Provost with had side-by-side seating and was powered by a 2,500lbf (11.1kN) Pratt & Whitney JT15D-4 turbofan which provided a maximum speed of 396kt (733km/h) at 25,000ft (7,620m) and a maximum rate of climb of 3,800ft/min (1,158m/min). It could sustain a 2.9g

The Scottish Aviation Don was an attractive design intended to replace the Bulldog in the strongly competitive basic trainer market increasingly dominated by turboprops and small turbofans. *Scottish Aviation via Joe Cherrie*

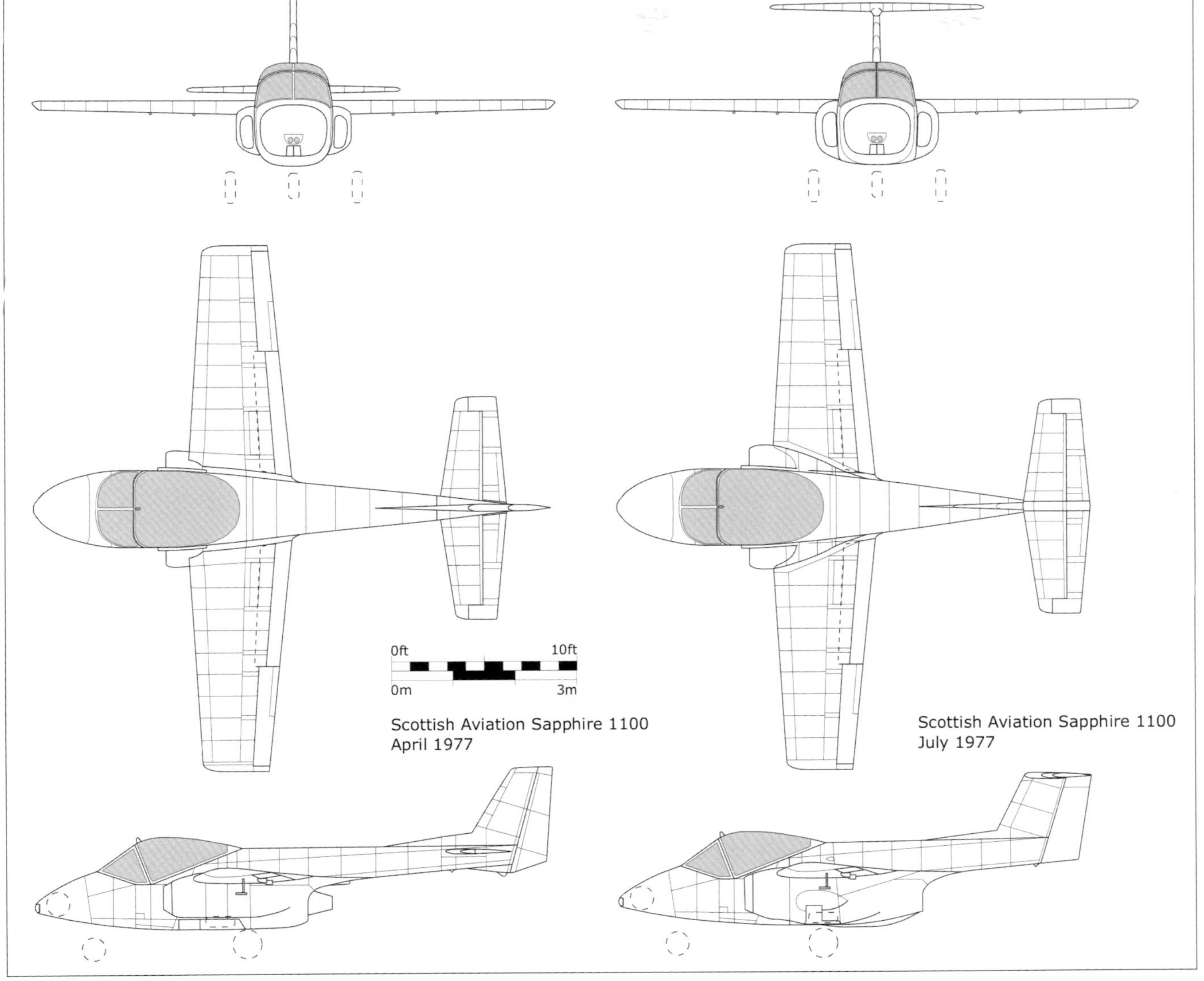

Scottish Aviation studied numerous layouts for the Sapphire 1100, before settling on the final design with a T-tail and a longer engine nacelle in July 1977. *Author*

turn at 10,000ft (3,050m) and the turbofan was estimated to provide a 40 to 50 percent fuel saving compared to the Jet Provost. The breakeven point was around 400 aircraft, far beyond the likely RAF requirements for 175 aircraft, so export orders were essential. It was also thought that the design might be attractive to nations looking to licence-build the aircraft to build up an indigenous industrial capability. By 1984 the turbofan powered P.164 designs had acquired tandem seating to satisfy AST.412 and resembled a smaller Hawk but retained the JT15D.

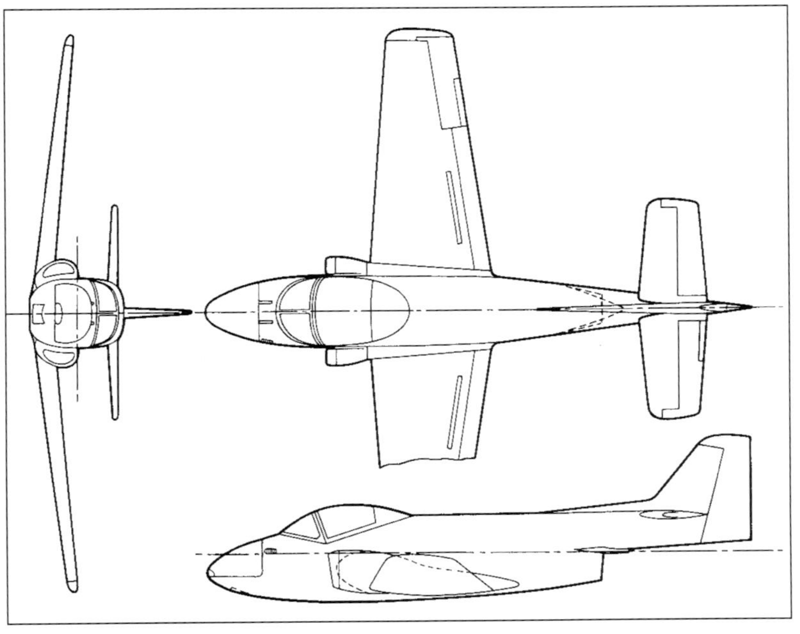

The Jet Provost was a sound design but its 1950s-era Viper turbojet was thirsty. Following the increase in fuel prices following the 1973 Oil Shock, BAe decided to modify the rear fuselage for a fuel efficient Garret TFE 731-2 turbofan to create the Eaglet. *Author's Collection*

The Eaglet married the wings and forward fuselage of the Jet Provost T.5 with a new rear fuselage incorporating a shorter jet exhaust. *Author's Collection*

Above: The P.164 series comprised several designs. This is one of the earlier studies based on further development of the Jet Provost formula with side-by-side seating and a similar overall design. *Author's Collection*

By the time that AST.412 had been finalised, BAe had thoroughly revised the P.164 as the RAF firmly rejected the side-by-side cockpit layout and wanted cockpit layout and systems commonality with the Hawk. The resulting P.164-108 strongly resembled the Hawk. *Author's Collection*

Replacing the Jet Provost

In late 1981 the Air Staff began planning the replacement of the Jet Provost during the early 1990s. The Commander-in-Chief of Support Command, Air Marshal Sir Michael Beavis, outlined the available options; conserving the Jet Provost until 1988 if a reduced annual 120 flying hour syllabus proved feasible, refurbishing 82 T.3As and 43 T.5As to last until 2000 would cost £60 million plus operating costs of £1.14 billion. Buying 120 new Embraer EMB-312 Tucanos would cost £76.9 million plus running costs for 102 operational aircraft to 2000 of £558 million, but the Pilatus PC-7 would cost £65.9 million and £405 million respectively. Buying from abroad offered substantial savings. BAe Brough's turbofan-powered P.164-12 for example would cost £136.8 million with running costs of £669.8 million, plus £45 million in development costs. In the short term the Jet Provost T.5s needed refurbishment; the discovery of fatigue cracks in several tail fins in April 1980 required repairs and fatigue life was extended from 1982 by fitting 38 spare and 20 new sets of wings, but a major refurbishment to extend their lives by another 20 years was unfeasible. The experimental 120 hour Jet Provost/86 hour Hawk syllabus was evaluated but the outcome was unsatisfactory and the original 140/90 hour syllabus was retained.

The Firecracker was not on Beavis' list and NDN's request to the MoD for a formal assessment by the A&AEE had been turned down, although they had secured a joint Firecracker/Hawk bid to Greece in cooperation with BAe. Firecracker Aircraft were now planning to fit the ubiquitous Pratt & Whitney Canada PT6A turboprop and began a press campaign pointing out its cheaper cost than either the EMB-312 or the PC-7. Pilatus too engaged in subtle lobbying; test pilot Bob Cole had been an RAF instructor and his assessment of the PC-7 also appeared in the newspapers. For the first time the selection of a trainer was to be a very public affair in the newspapers and in Parliament, MoD keenly applying Public Relations to defend its decisions.

During 1983 the Air Force Board agreed that a new aircraft was required. The preferred in-service date of 1986 could only be met by an off-the-shelf purchase of a turboprop type with the minimum of changes and developing a new aircraft would push the in-service date back to 1989. The after effects of the 'Oil Shock' made all-through jet training seem rather expensive and although for a time aircraft designers saw the lightweight turbofan as a possible solution, it was the turboprop that emerged as the ideal engine with good throttle response and good fuel economy.

There were, however, worries that a turboprop trainer might lead to more student wastage at the advanced training stage and the Assistant Chief of the Air Staff (Operations), Air Vice-Marshal John W Price, argued for a Bulldog-Hawk syllabus instead. This would entail setting up an additional Advanced Flying Training School, however, as Valley lacked growth capacity and further Hawk orders had already been postponed. A foreign purchase was likely but industrial and political factors meant that UK construction was essential, even at the risk of increasing the cost. This would require offset deals and any foreign deal ideally required *quid pro quo* that they would buy Hawks in return.

For the first time since the 1940s, tandem seating was favoured for a basic trainer by both aircraft designers and air forces. The CFS still preferred the side-by-side layout for elementary training. It was easier for the instructor to observe the student and to build a rapport between them and enabled economy in the provision of flying instruments. The negative was that some students were prone to 'empty seat syndrome' on their first solo finding an empty seat beside them. It was found that tandem seating provided a better all-round view for the student, improved their weapon aiming skills and they were no longer distracted by the instructor's actions. For the aircraft designer it offered simpler ergonomics and a slimmer fuselage for higher speed. Negatives were the greater risk of the student mis-selecting switches as the instructor could no longer monitor the student's instrument panel and the instructor needed to use precise dialogue over the intercom to avoid unintentional mistakes.

AST.412: The Contenders

The Air Staff Target AST.412 was agreed on 30th November 1983 for 155 basic training aircraft with an in service date of 1989. A supplementary war role with provision for underwing stores was added to protect the MoD's freedom of action in the procurement process by identifying the AST.412 trainer as a 'warlike store' and thereby making the programme Top Secret. The required performance and handling characteristics had to be forgiving of mistakes but sufficiently demanding to enable students to develop their potential during a 140 hour syllabus of basic flying training. It had to be suitable for spinning and aerobatics, instrument flying, formation flying, medium and low-altitude navigation training and night flying including basic formation flying. The maximum speed was to be 210kt (388km/h) at sea level with a stalling speed no greater than 60kt (111km/h), a climb to 15,000ft (4,570m) within seven minutes and a service ceiling of at least 25,000ft (7,620m). The take-off and landing distances had to suit a 2,000ft (610m) runway with an undercarriage capable of sustaining a descent of 13ft/sec (4m/sec). Both turboprop and turbofan engines were permissible. Tandem seating with ejection seats was required and the avionics and instrument panels should mirror those fitted to the Hawk as much as possible. The airframe had to be fully stressed to +6g/-3g which caused problems. The Controller Air pointed out that in practice this meant +6.7/-3.4g but nearly all the tenders were designed to civilian FAR 23 regulations for normal accelerations of +6/-3g which in practice would restrict flight clearance to +5.2/-2.2g, limits regularly exceed by the Jet Provost. In addition, a 12,000 hour fatigue life was required and the manufacturers had done little fatigue testing to such stringent limits and this seriously narrowed the likely contenders and would result in expensive redesign.

Pictured is the first prototype of the SOCATA (then part of Aérospatiale) TB 30 Epsilon armed with four cannon pods and sporting the modifications revealed to be necessary following early fight testing; a new swept tailfin, a larger tailplane supplemented by a ventral strake and with elliptical wingtips. In a similar requirement to that of AST.412, the French *Armée de l'Air* stipulated a tandem cockpit and instrument panel layout designed to aid transition to the Dassault/Dornier Alpha Jet. *Author's Collection*

The Australian Aircraft Consortium A20 Wamira II was a proposed development of the A10 Wamira which was being developed for the Royal Australian Air Force with a new fuselage with tandem seating to meet AST.412. Teaming with Westland failed to lead to an order and the Australians would later buy the Pilatus PC-9. *Leonardo via Jeremy Graham*

A full scale mock-up of the A20's new tandem cockpit was constructed at Westland's factory at Weston-super-Mare. The cockpit was tailored to the requirements of AST.412 with a similar layout and instruments as the Hawk T.1. *Leonardo via Jeremy Graham*

Despite the improvements in speed gained by having a narrower fuselage, the assessors felt that the estimated 250kt (444km/h) never exceed speed was optimistic and was in any case below the minimum requirement. *Leonardo via Jeremy Graham*

Invitations to tender were issued to industry in September 1983 and 22 responses were received – the Finnish manufacturer Valmet's late submission of the L-80TP being rejected. Most of the initial tenders from non-British companies were partnered with British-based agents with the potential British workshare outlined, some already had partners in mind but others would take a little while to firm up.

Aérospatiale submitted the Epsilon TP, a projected development of the basic TB 30B piston-powered trainer and surprisingly for a French company, offering BAe the lead partnership position. The selected engine was a 350shp 9260(kW) Allison 250B-17C turboprop, somewhat lower in power than all the other competing designs. The evaluators rejected the aircraft; it was just too small for the RAF role with a cramped cockpit which would need significant modification to accommodate ejection seats. The undercarriage, bird strike protection and oxygen supply would also require modifications which would further increase the weight at the expense of climbing performance. The Epsilon TP emerged as the Turbomeca Arrius-powered Omega in November 1985, but only the prototype was built.

The Australian Aircraft Consortium (AAC) submitted the A20 Wamira II developed from the A10 Wamira which was being developed for the Royal Australian Air Force and had a new fuselage with tandem seating. It was slightly more expensive than the Pilatus PC-9 and despite the improvements gained by having a narrower fuselage compared to the A.10, the estimated 250kt (444km/h) never exceed speed was below the minimum limits of AST.412 and the assessors felt that the estimated improvement of the slimmer fuselage was optimistic. AAC offered a 50 percent share with a UK company, later confirmed after much discussion as Westland which pleased the MoD as they saw this a chance to boost helicopter sales, in particular the Lynx, to Australia and the Pacific region. It would also secure 300 jobs at Westland's Weston-super-Mare factory at a time when helicopter production was declining. It seems that AAC had accepted that any NATO or European orders for the A20 would also have been built by Westland. Westland seems not to have had a design role in the new A20 fuselage, but they were involved in the selection and fitting of specific equipment to meet the AST.412 requirements. A full scale mock-up of the cockpit and forward fuselage was also built.

Beechcraft partnered with Eagle Aircraft Services to offer an improved T-34C-1 Mentor, the T-34FBT with a possible production licence for Short Brothers. The T-34C had been in US Navy service since 1978 but the basic design dated back to 1948 and its un-stepped tandem seating and lack of ejection seats was dated. Even before the official invitation to tender a T-34C, N2067A, had been demonstrated to the CFS at Leeming in May 1983. The assessors found that the performance was below the requirements and the airframe would need extensive modifications to meet the strength and fatigue targets and was comparatively expensive.

BAe Brough continued to refine the P.164, offering the turbofan-powered P.164-108 and the PT6A-powered P.164-109, also known as the New Basic Trainer NBT 108 and NBT 109 respectively. Both had stepped tandem cockpits and cost half as much again as the PC-9 but were designed to UK standard requirements and offered a national solution – excepting the engines from Pratt & Whitney Canada; the P.164-108's 2,293lbf (10.1kN) JT15D-40 and the P.164-109's 750shp (559kW) PT6A-25C. The P.164-108A was also offered, powered by a turbofan variant of the new Rolls-Royce/Turbomeca RTM.322 which had been developed as a turboshaft for medium-lift helicopters like the EH101 Merlin. The 2,338lbf (10.3kN) RTM.322-20 would increase the development costs and risk, but would meet the performance requirements, weight and drag being cut by using a smaller wing.

Turboprops had been king in the trainer market for a decade due to their lower operating costs, so it was no surprise that the RAF and MoD also preferred the turboprop option. The P.164-109 with a Pratt & Whitney Canada PT6A engine looked remarkably similar to the competition. *Author's Collection*

Caproni Vizzola teamed with agents Charlotte Aircraft to offer the C.22J, which had been developed from Caproni-Vizzola's previous series of sailplanes and had high aspect ratio wings. The design proved unsuitable due to its side-by-side seating, lack of ejection seats, inadequate fuel supply and it had the poorest climb performance of all the submissions. It was however the cheapest of the turbofan-powered entries. Caproni also planned a tandem-seat trainer and single-seat variants for the light attack/reconnaissance and anti-helicopter roles, the latter armed with modified Shorts Blowpipe missiles. Only two prototypes were built and no production orders were ever forthcoming.

CASA offered the C-101BB Aviojet which had been a recent success in Latin America but was expensive and too advanced in performance to be a basic trainer. The Royal Aircraft Establishment (RAE) also had doubts about the fatigue life to meet AST.412. CASA were offering British industry a 60 percent production workshare.

The most surprising contender was from DK Aviation, offering the Romanian-built ICA-Brasov IAR 825TP Triumpf (Triumph). The IAR 825 had been intended for the Romanian Air Force and was developed from the IAR-823 two/five-seat trainer and touring light aircraft with a new tandem cockpit with un-stepped seating and powered by a 680shp (570kW) PT6A-15AG. The prototype YR-IGB – the only IAR-825 ever built – made its maiden flight on 12th June 1982. The assessors found it inadequate in most respects and had serious doubts about its airworthiness clearance.

Edgley Aircraft proposed their EA 21 (also known as EAX) development of the Optica with a turboprop-powered ducted-fan but this proposal was not considered in any depth. Miles also proposed the Merlin and the Martlet, further attempts to revive the M.100 Student. The Merlin had a modified fuselage for tandem seating and was powered by a Garrett F109 turbofan, while the Martlet had a ducted-fan. No detailed information was supplied for the assessment and it was unlikely either would have been seriously considered given the numerous rejections of the Student since the 1950s and their demise effectively ended the saga of the Miles Student.

Embraer in partnership with its UK market agent CSE Aviation offered the EMB.312 Tucano. The Tucano had been developed for the Brazilian Air Force to replace the Cessna T-37 – a contemporary of the Jet Provost – and was due to enter service during 1983. Embraer proposed a collaboration with Short Brothers with a full production licence, production being carried out by a subsidiary, the Shorts Light Aircraft Company. The main areas of concern were the fatigue life,

Proof that designing a basic trainer was not simple despite the aircraft's inherent simplicity was the Fairchild T-46A Eaglet. The MoD were already worried about its high cost when it was submitted by Fairchild to AST.412. Within a couple of years the development programme had been delayed and costs ballooned so high that the USAF cancelled the entire programme in 1986. The USAF briefly considered using a variant of the T-45A Goshawk but found its operating costs too expensive for the basic training role. *Author's Collection*

structural strength and bird strike resistance. A stronger airframe would be heavier and erode what was already poor climbing performance and acceleration but it was a modern design with a cockpit layout similar to the Hawk and had ejection seats and partnering with Shorts would provide design and manufacturing support.

Fairchild tendered their new T-46A Eaglet which had been designed for the USAF's Next Generation Trainer to replace the Cessna T-37. The T-46A retained side-by-side seating and was powered two 1,330lbf (5.9kN) Garrett F109-GA-100 turbofans. It had insufficient fuel capacity to achieve even the low-altitude AST.412 sortie, though more fuel could have been added. It was very expensive at £345 million (twice the cost of the PC-9) if licence-built or slightly less if built by Fairchild. The USAF on 2nd July 1982 had ordered two prototypes with options for the first 54 of up to 650 production aircraft. The prototype first flew on 15th October 1985, protracted development having delayed the first flight by six months and the unit cost doubled to $3 million. The cost issues led to the controversial cancellation of the programme in 1986 and meant the end of Fairchild as an aircraft producer. It was proof that designing a cheap and effective basic trainer was still not easy to achieve.

NDN Aircraft were eager to submit the PT6A-powered Turbo-Firecracker, having been waiting for a chance like AST.412 since 1978. The RAE and the MoD assessors were doubtful about the level of expertise within the company, particularly in fatigue design and structural testing and collaboration with an experienced company was essential, although it was recognised that this would increase the cost, which would negate the main selling point that had made the Turbo-Firecracker attractive. The prototype, G-SFTR, made its maiden flight on 5th September 1983 at the Isle of Wight Airport, Sandown, flown by Desmond Norman and Squadron Leader John Davy of Specialist Flying Training who had ordered three aircraft. With Westland and BAe pitching their bids with other competitors, Firecracker allied with Hunting Aviation and founded Hunting Firecracker Aircraft Ltd. to develop and market the aircraft.

There were two Pilatus products on offer, the PC-7 and the newer PC-9 which was then in development as a private venture. Pilatus in cooperation with Britten Norman was offering the proven PC-7. The PC-9 was most attractive being a new design with a stepped tandem cockpit and ejection seats and set the benchmark for the entire assessment. There was a third option, Marshall Aerospace in Cambridge offered the MC-7, combining the PC-7's engine and wing with the new PC-9 fuselage. This hybrid offered too many compromises in performance, however, with no real savings over the PC-9 and was rejected. Interestingly, a decade later Pilatus would develop the PC-7 Mk.II with a stepped cockpit for a South African requirement.

Rhein-Flugzeugbau offered the Fanhawk variant of their Fantrainer with its novel design using a mid-fuselage ducted fan. It had good performance but the complex structure gave inadequate fatigue life and there were doubts whether it could be economically developed to meet AST.412. A 65 percent production workshare was offered.

The SIAI-Marchetti S.211 was a turbofan-powered aircraft and had been flying for three years and was seen as less of a development risk. There were some doubts, however, about meeting the structural strength requirements and the use of complex manufacturing techniques would make any structural modifications expensive. It was also an expensive aircraft to operate.

Desmond Norman had always intended to fit a turboprop to the Firecracker. G-SFTS and G-SFTR were the two Turbo Firecrackers ordered by Specialist Flying Training, the only order that NDN Aircraft received for the type. *Author's Collection*

Table 9.1 – AST.412 Contenders

	Aerospatialé Epsilon TP	AAC A10 Wamira	AAC A20 Wamira II	Beech T-34C-1	BAe P.164-108	BAe P.164-108A	BAe P.164-109	Caproni C22J	CASA C-101BB Aviojet	Embraer EMB-312 Tucano
Wingspan	25ft 11.8in (7.92m)	36ft 1in (11m)	36ft 1in (11m)	33ft 4in (10.16m)	28ft 2in (8.59m)	26ft 10in (8.45m)	32.8ft	32ft 10in (10m)	34ft 9.3in (10.6m)	36ft 6.5in (11.14m)
Length	26ft 10in (8.17m)	33ft 6in (10.2m)	33ft 6in (10.2m)	28ft 8.5in (8.75m)	30ft 9in (9.41m)	30ft 9in (9.41m)	32ft 6in (m)	20ft 4in (6.19m)	40ft 2.25in (12.25m)	32ft 4.25in (9.86m)
Wing Area	96.88ft^2 (9m^2)	215.3ft^2 (20m^2)	215.3ft^2 (20m^2)	179.9ft^2 (16.71m^2)	145ft^2 (13.47m^2)	132ft^2 (12.26m^2)	180ft^2 (16.72m^2)	94.2ft^2 (8.75m^2)	215.3ft^2 (20m^2)	208.82ft^2 (19.4m^2)
Normal TO Weight	2,867lb (1,300kg)	4,850lb (2,200kg)	4,619lb (2,095kg)	4,300lb (1,950kg)	6,505lb (2,950kg)	5,825lb (2,642kg)	5,068lb (2,298kg)	2,502lb (1,135kg) MTOW	10,692lb (4,850kg)	5,622lb (2,550kg)
Powerplant	350shp (260kW) Allison 250B-17C	750shp (559kW) P&WC PT6A-25C	750shp (559kW) P&WC PT6A-25C	715shp (533kW) P&WC PT6A-25	2,293lbf (10.1kN) P&WC JT15D-4C	2,338lbf (10.3kN) RTM.322-20	750shp (559kW) P&WC PT6A-25C	2x 286lbf (1.2kN) Microturbo TSR 18-1	3,700lb (16.4kN) Garrett TFE-731-3-1J	750shp (559kW) P&WC PT6A-25C
Max Speed/Height at SL	216kt (400km/h)	222kt (411km/h)	233kt (431km/h)	204kt (377km/h)	345kt (638km/h)	345kt (638km/h)	240kt (444km/h)	270kt (500km/h)	372kt (688km/h)	226kt (418km/h)
Service Ceiling	32,000ft (9,750m)	31,800ft (9,700m)	32,600ft (9,940m)	29,000ft (8,840m)	35,000ft (10,670m)	36,000ft (10,970m)	29,700ft (9,050m)	27,900ft (8,500m)	40,025ft (12,200m)	30,000ft (9,150m)
	Fairchild T-46A	**NDN-1T Turbo-Firecracker**	**IAR-825 Triumpf**	**Marshalls/ Pilatus MC-7**	**Pilatus PC-7**	**Pilatus PC-9**	**RFB Fanhawk**	**SIAI-Marchetti S.211**	**Shorts Tucano T.1**	
Wingspan	38ft 7.75in (11.77m)	26ft 97.92m)	32ft 10in (10m)	34ft 1.5in (10.4m)	34ft 1.5in (10.4m)	33ft 2.5in (10.12m)	31ft 11in (9.74m)	27ft 4.75in (8.43m)	37ft (11.28m)	
Length	29ft 6in (8.99m)	27ft 4in (8.33m)	29ft 6in (8.99m)	33ft 4.75in (10.17m)	32ft 0.75in (9.77m)	33ft 4.75in (10.17m)	30ft 2in (9.2m)	30ft 6.5in (9.31m)	32ft 4.25in (9.86m)	
Wing Area	160.9ft^2 (14.95m^2)	128ft^2 (11.89m^2)	160ft^2 (15m^2)	179.7ft^2 (16.6m^2)	179.7ft^2 (16.6m^2)	175.3ft^2 (16.29m^2)	150.7ft^2 (14m^2)	135.63ft^2 (12.6m^2)	208.82ft^2 (19.4m^2)	
Normal TO Weight	6,805lb (3,086kg)	3,600lb (1,633kg) MTOW	3,749lb (1,700kg)	4,410lb (2,000kg)	4,188lb (1,900kg)	4,960lb (2,250kg)	3,320lb (1,505kg)	6,063lb (2,750kg)q	5,952lb (2,700kg)	
Powerplant	2x 1,330lbf (5.9kN) Garrett F109-GA-100	715shp (533kW) P&WC PT6A-25	680shp (507kW) P&WC PT6A-15AG	600shp (447kW) P&WC PT6A-25C	650shp (485kW) P&WC PT6A-25A	950shp (708kW) P&WC PT6A-62	650shp (485kW) Allison 250C-30	2,500lbf (11.1kN) P&WC JT15D-4D	1,100shp (820kW) Garrett TPE-331-12B	
Max Speed/Height at SL	330kt (611km/h)	218kt (403km/h)	216kt (400km/h)	?	202kt (374km/h)	270kt (500km/h)	210kt (388km/h)	330kt (611km/h)	273kt (505km/h) at 10,000ft (3,5050m)	
Service Ceiling	46,500ft (14,200m)	27,100ft (8,260m)	30,000ft (9,000m)	?	31,990ft (9,750m)	40,025ft (12,200m)	25,000ft (7,620m)	40,025ft (12,200m)	34,000ft (10,365m)	

The result was four possible contenders that were publicly announced in March 1984; the PC-9, A20 Wamira II and the two NBT designs. In terms of capital and development costs the BAe aircraft were the most expensive at £215-£775 million, the A20 costing £170 million and the PC-9 was the cheapest at £155 million. The PC-9 offered the best choice being comparatively low cost and was the closest to fulfilling AST.412. Pilatus even offered to provide fatigue testing to the AST.412 requirements at no extra cost. There was also a list of also-rans that might be considered if further development effort could remedy their structural shortcomings; the S-211 (soon discarded due to its high operating costs), Tucano, PC-7 and the Turbo-Firecracker. While the MoD decided how to pay for AST.412 at a time of financial stringency, BAe saw which way the wind was blowing and ditched the P.164 designs in favour of a partnership with Pilatus for the PC-9, partly in response to Swiss interest in the Hawk. In cooperation with Shorts, Embraer had begun to modify the EMB-312 with a stronger structure, revised wing leading edges for improved bird strike protection, a revised canopy and a new ventral airbrake. A new four-blade Dowty propeller would also improve the climbing performance. This was sufficient to bring the Tucano back into the list of top contenders.

Choosing a Winner: Performance or Political?

Specification T.301D&P was issued on 30th May 1984 and the top three contenders were subjected to flying assessments by the A&AEE. One major change in the specification was an increase in speed to 240kt (444km/h) at sea level – although designs that met the original 210kt (388km/h) would still be considered – and at least 170kt (314km/h) at 20,000ft (6,096m). A standard EMB-312 PP-ZDK had been assessed at CSE Aviation's Kidlington base in September 1982 by Wing Commander R S Burrows. Burrows declared that the Tucano more suited to intermediate and advanced training. The main criticisms were inadequate pre-stall warning, high rolling stick forces with a poor maximum roll rate and the cockpit was cluttered. Between July and September 1984 the A&AEE and two CFS instructors carried out assessments on the Tucano, PC-9 and the Turbo-Firecracker. None were completely representative of the offered RAF standard; a standard EMB-312 Tucano with the original PT6A, the Turbo-Firecracker lacked the planned assisted escape system and the 750shp (559kW) PT6A-25C and the PC-9 was the first prototype which had only been flying for six months. The PC-9 gave a good account of itself, excluding the inevitable prototype snags at such an early stage of development. The Tucano's assessment mirrored Burrows' earlier informal findings but was deemed adequately suitable to meet AST.412 for the basic training role. The Turbo-Firecracker was underpowered and suffered worst from the similar aerodynamic issues affecting all three airframes. It was unacceptable without a major redesign, whereas the Tucano and PC-9 could be brought up to acceptable standard, the latter being considered the best choice due to higher performance, the more extensive flight envelope and superior stalling and landing characteristics. The Turbo-Firecracker was now out of contention. So was the A20 Wamira II. Being developed alongside the A10, the third Wamira prototype was to be the first A20 and was scheduled to fly during 1985, somewhat behind its off-the-shelf

PP-ZTC was the prototype of the UK-spec Tucano with the Garrett TPE-331-10 turboprop. First flown on 14th February 1986, it conducted a brief test programme in Brazil before being airlifted by Shorts Belfast to Belfast, Northern Ireland, where it continued its test programme as G-BUTC (briefly being marked G-14-007). *Author's Collection*

The Pilatus PC-9 was a brand new aircraft, the prototype HB-HPA had only been flying for six months at the time of the AST.412 selection process. HB-HPA is seen behind the second prototype HB-HPB on the occasion of the latter's first flight. *Author's Collection*

competitors. The estimated performance could still not fully meet AST.412 and its relatively high cost also counted against it.

Now the political factors came into play. For Shorts, the Tucano deal offered a further boost after winning a USAF order for C-123A Sherpa transports and Embraer was offering civil and military collaboration which would boost the company's privatisation strategy (Shorts was sold to Bombardier Aerospace in 1989). Shorts had often been awarded contracts in the past to keep its Belfast workers employed in a high unemployment area. This still applied as local unemployment rose to around 20 percent, but making the company attractive to potential buyers was now the government's prime motivation. The Foreign Secretary, Geoffrey Howe, strongly pressed the Defence Secretary, Michael Heseltine, to buy the Tucano. Half of the UK's visible trade to Latin America went to Brazil, especially defence exports, so an order would consolidate this position and Shorts could tap into Brazilian expertise in exporting to third-world countries and could lead to better prospects for other aircraft like the BAe 146. There would also be important prestige for Brazil; supplying the RAF signified that its aerospace industry had come of age. Politically, there were considerable efforts underway to improve relations with Brazil following the Falklands War and on the debt position and Brazil was also an important long-term ally. The political factors in favour of the PC-9 were potential defence sales to Switzerland including Hawks to replace their de Havilland Vampire trainers, Hawk 200 to replace Hawker Hunters, Javelin and LAW 80 anti-tank weapons and Land Rover vehicles.

All the leading AST.412 contenders were powered by the Pratt & Whitney Canada PT6A, a win-win situation for the company. The American Garrett company began pushing its 1,100shp (820.3kW) TPE-331 engine and Rolls-Royce signed a Memorandum of Understanding to act as major sub-contractor for up to a third of the engine, including third country sales. Pratt & Whitney Canada failed to offer a similar deal and some of the proposals, including the Wamira II, were modified with the TPE-331 as an alternative, especially to meet the higher speed requirements of Specification T.301. Although Embraer and Shorts initially resisted the change, despite the new Dowty propeller more power was needed to improve the performance of the heavier revised Tucano and so the TPE-331 was eventually selected. It was noted that Embraer were happy to incorporate equipment from non-Brazilian origins to satisfy their customers. In terms of economics, Shorts estimated a total lifetime saving of £60 million compared to the PC-9, a figure which was very attractive to the MoD.

The Royal Australian Air Force's Roulettes display team present a neat line of PC-9s. The PC-9 was the pilot's preferred choice but there is no doubt that the Tucano is an equally fine aircraft and both types have illustrious histories of further development and sales success. *Author's Collection*

The cockpit of the Tucano was to be as similar as possible in terms of layout and avionics to the Hawk T.1 to enable a smooth progression by the student to the jet-powered advanced trainer. *Author's Collection*

Following these refinements the MoD requested final bids by 31st January 1985 from Embraer and Pilatus and, surprisingly, the Hunting-Firecracker and AAC-Westland teams were also included in this final round despite falling out of contention only a couple of months earlier. Norman continued to market the Turbo-Firecracker but no further orders ever materialised and the Norman Aircraft Company (as NDN had become in 1985) went into receivership in 1988.

The final decision announced by Heseltine to purchase 130 Tucanos rather than the PC-9 was heavily debated afterwards. The government publicly insisted that there had been no political considerations and that the selection had been made purely on technical and cost grounds. While this was partly true there were clearly other political factors at play. But it could not be denied that Brazil had made a significant breakthrough in being the first developing country to win a major contract for a NATO member. The PC-9 was slightly superior and required less modification to meet AST.412, but the Tucano soon proved popular with students and instructors and provided the perfect complement to the Hawk in terms of performance and capability. The industrial and political impacts of choosing the Tucano proved to be slight; BAe's partnership with Pilatus resulted in thirty Warton-assembled PC-9s being included in the *Al Yamamah 1* deal with Saudi Arabia for Hawks and the Tornado ADV and the Swiss still purchased the Hawk and Brazil also brought Westland Lynx naval helicopters. BAe also undertook PC-9 stalling spinning clearance trials with full loads on the six wing hardpoints on behalf of Pilatus. AST.412's demanding fatigue and stress limits added additional expense and delay but the result lasted the RAF for thirty years of hard service. Developed versions of both types still dominate the turboprop trainer market today. Ultimately the PC-9 has had the last laugh as its American-built Beechcraft T-6 Texan II derivative has now replaced the Tucano in RAF service via Affinity Flight Training Systems.

One PC-9 did see service with the MoD. ZG969 was acquired in July 1989 as a chase plane, nicknamed 'Percy' it was operated by BAE Systems until 2016. This photograph shows ZG969 at the Royal International Air Tattoo at Fairford in July 1991. *Terry Panopalis Collection*

The Tucano

The Garrett-engined prototype, registered PP-ZTC, was first flown 14th February 1986 by test pilot Gilberto P Schittini and conducted a brief test programme before being airlifted to Belfast – fittingly in a Shorts Belfast transport operated by HeavyLift Cargo Airlines – where it was reassembled and continued the test programme as G-14-007 and later G-BUTC. The trials showed no problems with the TPE-331-10 (production aircraft received the TPE-331-12B) with the four-blade Dowty propeller; the spinning characteristics were different but satisfactory and several aspects of the flying characteristics had been improved, notably the rate of climb. The first of 130 Shorts-built aircraft, ZF135, flew on 30th December 1986, the last being delivered on 25th January 1993 (the S.312 designation has often been applied to the Shorts-built aircraft but this designation is in fact erroneous). The first ten aircraft incorporated Embraer-built components but the extensive changes to meet AST.412 meant that the Shorts Tucano shared no common structural parts or equipment with the EMB-312. Shorts had made one final change with reprofiled wing tips to enable a sustained 2g turn at 20,000ft (6,096m) in level flight.

The CFS at Scampton was the first to receive the Tucano T.1 in June 1988, running the Tucano Course Design Team to devise the training syllabus. Gradually No 1 Flying Training School (FTS) at Linton-on-Ouse, No 3 FTS at Cranwell and No 6 FTS at Finningley were re-equipped. In 2000, the Tucano T.1 fleet was centralised at No 1 FTS who retired the last aircraft in October 2019, its training task being taken on by the Affinity-supplied Texan T.1. The Tucano had been recommended to replace the A&AEE's North American Harvard photographic chase planes, but this failed to come to fruition. Although Embraer had already developed a weapons capability for the EMB-312, during spring 1991 Shorts trialled an ML Aviation stores management system to widen the range of machine gun and rocket pods and bombs that could be fitted for the export market. The only export customers for the Shorts-built Tucano were Kenya with twelve T.51s and Kuwait with sixteen T.52s, somewhat short of the 75 exports originally hoped for.

Shorts Tucano T.1 ZF139, one of the first production batch of 130 Tucanos for the RAF. *Author's Collection*

The Tucano production line at Short Brothers, in the foreground ZF212 is nearing completion and behind is the third production aircraft ZF137, presumably being serviced by the Shorts engineers. *Author's Collection*

The Chipmunk and Jet Provost became stalwarts of the training syllabus and finding a suitable replacement was not easy. Both the Bulldog and Tucano courted publicity and controversy during their development but this was soon forgotten as both aircraft became popular and worthy successors, being superb training platforms and going on to serve as long as their predecessors.

Tucano T.1 ZF446 of No 1 FTS at Linton-on-Ouse in the display colour scheme for the 2004 season. Following trials, in 1998 all RAF training aircraft were painted black, the trials having discovered that black was the most conspicuous colour against sky or ground to mitigate the hazards of mid-air collisions. Strobe lights were also fitted at the same time.
MoD/Open Government Licence, 2004

10 Rotary-Wing Trainers

The RAF's first rotary wing aircraft entered service in 1935, when it brought six Cierva C.30 autogiros for the School of Army Co-Operation, followed by five C.40 autogiros in 1939. The first helicopters in British military service arrived due to the need to provide convoys with airborne anti-submarine cover during the Second World War. During a visit to the United States during 1942, the former Cierva Chief Test Pilot, Wing Commander Reginald Brie, witnessed a demonstration of the Sikorsky US-300 helicopter and persuaded Igor Sikorsky to let him fly the improved YR-4. Brie saw that the YR-4 had potential for use in anti-submarine warfare (ASW) and he persuaded the British Air Commission to order two for the Fleet Air Arm (FAA), with the RAF also receiving five. The R-4 Hoverfly proved unsuitable for its intended role aboard merchant ships and the RAF's 45 R-4B Hoverfly Mk.II helicopters saw little operational use beyond radar calibration with No 529 Squadron and the majority were used for training and trials. With the need to train helicopter pilots becoming apparent, the Helicopter Training Flight was formed at Andover as part of No 43 Operational Training Unit (OTU), which was responsible for training Air Observation Post (AOP) aircrews. The first course began on 5th February 1945 using nine Hoverflies and five instructors who had been trained in the USA, joined by two graduates of the first course who were selected for instructor training. The syllabus was short with just six hours of instruction. The Flight became an independent unit two months later but was disbanded on 16th January 1946. The Hoverfly was deemed to have limited utility and the RAF largely abandoned the helicopter. The Navy was more enthusiastic, however, and by the early 1950s was the largest British military user and began to gain practical experience in rotary-wing aviation and training. Basic training however was largely left to the helicopter manufacturers to provide with their own instructors. Belatedly the requirements for casualty evacuation and troop transportation in Malaya during Operation FIREDOG forced the RAF to reconsider the helicopter but the small numbers of aircraft and qualified pilots and crew hampered an expansion in training. The RAF had no option but to rely on civilian contractors and the Central Flying School (CFS) until enough critical mass of airframes and funding could enable fully professional military training. With all three Services, the RAF, Navy and the Army, operating helicopters the desire to rationalise training was attractive in terms of economics but harder to achieve due to rivalries and politicking. Rationalised training was eventually achieved and today still remains the central tenet of helicopter training, but it has also returned to its origins in being provided by private companies.

The Sud Aviation SA 341 Gazelle light observation helicopter became the standard training helicopter for all three British Armed Forces. Despite this, a common training system for all British military helicopter pilots proved an elusive dream for five decades. Gazelle HT.2 XW890 was used by 705 NAS for basic helicopter training for the Royal Navy from 1974 until 1995. *Terry Panopalis Collection*

A mass take-off of Fleet Air Arm Westland Dragonfly HR.3s in 1952. The type was used by 705 NAS for basic helicopter training. *Author's Collection*

The Navy Takes the Lead

As outlined above, the Royal Navy were early and enthusiastic adopters of the helicopter. In February 1945, 771 Naval Air Squadron (NAS) had received the R-4 Hoverfly as part of its Fleet Requirements role, flying a variety of aircraft on target towing and general duties in addition to carrying out evaluations. On 1st February 1947 Lieutenant K Reed made the first deck landing on a Royal Navy warship when he landed a Hoverfly aboard the battleship HMS *Vanguard* off Portland. Further evaluations of helicopter operations at sea in May 1947 saw the helicopter element of 771 NAS forming 705 NAS. Since 1948, Westland had been licence-building the Sikorsky S-51 Dragonfly powered by a 520hp (387kW) Alvis Leonides 50 radial engine for the Royal Navy for transport duties. With the Dragonfly HR.1, 705 NAS began a programme of deck landing trials during 1950. The Admiralty began considering future ASW helicopters and in mid-1952 issued Naval Staff Requirement NA.43 for a helicopter capable of carrying out ASW search and strike roles carrying a homing torpedo and dipping sonar. As an interim solution, fifteen Sikorsky S-55 HAS.22 helicopters were acquired from – and funded by – the United States under the Mutual Defence Aid Plan (MDAP). These developments not only increased the scope of the evaluation work undertaken by 705 NAS but the increased requirement for trained operational pilots as new frontline squadrons were formed. Given the Navy's small helicopter fleet, 705 NAS became responsible for all things rotary; including basic flying training and training crewmen and groundcrew in addition to trials and communications work. Basic flying training was carried out with the improved Dragonfly HR.3 with all-metal rotor blades and hydraulic-powered flying controls. The FAA began looking for a simple and robust basic helicopter trainer to free it from reliance on civilian training. Rejecting the Sycamore and Skeeter, they again turned to the United States for equipment, ordering

The Hiller HT.1 was identical to the US Navy's HTE.2 light helicopter. Delivered on 2nd April 1953, XB474 is seen here in 1961 in service with 705 NAS at Lee-on-Solent. It was sold for civilian use in August 1964. *Terry Panopalis Collection*

The Hiller HT.2 was equivalent to the US Army's Hiller OH-23G variant. XS165 was delivered to the FAA on 17 December 1962, being sold for civilian use in October 1976. In the background of this October 1969 photograph can be seen Westland Wessex HAS.3 XM838 belonging to 737 NAS, the Air Anti-Submarine School. *Terry Panopalis Collection*

20 Hiller Type 360 helicopters, being essentially the HTE-2 variant then in use with the United States Navy. Designated the Hiller HT.1, they were funded by MDAP and delivered during 1953. The HT.1 was replaced in May 1962 by 21 Hiller HT.2 which were based on the US Army's OH-23G variant with a more powerful 360hp (268kW) Lycoming VO-540 piston engine and three seats in the cockpit. The HT.2s were joined by examples of the Whirlwind HAR.1 and HAR.3 for advanced training.

The RAF's Rotary Beginnings – Forged in Malaya

The aerial element of Operation FIREDOG during the Malayan Emergency in the early 1950s soon proved the worth of the helicopter, particularly for casualty evacuation. The Far East Air Force (FEAF) Casualty Evacuation Flight was formed in 1949 but few trained pilots or suitable helicopters existed within the RAF. Since 1948, Westland had been licence-building the Sikorsky S-51 Dragonfly powered by a 520hp (387kW) Alvis Leonides 50 radial engine for the Royal Navy for transport duties. The Dragonfly was pressed into service with the FEAF Casualty Evacuation Flight, the first of three HC.2s making the first casualty evacuation on 19th June 1950. The lack of trained manpower was a problem, the initial four pilots were only given brief hovering practice. Operations soon revealed that a crewman was required to assist the pilot and two groundcrew volunteers were selected. In recognition of their performance in this dangerous role without any formal training, Sergeant Jack Christopher Bowman and Flight Sergeant Alexander Moss were awarded the Air Force Medal and the Distinguished Flying Medal respectively. The provision of dedicated trained helicopter crewmen would take another decade to come to fruition.

The Bristol Sycamore HR.14 had been ordered for search-and-rescue operations but proved less than successful in that role. CFS(H) found itself using them for advanced flying training in the absence of anything better that could be spared from the RAF's small fleet of helicopters. One unusual characteristic was the centrally-located collective lever, which made it difficult to fly from the left hand seat, occupied by the instructor. Sycamore HR.14 XF266 seen here at Singapore was not assigned to the CFS(H), but illustrates the type well. *Terry Panopalis Collection*

Some RAF pilots were sent to 705 NAS for training, but from 1950 training contracts were issued to Air Service Training Limited at Hamble, the Bristol Aeroplane Company at Filton and Westland Aircraft at Yeovil to train small batches of no more than ten students per year, Westland providing a 50 hour flying syllabus. The lack of training capacity was a constant problem; in the summer of 1952 the Chief of Air Staff, Marshal of the RAF Sir John Slessor, asked whether six pilots could be trained to enable a squadron of Westland S-55 Whirlwinds to be formed; the response was negative due to the lack of pilots. In September 1952, the Army offered to post two experienced NCOs to help alleviate the shortage of trained operational RAF pilots. The quality of the civilian training varied and this became tragically apparent when Bristol Type 171 Sycamore HR.12 WV782 crashed during landing at a public evening display at the St. Austell Speedway on 19th September 1952, killing the co-pilot and a spectator and injuring several others. Relying on civilian instructors was also depriving the Services from obtaining their own experience. Flying Training Command grew increasingly concerned and a working party was created in co-operation with the Navy. With around 40 pilots required annually for both services a common training commitment seemed attractive but the Admiralty insisted on retaining their own operational training given their specialist carrier-based and ASW operations. Initial hopes that civilian schools could meet the increased training requirement were soon dashed and instead it was proposed to establish a Helicopter Training Unit within Flying Training Command, the latter agreeing that the new unit should be part of the CFS. The initial proposal was to use three Saunders-Roe (Saro) Skeeters or Sycamores and two Dragonflies to train 25 pilots annually. Using Sycamores would increase the capital cost to £159,040 and the annual running costs by £55,780, the cost per hour rising from £52 to £85 with the Sycamore, compared to Bristol's offer to train 35 pilots annually for £61 per hour and the £25 then being paid to Westland. Some draft requirements for a simple lightweight basic training helicopter had already been gathered; it needed to have an enclosed cabin with side-by-side seating, an all-up weight of 4,000lb (1,814kg) with a 300lb (136kg) payload, a 300-400hp (223-298kW) piston engine for a service ceiling of 12,000-15,000ft (3,655-4,570m) and a rotor ground clearance of 7ft (2.1m). It had to have a speed range of 0-30kt (0-55km/h) forwards, 0-15kt (0-27km/h) backwards and 0-20kt (37km/h) sideways and an endurance of at least 2.5 hours. The most realistic choice remained the Skeeter or Sycamore simply because both were available. Regardless of the arguments over which type to choose, frustrated by the delays and the dissipation of their hard won operational experience, FEAF Headquarters in July 1953 pressed the Air Ministry for a joint helicopter school.

The Sycamore offered good visibility for the two pilots, this example is one of the later HR.14s with the extensively bulged cabin windows which allowed good visibility for search and rescue missions and vitally, allowed a litter to be carried across the cabin. *Author's Collection*

The Arrival of the CFS(H)

Delayed by the lack of available helicopters, the CFS Helicopter Development Unit (CFS(H)) formed at Middle Wallop in May 1954 under the command of Flight Lieutenant J R Dowling. Dowling and the other two instructors had all served with No 194 Squadron in Malaya flying casualty evacuation and transport missions. The terms of reference for the new unit were to; develop the instructional technique, develop handling techniques and become the authority on helicopter flying, train a nucleus of flying instructors and finally to compile comprehensive notes on flying instruction. The unit received two improved Dragonfly HC.4s with a metal three-blade main rotor, hydraulic-powered flying controls and a 540hp (402kW) Alvis Leonides 524/1 engine. The unit was almost immediately pressed into supporting HRH Princess Margaret's nine-day tour of West Germany, however, signalling the beginning of an increasing and distracting VIP transport task, until one of the Dragonflies – and later two Westland Whirlwind HAR.2s – were finally assigned to the Queen's Flight. With the lack of any other centralised authority within the RAF, by 1956 the CFS was the focal point of helicopter experience and even the new Joint Experimental Helicopter Unit found itself agreeing with this view.

From the beginning all prospective Qualified Helicopter Instructors (QHI) who were not QFIs already, first underwent Qualified Flying Instructor (QFI) training on the Percival Provost T.1. Other CFS QFIs provided invaluable input into the training syllabus intended to convert fixed-wing pilots onto helicopters. By August 1954, the syllabus was complete and the first trial course began which included some notable pupils such as the CFS Commandant and his personal assistant, South Cerney's Station Commander and the CFS Examining Wing's commanding officer. Following the success of this initial course the first formal intake was admitted and Flight Lieutenant Shafe was the first QHI to graduate in early 1955. The course comprised 50 flying hours on the Dragonfly HC.4 followed by ten hours on the Sycamore HR.12, which had been transferred from the joint RAF/Royal Navy Anti-Submarine Warfare Development Unit at St Mawgan.

Later the CFS(H) received several Sycamore HR.14s which had proved unsuited for its intended search-and-rescue (SAR) role. One unusual characteristic of the Sycamore HR.14 was its centrally-located collective lever and the QHI was expected to be able to fly it from the left hand seat, something pilots even today would find very difficult.

Tri-Service Training: Round One

The earlier calls for a joint school were hard to ignore as additions to the RAF's Korean War expansion scheme Plan K would see the RAF's helicopter fleet increasing to 82 and the Army would have 100 AOP/light liaison helicopters by 1959. Slessor asked the Vice Chief of the Air Staff, Air Chief Marshal Sir John W Baker to consider a training organisation suitable for all three Services. The resulting Air Council paper was ready by April 1954. The estimated need was between 30-40 pilots annually for each of the three Services. The proposed syllabus was 25-30 hours of basic training using the Skeeter or the FAA's Hiller HT.1s and 25-30 hours on the Sycamore or Dragonfly. The paper's three options reflected the likely Service politics – especially since neither the Admiralty or the War Office had yet been consulted! Scheme I would see the Navy training its own pilots while Army pilots would receive basic training at the Light Aircraft School at Middle Wallop using RAF and Army instructors and the RAF would contract Bristol for its training with operational training left to the squadrons for a total estimated annual cost of £156,000. Scheme II had the same provisions for the Navy and Army but the RAF would set up a Helicopter School with Sycamores and ultra-light helicopters with annual costs of £176,000. Scheme III was the joint training for all three Services with a pooled Hiller and Sycamore fleet and a common basic training syllabus which would require a £577,000 capital outlay plus £457,000 annually. The joint school was vastly more efficient and the annual cost of training each pilot was £3,800, compared with £3,900 charged by Bristol. The capital costs still had to be borne but the recommendation was to approach the Admiralty and War Office with the aim of forming a school in 1955. Not everybody was happy. The Air Ministry's finance branch felt that the costs were high and that to compensate helicopter crews should serve least two tours or even as much as ten years in the transport and communications role.

Air Commodore A Earle, the Director of Policy, in a minute exposed another deeper criticism, the inter-service rivalry trying to stop the Army's plans to revive its independent Army Air Corps (AAC) (which was accomplished in 1957); "both these schemes admit the existence of an independent Army air force whereas, unless the current Air Council/Army Council arguments on "aircraft for the Army" result in complete victory for the Army, all aircraft flown by Army pilots remain RAF aircraft in RAF units and the training of Army pilots remains an RAF responsibility." The Assistant Chief of the Air Staff (Tactics and Requirements), Air Vice-Marshal Laurence F Sinclair, had the previous month complained to Earle that Skeeters should not be supplied to the Army's 1906 Flight responsible for training at Middle Wallop, for fear of duplicating CFS(H).

The Assistant Chief of the Air Staff (Policy), Air Vice-Marshal C Edward Chilton even had to step in to stop the Air Council from invoking the Inskip Award to prevent the Navy from operating training helicopters; "on grounds of common sense I am afraid I must agree... the Inskip Report does not deal with the training aspect in any detail, and even if it did doubt it would carry much weight applied at this stage to helicopters, particularly as the Admiralty have a helicopter training organisation in being and we have not." The Inskip Award had been devised by the Minister for the Coordination of Defence, Sir Thomas Inskip, as far back as 1937 to maintain the allocation of the maritime patrol role with RAF Coastal Command and preventing the FAA from operating frontline aircraft from shore bases. Indeed, during 1954 the Inskip award had defeated an attempt by the Admiralty to take over Coastal Command. In the event the Admiralty declined to participate and by November the Joint School was recast as a joint RAF/Army venture, although the Deputy Chief of the Air Staff, Air Marshal Sir Thomas G Pike, still wanted to use an order for the Skeeter as a political tool to thwart the establishment of the AAC. While the immediate needs of both Services were relatively clear, requirements beyond 1960 were dismissed as 'pure crystal gazing,' which made any attempts at establishing a long-term training organisation more difficult.

Tentative Steps

Throughout all this infighting, the CFS(H) was struggling with a handful of helicopters – often depleted by being seconded to transport VIPs – and lacking the necessary authority to exercise control of flying standards throughout the RAF's units. As a result the accident rate was high. All groundcrews were still trained by civilian contractors too. Requests for replacement helicopters in Malaya stifled any attempts to expand the CFS(H) or indeed other UK-based operational units and the civilian training contracts were extended to compensate and were still considered cheaper. Air Service Training was providing 20 hours of basic training on the Hiller Model 360, Westland provided two courses with 30 hours of advanced training for Whirlwind pilots and 20 hours on the Dragonfly, while Bristol had a ten hour syllabus on the Sycamore. Not until December 1955 was CFS(H) in a position to sit down with the industry to work on a common syllabus before the existing contracts were due to expire during 1956. Growing increasingly concerned about the reliance on civilian schools, the Air Ministry in June 1956 proposed approaching the Admiralty and asking them to provide basic training for their pilots but the protracted talks had reached no agreement by December 1957.

During 1957 the civilian contracts were finally cancelled and CFS(H) became responsible for RAF and AAC pilot training, as well as QHI training and helicopter standardisation for all three Services. In addition, informal Staff Officer familiarisation courses were run to enable senior officers to gain a first-hand appreciation of rotary wing aviation. The CFS(H) made several breakthroughs in helicopter flying training. Practicing autorotation was essential to enable pilots to make a safe recovery in the event of an engine failure. The standard method was to practice with the engine idling, but this was problematic because the linkage between the collective lever and the throttle prevented the collective being raised fully to cushion the touchdown without violently re-engaging the engine, which could have potentially disastrous results. Following extensive trials, by April 1955 the CFS(H) was teaching a safe method of 'engine-off' autorotation covering any combination of altitude and airspeed. In October 1955, the CFS(H) hosted the first Helicopter Instructional Technique Conference, attended by representatives from Headquarters No 23 Group, Flying Training Command, the Army, Navy and civilian operators. In September 1956, the unit flew a Sycamore HR.12 every night of the week-long Woolwich Tattoo after both the Army and Royal Navy had declined the offer (perhaps understandably following the fatal crash of WV782). Although proving safe helicopter flying at night was possible, formal night flying and instrument flight training did not begin until 1959.

Without any Operational Conversion Unit (OCU), Fighter Command had to devise and operate its own training syllabus for its SAR helicopter squadrons equipped with the Sycamore HR.14. They devised a syllabus of ground training and pre-operational training of 25 flying hours for new pilots (only fifteen hours for pilots who had completed one tour) which included navigation and winching exercises to reach the operational standard.

Tri-Service Training: Round Two

Following political pressure to co-operate, a joint committee was formed in early 1954 to study a joint school for basic and advanced training and the use of civil contractors was finally abandoned. The annual training requirement was 45 for the Navy (although in 1958 the Navy had required 60 pilots), 33 for the Army and 30 for the RAF. Despite having been the leaders in training, the RAF now discovered during the discussions that the rapid turnover of FAA personnel had actually hampered its training organisation and instructor training so much that CFS(H) was tasked with creating the syllabus and would train the required nine instructors. The pooled helicopter fleet would comprise ten Skeeters or Hillers, two Sycamores and eight Whirlwinds. The main argument, however, was over the location of the school. The RAF wanted to continue to use South Cerney in Gloucestershire but the Navy wanted to concentrate most of its helicopters at Culdrose in Cornwall. The Joint Committee in its report wisely reported the options and left the decision to ministerial haggling. The Secretary of State wrote to The Earl of Selkirk, the First Lord of the Admiralty, to reassure the Navy that a joint school was feasible but that Culdrose – the busiest naval air station in the country – was completely unacceptable to the RAF on the grounds of airspace congestion and the prevailing weather conditions in Cornwall. The proposal again died.

The Westland Whirlwind became the backbone of the RAF and FAA's helicopter transport capability throughout the 1960s. The Whirlwind HAR.10 was powered by a de Havilland Gnome Mk101 turboshaft and was used as an advanced trainer by CFS(H) and its successor No 2 FTS. Whirlwind HAR.10 XP360 is seen here on a practice SAR sortie. *Blue Envoy Collection*

By August 1961, the CFS(H) had expanded to become a squadron and expanded further following a move to Tern Hill to become the CFS Helicopter Wing with two squadrons; a Training Squadron conducting basic and advanced pilot and QHI training and the Standards Squadron responsible for QHI re-categorisations and maintaining standards across all three Services. In early 1962, the Training Squadron was split into 1 Squadron for basic pilot and QHI training and 2 Squadron for advanced pilot/QHI training with the Standards Squadron becoming 3 Squadron. Having already acquired single examples of the Westland Whirlwind HC.2 and HC.4 for advanced training, the unit received its first turbine-engined helicopter during November 1961, a Whirlwind HAR.10 powered by a 1,050shp (782kW) de Havilland Gnome 101 turboshaft and eventually a fleet of sixteen were used for advanced training.

Saro Skeeter

By 1953 the Air Staff was looking for a new basic training helicopter and considered that the Skeeter was potentially suitable. Beginning life as the Cierva W.14, the Skeeter had suffered a long and tortuous development due to ground resonance and poor reliability. The prototype W.14 Mk.1, G-AJCJ, was first flown on 10th October 1948 and soon attracted military interest. Following its purchase of Cierva, Saunders-Roe continued development as the Skeeter. The Mk.5 with a 180hp (134kW) Blackburn Bombardier 702 engine was the first successful variant, largely curing the resonance problems suffered by the earlier marks. The prototype, G-AMTZ, was loaned to CFS(H) for evaluation as XG303 but was judged to be underpowered and to have undesirable control characteristics during simulated engine failures and low-speed flight which made it unsuitable for the training role. The Air Ministry now considered evaluating the American Hiller Model 360 or the French Sud-Ouest SO.1221 Djinn as alternatives. The Skeeter Mk.6 received a variety of modifications; a 200hp (149kW) de Havilland Gipsy Major Mk.130 engine, cyclic and collective pitch controls that could be operated independently, an electrical longitudinal/lateral trim system, a larger 6ft (1.8m) diameter tail rotor and an engine cut-out device to allow the collective pitch level to be fully raised during autorotation. G-AMTZ was converted and joined by three new-build helicopters, XJ355, XK773 and XK994, which underwent trials at the Aeroplane and Armament Experimental Establishment (A&AEE) and XK773 was evaluated by the CFS(H) during the summer of 1956. This evaluation was cut short when XK773 was written off on 21st June after a rotor blade struck the ground and the helicopter overturned. But during the 27 flying hours obtained, it had shown sufficient improvements to make it more suited for training.

Specification H.163P was issued on 29th August 1955 covering the Skeeter AOP.10 for the observation role with the AAC and the dual-control equipped T.11 for the RAF as a basic helicopter trainer. Both marks were essentially identical except that the T.11 had dual-controls with a cyclic bias trim switch on both control columns and different radios. Three AOP.10s and one T.11 were ordered for evaluation. The sole T.11, XK749, was intended to complete the CFS(H) evaluation, which was inconclusive following the loss of XK773. The relative success of the T.11 evaluation resulted in Specification H.163P2 being issued on 15th April 1957 for series production of the Skeeter AOP.12 and T.13. Minor improvements had been made to the design, known as the Skeeter 7B, and a 215hp de Havilland Gipsy Major Mk.140 engine was fitted. The specification called for the T.13 to have sufficient endurance for two 45 minute training sorties, including take-off and landing and ten minutes hovering within ground effect with 20 percent fuel remaining at the end of the sortie. The vertical rate of climb from sea level up to 4,000ft (1,219m) was to be at least 180ft/min (55m/min). A total of 64 AOP.12s were built and entered service in June 1958 with the AAC. The Air Staff had ordered 27 T.13s but these were later cancelled due to production delays. The CFS(H) later received three transferred AOP.12s, XM556, XM564 and XN339, which following modifications for dual-control use, rather confusingly, adopted the T.13 designation.

The Light Helicopters

By the early 1960s the Army was looking for a replacement for its Skeeter fleet and selected the Saro P.531. The P.531 was developed to fulfil a Joint Services Requirement for a turbine-powered general purpose helicopter with full tropical performance. With government encouragement to rationalise the aircraft industry, Westland by 1960 had acquired the helicopter divisions of Bristol, Fairey and Saunders-Roe. While further development of the P.531 as the Westland Scout to meet Specification H.201D continued, the AAC acquired seventeen Sud-Est SE 3130B Alouette II in 1961 as an interim replacement. But the Army also desired a small and basic Unit Light Helicopter to provide units down to battalion level with their own battlefield observation and liaison capability and issued GSOR.1124 and Specification H.240T. This shift towards simple helicopters was also partly driven by a lack of pilot recruits from the line regiments. The RAF soon became interested too, seeing such a helicopter as a suitable type to replace CFS(H)'s Sycamores.

In response to the requirement Short Brothers began design work on the PD.66, PD.67 and PD.68 projects, the latter two in co-operation with Hiller. Shorts and Hiller tendered the Hiller 12E, Brantly in partnership with British Executive Air Services (and its sister company British Executive and General Aviation Limited) submitted the B-2B and Hughes teamed with Westland to offer their Model 269A.

The Bell 47 is perhaps one of the most well-known helicopters ever made. Licence-built versions by Agusta and Westland were used by the Army Air Corps as the Sioux AH.1 and the RAF as the Sioux HT.2. This example is G17-1 on its delivery flight to Westland's factory at Weston-super-Mare. *Author's Collection*

British Executive Air Services supplied a Brantly for evaluation from its own fleet. The outcome was positive but the company managed to sour its relations with the Ministry of Aviation and Westland stepped in with a competing proposal to build the B-2B under licence. Eventually Westland tendered the Bell 47G-3B-1 in co-operation with the Italian company Agusta to Specification AH.247T, which had superseded the earlier H.240T specifications. Westland had already provided sixteen similar Bell 47G-4A helicopters to Bristow Helicopters who were contracted to train Army pilots at Middle Wallop (the company's founder, Lieutenant Alan Bristow, had been an FAA Hoverfly pilot) Following an evaluation by the A&AEE at Boscombe Down and in Libya during 1962 and 1963, the Bell 47G was selected and 50 Sioux AH.1 were brought from Agusta, with the remaining 216 built by Westland. The Air Staff placed an order for fifteen Sioux HT.2 of basically similar standard to the AH.1 and these remained in service with the CFS(H) until December 1973.

The Anglo-French Generation

Both Britain and France during the early the early 1960s were formulating requirements for a new generation of turbine-powered helicopters to replace their current equipment, which is most cases had design origins going back to the late 1940s and included licence-built American designs. Unable to afford the development of multiple types and seeing that both nations had common requirements, a programme of collaborative development was agreed. The resulting Anglo-French Helicopter Agreement signed in January 1967 covered the development of the Sud Aviation SA 330 Puma tactical transport helicopter, Sud Aviation SA 341 Gazelle lightweight observation helicopter and the Westland WG.13 Lynx battlefield utility and shipborne ASW helicopter. The SA 341 and the WG.13 were seen ideal replacements for the Sioux HT.2, Hiller HT.2 and the Whirlwind HAR.4 and HAR.10 respectively.

Brantly in partnership with British Executive Air Services (and its sister company Beagle) tendered the Brantly B-2B to meet Specification H.240T for a battlefield observation and liaison helicopter capable of use for basic flying training. *Terry Panopalis Collection*

Gazelle HT.3 XW902 in flight over rugged terrain. XW902 served with CFS(H) and its successor No 2 FTS in the training role before being assigned to No 18 Squadron in 1994. This allowed the squadron's Chinook crews to obtain their continuation training on a cheaper to run helicopter. XW902 was auctioned to private ownership in 2013. *Blue Envoy Collection*

Influenced by the experiences of the US Army in Vietnam, the Army wanted a Light Observation Helicopter and the Land/Air Warfare Directorate issued General Staff Requirement GSOR.3336. Sud Aviation keenly promoted their new X-300 design (soon to become the SA 340) and Westland in co-operation with Hughes offered the Model 500 as used by the US Army as the OH-6 Cayuse. Both the RAF and the FAA saw the proposed requirements as ideal for a new basic training helicopter and in 1965 the requirements were expanded to include the needs of all three services as NGASR.3336. The SA 340 was selected under the Anglo-French Helicopter Agreement and the prototype SA 340, F-WOFH, made its maiden flight on 7th April 1967. Following several production refinements and a new shrouded fenestron tail rotor, the design became the SA 341 Gazelle. Under the production agreement, Westland initially gained a 65 percent workshare and assembled all the British Gazelles at Yeovil, the production line later being moved to Weston-super-Mare. With nearly identical specifications, all three British variants were built in joint production batches. The SA 341C Gazelle HT.2 for the Royal Navy had dual controls and 40 were delivered during 1974 for use by 705 NAS at Culdrose. These became well-known to the public, being used between 1975 and 1992 by the unit's *Sharks* helicopter display team. The SA 341D Gazelle HT.3 for the RAF was of very similar standard and 29 were delivered from 16th July 1973 to the CFS(H).

The Gazelle HT.2 was the mount of the Royal Navy's *Sharks* display team between its formation as part of 705 NAS in 1975 and its disbandment in 1992. Following a mid-air collision in June 1977, the team size was reduced to four aircraft. In this formation are Gazelle HT.2s; XX431, XW854, XW891 and XZ938. Despite the demise of the *Sharks*, 705 NAS continued a display a pair of Gazelles until 1996, when the Gazelles were retired. *Blue Envoy Collection*

The AAC had no dedicated trainer Gazelle variant and used its standard AH.1 helicopters for training. The example shown here is AH.1 ZB689. *Blue Envoy Collection*

Students posted to CFS(H) would first complete their fixed-wing 145 flying hours syllabus to gain their wings on the Jet Provost before taking the 90 flying hour Gazelle syllabus. Several HT.3s were later passed to No 7 Squadron and No 18 Squadron equipped with the Boeing Vertol CH-47 Chinook for route reconnoitring and to provide relatively cheap continuation and standards training. The AAC used standard SA 341B Gazelle AH.1 helicopters for training with the Advanced Rotary Wing Squadron, later re-designated the Rotary Wing Conversion Flight, at Middle Wallop.

During 1965 Land/Air Warfare Directorate also issued GSOR.3335 to replace the Westland Scout. Westland offered its WG.13 design which it had refined from the WG.3A tactical transport project of 1963. The number of variants expanded as both partner's navies looked to replace their Westland Wasp and SE 319B Alouette III light ASW helicopters and the French also wanted an armed reconnaissance helicopter. The RAF also joined the list in May 1966, wanting a replacement for the Whirlwind HAR.10 in the SAR and advanced helicopter training roles. The amended NGASR.3335 was issued in January 1968 to cover the development of the WG.13 for all three Services and two trainer prototypes were among the seventeen prototypes planned. Development was delayed by several technical problems and suffered from increasing costs and unit prices, the French cancelling their armed variant in 1968 and the Army and Royal Navy agreeing to economies in the required equipment. Development delays also affected the new 900shp (671kW) Bristol Siddeley BS.360 Gem turboshaft. By 1972 however, the BS.360 Gem was making good progress and the trials programme using five development batch aircraft had begun. In June, Specification 277P was issued to cover development of the Lynx HT.3 trainer. The airframe was identical to the AH.1 utility transport being developed for the AAC. Further economies, however, reduced the order from 24 to thirteen HT.3s, being assigned serial numbers XZ605 to XZ617. The forthcoming 1975 Defence Review led to further cuts and a change of policy which would see the Gazelle HT.3 being used for both basic and advanced training. Therefore, the Lynx HT.3 order was cancelled and the production batch re-assigned as standard AH.1s for the AAC.

What might have been. A Lynx HT.3 duo from No 2 FTS conducting a low-level training sortie accompanied by one the School's Gazelle HT.3s. The order for thirteen Lynx HT.3 was cancelled in 1974 due to defence budget cuts and the airframes completed to AH.1 standard for the Army Air Corps. *Lucano Alviani*

The Wessex HU.5 was used by 707 NAS for operational training. Here seven Wessex are landing onto HMS *Hermes* in 1977. At this time the ship was transitioning from her Commando amphibious helicopter assault role, which 707 NAS are seen practicing here, to an anti-submarine role. *FAA/ Terry Panopalis Collection*

Operational Training

During the 1950s it was common for students to graduate from basic helicopter flying training and be posted directly to a squadron, where they might expect to receive only a couple of weeks of familiarisation sorties before being declared operational, even in Malaya where operational flying meant sorties under the risk of ground fire. Gradually during the 1960s this situation improved as helicopters became available for operational training as well as specialist courses.

Operational conversion flying for Transport Command's tactical transport fleet was rationalised in August 1964 with the formation of the Short Range Conversion Unit at Odiham. It was equipped with the Bristol Type 193 Belvedere HC.1 heavy lift helicopter, Westland Wessex HC.2 tactical transport helicopter and the Scottish Aviation Twin Pioneer CC.1 tactical transport aircraft. On 1st July 1967, the unit became the Helicopter Operational Conversion Flight before being expanded as the Air Training Squadron in May 1971, including a new Standards Flight. Although primarily intended as a training unit for the Wessex, it received the RAF's first two production Puma HC.1 tactical transport helicopters on 29th January 1971 and became No 240 OCU on 29th December. The unit also introduced the Chinook HC.1 into RAF service during January 1981, the unit two months' previously having separated its Wessex element to Benson as the type's training requirements reduced as the Wessex fleet slowly reduced in size. On 1st October 1993, No 240 OCU disbanded to form No 27 (Reserve) Squadron, which from January 1998 became a Chinook-only OCU. The FAA also used the Wessex, 707 NAS conducting advanced and operational training for the Wessex HU.5 fleet used for carrying commandos for amphibious assault operations between December 1964 and September 1985, handing over the responsibility to 771 NAS which also provided SAR coverage along the South coast. For the AAC, the School of Army Aviation remained responsible for providing advanced and operational training with 670 and 671 Squadrons AAC, using standard Gazelle AH.1 helicopters After over two decades of operations, the CFS(H) was disbanded at Tern Hill on 31st March 1976 and its task absorbed by No 2 Flying Training School (FTS) and in September moving to Shawbury, Shropshire. During 1976 No 2 FTS replaced its Whirlwind HAR.10s with Wessex HC.2 for advanced pilot training and aircrew training.

Wessex HAS.3 XS121 served with 737 NAS following its conversion from HAS.1 standard. It was lost on 16th February 1972 when it ditched in English Channel off Portland, its home base. 737 NAS had reformed in August 1959 as the Air Anti-Submarine School, providing operational training to Wessex crews. In June 1970 the squadron also became the parent for Wessex Flights aboard the remaining *County*-class destroyers, the remainder of the unit converting to the Sea King HAS.1 The squadron disbanded in September 1983. *Author's Collection*

Tri-Service Training: Round Three

Before the disbandment of CFS(H), the proposals for a combined helicopter school that had been circulating around Whitehall since 1952 had come back to life. The Defence and External Affairs Sub-Committee of the Select Committee of Expenditure had recommended rationalisation but a working party in December 1973 had concluded against the proposal. Under further pressure from the Sub-Committee Rear Admiral P W Hearn, the Chairman of The Defence Training Committee and the Assistant Chief of Personnel and Logistics, formed another working party in May 1975. The resulting report in December proposed consolidating all basic fixed-wing training at Leeming (either with or without the AAC's Chipmunk T.10 fleet) and all basic rotary-wing training at either Tern Hill or Shawbury on Whirlwinds and Gazelles and a separate RAF advanced course at Middle Wallop or Shawbury, supported by a civilian maintenance contract. Other advanced and operational training was not included in the study.

One problem was the lack of aircraft; 67 Gazelles were required but the pooled Navy HT.2 and RAF HT.3 fleet would only provide 54 airframes and ordering more Gazelles was resisted due to the cost and the impending closure of the Westland production line by 1978. The fixed-wing fleet fared little better; 42 Scottish Aviation Bulldogs were required but the Royal Navy Elementary Flying Training School, part of No 2 FTS, only had 19 requiring either the RAF to make available and transfer Bulldogs from other training units, or to accept a mixed fleet of Bulldogs and Chipmunks. By December 1976, further revisions to the plan had reduced the Gazelle requirement to 32 and a revised pool of 31 FAA, five RAF and two AAC Gazelles was proposed. The RAF felt that the Gazelle would only be suitable for training until 1990 but the FAA and AAC saw no obstacle in operating them until 1995 at least.

The AAC feared that losing its fixed wing training role would mean the closure of Middle Wallop and resisted centralisation at Leeming. The RAF were also concerned that only providing piston-engine fixed wing training for helicopter pilots broke the central tenet since 1957 of providing all pilots with jet aircraft experience. They were worried this lack of experience might create a second-class helicopter pilot community within the RAF. Training officer cadets away from Cranwell was another broken tradition for the RAF. Since 1970, the whole training syllabus had been arranged around the minimum number of stages, minimum number of aircraft types, the maximum amount of time spent on less expensive aircraft and simulators used to the limit of their capacity to ensure the maximum economy. The potential savings of £100,000 annually seemed a poor return for disrupting the entire training pattern. Basing also proved problematic, as Leeming was earmarked for a large Iraqi Air Force training contract and although a Tern Hill and Shawbury combination looked the most practical and economical solution, Tern Hill had already been transferred to the Army in 1976 for conversion into a barracks. Every Service lost something and had to make serious compromises within the proposals, but it proved hard to quantify the long-term cost savings to encourage all sides to reach an agreement. Rationalisation had again proved impossible.

The Bell 214EP Griffin HT.1 was used between 1996 and 2018 to train SAR crews, initially with SARTU and later No 202 (Reserve) Squadron. Here ZJ240 is conducting a training exercise with a helicopter crewman about to be lowered on the winch. *MoD/Open Government Licence, 2017*

Training to Rescue

Specialist helicopter roles such as SAR also became a training focus. In 1961, 771 NAS was reformed out of 700 NAS, the Intensive Flying Trials Unit, as a helicopter trials and training unit and also using the Dragonfly and Whirlwind for training aircrews in the SAR role. Before its disbandment on 1st December 1964, the squadron had pioneered several SAR techniques including; helicopter in-flight refuelling, hi-line transfer, diver dropping and cliff winching techniques. Paralleling this effort, CFS(H) had formed a detachment at Valley in April 1962 to teach SAR techniques to RAF Whirlwind HAR.10 and Wessex HAR.2 aircrews and to provide students with experience of mountain flying during the basic training phase. The Flight became the Search and Rescue Training Unit (SARTU) in 1979 with six Wessex HC.2. Only aircrew rated as above average on leaving No 2 FTS were eligible for posting to SARTU's demanding course which included cliff rescues and winching people from the pitching decks of RAF launches in the Irish Sea. The graduates were then posted to No 22 Squadron, also located at Valley. During 1978 the RAF had begun receiving the more capable Westland Sea King HAR.3 to replace the remaining Whirlwind HAR.10s and a new Sea King Training Unit was formed at Culdrose. This was soon merged with 706 NAS and carried out joint Sea King training and use of the Navy's Sea King flight simulators, although the RAF element became independent in 1982 and finally broke away when an independent Sea King OTU was formed at RAF St Mawgan in 1993 (becoming No 203 (Reserve) Squadron in 1996), which acquired its own flight simulator facility in 1997.

Until this point, the provision of simulators had been a patchwork affair and the RAF often did not provide the necessary resources. As mentioned above, Sea King training relied on the FAA's simulator facilities at Culdrose. A Chinook simulator was acquired in 1985 from British Airways under a fifteen year contract. British Airways paid for the relocation from Dyce Airport to Farnborough and the modifications to bring the simulator to Chinook HC.1 standard and recouped the costs by charging the MoD an hourly rate for training time, other operators being able to also buy training time when the RAF was not using it. The RAF also brought training time on a Norwegian Puma simulator with modified software to emulate the Puma HC.1. These experiences led to a refined and more successful public/private partnership to provide three Chinook, one Puma and two EH101 Merlin simulators at a new facility constructed at Benson. The unit began training Qualified Helicopter Navigator Instructors (QHNIs) in 1992, which proved useful when the training of navigators was expanded after the MoD's *Harding Report* which recommended substituting some Chinook co-pilots with navigators. Eventually navigators would total a third of the Chinook pilot establishment.

The Chinook HC.2 flight simulator facility at Benson. *MoD/Open Government Licence, 2006*

This photograph of the DHFS flightline at Shawbury in December 1998 shows five of the Aèrospatiale Squirrel AS 350BB HT.1 supplied by contractor FBS Limited the previous year. *MoD/Open Government Licence, 2012*

Tri-Service Training Becomes a Reality: The Defence Helicopter Flying School

Presaging the future UK Military Flying Training System (UKMFTS) public finance initiative, helicopter training for all three Services was finally rationalised under the Defence Helicopter Flying School (DHFS). This was a result of the *Frontline First: The Defence Costs Study*, published by the MoD in July 1994, which recommended amalgamating helicopter flying training and increasing the use of civilian instructors. The DHFS was to be run by a private contractor and in October 1996 the fifteen year private finance initiative contract was awarded to FBS Limited (becoming FBS Heliservices in 2001), a consortium comprising Flight Refuelling Aviation (FRA – later rebranded as Cobham), Bristow Helicopters and Serco (who departed from the contract during 1998). The contract included the provision of the helicopters (which would receive military serials), 40 percent of the instructors and the engineering support (the latter building on existing contracts). The government expected the DHFS to save £80 million over the fifteen year contract period.

The DHFS was formed on 1st April 1997 at Shawbury, replacing the disbanded No 2 FTS and combining the training units of all three Services; 660 Squadron AAC becoming the Single-Engine Basic Rotary Wing Squadron, 705 NAS becoming the Single-Engine Advanced Rotary Wing Squadron, No 60 (Reserve) Squadron becoming the Multi-Engine Advanced Rotary Wing Squadron and the SARTU at Valley was also incorporated. CFS(H), which had been already been resurrected, remained at Shawbury to provide and train the instructors. FBS supplied 26 Aérospatiale Squirrel AS 350BB HT.1 helicopters as basic and advanced trainers. These were joined by twelve modified Squirrel HT.2 fitted with Night Vision Goggles, GPS, a Brightstar searchlight and a ventral cargo hook for specialised AAC training with 670 Squadron AAC at Middle Wallop. Twelve Bell 214EP Griffin HT.1 were used by 60 (Reserve) Squadron for advanced pilot training and by SARTU on their Qualified Helicopter Crewman Instructor Course. SARTU also obtained specialist ground school training equipment including a physical simulator, called the Parrot, using the fuselage of an old Bell 212 fitted with a winch and hydraulics to simulate a range of different terrains for practice, ranging from undulating terrain through to a simulated boat pitching up and down. After this ground school phase the students' progressed to dry winching over land before undertaking their first simulated rescue from the deck of an RAF launch.

Airbus Helicopters Juno HT.1 ZM506 coming into land at Shawbury. The Juno is used for both basic and advanced pilot training. *MoD/Open Government Licence, 2018*

While the MoD deliberated about the helicopter portion of UKMFTS, the initial contract expired in April 2012 and FBS Heliservices received an interim £193 million four-year contract. In 2016 the MoD finally selected Ascent Flight Training and they sub-contracted Airbus Helicopters to provide and maintain the helicopters with Babcock and Lockheed Martin supplying infrastructure and ground-based training equipment. Airbus supplied 29 EC135T3 Juno HT.1 helicopters for the basic and advanced training role and three H145 Jupiter HT.1 to replace the Bell 214EP Griffin HT.1 in the SAR training role. The reduced number of Jupiter HT.1s partly reflected the reduced training requirement following the government's privatisation of SAR helicopter services in 2013. The first examples of the Juno HT.1 and Jupiter HT.1 were delivered on 3rd April 2017 and by April 2018 had replaced the FBS Heliservices fleet. In early 2020 Airbus invested £183 million to supply four additional Juno HT.1s, the Juno fleet having already amassed 25,000 flying hours.

Organisationally, the DHFS under UKMTFS was revised with two Wings; 2 Maritime Air Wing comprising 660 Squadron AAC and 705 NAS at Shawbury providing basic flying training alongside No 202 (Reserve) Squadron (the former SARTU) at Valley; and 7 (Training) Regiment comprised of No 60 (R) Squadron and 670 Squadron AAC also at Shawbury providing advanced flying training. The planned annual output is 286 students per year with four six-month courses running annually, split equally between 705 NAS and 660 Squadron AAC. No 202 (R) Squadron trains all RAF and FAA pilots and winchmen destined for the SAR role. The Royal Navy's students are first graded by 727 NAS at Yeovilton on the Grob G115E Tutor T.1 before passing on to 703 NAS at the Defence Elementary Training School at Barkston Heath where students for all three Services receive their fixed-wing basic training before arrival at Shawbury. The helicopter training syllabus begins with basic rotary-wing skills, emergency handling which includes engine-off landings, the advanced phase covers non-procedural instrument flying, basic night flying, low-level and formation flying, mountain flying and FAA students also receive an introduction to winching operations.

The Airbus Helicopters Jupiter HT.1 is used for advanced training, replacing the Griffin HT.1 in the helicopter crewman training role with No 202 (Reserve) Squadron.
MoD/Open Government Licence, 2017

Since July 2015 the RAF's graduates have progressed to No 28 (Reserve) Squadron at Benson, which serves as the OCU for the support helicopter fleet of Pumas and Chinooks. Naval graduates progress to either 824 NAS with the Leonardo Merlin HM.2 or 825 NAS with the Leonardo Wildcat HMA.2 for operational training. The Army's graduates progress to 671 Squadron AAC for conversion training on the Leonardo Wildcat AH.1 or 673 Squadron AAC on the Westland WAH-64 Apache AH.1. The AAC also runs the Aviation Command and Tactics Trainer (ACTT) located at Middle Wallop for procedural mission command training of pilots during the Operational Training Phase of the Army Pilots Course, but is also sometimes used for mission specific training at Squadron level. Since 1999 all frontline helicopter units of all the Services have been under the unified command of the Joint Helicopter Command, which is directly responsible to the Chief of the General Staff. On 14th May 2020 No 22 Squadron was reformed at Benson as the operational testing and evaluation squadron for Joint Helicopter Command. As well carrying out its operational evaluations of the entire helicopter fleet (Chinook, Puma, Apache, Wildcat, Merlin), it is also responsible for training Qualified Warfare Instructors for the individual units.

Helicopter training has come a long way since the initial steps taken by No 43 OTU where the instructors had to teach themselves from the operating manuals in order to begin teaching their first students in what was a new form of aviation. For much of the post-war period the helicopter training community had to fight against shortages of helicopters, manpower, money and expertise. Being a different form of aviation with different pilot and aircrew skills, it did not easily fit within the traditional training pattern. It may seem incredible with hindsight that it took forty years of negotiations and bargaining to deliver a centralised training system. Some of the delay was undoubtably due to jealous Service rivalries and turf wars but the unwillingness to purchase adequate numbers of frontline helicopters prevented the cost benefits of rationalisation being achieved due to lack of spare airframes and heavy operational commitments. The formation of the DHFS, however, became the organisational blueprint of the future of British military air training.

On 14th September 2016 a special formation of Chinooks celebrated the 100th anniversary of Nos 18, 27 and 28 Squadrons. No 28 (Reserve) Squadron at Benson serves as the OCU for the support helicopter fleet of Pumas and Chinooks, while No 27 (Reserve) Squadron had briefly been the Wessex OCU before the type was retired in 1998.
MoD/Open Government Licence, 2016

11 Training the Navigators and Aircrews

'From time to time the term "Air Staff modification" crops up and almost on an equal number of occasions I refute the charge and say that we have little or nothing to do with it.'
Air Vice-Marshal John Boothman, Assistant Chief of the Air Staff (Tactics and Requirements) to the Controller of Supplies (Air), Air Chief Marshal Sir William Alec Coryton, 25th November 1946

'For some time we have been concerned with the magnitude of the speed difference between Basic Navigation training aircraft and future jet aircraft.'
Air Commodore William S Hebden, Director of Flying Training, January 1952

'I felt you may of left the meeting last week with the impression that, although the firm had offered every possible permutation and combination of aircraft, the Air Staff, in their usual prima donna-ish fashion, felt that none suited them. Let me hasten to assure you that the situation is not quite as bad as that.'
Air Commodore Ian Esplin to James A R Kay, Hawker Siddeley Group Ltd., July 1960

Every member of an aircrew required training for his specialist role. The pilot and the navigator received the lion's share of specialist training aircraft but flight engineers, radio operators (signallers), radar operators, bomb aimers and air electronics operators (AEO) also had to learn how to perform their duties and operate their equipment under operational conditions in the air. This chapter will deal with these specialist areas and the multi-engine crew trainers developed to train the crew as a collective unit. Alongside dedicated navigation trainers for the basic training phase were crew trainers for students destined to serve with Bomber or Transport Command. These enabled pilots, navigators, signallers and bomb aimers to be trained together for greater economy and to build team cohesion as they learnt how to work together as a crew. Operational conversion crew trainers specifically intended for the V-Bombers and bomb aimer training has already been covered in Chapter Six so will not be discussed in depth here.

The majority of RAF navigators who served during the Second World War were trained on the Airspeed Oxford and Avro Anson, both at home and overseas under the British Commonwealth Air Training Plan. In response to criticisms regarding the standard of training at Navigator and Air Observer training schools, the Bombing and Gunnery Schools added navigation training to their syllabuses during late 1940, becoming Air Observer Schools in the process. On 14th August 1942, the Central Navigation School (CNS) was formed at Cranage from No 2 School of Navigation to run a special six to eight month-long course to train specialist navigation officers in long-distance navigation and became responsible for training instructors and the development of techniques and equipment. In October 1944 the CNS flew modified Avro Lancaster Mk.I PD328, named *Aries*, on a circumnavigation of the world, the first British military aircraft to accomplish this feat. Other *Aries* flights would follow in the post-war years using modified aircraft including an Avro Lincoln and an Armstrong Siddeley AW.660 Argosy. During early 1944 as the demand for aircrew lessened, standards were raised and the new Pilot, Navigator, Bomb Aimer Scheme was introduced which gave navigators and bomb aimers the same status as pilots for the first time. At the same time a new training syllabus was devised and maintained by the newly formed Air Navigation and Bombing School at Jurby. On 28th October 1944, the Empire Air Navigation School was formed at Shawbury (alongside the recently moved CNS) to provide instruction and development of advanced navigation techniques. Overseas training continued post-war with training in Southern Rhodesia lasting until 1953 and in Canada until 1957. This solved airspace and school capacity problems but did require a degree of refresher training to enable new graduates to gain experience of the vagaries of the weather over the British Isles and Northern Europe.

Navigator training had been improved by wartime experience and was highly specialised and required multi-engine trainers with a large enough cabin to seat several students along with an instructor as well as room for their plotting tables and equipment and sufficient astrodomes for sextant practice.

The two-seat night-fighters of the Second World War gained increased capabilities post-war as jet engines and more advanced radars were developed and the introduction of guided air-to-air missiles enabled them to operate in all weathers by day and night and were (relatively briefly) classified as All-Weather fighters. The navigators destined to join this force had to not only learn the skills of navigation but also how to operate the radar in all types of weather conditions by day and night. As two-man aircrew increased as a proportion of the frontline fighter and strike aircraft force, the traditional navigator morphed into the systems-oriented weapons systems officers of today. As increasing use was made of the electromagnetic spectrum, whether for communications or radar, new training roles mirrored new ways to use this invisible force. The wireless operator/gunner of the Second World War became a specialist as a Signaller and then as an AEO to operate a variety of radio equipment, including electronic countermeasures. As electronic warfare and signals intelligence (SIGINT) grew in importance operators required training on how to effectively locate, record and interpret electromagnetic emissions for analysis by intelligence teams. In the early post-war years the training fleet was mainly comprised of stalwarts from the pre-war era; the Avro Anson and the Vickers Wellington, backed up by smaller numbers of Airspeed Oxfords. Their replacement would occupy development efforts during the 1950s as would the task of finding aircraft suitable for the jet age.

Faithful Annie Serves On

Since its entry into RAF service in March 1936 as a coastal maritime reconnaissance aircraft, A V Roe had continually modified the Type 652A Anson to fulfil a wide range of roles including radio, navigation and crew training. During the latter war years, two navigation trainer variants based on the Anson Mk.X had been proposed but abandoned; the six-seat Mk.XV in Series I and Series II versions, the latter featuring an hydraulically-retracted undercarriage; the three-seat Mk.XVI also equipped as a bombing trainer and fitted with Armstrong Siddeley Cheetah XV engines, Rotol variable-pitch propellers and a hydraulically-retracted undercarriage.

The Avro Type 652A Anson had been a training workhorse throughout the Second World War and in the early post-war years the only credible solution was new Ansons. The Anson T.20 was specially developed for use Southern Rhodesia. VS504 served with No 3 FTS and was lost while returning to Britain when an engine failed and the aircraft belly landed near Saras in Sudan on 23rd August 1951. *Author's Collection*

The prototype radio operator trainer Anson T.22 VM306 was completed in June 1948. Following a long career with the A&AEE, the aircraft was finally struck off charge on 28th January 1960. *Blue Envoy Collection*

Shortly after the war ended the Air Staff had released Operational Requirements OR.212 and OR.224 for navigation and radio trainer variants of the Avro Anson XIX Series 2 for post-war use and three specifications were issued during 1947. Specification T.24/46 called for a tropicalised navigation trainer for use in Southern Rhodesia and resulted in the T.20 which featured a transparent nose and underwing bomb racks for sixteen 8.5lb (3.8kg) practice bombs to allow the training of bomb aimers. Accommodation was provided for a pilot, a student radio operator and an instructor and three navigation positions for two students and an instructor. Navigation equipment included Rebecca Mk.4 homing equipment and TR.1143A, T.1154/R.1155 radio sets and desert survival gear was also stowed aboard. Specification T.25/46 for a UK-based navigation trainer resulted in the T.21, essentially identical to the T.20 but lacking any provision for bomb aiming. Lastly, Specification T.26/46 for a radio operator trainer led to the T.22 which could accommodate three students with an instructor and was equipped with TR.1143A and T.1154/R.1155 transmitters and receivers as well as IFF and Rebecca Mk.4.

The prototype Anson T.20, VM305, was first flown on 5th August 1947 and the type entered service with No 3 Air Navigation School (ANS) at Thornhill, Southern Rhodesia, in April 1948. A total of 53 T.20s were built and after withdrawal by 1953 many returned to the UK to equip several schools. The prototype Anson T.21, VS562, was first flown during May 1948 and was followed by 252 production aircraft which became the main basic navigation trainer until the late 1950s. Following their training duty, 27 Ansons were later stripped of their navigational fittings and used for communications and transport duties redesignated as the C.21 well into the 1960s. The prototype T.22, VM306, flew on 21st June 1948 and 54 production aircraft were built. The last T.21, WJ561, having the honour of being the 11,020th and final Anson to be built, being delivered on 27th May 1952.

Wartime Bomber, Peacetime Trainer

The Vickers Type 440 Wellington Mk.X had entered service during the Second World War as an improved Wellington Mk.III medium bomber powered by two 1,615hp (1,204kW) Bristol Hercules XVI radial engines and using the newer DTD646 light alloy to save structural weight. From 1946, 270 Mk.X bombers were converted by Boulton Paul as advanced multi-engine and navigation trainers, being redesignated as the T.X (later the T.10 when the RAF switched to Arabic numerals). The turrets were removed and faired over (some retained the rear turret for gunnery training) but the bomb aiming position was retained to train bomb aimers. The airframes were completely stripped by Boulton Paul and overhauled and re-covered with new fabric skins.

Converted by Boulton Paul, Wellington T.10 NA928 served with No 1 ANS at Hullavington. *Crown Copyright*

The smart all-silver finish of Wellington T.10 NC982 on the strength of No 5 ANS cannot hide its obvious 1930s bomber origins. NC982 is seen here during the Daily Express 50 Years of Flying Exhibition at Hendon during 19-20 July 1951 to mark the Golden Jubilee of the Royal Aero Club. *Terry Panopalis Collection*

In early 1946 design work began on another conversion as the Type 619 Wellington T.19. This was to be an interim solution to the need for crew trainers with modest improvements with the Air Ministry planning that RAF Maintenance Units would complete up to 1,000 conversions. But in July 1946 the Ministry of Supply's (MoS) RD Equipment (RDQ) visited Weybridge and demanded so many changes that it turned into virtually a rebuild of the interior with complete stripping and rebuilding of the radio and navigation stations, additional oxygen supplies, an extra escape hatch and an extra dinghy. These modifications were based on an earlier aborted crew trainer development of the larger Vickers Warwick. The Air Ministry protested that they did not want such a complicated and expensive conversion but Vickers and RDQ countered that they had put a lot of effort into the work and did not wish to see it wasted. The Air Ministry grumpily responded that they would rather continue to receive the cheaper T.10 conversions. The impasse continued until November, RDQ again trying to persuade the Air Ministry to accept a rebuilt Wellington and Vickers argued that it would take less manhours to complete the design work but they carefully ignored the impact of the increased conversion costs. Air Vice-Marshal John Boothman, the Assistant Chief of the Air Staff (Tactics and Requirements) (ACAS(TR)) wrote a formal complaint to Air Chief Marshal Sir William Alec Coryton, the Controller of Supplies (Air) at the MoS, to put on record that the MoS rather than the Air Ministry was at fault for increasing the cost for no good reason. The result was a heavily reduced T.19 conversion programme; today it is unclear how many were actually completed by the Maintenance Units. Boulton Paul continued to deliver T.10 conversions until the last was handed over on 20th March 1952. The T.10 remained in service until March 1953 and several were transferred to France and Greece to help rebuild their training organisations.

Replacing the Wellington

While the disagreement over the Wellington T.19 rumbled on the Air Staff were already considering a requirement for an aircraft suitable for training crews to operate future jet-powered bombers; the English Electric Canberra was then in the design phase and Specification B.35/46 for a medium-range bomber capable of carrying a nuclear bomb was about to be issued. A draft specification for an Intermediate Trainer included a maximum speed of 200kt (370km/h), a service ceiling of 25,000ft (7,620m) and a range of 1,300nm (2,410km) with provision for overload tanks for an additional 430nm (800km). Accommodation was to be provided for two pilots, three navigators, two signallers and an instructor with equipment for radar-guided blind bombing, visual bombing and photography. On 11th October 1946, Boothman as ACAS(TR) chaired a meeting to discuss the future crew trainer. It was hard to foresee exactly what the crew trainer of the future would look like and the meeting discussed all the implications; whether visual bomb aiming at high speed was feasible, what navigation techniques might be required, whether the defensive gun was really dead and – rather presciently – whether future high-altitude defences would force the bombers back to low-level flight. Boothman pointed out that gunnery training was not likely to be required for bomber crews, but possibly would be for maritime reconnaissance aircraft. New training requirements identified included; operating pressurised cabins, jet engine handling for the pilots and high-altitude navigational techniques. Air Vice-Marshal Thomas Williams, the Assistant Chief of the Air Staff (Operations), argued that operational bombers could be used for conversion training if they were fitted with suitable flying controls and navigation equipment, with the students occupying the co-pilot's seat and providing an additional navigator's seat. This option was indeed followed for the V-bombers resulting from B.35/46 but for the previous training phases a more economical solution was still required. Three potential types were identified; a replacement for the Anson and Wellington – for which Boothman suggested the Vickers Viking airliner; a variant of the Canberra for advanced training and a basic type suited to grass airfields for reservists, the Cunliffe-Owen Concordia feederliner being suggested. Of these, only the first type would be developed (the Canberra T.4 was a pilot conversion trainer only, see Chapter Six).

Operational Requirement OR.249 was issued in 1948 for a Crew Training Aircraft to replace the Wellington T.10 by 1952 for use by day and night for air navigation, bomb aiming, pilot and signals training. The specified cruising speed was 200kt (370km/h) at 10,000ft (3,050m), a service ceiling of 25,000ft (7,620m) and a still air range of 1,500nm (2,780km) at 10,000ft (3,050m). The aircraft had to accommodate two pilots, three navigators or bomb aimers (one being an instructor) and two signallers (one of these being an instructor). The aircraft was to be equipped with H2S Mk.4A radar with provision to fit the H2S Mk.9 radar and the Navigation and Bombing Computer Mk.2 when they became available. Both navigational stations were to be similar to those specified for the Vickers Valiant bomber and fitted with the latest equipment – Gee, Rebecca, automatic radio compass, air and ground position indicators for H2S Mk.IV, Drift Sight Mk.VII, master clock, gyro stabilised compass master indicator. The two signallers would sit side-by-side with one complete radio installation. The ventral visual bomb aiming station was a dual station for an instructor and student lying prone with a view from the horizon to 15° behind vertically and up to 20° on either side to enable suitable drift settings on the bombsight which could be either the Mk.XIV, Stabilising Automatic Bomb Sight or Low Level Mk. III bombsights. Internal stowage would be provided for 32 25lb (11.3kg) or 11.5lb (5.2kg) practice bombs, twelve photoflashes or reconnaissance flares and 25 smoke and flame floats either stowed on light series racks or released from within the cabin via the flare chute. A gun turret had been included in the first draft but was quickly removed from the specification.

The aircraft had to be a conversion from an existing type to reduce the development cost. The Concordia was again suggested but quickly rejected as it could not meet the load and range requirements. The Airspeed Ambassador easily met the performance requirements but providing a suitable bomb aiming station and internal bomb stowage was difficult and was expensive at £125,000 per aircraft. The Vickers Valetta C.1 – the military transport variant of the Viking – was the favoured choice with the Ambassador being a close runner-up and Specification T.13/48 was issued on 14th September 1948 to cover the development. The result would be a much revised version of the Valetta. The commercial origins of the main cabin meant there was ample internal space and by limiting the payload and extending the wing span by 6ft 3in (1.9m) the aircraft could reach the altitude requirements. To give a good forward view for bomb aimer it would be necessary to either extend the nose or locate the station in an enlarged luggage compartment below the cockpit. The second option was adopted, the after portion of the pannier serving as the bomb bay for 24 practice bombs. The aircraft also gained a tricycle undercarriage, the nosewheels being fitted with mudguards to prevent mud obscuring the bomb aiming windows during take offs from grass strips. The wireless station was fitted behind the pilots' seats and the pannier, the signallers facing aft, and the navigation station was behind the wing spar. The planned H2S Mk.4 radar was never fitted. Although it had proved possible to fit a smaller 3ft (91cm) diameter scanner into the nose with the extra weight offset by a reduced fuel load, the cancellation of the scanner that was also intended for the Canberra saw the requirement removed. Attempts were made later to reinstate a radar capability with the later H2S Mk.9 radar but this proved impossible (see Chapter Six). At a cost of £56,000 per aircraft the MoS complained about the expensive price relative to the cheaper – and much inferior – Wellington T.10 conversion, but financial approval was obtained.

The Vickers Varsity was the first purpose-built post-war crew trainer. Here the prototype VX828 takes off from Wisley. Clearly visible is the ventral pannier which contained the bomb-aiming position and a bay for practice bombs. A dielectric nosecone is fitted, intended for a H2S Mk.4A bombing radar which was later removed from the requirements. ***Blue Envoy Collection***

The first Type 648 prototype, VX828, first flew on 17th July 1949 at Wisley in the hands of Chief Test Pilot Maurice 'Mutt' Summers accompanied by Gabe 'Jock' Bryce and was followed by the second prototype, VX835, on 29th January 1950. By then the aircraft had been named Varsity, one alternative proposal having been Vulcan. The third prototype,VX838, was later cancelled. Trials at the Aeroplane and Armament Experimental Establishment (A&AEE) at Boscombe Down, including tropical trials at Khartoum in Sudan went well, with only the proposed H2S radar fit and the loading of practice bombs being criticised; the low ground clearance meant that armourers frequently scorched their backs or limbs on the aircraft's hot skin in the tropics. The first Type 668 production Varsity T.1, WF324, flew on 21st May 1951 and from 1st October No 201 AFS at Swinderby began replacing its Wellingtons, beginning its first course with the Varsity in late November. A total of 163 were built, another 50 being cancelled in December 1952 and two were sold on to Sweden as trials aircraft. Production was moved from Weybridge to Hurn during 1951 to make way for the growing Viscount airliner production line. The Varsity was also offered in the maritime reconnaissance role (see Chapter Thirteen) and in 1948 Vickers had proposed two further developments; a military transport with a revised flat cabin floor and the VC.3 24/37-seat airliner, but both remained on the drawing board.

The Varsity would go on to serve with many training units, including the RAF College and the Central Flying School (CFS), as advanced multi-engine pilot trainers as well as its usual navigation and signals training role. The utilisation was high during the peak of training crews for the V-Force and Coastal Command which totalled 3,000 aircrew annually; in January 1952 No 201 AFS clocked up 1,117 flying hours in three weeks with ten aircraft – one of which completed 25 landings in four hours. The success of the Varsity saw the training wastage rate quickly reduced by 50 percent following its introduction into service. With a maximum range of 2,156nm (3,994km), training flights were undertaken to Cyprus and North Africa and transit flights were made to the Far East. No 1 Air Navigation School (ANS) and No 2 ANS used the type for navigator training, the latter unit during the 1960s providing the basic navigation syllabus while No 1 ANS used the Varsity on a four-month long 'slow' advanced training stream for non-fast jet navigators. No 4 Flying Training School (FTS) at Valley used a small number for advanced multi-engine pilot training, this task passing to No 5 FTS at Oakington in 1960.

The Varsity was also used as an advanced twin-engined pilot trainer. Varsity T.1 WF377 was delivered to the RAF on 5th March 1952, and ended its flying career with the CFS at Little Rissington, as seen here in June 1973. Just under two years later it was sold for scrapping. *Bob Woolnough*

The Varsity also trained AEOs. This is Varsity T.1 WJ909 of the Air Electronics School at Topcliffe seen on display at Acklington in September 1964. This aircraft had a long RAF career between October 1951 and March 1976. *Mike Hines*

The Varsity was also used to train SIGINT operators with Nos 192 and 51 Squadrons, including 'Baby Crawl' training exercises along the Inner German Border and other Varsities served with the Electronic Warfare Support Unit and its successors for trials and training work. One of these Varsities, WL687 was given an extensive modification by the Radar Research Establishment at Defford during 1954-55 with the assistance of Vickers as a trials aircraft for the ARI.18058 Breton S-band direction-finding receiver. An improved navigation suite including Blue Shadow sideways-looking radar and Green Satin doppler radar was also fitted, the complexity of the work was reflected in the eleven months taken to complete the conversion. In November 1955 work began on converting WL686 as a trainer for Special Operators. The navigator's position was moved forwards to allow five stations for the students and AN/APA-17 direction finding antennas were fitted in the nose radome and in a thimble randome under the rear fuselage. The five stations were equipped with a mix of metric and centimetric intercept equipment. The demanding training syllabus required 60 flying hours and in mid-1956 WL686 began flying training sorties and by 1957 had largely removed the backlog to provide a sufficient number of trained operators for the new de Havilland Comet 2Rs then entering service in the electronic intelligence gathering role. In 1958 WL687 was given a similar conversion for training duties but equipped with ARI.18050, ARI.18058, CRT-2 and ALA-6 direction finding receivers. WL686 was also upgraded with one ALA-6 receiver replacing one of its APA-17 and during the 1960s WJ911 was converted to replacing the ageing WL686. Lacking space for sufficient equipment one Varsity operated in the L-band and S-band search role and the other in the X-band. The initial stage of training was to fly up and down the East Coast with the students locating and identifying the RAF's air defence radars. The two Varsities were retired during the early 1970s.

In 1968 No 5 FTS was given a secondary wartime role for inshore maritime reconnaissance patrols and some training sorties were undertaken. Despite the Varsity lacking suitable low-altitude navigation equipment or any kind of submarine detection equipment and its inability to carry anti-submarine weaponry, Varsities were still being declared to NATO with this secondary wartime role right up until their retirement. The Varsity was also used for experimental work, including the development of automatic landing devices at the Royal Aircraft Establishment (RAE). Another surprising use for the Varsity was to sample radioactive clouds following tests of British nuclear weapons in Australia during 1956 and 1957. In February 1956 six Varsities were assigned to Task Force 308/5 for Operation Mosaic off the Montebello Islands during May and June and Operation Buffalo at Maralinga in September and October 1956. During the latter trials, the Varsities carried out ground contamination surveys along the coastline from Onslow to Darwin and cloud-tracking. At least two Varsities were issued to No 1439 Flight in 1957 for Operation Antler at Maralinga during September and October 1957. The last Varsity would not retire from training service until 1974 with No 5 FTS having run 102 courses since March 1962 and the last Varsity was retired in May 1976.

Varsities travelled far and wide. No 115 Squadron used the type as part of its radar and landing aids calibration fleet from 1958 to 1970. Here WJ946 is seen visiting Gatow in Berlin on 15th June 1967 to conduct a calibration. *Ralf Manteufel*

Varsity T.1 WF417 is seen here at the Royal Aircraft Establishment's airfield at Thurleigh in June 1957 when it was being used as a trials aircraft by the Blind Landing Experimental Unit. WF417 made its first fully automatic landing approach and landing with the Autoland system on 11th November 1954. The information boards and lines shown were highlighting the various receiver antennas of the Autoland equipment. *Peter Berry via ABPic*

The Valetta Flying Classroom

The concept of the flying classroom dated back to 1939 when Scottish Aviation used four second-hand Fokker F.XXXVI and F.XXII airliners as observer, navigation and radio flying classrooms when it operated No 1 Air Observers Navigation School at Prestwick. The aircraft would frequently carry over 20 students (no less than 33 were recorded on one sortie!) plus instructors packed into the cabin. Post-war the concept was picked up again for the elementary stage of navigation training under Operational Requirement OR.269. Again the Valetta was considered suitable due to its spacious cabin and Specification T.1/49 was issued on 26th August 1949 to cover development. The cabin was configured for ten positions for students facing aft with each station equipped with a Gee Mk.2 indicator repeater, Rebecca Mk.4 homing, an air speed indicator and altimeter, a variation setting corrector, a drift sight, radio compass and a clock. Two seats were provided for the instructors and along the roof of the cabin five astrodomes were provided for the use of sextants. The prototype Type 664 Valetta T.3, VX564, made its maiden flight on 31st August 1950. A final conference on 20th September 1950 approved the equipment installations subject to flight trials at the Telecommunications Research Establishment at Defford, which were conducted the following month. Production totalled 39 aircraft and they replaced the Wellingtons of No 201 AFS and later served with all five Air Navigation Schools, in particular with No 1 ANS at Topcliffe and by 1965 all were with No 2 ANS at Hullavington to provide a 28 flying hour basic syllabus, students then passing onto that unit's Varsities.

Vickers Valetta T.3 VX564 of the Royal Air Force College is seen here on the apron at Cranwell on 20th May 1962. The line of five astrodomes are the prominent identifying feature of the T.3. Following retirement, it was relegated to Cranwell's fire dump in March 1967. *Ian Macfarlane*

Eighteen were later converted to T.4 standard with AI.17 airborne interception radar to train student navigators destined for the Gloster Javelin all-weather fighter (see below). Near the end of their operational lives in late 1960, the RAF College at Cranwell proposed converting six T.4s back to T.3 standard to replace its Varsity T.1s to meet the increased training demand. At this time the RAF College was taking biannual intakes of ten students each onto the three-year 166 flying hour syllabus, the aim being to bring the students up to ANS basic training standards. Marshall of Cambridge mocked-up a conversion which removed the AI.17 radar and Gee Mk.2 and added a second Gee Mk.3, two drift recorders, Rebecca Mk.4, positions for two student navigators seated side-by-side along with an occasional seat for the instructor on the main spar, a periscopic sextant mounting and a second astrodome. The conversion would cost £5,250 per aircraft and take eight weeks. The Air Ministry were unconvinced by the need and the project went no further and the T.4s were released for scrapping.

Intermediate Navigation Trainer

Flying Training Command wanted a more direct Avro Anson replacement for the intermediate training phase and Operational Requirement OR.312 was formulated in December 1951. The aircraft would sit between the Valetta T.3 used to teach the basic elements of navigation and the crew training Varsity and would be used to teach students the skills to navigate a light aircraft using all aids available and to accustom them to responsibilities of navigating before progressing to a larger and more advanced crew trainer. It would also have dual controls for pilot conversion and checking of staff pilots and was initially planned for elementary bombing training as well. Accommodation was required for a pilot, an instructor, two students and a signaller. Provision for worldwide operation was required. The performance requirements were quite basic; a ceiling of 15,000ft (4,570m) and a cruising speed no less than 115kt (212km/h) to allow the effective use of a bombsight. Equipment was to include provision for a vertical F.24 camera and light series carriers for sixteen practice bombs. Initially the first aircraft was wanted as soon as October 1952 but this date was relaxed and the bomb aimer training role was later deleted.

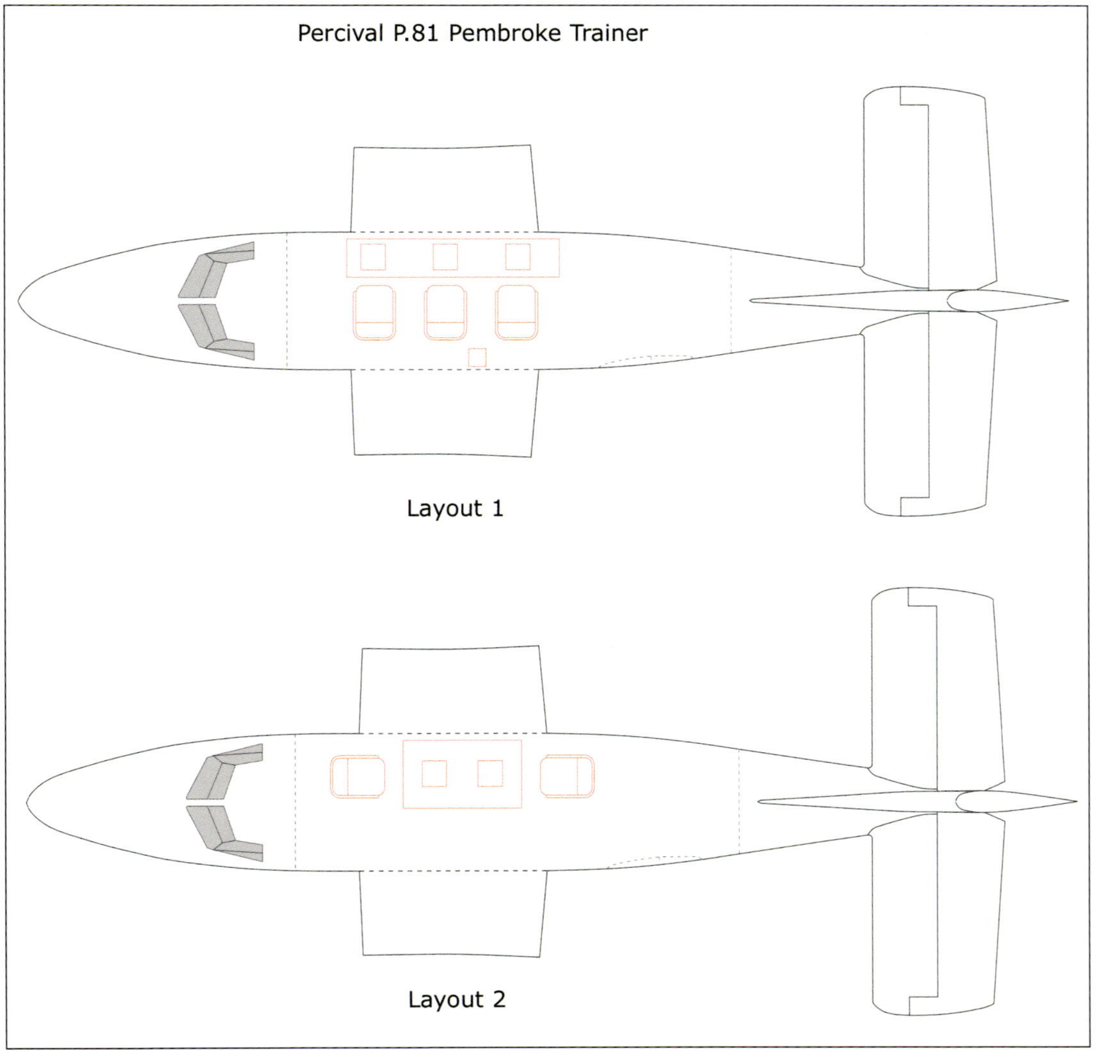

The Percival P.81 was a Pembroke variant intended as an Intermediate Navigation Trainer to meet OR.312. Two internal layouts, based on those used in the similar P.50 Sea Prince T.1 were offered with either two or three positions for the students and instructor. *Author*

Initial discussions identified that a variant of the Percival P.66 Pembroke C.1 transport would be suitable. The P.66 was a military development of the P.50 Prince eight-seat feederliner developed during 1947, which had achieved some commercial success with smaller operators and as a surveying aircraft. In June 1949 Percival Aircraft Limited had issued a brochure for the P.57 Prince Military Trainer as a flying classroom for no less than six training roles; radio and navigation, bomb aimer, solo crew, multi-engine pilot, bombing and gunnery and, finally, photography. The variants were very similar to the standard P.50, the two bombing training variants having the glazed nose of the P.54 Survey Prince and a Mk.XIV bombsight and an external light series carrier for four practice or smoke bombs; the second version added a Boulton Paul gun turret and an aft facing G.45 gun camera. The radio and navigation training variant would have an astrodome and positions for an instructor and three students in the cabin with the necessary navigational and radio equipment. The RAF had shown interest, but their requirements had already led to the larger Varsity; the Fleet Air Arm did procure the basic P.57 concept, however, as a flying classroom trainer for observer training (see Chapter Twelve).

RAF interest in the Prince for the communications role had meanwhile resulted in the larger and heavier P.66 Pembroke with 550hp (410kW) Alvis Leonides 127 engines. A total of 49 were eventually brought, six being fitted as survey/photoreconnaissance aircraft for the Far East. The MoS assessment confirmed the Pembroke's suitability as a navigation trainer, Percival having responded with the P.81 with an increased wingspan. But while the airframes could be delivered from December 1952, shortages of engines and some of the training equipment (including the Low Level Radio Altimeter Mk.5, IFF Mk.10 and lightweight radio sets) would delay delivery until September 1953 and even then some of the equipment would still be missing. Percival then proposed delivering an interim batch of up to 25 P.50 Princes by March 1953 but the MoS now proposed using 35 stored Handley Page Reading HPR.1 Marathons instead. Air Commodore Glynn Silyn-Roberts, the Deputy Director of Military Aircraft Research and Development, confirmed that the Air Ministry was happy to order either the Pembroke or the Marathon, whichever was the cheaper to run. Despite Specification T.121D&P having been written up for the Pembroke, there were now second thoughts and progress slowed, the P.81 being quietly dropped as attention shifted to the Marathon.

The Marathon had been developed as a four-engined 14-seat feederliner by George Miles during 1943, subsequently winning the Brabazon Committee's Type VA requirement. The Marathon emerged as a high-wing aircraft with tricycle undercarriage and powered by four 330hp (246kW) de Havilland Gipsy Queen 71 engines. The prototype, G-AGPD (initially flown under the B Condition marking of U10), made its maiden flight at Woodley on 19th May 1946 but the Marathon was dogged with bad luck. Even before it had flown the Treasury were concerned about the high production cost, which threatened a potential order for 40 for the British European Airways Corporation (BEA), although Miles wanted an order for 50 to enable a more economic production run. By December 1946 no official order was forthcoming but Miles tentatively ordered materials for the first 25 aircraft before the official order was finally placed on 17th February 1947. MAP's stipulated price of £32,000 per airframe was below Miles' offer of £40,000 and incurred a financial loss due to the production cost of £37,500. By the end of 1947 Miles Aircraft entered receivership and Handley Page acquired the Woodley site as Handley Page Reading and continued the Marathon programme, securing the order for 50 aircraft divided between BEA and companies affiliated to the British Overseas Airways Corporation. Neither customer really wanted the aircraft and they wriggled out of the contracts leaving 40 completed, but surplus, aircraft. The MoS now had to find a use for them. At this time the Air Ministry had raised OR.307 for an Airborne Interception radar trainer, OR.312 for an intermediate navigation trainer and OR.313 for a maritime reconnaissance crew trainer and the Marathon could be adapted to any of these. The Valetta and Varsity had already been earmarked for first and last of these requirements, so the Air Ministry was forced to accept 35 converted Marathons to fulfil OR.312 and Specification T.130D&P was issued to cover the conversion on 11 September 1952.

The second prototype Miles M.60 Marathon was first flown as G-AILH on 27 February 1947 but had been allocated serial VX229 as the aircraft was owned by the MoS. In 1952 the serial was finally applied as it became the prototype for the Marathon T.11. The astrodome was mocked-up on the aircraft and it was used for a series of handling flights, tropical trials and as avionics trials with the Telecommunications Research Establishment. In 1953 it was used for trials in connection with the Blue Jay air-to-air missile before being scrapped in 1957. *Blue Envoy Collection*

The changes to the Marathon included three rearward-facing navigation stations for the students, a signaller's position, provision of two astrodomes and two bulged windows in the cabin, and the equipment included Rebecca Mk.4, Gee Mk.2 and radio compasses. Space was reserved for a vertical camera and although bomb aiming was not required for the converted aircraft, any future new production aircraft may have received a glazed nose position. The conversion was not an easy process. All the aircraft were at varying stages of civil modification (there were a total of 400 modifications noted!) and needed to be brought a standard specification before work could begin on the modifications necessary for OR.312. There were also wing skin wrinkling problems, cured by redesigning the leading-edge and repairs with straps fitted over the main spar in line with the flanges of the front and rear ribs to achieve a 2,000 hour fatigue life. The stored airframes had a mix of 380hp (283kW) Gipsy Queen 70-3 or 340hp (253kW) Gipsy Queen 70-4 engines which were no longer in production, so they had to be replaced by new 330hp (246kW) Gipsy Queen 71-2 engines.

The first accepted Marathon T.11 was XA250, the former G-ALVW, which flew on 29th August 1952 but the first fully converted aircraft was XA260, formerly G-AMEP, did not fly until August 1953 (there is some ambiguity about the designation with confusion between T.1 and T.11, Marks 1-10 were reserved for civil variants and the servicing manuals and official documents are consistent with the use of T.11). By October 1952 it had been decided to continue running the Ansons until at least 1960, but the Air Staff had no choice but to find some use for the Marathons then being converted and one possible use was for refresher training for navigators trained in Canada. Following conversion the aircraft were delivered to No 10 Maintenance Unit at Hullavington before being issued to No 1 ANS based at the same airfield from January 1954, being used for two months until the school disbanded. The Marathons were then passed to No 2 ANS at Thorney Island. Following the cessation of navigator training in Canada, in March 1957 No 1 ANS reformed at Topcliffe with the surviving Marathons, using them until 29th July 1958 alongside four Valetta T.3s and a fast jet navigator fleet of nine Vampire NF.10s and two Vampire T.11s. Five Marathons were never issued and remained in storage at Hullavington and two conversions had been halted and completed as airliners for Japanese Far Eastern Airlines in February 1954. The surviving Marathons were sold off but all attempts at civil conversions for passenger or survey use were abandoned and most were acquired for scrap simply for their Gipsy Queen 71-2 engines. Some use had been obtained from the Marathon but in reality the desire to find a use for these surplus aircraft had forced the Air Ministry to persevere with a requirement that was not really needed and wasted resources on a conversion programme that could not salvage the investment already lost on the Marathon.

The Miles M.69 Marathon II had Armstrong Siddeley Mamba turboprops and full cabin pressurisation but also failed to attract commercial interest. The prototype G-AHXU was issued military serial VX231 for trials and was served for a brief period during 1953-54 at the Empire Test Pilot's School. *Terry Panopalis Collection*

All-weather Radar Operator Trainers

Airborne Interception (AI) radar had been introduced during the autumn of 1940 in night-fighters and during the war the radar operators were initially trained using operational aircraft. The first dedicated AI trainer was developed during the autumn of 1944, the Type 487 Wellington T.XVII aircraft were converted GR.XI anti-submarine aircraft intended for Coastal Command fitted with the nose radome and AI.10 radar from the de Havilland Mosquito NF.XVII, which replaced the nose turret. These nine T.XVII conversions were followed by 80 Type 490 Wellington T.XVIIIs built at Vickers' Blackpool factory based on the airframe of the GR.XIII torpedo-bomber and equipped with the American SCR 720 radar. The radio operator and navigator's compartments were modified to accommodate four students and an instructor. These aircraft were used until the early 1950s by units like the Central Fighter Establishment.

Early post-war advanced AI training made use of another aircraft conversion. The Bristol Type 164 Brigand had been developed to Specification H.7/42 as a torpedo-fighter. The original requirement had passed by the time it entered service as the Brigand B.1 as a light bomber in 1946. Production ended in 1949 and a search was made for other suitable uses for the aircraft. Due to the Brigand's maximum speed of 358mph (576km/h) at 16,000ft (4,785m) and its spacious three-man cockpit it was considered suitable for conversion as a radar trainer for night-fighter navigators. The resulting Brigand T.4 had an AI.10 set in the nose and the former navigator and radio operator positions were fitted with radar consoles for an instructor and pupil. The rear cockpit canopy was also blacked out to simulate night-time conditions during daytime training sorties. A total of nine new-build and 33 B.1 conversions – many of which were carried out by Flight Refuelling Limited – were completed and issued from July 1951 to No 228 Operational Conversion Unit (OCU) at Leeming – disbanding and reforming the following year as No 238 OCU.

The transfer of bombing and advanced AI training from the Air Navigation Schools (ANS) to the to OCUs in early 1952 resulted in increased utilisation of the Brigands and additional aircraft were required to cope. A proposal to convert the similar Bristol Type 166 Buckmaster advanced trainer was abandoned as the different forward fuselage and cockpit required more extensive modifications which would have overloaded an already busy design office at Filton. The wartime AI.10 set was also showing its age as newer Gloster Meteor NF.12 and de Havilland Venom NF.3. night-fighters received the more modern American AN/APS-57 radar (designated in British service as the AI.21).

The Bristol Brigand T.4 prototype RH798 shows two of its distinguishing features; the dielectric radome for the AI.10 radar and the blacked out rear cockpit canopy so that the student navigator and instructor could work in darkness. *Bristol via Tony Buttler*

Brigand T.4 VS837 on a training sortie in early 1952 with the Airborne Interception School, which had formed out of No 228 OCU and later that year became No 238 OCU. The darkened rear cockpit meant that all-weather and night interceptions could be practiced in safety by day. *Tony Buttler Collection*

Brigand T.4 WA560 had an unusual history. Built as Brigand B.1 RH821, it was one of two aircraft delivered to the Royal Pakistan Air Force in 1949 for evaluation. On return to the UK the aircraft was overhauled by Bristol and issued to the RAF as WA560. It was converted to T.4 standard in early 1951 and struck off charge on 28th May 1957. *Frank Hudson*

The Bristol Buckmaster was developed as an advanced twin-engine trainer to Specification T.13/43 and 110 aircraft were built using parts from cancelled Buckingham bombers. The fastest trainer in the RAF on its introduction, they were issued to No 228 OCU to aid pilot conversion to the Brigand. They also performed this duty with No 238 OCU. An AI trainer conversion was considered but proved too much for Bristol's stretched design office resources. Buckmaster T.1 RP246 seen here served with the Empire Central Flying School in 1946. *Blue Envoy Collection*

The Brigand T.5 was almost identical externally to the T.4 but had the American AN/APS-57 radar, designated AI.21 in British service. WA566 seen in the foreground of this row of Brigands belonging to No 238 OCU was one of 21 T.5 conversions. *Tony Buttler Collection*

Marshall of Cambridge began the Brigand T.5 conversion programme from February 1953, converting most of the T.4s and eight B.1s with the AI.21 inside a longer nose radome. The 45 flying hour basic training syllabus was flown during the daytime, hence the blacked out rear cockpit canopy and the students practiced against Boulton Paul Balliol T.2 and Supermarine Spitfire LF.16E flying targets. By the time of its disbandment in March 1958, No 238 OCU had trained around 600 radar navigators on the Brigand. The unit had also undertaken standardisation training with the night-fighter squadrons assigned to Fighter Command and RAF Germany and had trained Egyptian, Israeli and Syrian Meteor night-fighter crews. A couple of Brigand T.5s also served as radar trainers with the Maritime Training Unit, No 236 OCU. The main drawback of the Brigand was that only one student could be trained at a time, this lead to the introduction of a larger 'flying classroom' for the basic phase before the students moved onto the Meteor NF.14, which replaced the ageing Brigands for advanced training.

In June 1952 Operational Requirement OR.307 was drafted for a flying classroom AI trainer with the capability to carry four students and one instructor. The aircraft needed an endurance of four hours and an operating ceiling of at least 18,000ft (5,485m) (ideally 20,000ft (6,100m)) to prevent radar wave ground return effects from confusing the student operators. The American AN/APQ-43 radar was specified until the new long-range X-band AI.18 radar was ready and the desired in-service date was early 1956. Later the AI.17 set (a development from the AI.10) was selected instead of the APQ-43, which with its two scanner dishes was both cumbersome and heavy and it proved difficult to engineer sufficient repeaters to present the radar scope image at the students' positions. The Vickers Valetta transport had already been modified as a flying classroom for the navigation training role as the Valetta T.3 and was quickly identified as the best solution, although the Varsity T.1 was also considered for conversion. Other potential aircraft examined by the Ministry of Supply's (MoS) Director of R&D Projects, Mr A S Crouch, were the Percival Pembroke and the Handley Page (Reading) HPR.1 Marathon (formerly the Miles M.60). It was soon found that neither could meet the altitude requirement without new engines; Alvis Leonides Major radial engines and Armstrong Siddeley Mamba turboprops respectively. The substantial redesign required led to both aircraft being quickly rejected. An MoS team visited Weybridge in September 1952 to discuss the Valetta conversion. The main changes would entail modifying the nose for the radar and fitting the five new stations equipped with radar repeaters in the cabin. The two Bristol Hercules 230 engines were swapped for the Hercules 270 which had two additional generators for an increased electricity supply. Financial problems slowed progress as the Air Ministry dragged their heels over the £21,000 development cost, but Marshall's eventually received a contract to carry out a trial installation in Valetta T.3 WJ465. This aircraft flew as the Type 743 Valetta T.4 prototype on 15th March 1956. A total of eighteen Valetta T.3 trainers were converted, the last two being an additional order. These served with Nos 1 and 2 ANS as well as No 238 OCU.

The Canberra T.11 was another modification to the ubiquitous airframe. Boulton Paul modified the B.2 bombers with an ungainly nose radome containing an AI.17E radar. WH714 was used by No 228 OCU from its conversion until it was struck off charge in June 1968 following an accident during taxying when the brakes failed and the aircraft ran into a hedge at Binbrook. *Author's Collection*

Another spike in the training demand during 1956, resulting from the introduction of the Gloster Javelin FAW.1 all-weather fighter, led to proposals to convert three Valetta C.1 transports as additional aircraft and there was a tentative plan to fit the Varsity with either AI.17 or AI.21 radar, but both schemes were soon abandoned. During 1957 to 1959, No 238 OCU operated the Javelin Mobile Conversion Unit which toured the squadrons re-equipping with the Javelin, giving the crews radar practice aboard a Valetta T.4 before they carried out training interceptions on their own Javelins. The Valetta T.4s ended their operational life with No 2 ANS in 1967 as the Hawker Siddeley Dominie T.1 entered service.

As already mentioned, the advanced training phase took place on the Meteor NF.14 night-fighter from 1958 onwards, the main drawback being that an instructor could not be carried with the student. As befits British military procurement, the ideal solution took nearly a decade to come to fruition. In July 1949 the Assistant Chief of the Air Staff (Operational Requirements) (ACAS(OR)), Air Vice-Marshal Claude Pelly had called for a draft Operational Requirement for a jet-powered AI radar trainer and the English Electric Canberra was quickly identified as being ideal with performance representative of a fighter and with enough room in the cockpit for up to two students and an instructor as well as the pilot. The draft requirements circulated around Fighter Command

Canberra B.2 WH903 returned to RAF service on 26th August 1958 following its T.11 conversion. WH903 is pictured here in May 1968, two years after its conversion to radar-less T.19 standard, during its time with No 85 Squadron. *Terry Panopalis Collection*

Canberra B.2 WK106 was converted to T.11 standard, losing its radar to become a T.19 in 1968 and being passed to No 100 Squadron, whose colourful chequerboard and skull and crossbones adorn the tailfin. WK106 was scrapped in 1977. *Terry Panopalis Collection*

and the MoS before the Vice Chief of the Air Staff, Air Chief Marshal Sir Ralph Cochrane in March 1951 stated that the Canberra should be dropped and both Fighter Command and the Assistant Chief of the Air Staff (Training) were told to go away and prepare a stronger case. Obviously this proved impossible as in May Air Marshal Sir Basil Embry, the Air Officer Commanding Fighter Command, declared that there were no further AI trainer requirements. There the matter rested until 1954 when the need arose for an intermediate solution between the Valetta T.4 and the Meteor NF.14 and a Canberra conversion was again proposed. The MoS agreed with the proposal and Specification T.182D was issued for the conversion of B.2 bombers as the T.11 Airborne Interception Trainer. Development was contracted to Boulton Paul, who had already carried out several experimental Canberra conversions including fitting AI.18 radars for research and trials. Even so, the programme took time to complete. An AI.17E radar was fitted in an elongated nose radome and new stations provided for the student and instructor behind the pilot's cockpit. Although twelve conversions were requested, three aircraft were later cancelled and the first of the completed conversions, WJ610 (which had been the first production B.2) flew on 11th August 1958. The T.11 fleet was issued to No 228 OCU and used until its disbandment in January 1967 as the Javelin fleet retired. The T.11s were then assigned to No 85 Squadron and then the newly reformed No 100 Squadron and used for the other side of the training process – being flown as radar targets by these target facilities units and for target towing. In the process the eight survivors lost their radars and were re-designated as the T.19.

Eight Canberra T.11 airframes had their AI.17E radars removed during the late 1960s to serve as T.19 electronically silent flying targets. T.19 WJ975 is seen here in July 1977 while serving with No 100 Squadron. Retired in 1980, the aircraft now resides with AeroVenture South Yorkshire Aircraft Museum, Doncaster. *Terry Panopalis Collection*

Fast-Jet Navigators

As early as 1951 consideration had been given to jet-powered crew trainers for Bomber Command but the cost and lack of suitable military or civilian designs for conversion prevented any developments in this area (see Chapter Six). By 1953, however, the need to provide navigators destined for all-weather fighters and Canberras with experience of high-altitude, high-speed flight became increasingly evident. The Vampire NF.10 night-fighter had entered service in July 1951 but by 1953 was already being phased out in favour of the Gloster Meteor NF.11 and NF.12. The stored NF.10s also offered a cheap and economical solution for the refresher training of Canadian-trained navigators instead of using the Marathon. The syllabus would consist of high-speed, high altitude familiarisation flights over the UK (and its changeable weather!) as well as timing, tracking and rapid fixing Gee Mk.3 exercises and VHF 'let downs' and approaches. Airwork Limited were awarded a contract to convert 36 NF.10s, replacing the AI.10 radar with concrete ballast and fitting Rebecca Mk.4. The cannon were retained to maintain the centre of gravity. A clear-view canopy from the Venom NF.2A was also fitted, although ejection seats were not.

The fifth conversion, WM711, was assessed by the A&AEE in May 1955, who carried out flight trials, a magnetic survey of compass positions and checked the operation of the Gee Mk.3 and VHF. Following these it recommended providing a folding plotting table for the navigator, moving the Gee indicator which was difficult to see being mounted behind the pilot's headrest facing starboard, and removing some metal items on the instrumental panel which affected the compass. The trials noted that the navigator's view of the flight instruments was not good and that the lack of a height adjustable seat made map reading difficult due to the limited field of vision outside. The Central Navigation and Control School at Shawbury received its first NF(T).10s in May 1954 and became the major user until September 1959. Others served with No 2 ANS at Thorney Island until July 1959 and with No 1 ANS at Topcliffe from May 1957 for two years. At the end of their RAF service many still had low airframe hours and thirty were refurbished by de Havilland for export to India as NF.54 night-fighters.

During the summer of 1957, Flying Training Command examined a proposal to use twenty Canberra B.2 bombers for navigator training instead of the Vampires. The Canberra could carry an instructor as well as a student and could replace the 20 hours of Vampire training and some of the Varsity's 22 flying hours, which would improve the overall quality of the training. Air Vice-Marshal Wallace Kyle, the Assistant Chief of the Air Staff (Operational Requirements), warned that any substantial modifications could take up to four years to pass through the chain of Air Staff and MoS technical and policy committees and for Treasury approval. Even so, it was the additional £1 million of running costs annually that scuppered the plan. By February 1959, numbers of Meteor NF.14 night-fighters had become available to replace the Vampires and these were similarly converted with ballast replacing the radar and new UHF radios were installed. They entered service during the summer of 1959 as the NF(T).14 with Nos 1 and 2 ANS and the Central Navigation and Control School.

The Jet-Set Generation Trainer: Dominie

Despite the Canberra having been rejected due to its operating costs, the Air Ministry by November 1957 had been studying an outline requirement for a high-speed light passenger/crew training aircraft with the ability to carry two crew and five passengers (with a maximum capacity for ten passengers) over 1,500nm (2,778km) stage lengths at 400kt (740km/h). Such a type would replace the Anson,

The Gloster Meteor NF(T).14s replaced the Vampire NF(T).10 in the fast jet navigator training role. WS797 of No 1 ANS is seen here at Benson during the 1960s. *Terry Panopalis Collection*

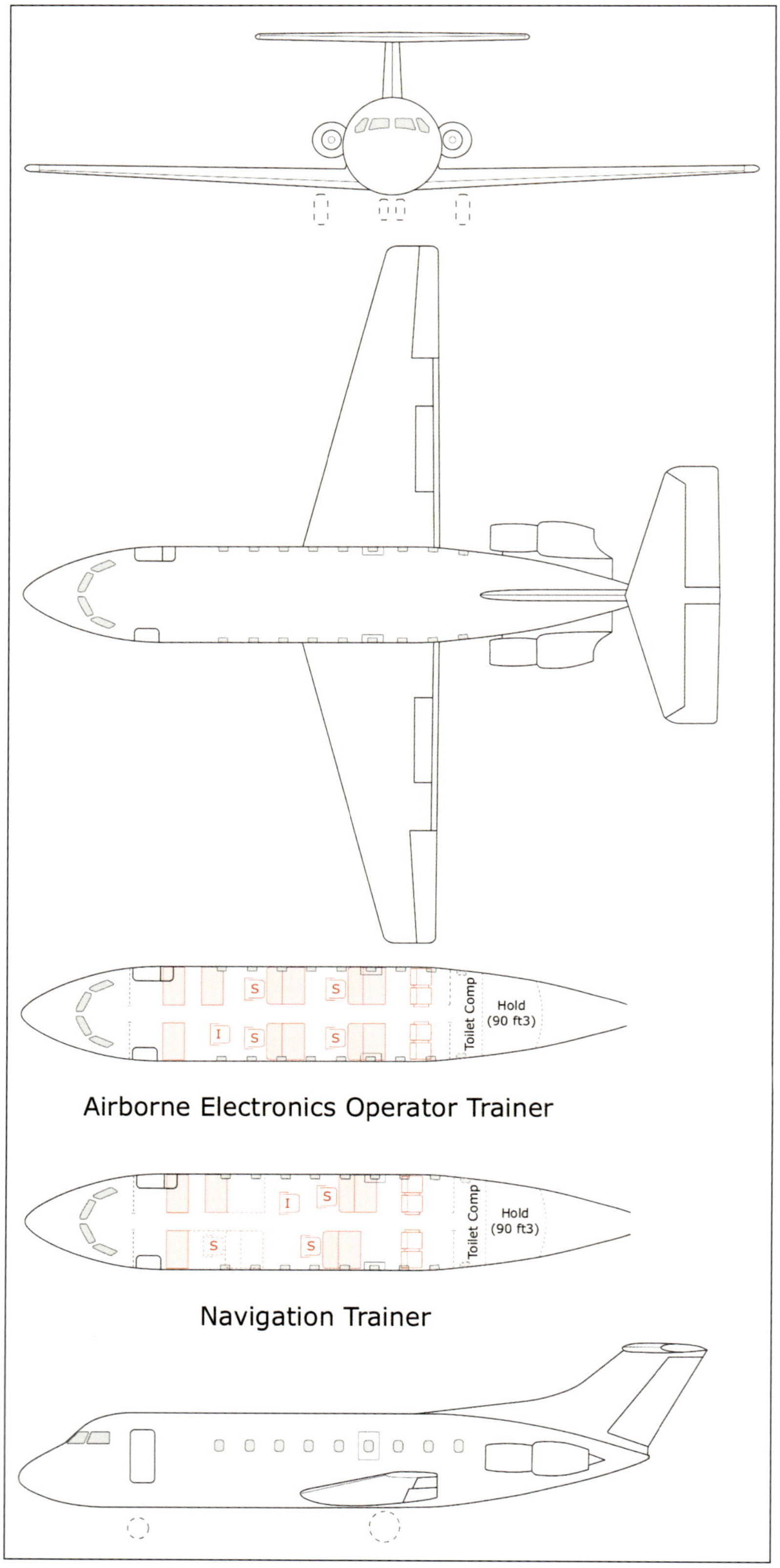

Soon after designing the DH.125 executive aircraft, de Havilland drew up the DH.126, a larger development suitable as a feederliner. This was offered to the RAF as a crew trainer. Example layouts were for four AEO students and an instructor or as a navigation trainer with two or three students and an instructor. *Author*

Pembroke and the de Havilland Devon which were, 'out of keeping with the present jet age.' There was no spare research and development money, but with Avro and Vickers keenly interested in the jet-powered executive aircraft market, it was decided not to draft a formal Operational Requirement but wait and see if either company would risk a private venture. Neither company showed any interest at this time and even in April 1960, when thoughts had turned to replacing the Varsity T.1, an Operational Requirement remained difficult to agree given the economic constraints. The Director of Operational Requirements, Air Commodore Thomas W Piper, went ahead regardless and assessed the likely contenders; the Handley Page Reading HPR.7 Dart Herald, Avro 748 Series 2, de Havilland DH.123, Dassault Communaute and the Lockheed CL-329 JetStar. All but the DH.123 were (or nearly) off-the-shelf purchases and the CL-329 had originally been developed as the T-40A utility aircraft and crew trainer for the United States Air Force (USAF), although in 1959 the USAF decided to purchase the smaller and cheaper North American T-39 Sabreliner instead. None of them fully met the likely requirements but the turboprop-powered Avro 748, Dart Herald and DH.123 with extra fuel and improved cabin pressurisation would meet all but the speed requirements. It was acknowledged that any changes for low-level flying and provision of navigation equipment would increase the cost.

Shortly afterwards, Hunting Percival's technical director, F H Pollicut, visited the Air Ministry to present their new H.107 59-seat feederliner powered by two Bristol Siddeley BS75 turbojets, which following the merger with the British Aircraft Corporation would emerge as the larger BAC 1-11 airliner. It could attain an altitude of 30,000ft (9,145m) with a cruising speed of 400kt (740km/h) and could carry three to five crew plus four passengers and as a flying classroom could seat ten students. In July, James A R Kay, one of the joint managing directors of Hawker Siddeley Aviation presented a range of options. Kay heavily pushed the Avro 761 65-seat feederliner designed as a Viscount replacement powered by two Rolls-Royce RB.163 Spey turbofans, which the Air Staff immediately felt was too large. Hawker Siddeley felt that the Avro 748 was the most economical choice but if the Air Staff really wanted a faster type they had the smaller BS75-powered 46/60-seat Avro 771 and the cheaper 50-seat 778, a development of the 748 with two RB.161 turbofans. Handley Page during 1961 had offered a navigation trainer variant of the HP.124 Military Herald tactical transport to meet a Royal Canadian Air Force (RCAF) requirement. The RCAF were also thinking in terms of a jet and so the two Rolls-Royce Dart R.Da.12 turboprops were replaced with Bristol Siddeley Viper turbojets, giving a speed of 350kt (648km/h) at 33,000ft (10,060m) and four hours endurance. Not to be left out, de Havilland offered their DH.126 30-seat feederliner which they had just begun to sketch out. Looking like an enlarged

Crew training enters the jet age. Prototype Hawker Siddeley Dominie T.1 XS709 is pictured here during an early test flight during 1962 fitted with an anti-spin parachute in an enlarged tailcone. XS709 is one of the few RAF trainer prototypes to survive, today being displayed at the RAF Museum, Cosford. *Terry Panopalis Collection*

DH.125, it was offered for VIP transportation and both as a navigation trainer with two pilots, an instructor and two students plus space for four passengers and as an electronic training aircraft with an instructor, four pupils and retaining space for four passengers.

All of these offerings were larger and more expensive than the Air Ministry desired and as designs still on the drawing board they would all require reasonably expensive research and development programmes. A team under Joe Goodwin at de Havilland's Hatfield design offices began work in 1961 on a six to eight-seat executive aircraft, a spiritual successor to the Dragon Rapide – indeed briefly receiving the moniker Jet Dragon – which more closely met what the Air Staff had in mind. The prototype DH.125, G-ARYA, was powered by two 3,000lbf (13.3kN) Bristol Siddeley Viper turbojets and first flew on 13th August 1962. Hawker Siddeley continued development on its take-over of de Havilland as the HS.125 and the Air Ministry quickly became very interested and Air Staff Target AST.375 was issued to replace the Meteors NF(T).14s. Specification T.233D&P was issued to Hawker Siddeley on 13th February 1963 and an order for 20 Series 2 aircraft with 3,100lbf (13.7kN) Viper 301 engines was placed soon after for a cost of £5.57 million. The cabin was arranged with two rearward-facing navigational stations for the pupils and a seat for an instructor in addition to the pilot and a signaller. In addition to the Ekco E190 weather-avoidance radar and the navigation equipment, an accident recording device and a crash locator beacon was also fitted.

The prototype, XS709, first flew on 30th December 1964. A total of 21 names with navigational, educational and geographic connotations and alliteration with the first letters of both de Havilland and Hawker were proposed, the chosen name of Dominie narrowly pipping Don – itself a former de Havilland trainer. The first Dominie T.1 was delivered to No 1 ANS at Stradishall in December 1965 Others were issued to the RAF College at Cranwell and the College of Air Warfare. Eleven Dominies replaced No 1 ANS's twelve Meteor NF(T).14s, taking over the advanced course and also replacing eight of the School's Varsity T.1s. At the time of its introduction,

Early production Dominie XS711 was delivered to the RAF in November 1965, being issued to No 1 ANS. The original silver and red colour scheme was short-lived and arguably not as attractive as the later white-red-grey colours which the Dominie wore for the majority of its career. *Terry Panopalis Collection*

Above: Dominie T.1 XS712 is seen here at Hawker Siddeley's factory at Hatfield in March 1968. At this time it was serving with No 1 ANS. Delivered in August 1965, XS712 was withdrawn from service on 20th January 2011 and today is a ground instructional airframe at the BAE Systems R J Mitchell Aircraft Maintenance Academy at Humberside Airport. *Ken Haynes*

Left: Dominie T.1 XS713 was serving with No 6 FTS when this photograph was taken at Leuchars on 23rd September 1989. *Steve Ryle*

Flying Training Command's maximum capacity was 102 navigator students on its main and refresher courses and they were planning for future rationalisation of the training schools by the end of the 1960s. In August 1970 No 1 ANS and the Varsity-equipped No 2 ANS were disbanded and reformed into No 6 FTS at Finningley which was soon also responsible for AEO training and took over the RAF College's Staff Navigation courses. It also used Jet Provosts, including the modified T.5s (unofficially called the T.5B) with tip tanks reinstated for low-level fast jet navigator training. The growing importance of two-seat combat aircraft as a proportion of the frontline force saw the navigator being renamed the weapon system officer by the 1990s. The Dominies were also increasingly used for signaller and air loadmaster training. Between 1992 and 1996 eleven Dominies were upgraded to T.2 standard by Marshalls Aerospace and Racal with upgraded training stations (now forward-facing) and the addition of Thorn Searchwater radar in a new 12in (30cm) longer nose radome for improved ground-mapping radar training.

Multi-Purpose Trainer: The Jetstream Blows In

With the Dominie being developed for the fast jet navigator phase of the training syllabus, the Air Staff turned their attention to finding a replacement for the Varsity. A programme of refurbishment had begun in 1965 but the service life would expire in the early 1970s and a draft of Air Staff Requirement ASR.390 was circulated in March 1967. The aircraft would ideally be an off-the-shelf purchase with minimal changes to avoid expensive development costs and had to be suitable to train multi-engine pilots, navigators, AEOs and flight engineers and had to enter service by June 1972. In addition to the pilot and an instructor, there would be space in the cabin for four student navigators in the navigation training role or in the aircrew training role the pilot would be joined by a navigator and two instructors (one flight engineer and one AEO) and two engineer and two AEO students. The maximum speed range was 250kt (462km/h) at sea level to Mach 0.6 (735km/h) at 25,000ft (7,620m) with sufficient fuel and reserves for two one-hour sorties or 1,300nm (2,408km) stage lengths. The aircraft was to have a ten-year service life without any major structural modifications. In addition, two pilot flight simulators were required, but existing navigation, AEO and air engineer training simulators would be modified. Discussions were also held with the RCAF who still had a similar requirement and had evaluated the Dominie in 1963. The new Ministry of Technology (Mintech) agreed with an off-the-shelf solution but they were concerned that equipment integration would still be expensive.

The selection process would prove to be tortuous. In 1965 Handley Page followed de Havilland in focusing on the business executive market, especially within the USA, with a twelve-seat design powered by two 840shp (626kW) Turbomeca Astazou XIV turboprops, the HP.137 Jetstream. Scottish Aviation Ltd. at Prestwick were brought in as partners to produce the wings. The prototype, G-ATXH had flown at Radlett on 18th August 1967, so qualified as an off-the-shelf type. Shortly afterwards, Handley Page re-engined the Jetstream Series 1 with the more powerful (and less temperamental) Garrett TPE-331 for the US-market and secured an order from the USAF for eleven Series 3M aircraft as the C-10A for personnel and cargo transport. The Jetstream's troubled development programme due to problems with the Astazou XIV – soon abandoned for the 965shp (720kW) Astazou XVI – hastened Handley Page's demise, the resulting £13 million development costs being £10 million more than originally forecast. Falling into bankruptcy, the C-10A order was cancelled and the company's assets placed up for disposal. Handley Page had been in an awkward situation; its founder and Chairman, Sir Frederick Handley Page, had resisted the Ministry of Aviation's (MoA) rationalisation policy and during 1962 he had rejected an undervalued share price offer from Hawker Siddeley Aviation. The company began to lose out on Ministry contracts on Victor B.2 production and tanker conversions which worsened the financial situation. The Air Staff had wanted the HP.124 Military Dart Herald tactical transport but in February 1962 had been forced by the government to buy the Hawker Siddeley HS.780 Andover based on the Avro 748 instead. This anti-Handley Page atmosphere now affected ASR.390, the Air Staff clearly wanting a variant of the Jetstream and basing their requirements around it, but never feeling able to openly state that they wanted to buy the Jetstream. A Mintech official in September 1968 admitted that a competitive tender would see both Hawker Siddeley and BAC applying political pressure against a Jetstream order.

Another complication was that the Air Staff had already claimed that only a jet-powered aircraft could meet the performance requirements for training navigators for strategic and tactical bombers when they justified buying the Dominie, leading Mintech to now question whether a turboprop-powered aircraft would actually be of any use for advanced pilot and crew training. Mintech argued that ordering more Dominies was the best solution, adding that a Jetstream trainer would require a gross weight of 15,500lb (7,030kg) to enable a sufficient payload, a figure higher than planned for the C-10A variant. Other types put forward by Mintech were converted Armstrong Whitworth Argosy C.1 transports or the Avro 748. No decision was reached, ASR.390 was in abeyance and Handley Page's collapse soon after seemed to end the matter.

The Avro 748 was never selected for aircrew training, but HS.780 Andover XS606 was issued to the Empire Test Pilot's School in 1975 following retirement from the tactical transport role. Withdrawn from use in late 2012, it was sold for civil use and was destroyed in an accident taking off from Malakai Airport, Sudan, on 10th November 2015. *Terry Panopalis Collection*

The second production Jetstream T.1 XX476. It was one of the surplus ex-RAF aircraft that were converted to T.2 standard in 1976 for the FAA as observer trainers. The aircraft was retired in 2010 and today is preserved at Hermeskeil Air Museum in Germany. *Blue Envoy Collection*

Multi-Purpose Trainer: The Jetstream Returns

In fact the Jetstream was not dead and neither was the need to replace the Varsity. Scottish Aviation had acquired the Jetstream programme, setting up a subsidiary Jetstream Ltd., to secure the future of their own badly hit company and restarted production with the understanding that the RAF would place an order. ASR.398 was issued for a Varsity replacement for the navigator training role. A survey of available off-the-shelf twin turboprop-engined aircraft with pressurised cabins identified two favourable options; the Jetstream 200 (formerly the Series 2) and the North American Rockwell Model 690 Turbo Commander. Several other types were rejected following the survey; the Avro 748 was judged to be too large, the Beechcraft Model C90 King Air had been favoured by the CFS but was expensive, as was the Swearingen Merlin III business aircraft. The new six-seat Piper PA 31T Cheyenne was too small for the role and while the slightly larger eight-seat Cessna 421B Golden Eagle was considered to be suitable, it did not make the shortlist.

It was decided to hold comparative trials of the Jetstream and the Turbo Commander at A&AEE Boscombe Down in August 1971. The prototype Jetstream 200 G-AXFV was joined by the fourth production Turbo Commander N9203N for a full flying and performance assessment covering handling for pilot training, suitability of the cabin for modification and serviceability. The Turbo Commander was found to be very pleasant to fly with excellent handling qualities and good safety margins. With the full avionics specified to ASR.398 the A&AEE felt that with a few minor changes it would have very good potential and that students trained on the Scottish Aviation Bulldog (note at this time the Bulldog had not yet officially been ordered for the RAF) or the Jet Provost would have no problem converting to it. Despite having a standard seven-seat arrangement and a maximum capacity of eleven it was found that fitting seven airmen, their equipment plus a dinghy would be difficult but could be accomplished. The prototype Jetstream 200 gave a slightly poorer impression, G-AXFV having been hurriedly readied for the Paris Air Show and following heavy use in demonstrations, certification trials and the London-Victoria Air Race the exterior finish was poor and it lacked any interior trim. The cockpit view was found to be poor for the training role and the handling was more demanding, suitable for pilots trained on the Jet Provost but less so for those coming straight from the Bulldog, which offered more realistic handling for conversion onto operational types. With modifications to the cockpit windows, the stall warning 'stick pusher' and the addition of a yaw damper it was considered that the Jetstream would be suitable. It was inevitable that the desire to support Scottish Aviation following its purchase of the Jetstream programme would decide the order.

Specification 283D&P was issued for the Jetstream 200 Model 201 on 27th June 1972. The cruising speed was to be not less than 200kt (370km/h) with a service ceiling not less than 25,000ft (7,620m) at all weights up to the take-off weight of 12,500lb (5,669kg) at maximum continuous power. The aircraft was to be capable of climbing to 15,000ft (4,570m) within twelve minutes. An order was placed for 26 aircraft for a cost of around £9 million. The first seven aircraft were converted from stored Handley Page-built airframes, the next fourteen were unfinished airframes completed by Scottish Aviation and the remaining five were new-builds. The first aircraft to fly was XX475 (formerly G-AWVJ) on 13th April 1973 and deliveries to the CFS began on 26th June and No 5 FTS at Oakington on 12th December. Twelve months later No 5 FTS was disbanded and the Jetstreams were passed to 6 FTS. Then the effects of the Defence Review which drastically reduced Transport Command's size resulting a decline in navigator requirements and all of the Jetstreams were placed in storage by the end of 1975 as the Dominie took over crew training. The Royal Navy saw this as an opportunity to acquire fourteen converted for observer training as the Jetstream T.2 (see Chapter Twelve).

The remaining Jetstreams were reassigned from November 1976 for the advanced multi-engine pilot training role with the Multi-Engine Training Squadron (METS), part of No 3 FTS at Leeming. The METS syllabus lasted for 20 weeks and was composed of 45 hours on the simulator and 47 hours on the Jetstream. Courses were also run for students re-streamed from fast jet or rotary wing courses. With hindsight it is surprising that asymmetric flying training, both during the training syllabus and on frontline squadrons, for all multi-engined types still relied on the rather hazardous course of actually shutting down one engine well into the 1980s despite many accidents throughout the post-war period, many of which were sadly fatal. METS had several changes of parent unit; in 1979 it transferred to No 6 FTS at Finningley, in June 1992 became No 45 (Reserve) Squadron and then in September 1995 was returned to No 3 FTS at Cranwell.

Rear Crew Training: The Argosy's Final Mission

The Jetstream was not to be the only Varsity replacement. In 1970 the Air Force Board had agreed to Mintech's earlier suggestion to replace the Varsity with converted Argosy C.1 transports which were being replaced by the Lockheed C-130K Hercules. A draft of ASR.399 focused on the crew training role was circulated in July 1971 to replace the Varsity by 1974 when its structural life would expire and the Hercules had fully supplanted the Argosy. Hawker Siddeley received a contract to undertake the Argosy T.2 conversions. The main external difference was a larger radar radome for an ASV.21E radar for navigator training. To reduce costs only surplus radar equipment could be used, making the ASV.21 ideal as it was also fitted to the Nimrod and offered good performance for training. Additionally, like the Varsity before it, the plan was to declare these converted Argosies to NATO with a secondary wartime maritime reconnaissance role. Several other radars had been considered; the Blue Parrot fitted to the Blackburn Buccaneer was similar to ASV.21 but spare sets were difficult to obtain and the commercial Ekco E160, E190, E290 and E390 series weather radars were deemed unsuitable, although their new manufacturer, Mullard Equipment Limited, did propose to develop a new radar. Even the 1950s vintage H2S Mk.9 and the Marconi ARI.5955 fitted to Westland Wessex HAS.3 anti-submarine helicopters had briefly been considered. The spacious cabin had ample room for the training stations. The other external distinguishing feature was a larger supply aimer's window. Fourteen Argosy conversions were ordered for an establishment of twelve at No 6 FTS with two reserves, the cost being £5.5 million. In addition, two further Argosys would be converted to T.1 standard for crew familiarisation training.

Then in the summer of 1973 Flying Training Command proposed ordering new HS.125-600 aircraft instead. The HS.125-600 was powered by the more powerful 3,700lbf (16.4kN) Viper 601-22 and two of these had already been ordered for the VIP transport role with No 32 Squadron. The two choices were now compared in detail. The HS.125 offered a smaller cabin and its E190 radar had already been rejected, despite Flying Training Command now contradicting its earlier policy and claiming that was superior to the ASV.21 for training. For training flight engineers the HS.125 was derided as 'useless' and the AEO students would have little more than a Morse key when the Argosy offered full radar training capability and the future potential for electronic warfare simulation equipment. The flight performance was greater but this was less of an advantage for basic training. Comparing acquisition and running costs to 1988/89, twelve Argosies would cost an estimated £25.28 million, eleven HS.125-600 would cost £31.25 million and operating nine would still cost £26.88 million. The Air Staff argued that Strike Command, Technical Training Command, the Operational Conversion Units (OCUs), the Ministry of Defence (MoD) and the Radar Research Establishment all favoured the Argosy. Cancelling the Argosy conversion would waste £200-300,000 already spent and getting a new operational requirement approved for the HS.125-600 would take at least three years of endless committees and there was no guarantee that it would be chosen if another round of technical assessments were required. Faced with such opposition the proposal was dropped.

By October 1974, however, further problems were looming. The forthcoming Defence Review demanded heavy savings and as mentioned earlier, the long-range transport fleet was to be drastically reduced. At that time 25 percent of all navigator graduates were destined for fast jets, in future it would be 45 percent. Students received 165 hours on the simulator but the 149.5 flying hours would be reduced to 100 and would use spare Dominie capacity to enable the Argosy conversions to be cancelled. The AEO students were receiving 60 hours in the Varsity and 204 hours on the simulator, the Argosy would be replaced by equipping the spare seat in the Dominie with a table, Morse key and a HF618T controller for a reduced 48 hour course flown conjointly with navigation training sorties. What the Dominie could not provide, but the Argosy would have, was airborne maritime training, photography, ship recognition and air-to-ship communications below 100ft (30.5m) altitude. Air engineer students were receiving 51 hours in the Varsity alongside the AEO students. Instead of using the Argosy, it was proposed to fit the Dominie with a seat between the pilots so the student could observe and reach the centre console, flying 25 hours during normal navigation training sorties. The current Argosy flight simulator planned for No 6 FTS would be used, the course being reduced from 50 weeks to 45.

For navigator radar training, it was planned to introduce the Radar Videotape Recorder (RVR) which offered a far more economical solution using video tapes to teach the students how to interpret the likely radar returns on the scope. The RVR would also replace the Hastings T.5s of the Radar Flight of No 230 OCU, despite that unit's recently increased utilisation to meet Buccaneer training requirements and the fact that the RVR was unproven – luckily it soon proved a success following its introduction. In addition, the Dominies of No 6 FTS took on the flying portion of the syllabus. The impact for Coastal Command's first tourists was less as they could gain operational experience sitting alongside an experienced first navigator. The current Jet Provost T.5B and the Argosy with its ASV.21 radar were recognised as being limited training tools for the forthcoming Panavia Tornado GR.1 and more OCU flying hours would be needed. The prospects of saving up to £19 million by cancelling the Argosy and its limited future capability for training students to operate modern avionics meant that cancellation was seen as the best option, being described by an Air Staff officer as, 'an over-insurance and one that is unaffordable.'

During all these deliberations Hawker Siddeley had pressed on with conversion work and the first Argosy T.2, XP442 was flown on 30th October 1975. Shortly afterwards the programme was cancelled. However, by this time, the first four T.2 conversions (XP442, XP446, XP447 and XR136) had their structural changes for the larger radome and supply aimer's window completed, but only two had been completely outfitted internally. Argosy C.1 XP411 in addition had become the first T.1. The defence review hit Hawker Siddeley hard, also losing Victor K.2 tanker conversions, eight Nimrod MR.2 upgrades, Comet and Victor K.1 servicing contracts as both fleets were retired and the MoD never informed the company about the loss of potential future orders for 35 Hawks and twelve Sea Harriers.

New Roles Replace the Old

The post-Cold War defence cuts further reduced demand for aircrews and broadened the skills needed to operate increasingly more sophisticated avionics, the title of navigator becoming weapon system officer to reflect the change of role emphasis. Beyond the high-end world of the fast jets the emergence of modern glass cockpits and navigational aids such as GPS took a long time to filter through. Much of the transport fleet still relied on the old methods and retained its original 1960s-era equipment well into the 1990s. The Falklands War saw aids like Omega being hastily fitted for the long trans-oceanic flights and during the First Gulf War's Operation Granby the Hercules navigators were reliant on the timeless compass, map, stopwatch and 'Mark One eyeball' for tactical navigation. By the 21st Century, navigation training was becoming partially outsourced to private contractors in line with the rest of the training system and the MoD's *Frontline First: Defence Costs Study* in 1994 had opened the way but by 2000 the MoD was planning the UK Military Flying Training System (UKMFTS), a 25-year Private Finance Initiative contract covering elementary, basic, advanced, fast jet, multi-engine and helicopter pilot training and aircrew training as well as providing the aircraft and facilities for all three Services.

In the meantime, the last Jetstream T.1s of No 45 (R) Squadron had been replaced in 2004 by seven Beechcraft King Air B200 aircraft supplied by Serco. These aircraft had traditional analogue cockpits and so were joined by three B200GT aircraft in 2008 equipped with modern glass cockpits, an increasingly important feature for students destined to fly modern transports like the Airbus A400M Atlas C.1. The King Airs were used for the 30 hour Multi-Engine Lead-In (MELIN) course as well as familiarisation and air experience for trainee rear crew and Weapon Systems Operators.

Armstrong Whitworth C.1 XP442 was the first T.2 conversion completed. The larger nose radome for the ASV.21E radar and enlarged supper aimer's window are clues to its conversion. It flew in its new guise shortly before the programme was cancelled. XP442 ended its days as ground instructional airframe 8454M with No 1 School of Technical Training at Halton, where it is seen here in March 1979. It was scrapped in 1990. *Robin A Walker*

The Jetstream T.1s were replaced in 2004 by seven Beechcraft King Air B200 aircraft supplied by contractor Serco. *MoD/Open Government Licence, 2010*

During the summer of 1995, No 6 FTS's Dominies transferred to No 3 FTS at Cranwell, becoming No 55 (Reserve) Squadron, operating ab initio and refresher courses for weapon system officers, weapon system operators, air loadmasters and air engineers. The increasing adoption of modern glass cockpits and the retirement of older transport aircraft meant that the traditional air engineer was no longer required and that course was halted in 2005. The cancellation of the Nimrod MRA.4, reduction in the number of Tornado GR.4s and impending retirement of the Tornado F.3 laid down in the 2010 Strategic Defence and Security Review resulted a severe downturn of training requirements. The weapons system officer course was stopped and the sensor operator conversion course suspended, the Dominie T.2 retiring on 20th January 2011 as surplus to requirements and No 55 (R) Squadron disbanding. These two training roles were eventually restarted when demand for replacements reached a sustainable level and the task passed to 750 Naval Air Squadron, which was training naval observers and systems operators at Culdrose using the Beechcraft King Air 350 Avenger T.1.

At the end of 2006 the Ascent consortium, which included Lockheed Martin and the VT Group, was awarded the UKMFTS contract and in 2012 Ascent selected Elbit Systems and KBR operating as Affinity Flight Training Systems as the sub-contractor to supply the aircraft, selecting the Embraer EMB-500 Phenom 100 very light business jet for the multi-engine and aircrew training requirements as part of its bid. Affinity has supplied five Phenoms to No 45 (R) Squadron at Cranwell, where Ascent has built a ground training facility containing simulators and synthetic training facilities, enabling the aircrew training syllabus for aircrew to be reduced to 40 flying hours and 20 synthetic hours. In production since 2008, the Phenom is a thoroughly modern design with a glass cockpit based on Garmin 3000 avionics and can be used to train two student pilots and four aircrew students in the cabin along with an instructor; the first was delivered to the RAF in July 2018.

The need for specialised aircrew training has not gone away but its scope and manpower requirements are very much smaller, a dozen Phenoms and Avengers now fulfilling a task once performed by hundreds of aircraft, but still upholding the tradition of using modified variants of off-the-shelf aircraft and evolving to keep abreast of technical advances.

King Air B200 ZK454 in the markings of No 45 (Reserve) Squadron in February 2011. The King Airs were used for advanced multi-engine pilot training. *MoD/Open Government Licence, 2011*

12 Maritime Trainers

'I think our recent experience with the Varsity/Shackleton controversy has shown that nothing very far short of the front line Coastal aircraft is suitable as an M.R. trainer.'
Air Vice Marshal Geoffrey Tuttle, Assistant Chief of the Air Staff (Operational Requirements), March 1953

Bomber Command required aircraft suitable for operational conversion training to train its crews to penetrate enemy airspace, navigate to high levels of accuracy and drop their weapons accurately and its needs had shaped the development of many of the multi-engined trainers, including the Vickers Varsity. Coastal Command's aircrews aboard its maritime patrol aircraft had an equally arduous duty and a wide range of equipment to master. The Fleet Air Arm (FAA) operated anti-submarine aircraft from aircraft carriers and had very similar training and operational requirements, indeed the FAA would co-operate closely with joint training units. The observers faced the task of long hours staring at the sea to spot ships, submarines and wrecked mariners in distress regardless of whether the sea was calm or rough. But new methods of detection had to be mastered too; air-to-surface-vessel radar (ASV), magnetic anomaly detection, Autolycus equipment capable of 'smelling' the diesel fumes from a submarine's engines, infra-red detectors and passive and active sonobuoys – miniature disposable hydrophones and sonars to listen for submarines. Most of these roles did not require a purpose-built aircraft, but would require conversion of suitable airframes and, as ever, the process of procurement was not always smooth.

Maritime Reconnaissance Trainers

The maritime reconnaissance role undertaken by Coastal Command required observers trained not only in visual observation but who could also operate radars and sonobuoy receivers. The training could be conducted in a flying classroom but operational conversion trainers were also required; the students had to learn how to operate effectively as a team before they could be posted to operational squadrons. Coastal Command was rapidly becoming a land-based force, although Short Sunderlands remained in service until 1959 and new flying boats were mooted until the mid-1950s. Avro Lancaster GR.3 (later redesignated MR.3) conversions were an interim solution until the Avro Shackleton MR.1 arrived in greater numbers from 1951 onwards, supplemented during 1952-57 by Lockheed Neptune MR.1s supplied by America under the Mutual Defense Aid Plan. Finding a suitable replacement for the Shackleton was complicated by cuts in defence spending and overly ambitious requirements, but the Hawker Siddeley HS.801 Nimrod MR.1 finally entered service in 1969 and with constant upgrading remained in service until 2010. The School of General Reconnaissance for observer training had only lasted eighteen months before its disbandment on 5th September 1947 and not until April 1951 did the school re-emerge as the School of Maritime Reconnaissance at St Mawgan. In September 1956 it became the Maritime Operational Training Unit and in July 1970 became No 236 OCU. Another training unit dedicated to anti-submarine warfare (ASW) techniques and tactics was the Joint Anti-Submarine School, formed at Ballykelly on 19th November 1945 and which had a long career as a joint RAF and FAA unit, becoming the Joint Maritime Operational Training School in March 1970, absorbing the Air-Sea Warfare Development Unit – which had been formed in 1948.

One of the first requirements for the new School of Maritime Reconnaissance was a suitable crew trainer. During 1950 Coastal Command had looked at several types as a short-range maritime patrol aircraft; the Airspeed Ambassador, Bristol Freighter and the Vickers Varsity – all of which had also been discussed for other training requirements. The Ambassador had been redesigned as the AS.69 and several Varsity designs had been proposed but neither aircraft had been found suitable; the Varsity

The 'Mighty Hunter', Hawker Siddeley Nimrod MR.1 XV241 illustrates the advanced aircraft that were developed for maritime patrol and anti-submarine duties during the Cold War. A crew of pilots, navigators and observers trained in operating radar and sonobuoys had to be trained to high standards. By the 1950s it was clear that the most economical method of training was to use frontline aircraft. *Author's Collection*

lacking the ability to carry the necessary payload and the AS.69 having superior range and payload but requiring more extensive and expensive redesign and development. These concerns were just as valid as the aircraft were reassessed for the training role in mid-1951, the Varsity being favoured but with concerns that additional orders would affect the production of Valiant bombers, which at this time was probably one of the most important production programmes for the RAF. To this list of contenders were added the 35 stored HPR.1 Marathon airliners awaiting a role and the Percival P.50 Prince and P.66 Pembroke. These three smaller aircraft were quickly ruled out as they could not carry all the required equipment and their high-wing layout made ditching into the sea following an engine failure highly dangerous. Using a variant of the Shackleton was ruled out due to its expensive price and Coastal Command felt that the type was too uneconomic to operate for training duties. During mid-1952 the MoS also assessed the Avro Lancaster GR.3, Lincoln B.1, York, Douglas Dakota C.4, Bristol Freighter (again) and the Vickers Valetta for their potential to be converted. Yet again the Varsity was declared the best choice on offer. Until a dedicated trainer could be developed the School began its training syllabus with the Lancaster GR.3, subsequently earning the honour of being the last Lancasters in RAF service.

While the Air Ministry and the MoS argued over Vickers's production and design capacity, the draft Operational Requirement OR.317 was written around the Varsity and Vickers began design work based on its earlier short-range maritime reconnaissance studies. The Varsity was to carry a flight crew of a pilot and signaller along with an instructor and four students for navigational and bombing training with six hours endurance or carrying six students as a sonobuoy, ASV radar, anti-submarine and bombing trainer with four hours endurance. The ASV.13A radar from the Shackleton would be fitted in a retractable ventral radome behind the nosewheel undercarriage bay. For the students there would be a tactical navigation position, a routine navigation/sonobuoy position and two sonobuoy positions, all three of the latter having an ARI.5487 receiver and indicator. Navigation equipment would include Gee Mk.2 and LORAN as well as Rebecca Mk.4. The ASV and search receiver station comprised three positions; the first having an American AN/APR-4 metric search receiver, an AN/APA-17 with two receivers for direction finding and a Type 211 repeater for the ASV.13; the second position had the ASV.13 Type 211 indicator; the third position was identical to the first except for AN/APR-9 centimetric search receiver instead of the APR-4. The bomb aimer's position would have a Low Level Mk.3 bombsight and two light series carriers would be fitted for 24 practice bombs. The two flare chutes in the cabin (one could be removed) would be used to launch 42 flame floats or twelve photo-flashes for night photography. Five multi-barrel dischargers would fire illuminating flares. For the lighter four-student sortie the Varsity would carry six directional sonobuoys with twelve non-directional sonobuoys launched via the flare chutes. Photographic equipment included an F.24 camera for vertical photography and either a rear-facing F.24 or FX.97 for day and night oblique photography respectively and a hand-held K.20 camera in the cabin for photographing ships and surfaced submarines. Provision for depth charges, Mk.30 Dealer-B homing torpedoes and a gun turret was quickly abandoned as the additional payload would require strengthened wings which would overload the Vickers design team even further.

The Varsity was initially the favoured maritime reconnaissance trainer but was simply too small for all the necessary equipment. Varsity T.1 WF410 seen here was used by No 2 ANS for advanced navigation training and previously had been assigned to the RAF College at Cranwell. Following retirement in 1971 it was used as teaching aid at Bristol Polytechnic before sadly being burned on Lulsgate fire dump in 2004. *Blue Envoy Collection*

By October 1952 Coastal Command seemed satisfied with the Varsity but ACAS(OR), Air Vice-Marshal Geoffrey Tuttle, was less convinced. The Varsity had been stretched to its structural limits to take all the required equipment and the take-off weight and endurance were now marginal. There was no chance of fitting future operational equipment such as the Autolycus diesel exhaust detector, the Yellow Duckling infra-red detector, a Magnetic Anomaly Detector (MAD) or the Blue Silk Doppler navigation radar. There were also worries about twin-engine reliability over the sea. It is surprising that having been rejected already for precisely the same reasons barely two years earlier that the Varsity had been reconsidered when the limitations were already known. Tuttle was convinced that only the Shackleton could take all the necessary equipment and suggested using earlier MR.1 aircraft released as improved marks began to re-equip the squadrons. Coastal Command were against the increased operating costs but in February 1953 the Deputy Chief of the Air Staff, Air Marshal Sir Ronald Ivelaw-Chapman, ruled that the Varsity was a non-starter and in July 1954 authority was given to order more Shackleton MR.3s to release MR.1s for training. Greater use was also made of ground-based radar and sonobuoy training simulators which saved flying hours and reduced the need to fly to Ballykelly in Northern Ireland to train with Royal Navy submarines as live targets.

Avro's Langar works began planning the T.4 conversion from the MR.1 and one aircraft, VP259, was selected to mock-up the conversion. The requirement to fit Blue Silk was dropped in early 1956 as it had been decided that no specialist skill was required to use it and the higher standard of compass calibration and aerial alignment required would affect the pace of the flying training programme. Kelvin Hughes was asked to develop a modification to fit two additional ASV.13 radar indicators at the training station. Other equipment

The Avro Shackleton T.4s were conversions of MR.1 airframes and looked almost identical, retaining the undernose ASV.13A radar radome but losing the dorsal gun turret. WB829 served with No 236 OCU from 14th December 1951 until May 1957 when the port overwing escape hatch blew out on take-off and damaged the tailplane. This photograph shows WB829 being prepared for a sortie later in its career when the OCU had become the Maritime Operational Training Unit at Kinloss. After repair and storage, WB829 was delivered to Seletar, Singapore in May 1959 but was grounded on arrival following fatigue life expiry of the wing spar. *Dave Welch*

included Green Salad UHF homing and Orange Harvest passive radar detection. Avro even offered to retain the original dorsal turret for gunnery practice, though this was not taken up. Delays in MR.3 production affected the conversion schedules, Coastal Command being eager to replace the School of Maritime Reconnaissance's Lancasters but equally unwilling to reduce their frontline strength by releasing the MR.1s too soon. The initial plan for 24 conversions was reduced to seventeen; all served with the School and its subsequent incarnations until the last was retired in the late 1960s. The later Shackleton T.2 was a conversion of MR.2 airframes with the additional training stations replacing the bunks in the rear of the cabin. Ten conversions were carried out (two more were cancelled) at Langar and were issued to the frontline squadrons, No 236 OCU and the Joint Maritime Operational Training School.

The Shackleton T.4 was fully equipped and was effectively a frontline ASW aircraft with additional equipment consoles for the students. WB844 is seen here in 1959 with the Maritime Operational Training Unit. It ended its days as a ground instructional aircraft in 1968 at the No 2 School of Technical Training at Cosford. The airframe was later scrapped. *Bill Lewis via Air Britain*

In late 1953 Percival had proposed a short-range maritime reconnaissance and training aircraft which immediately caught the interest of Coastal Command who were at that time looking again at an inshore anti-submarine and anti-motor torpedo boat aircraft. A group of Staff officers visited Luton to discuss the proposals. The aircraft had eight to ten hours endurance, the crew comprised a pilot, navigator and a signaller and the weapons bay could hold four 250lb depth charges or one Dealer-B homing torpedo as well as four directional sonobuoys. The aircraft was also equipped with MAD, two directional sonobuoy indicators and ASV.19 radar. The officers from Coastal Command were impressed with the proposals for the inshore role, but they recognised that it would be far too small as a trainer. In the event the inshore ASW requirement was handed to helicopters.

After experiencing the battle to convince Coastal Command to accept the more expensive but realistic Shackleton for its training requirements, Tuttle argued that only operational aircraft were suitable for maritime reconnaissance training and he could not believe that "it would be worth paying the enormous research and development costs necessary to develop a separate type." That policy has been followed ever since, no operational trainer variant of the Nimrod was developed and No 236 OCU used standard aircraft alongside a series of systems simulators for the various sensors. The rapid retirement of Nimrod in 2010 led to not only a capability gap but a potential skills gap too. This resulted in the Project Seedcorn in 2012 which saw experienced maritime operators being sent to allied and partner air forces around the world to maintain skills until a replacement for the Nimrod was selected. In 2015 this was announced as the Boeing P-8A Poseidon MRA.1. Project Seedcorn included sending twelve instructors sent to Patrol Squadron VP-30 based at Naval Air Station Jacksonville, Florida. VP-30 is the Fleet Replacement Squadron that trains USN and NATO/Allied air and ground crews on the P-8A Poseidon as well as its predecessor, the Lockheed P-3C Orion and AP-3E Aries, a commitment totalling 600 students annually. It was here that the first RAF Poseidon squadron, No 120, began training in January 2019. The support contract includes a commitment for VP-30 to provide training for three years until 2022, by which time the Lossiemouth base and the second squadron, No 201, should be become operational with full operating capability scheduled for 2024.

RAF Coastal Command was only a few years away from entering the jet age with the Hawker Siddeley Nimrod MR.1 when Shackleton T.4 WB858 of the Maritime Operational Training Unit was photographed visiting Odiham on 6th September 1966 for a Battle of Britain open day. WB858 was withdrawn from use in June 1968. *Robin A Walker*

The first RAF Boeing P-8A Poseidon MRA.1, ZP801, during the delivery ceremony at Naval Air Station Jacksonville, Florida on 31st October 2019 where the initial flight training also took place. Following the retirement of Nimrod, specialist aircrew skills were maintained with close liaison and exchange tours with allied forces such as the US Navy under Project Seedcorn. *MoD/Open Government Licence, 2019*

There will be no dedicated OCU, both No 120 Squadron (reformed in April 2018) and No 201 Squadron at Lossiemouth will be frontline units. Two Operational Flight Trainer simulators are part a new £100 million facility at Lossiemouth being built by Boeing Defence UK, the first being delivered in August 2020. The simulators provide training specifically for the pilots but will be linked to the specialist mission simulators used by the rear crew members, allowing the crews to train together.

FAA Observer Training

The FAA had similar training requirements for their anti-submarine aircraft observers as Coastal Command had for their own aircrews, so unsurprisingly there was an element of joint training; for example the Joint Anti-Submarine School had FAA elements at Eglinton with 719 and 737 (Naval Air Squadrons (NAS). Being predominantly equipped for operations from aircraft carriers (the Inskip Award of 1937 had prevented the FAA from operating frontline aircraft from shore bases to preserve RAF Coastal Command's role) it was inevitable that its first ASW aircraft would be carrier-based and that these would also be used for training. The Fairey Barracuda had been designed as a carrier-based torpedo-bomber/reconnaissance aircraft capable of dive-bombing but during the latter part of the Second World War had taken on ASW role with the addition of ASV Mk.X radar and sonobuoys. When the war ended these surplus Barracudas became available for training, in particular with 719 and 744 NASs at Eglinton who operated the basic and advanced phases of the anti-submarine training syllabus respectively. Twelve aircraft from 744 NAS enabled the frontline 815 NAS to reform in December 1947. As the Fairey Firefly supplanted the Barracuda in frontline and training roles some of the redesignated TR.3 aircraft were used by 750 NAS at St Merryn until 1953 for basic observer training.

The Fairey Firefly had begun life as a two-seat carrier-based fighter but during the late 1940s it had been adapted for ASW carrying radar and sonobuoys with the former navigator's position used by the observer and equipped with radar and sonobuoy receivers. The Firefly Mk.5 was a multi-role variant capable of easy conversion to the fighter,

The Fairey Firefly AS.7 was soon superseded in frontline use as an anti-submarine aircraft and instead was widely used for training. WM770 had been delivered in January 1953 and had served with 719 and 796 NAS training observers and is seen here at Lossiemouth on 21 July 1962. The aircraft was sold for scrap in March 1964. *Mike Hines*

A flight of Firefly T.7s from 750 NAS on a training sortie in 1953. The student observer and instructor can be clearly seen sitting in the rear cockpits. *Terry Panopalis Collection*

night-fighter and ASW roles. In the latter role (designated as the AS.5) it was fitted with American-supplied sonobuoys and AN/APS-4 ASH (Air-Surface, Model H) radar. The AS.6 differed in having the equivalent British sonobuoy and radar equipment. The Firefly T.3 was produced to train observers and – like the T.1 and T.2 variants produced for pilot training – was converted from surplus FR.I fighters and retained the original flush rear cockpit for the student observer. The T.3 retained the FR.I's ASH radar but the four 20mm Hispano cannon were removed. Around fifty T.3s were produced and were used by 796 NAS at St Merryn between July 1950 and June 1953 on the advanced phase of the observer training course. Others saw service with five Royal Navy Volunteer Reserve squadrons. The T.3 was replaced by the three-seat Firefly T.7. The AS.7 had been developed for the ASW search role as an interim type until the new Fairey Gannet entered service. It lacked any weapons capability and carried two observers in the rear cockpit which gained a large, bulged canopy. The T.7 was identical except for the lack of an arrester hook and its two-seat rear cockpit enabled an instructor to fly with a student. A total of 151 Mk.7 aircraft were built by Fairey at Hayes and Heaton Chapel with 43 being completed as the T.7. With the advent of the Gannet many of the AS.7s were also issued directly to training units, which included; the Naval Air Anti-Submarine School at Eglinton, 719 NAS; 750 and 796 NASs at St Merryn and 766 NAS briefly used the type on its Phase 1 Operational Flying Course. The other element of the Naval Air Anti-Submarine School, 737 NAS, used the armed Firefly T.2 trainer and standard AS.5 aircraft for weapons training.

When the Fairey Gannet was developed to Specification GR.17/45 for a carrier-based ASW aircraft, an operational conversion training variant was also planned, Specification T.117D being issued on 9th April 1952. The Gannet T.2 had the forward observer's cockpit modified for an instructor with a duplicated set of flying controls and a periscope. The retractable ASV.19 radar radome and associated equipment was removed and the rear cockpit could accommodate either a radio operator or two passengers. The first aircraft, WN365, was converted from a standard AS.1 and made its maiden flight on 16th August 1954. A total of 34 were built, another eight received the more powerful Armstrong Siddeley Double Mamba 101 turboprop as fitted to the improved AS.4 variant to become the T.5. The first, XG882, made its maiden flight on 1st March 1957. These Gannet trainers soon replaced the Fireflies with 719, 737 and 796 NAS – 737 NAS becoming the first to receive the T.2 in February 1955 – and were issued in ones and twos to all the frontline Gannet squadrons. The T.5s used by 849 NAS equipped with the Airborne Early Warning (AEW) configured Gannet AEW.3 for check flights and standards training were the last Gannet trainers to retire in 1978. Export Gannet users also received small numbers of trainer; the Royal Australian Navy receiving three T.2s, the West German Marineflieger had one T.5 and Indonesia received two T.2s upgraded to T.5 standard. The first batch of Indonesian pilots were trained by Fairey at White Waltham using WN365 which Fairey had converted to T.5 standard and were using as a company communications aircraft as G-APYO. It later re-joined the FAA as XT752.

Fairey Gannet T.2 XA508 was delivered in February 1955 but only two years later became a ground instructional airframe. Donated to the Fleet Air Arm Museum at Yeovilton in 1975, XA508 is today the only surviving T.2 and is on display at the Midland Air Museum, Coventry Airport. *Robin A Walker*

Gannet T.5 XT752 is seen here in September 1968 with the HQ Flight of 849 NAS, which was equipped with the AEW.3 variant, providing pilots with continuation training. This aircraft had begun life as AS.1 WN365, before being converted into the prototype T.2 before being further altered as a T.5 and used by Fairey as a demonstrator registered as G-APYO. It was then sold to the Indonesian Navy before returning to FAA service on 2 March 1965 with new serial XT752. Today the aircraft is the sole airworthy Gannet in the world, based at New Richmond Regional Airport, Wisconsin, USA. *Terry Panopalis Collection*

Gannet T.5 XG686 was another of the trainers which saw service with 849 NAS, being assigned to them at Culdrose in July 1964. In May 1970 it was broken up as a spares source. *Robin A Walker*

This long line of Sea Princes in August 1952 features some fitted with the thimble nose radome for the AN/APS-4 ASH radar. *Terry Panopalis Collection*

The Prince Goes to Sea

During 1947 Percival Aircraft had developed the P.50 Prince as an eight-seat small airliner and had achieved some commercial success both as a passenger aircraft and as a surveying aircraft. In June 1949 Percival issued a brochure for the P.57 Prince Military Trainer as a flying classroom for a range of training roles; radio and navigation training, bomb aimer training, solo crew training, twin-engined pilot training, bombing and gunnery training and photographic training. The RAF soon showed interest but their equipment and training sortie requirements required a larger aircraft, the Vickers Varsity. But the P.57 proved amply suitable for the FAA's Operational Requirement NR/A20 for a flying classroom for radar, radio and navigation training. The fact that the Admiralty and had already selected the Prince for the communications role was an added bonus. An order for three P.57 Sea Prince C.1 transports and eighteen Sea Prince T.1 trainers was placed on 25th October 1949. These were later increased by orders for four C.2 VIP transports and 23 more T.1s and Specification T.17/49 was issued on 10th March 1950 to cover development.

The P.57 received a longer nose cone for the AN/APS-4 ASH radar, increasing the length to 46ft 4in (14.12m), but least four aircraft (including the prototype) received a thimble radome which could be removed and fitted with a blanking plate. The Sea Prince T.1 could accommodate a pilot, an instructor and three students and was designed to be used for four roles; the 'X1' version was the basic ASV radar trainer, the 'X2' was a communications trainer with two additional ARI.5669 HF radios as well as the standard TR.1936 VHF set, the 'Y' anti-submarine trainer only carried two students and the 'F' version was used for radar and sonobuoy training. The last two versions were fitted with two ARI.5487 sonobuoy receivers and had two light series carriers for eight sonobuoys – the 'Y' version was originally intended to have internal launch chutes for eight Mk.1 sonobouys replacing the third student's position but the use of larger American sonobuoys prevented this. A proposed AI trainer using the AN/APS-57 radar and a blacked out cabin was later cancelled. The increased gross weight of 11,850lb (5,375kg) resulted in the use of new twin-wheel main undercarriage legs, which required longer engine nacelles.

The prototype, WF118, first flew from Luton on 28th June 1951 and in August went to Farnborough for radio and radar trials. The second aircraft, WF119, was also extensively used for trials work,

Sea Prince T.1 WP311 was completed with a thimble nose radome, but is seen here following the fitting of a standard nose cone during its time with the RNAS Bramcote Station Flight in 1957. WP311 was scrapped in 1961. *Terry Panopalis Collection*

Out with the old and in with the new. Percival Sea Prince T.1 WP308 is seen here in formation with a Scottish Aviation Jetstream T.2 on 23rd March 1979. WP308 had been delivered to 750 NAS in February 1953, in whose service it remained when it made the last operational Sea Prince flight on 1st May 1979. *Blue Envoy Collection*

including trials of the Autolycus equipment. The last production aircraft, WP321, was delivered in April 1953 and the type served mainly with 750 NAS at Culdrose for observer training but was also issued to several other schools and units during a long career. In 1961 WF122 was converted as an ECM trainer for 831 NAS at Watton, serving in this role until 1966. Replacement for the Sea Prince was slow in materialising and following the discovery of cracks in the wing spars several aircraft received new steel spars to extend their lives until April 1979 when 750 NAS completed its final course using the Sea Prince.

The Navy had been offered several other Sea Prince variants; the P.77 of October 1950 with an arrester hook to allow operations from aircraft carriers in the transport role, but lacking a folding tail fin and outer-wing sections which would be required for effective operations aboard carriers, two P.75 AEW variants with a retractable ventral radar scanner in early 1951 and in February 1954 a stripped out T.1 with just a pilot to enable it to carry 2,539lb (1,151kg) of urgently needed freight, such as spare parts from the UK to Malta and other European bases.

Fleet Air Arm Radar Trainers

The FAA introduced its first jet all-weather fighter, the de Havilland DH.112 Sea Venom FAW.20 equipped with AI.10 radar in March 1954, followed by the FAW.21 with the AI.21 radar and, after much delay, the DH.110 Sea Vixen FAW.1 with the AI.18 radar in July 1959. The introduction of all-weather fighters required the FAA to create suitable advanced and operational training syllabuses. The result was the formation of 766 NAS at Yeovilton as the All Weather Fighter Training unit and 736 NAS at Lossiemouth as the Sea Venom Operational Flying School as part of the Naval Air Fighting School. Both squadrons used Sea Venom fighters and Vampire T.22 trainers until sufficient examples of the Sea Vixen FAW.1 became available for the training units. The Sea Venom was retired from the FAA's frontline fighter squadrons in 1961 but continued to see use in the operational training role until 1970 with some being issued to 750 NAS, the Observer School at Culdrose, for advanced radar training.

During the late 1960s the improved Sea Vixen FAW.2 replaced the FAW.1 with the training units. At Yeovilton, 890 NAS reformed on 14th August 1967 with six FAW.2s for operational trials and training on the type. From December 1969 its aircraft were maintained by Airwork Ltd., who also ran the Fleet Requirements Unit (FRU) which provided target towing aircraft among other duties. In October 1970 the FRU took on 890 NAS's Fleet Requirements duties and its Sea Vixens. By this time the McDonnell Douglas F-4 Phantom FG.1 had supplanted the Sea Vixen and the drawdown of the Royal Navy's fixed-wing carrier-based squadrons had gathered pace following the defence reviews of the late 1960s. The FRU continued to use its Sea Vixens for radar training and on 1st December 1972 Airwork's two separate contract-run entities were rationalised; the FRU and the Air Direction Training Unit became the Fleet Requirements and Air Direction Training Unit (FRADTU). Finally, in January 1974 the Sea Vixens – which were the last remaining flying examples – were retired due to their high operating cost.

Canberra T.22 WT510 began its life as a PR.7 photo-reconnaissance aircraft delivered to the RAF on 31st December 1954. WT510 was transferred to the Royal Navy in February 1971 and became the prototype T.22 conversion. It first flew in this configuration on 28th June 1973 and following A&AEE trials was issued to the FRADTU on 27th March 1974. The aircraft was retired in July 1985 and scrapped in 1991-93. *Terry Panopalis Collection*

The Sea Vixens were replaced by the English Electric Canberra T.22, a conversion of seven surplus ex-RAF PR.7 reconnaissance aircraft to meet Naval Staff Requirement NSR.6642 and Specification 279D&P. Although the converted Canberra T.22 was fitted with Ferranti Blue Parrot surface-search and strike radar and the specification had included the roles of AI training and aircrew training, the FRADTU Canberra T.22s were never used for training Buccaneer navigators and were used as silent targets, for radar calibration and missile simulation. The first aircraft converted by BAC, WT510, made its first flight on 28th July 1973. FRADTU carried out radar calibration and simulated anti-ship missiles in the Air Direction role testing the Royal Navy's air defences until 1983 when Airwork's contract came up for renewal and the MoD became very interested in achieving increased cost efficiencies. Flight Refuelling Limited's tender was selected and from 1985 they began using Dassault Falcon 20 business jets fitted with the necessary electronic warfare equipment and the Canberra T.22s were retired.

Jetstreams and Avengers

The badly needed replacement for the Sea Prince T.1 was the Scottish Aviation Jetstream T.2. The HP.137 Jetstream had been developed as a turboprop-powered executive transport but had quickly attracted the RAF's attention as a multi-role crew trainer and the first of 26 Jetstream T.1 aircraft entered service in 1973. The 1975 Defence Review shortly afterwards drastically reduced Transport Command's size and the resulting decline in multi-engine pilot and navigator requirements saw the new fleet placed in storage. The FAA now saw an opportunity to acquire several of these to replace the Sea Prince under Naval Staff Requirement NSR.6675. Evaluation trials were carried out with XX497 at 750 NAS in January 1976 and the success of this led to the issuing of Specification 291 to cover the pricing of the conversion costs for fourteen airframes. The conversion saw the addition of a MEL E190 radar in a new thimble nose radome. Although not a dedicated surface search radar, the weather warning E190 radar had the virtue of being available as it was

The MEL E190 radar fitted to the Jetstream T.2 was a weather warning set, not a dedicated surface search radar, but had the virtue of being available as it was also fitted to the RAF's HS.125 Dominie T.1 navigation trainers. XX480 first flew following conversion to T.2 standard on 13th February 1979 and was retired in April 1996. *Terry Panopalis Collection*

also used by the RAF's Hawker Siddeley HS.125 Dominie T.1 navigation trainers. The Jetstream T.2 equipped 750 NAS, with the first delivery of XX480 on 21st October 1978 and the first course to completely use the Jetstream was completed in April 1980. These were later joined by two additional T.2 conversions and four T.3 aircraft converted from Series 31 airframes with Garrett TPE331 turboprops and a Racal ASR360 surveillance radar in a ventral radome, which was more suitable for training observers destined for the Westland Lynx HAS.8 and EHI101 Merlin HM.1 ASW helicopters. Two similar Jetstream 31 conversions for radar training with nose radomes were included in the *Al Yamamah 1* deal with Saudi Arabia signed in 1985, one of which was written off in 1989 following a possible engine failure during a landing approach at Dharan.

The Jetstreams were retired in 2009 and were replaced by private contractor aircraft under the UK Military Flying Training System (UKMFTS). The Affinity consortium supplied four Beechcraft King Air B350 aircraft, designated as the Avenger T.1 (commemorating the Grumman Avenger torpedo-bomber), for 750 NAS. The Avenger is equipped with both ground and air-based avionics able to simulate a range of sensors including radars, electronic support measures and tactical data links. Graduates from 750 NAS progress onto operational training with either 824 NAS on the Merlin HM.2 or 825 NAS on the Leonardo Wildcat HMA.2. Since the retirement of the RAF's Dominie T.2 fleet in February 2011, the unit has also taken on the training of RAF weapon systems officers and weapon systems operators as part of UKMFTS.

The Jetstream T.3s were converted from Series 31 airframes powered by Garrett TPE331 turboprops and were fitted with a Racal ASR360 radar in a ventral radome which provided 360° coverage. This was a great advantage in training observers destined for the Lynx and Merlin helicopter fleets with modern surveillance radars with 360° coverage. *Blue Envoy Collection*

13 The PFI Generation

Today the majority of flying training for the armed services is conducted in partnership with private companies and the advanced and operational training conducted by the RAF is subject to private contractor support for servicing and spares supply. It is not unusual today to see private contractors on the flightline keeping aircraft operational even in combat zones. The UK Military Flying Training System (UKMFTS) came into existence in 2002 and was the culmination of previous developments. As we have already seen in Chapter Ten, helicopter training adopted the model of private contractor-supplied assets and centralised multi-service training during the mid-1990s and in Chapter Eight we saw how BAE Systems gained the contract to supply Hawk T.2 trainers for the Advanced Jet Trainer (AJT) portion of UKMFTS in 2003. Although challenging and at times problematic, this model is now common to many Western air forces and looks set to expand as increased pressures on defence expenditures remain very likely. The desire for 'more for less' has resulted in changes in operational flying training too. Eurofighter Typhoons and Lockheed F-35B Lightnings (note that the MoD decided to drop the II from the name) are expensive to fly and therefore much of the operational conversion training is now carried out on simulators before a pilot ever sits in the aircraft. These simulators are a far cry from their 1950s antecedents with realistic visual depictions of terrain and flight and more importantly the application of artificial intelligence to provide a level of adversary training that was previously unthinkable without flying against another human pilot.

Multinational Solutions

During the Second World War the training of pilots and aircrew had been multinational, conducted across the Commonwealth and in the USA. The post-war reductions saw training returning to the UK, although pilots and navigators were still sent to Southern Rhodesia and Canada in some numbers until the mid-1950s. With the formation of the North Atlantic Treaty Organisation (NATO) in 1949, co-operation increased as the members began to share doctrines, experience and equipment. While the dream of using common training aircraft largely never came to fruition, smaller scale co-operation emerged. When the Netherlands bought the Westland Wasp HAS.1 anti-submarine helicopter to equip its Dutch-built *Leander*-class frigates in the 1960s, they proposed a common pool of helicopters with the Royal Navy and a joint supply and training organisation. While these plans did not materialise,

BAE Systems Hawk T.2 XK037 during a training sortie on the Mach Loop in May 2018. The markings are of No IV (Reserve) Squadron, one of the shadow squadrons belonging to No 4 FTS. *Chris Gibson*

the first six Dutch pilots were sent to 706 Naval Air Squadron (NAS), the Advanced Helicopter Training School at Culdrose in 1966. The United States Air Force (USAF) formed the most important training relationships with several Northern European NATO members as the USA provided two things in short supply in the region; large areas of unrestricted airspace and good weather conditions all-year round. In 1974 the Ministry of Defence (MoD), while trying to grapple with the problems of centralising helicopter flying training, declined to participate in a NATO working group to consider joint basic helicopter pilot training with either new facilities in Europe or Canada or continued reliance on the US Army's Aviation School at Fort Rucker, Alabama. Only West Germany, Denmark and Norway participated, all of whom were already reliant on US training facilities. The RAF was not opposed to co-operation where there was beneficial mutual interest. In 1979 it agreed to the formation of the Tri-national Tornado Training Establishment at Cottesmore to train aircrews for all three partner nations. This agreement lasted until the changing post-Cold War environment saw it disbanded in 1999 in favour of nationally-based operational conversion training.

The UK participates in the Euro-NATO Joint Jet Pilot Training Scheme (ENJJPTS). This scheme commenced in October 1981 to train fighter pilots with reduced costs and improved effectiveness, standardisation and rationalisation. Because of the urgency at the time of its formation, ENJJPTS simply expanded the USAF's 80th Flying Training Wing's operations at Sheppard Air Force Base, Texas, which had been training German and Dutch pilots. A longer-term solution to relocate the ENJJPTS to Spain or Turkey to avoid reliance on the USA was later deemed too expensive as the Cold War thawed out. In 1988 Requests for Information were issued to industry to offer solutions. British Aerospace (BAe) outlined a concept built around the Eurofighter partners to supply the Pilatus PC-9 and the Hawk along with flying simulators. The NATO 'customers' would pay an 'asset use' charge for the facilities and equipment and provide their own military instructors. In May 1989, the ENJJPTS created the Aircraft and Equipment Selection Working Group to choose the ideal training aircraft but NATO soon abandoned these ideas as they had no concrete funding for new aircraft. At the time of writing, the 80th Flying Training Wing is still running the ENNJPTS and has trained over 7,500 pilots, providing all fighter pilot training for Belgium, Denmark, Germany, the Netherlands and Norway.

During the late 1990s the UK joined with Canada, Denmark, Italy and Singapore to form the NATO Flight Training in Canada (NFTC) programme to secure more cost effective training. Bombardier Aerospace in 1994 had made the initial unsolicited proposal for a NATO flight training school and unexpectedly the Canadian government approved a contract in 1997, partly because it could not afford to replace their ageing Canadair CT-114 Tutors. NFTC was provided by an industrial team led by Bombardier Aerospace which included BAE Systems, Raytheon, CAE Electronics (who became the prime contractor in October 2015) and other locally-based companies to provide the aircraft, training materials, simulators and support services. The Project Director was John Cockbourn, a former British Aircraft Corporation/BAe test pilot who test flew the Jaguar, was the Senior Avionics Development Test pilot for Tornado, which involved rigorous testing of the automatic terrain following navigation system and finally becoming the Project Pilot for Tornado ADV before ending his flying career and entering management role, including a period with Ferranti on their Head-Up Display programme.

The choice of aircraft was identical to BAe's earlier ENJJPTS proposal; the Beechcraft CT-156 Harvard II (the T-6 Texan II, a developed Pilatus PC-9) for basic training and the Hawk Mk.115 CT-155 for the advanced phase. The Hawk Mk.115 was an improved Hawk Series 100 with a modified cockpit with two multi-function displays. The first Hawks were delivered in 2000 and the programme became fully operational in July 2006, the course consisting of 95 flying hours of basic training on the CT-156 at 2 Canadian Forces Flying Training School at Canadian Forces Base Moose Jaw, Saskatchewan. The pilots are then streamed for fast jets, multi-engine or helicopters. Fast jet and instructor students receive another 45 hours on the CT-156 before going to 4 Wing at Canadian Forces Base Cold Lake, Alberta, for 70 hours on the CT-156 to earn their wings. The UK involvement in ENJJPTS and NFTC has only supplied a relatively small proportion of undergraduate and postgraduate pilots, but has been invaluable for providing experience and skills in co-operating with pilots from other partner nations.

Enter the Private Provider

The concept of the Private Finance Initiative (PFI) arose during the mid-1990s as a government policy where previously state-run services would be conducted or supported by private industry, the government avoiding upfront capital costs but paying fees over the duration of the contract. Of course the concept of civilian operators was nothing new in flying training. The 1930s expansion plan had relied on civilian flying schools operating Elementary Flying Training Schools and some of these continued to be operated by private companies until the late 1940s. During the Korean War the Air Ministry again turned to civilian flying schools to run five Basic Flying Training Schools and two Basic Air Navigation Schools to increase the RAF's training capacity and provide refresher training. At the same time, Flight Refuelling Limited was contracted for the organisation and support operations for No 210 Advanced Flying School at the company's airfield at Tarrant Rushton. The RAF and Fleet Air Arm (FAA) also relied on civilian schools for rotary winged flying training for much of the 1950s. It would be thirty years before budget pressures and wider changes within government policy saw the private sector re-enter the

Slingsby T67 Firefly G-BWXA is seen here in Slingsby Aviation Ltd colours in 1996. G-BWXA was later operated by Babcock Support Services for Royal Navy flight grading as part of the Joint Elementary Flying Training School. The Firefly was the first training aircraft to be contracted from a private operator to provide training services to the MoD. *Author's Collection*

Based on the Fournier RF-6B but with a new glassfibre reinforced plastic structure, the Firefly became a success in the military training market, especially when it was selected by the USAF as the T-67. *Author's Collection*

field. One early sign of this re-emergence was the awarding of a contract for the operation of No 1 Flying Training School (FTS) at Linton-on-Ouse to Airwork Limited in 1984. From the mid-1980s until 2014, BAe was contracted to operate the North Sea ACMI Range with a debriefing facility at Waddington. The Air Combat Manoeuvring Instrumentation (ACMI) Range was a calibrated area in which military aircraft were reliably tracked for scoring bomb aiming, kill notification in aerial combat and safety. The range was used to conduct training missions and NATO flying exercises. Today the use of ACMI pods that use GPS for precise location tracking and record in-flight data for subsequent analysis and which can be carried on a missile pylon have largely replaced expensive calibrated fixed range facilities.

Given the historical precedents it was unsurprising that elementary and grading flying training were the first areas to be privatised. In 1993 Hunting Aviation (part of the Hunting Group that had once included Percival Aircraft) beat a FLS Aerospace tender with the FLS Spirit 160 to secure the contract to operate a fleet of eighteen civil-registered Slingsby T67M120 Fireflies for the Joint Elementary Flying Training School (JEFTS) at Topcliffe. The T67 was a development of the Fournier RF-6B built under licence with a glassfibre reinforced plastic structure replacing the original wooden construction and the T67M was aimed at the military training market. A big success for Slingsby was the selection of the T67M260 by the USAF as the T-3A Firefly, although this was marred by four accidents (three of them fatal) which saw the T-3A fleet grounded in 1997 and scrapped in 2006. Despite this setback Fireflies have been used for military training in Bahrain, Belize, Canada, Hong Kong, Jordan and the Netherlands.

Grob G115D2 G-BVHC was one of five Herons operated by VT Aerospace to provide elementary training for the Royal Navy student pilots during the 1990s. *Author's Collection*

The JEFTS was formed on 1st April 1993 and merged the former Elementary Flying Training Squadron at Swinderby, which still had the venerable de Havilland Chipmunk T.10, with 1 FTS which was the Royal Navy Elementary Flying Training School. The JEFTS moved to Barkston Heath on 1st April 1995 and became a tri-Service unit when the Army Air Corps (AAC) joined in 1996. In July 2003, the RAF moved its elementary training to the University Air Squadrons (UAS), the School becoming the Defence Elementary Flying Training School with the FAA and AAC elements becoming 703 NAS and 674 Squadron (AAC) respectively. In 2009 the Fireflies were replaced by the Grob G 115E Tutor T.1 operated by Vosper Thornycroft Aerospace. Hunting Aviation also won a contract in 1996 to supply two Shorts Skyvan 3M aircraft for Army parachute training, carrying up to fourteen parachutists at a time.

A similar contract was issued to Short Brothers (privatised itself in 1989 and sold to Bombardier, Bombardier Defence Services being later renamed Vosper Thornycroft Aerospace) to supply and maintain five Grob G115D2 Herons, again civilian-registered, to the Naval Flying Grading Flight at Roborough to replace its Chipmunks. The G115D was an aerobatic variant of the German manufacturer's popular light aircraft and Shorts bought five of the six G 115D2s built. In 2001, the Royal Naval Flying Training Flight as 727 NAS took up the grading and elementary training roles, based at Yeovilton with five Grob G115E Tutor T.1s and five QFIs supplied by Babcock International.

Tutoring the Cadets

The same contract model was applied to replace all the remaining Scottish Aviation Bulldogs then in use by the UASs, the Air Experience Flights (AEFs) and the Central Flying School (CFS). The MoD examined suitable replacements and in June 1998 selected another variant of the Grob G115 family, the G115E which was designated the Tutor T.1, recalling the famous interwar Avro biplane trainer. The G115E had additional carbonfibre composites in the structure which saved 88lb (40kg) and was rated at +6/-3g with a service life of 24,000 hours. The 186hp (139kW) Lycoming AEIO-360-B1F/B piston engine has a three-blade variable pitch propeller. Avionics included a UHF radio, Bendix-King navigation/communications/glide slope transceiver and a VOR receiver. One feature that helped with student progression was that the flight instruments were on the right-hand side of the instrument panel so that the student could get used to flying with the control wheel in the right hand and the throttle in the left hand, the layout used in the basic and advanced trainers and frontline fighters to follow. The following month Bombardier Defence Services (later renamed VT Aerospace, later still becoming Babcock) was awarded a ten-year PFI contract to supply and maintain 90 Tutor T.1s to provide around 10,000 flying hours annually for the UASs and 20,000 hours for the AEFs. This large order restarted the Grob production line which had been closed due to lack of orders. All the Tutors had civil registrations but carried RAF roundels and fin flashes. The CFS received its first Tutor T.1 on 13th September 1999 and the Cambridge UAS received its first aircraft

Every RAF, FAA or AAC student pilot during the first two decades of the 21st century began their flying training with this view – the cockpit of a Grob 115E Tutor T.1. Although an analogue cockpit it offers a far more comprehensive instrument panel compared to that offered by the DHC Chipmunk in 1950. *MoD/Open Government Licence, 2011*

the following day. The last unit to re-equip was No 10 AEF at Woodvale which replaced its Bulldogs during 2001 and over 250,000 flying hours had been accumulated across the fleet by 2007. The elementary flying syllabus flown by Nos 1, 2 and 3 Elementary Flying Training Schools was four months long – in 2008 these units were renumbered No 16 (Reserve), No 57 (R) and No 85 (R) squadrons respectively. The fifteen UASs have capacity for around 75 students each, providing them with 15 flying hours a year. The AEFs provide air experience for cadets from the Air Training Corps and the Combined Cadet Force. The CFS's No 115 (R) Squadron used its Tutors for instructor and weapon system officer training at Cranwell. VT Aerospace acquired 23 upgraded G115EA trainers with improved avionics and GPS navigation in April 2009 to use for the remainder of its contract (at that time the Tutor fleet was actually the second most numerous in RAF service behind the Panavia Tornado GR.4). The loss of three Tutors during 2009, two from Wales UAS and one from Oxford UAS with the loss of three teenage cadets and their instructors resulted in an urgent operational requirement to fit traffic advisory service equipment to the entire fleet. The £2.8 million upgrade was completed in December 2011, nine months ahead of schedule.

Tutor T.1 G-BYXN performing aerobatics over its home at Cranwell. As civilian-owned aircraft the Tutor fleet never received MoD-issued serial numbers but they did carry RAF roundels. In 2017 this aircraft was one of 28 sold to the Ilmavoimat (Finnish Air Force). *MoD/Open Government Licence, 2004*

Tutor T.1 G-BYUC flies past the famous main block of the RAF College at Cranwell. Surprisingly, after 2009 the Tutor fleet was briefly the second largest flown by RAF pilots behind the Panavia Tornado GR.4. *MoD/Open Government Licence, 2002*

During 2020, the MoD began a new training aircraft colour scheme trial to determine a conspicuous colour for its remaining Tutors to improve safety by reducing the risk of mid-air collisions. Following a series of collisions during the 1990s the RAF settled on all-over black for all its training aircraft as it was found that this colour made the aircraft standout against the sky or land. The problem is that the Tutor with its carbonfibre composite construction has a limited choice of suitable paints and they have been operated in an all-over white colour since their introduction in 1999 (the JEFTS Fireflies were all painted yellow for the same reason). The first Tutor, G-BYXH of No 3 FTS, emerged in April with yellow fuselage and wings with black undersides and conducted visibility trials over the summer at Boscombe Down before heading to Cranwell for further tests. If accepted it is likely that the entire Tutor fleet, and possibly the Prefect T.1s will be repainted as aircraft are cycled through for maintenance.

The Expansion of Contracts

The next major development was the creation of the Defence Helicopter Flying School (DHFS) operated by FBS Limited (becoming FBS Heliservices in 2001) in October 1996 with a fifteen year contract in response to an MoD report on defence costs two years earlier. FBS supplied 26 Aérospatiale Squirrel AS 350BB HT.1 helicopters as basic and advanced trainers for 660 Squadron AAC and 705 NAS and twelve modified Squirrel HT.2 with GPS and nocturnal operations equipment for specialised training with 670 Squadron AAC. FBS also supplied twelve Bell 214EP Griffin HT.1 for No 60 (Reserve) Squadron for advanced training and the Search and Rescue Training Unit for their Qualified Helicopter Crewman Instructor course (for the full story see Chapter Ten).

In February 2000 the BAE Systems designed and operated Hawk Synthetic Training Facility was opened under another PFI deal; a £60 million contract for eighteen years with the MoD only paying for the use of the facility. The modern digital simulators feature visual displays and there are two networked full-dome simulators with two target projects to insert enemy and friendly aircraft into the field of view. Students would spend 60 hours in the facility, far more time than the 27 hours allocated to the original analogue Hawk simulators.

A System Emerges

The contract system proved fairly successful despite some teething troubles, but they were essentially *ad hoc* responses to meet a particular need. The MoD's 1994 study had recommended centralising multi-engine pilot training with a private provider and proposals were sought in February 1999 but soon the plan was abandoned. Despite this, it was becoming clear that a properly structured organisation was required to cover the entire training syllabus to achieve real efficiencies, not only in terms of costs, but also of operations and quality. The piecemeal awarding of contracts was hard to manage and was causing delays and gaps within the training system. The result was UKMFTS, a 25-year PFI contract covering elementary, basic, advanced, fast jet, multi-engine and helicopter pilot training and aircrew training as well as providing the aircraft and facilities for all three Services. Four consortia submitted bids; BAE Systems partnered with Serco and Bombardier; Rolls-Royce partnered with Lockheed Martin and the Vosper Thornycroft Group; Boeing and Thales; Kellogg Brown & Root with EG&G and Lear Siegler. BAE Systems pulled out of the bidding process in April 2004 as they had been awarded AJT portion of UKMFTS to supply the Hawk Mk.128 in July 2003, in what had been a politically controversial decision by the government not to pursue a competitive tender process despite a potentially cheaper bid from Alenia Aermacchi. At the end of 2006 the Ascent Flight Training consortium, which included Lockheed Martin and the VT Group, was awarded the contract worth £6 billion. Ascent had until 2012 to create a new centralised training organisation and began searching for contractors to supply the aircraft and helicopters required. The Strategic Defence and Security Review in 2010 delayed the bidding process due to shifting training commitments and new tenders were submitted at the end of 2012 based around a requirement to handle 230 students annually. A consortium led by BAE Systems which included Babcock International and Pilatus offered the Grob G115E Tutor T.1, Pilatus PC-21 and the Cessna Citation Mustang for the elementary, basic and multi-engine training phases. EADS Cassidian, CAE and Cobham offered the Grob G 120TP and the Beechcraft T-6C Texan II. Elbit Systems and KBR operating as Affinity Flight Training Systems tendered the same Grob and T-6C package alongside the Embraer EMB-500 Phenom 100 for the multi-engine phase and secured the contract.

The Grob G 120TP Prefect T.1 elementary trainer, of which 23 were supplied, began re-equipping the elements of the former Defence Elementary Flying Training School, 703 NAS and 674 Squadron AAC, alongside No 57 (R) Squadron at Cranwell. Cranwell is the location of Ascent's ground training facility containing simulators and synthetic training equipment (all Cranwell-based units and facilities belong to No 3 FTS). These facilities have been key in enabling training to be conducted by fewer aircraft to reduce costs. Another important factor has been fitting all the aircraft with digital systems and glass-cockpit displays for commonality with frontline types. Also at Cranwell is No 45 (Reserve) Squadron with five Phenom 100s (unusually not acquiring a service name from the MoD) for multi-engine and rear aircrew training. Although delayed by certification issues, the Phenoms have replaced the previous Beechcraft King Air B200 aircraft operated by contractor Serco at Cranwell and are equipped with a glass cockpit based on Garmin 3000 avionics and can be used to train two student pilots and four aircrew students in the cabin along with an instructor. Ascent has used four King Air 350ERs as the Avenger T.1 since 2011 to provide Stage 1 Observer and Weapon Systems Operator training at 750 NAS at Culdrose.

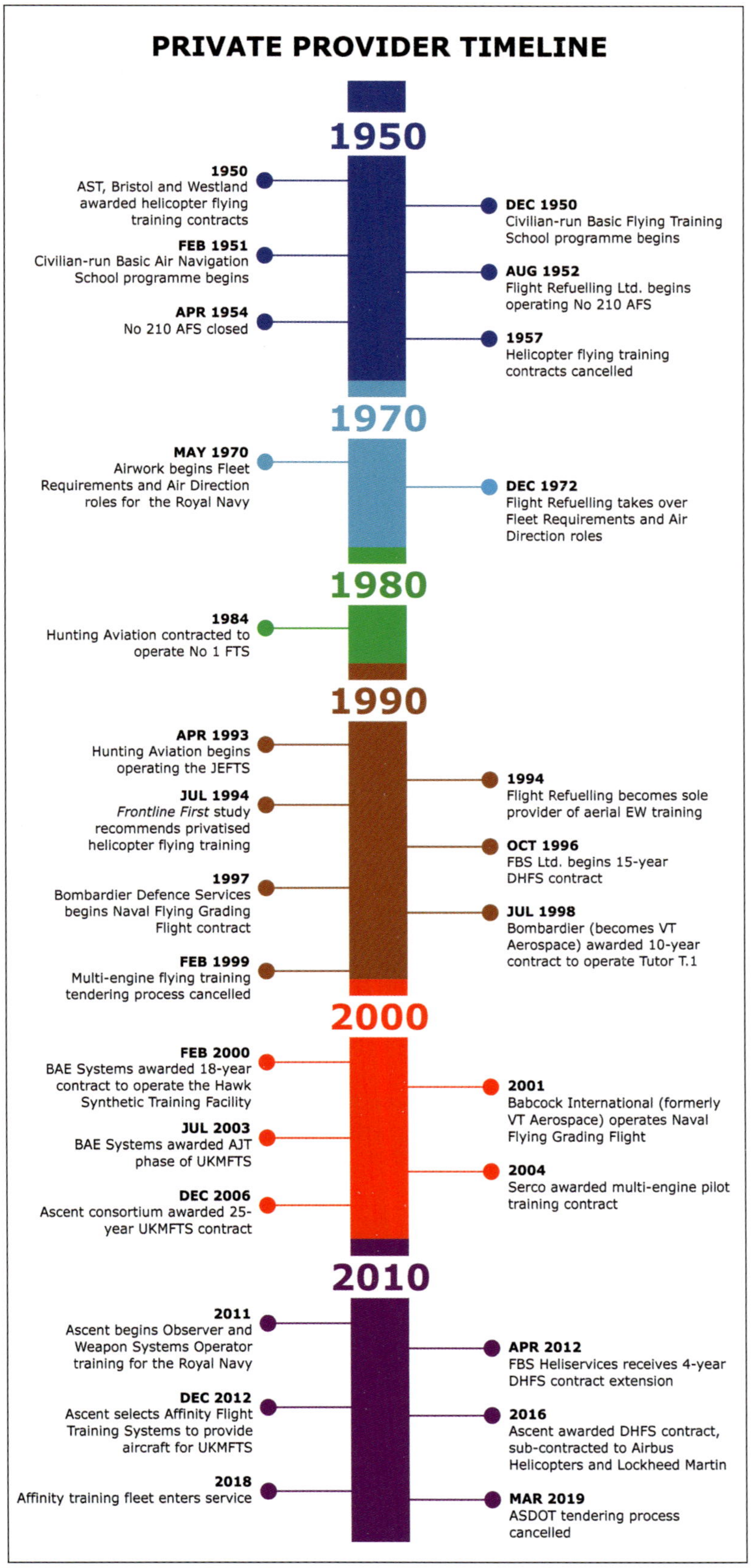

Left: The Grob G.120TP Prefect T.1 provides a modern 'glass' cockpit environment for to give student pilots experience of digital displays right from the elementary training phase, in contrast to the Prefect T.1. *Grob Aircraft AG/WikiCommons*

Below left: The Phenom 100 provides a modern glass cockpit with Garmin 3000 avionics and enables the student pilots to become familiar with such technology before they progress to the Airbus A400M Atlas C.1 and Boeing P-8 Poseidon MRA.1. *MoD/Open Government Licence, 2018*

Below: The cabin of the Phenom 100 is perhaps the most luxurious ever experienced by RAF students and a far cry from the days of clambering over wing spars and draughty fabric-covered fuselages in the early post-war period. *MoD/Open Government Licence, 2018*

The Embraer Phenom 100 is the second product of this Brazilian company to enter RAF service as a trainer. The five aircraft supplied by Affinity Flight Training Systems serve with No 45 (Reserve) Squadron at Cranwell. *MoD/Open Government Licence, 2018*

The Advanced Jet Training phase of UKMFTS was separately awarded to BAE Systems with the new Hawk T.2. ZK032 and ZK025 of No 4 FTS are seen here flying over Anglesey. The wingtip rails for AAMs are the obvious identifying feature, seen here carrying ACMI pods. *MoD/Open Government Licence, 2010*

Basic Fast Jet Training with the Shorts Tucano with No 1 FTS at Linton-on-Ouse has been replaced by No 72 (Reserve) Squadron as part of 4 FTS at Valley with fourteen Texan T.1s (note that the RAF has kept the Texan name for its second generation T-6s, despite its original T-6s being Harvards, a name Canada rekindled with its Texan IIs). The first Texans arrived at Valley on 16 February 2018 and the first course began in September 2019. Advanced fast jet training is also carried out by No 4 FTS at Valley by No IV (Reserve) and No 25 Squadrons using the 28 Hawk T.2s as supplied by BAE Systems. Delays and problems at Valley have caused a shortage of new fast pilot graduates and these effects are still being felt as the Typhoon and Lightning fleets continue to expand. After much delay, in 2016 the MoD selected Ascent Flight Training to run the DHFS. The supply and maintenance of the helicopters was sub-contracted to Airbus Helicopters with Babcock and Lockheed Martin supplying the infrastructure and ground-based training equipment. Airbus has provided 29 EC135T3 Juno HT.1 helicopters for the basic and advanced training phases with three H145 Jupiter HT.1 to replace the Bell 214EP Griffin HT.1 in the SAR training role. In early 2020 Airbus supplied another four Juno HT.1s.

Nearly forty years after the RAF assessed the Pilatus PC-9, its American descendant, the Beechcraft T-6C Texan II replaced the Tucano in 2018. The original ten aircraft supplied by Affinity Flight Training Systems have since been joined by four more. They are all based with No 72 (Reserve) Squadron at Valley. *MoD*

The Empire Test Pilots School at Boscombe Down, now controlled by the privatised defence company QinetiQ uses a mixture of Hawk T.1 and Alpha Jets. In 2017 it ordered two Pilatus PC-21 as part of its fleet modernisation due to the type's performance and capabilities and its low running costs.

With the cancellation of ASDOT the Hawk T.1 fleet of No 100 Squadron is likely solider on until at least 2030 flying as enemy Red Air targets for dissimilar combat. Hawk T.1 XX349 is seen here on 16th June 2002 during its time with the squadron. It was scrapped in 2015 but the cockpit survives with the Scampton Fire Section as a training aid. *Author's Collection*

Air Support to Defence Operational Training (ASDOT)

The next stage of the MoD's plan was to hand over operational training for all three Services to private contractors. In June 2016, the MoD released its outline programme which would include; air-to-air and air-to-surface combat training, Joint Terminal Attack Controller/Forward Air Controller training, electronic warfare (EW) training, air traffic control and aerospace battle management training, ground-based air defence and live gunnery training. The initial ten-year contract was worth £700 million (potentially up to £1.5 billion for fifteen years) for up to 6,000 hours annually and was due to begin during 2020. The new training aircraft would replace the current EW training Dassault Falcon 20s operated by Cobham Aviation Services, who had begun operating Fleet Requirements contracts as Flight Refuelling Limited in 1985 and became the sole providers of EW training in 1994. The successful contractor would also have to provide its own Red Air aggressor capability to act as adversaries to replace the Hawk T.1s of 736 NAS and

Hawk T.1A XX159 and Flight Refuelling Aviation operated Falcon 20 G-FRAL on an exercise sortie with the Royal Navy. The Hawk will mimic a fast sea-skimming anti-ship missile launched from the Falcon as a Red Air strike aircraft, which will use its EW pods in an attempt to mask the incoming Hawk in order to provide realistic combat conditions for the warship crews. *MoD/Open Government Licence, 2010*

A Typhoon T.3 of No 29 (Reserve) Squadron, the Typhoon OCU, flying over its base at Coningsby. Getting into the Typhoon or the F-35 Lightning is the dream for any student pilot wishing to fly fighters. *MoD/Open Government Licence, 2008*

No 100 Squadron. The MoD was keen for the Red Air aircraft to be something not in RAF use to offer unfamiliar capabilities to test the students. When the Hawks of 736 NAS co-operate with Cobham's Falcon 20s, the nimble Hawks are used to mimic fast sea-skimming anti-ship missiles. Other private providers are also used to provide threat simulation. For example, Hawker Hunter Aviation uses a small fleet of ex-Swiss Hawker Hunter F.58s as threat simulators and as equipment test and trials platforms for MoD and NATO member contracts. The four bidding consortia for ASDOT were; Babcock Aerospace with Elbit Systems Limited; Cobham Aviation Services with Draken International, 3SDL and QinetiQ; Leonardo with Red Aces (who carry out similar contracts in Canada) and Inzpire; and finally Thales UK who at one point were partnered with Draken International. But in March 2019 the MoD announced the cancellation of ASDOT. It is unclear whether this is a permanent decision, but it is unlikely that the programme will not go ahead in some form as the Hawk T.1s and Typhoon FGR.4 Tranche 1 aggressor fleets are scheduled for retirement by 2023 and 2025 respectively under the latest plans within the Command Paper, *Defence in a Competitive Age* published in March 2021.

Training to Operate

The RAF is still responsible, at the time of writing, for its operational conversion training, although Personnel and Training Command is now defunct, having merged with Strike Command in 2007 to form a single Air Command. The CFS maintains its traditional role of training the instructors, since 1995 training all instructors for all pilot and aircrew training roles, examining students and auditing the flying training system (UKMFTS) to ensure that standards are maintained. It also remains the parent unit of the *Red Arrows* display team. With the retirement of the Tornado in 2019, numerically the Typhoon is the most important frontline combat asset with the F-35B Lightning fleet continuing to grow and come into frontline service. The fourth-generation fighter capabilities the Typhoon promised throughout its inception have driven many of the modernising developments over the last decade. The cornerstone of UKMFTS was to provide modern training aircraft equipped with suitable glass cockpits and avionics so that students could jump out of the Hawk and still feel familiar in a Typhoon or a Lightning. A fully combat-capable Typhoon two-seat conversion trainer was developed alongside the standard fighter and entered service with all four partner nations, the UK, Germany, Italy and Spain. The RAF received 37 two-seaters. By 2020, all the original Tranche 1 Typhoon T.2 trainers had been retired and reduced to spares sources, but the T.3 upgraded to later Tranche 3 standards remains in service.

Typhoon T.3 ZJ814 of No 3 Squadron roaring into the sky on a training sortie during Exercise Taurus Mountain 3 in 2012. Delivered to the RAF on 22nd November 2006, the aircraft had a short life, being reduced to produce (scrapped in old parlance) in 2018, the fate of all sixteen of the original T.2 airframes. *MoD/Open Government Licence, 2012*

In December 2020 two Typhoon T.3s of No 12 Squadron were used for a special VIP flight as part of a capability demonstration. They carried the Qatari Deputy Prime Minister and the Minister of State for Defence aloft and during the sortie took on fuel from an Airbus Voyager tanker. No 12 Squadron is the first joint squadron since the Second World War, having Qatar Emiri Air Force pilots and engineers embedded within the unit as that air force works up on the Typhoon. ***MoD/Open Government Licence, 2020***

The introduction of the Typhoon into RAF service during 2003 saw a new pioneering development. Both the Operational Evaluation Unit, No 17 Squadron, and the Operational Conversion Unit (OCU), No 29 Squadron, were formed at BAE System's Warton site under 'Case White' to train the initial cadre of 16 pilots and 248 ground crews. This arrangement ensured that both units had on-site manufacturers support as well as allowing two-way conversations with the development team. In 2004 they moved to Coningsby as the core of the future Typhoon force. By 2020 29 Squadron had eighteen aircraft – a mix of FGR.4s and T.3s – and 25 QFIs and runs three to four six-month courses concurrently and trains 1,000 ground crews annually as part of the Typhoon Training Facility. Although it has been hampered by low pilot turnout from the fast jet schools at Valley, the OCU provides sufficient training to get a pilot combat ready within six months, a task that used to take eighteen months. Being a multi-role fighter, the pilot must be trained in the full range of air-to-air and air-to-ground missions.

Perhaps surprising to older generations of pilots, 70 percent of the training is synthetic using a cockpit trainer, a full 360° dome simulator and the ASTA Full Mission Simulator. The current simulators are being replaced from April 2021 by BAE Systems. The new system will comprise three full mission simulators and three operational mission trainers at Coningsby and two of each at Lossiemouth. The new system uses virtual reality and gaming technology to enable a 50/50 mix of synthetic and real flying for the 20 missions for the students each month. The Defence Operational Training Capability (Air) requirement will see these simulators networked together with similar facilities for the Lightning at Marham and the Airborne Early Warning simulators at Waddington. The equipment will also be exported to Qatar and a potential customer is Saudi Arabia. A new Sceptre mission planning and debriefing system will replace the current equipment from November 2020 and is similar to equipment already used by AAC and FAA Leonardo Wildcat helicopter crews. Sceptre uses 3D imaging to show potential hazards and conflict detection and uses real-time weather information and intelligence information. Qatar and Saudi Arabia are again export buyers. A new capability called Gladiator was announced in May 2019. The system supplied by Boeing Defence UK allows multiple Typhoon and Lightning pilots to synthetically fly together and experience the same battlefield environment and threats simultaneously. For the first time an entire exercise can be flown without a single aircraft having to leave the ground and with all the reductions in costs that brings. Further investment in synthetic training facilities and changes in the way simulators are used for training and mission planning has been outlined in March 2021 Command Paper, *Defence in a Competitive Age*, in the pursuit of further efficiencies within the training programme.

A former Tornado unit, No IX (Bomber) Squadron, reformed at Lossiemouth in 2019 for the Northern Quick Reaction Alert (QRA) role with several of the remaining Tranche 1 Typhoons. In addition the squadron was to provide the RAF with an Red Air aggressor training capability, doubtless due to the cancellation of ASDOT. The decision in the Command Paper, *Defence in a Competitive Age*, to retire the last Tranche 1 Typhoons by 2025 puts this in doubt, however. On 24th July 2018, No 12 Squadron formed at Coningsby as a special joint RAF-Qatar Emiri Air Force unit, providing training to the latter's pilots and ground crew before their first squadron becomes operational on the Typhoon. Eventually the unit will transfer to Qatar and will return to Britain in 2022. Originally the plan was for the squadron to swap its latest Tranche 3 Typhoons for Tranche 1s alongside No IX Squadron in the joint QRA/aggressor role, but again the pending retirement of the older Typhoons means that this is unlikely to happen. In addition, there have been discussions between the Qatar Emiri Air Force and the MoD to form another joint squadron to operate Qatar's new Hawk fleet.

The F-35B Lightning will be operated by a joint RAF/FAA force and No 207 Squadron formed at Marham on 1st August 2019 as the OCU. The initial work to train the instructors was undertaken with the US Marine Corps VMFAT-501 'Warlords' at Beaufort, South Carolina, to enable No 617 Squadron to form in 2018. The training to enable the successful first Short Take-Off and Vertical Landings aboard the new aircraft carrier HMS *Queen Elizabeth* at the end of 2018 relied heavily on simulator time as well as practice flights with VFMAT-501. HMS *Queen Elizabeth's* debut operational deployment in 2021 will bring together Royal Navy, RAF and US Marine Corps experience with a joint F-35B force. Without a dedicated conversion trainer, future Lightning pilots must master the type flying the simulator before sitting in the cockpit of a real F-35B. An indication of the emphasis on synthetic flying is that whenever HMS *Queen Elizabeth* or HMS *Prince of Wales* are on operational deployments, they will carry four full mission simulators to enable four pilots to train simultaneously to maintain standards and offering the ability to fly their operational missions before setting off on the real thing.

Whether or not you agree that PFI deals have provided value for money and provided a robust supply train of enough suitably well-trained pilots and aircrews, there is no doubt that the Treasury and MoD would never have taken steps to renew the entire training fleet in such a coordinated purchase due to capital costs involved. The contract system means that the RAF is assured to always keep up to date with modern aircraft and simulators as the providers and contracts are renewed or changed every thirty years or so. The structure of UKMFTS provides a centralised training organisation but it has not been a radical change, the RAF having providing basic and advanced flying training to FAA and AAC pilots for many decades, but has built on the growing concept of centralisation, for example in elementary and helicopter training, over the last 30 years. There will always be a challenge to guarantee the quality provided by private contractors and to balance the mix between real and synthetic flying training, but there is little alternative while the size of the armed forces and their budgets are likely to continue to shrink with the training demands contracting at a corresponding pace. There is no doubt that the RAF pilots and crews of today are as well, if not better, trained than many of their forebears.

The F-35B requires the piloting skill of vertical landing. The development of cockpit controls during the transition and landing phases has built on Harrier experience and is now an intuitive 'throttle and stick' system to reduce cockpit workload and potential errors. This F-35B is landing aboard HMS *Queen Elizabeth* during the ships' WESTLANT 19 deployment as the RAF's F-35 pilots began V/STOL operations onto the deck.
MoD/Open Government Licence, 2019

Conclusion: Imprimis Praecepta

Like the Latin motto of the Central Flying School, teaching is everlasting and as long as a human is required to fly an aircraft some form of training will be required. When we began our journey at the start of this book a student pilot in 1945 might have progressed from the venerable de Havilland Tiger Moth, perhaps in chilly Canada or the hot veldt of South Africa. If they were lucky after earning their wings, they might be posted to fly the new de Havilland Vampire. Having been handed the pilots notes, while a few groundcrew 'erks' sat on his tailbooms to show him the correct landing attitude he would then simply be told by his instructor to get airborne. Training today's fighter

This impressive line-up of the RAF training aircraft then in service during the late 1980s represents many of the most important British post-war training aircraft that have shaped thousands of RAF service careers. *Blue Envoy Collection*

pilot costs tens of thousands of pounds and takes several years to accomplish. The student will have to fly many simulated missions in an array of specialised flight simulators before they get their hands on a Eurofighter Typhoon or an F-35 Lightning. Today's transport pilots need similar cognitive skills to the fighter pilots, they also have Head-Up-Displays and 'glass' cockpits and landing an Airbus A400M Atlas on a rough field strip is just as demanding as it was for their forebears flying Blackburn Beverleys and Douglas Dakotas.

Unsurprisingly as aviation technology has advanced the training aircraft and methods have had to evolve, keeping in-step with changes to frontline equipment. As we have seen the Air Ministry has sometimes been too ambitious and sometimes too cautious in specifying the equipment it needed and formulating the best ways of operating it. No stone was left unturned; vertical take-off and landing, supersonics, variable-geometry wings, fly-by-wire and simulators. All of these innovations were adopted so that student pilots could master their application and learn how to get the best from them in operational flying. Much is often written about the dichotomy between the ministries and industry; it is true that there were frictions between both sides of the procurement process. This book has highlighted the differences but also the symbiotic relationship under which both sides shared concepts and strategies. Eventually an objective view would accept what might at first seem like radical ideas, even if funding and experience would actually dictate when the adoption of new ideas or equipment would happen.

Today the Services are merely customers to industry providers. This is perhaps the major shift throughout the events of this book, a change that has not been without criticism or problems, but one that with ever increasing aviation and defence costs was perhaps inevitable. The UK Military Flying Training System is perhaps only the second time a coherent training organisation has provided the training for every branch and type of military pilot and aircrew since the formation of the original Central Flying School in 1912. Such a financial model enables the Ministry of Defence to procure a new completely new training fleet every 30 years. The only downside is that the training aircraft offered at the next contract renewal will be existing off-the-shelf solutions, there will be no scope – or money – for the kind of in-depth studies and requirements process and British aviation industry expertise that led to cutting-edge designs such as the Jet Provost, Gnat or Hawk. The chances of British military pilots in the second half of this century being trained on aircraft produced in Britain are small.

But will we even need pilot trainers in the future? Although the RAF is increasingly becoming a user of unmanned aerial vehicles and investing in optionally-manned and unmanned elements for the Future Combat Air System to replace Typhoon, the day when all pilots hang-up their flying helmets for good is not yet near. Future pilots will certainly be trained in advanced virtual reality environments, pitted against artificial intelligence aggressors in scenarios that would be impossible to recreate safely or economically in flying exercises. But the simulators will never entirely replace flying hours and every pilot will need to master good piloting skills and airmanship in humble piston-engined trainers before they can earn their wings. The only difference is the proportion of the training time, the simulators due to their capability and lower operating costs have inevitably eaten away at expensive flying hours. Tomorrow's pilots will following a well-trod path from their great-great forebears who first arrived at the gates of Upavon to join the Central Flying School in 1912.

Bibliography and Source Notes

During the research for this book a great deal of primary source material was consulted, including documents held by The National Archives at Kew, museums and individuals as noted in the acknowledgments.

There is not space here to list every file but the following File Divisions were consulted at Kew:

AIR 2, 8, 10, 20, 64 and 77

AVIA 6, 18, 53, 54, 55, 65 and 69

T 225

Good secondary sources are important starting points for further research and for cross-checking other sources. Listed here are the most important ones that were consulted:

Amos, Peter, *Miles Aircraft – The Wartime Years 1939 to 1945*, Air-Britain, 2012

Amos, Peter, *Miles Aircraft – The Post War Years 1945 to 1948*, Air-Britain, 2016

Andrews, C F and Morgan, E B, *Vickers Aircraft since 1908* (2nd *Ed.)*, Putnam, 1988

Burke, Damien, *TSR.2 Britain's Lost Bomber*, Crowood Press, 2010

Buttler, Tony, *British Secret Projects, Vol.1: Jet Fighters since 1950*, Midland Publishing, 2000

Buttler, Tony, *British Secret Projects, Vol.2: Jet Bombers since 1949*, Midland Publishing, 2000

Carbonel, Jean-Christophe, *French Secret Projects, Vol.2: Cold War Bombers, Patrol and Assault Aircraft*, Crécy Publishing, 2017

Flintham, Vic, *Aircraft in British Military Service*, Airlife Publishing, 1998

Fraser-Mitchell, Harry, The Hawk Story, *Journal of Aeronautical History*, Paper No. 2013/01

Gearing, David W, *On the Wings of a Gull: Percival and Hunting Aircraft*, Air-Britain, 2012

James, Derek N, *Westland Aircraft since 1915*, Putnam, 1991

Jefford, C G Wing Commander (Ed.), The Helicopter in the RAF, *Royal Air Force Historical Society Journal*, No.25, 2001

Jefford, C G Wing Commander (Ed.), The Canberra in the RAF, *Royal Air Force Historical Society Journal*, 2009

Jones, Barry, *V-Bombers Valiant, Vulcan and Victor*, Crowood Press, 2007

Laming, Tim, *Training the High Fliers*, Arms and Armour Press, 1993

Longworth, James H, *Test Flying in Lancashire from Samlesbury and Warton Aerodromes, Vol 2: From the 1960s into the 1980s*, BAE Systems Heritage, 2013

Longworth, James H, *Test Flying in Lancashire from Samlesbury and Warton Aerodromes, Vol 2: From the 1980s into the New Millennium*, BAE Systems Heritage, 2014

McLelland, Tim, *The Avro Vulcan*, Crécy Publishing, 2007

Meekcoms, K J and Morgan, Eric B, *The British Aircraft Specifications File*, Air-Britain, 1994

Michell, Simon (Ed.), *Jane's Civil and Military Aircraft Upgrades 1993-94 (1st Ed.)*, Jane's Information Group, 1992

Petit, Martin H. et al, *British Military Aircraft Serials and Markings*, British Aviation Research Group, 1980

Sturtivant, Ray, *History of British Military Training Aircraft*, Foulis/Haynes Publishing, 1987

Sturtivant, Ray and Hamlin, John, *Flying Training and Support Units since 1912*, Air-Britain, 2007

Taylor, H A, *Fairey Aircraft since 1915*, Putnam, 1974

Taylor, Michael (Ed.), *Brassey's World Aircraft & Systems Directory 1996/97 (1st Ed.)*, Brassey's Publishing, 1996

Watkins, David, *History of the de Havilland Vampire*, Fonthill Media, 2013

Wenham, Tom, *False Dawn: The Beagle Aircraft Story*, Air-Britain, 2015

Wenham, Tom, *Scottish Aviation Bulldog: Trainer for the World*, Air-Britain, 2019

Various issues of the following periodicals and magazines were also consulted:

Aeroplane Monthly

Aeromilitaria, Air-Britain

Air International

Aviation World, Air-Britain

Flight

Flight International

Glossary

AAC	Army Air Corps
A&AEE	Aeroplane and Armament Experimental Establishment
ACAS(OR)	Assistant Chief of the Air Staff (Operational Requirements)
ACAS(P)	Assistant Chief of the Air Staff (Policy)
ACAS(T)	Assistant Chief of the Air Staff (Training)
ACAS(TR)	Assistant Chief of the Air Staff (Tactics and Requirements)
ACMI	Air Combat Manoeuvring Instrumentation
AEO	Air Electronics Operator
AEF	Air Experience Flight
AFS	Advanced Flying School
AI	Airborne Interception Radar
AMSO	Air Member for Supply and Organisation
ANS	Air Navigation School
AOP	Airborne Observation Post
ASR	Air Staff Requirement
AST	Air Staff Target
ASV	Air-to-Surface-Vessel Radar
ASW	Anti-Submarine Warfare
AUW	All-Up Weight
B-Conditions	A British identity marking for experimental flight testing
BFTS	Basic Flying Training School
CFS	Central Flying School
CFS(H)	Central Flying School Helicopter Development Unit
DHFS	Defence Helicopter Flying School
DRPC	Defence Research Policy Committee
EFTS	Elementary Flying Training School
FAA	Fleet Air Arm
FEAF	Far East Air Force
FTS	Flying Training School
GPS	Global Positioning System
GSOR	General Staff Operational Requirement
HDU	Helicopter Development Unit
IAS	Indicated Air Speed
IFIS	Integrated Flight Instrument System
ILS	Instrument Landing System
MDAP	Mutual Defense Aid Plan
NAS	Naval Air Squadron
NBC	Navigation and Bombing Computer
NGASR	Naval General Air Staff Requirement
OCU	Operational Conversion Unit
OTU	Operational Training Unit
QFI	Qualified Flight Instructor
QHI	Qualified Helicopter Instructor
QHNI	Qualified Helicopter Navigator Instructor
RAE	Royal Aircraft Establishment
RAF	Royal Air Force
RAAF	Royal Australian Air Force
RCAF	Royal Canadian Air Force
RFS	Reserve Flying School
RN	Royal Navy
RNAS	Royal Naval Air Station
SAR	Search-and-Rescue
SARTU	Search and Rescue Training Unit
SBAC	Society of British Aircraft Constructors
TACAN	Tactical Air Navigation
UAS	University Air Squadron
UKMFTS	UK Military Flying Training System

Index

AIRCRAFT

ORGANISATIONS

PEOPLE

PLACES

SPECIFICATIONS